GPU Gems

GPU Gems

Programming Techniques, Tips, and Tricks for Real-Time Graphics

Edited by Randima Fernando

✦ Addison-Wesley

Boston • San Francisco • New York • Toronto • Montreal
London • Munich • Paris • Madrid
Capetown • Sydney • Tokyo • Singapore • Mexico City

The publisher offers discounts on this book when ordered in quantity for bulk purchases and special sales. For more information, please contact:

> U.S. Corporate and Government Sales
> (800) 382-3419
> corpsales@pearsontechgroup.com

For sales outside of the U.S., please contact:

> International Sales
> (317) 581-3793
> international@pearsontechgroup.com

Visit Addison-Wesley on the Web: www.awprofessional.com

Library of Congress Control Number: 2004100582

ISBN 0-321-22832-4
Text printed on recycled paper
3 4 5 6 7 8 9 10 11—QWT—0807060504
Second printing, May 2004

To those who have brought us where we are,

and to those who will take us where we are going

Contents

PART I   NATURAL EFFECTS   1

Chapter 1
Effective Water Simulation from Physical Models 5
Mark Finch, Cyan Worlds

Chapter 5
Implementing Improved Perlin Noise 73
Ken Perlin, New York University

Chapter 6
Fire in the "Vulcan" Demo 87
Hubert Nguyen, NVIDIA

Chapter 7
Rendering Countless Blades of Waving Grass 107
Kurt Pelzer, Piranha Bytes

Chapter 8
Simulating Diffraction 123
Jos Stam, Alias Systems

PART II LIGHTING AND SHADOWS   133

Chapter 9
Efficient Shadow Volume Rendering 137
Morgan McGuire, Brown University

Chapter 10
Cinematic Lighting 167

Fabio Pellacini, Pixar Animation Studios
Kiril Vidimce, Pixar Animation Studios

Chapter 11
Shadow Map Antialiasing 185

Michael Bunnell, NVIDIA
Fabio Pellacini, Pixar Animation Studios

Chapter 12
Omnidirectional Shadow Mapping 193
Philipp S. Gerasimov, iXBT.com

Chapter 13
Generating Soft Shadows Using Occlusion Interval Maps 205
William Donnelly, University of Waterloo
Joe Demers, NVIDIA

Chapter 14
Perspective Shadow Maps: Care and Feeding............ 217
Simon Kozlov, SoftLab-NSK

Chapter 15
Managing Visibility for Per-Pixel Lighting............... 245
John O'Rorke, Monolith Productions

Chapter 26
The OpenEXR Image File Format 425

Florian Kainz, Industrial Light & Magic
Rod Bogart, Industrial Light & Magic
Drew Hess, Industrial Light & Magic

Chapter 27
A Framework for Image Processing 445

Frank Jargstorff, NVIDIA

Chapter 32
An Introduction to Shader Interfaces. 537
Matt Pharr, NVIDIA

Chapter 33
Converting Production RenderMan Shaders to Real-Time 551
Stephen Marshall, Sony Pictures Imageworks

PART VI   BEYOND TRIANGLES   617

Chapter 37
A Toolkit for Computation on GPUs 621
Ian Buck, Stanford University
Tim Purcell, Stanford University

Chapter 38
Fast Fluid Dynamics Simulation on the GPU 637
Mark J. Harris, University of North Carolina at Chapel Hill

Chapter 39
Volume Rendering Techniques. 667
Milan Ikits, University of Utah
Joe Kniss, University of Utah
Aaron Lefohn, University of California, Davis
Charles Hansen, University of Utah

Chapter 42
Deformers

Eugene d'Eon, University of Waterloo

Foreword

Now is an excellent time to be working in the field of computer graphics. Over the past five years, GPU technology has advanced in astounding ways, and at an explosive pace. The rendering rate, as measured in pixels per second, has been approximately doubling every six months during those five years. A factor of two is certainly exciting enough, but more exciting is the wonder of compounding. Five years represents the doubling of performance ten times—that's two to the tenth power, a factor of one thousand!

Not only has performance increased, but also the quality of computation and the flexibility of graphics programming have steadily improved during that same time. Five years ago, PCs and computer workstations had graphics accelerators, not graphics processing units (GPUs). The implication was that a graphics accelerator does simply that: it accelerates graphics. Furthermore, the word *accelerator* implied that the computer would perform exactly the same rendering operations as before, only faster. As graphics accelerators were replaced by GPUs, we abandoned the old concept of graphics acceleration. We advanced to graphics *processing*, embracing the idea of processors that enable new graphics algorithms and effects.

We have entered the era of programmable GPUs. The graphics hardware pipeline, which had not previously changed significantly in twenty years, was broken down to its component, hard-wired elements and rebuilt out of programmable, parallel-pipelined processors. In a hard-wired pipeline, triangle vertices are transformed and lit, triangles are rasterized, and pixels are shaded with diffuse lighting, specular exponentiation, fog blending, and frame-buffer blending. In a programmable pipeline, each of these operations is abstracted to its component memory accesses and mathematical operations. A programmer can still write a program that calculates the same results as a hard-wired pipeline (and in fact, such a program is often the first one a student programmer writes for a programmable processor!), but the opportunity presented is so much greater than this.

The first effects of fast, programmable GPUs are subtle. Previously difficult graphics problems become much more tractable through the application of one thousand-fold performance increases. Offline rendering techniques become more practical for interactive applications. Historically, brute force has been a popular algorithmic approach; simply casting a graphics problem in a way that it can run on a GPU is an unsubtle application of brute force—it works, but it leaves opportunity on the table. Beyond that, algorithm development gets more interesting. Graphics programmers can now experiment with new algorithms and techniques that would not have been practical on a slower, single-threaded serial processor such as a CPU. The parallel-stream-processing nature of the GPU, coupled with flexibility and programmability, allows new algorithms to be developed and invites experimentation. Any computationally demanding problem—not just graphics—that can take advantage of large-scale parallelism, larger memory bandwidth, and geometric performance growth is a good candidate for GPU implementation. As an industry, we're still learning which problems will benefit most from GPU solutions.

The true beneficiaries of the programmable GPU revolution are the computer graphics algorithm designer, the researcher, the application developer, and ultimately the end user or consumer—the gamer, the moviegoer, and so on. *GPU Gems* is a timely book, as the GPU programming field is young and vibrant, and many developers are reinventing the same techniques again and again. This volume contains straightforward applications of known techniques to a structure more amenable to GPU execution, as well as innovative new algorithms and effects that were not previously possible.

At this time in the history of GPU programming, many problems remain unsolved and many challenges remain unmet. Consequently, this first volume of *GPU Gems* is a compendium of approaches and examples of work carried out so far, rather than a cookbook of completed effects to be plugged into applications. This collection will allow programmers to benefit from the exciting progress already made, and it will enable tomorrow's developers to stand on the shoulders of giants, the pioneers of programming GPUs. It's up to you to take the next steps of innovation!

David Kirk
Chief Scientist
NVIDIA Corporation

Preface

This book is an extensive and practical collection of articles about real-time computer graphics, accumulating the knowledge and experience of experts in both industry and academia. Building, in the same style, upon the wealth of the great "Gems" books already available, *GPU Gems* is a collection of short chapters. However, a number of key characteristics make this book unique and valuable to today's developers as they attempt to harness the ever-increasing power of the graphics processing unit (GPU).

First and foremost, this book focuses squarely on real-time programmable graphics—specifically, on techniques relevant to GPUs. Each chapter was carefully selected to present ideas and techniques that are directly useful in interactive applications, such as computer games. The chapters provide insight and understanding, rather than focusing on low-level API calls or specific mathematical tricks. Furthermore, each chapter is packed with numerous full-color diagrams and images to illustrate and drive home key concepts. Finally, the experience and diversity of the contributors help readers gain a broad understanding, as well as a certain confidence that the advice they are getting comes from experts in the field.

NVIDIA's strongest asset is its people: the depth and quality of their collective expertise inspired the initial idea for *GPU Gems*. With so much knowledge and expertise at hand, we felt that the thoughts and insights of the teams that brought us many recent advances in real-time graphics would make for a wonderfully instructive book. So, we started the project with an internal call for participation.

Having the good fortune to work with people from leading game development houses, tool developers, film studios, and academic institutions who are shaping the future of real-time computer graphics, we also wanted to highlight their real-world contributions in *GPU Gems*. Hence, a wider, public call for participation allowed us to coalesce a great amount of talent and refreshing perspective into this volume.

Whether you're creating new effects, architecting a graphics engine, or squeezing out the last bits of performance, we hope that this book provides valuable guidance and saves you from some of the challenges the authors faced on their own projects. All of us who worked on *GPU Gems* hope that it will help you to adopt new ideas and take your projects to the next level of graphical realism.

Our Intended Audience

This book provides intermediate and advanced readers with useful information that will help them in their projects. Focusing beyond the fundamentals of high-level shading, *GPU Gems* looks at how to take existing projects further by removing the mystery behind complex effects and advanced GPU programming. With the rapid evolution of real-time shading languages, the collection of algorithms available to real-time graphics developers is larger than ever. By compiling and distributing the information in this book, our goal is to make high-quality, high-performance graphics more accessible to a wider audience that includes game developers, technical directors, professors, and students.

Trying the Examples

Many of the chapters in this book include code samples to make their subject matter more concrete. The authors used whichever shading language they wanted, so the code samples ended up in DirectX 9's High-Level Shader Language (HLSL) or Cg, which were the only two high-level shading languages widely in use during this project. Almost everything that is presented can be applied to either language, as well as to languages that came later, such as the OpenGL Shading Language. The code samples are available on the CD that accompanies this book, along with standalone examples wherever possible. This makes it easy for you to integrate or experiment with the various examples. Updated sample code, as well as additional supplementary materials, is available at the book's Web site: **http://developer.nvidia.com/GPUGems/**.

Acknowledgments

A project the size of *GPU Gems* cannot succeed without the efforts of many people. First, I would like to thank the contributors, without whom this book would not exist. It has been my privilege to work with such an experienced and capable group of people. But part of the challenge when working with a group of this caliber is that everyone is also exceptionally busy. I am grateful to them for taking the time to work on the project, and for putting in the effort to produce superlative results. Thanks also go to their respective organizations for allowing them to participate in *GPU Gems*. Our appreciation also goes to those who responded to our call for participation and presented worthy proposals for consideration.

The section editors—Kevin Bjorke, Cem Cebenoyan, Sim Dietrich, Simon Green, Juan Guardado, and John Spitzer—contributed enormously by iterating with the authors, helping to shape the manuscript, and tracking down articles to keep them on schedule. I'm grateful to all of them for volunteering to assist with this project. Chris Seitz was also instrumental in the success of this project, taking care of legal issues, reviewing chapters, and always being ready to take a few moments to discuss project concerns with me.

Each chapter underwent an extensive review process, involving comments from peer reviewers, editors, and external reviewers. The contributors and section editors did a wonderful job critiquing and helping to improve the book's content. In particular, I'd like to thank Matt Pharr (who spent weekends above and beyond the call of duty to help review several chapters—in addition to writing three!) and Kevin Bjorke (who was a section editor in addition to writing and contributing to several chapters). Larry Gritz, Eric Haines, and Matthias Wloka were kind enough to serve as critical external reviewers and provided a wealth of insightful comments. Thanks also to our anonymous external reviewers, who did well to tackle the massive amount of material they were given.

Caroline Lie, Spender Yuen, Dana Chan, and Melvin Chong provided their expertise to create the book's cover, template, and diagrams. I would particularly like to thank Spender for his patience as we worked through the more than 100 diagrams in the book (in addition to over 200 screenshots). Catherine Kilkenny, Debra Valentine, and Teresa Saffaie helped improve and clarify the writing. David Kirk lent his insight to produce the book's foreword.

Christopher Keane did a fantastic job of pulling the manuscript through copyediting and composition. Many thanks go to Jacquelyn Doucette, John Fuller, Bernard Gaffney, Curt Johnson, Heather Mullane, and the other folks at Addison-Wesley for their help in this project from start to finish. In particular, Peter Gordon's encouragement and deadlines helped us keep the book on schedule.

From architecting GPUs to helping developers create exciting new content, there are innumerable steps that take place at NVIDIA before the knowledge contained in this book can be useful to the graphics community. Therefore, I'd like to thank everyone at NVIDIA, because without their hard work there wouldn't be an opportunity to do a project like *GPU Gems*. Specific thanks to Mark Daly, Dan Vivoli, and Jen-Hsun Huang for providing the teams and resources to make it all happen.

Finally, I would like to thank my parents and sister for their extraordinary support, and for making it possible for me to have such exceptional opportunities.

Given the unique combination of effort, creativity, and care that so many talented people contributed to *GPU Gems*, I'm sure this book will serve you well.

Randima (Randy) Fernando
NVIDIA Corporation

Contributors

Curtis Beeson, NVIDIA

Curtis Beeson moved from SGI to NVIDIA's Demo Team more than five years ago; he focuses on the art path, the object model, and the DirectX renderer of the NVIDIA demo engine. He began working in 3D while attending Carnegie Mellon University, where he generated environments for playback on head-mounted displays at resolutions that left users legally blind. Curtis specializes in the art path and object model of the NVIDIA Demo Team's scenegraph API—while fighting the urge to succumb to the dark offerings of management in marketing.

Kevin Bjorke, NVIDIA

Kevin Bjorke works in the Developer Technology group developing and promoting next-generation art tools and entertainments, with a particular eye toward the possibilities inherent in programmable shading hardware. Before joining NVIDIA, he worked extensively in the film, television, and game industries, supervising development and imagery for *Final Fantasy: The Spirits Within* and *The Animatrix*; performing numerous technical director and layout animation duties on *Toy Story* and *A Bug's Life*; developing games on just about every commercial platform; producing theme park rides; animating too many TV commercials; and booking daytime TV talk shows. He attended several colleges, eventually graduating from the California Institute of the Arts film school. Kevin has been a regular speaker at SIGGRAPH, GDC, and similar events for the past decade.

Rod Bogart, Industrial Light & Magic

Rod Bogart came to Industrial Light & Magic (ILM) in 1995 after spending three years as a software engineer at Pacific Data Images. His early work in camera tracking is published in *Graphics Gems II*. At ILM, Rod developed the core engine of the interactive compositing tools, and he oversaw much of the design and implementation of ILM's other image-processing and image-viewing techniques.

Ian Buck, Stanford University

 Ian Buck is completing his Ph.D. in computer science at the Stanford University Graphics Lab, researching general-purpose computing models for GPUs. His research focuses on programming language design for graphics hardware, as well as general-computing applications that map to graphics hardware architectures. Ian received his B.S.E. in computer science from Princeton University in 1999 and is a recipient of Stanford School of Engineering and NVIDIA fellowships.

Michael Bunnell, NVIDIA

 Michael Bunnell graduated from Southern Methodist University with degrees in computer science and electrical engineering. He wrote the Megamax C compiler for the Macintosh, Atari ST, and Apple IIGS before co-founding what is now LynuxWorks. After working on real-time operating systems for nine years, he moved to Silicon Graphics, focusing on image processing and on video and graphics software. Next, he worked at Gigapixel, then at 3dfx, and now he works at NVIDIA, where, interestingly enough, he is developing compilers again—this time, shader compilers.

Cem Cebenoyan, NVIDIA

 Cem Cebenoyan is a software engineer working in the Developer Technology group. He spends his days researching graphics techniques and helping game developers get the most out of graphics hardware. He has spoken at past Game Developer Conferences on character animation, graphics performance, and nonphotorealistic rendering. Before joining NVIDIA, Cem was a student/research assistant in the Graphics, Visualization, and Usability Lab at the Georgia Institute of Technology.

Joe Demers, NVIDIA

 Joe Demers received a B.S. from Carnegie Mellon University and an M.S. from the University of Southern California. He worked on Nendo, a simple but powerful 3D modeling and painting package from Nichimen Graphics, and on numerous demos at NVIDIA, where he has worked since 1999.

Eugene d'Eon, University of Waterloo

Eugene d'Eon recently completed a B.S. in applied mathematics and computer science at the University of Waterloo. He currently resides in California, working on the Demo Team at NVIDIA. He can occasionally be found in the office playing piano late at night.

Sim Dietrich, NVIDIA

Sim Dietrich manages the U.S. Developer Technology team at NVIDIA. Sim has written chapters for *Game Programming Gems 1* and *Game Programming Gems 2* and served as editor of the Graphics Display section of *Gems 2*. Sim was a key contributor to the CgFX effort, bringing real-time shaders to 3ds max, Maya, and Softimage|XSI for the first time. Sim's interests include new shadow techniques and improving graphics workflow through efforts such as Cg and CgFX.

William Donnelly, University of Waterloo

William Donnelly is an undergraduate student in mathematics and computer science at the University of Waterloo in Ontario. He has completed internships with Okino Computer Graphics, writing extensions to the NuGraf ray tracer, and with NVIDIA, creating real-time graphics demos for the GeForce FX. He has been destined for computer graphics ever since his dreams were shattered at the age of eight upon discovering that Lego set building was not a viable career path.

Randima Fernando, NVIDIA

Randima (Randy) Fernando has loved computer graphics from the age of eight. Working in NVIDIA's Developer Technology group, he helps teach developers how to take advantage of the latest GPU technology. Randy has a B.S. in computer science and an M.S. in computer graphics, both from Cornell University. He has been published in SIGGRAPH and is the co-author (along with Mark Kilgard) of *The Cg Tutorial: The Definitive Guide to Programmable Real-Time Graphics.*

Mark Finch, Cyan Worlds

Mark Finch has a B.S. in physics from Georgia Institute of Technology and an M.S. in computer science from the University of North Carolina at Chapel Hill. His professional graphics work started when he did image processing and rendering for the Star Wars program, but he soon moved to game programming, which he finds equally challenging and more constructive. He is currently the graphics programmer behind Cyan's *Uru* project.

Philipp S. Gerasimov, iXBT.com

Philipp Gerasimov is a Russian 3D programmer and game designer. He is currently working on the creation of RightMark 3D, an open-source 3D hardware benchmark by iXBT.

R. Steven Glanville, NVIDIA

Steve Glanville received his Ph.D. in computer science from UC Berkeley in 1977. In 1978, he founded Silicon Valley Software and served as president for 15 years, where he developed C and FORTRAN compilers. After spending too many years attending SIGGRAPH, in 1995 he finally made the switch to graphics and began developing OpenGL drivers. His past eventually caught up with him, however, and he is now one of the principal designers and implementers of the Cg language at NVIDIA.

Simon Green, NVIDIA

Simon Green is an engineer in the Developer Technology group at NVIDIA. After graduating from Reading University, England, with a degree in computer science, Simon worked in the video game industry for two years before emigrating to the United States to work for Silicon Graphics. He has presented at the Game Developer and Apple World Wide Developer conferences. His interests include OpenGL, cellular automata, image-based rendering, and analog synthesizers. He spends his time at NVIDIA thinking up new and interesting ways to abuse graphics hardware.

Juan Guardado, NVIDIA

In between riding camelback through the Sahara and lounging on the Brazilian coast, Juan Guardado enjoys contributing graphics technologies to the computer game industry. After graduating from McGill University with a bachelor's degree in computer engineering, he joined Matrox Graphics, where his work culminated in the development of hardware-accelerated displacement mapping. He now works at NVIDIA with the Developer Technology team based in the United Kingdom. He has given numerous talks at industry events, including GDC (U.S. and Europe), and he has been published in *ShaderX* and in *Gamasutra* online magazine.

Charles Hansen, University of Utah

Charles Hansen received a B.S. in computer science from Memphis State University in 1981 and a Ph.D. in computer science from the University of Utah in 1987. He is currently an associate professor of computer science at the University of Utah. From 1989 to 1997, he was a technical staff member in the Advanced Computing Laboratory (ACL) located at Los Alamos National Laboratory, where he formed and directed the visualization efforts of the ACL. He was a Bourse Chateaubriand Postdoctoral Fellow at INRIA Rocquencourt, France, in 1987 and 1988. His research interests include large-scale scientific visualization and computer graphics.

Mark J. Harris, University of North Carolina at Chapel Hill

Mark Harris received a B.S. from the University of Notre Dame in 1998 and a Ph.D. in computer science from the University of North Carolina at Chapel Hill in 2003. At UNC, Mark's research covered a wide variety of computer graphics topics, including real-time cloud simulation and rendering, general-purpose computation on GPUs, global illumination, non-photorealistic rendering, and virtual environments. During his graduate studies, Mark worked briefly at Intel, iROCK Games, and NVIDIA. Mark now works with NVIDIA's Developer Technology team based in the United Kingdom.

Drew Hess, Industrial Light & Magic

Drew Hess is a software developer in the Software Research and Development department at Industrial Light & Magic. In a past life, he was a member of the IA-64 architecture team at Intel Corporation. Drew received a B.S. in computer engineering from the University of Illinois at Urbana-Champaign and an M.S. in computer science from Stanford University.

Milan Ikits, University of Utah

 Milan Ikits is a Ph.D. candidate in the School of Computing at the University of Utah and a research assistant at the Scientific Computing and Imaging Institute. His current research interests lie in the areas of computer graphics, scientific visualization, immersive environments, and human-computer interaction. He received a diploma in computer science from the Budapest University of Technology and Economics in 1997. Milan is the creator of the popular OpenGL Extension Wrangler library (GLEW).

Greg James, NVIDIA

 Growing up in a house where 3D graphics movies and computers were left unlocked and out in plain sight, it's no wonder that Greg James became addicted to graphics at an early age. Attempts to cure him using respectable math and science have failed, but he did come away with a B.S. in physics and a minor in studio art in 1995. Fortunately, Greg has found a safe environment with the developer community outreach program at NVIDIA, where he helps himself and others work through their afflictions. He has developed and contributed to visual effects in many games. Among these are the reflective water animation in *Morrowind*, the glow in *Tron 2.0*, and a volume translucency effect for an upcoming title. His works have appeared in various computer graphics and physics publications, and he is particularly excited by the combination of physics and computer graphics.

Frank Jargstorff, NVIDIA

 Frank Jargstorff is a software engineer working on the Developer Technology team. He works on tools for digital content creation and helps DCC companies integrate new technologies into their products. Before joining NVIDIA, he worked for IBM, CoCreate, and Fraunhofer Research on topics ranging from streaming 3D to mainframe operating systems. Frank received his degree in computer science in 1997 from the University of Tübingen, Germany.

Alexandre Jean Claude, Softimage

 Alexandre Jean Claude currently works as the team lead for rendering and pipeline at Softimage. For the past few years, he has focused on game development pipelines and hardware-rendering technologies. He graduated from the Université du Québec à Montréal in computer science.

Florian Kainz, Industrial Light & Magic

Florian Kainz joined Industrial Light & Magic (ILM) in 1995 as a member of the research and development group. In his current role of computer graphics principal engineer, he leads the team that is responsible for the core architecture of ILM's in-house computer animation system. Kainz has worked on developing particle, fur, and implicit surface renderers, as well as a network protocol that forms the basis of a fault-tolerant, distributed batch-processing system. Kainz is one of the authors of the OpenEXR file format. Before joining ILM, Kainz worked as a software engineer for Steiner Film in Munich, Germany, and for Twenty-Five Frames in Singapore, writing image-processing and 3D rendering software. He received a degree in computer science in 1992 from the Technical University in Munich, Germany.

Joe Kniss, University of Utah

Joe Kniss received a B.S. in 1999 from Idaho State University and an M.S. in computer science from the University of Utah in 2002. He is currently pursuing a Ph.D. in computer science at the University of Utah, where he is a member of the Scientific Computing and Imaging Institute. His research interests include computer graphics, light transport in participating media, human-computer interaction, and immersive environments.

Simon Kozlov, SoftLab-NSK

Simon Kozlov graduated from Novosibirsk State University in June 2003, specializing in physics and computer science. Since 2001, Simon has worked at SoftLab-NSK, a game developer in Russia. Simon's current project is *Rig 'n' Roll*, a truck simulation game.

Aaron Lefohn, University of California, Davis

Aaron Lefohn is a Ph.D. student in the computer science department at the University of California at Davis and a graphics software engineer at Pixar Animation Studios. His research interests include general computation with graphics hardware, photorealistic rendering, and physically based animation. Aaron received an M.S. in computer science from the University of Utah in 2003, an M.S. in theoretical chemistry from the University of Utah in 2001, and a B.A. in chemistry from Whitman College in 1997. Aaron is an NSF graduate fellow in computer science.

Jörn Loviscach, Hochschule Bremen

Jörn Loviscach published many articles in popular computing magazines about programming and electronic music before receiving his doctorate degree in mathematical physics in 1993. He later worked at several computer magazines, becoming deputy editor-in-chief of the German computer magazine *c't*. He remained in this position for three years before accepting a professorship at Hochschule Bremen (University of Applied Sciences) in 2000, where he now teaches and researches in the field of computer graphics.

Stephen Marshall, Sony Pictures Imageworks

Stephen Marshall has worked as a software engineer at Sony Pictures Imageworks and currently is an effects technical director. Before joining Imageworks, Stephen was a developer in Engineering Animation's software and litigation animation divisions.

Christopher Maughan, NVIDIA

Chris Maughan has worked in the graphics hardware industry for 10 years. He began his career working on a video digitizer product for a startup company, soon followed by a move to 3Dlabs, where he wrote the first OpenGL device driver for Windows 95, in collaboration with Microsoft. Chris then developed the company's DirectX driver, staying for five years before leaving to join NVIDIA. At NVIDIA, he works in the Developer Technology group, focusing on providing tools and sample software for game developers. Chris works from home in York, in the north of England, where he lives with his wife, Stacey. He's still trying to figure out what he did right to get the girl, the job, and the location.

David McAllister, NVIDIA

David McAllister has been a computer graphics architect for NVIDIA since 2000. He received a Ph.D. in computer science from the University of North Carolina at Chapel Hill in 2002, where he did research in image-based rendering, reflectance measurement and representation, and graphics hardware. He spent the summer of 1997 at Hewlett-Packard working on the PixelFlow graphics supercomputer. David worked at Evans & Sutherland from 1989 to 1996 and received a B.S. from the University of Utah in 1995. David lives in Salt Lake City, Utah.

Morgan McGuire, Brown University

Morgan McGuire leads the Games Research Group at Brown University. His Ph.D. research is on real-time global illumination models for games. He has received master's degrees from MIT and Brown University, and he is the project manager for the Open Source G3D library at graphics3d.com.

Hubert Nguyen, NVIDIA

Hubert Nguyen is a software engineer at NVIDIA working on the Demo Team. He spends his time searching for novel effects that show off the features of NVIDIA's latest GPUs. He has spoken at past Game Developer Conferences on the techniques used to create NVIDIA demos. Before joining NVIDIA, Hubert was an engineer at 3dfx Interactive, the creators of Voodoo graphics. Prior to 3dfx, Hubert was part of the R&D department of Cryo Interactive (Paris, France). Hubert started to develop 3D graphics programs when he was involved in the European demoscene. He holds a bachelor's degree in computer science.

John O'Rorke, Monolith Productions

John O'Rorke has been creating games since the age of six. During high school, he worked after school with Hewlett-Packard in their firmware division and then attended the DigiPen Institute of Technology. He is currently an engine architect at Monolith Productions, where he has worked on *Aliens vs. Predator 2, Tron 2.0, No One Lives Forever 2: A Spy in H.A.R.M.'s Way*, and is currently developing engine technology for future products.

Fabio Pellacini, Pixar Animation Studios

Fabio Pellacini was born in Italy, where he spent the first 24 years of his life. During this time, he received a Laurea degree in physics from University of Parma and worked one year for Milestone building a physics engine. Following this experience, he decided to pursue his interests in computer graphics by moving to the United States, where he received a Ph.D. in computer graphics from Cornell University and published a few papers (four of which luckily got accepted to SIGGRAPH). These days he is spending his time in a dark office at Pixar Animation Studios designing and implementing the next generation of lighting technology for the studio.

Kurt Pelzer, Piranha Bytes

Kurt Pelzer is a senior software engineer at Piranha Bytes, where he worked on the PC game *Gothic*, the top-selling *Gothic II* (awarded "RPG of the Year" in Germany during 2001 and 2002, respectively), and the add-on *Gothic II: The Night of the Raven*. Previously, he was a senior programmer at Codecult and developed several real-time simulations and technology demos built on Codecult's high-end 3D engine Codecreatures (for example, a simulation of the Shanghai TRANSRAPID track for SIEMENS AG, and the well-known *Codecreatures Benchmark Pro*). He has published in *ShaderX 2* and *Game Programming Gems 4*.

Ken Perlin, New York University

Ken Perlin, a professor in the NYU Department of Computer Science, directs the Media Research Laboratory and Center for Advanced Technology. He has received an Academy Award for his procedural texturing algorithms (widely used in games and films), the New York City Mayor's Award for Excellence in Science and Technology, the Sokol Faculty Award for outstanding NYU science faculty, and a National Science Foundation Presidential Young Investigator Award. Ken received a Ph.D. in computer science from NYU and a B.A. in theoretical mathematics from Harvard. He has headed software development at R/GA and Mathematical Applications Group, Inc., and has worked on various films, starting with *Tron*. He serves on the board of directors of the New York Software Industry Association.

Matt Pharr, NVIDIA

Matt Pharr is a member of the technical staff at NVIDIA, where he works on issues related to high-quality interactive graphics, programmable shading, and language features in the Cg group. Previously, he was a co-founder of Exluna, which developed offline rendering software, and was investigating advanced shading algorithms for graphics hardware. He was a Ph.D. student in the Stanford University Graphics Lab, where he researched systems issues for rendering and the theoretical foundations of rendering; he published a series of SIGGRAPH papers on these topics. With Greg Humphreys, he is the author of the book *Physically-Based Rendering: From Theory to Implementation*, which will be published in 2004.

Fabio Policarpo, Paralelo Computação Ltda.

Fabio Policarpo graduated from UFF Federal University in Rio de Janeiro and has written books and applications for classical and real-time computer graphics. Fabio has coauthored the books *The Computer Image*, *3D Games Volume 1*, and *3D Games Volume 2*, with Alan Watt (both published by Addison-Wesley).

Tim Purcell, Stanford University

Tim Purcell is finishing his Ph.D. in computer science at Stanford University. He received a B.S. in computer science from the University of Utah in 1998 and an M.S. in computer science from Stanford University in 2001. He is a recipient of the National Science Foundation Graduate Research Fellowship and is an NVIDIA fellowship winner. His current research interests include stream programming, ray tracing, and leveraging GPUs for general-purpose computation.

Daniel Sánchez-Crespo, Universitat Pompeu Fabra

Daniel Sánchez-Crespo is one of the leading voices in game research in Spain and Europe. His academic career started in 1997, working as a researcher on user interfaces and virtual reality at Universitat Politècnica de Catalunya in Barcelona, Spain. By 2001, he had founded Europe's first master's degree in video game creation, held at Universitat Pompeu Fabra, where he still teaches and serves as the degree's director. He's written three books, most recently *Core Techniques and Algorithms in Game Programming*, published by New Riders/Prentice-Hall. His latest venture is Novarama, a game development studio focused on new forms of entertainment for the masses and recently recognized as Spain's third most innovative company for 2003.

Dean Sekulic, Croteam

With a couple of his best friends, Dean Sekulic founded Croteam in 1993, right after he realized that making computer games could be more fun than just playing them. For the last couple of years, he has specialized in coding sound and vision. He also graduated from Zagreb University of Business Informatics and Computer Design in 1996, and with a little luck, he hopes to stay in computer game programming for the next one or two hundred years.

John Spitzer, NVIDIA

John Spitzer is director of European Developer Technology at NVIDIA, where he oversees development of tools, technology, art, and educational materials for the 3D software development community. John collaborates with game developers on a daily basis, evaluating the technology in their games and assisting in the implementation of advanced visual effects. John has participated in a number of industry standards committees relating to 3D graphics, including the OpenGL Architectural Review Board (ARB), and is a founding member and chair of the SPEC OpenGL Performance Characterization (SPECopc) organization. While serving on SPECopc, John defined, designed, and implemented the industry-standard SPECglperf benchmark. John presents at many developer educational events each year on topics ranging from performance optimization to advanced shading techniques. John holds bachelor's and master's degrees in computer science from Rice University.

Jos Stam, Alias Systems

Jos Stam is a research scientist at Alias Systems. He holds a Ph.D. in computer science from the University of Toronto and is interested in most areas of computer graphics. He is a regular contributor at SIGGRAPH and other conferences. His best research has been in the areas of physics-based animation, rendering, texture mapping, and subdivision surfaces.

Marc Stevens, Softimage

Marc Stevens holds a master's degree in computer science from Brown University and has over 12 years experience in the graphics industry. Marc is currently employed by Softimage/AVID, where he has held various positions over the past nine years in software development. He was one of the principal architects of Softimage|XSI and is now the director of Research and Development and Special Projects for Softimage.

Thilaka S. Sumanaweera, Siemens Medical Solutions USA, Inc.

 Thilaka Sumanaweera has been having fun with first GL and then OpenGL since the late 1980s, creating applications—ranging from 2D to 4D—in computer vision, image processing, and medical imaging. He received his Ph.D. in electrical engineering from Stanford University in 1992 and then joined Radiological Sciences Laboratory at Stanford's Radiology Department as a post-doc and a research associate developing CT/MRI image fusion and image-guided neurosurgery. Currently a fellow at Siemens Medical Solutions USA, Inc., Ultrasound Division, he holds many patents for techniques related to medical imaging and visualization and has published extensively in medical journals.

Kiril Vidimce, Pixar Animation Studios

 Kiril Vidimce is a graphics software engineer in Pixar's Research & Development group and is working on their next-generation renderer. Previously, he was locked down in the Visualization Lab at Mississippi State University working under the guidance of Professor David Banks and producing 3D graphics and publications. Kiril's work has been published at SIGGRAPH, IEEE Visualization, IEEE Computer Graphics & Applications, and Graphics Interfaces. In his spare time and in between paper deadlines, he also managed to complete B.S. degrees in computer science and mathematics and internships at SGI, SRI, and Caltech. Originally from Macedonia's capital and largest city, Skopje, he now resides in San Francisco, California.

PART I
NATURAL EFFECTS

Special effects have differentiated real-time applications throughout the history of consumer-level graphics accelerators, and more important, they have helped immerse users into the virtual settings envisioned by designers. In games and in visualization applications, special effects greatly enhance the user's experience, portraying environments from the surreal to the photorealistic. Good special effects convince users to suspend their disbelief and become absorbed in the story or setting. This part of the book collects numerous practical techniques for creating natural effects that have traditionally been difficult to render properly and robustly.

Water animation and lighting are some of the most difficult tasks in computer graphics, and two chapters are dedicated to water rendering. **Chapter 1, "Effective Water Simulation from Physical Models"** by **Mark Finch** of Cyan Worlds—creators of classic games such as *Myst*—explores animating and lighting water surfaces and provides useful tricks for improving reflections. In **Chapter 2, "Rendering Water Caustics," Daniel Sánchez-Crespo** and I show how to incorporate convincing caustics using a similar basis for water animation.

In **Chapter 3, "Skin in the 'Dawn' Demo," Curtis Beeson** and **Kevin Bjorke** detail the shading techniques used for the fairy in the "Dawn" demo, which was written for the launch of the NVIDIA GeForce FX 5800 GPU. The chapter provides valuable insights into the development process—especially the critical shading decisions influenced by the design goals—when NVIDIA created this cinematic-quality demo that is now synonymous with photorealistic, real-time rendering.

Chapter 4, "Animation in the 'Dawn' Demo," goes on to describe how Dawn was brought to life. **Curtis Beeson** explains how the programmers were able to give the artists control over blend shapes to create a diverse range of expressions. The chapter also discusses the various trade-offs that were made to perform the animation in real time.

The versatility of **Ken Perlin's** Academy Award–winning Noise algorithm has been shown repeatedly in real-time and offline computer graphics, starting from its first use in the film *Tron*. In **Chapter 5, "Implementing Improved Perlin**

Noise," Ken elaborates on recent advancements, as described at SIGGRAPH 2002, which correct two particular defects of Ken's original work. The chapter also provides an efficient and robust framework for an implementation of Noise on modern programmable graphics hardware.

In **Chapter 6, "Fire in the 'Vulcan' Demo," Hubert Nguyen** describes the fire rendering used in the GeForce FX 5900 launch demo, "Vulcan." Though the effect, like most of the others in this part of the book, is not a true physical simulation, it does follow in the steps of offline techniques such as the one used in *The Lord of the Rings*. The realistic and convincing fiery imagery is made possible through some enhancements to overcome the performance limitations when rasterizing mass amounts of particles. Rounding off the focus on the natural elements is **Chapter 7, "Rendering Countless Blades of Waving Grass." Kurt Pelzer** tackles the challenge of depicting vast fields of waving grass using a tried and tested method whose first incarnation was seen in the "Codecreatures" real-time demo. He expands on this technique to enable higher-performance rendering that better suits the needs of a game engine, and he details the content-creation requirements.

Finally, in **Chapter 8, "Simulating Diffraction," Jos Stam** considers submicron-scale detail, such as the grooves on compact discs. The chapter describes a simplification of Jos's diffraction lighting model, first presented at SIGGRAPH 1999. The model has its foundations on the physical properties of light, which when modeled as a wave, can create colorful interference patterns.

Juan Guardado, NVIDIA

Chapter 1

Effective Water Simulation from Physical Models

Mark Finch
Cyan Worlds

This chapter describes a system for simulating and rendering large bodies of water on the GPU. The system combines geometric undulations of a base mesh with generation of a dynamic normal map. The system has proven suitable for real-time game scenarios, having been used extensively in Cyan Worlds' *Uru: Ages Beyond Myst*, as shown in Figure 1-1.

1.1 Goals and Scope

Real-time rendering techniques have been migrating from the offline-rendering world over the last few years. Fast Fourier Transform (FFT) techniques, as outlined in Tessendorf 2001, produce incredible realism for sufficiently large sampling grids, and moderate-size grids may be processed in real time on consumer-level PCs. Voxel-based solutions to simplified forms of the Navier-Stokes equations are also viable (Yann 2003). Although we have not reached the point of cutting-edge, offline fluid simulations, as in Enright et al. 2002, the gap is closing. By the time this chapter is published, FFT libraries will likely be available for vertex and pixel shaders, but as of this writing, even real-time versions of these techniques are limited to implementation on the CPU.

Figure 1-1. Tranquil Pond
A scene from Uru: Ages Beyond Myst

At the same time, water simulation models simple enough to run on the GPU have been evolving upward as well. Isidoro et al. 2002 describes summing four sine waves in a vertex shader to compute surface height and orientation. Laeuchli 2002 presents a shader calculating surface height using three Gerstner waves.

We start with summing simple sine functions, then progress to slightly more complicated functions, as appropriate. We also extend the technique into the realm of pixel shaders, using a sum of periodic wave functions to create a dynamic tiling bump map to capture the finer details of the water surface.

This chapter focuses on explaining the physical significance of the system parameters, showing that approximating a water surface with a sum of sine waves is not as ad hoc as often presented. We pay special attention to the math that takes us from the underlying model to the actual implementation; the math is key to extending the implementation.

This system is designed for bodies of water ranging from a small pond to the ocean as viewed from a cove or island. Although not a rigorous physical simulation, it does deliver convincing, flexible, and dynamic renderings of water. Because the simulation runs entirely on the GPU, it entails no struggle over CPU usage with either artificial intelligence (AI) or physics processes. Because the system parameters do have a physical basis, they are easier to script than if they were found by trial and error. Making the system as a whole dynamic—in addition to its component waves—adds an extra level of life.

1.2 The Sum of Sines Approximation

We run two surface simulations: one for the geometric undulation of the surface mesh, and one for the ripples in the normal map on that mesh. Both simulations are essentially the same. The height of the water surface is represented by the sum of simple periodic waves. We start with summing sine functions and move to more interesting wave shapes as we go.

The *sum of sines* gives a continuous function describing the height and surface orientation of the water at all points. In processing vertices, we sample that function based on the horizontal position of each vertex, conforming the mesh to the limits of its tessellation to the continuous water surface. Below the resolution of the geometry, we continue the technique into texture space. We generate a normal map for the surface by sampling the normals of a sum of sines approximation through simple pixel shader operations in rendering to a render target texture. Rendering our normal map for each frame allows our limited set of sine waves to move independently, greatly enhancing the realism of the rendering.

In fact, the fine waves in our water texture dominate the realism of our simulation. The geometric undulations of our wave surface provide a subtler framework on which to present that texture. As such, we have different criteria for selecting geometric versus texture waves.

1.2.1 Selecting the Waves

We need a set of parameters to define each wave. As shown in Figure 1-2, the parameters are:

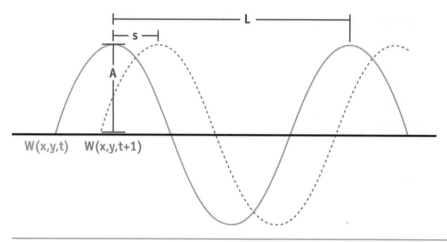

Figure 1-2. The Parameters of a Single Wave Function

- Wavelength (L): the crest-to-crest distance between waves in world space. Wavelength L relates to frequency w as $w = 2\pi/L$.

- Amplitude (A): the height from the water plane to the wave crest.

- Speed (S): the distance the crest moves forward per second. It is convenient to express speed as phase-constant φ, where $\varphi = S \times 2\pi/L$.

- Direction (D): the horizontal vector perpendicular to the wave front along which the crest travels.

Then the state of each wave as a function of horizontal position (x, y) and time (t) is defined as:

$$W_i\left(x, y, t\right) = A_i \times \sin\left(\mathbf{D}_i \cdot \left(x, y\right) \times w_i + t \times \varphi_i\right). \tag{1}$$

And the total surface is:

$$H\left(x, y, t\right) = \sum\left(A_i \times \sin\left(\mathbf{D}_i \cdot \left(x, y\right) \times w_i + t \times \varphi_i\right)\right), \tag{2}$$

over all waves i.

To provide variation in the dynamics of the scene, we will randomly generate these wave parameters within constraints. Over time, we will continuously fade one wave out and then fade it back in with a different set of parameters. As it turns out, these parameters are interdependent. Care must be taken to generate an entire set of parameters for each wave that combine in a convincing manner.

1.2.2 Normals and Tangents

Because we have an explicit function for our surface, we can calculate the surface orientation at any given point directly, rather than depend on finite-differencing techniques. Our binormal **B** and tangent **T** vectors are the partial derivatives in the x and y directions, respectively. For any (x, y) in the 2D horizontal plane, the 3D position **P** on the surface is:

$$\mathbf{P}\left(x, y, t\right) = \left(x, y, H\left(x, y, t\right)\right). \tag{3}$$

The partial derivative in the x direction is then:

$$\mathbf{B}\left(x, y\right) = \left(\frac{\partial x}{\partial x}, \frac{\partial y}{\partial x}, \frac{\partial}{\partial x}\left(H\left(x, y, t\right)\right)\right) \tag{4a}$$

$$\mathbf{B}\left(x, y\right) = \left(1, 0, \frac{\partial}{\partial x}\left(H\left(x, y, t\right)\right)\right). \tag{4b}$$

Similarly, the tangent vector is:

$$\mathbf{T}\left(x, y\right) = \left(\frac{\partial x}{\partial y}, \frac{\partial y}{\partial y}, \frac{\partial}{\partial y}\left(H\left(x, y, t\right)\right)\right) \tag{5a}$$

$$\mathbf{T}\left(x, y\right) = \left(0, 1, \frac{\partial}{\partial y}\left(H\left(x, y, t\right)\right)\right). \tag{5b}$$

The normal is given by the cross product of the binormal and tangent, as:

$$\mathbf{N}\left(x, y\right) = \mathbf{B}\left(x, y\right) \times \mathbf{T}\left(x, y\right) \tag{6a}$$

$$\mathbf{N}\left(x, y\right) = \left(-\frac{\partial}{\partial x}\left(H\left(x, y, t\right)\right), \ -\frac{\partial}{\partial y}\left(H\left(x, y, t\right)\right), 1\right). \tag{6b}$$

Before putting in the partials of our function H, note how convenient the formulas in Equations 3–6 happen to be. The evaluation of two partial derivatives has given us the nine components of the tangent-space basis. This is a direct consequence of our using a height field to approximate our surface. That is, $\mathbf{P}(x, y).x = x$ and $\mathbf{P}(x, y).y = y$, which become the zeros and ones in the partial derivatives. It is only valid for such a height field, but is general for any function $H(x, y, t)$ we choose.

For the height function described in Section 1.2.1, the partial derivatives are particularly convenient to compute. Because the derivative of a sum is the sum of the derivatives:

$$\frac{\partial}{\partial x}\big(H(x,y,t)\big) = \sum\left[\frac{\partial}{\partial x}\big(W_i(x,y,t)\big)\right] \tag{7}$$

$$= \sum\big(w_i \times \mathbf{D}_i.x \times A_i \times \cos\big(\mathbf{D}_i \cdot (x,y) \times w_i + t \times \varphi_i\big)\big),$$

over all waves i.

A common complaint about waves generated by summing sine waves directly is that they have too much "roll," that real waves have sharper peaks and wider troughs. As it turns out, there is a simple variant of the sine function that quite controllably gives this effect. We offset our sine function to be nonnegative and raise it to an exponent k. The function and its partial derivative with respect to x are:

$$W_i(x,y,t) = 2A_i \times \left(\frac{\sin\big(\mathbf{D}_i \cdot (x,y) \times w_i + t \times \varphi_i\big) + 1}{2}\right)^k, \tag{8a}$$

$$\frac{\partial}{\partial x}\big(W_i(x,y,t)\big) = k \times \mathbf{D}_i.x \times w_i \times A_i \times \left(\frac{\sin\big(\mathbf{D}_i \cdot (x,y) \times w_i + t \times \varphi_i\big) + 1}{2}\right)^{k-1}$$

$$\times \cos\big(\mathbf{D}_i \cdot (x,y) \times w_i + t \times \varphi_i\big). \tag{8b}$$

Figure 1-3 shows the wave shapes generated as a function of the power constant k. This is the function we actually use for our texture waves, but for simplicity, we continue to express the waves in terms of our simple sum of sines, and we note where we must account for our change in underlying wave shape.

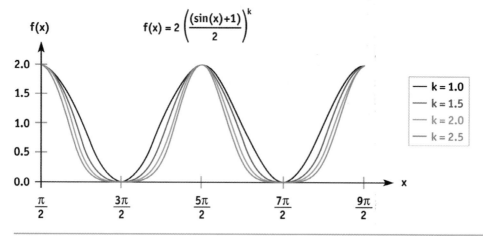

Figure 1-3. Various Wave Shapes
As the exponent k is raised above 1, the peaks sharpen and the valleys flatten.

The Gerstner wave function is:

$$\mathbf{P}(x, y, t) = \begin{pmatrix} x + \sum \left(Q_i A_i \times \mathbf{D}_i.x \times \cos\left(w_i \mathbf{D}_i \cdot (x, y) + \varphi_i t \right) \right), \\ y + \sum \left(Q_i A_i \times \mathbf{D}_i.y \times \cos\left(w_i \mathbf{D}_i \cdot (x, y) + \varphi_i t \right) \right), \\ \sum \left(A_i \sin\left(w_i \mathbf{D}_i \cdot (x, y) + \varphi_i t \right) \right) \end{pmatrix}. \quad (9)$$

Here Q_i is a parameter that controls the steepness of the waves. For a single wave i, Q_i of 0 gives the usual rolling sine wave, and $Q_i = 1/(w_i A_i)$ gives a sharp crest. Larger values of Q_i should be avoided, because they will cause loops to form above the wave crests. In fact, we can leave the specification of Q as a "steepness" parameter for the production artist, allowing a range of 0 to 1, and using $Q_i = Q/(w_i A_i \times numWaves)$ to vary from totally smooth waves to the sharpest waves we can produce.

Note that the only difference between Equations 3 and 9 is the lateral movement of the vertices. The height is the same. This means that we no longer have a strict height function. That is, $\mathbf{P}(x, y, t).x \neq x$. However, the function is still easily differentiable and has some convenient cancellation of terms. Mercifully saving the derivation as an exercise for the reader, we see that the tangent-space basis vectors are:

$$\mathbf{B} = \begin{pmatrix} 1 - \sum \left(Q_i \times \mathbf{D}_i.x^2 \times WA \times S() \right), \\ -\sum \left(Q_i \times \mathbf{D}_i.x \times \mathbf{D}_i.y \times WA \times S() \right), \\ \sum \left(\mathbf{D}_i.x \times WA \times C() \right) \end{pmatrix}, \quad (10)$$

$$\mathbf{T} = \begin{pmatrix} -\sum \left(Q_i \times \mathbf{D}_i.x \times \mathbf{D}_i.y \times WA \times S() \right), \\ 1 - \sum \left(Q_i \times \mathbf{D}_i.y^2 \times WA \times S() \right), \\ \sum \left(\mathbf{D}_i.y \times WA \times C() \right) \end{pmatrix}, \quad (11)$$

$$\mathbf{N} = \begin{pmatrix} -\sum \left(\mathbf{D}_i.x \times WA \times C() \right), \\ -\sum \left(\mathbf{D}_i.y \times WA \times C() \right), \\ 1 - \sum \left(Q_i \times WA \times S() \right) \end{pmatrix}, \quad (12)$$

where:

$WA = w_i \times A_i$,

$S() = \sin\left(w_i \times \mathbf{D}_i \cdot \mathbf{P} + \varphi_i t \right)$, and

$C() = \cos\left(w_i \times \mathbf{D}_i \cdot \mathbf{P} + \varphi_i t \right)$.

These equations aren't as clean as Equations 4b, 5b, and 6b, but they turn out to be quite efficient to compute.

A closer look at the z component of the normal proves interesting in the context of forming loops at wave crests. While Tessendorf (2001) derives his "choppiness" effect from the Navier-Stokes description of fluid dynamics and the "Lie Transform Technique," the end result is a variant of Gerstner waves expressed in the frequency domain. In the frequency domain, looping at wave tops can be avoided and detected, but in the spatial domain, we can see clearly what is going on. When the sum $Q_i \times w_i \times A_i$ is greater than 1, the z component of our normal can go negative at the peaks, as our wave loops over itself. As long as we select our Q_i such that this sum is always less than or equal to 1, we will form sharp peaks but never loops.

Wavelength and Speed

We begin by selecting appropriate wavelengths. Rather than pursue real-world distributions, we would like to maximize the effect of the few waves we can afford. The superpositioning of waves of similar lengths highlights the dynamism of the water surface. So we select a median wavelength and generate random wavelengths between half and double that length. The median wavelength is scripted in the authoring process, and it can vary over time. For example, the waves may be significantly larger during a storm than while the scene is sunny and calm. Note that we cannot change the wavelength of an active wave. Even if it were changed gradually, the crests of the wave would expand away from or contract toward the origin, a very unnatural look. Therefore, we change the current average wavelength, and as waves die out over time, they will be reborn based on the new length. The same is true for direction.

Given a wavelength, we can easily calculate the speed at which it progresses across the surface. The dispersion relation for water (Tessendorf 2001), ignoring higher-order terms, gives:

$$w = \sqrt{g \times \frac{2\pi}{L}},$$

(13)

where w is the frequency and g is the gravitational constant consistent with whatever units we are using (such as 9.8 m/s^2), and L is the crest-to-crest length of the wave.

Amplitude

How to handle the amplitude is a matter of opinion. Although derivations of wave amplitude as a function of wavelength and current weather conditions probably exist, we use a constant (or scripted) ratio, specified at authoring time. More exactly, along with a median wavelength, the artist specifies a median amplitude. For a wave of any size, the ratio of its amplitude to its wavelength will match the ratio of the median amplitude to the median wavelength.

Direction

The direction along which a wave travels is completely independent of the other parameters, so we are free to select a direction for each wave based on any criteria we choose. As mentioned previously, we begin with a constant vector that is roughly the wind direction. We then choose randomly from directions within a constant angle of the wind direction. That constant angle is specified at content-creation time, or it may be scripted.

1.2.4 Texture Waves

The waves we sum into our texture have the same parameterization as their vertex cousins, but with different constraints. First, in the texture it is much more important to capture a broad spectrum of frequencies. Second, patterns are more prone to form in the texture, breaking the natural look of the ripples. Third, only certain wave directions for a given wavelength will preserve tiling of the overall texture. Also, note that all quantities here are in units of texels, rather than world-space distance.

We currently use about 15 waves of varying frequency and orientation, taking from two to four passes. Four passes may sound excessive, but they are into a 256×256 render-target texture, rather than over the main frame buffer. In practice, the hit from the fill rate of generating the normal map is negligible.

Wavelength and Speed

Again, we start by selecting wavelengths. We are limited in the range of wavelengths the texture will hold. Obviously, the sine wave must repeat at least once if the texture is to tile. That sets the maximum wavelength at *TEXSIZE*, where *TEXSIZE* is the dimension of the target texture. The waves will degrade into sawtooth patterns as the wavelength approaches 4 texels, so we limit the minimum wavelength to 4 texels. Also, longer wavelengths are already approximated by the geometric undulation, so we favor shorter wavelengths in our selection. We typically select wavelengths between about 4 and 32 texels. With the bump map tiling every 50 feet, a wavelength of 32 texels corresponds to about 6 feet. This leaves geometric wavelengths ranging upward from about 4 feet, and texture wavelengths ranging downward from about 6 feet, with just a little overlap.

The wave speed calculation is identical to the geometric form. The exponent in Equations 8a and 8b controls the sharpness of the wave crests.

Amplitude and Precision

We determine the amplitude of each wave as we did with geometric waves, keeping amplitude over wavelength a constant ratio, *kAmpOverLen*. This leads to an interesting optimization.

Remember that we are not concerned with the height function here; we are only building a normal map. Our lookup texture contains cos($2\pi u$), where u is the texture coordinate ranging from 0 to 1. We store the raw cosine values in our lookup texture rather than in the normals because it is actually easier to convert the cosine into a rotated normal than to store normals and try to rotate them with the texture.

We evaluate the normal of our sum of sines by rendering our lookup texture into a render target. Expressing Equation 7 in terms of *u-v* space, we have:

$$\frac{\partial}{\partial u} W_i = \mathbf{D}_i.x \times w_i \times A_i \times \cos\left(\mathbf{D}_i \cdot (u, v) + \varphi_i t\right), \qquad (14)$$

where u and v vary from 0 to 1 over the render target. We calculate the inner term, $\mathbf{D}_i \cdot (u, v) + \varphi_i t$, in the vertex shader, passing the result as the u coordinate for the texture lookup in the pixel shader. The outer terms, $\mathbf{D}_i.x \times w_i \times A_i$ and $\mathbf{D}_i.y \times w_i \times A_i$, are passed in as constants. The resulting pixel shader is then a constant times a texture lookup per wave. We note that to use the sharper-crested wave function in Equation 8a, we simply fill in our lookup table with:

$$\left(\frac{\sin(2\pi u) + 1}{2}\right)^{k-1} \times \cos(2\pi u),$$

instead of cos($2\pi u$), and pass in $\mathbf{D}_i \times w_i \times A_i \times k$ as the outer term.

Using a lookup table here currently provides both speed and flexibility. But just as the relative rates of increase in processor speed versus memory access time have pushed lookup tables on the CPU side out of favor, we can expect the same evolution on the GPU. Looking forward, we expect to be much more discriminating about when we choose a lookup texture over direct arithmetic calculation. In particular, by using a lookup table here, we must regenerate the lookup table to change the sharpness of the waves.

Unlike our approach to the composition of geometric normals in the vertex shader, in creating texture waves we are very concerned with precision. Each component of the output normal must be represented as a biased, signed, fixed-point value with 8 bits of precision. If the surface gets very steep, the x or y component will be larger than the z component and will saturate at 1. If the surface is always shallow, the x and y components will always be close to 0 and suffer quantization errors. In this work, we expect the latter case. If we can establish tight bounds on values for the x and y components, we can scale the normals in the texture to maximize the available precision, and then "un-scale" them when we use them.

Examining the x component of the generated normal, we first see that both the cosine function and the x component of the direction vector range over the interval $[-1..1]$. The product of the frequency and the amplitude is problematic, because the frequency and amplitude are different for each wave.

Expressing Equation 7 with the frequency in terms of wavelength, we have:

$$\frac{\partial}{\partial x} W_i = 2\pi \times \frac{A_i}{L_i} \times \mathbf{D}_i.x \times \cos(\dots).$$

Whereas the height is dominated by waves of greater amplitude, the surface orientation is dominated by waves with greater ratios of amplitude to wavelength.

We first use this result to justify having a constant ratio of amplitude to wavelength across all our waves, reasoning that because we have a very limited number of waves, we choose to omit those of smaller ratios. Second, because of that constant ratio, we know that the x and y components of our waves are limited to having absolute values less than $kAmpOverLen \times 2\pi$, and the total is limited to $numWaves \times kAmpOverLen \times 2\pi$. So to preserve resolution during summation, we accumulate:

$$\frac{1}{numWaves} \times \mathbf{D}_i.x \times \cos(\dots)$$

and scale by $numWaves \times 2\pi \times kAmpOverLen$ when we use them.

Direction and Tiling

If the render target has enough resolution to be used without tiling, we can accumulate arbitrary sine functions into it. In fact, we can accumulate arbitrary normal maps into it. For example, we might overlay a turbulent distortion following the movements of a character within the scene. Alternately, we might begin with a more complex function than a single sine wave, getting more wave complexity with the accumulation of fewer "wave" functions. Keep in mind that the power of this technique is in the relative motion of the waves. A complex wave pattern moving as a unit has less realism and impact than simpler waves moving independently.

These additions are relatively straightforward. Getting the render target to tile, however, imposes some constraints on the wave functions we accumulate. In particular, note that a major appeal of circular waves is that they form no repeating patterns. If we want our texture to tile, we need our waves to form repeating patterns, so we limit ourselves to directional waves.

Obviously, a tiling of a texture will tile itself only if the texture is repeated an integer number of times. Also, for a sine wave of given wavelength that tiles, only certain rotations of the texture will still tile. Less obvious, but equally true, is that if each of the rotated sine functions we add in will tile, then the sum of those sine functions also tiles.

Because we rotate and scale the sine functions through the texture transform, we can ensure that both conditions for tiling are met by making certain that the scaled rotation elements of the texture transform are integers. We then translate the wave by adding a phase component into the transform's translation. Note that because the texture is really 1D, we need concern ourselves only with the transformed u coordinate.

1.3 Authoring

We briefly discuss in this section how the water system is placed and modeled offline. Through the modeling of the water mesh, the content author controls the simulation down to the level of the vertex. See Figure 1-6.

In our implementation, the mesh data is limited to the tessellation of the mesh, the horizontal positions of each vertex in the mesh, the vertical position of the *bottom* of the body of water below the vertex, and an RGBA color. Texture coordinates may be explicitly specified or generated on the fly. See Figure 1-7.

First, we discuss using the depth of the water at a vertex as an input parameter, from which the shader can automatically modify its behavior in the delicate areas where water meets shore. We also cover some vertex-level system overrides that have proven particularly useful. To prevent aliasing artifacts, we automatically filter out waves for which the sampling frequency of the mesh is insufficient. Finally, we comment on the

Figure 1-6. Ocean and Pond Water
(a) Ocean water scene and (c) pond water scene, with the normal maps (b) and (d) used for the rendering of each water surface.

additional input data necessary when the texture mapping is explicitly specified at content-creation time, rather than implicitly based on a planar mapping over position.

1.3.1 Using Depth

Because the height of the water will be computed, the z component of the vertex position might go unused. We could take advantage of this to compress our vertices, but we choose rather to encode the water depth in the z component instead. More precisely, we put the height of the bottom of the water body in the vertex z component, pass in the height of the water table as a constant, and have the depth of the water available with a subtraction. Again, this assumes a constant-height water table. To model something like a river flowing downhill, we need an explicit 3D position as well as a depth

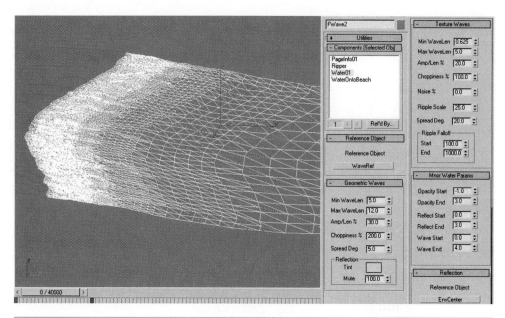

Figure 1-7. The User Interface of the 3ds max Authoring Tool
This screen shot shows many of the parameters available to the production artist. Note also that the water mesh is more highly tessellated near the shore, and that it conforms to the bottom of the ocean, rather than the surface.

for each vertex. In such a case, the depth may be calculated offline using a simple ray cast from water surface to riverbed, or it can be explicitly authored as a vertex color, but in any case, the depth must be passed in as an additional part of the vertex data.

We use the water depth to control the opacity of the water, the strength of the reflection, and the amplitude of the geometric waves. For example, one pair of input parameter for the system is a depth at which the water is transparent and a depth at which it is at maximum opacity. This might let the water go from transparent to maximum opacity as the depth goes from 0 at the shore to 3 feet deep. This is a very crude modeling of the fact that shallow water tints the bottom less than deep water does. Having the depth of the water available also allows for more sophisticated modeling of light transmission effects.

Attenuating the amplitude of the geometric waves based on depth is as much a matter of practicality as physical modeling. Attenuating out the waves where the water mesh meets the water plane allows for water vertices to be "fixed" where the mesh meets steep banks. It also gives a gradual die-off of waves coming onto a shallow shore. Because we constrain our vertices never to go below their input height, attenuating the waves to zero slightly above the water plane allows waves to lap up onto the shore, while enabling us to control how far up the shore they can go.

1.3.2 Overrides

For the most part, the system "just works," processing all vertices identically. But there are valid occasions for the content author to override the system behavior on a per-vertex basis. We encode these overrides as the RGB vertex color. Left at their defaults of white, these overrides pass all control to the simulation. Bringing down a channel to zero modulates an effect.

The red component governs the overall transparency, making the water surface completely transparent when red goes to zero. Green modulates the strength of the reflection on the surface, making the water surface matte when green is zero. Blue limits the opacity attenuation based on viewing angle, which affects the Fresnel term. An alternate use of one of these colors would be to scale the horizontal components of the calculated per-pixel normal. This would allow some areas of the water to be rougher than others, an effect often seen in bays.

1.3.3 Edge-Length Filtering

If you are already familiar with signal-processing theory, then you readily appreciate that the shortest wavelength we can use to undulate our mesh depends on how finely tessellated the mesh is. From the Nyquist theorem, we need our vertices to be separated by at most half the shortest wavelength we are using. If that doesn't seem obvious, refer to Figure 1-8, which gives an intuitive, if nonrigorous, explanation of the concept. As long as the edges of the triangles in the mesh are short compared to the wavelengths in our height function, the surface will look good. When the edge lengths get as long as, or longer than, half the shortest wavelengths in our function, we see objectionable artifacts.

One reasonable and common approach is to decide in advance what the shortest wavelength in our height function will be and then tessellate the mesh so that all edges are somewhat shorter than that wavelength. In this work we take another approach: We look at the edge lengths in the neighborhood of a vertex and then filter out waves that are "too short" to be represented well in that neighborhood.

This technique has two immediate benefits. First, any wavelengths can be fed into the vertex processing unit without undesirable artifacts, regardless of the tessellation of the mesh. This allows the simulation to generate wavelengths solely based on the current

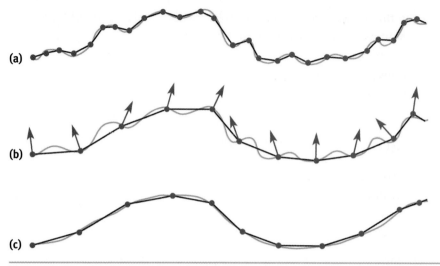

Figure 1-8. Matching Wave Frequencies to Tessellation
(a) A highly tessellated mesh adequately representing a mix of high- and low-frequency waves. (b) The same waves, poorly represented by a lower tessellation. Note especially that while the surface itself is okay, the normals generated from this undersampling are horrible. (c) The low-tessellation mesh doing a good job again, after we filtered out the high-frequency wave, leaving the low-frequency wave intact.

weather conditions. Any wavelengths too small to undulate the mesh are filtered out with an attenuation value that goes from 1 when the wavelength is 4 times the edge length, to 0 when the wavelength is twice the edge length. Second, the mesh need not be uniformly tessellated. More triangles may be devoted to areas of interest. Those areas of less importance, with fewer triangles and longer edges, will be flatter, but they will have no objectionable artifacts. An example would be modeling a cove heavily tessellated near the shore, using larger and larger triangles as the water extends out to the horizon.

1.3.4 Texture Coordinates

Usually, texture coordinates need not be specified. They are easily derived from the vertex position, based on a scale value that specifies the world-space distance that a single tile of the normal map covers.

In some cases, however, explicit texture coordinates can be useful. One example is having the water flow along a winding river. In this case, the explicit texture coordinates must be augmented with tangent-space vectors, to transform the bump-map normals from the space of the texture as it twists through bends into world space. These values are automatically calculated offline from the partial derivatives of the position with respect to texture coordinate, as is standard with bump maps. The section "Per-Pixel Lighting" in Engel 2002 gives a practical description of generating tangent-space basis vectors using DirectX.

1.4 Runtime Processing

Let's consider the processing in the vertex and pixel shaders here at a high level. Refer to the accompanying source code for specifics. With the explanations from the previous sections behind us, the processing is fairly straightforward. Only one subtle issue remains unexplored.

Having a dynamic, undulating geometric surface, and a complex normal map of interacting waves, we need only to generate appropriate bump-environment mapping parameters to tie the two together. Those parameters are the transform to take our normals from texture space to world space, and an eye vector to reflect off our surface into our cubic environment map. We derive those first and then walk through the vertex and pixel processing.

1.4.1 Bump-Environment Mapping Parameters

Tangent-Space Basis Vectors

We can compute space basis vectors from the partial derivatives of our water surface function. Equations 10, 11, and 12 give us the binormal $\mathbf{B}$, the tangent $\mathbf{T}$, and the normal $\mathbf{N}$.

We stack those values into three vectors (that is, output texture coordinates) to be used as a row-major matrix, so our matrix will be:

$$Surf2World = \begin{pmatrix} \mathbf{B}_x & \mathbf{T}_x & \mathbf{N}_x \\ \mathbf{B}_y & \mathbf{T}_y & \mathbf{N}_y \\ \mathbf{B}_z & \mathbf{T}_z & \mathbf{N}_z \end{pmatrix}.$$

Except for where we got the basis vectors, this is the usual transform for bump mapping. It accounts for our surface being wavy, not flat, transforming from the undulating surface space into world space. If the texture coordinates for our normal map are implicit—that is, derived from the vertex position—then we can assume that there is no rotation between texture space and world space, and we are done. If we have explicit texture coordinates, however, we must take into account the rotations as the texture twists along the river.

Having computed $\partial P/\partial u$ and $\partial P/\partial v$ offline, we use these to form a rotation matrix to transform our texture-space normals into surface-space normals.

$$Tex2Surf = \begin{pmatrix} \partial P/\partial u.x & \partial P/\partial v.x & 0 \\ \partial P/\partial u.y & \partial P/\partial v.y & 0 \\ 0 & 0 & 1 \end{pmatrix}$$

This is clearly a rotation in the horizontal plane, which we expect because we collapsed the water mesh to $z = 0$ before computing the gradients. In the more general case where the base surface is not flat, this would be a full 3×3 matrix. In either case, order is important, so our concatenated matrix is $Surf2World \times Tex2Surf$.

If we want to rescale the x and y components of our normals, we must take one final step. We might want to rescale the components because we had scaled them to maximize precision when we wrote them to the normal map. Or we might want to rescale them based on their distance from the camera, to counter aliasing. In either case, we want the scale to be applied to the x and y components of the raw normal values, before either of the preceding transforms. Then, assuming a uniform scale factor s, our scale matrix and final transform are:

$$Rescale = \begin{pmatrix} s & 0 & 0 \\ 0 & s & 0 \\ 0 & 0 & 1 \end{pmatrix},$$

$$FinalMatrix = Surf2World \times Tex2Surf \times Rescale.$$

Eye Vector

We typically use the eye-space position of the vertex as the eye vector on which we base our lookup into the environment map. This effectively treats the scene in the environment map as infinitely far away.

If all that is reflected in the water is more or less infinitely far away—for example, a sky dome—then this approximation is perfect. For smaller bodies of water, however, where the reflections show the objects on the opposite shore, we would like something better.

Rather than at an infinite distance, we would like to assume the reflected features are at a uniform distance from the center of our pool. That is, we will project the environment map onto a sphere of the same radius as our pool, centered about our pool. Brennan 2002 describes a very clever and efficient approximation for this. We offer an alternate approach.

Figure 1-9 gives an intuitive feel for the problem as well as the solution. Given an environment map generated from point **C**, the camera is now at point **E** looking at a vertex at point **P**. We would like our eye vector to pass from **E** through **P** and see the object at **A** in the environment map. But the eye vector is actually relative to the point from which the environment map was generated, so we would sample the environment map at point **B**.

We would like to calculate an eye vector that will take us from **C** to **A**. We can find **A** as the point where our original eye vector intersects the sphere, and then our corrected eye vector is **A** − **C**. Because **A** is on the sphere of radius r, and $\mathbf{A} = \mathbf{E} + (\mathbf{P} - \mathbf{E})t$, we have:

$$r^2 = \left| \mathbf{A} - \mathbf{C} \right|^2$$

$$r^2 = \left| \mathbf{E} + (\mathbf{P} - \mathbf{E})t - \mathbf{C} \right|^2$$

$$r^2 = \left| (\mathbf{P} - \mathbf{E})t - (\mathbf{E} - \mathbf{C}) \right|^2 .$$

This expands out to:

$$0 = (\mathbf{P} - \mathbf{E})^2 \cdot t^2 - 2(\mathbf{P} - \mathbf{E})(\mathbf{E} - \mathbf{C}) \cdot t + (\mathbf{E} - \mathbf{C})^2 - r^2 .$$

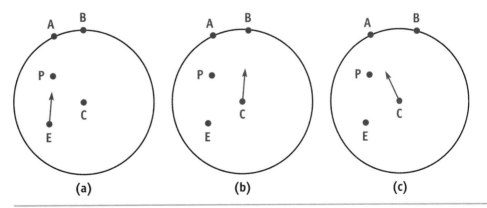

Figure 1-9. Correction of the Eye Vector
(a) A natural eye vector. (b) The result of using a natural eye vector. (c) The corrected eye vector.

We solve for t using the quadratic equation, giving:

$$t = \frac{2\,(\mathbf{P} - \mathbf{E})(\mathbf{E} - \mathbf{C}) \pm \sqrt{\left(4\left((\mathbf{P} - \mathbf{E}) \cdot (\mathbf{E} - \mathbf{C})\right)^2 - 4\,(\mathbf{P} - \mathbf{E})^2\left((\mathbf{E} - \mathbf{C})^2 - r^2\right)\right)}}{2\,(\mathbf{P} - \mathbf{E})^2}.$$

Here we make some substitutions:

$$\mathbf{D} = \frac{(\mathbf{P} - \mathbf{E})}{|\mathbf{P} - \mathbf{E}|} \qquad \textit{Original eye vector, normalized}$$

$$\mathbf{F} = (\mathbf{E} - \mathbf{C}) \qquad \textit{Vector from camera position to environment map center}$$

$$\mathbf{G} = \mathbf{F}^2 - r^2 \qquad \textit{Convenient collection of constants}$$

Substituting in and discarding the lesser root gives us:

$$t = \frac{2\mathbf{D} \cdot \mathbf{F} + \sqrt{4\,(\mathbf{D} \cdot \mathbf{F})^2 - 4\mathbf{D}^2 \cdot \mathbf{G}}}{2\mathbf{D}^2}.$$

Canceling our 2s and recognizing that $\mathbf{D}^2 = 1$ (it's normalized), gives us:

$$t = \mathbf{D} \cdot \mathbf{F} + \sqrt{(\mathbf{D} \cdot \mathbf{F})^2 - \mathbf{G}}$$

and

$$\mathbf{A} - \mathbf{C} = \mathbf{E} + \left(\mathbf{D} \cdot \mathbf{F} + \sqrt{(\mathbf{D} \cdot \mathbf{F})^2 - \mathbf{G}}\right) \times \mathbf{D}.$$

We already have $\mathbf{D}$, the normalized eye vector, because we use it for attenuating the water opacity based on viewing angle. $\mathbf{F}$ and $\mathbf{G}$ are constants. So calculating t and our corrected eye vector, although it started out ugly, requires only five arithmetic operations. This underlines a powerful point made in Fernando and Kilgard 2003, namely, that collapsing values that are constant over a mesh into shader constants can bring about dramatic and surprising optimizations within the shader code.

Because we have essentially intersected a ray with a sphere, this method will obviously fail if that ray does not intersect the sphere. This possibility doesn't especially concern us, however. There will always be a real root if either the eye position or the vertex position lies within the sphere, and since the sphere encompasses the scenery *around* the body of water, it is safe to constrain the water vertices to lie within the sphere.

Note that where the surroundings reflected off a body of water are not well approximated by a mapping onto a sphere, or where the surroundings are too dynamic to be captured by a static environment map, a projective method such as the one described in Vlachos et al. 2002 might be preferable.

1.4.2 Vertex and Pixel Processing

We begin by evaluating the sine and cosine functions for each of our four geometric waves.

Before summing them, we subtract our input vertex Z from our water-table height constant to get the depth of the water at this vertex. That depth forms our first wave-height attenuation factor by some form of interpolation between input constant depths.

Because we have stored the minimum edge length in the neighborhood of this vertex, we now use that to attenuate the heights of the waves independently, based on wave-length. That attenuation will filter out waves as the edge length gets as long as a fraction of the wavelength.

Explicit texture coordinates are passed through as is. Implicit coordinates are simply a scaling of the x and y positions of the vertex. The transformation from texture space to world space is calculated as described in Section 1.4.1. The scale value used is the input constant $numWaves \times 2\pi \times kAmpOverLen$, as described in the "Amplitude and Precision" subsection of Section 1.2.4. The scale value is modulated by another scale factor that goes to zero with increasing distance from the vertex to the eye. This causes the normal to collapse to the geometric surface normal in the distance, where the normal map texels are much smaller than pixels. The eye vector is computed as the final piece needed for bump environment mapping.

We emit two colors per vertex. The first is the color of the water proper. The second will tint the reflections off the water. The opacity of the water proper is modulated first as a function of depth, generally getting more transparent in shallows. Then it is modulated based on the viewing angle, so that the water is more transparent when viewed straight on than when viewed at a glancing angle. A per-pixel Fresnel term, as well as other more sophisticated effects, could be calculated by passing the view vector into the pixel shader, rather than computing the attenuation at the vertex level. The reflection color is also modulated based on depth and viewing angle, but independently to provide separate controls for when and how transparent the reflection gets.

In the pixel processing stage, there is little left to do. A simple bump lookup into an environment map gives the reflection color. We currently look up into a cubic environment map, but the projected planar environment maps described in Vlachos et al. 2002 would be preferable in many situations. The reflected color is modulated and added to the color of the water proper. The pixel is emitted and alpha-blended to the frame buffer.

1.5 Conclusion

Water simulation makes an interesting topic in the context of vertex and pixel shaders, partly because it leverages such distinct techniques into a cohesive system. The work described here combines enhanced bump environment mapping with the evaluation of complex functions in both vertex and pixel shaders. We hope this chapter will prove useful in two ways: First, by detailing the physics and math behind what is frequently thought of as an ad hoc system, we hope we have shown how the system itself becomes more extensible. More and better wave functions on the geometric as well as the texture side could considerably improve the system, but only with an understanding of how the original waves were used. Second, the system as described generates a robust, dynamic, controllable, and realistic water surface with minimal resources. The system requires only vs.1.0 and ps.1.0 support. On current and future hardware, that leaves a lot of resources to carry forward with more sophisticated effects in areas such as light transport and reaction to other objects.

1.6 References

Jeff Landers has a good bibliography of water techniques on the Darwin 3D Web site:
http://www.darwin3d.com/vsearch/FluidSim.txt

And another good one, on the Virtual Terrain Project Web site:
http://www.vterrain.org/Water/index.html

Brennan, Chris. 2002. "Accurate Reflections and Refractions by Adjusting for Object Distance." In *ShaderX*, edited by Wolfgang Engel. Wordware. **http://www.shaderx.com**

Engel, Wolfgang. 2002. "Programming Pixel Shaders." In *ShaderX*, edited by Wolfgang Engel. Wordware. **http://www.shaderx.com**

Enright, Douglas, Stephen Marschner, and Ronald Fedkiw. 2002. "Animation and Rendering of Complex Water Surfaces." In *Proceedings of SIGGRAPH 2002*. Available online at **http://graphics.stanford.edu/papers/water-sg02/water.pdf**

Fernando, Randima, and Mark J. Kilgard. 2003. *The Cg Tutorial*. Addison-Wesley.

Isidoro, John, Alex Vlachos, and Chris Brennan 2002. "Rendering Ocean Water." In *ShaderX*, edited by Wolfgang Engel. Wordware. **http://www.shaderx.com**

Laeuchli, Jesse. 2002. "Simple Gerstner Wave Cg Shader." Online article. Available online at **http://www.cgshaders.org/shaders/show.php?id=46**

Tessendorf, Jerry. 2001. "Simulating Ocean Water." In *Proceedings of SIGGRAPH 2001*. Course slides available online at **http://online.cs.nps.navy.mil/DistanceEducation/online.siggraph.org/2001/Courses/47_SimulatingNature/Presentation07.html**

Vlachos, Alex, John Isidoro, and Chris Oat. 2002. "Rippling Reflective and Refractive Water." In *ShaderX*, edited by Wolfgang Engel. Wordware. **http://www.shaderx.com**

Yann, L. 2003. "Realistic Water Rendering." E-lecture. Available online at **http://www.andyc.org/lecture/viewlog.php?log=Realistic%20Water%20Rendering,%20by%20Yann%20L**

Chapter 2

Rendering Water Caustics

Juan Guardado
NVIDIA

Daniel Sánchez-Crespo
Universitat Pompeu Fabra/Novarama Technology

2.1 Introduction

There is something hypnotic about the way water interacts with light: the subtle reflections and refractions, the way light bends to form dancing caustics on the bottom of the sea, and the infinitely varied look of the ocean surface. See Figure 2-1. These phenomena and their complexity have attracted many researchers from the fields of physics and, in recent years, computer graphics. Simulating and rendering realistic water is, like simulating fire, a fascinating task. It is not easy to achieve good results at interactive frame rates, and thus creative approaches must often be taken.

Caustics result from light rays reflecting or refracting from a curved surface and hence focusing only in certain areas of the receiving surface. This chapter explains an aesthetics-driven method for rendering underwater caustics in real time. Our purely aesthetics-driven approach simply leaves realism out of consideration. The result is a scene that looks good, but may not correctly simulate the physics of the setting. As we show in this chapter, the results of our approach look remarkably realistic, and the method can be implemented easily on most graphics hardware. This simplified approach has proven very successful in many fractal-related disciplines, such as mountain and cloud rendering or tree modeling.

The purpose of this chapter is to expose a new technique for rendering real-time caustics, describing the method from its physical foundations to its implementation details.

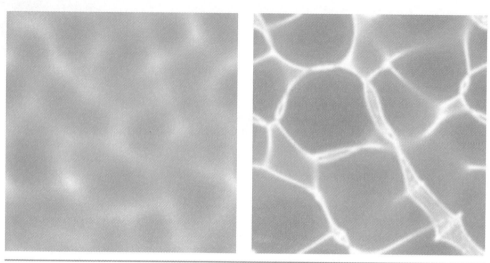

Figure 2-1. Examples of Water Caustics
Courtesy of Jos Stam

Because the technique is procedural, it yields elegantly to an implementation using a high-level shading language.

2.2 Computing Caustics

Computing underwater caustics accurately is a complex process: millions of individual photons are involved, with many interactions taking place. To simulate it properly, we must begin by shooting photons from the light source (for example, for a sea scene, the Sun). A fraction of these photons eventually collide with the ocean surface, which either reflects or refracts them. Let's forget about reflection for a moment and see how transmitted photons are refracted according to Snell's Law, which states that:

$$\eta_1 \sin \theta_1 = \eta_2 \sin \theta_2,$$

otherwise written as:

$$IOR = \frac{\eta_1}{\eta_2} = \frac{\sin \theta_2}{\sin \theta_1}.$$

In the preceding equations, η_1 and η_2 are the indices of refraction for the respective materials, and θ_1 and θ_2 are the incident and refraction angles, as shown in Figure 2-2. The index of refraction, IOR, can then simply be written as the ratio of the sines of the angles of the incident and refracted rays.

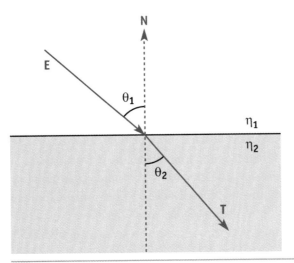

Figure 2-2. Computing Refraction
The incident ray (E) is bent to produce the transmitted ray (T) because of refraction from medium η_1 to medium η_2.

Snell's Law is not easy to code with this formulation, because it only imposes one restriction, making the computation of the refracted ray nontrivial. Assuming that the incident, transmitted, and surface normal rays are co-planar, a variety of coder-friendly formulas can be used, such as the one in Foley et al. 1996:

$$T = N\left[\frac{\eta_1}{\eta_2}(E \cdot N) \pm \sqrt{1 + \left(\frac{\eta_1}{\eta_2}\right)^2 \left((E \cdot N)^2 - 1\right)}\right] + \frac{\eta_1}{\eta_2}E.$$

Here T is the transmitted ray, N is the surface normal, E is the incident ray, and η_1, η_2 are the indices of refraction.

Once bent, photons advance through the water, their intensity attenuating as they get deeper. Eventually, some of these photons will strike the ocean floor, lighting it. Due to the ocean surface's waviness, photons entering the water from different paths can end up lighting the same area of the ocean floor. Whenever this happens, we see a bright spot created by the concentration of light in a caustic, similar to the way a lens focuses light.

From a simulation standpoint, caustics are usually computed by either forward or backward ray tracing. In forward ray tracing, photons are sent from light sources and followed through the scene, accumulating their contribution over discrete areas of the ground. The problem with this approach is that many photons do not even collide with the ocean surface, and from those that actually collide with it, very few actually contribute to caustic formation. Thus, it is a brute-force method, even with some speed-ups thanks to spatial subdivision.

Backward ray tracing works in the opposite direction. It begins at the ocean floor and traces rays backward in reverse chronological order, trying to compute the sum of all incoming lighting for a given point. Ideally, this would be achieved by solving the hemispherical integral of all light coming from above the point being lit. Still, for practical reasons, the result of the integral is resolved via Monte Carlo sampling. Thus, a beam of candidate rays is sent in all directions over the hemisphere, centered at the sampling point. Those that hit other objects (such as a whale, a ship, or a stone) are discarded. On the other hand, rays that hit the ocean surface definitely came from the outside, making them good candidates. Thus, they must be refracted, using the inverse of Snell's Law. These remaining rays must be propagated in the air, to test whether each hypothetical ray actually emanated from a light source or was simply a false hypothesis. Again, only those rays that actually end up hitting a light source do contribute to the caustic, and the rest of the rays are just discarded as false hypotheses.

Both approaches are thus very costly: only a tiny portion of the computation time actually contributes to the end result. In commercial caustic processors, it is common to see ratios of useful rays versus total rays of between 1 and 5 percent.

Real-time caustics were first explored by Jos Stam (Stam 1996). Stam's approach involved computing an animated caustic texture using wave theory, so it could be used to light the ground floor. This texture was additively blended with the object's base textures, giving a nice, convincing look, as shown in Figure 2-3.

Another interesting approach was explored by Lasse Staff Jensen and Robert Golias in their excellent Gamasutra paper (Jensen and Golias 2001). The paper covers not only caustics, but also a complete water animation and rendering framework. The platform is based upon Fast Fourier Transforms (FFTs) for wave function modeling. On top of that, their method handles reflection, refraction, and caustics in an attempt to reach physically accurate models for each one. It is unsurprising, then, that Jensen and Golias's approach to caustics tries to model the actual process: Rays are traced from the Sun to each vertex in the wave mesh. Those rays are refracted using Snell's Law, and thus new rays are created.

Figure 2-3. Caustics Created Using Jos Stam's Projective Caustic Texture

2.3 Our Approach

The algorithm we use to simulate underwater caustics is just a simplification of the backward Monte Carlo ray tracing idea explained in the previous section. We make some aggressive assumptions about good candidates for caustics, and we compute only a subset of the arriving rays. Thus, the method has very low computational cost, and it produces something that, although "incorrect" physically, very closely resembles a real caustic's look and behavior. The overall effect looks very convincing, and the superior image quality given by the caustics makes it worthwhile to implement.

To begin with, we assume that we are computing caustics at noon on the Equator. This implies that the Sun is directly above us. For the sake of our algorithm, we need to compute the angle of the sky covered by the Sun disk. The Sun is between 147 and 152 million kilometers away from Earth, depending on the time of year, and its diameter is 1.42 million kilometers, which yields an angle for the Sun disk of 0.53 degrees, as shown in Figure 2-4.

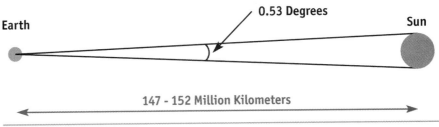

Figure 2-4. The Angle of the Sun Disk

The second assumption we make is that the ocean floor is lit by rays emanating vertically above the point of interest. The transparency of water is between 77 and 80 percent per linear meter, thus between 20 and 23 percent of incident light per meter is absorbed by the medium, which is spent heating it up. Logically, this means that caustics will be formed easily when light rays travel the shortest distance from the moment they enter the water to the moment they hit the ocean floor. Thus, caustics will be maximal for vertical rays and will not be as visible for rays entering water sideways. This is an aggressive assumption, but it is key to the success of the algorithm.

Our algorithm then works as follows. We start at the bottom of the sea, right after we have painted the ground plane. Then, a second, additive blended pass is used to render the caustic on top of that. To do so, we create a mesh with the same granularity as the wave mesh and which will be colored per-vertex with the caustic value: 0 means no lighting; 1 means a beam of very focused light hit the sea bottom. To construct this lighting, backward ray tracing is used: for each vertex of our mesh, we project it vertically until we reach the wave point located directly above it. Then, we compute the normal of the wave at that point, using finite differences. With the vector and the normal, and using Snell's Law (the index of refraction for water is 1.33), we can create secondary rays, which travel from the wave into the air. These rays are potential candidates for bringing illumination onto the ocean floor. To test them, we compute the angle between each one and the vertical. Because the Sun disk is very far away, we can simply use this angle as a measure of illumination: the closer to the vertical, the more light that comes from that direction into the ocean, as illustrated in Figure 2-5.

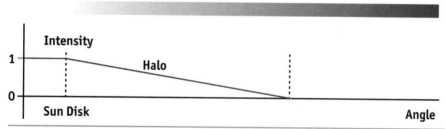

Figure 2-5. The Intensity of the Sun Disk Versus the Angle of Incidence

2.4 Implementation Using OpenGL

The initial implementation of the algorithm is just plain OpenGL code, with the only exception being the use of multipass texturing. A first pass renders the ocean floor as a regular textured quad. Then, the same floor is painted again using a fine mesh, which is lit per-vertex using our caustic generator, as shown in Figure 2-6b. For each vertex in the fine mesh, we shoot a ray vertically, collide it with the ocean surface, generate the bent ray using Snell's Law, and use that ray to perform a ray-quad test, which we use to index the texture map, as in Figure 2-6a. In the end, the operation is not very different from a planar environment mapping pass. The third and final pass renders the ocean waves using our waveform generator. These triangles will be textured with a planar environment map, so we get a nice sky reflection on them. Other effects, such as Fresnel's equation, can be implemented on top of that.

The pseudocode for this technique is as follows:

1. Paint the ocean floor.
2. For each vertex in the fine mesh:
   a. Send a vertical ray.
   b. Collide the ray with the ocean's mesh.
   c. Compute the refracted ray using Snell's Law in reverse.
   d. Use the refracted ray to compute texture coordinates for the "Sun" map.
   e. Apply texture coordinates to vertices in the finer mesh.
3. Render the ocean surface.

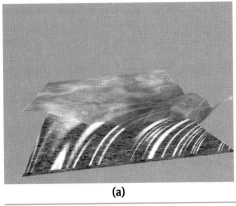 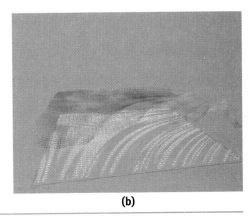

| (a) | (b) |

Figure 2-6. The OpenGL Implementation
(a) In solid rendering mode and (b) in wireframe mode.

2.5 Implementation Using a High-Level Shading Language

Implementing this technique fully on the GPU gives even better visual quality and improves its performance. A high-level shading language, such as Microsoft's HLSL or NVIDIA's Cg, allows us quickly to move all these computations to the GPU, using a C-like syntax. In fact, the same wave function previously executed on the CPU in the basic OpenGL implementation was simply copied into the pixel and vertex shaders using an include file, with only minor modifications to accommodate the vector-based structures in these high-level languages.

Calculating the caustics per-pixel instead of per-vertex improves the overall visual quality and decouples the effect from geometric complexity. Two approaches were considered when porting the technique to the GPU's pixel shaders, and both use the partial derivatives of the wave function to generate a normal, unlike the original method, which relies on finite differences.

The first method takes advantage of the fact that a procedural texture can be rendered in screen space, thereby saving render time when only a small portion of the pixels are visible. Unfortunately, this also means that when a large number of pixels are visible, a lot of work is being done for each one, even though the added detail may not be appreciable. Sometimes this large amount of work can slow down the frame rate enough to be undesirable, so another method is needed to overcome this limitation.

This second method renders in texture space to a fixed-resolution render target. Although rendering in texture space has the advantage of maintaining a constant workload at every frame, the benefit of rendering only visible pixels is lost. Additionally, it becomes difficult to gauge what render target resolution most adequately suits the current scene, to the point where relying on texture filtering may introduce the tell-tale bilinear filtering cross pattern if the texel-to-pixel ratio drops too low.

We can further optimize the algorithm by observing that there is little visual difference between refracting the incoming rays using Snell's Law and simply performing environment mapping based on the distance from the water surface to the floor surface along the wave normal. See Figure 2-7. As a result, vertical rays access the center of the texture, which is bright, while angled rays produce a progressively attenuated light source. Moreover, at larger depths, the relative size of the environment map—and hence the relative size of the light source—is reduced, creating sharper caustics that can also be attenuated by distance. Note that this approach allows us to have a nonuniform ground plane, and this variable depth can easily be encoded into a scalar component of a vertex attribute.

Figure 2-7. Environment Map of the Sun Overhead

The effect therefore calculates the normal of the wave function to trace the path of the ray to the intercept point on a plane—the ocean floor, in this example. To generate the normal, the partial derivatives of the wave function, in x and y, can easily be found.

Let's write the wave function used in the original approach as:

$$f(x, y) = -\sum_{i=1}^{i=octaves} \sqrt{x^2 + y^2} \, \frac{c_1 \cos\left(c_2 + 2^i c_3 xy\right)}{2^i},$$

where i indicates the number of octaves used to generate the wave; c_1, c_2, and c_3 are constants to give the wave frequency, amplitude, and speed, respectively; and x and y, which range from 0 to 1, inclusive, indicate a point on a unit square.

Applying the chain and product rules yields two functions, the partial derivatives, which are written as:[1]

$$\frac{\partial f(x, y)}{\partial x} = -\sum_{i=1}^{i=octaves} \sqrt{x^2 + y^2} \left(c_1 \sin\left(c_2 + 2^i c_3 xy\right) c_3 y\right) - \frac{c_1 \cos\left(c_2 + 2^i c_3 xy\right) x}{2^i \sqrt{x^2 + y^2}}$$

---

1. Note that c_1 can be factored outside the summation, as shown in the sample code.

and

$$\frac{\partial f(x, y)}{\partial y} = -\sum_{i=1}^{i=octaves} \sqrt{x^2 + y^2} \left(c_1 \sin\left(c_2 + 2^i c_3 xy\right) c_3 x \right) - \frac{c_1 \cos\left(c_2 + 2^i c_3 xy\right) y}{2^i \sqrt{x^2 + y^2}}.$$

The partial derivatives are actually components of the gradient vectors at the point where they are evaluated. Because the function actually represents height, or z, the partial derivative with respect to z is simply 1. The normal is then the cross product of the gradient vectors, which yields:

$$n = \left(-\frac{df}{dx} \quad -\frac{df}{dy} \quad 1 \right).$$

The last equation required to render the caustics is the line-plane intercept. We can calculate the distance from a point on a line to the interception point on the plane using:

$$d = \frac{D_{pl} - n_{pl} \cdot p_l}{v_l \cdot n_{pl}},$$

where D_{pl} is the distance from the water plane to the origin, n_{pl} is the normal of the ground plane, v_l is the vector describing the direction of the refracted light (effectively along the normal of the wave surface), and p_l is the intersection point of the refracted ray and the ocean floor. See Figure 2-8.

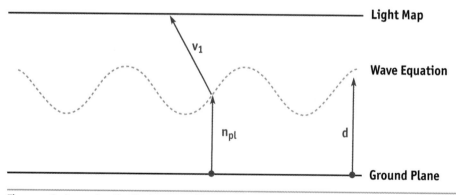

Figure 2-8. Accessing the Environment Map

Evidently the new calculations done per-pixel are quite complex, but given the flexibility of higher-level shading languages and the pixel-processing power available in current-generation hardware devices, they are trivial to implement and quick to render. The sample code in Listing 2-1 shows the implementation in Cg.

Listing 2-1. Code Sample for the Wave Function, the Gradient of the Wave Function, and the Line-Plane Intercept Equation

```
// Caustics
// Copyright (c) NVIDIA Corporation. All rights reserved.
//
// NOTE:
// This shader is based on the original work by Daniel Sanchez-Crespo
// of the Universitat Pompeu Fabra, Barcelona, Spain.

#define VTXSIZE 0.01f    // Amplitude
#define WAVESIZE 10.0f   // Frequency
#define FACTOR 1.0f
#define SPEED 2.0f
#define OCTAVES 5


// Example of the same wave function used in the vertex engine
float wave(float x,
           float y,
           float timer)
{
  float z = 0.0f;
  float octaves = OCTAVES;
  float factor = FACTOR;
  float d = sqrt(x * x + y * y);

  do {
    z -= factor * cos(timer * SPEED + (1/factor) * x * y * WAVESIZE);
    factor = factor/2;
    octaves--;
  } while (octaves > 0);

  return 2 * VTXSIZE * d * z;

}
```

```
// This is a derivative of the above wave function.
// It returns the d(wave)/dx and d(wave)/dy partial derivatives.
float2 gradwave(float x,
                float y,
                float timer)
{
  float dZx = 0.0f;
  float dZy = 0.0f;
  float octaves = OCTAVES;
  float factor = FACTOR;
  float d = sqrt(x * x + y * y);

  do {
    dZx += d * sin(timer * SPEED + (1/factor) * x * y * WAVESIZE) *
              y * WAVESIZE - factor *
              cos(timer * SPEED + (1/factor) * x * y * WAVESIZE) * x/d;
    dZy += d * sin(timer * SPEED + (1/factor) * x * y * WAVESIZE) *
              x * WAVESIZE - factor *
              cos(timer * SPEED + (1/factor) * x * y * WAVESIZE) * y/d;
    factor = factor/2;
    octaves--;
  } while (octaves > 0);

  return float2(2 * VTXSIZE * dZx, 2 * VTXSIZE * dZy);
}


float3 line_plane_intercept(float3 lineP,
                            float3 lineN,
                            float3 planeN,
                            float  planeD)
{
  // Unoptimized
  // float distance = (planeD - dot(planeN, lineP)) /
  //                   dot(lineN, planeN);
  // Optimized (assumes planeN always points up)
  float distance = (planeD - lineP.z) / lineN.z;
  return lineP + lineN * distance;
}
```

Once we have calculated the interception point, we can use this to fetch our caustic light map using a dependent texture read, and we can then add the caustic contribution to our ground texture, as shown in Listing 2-2.

Listing 2-2. Code Sample for the Final Render Pass, Showing the Dependent Texture Read Operations

```
float4 main(VS_OUTPUT vert,
            uniform sampler2D LightMap  : register(s0),
            uniform sampler2D GroundMap : register(s1),
            uniform float Timer) : COLOR
{
  // Generate a normal (line direction) from the gradient
  // of the wave function and intercept with the water plane.
  // We use screen-space z to attenuate the effect to avoid aliasing.
  float2 dxdy = gradwave(vert.Position.x, vert.Position.y, Timer);

  float3 intercept = line_plane_intercept(
                     vert.Position.xyz,
                     float3(dxdy, saturate(vert.Position.w)),
                     float3(0, 0, 1), -0.8);

  // OUTPUT
  float4 colour;
  colour.rgb = (float3)tex2D(LightMap, intercept.xy * 0.8);
  colour.rgb += (float3)tex2D(GroundMap, vert.uv);
  colour.a = 1;
  return colour;
}
```

The results in Figure 2-9 show the quality improvement achieved by doing the calculations per-pixel instead of per-vertex. As can be seen, a sufficiently large resolution texture has quality as good as screen-space rendering, without the performance impact when large numbers of pixels are displayed. Additionally, when using a render target texture, we can take advantage of automatic mipmap generation and anisotropic filtering to reduce aliasing of the caustics, which cannot be done when rendering to screen space.

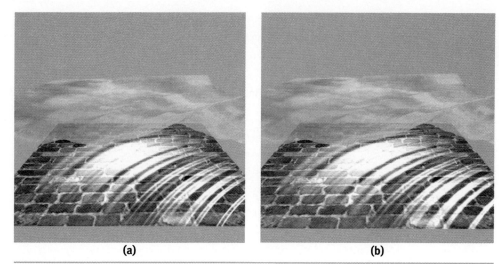

(a)   (b)

Figure 2-9. Rendered Caustics
(a) Using screen-space rendering and (b) render to texture.

2.6 Conclusion

The effect described in this chapter shows how a classic algorithm can be upgraded and enhanced to take advantage of shader-based techniques. As shader-processing power increases, the full Monte Carlo approach will eventually run entirely on graphics hardware, and thus computing physically correct caustics will become a reality.

For a complete, aesthetically pleasing model of underwater rendering, another effect worth investigating is *crepuscular rays*. This effect, also known as *god rays*, looks like visible rays of light, which are caused by reflections from underwater particles.

2.7 References

Foley, James, Andries van Dam, Steven Feiner, and John Hughes. 1996. *Computer Graphics: Principles and Practice,* 2nd ed. Addison-Wesley.

Jensen, Lasse Staff, and Robert Golias. 2001. "Deep-Water Animation and Rendering." Gamasutra article. Available online at
http://www.gamasutra.com/gdce/2001/jensen/jensen_01.htm

Stam, Jos. 1996. "Random Caustics: Wave Theory and Natural Textures Revisited." Technical sketch. In *Proceedings of SIGGRAPH 1996,* p. 151. Available online at
http://www.dgp.toronto.edu/people/stam/INRIA/caustics.html

Chapter 3

Skin in the "Dawn" Demo

Curtis Beeson
NVIDIA

Kevin Bjorke
NVIDIA

3.1 Introduction

"Dawn" is a demonstration that was created by NVIDIA to introduce the GeForce FX product line and illustrate how programmable shading could be used to create a realistic human character, as shown in Figure 3-1. The vertex shaders (described in Chapter 4, "Animation in the 'Dawn' Demo") deform a high-resolution mesh through indexed skinning and blend shapes, and they provide setup for the lighting model used in the fragment shaders. The skin and wing fragment shaders produce both range and detail that could not have been achieved before the introduction of programmable graphics hardware.[1]

This chapter discusses how programmable graphics hardware was used to light and accelerate the skin shader on the Dawn character in the demo.

3.2 Skin Shading

Skin is a difficult surface to simulate in computer graphics for a variety of reasons. Even the high-end production graphics used in movies are unable to simulate a photorealistic human character that can withstand close examination. Humans gain a great deal of

---

1. Concept and implementation with the help of Gary King and Alex Sakhartchouk of NVIDIA.

Figure 3-1. Dawn

information with nonverbal cues: the shifting of weight, the particular way of walking, facial expressions, and even the blush of someone's skin. Researchers have shown that babies recognize and gaze at facial expressions within moments of birth. We humans are therefore very perceptive when it comes to detecting irregularities in the way characters move and emote, and in the subtle coloring of their skin. Although few people may understand terms such as *subsurface scattering* and *rim lighting,* almost anybody can tell you when your rendering got them wrong.

In addition to shading issues, people may be quick to say that a skin shader looks like plastic because of the way the skin moves, so it is important to address the problems of character setup. Chapter 4 describes those techniques used in the "Dawn" demo for driving the body using accumulated indexed skinning, and for adding emotion to Dawn's face through blend targets. These techniques provide a passable approximation for Dawn and for the actions she needs to perform, but they might fail to fully describe the way skin slides, flexes, and sags over a real skeleton for other purposes. When creating a character, it's important to model both the rigging and the shading appropriately for the range of views that the observer will actually see.

3.3 Lighting the Scene

Once the skin is moving in as realistic a manner as possible, you can focus on the shading. The most straightforward way to break down the shading of a surface is to examine the lighting environment of the scene and then look at the skin's response to that light.

3.3.1 A High-Dynamic-Range Environment

We wanted to create our character and place her in a setting that defied the sort of flat, simple-looking shading that typifies traditional real-time graphics techniques. Older graphics architectures were built around the concepts of Gouraud and Phong shading, which describe all incoming light as radiating from infinitely small point, directional, and spot lights. The diffuse and specular responses of material surfaces were usually described using textures and equations that failed to describe a suitable range of light response.

One undesirable result of the previous approach is that scenes tended to lack the brightness range seen in the real world. A white piece of paper on the floor would be as bright as a white light source above; characters in complex environments often looked out of place because they were lit by discrete points instead of by their surroundings.

Paul Debevec has done a great deal of research in the area of high-dynamic-range image processing and manipulation to address exactly this problem. His work can be found in a variety of SIGGRAPH publications and is made more tangible through examples in his rendered films.[2] We sought to take advantage of the new programmable real-time graphics architectures to apply these concepts to a real-time character. In particular, we wished to have Dawn lit by the environment and to allow the bright spots to cause light to bleed and soften her silhouette edges.

Dawn being a fairy, we found a suitable woodsy area and took a number of calibrated pictures. We used an iPIX kit that included a tripod that locks at opposite angles, a digital camera, and a 183-degree fish-eye lens. In this case, the two hemispherical pictures were taken across several shutter speeds using one of the camera's built-in macros.

---

2. Much of Paul Debevec's work can be found at www.debevec.org.

This collection of images provides better information about the light intensities at each pixel, as opposed to the single pixel color produced at any individual shutter speed.

We used the iPIX software to stitch the corresponding hemispheres into a single panorama, and then we used Debevec's HDRShop software to create a high-dynamic-range panorama that encodes the light color and intensity of the environment at every given angle. See Figure 3-2. HDRShop can then create a diffuse lookup map that performs a convolution to create a diffuse or specular map for a surface with a given surface roughness (which in the past would have been modeled using a Phong exponent).

The diffuse map is a cube map, as shown in Figure 3-3, indexed using the surface normal of the mesh, and it stores a cosine-weighted average of the incoming light for that direction. Ignoring for now the fact that parts of the hemisphere may be occluded at a given point, this weighted average gives the appropriate value for computing diffuse reflection for points on the surface.

The specular map is also a cube map, as shown in Figure 3-4, and is indexed using the reflection vector (the way "usual" cube maps are used for reflections). This specular map is blurred based on the roughness factor to simulate the changing surface normal at any given point on the surface.

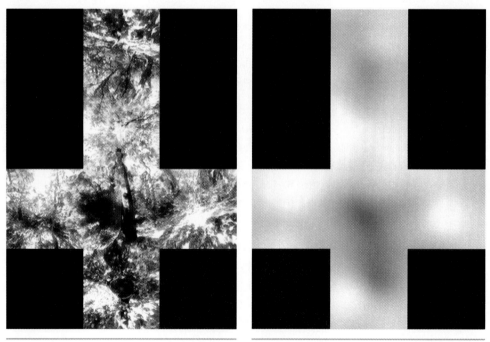

Figure 3-2. The Cube Map of the Environment   **Figure 3-3.** The Diffuse Cube Environment Map

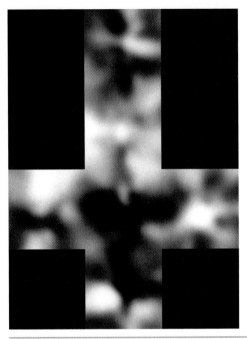

Figure 3-4. The Specular Cube Environment Map

3.3.2 The Occlusion Term

One problem with using environment maps to describe an environment or a lighting solution is that the mapped samples are really accurate for only a single point in space. The first side effect of this is that if the fairy walks around, the background appears to be "infinitely" far away. This was a suitable approximation for us, because the fairy is small and the background should look far away in this instance.[3]

The second side effect is that the diffuse and specular maps describe the incident light from the environment that was photographed, but they do nothing to describe the shadows introduced by simulated elements such as Dawn herself. Thus, it was necessary to develop a technique to incorporate this information.

Many real-time shadowing techniques produce hard shadows, and we wanted a particularly soft look. Thus, we generated an occlusion term that approximated what percentage of the hemisphere above each vertex was obstructed by other objects in the scene.[4]

3. One could interpolate between panoramas taken at different points or skew panoramas to simulate travel akin to *plenoptic modeling* (McMillan and Bishop 1995).
4. A similar technique is outlined in Chapter 17 of this book, "Ambient Occlusion."

This was done using a custom software tool that casts rays stochastically over that vertex's visible hemisphere and found collisions with other geometry. We used this technique in the "Dawn" demo and in the "Ogre" demo (content courtesy of Spellcraft Studio), though the results were then used differently. For Dawn, the occlusion term was kept constant for the vertices of her figure; her face used a blend of occlusion terms from the various morph targets.

Having reached the limits of what we could do on a prerelease GeForce FX 5800 (Dawn was created to be a launch demo for that product), we stopped shy of animating the occlusion term for every vertex on every frame, as we did for the Ogre character in Spellcraft Studio's "Yeah! The Movie" demo.

3.4 How Skin Responds to Light

Skin is unlike most surfaces that we model in computer graphics because it is composed of layers of semitranslucent epidermis, dermis, and subcutaneous tissue. *Subsurface scattering* is the term we give to the phenomenon whereby light enters the surface, scatters through the medium, and exits at another point. This effect can commonly be seen as an orange glow of light passing through the skin when you hold your hand up in front of the Sun. This scattering under the skin is important to skin's appearance at all angles and helps give it a soft, highly distinctive character. Unfortunately, this reality defies a common assumption in graphics APIs and architectures: namely, light at one point on an object doesn't affect reflection at other points.

In the past, some groups have tried to emulate skin's complexity using multiple, layered texture maps. In general this approach has proven to be difficult to manage and difficult for the texture artists to work with as they previsualize the final blended color. Instead, we used a single color map, with color variations added through the shading, as shown in Figure 3-5.

Furthermore, skin has extremely fine variations that affect its reflective properties. These have subtle effects on skin's appearance, particularly when the light is directly opposite the camera position—that is, edge and rim lighting. Real skin has tiny features such as vellus hairs and pores that catch the light. These details were too small for us to model explicitly, but we wanted a surface that still gave us an appropriate overall look. Adding a bump map provided some additional detail when seen in close-up—particularly for small wrinkles—but we wanted a soft appearance, not shiny, stippled plastic,

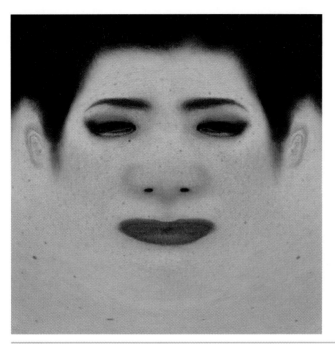

Figure 3-5. The Diffuse Color Map for the Front Half of Dawn's Head
Texture resolution is 1024×1024.

and we wanted the effects to be visible regardless of the size on screen (bump maps are usually visible only when seen up close).

We approximated both of these shading attributes by recognizing that we could model them as simple formulas based on the surface normal and the lighting or viewing vectors. In particular, along silhouette edges we sampled the lighting from *behind* Dawn, as indexed by the view vector—mixing the light coming "through" Dawn with her base skin tones to create the illusion of subsurface and edge-effect lighting, particularly for very bright areas in the background map. See Figure 3-6.

3.5 Implementation

The processes of lighting are split between the vertex and the fragment shaders. This is a *one-pass* lighting solution: no additional render passes or alpha blending is required to create the skin surface.

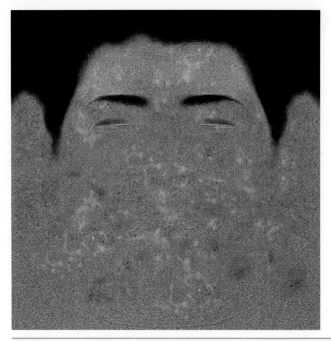

Figure 3-6. The Tangent-Space Normal Map (Bump Map) for the Front of Dawn's Head
With contrast enhanced. Texture resolution is 1024×1024.

3.5.1 The Vertex Shader

The primary functions of the vertex shader are to transform the coordinate into projection space and to perform those mathematical operations that are prohibitively expensive to compute in the fragment shader. As mentioned in Section 3.3.2, the vertex shader in the "Dawn" demo first applied morph targets (if any), and then skinned the mesh of over 180,000 vertices with a skeleton of 98 bones. See Chapter 4 for more.

For each vertex, we receive from the CPU application the data shown in Listing 3-1.[5]

The factors that are computed in the vertex shader and passed as interpolated values in the fragment shader include the world-space eye direction vector (`worldEyeDirection`), describing the direction from the viewer's eye to any given vertex; the 3×3 tangent to world-space matrix (`tangentToWorld`)[6]; and a variety of terms collectively called *blood transmission terms* (`bloodTransmission`). Listing 3-2 shows the data structure of the output vertices.

---

5. Much of the data and code in the vertex shader pertains to the skinning and morph targets described in Chapter 4 of this book, "Animation in the 'Dawn' Demo."

6. Only a 3×3 matrix is needed because surface vectors (such as the normal, binormal, and tangent) should not be translated in the way points are.

Listing 3-1. The Per-Vertex Data Received from the CPU Application

```
// Here is the PER-VERTEX data — we use 16 vectors,
// the maximum permitted by our graphics API
struct a2vConnector {
  float4 coord;                    // 3D location
  float4 normal;
  float4 tangent;
  float3 coordMorph0;              // 3D offset to target 0
  float4 normalMorph0;            // matching offset
  float3 coordMorph1;             // 3D offset to target 1
  float4 normalMorph1;            // matching offset
  float3 coordMorph2;             // 3D offset to target 2
  float4 normalMorph2;            // matching offset
  float3 coordMorph3;             // 3D offset to target 3
  float4 normalMorph3;            // matching offset
  float3 coordMorph4;             // 3D offset to target 4
  float4 normalMorph4;            // matching offset
  float4 boneWeight0_3;           // skull and neck bone
  float4 boneIndex0_3;            // indices and weights
  float4 skinColor_frontSpec;     // UV indices
};
```

Listing 3-2. The Data Structure of the Output Vertices

```
// Here is the data passed from the vertex shader
// to the fragment shader
struct v2fConnector {
  float4 HPOS                 : POSITION;
  float4 SkinUVST             : TEXCOORD0;
  float3 WorldEyeDir          : TEXCOORD2;
  float4 SkinSilhouetteVec    : TEXCOORD3;
  float3 WorldTanMatrixX      : TEXCOORD5;
  float3 WorldTanMatrixY      : TEXCOORD6;
  float3 WorldTanMatrixZ      : TEXCOORD7;
};
```

Because we are bump mapping, our fragment shader will have to find the world-space bumped normal, so we must provide it a way to get from the tangent-space bumped normal (provided by a texture map) into world space. The common way of doing bump mapping is to have the vertex shader pass the world-space normal, binormal, and tangent, and then to use these three vectors as a 3×3 matrix to rotate vectors from world space into tangent space for computation. In this case, the fragment shader will have to look into the lighting solution using the world-space vectors, so we map the transpose of this matrix (the transpose is the inverse for a rotation matrix), resulting in nine `MOV` instructions in the vertex shader to load the `WorldTanMatrixX`, `World-TanMatrixY`, and `WorldTanMatrixZ` terms.

Finally, the vertex shader blood transmission or "skin silhouette" terms are a `float4` vector, composed of the occlusion term; different variations on the expression $(\mathbf{N} \cdot \mathbf{V})$ (that is, the dot product of the surface normal and the view vector); and a rotation of the normal against the coordinate system of the cube map lighting. See Figure 3-7.

```
OUT.SkinSilhouetteVec = float4(objectNormal.w,
                               oneMinusVdotN * oneMinusVdotN,
                               oneMinusVdotN,
                               vecMul(G_DappleXf, worldNormal.xyz).z);
```

These steps provided just a few ways of parameterizing how near a silhouette the pixel was, and they gave us a toy box of values to play with while developing the fragment shader. Mathematically astute readers may notice that the $(\mathbf{N} \cdot \mathbf{V})$ terms may not interpolate correctly on large triangles via Gouraud (linear) shading. Fortunately for this specific case, Dawn is finely tessellated, and the camera needs to be *very* near her face before any error is apparent. This is a good example of using a shader that is highly specific to a particular model, to be seen in a range of predictable screen sizes. The $(\mathbf{N} \cdot \mathbf{V})$ could have been done in the fragment shader, but that would have made for a significantly more expensive (and hence slower) shader.

Note that all of the vertex shaders in the "Dawn" demo were procedurally generated. We assign fragment shaders in Maya, and we have a vertex shader generator that looks at the character setup (skeletons, morph targets, and so on) and the inputs requested by the fragment shader; it then generates the optimal vertex shader from a rules file using an A* search.[7]

Listing 3-3 is a sample annotated vertex shader, as used on Dawn's face area (incorporating both matrix skinning and shape blends, along with values used for the color calculations in the fragment shader).

---

7. A* is a variant brute-force search that uses an aggregate-cost metric to guide the search to converge on the optimal result.

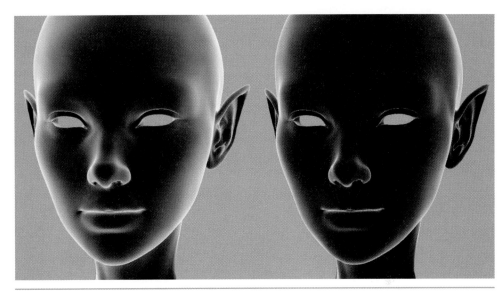

Figure 3-7. Dot Products Stored in `SkinSilhouetteVec`
On the left, $(1 - (\mathbf{N} \cdot \mathbf{V}))$; on the right, $(1 - (\mathbf{N} \cdot \mathbf{V}))^2$.

Listing 3-3. A Sample Vertex Shader for Dawn's Face

```
// Helper function:
// vecMul(matrix, float3) multiplies like a vector
// instead of like a point (no translate)
float3 vecMul(const float4x4 matrix, const float3 vec)
{
  return(float3(dot(vec, matrix._11_12_13),
                dot(vec, matrix._21_22_23),
                dot(vec, matrix._31_32_33))));
}

// The Vertex Shader for Dawn's Face
v2fConnector faceVertexShader(a2vConnector IN,
  const uniform float MorphWeight0,
  const uniform float MorphWeight1,
  const uniform float MorphWeight2,
  const uniform float MorphWeight3,
  const uniform float MorphWeight4,
  const uniform float4x4 BoneXf[8],
  const uniform float4   GlobalCamPos,
```

Listing 3-3 (*continued*). A Sample Vertex Shader for Dawn's Face

```
    const uniform float4x4 ViewXf,
    const uniform float4x4 G_DappleXf,
    const uniform float4x4 ProjXf)
{
  v2fConnector OUT;

  // The following large block is entirely
  // concerned with shape skinning.
  // First, do shape blending between the five
  // blend shapes ("morph targets")
  float4 objectCoord = IN.coord;
  objectCoord.xyz += (MorphWeight0 * IN.coordMorph0);
  objectCoord.xyz += (MorphWeight1 * IN.coordMorph1);
  objectCoord.xyz += (MorphWeight2 * IN.coordMorph2);
  objectCoord.xyz += (MorphWeight3 * IN.coordMorph3);
  objectCoord.xyz += (MorphWeight4 * IN.coordMorph4);

  // Now transform the entire head by the neck bone
  float4 worldCoord = IN.boneWeight0_3.x *
                      mul(BoneXf[IN.boneIndex0_3.x], objectCoord);
  worldCoord += (IN.boneWeight0_3.y *
                mul(BoneXf[IN.boneIndex0_3.y], objectCoord));
  worldCoord += (IN.boneWeight0_3.z *
                mul(BoneXf[IN.boneIndex0_3.z], objectCoord));
  worldCoord += (IN.boneWeight0_3.w *
                mul(BoneXf[IN.boneIndex0_3.w], objectCoord));

  // Repeat the previous skinning ops
  // on the surface normal
  float4 objectNormal = IN.normal;
  objectNormal += (MorphWeight0 * IN.normalMorph0);
  objectNormal += (MorphWeight1 * IN.normalMorph1);
  objectNormal += (MorphWeight2 * IN.normalMorph2);
  objectNormal += (MorphWeight3 * IN.normalMorph3);
  objectNormal += (MorphWeight4 * IN.normalMorph4);
  objectNormal.xyz = normalize(objectNormal.xyz);
  float3 worldNormal = IN.boneWeight0_3.x *
                      vecMul(BoneXf[IN.boneIndex0_3.x],
                             objectNormal.xyz));
```

Listing 3-3 (*continued*). A Sample Vertex Shader for Dawn's Face

```
worldNormal += (IN.boneWeight0_3.y *
                vecMul(BoneXf[IN.boneIndex0_3.y],
                    objectNormal.xyz));
worldNormal += (IN.boneWeight0_3.z *
                vecMul(BoneXf[IN.boneIndex0_3.z],
                    objectNormal.xyz));
worldNormal += (IN.boneWeight0_3.w *
                vecMul(BoneXf[IN.boneIndex0_3.w],
                    objectNormal.xyz));
worldNormal = normalize(worldNormal);

// Repeat the previous skinning ops
// on the orthonormalized surface tangent vector
float4 objectTangent = IN.tangent;
objectTangent.xyz = normalize(objectTangent.xyz -
                            dot(objectTangent.xyz,
                                objectNormal.xyz) *
                            objectNormal.xyz);
float4 worldTangent;
worldTangent.xyz = IN.boneWeight0_3.x *
                    vecMul(BoneXf[IN.boneIndex0_3.x],
                        objectTangent.xyz);
worldTangent.xyz += (IN.boneWeight0_3.y *
                    vecMul(BoneXf[IN.boneIndex0_3.y],
                        objectTangent.xyz));
worldTangent.xyz += (IN.boneWeight0_3.z *
                    vecMul(BoneXf[IN.boneIndex0_3.z],
                        objectTangent.xyz));
worldTangent.xyz += (IN.boneWeight0_3.w *
                    vecMul(BoneXf[IN.boneIndex0_3.w],
                        objectTangent.xyz));
worldTangent.xyz = normalize(worldTangent.xyz);
worldTangent.w = objectTangent.w;

// Now our deformations are done.
// Create a binormal vector as the cross product
// of the normal and tangent vectors
float3 worldBinormal = worldTangent.w *
                        normalize(cross(worldNormal,
                                    worldTangent.xyz));
```

Listing 3-3 (*continued*). A Sample Vertex Shader for Dawn's Face

```
// Reorder these values for output as a 3 x 3 matrix
// for bump mapping in the fragment shader
OUT.WorldTanMatrixX = float3(worldTangent.x,
                             worldBinormal.x, worldNormal.x);
OUT.WorldTanMatrixY = float3(worldTangent.y,
                             worldBinormal.y, worldNormal.y);
OUT.WorldTanMatrixZ = float3(worldTangent.z,
                             worldBinormal.z, worldNormal.z);

// The vectors are complete. Now use them
// to calculate some lighting values
float4 worldEyePos = GlobalCamPos;
OUT.WorldEyeDir = normalize(worldCoord.xyz - worldEyePos.xyz);
float4 eyespaceEyePos = {0.0f, 0.0f, 0.0f, 1.0f};
float4 eyespaceCoord = mul(ViewXf, worldCoord);
float3 eyespaceEyeVec = normalize(eyespaceEyePos.xyz -
                                  eyespaceCoord.xyz);
float3 eyespaceNormal = vecMul(ViewXf, worldNormal);
float VdotN = abs(dot(eyespaceEyeVec, eyespaceNormal));
float oneMinusVdotN = 1.0 - VdotN;
OUT.SkinUVST = IN.skinColor_frontSpec;
OUT.SkinSilhouetteVec = float4(objectNormal.w,
                              oneMinusVdotN * oneMinusVdotN,
                              oneMinusVdotN,
                              vecMul(G_DappleXf, worldNormal.xyz).z);
float4 hpos = mul(ProjXf, eyespaceCoord);
OUT.HPOS = hpos;
return OUT;
}
```

3.5.2 The Fragment Shader

Given the outputs of the vertex shader (and everywhere on Dawn's body, the vertex shaders output a consistent data structure), we can generate the actual textured colors.

Listing 3-4 shows the complete fragment shader as used by the face.

Listing 3-4. The Fragment Shader for Dawn's Face

```
float4 faceFragmentShader(v2fConnector IN,
  uniform sampler2D SkinColorFrontSpecMap,
  uniform sampler2D SkinNormSideSpecMap,    // xyz normal map
  uniform sampler2D SpecularColorShiftMap,  // and spec map in "w"
  uniform samplerCUBE DiffuseCubeMap,
  uniform samplerCUBE SpecularCubeMap,
  uniform samplerCUBE HilightCubeMap) : COLOR
{
  half4 normSideSpec tex2D(SkinNormSideSpecMap,
                           IN.SkinUVST.xy);
  half3 worldNormal;
  worldNormal.x = dot(normSideSpec.xyz, IN.WorldTanMatrixX);
  worldNormal.y = dot(normSideSpec.xyz, IN.WorldTanMatrixY);
  worldNormal.z = dot(normSideSpec.xyz, IN.WorldTanMatrixZ);
  fixed nDotV = dot(IN.WorldEyeDir, worldNormal);
  half4 skinColor = tex2D(SkinColorFrontSpecMap, IN.SkinUVST.xy);
  fixed3 diffuse = skinColor * texCUBE(DiffuseCubeMap, worldNormal);
  diffuse = diffuse * IN.SkinSilhouetteVec.x;
  fixed4 sideSpec = normSideSpec.w * texCUBE(SpecularCubeMap,
                                             worldNormal);
  fixed3 result = diffuse * IN.SkinSilhouetteVec.y + sideSpec;
  fixed3 hilite = 0.7 * IN.SkinSilhouetteVec.x *
                  IN.SkinSilhouetteVec.y *
                    texCUBE(HilightCubeMap, IN.WorldEyeDir);
  fixed reflVect = IN.WorldEyeDir * nDotV - (worldNormal * 2.0x);
  fixed4 reflColor = IN.SkinSilhouetteVec.w *
                        texCUBE(SpecularCubeMap, reflVect);
  result += (reflColor.xyz * 0.02);
  fixed hiLightAttenuator = tex2D(SpecularColorShiftMap,
                                  IN.SkinUVST.xy).x;
  result += (hilite * hiLightAttenuator);
  fixed haze = reflColor.w * hiLightAttenuator;
  return float4(result.xyz, haze);
}
```

First, we get bump-mapped surface normal. The texture stored in SkinNormSide-SpecMap contains tangent-space normals in its RGB components, and the specular map—a grayscale representing highlight intensities—is piggybacking in the alpha channel (we'll refer to the component RGB as xyz here for code clarity). By rotating the tangent-space `xyz` values against the `WorldTanMatrix`, we recast them in world coordinates—exactly what we need to perform our world-space lighting algorithm.

We then compare the newly calculated surface normal to the view direction. We use this nDotV value later.

```
half4 normSideSpec tex2D(SkinNormSideSpecMap,
                         IN.SkinUVST.xy);
half3 worldNormal;
worldNormal.x = dot(normSideSpec.xyz, IN.WorldTanMatrixX);
worldNormal.y = dot(normSideSpec.xyz, IN.WorldTanMatrixY);
worldNormal.z = dot(normSideSpec.xyz, IN.WorldTanMatrixZ);
fixed nDotV = dot(IN.WorldEyeDir, worldNormal);
```

Diffuse color is the skin texture map, multiplied by the preconvolved diffuse-lighting cube map. We modulate this a bit by the hemispherical occlusion term passed in `SkinSilhouetteVec`.

```
half4 skinColor = tex2D(SkinColorFrontSpecMap, IN.SkinUVST.xy);
fixed3 diffuse = skinColor * texCUBE(DiffuseCubeMap, worldNormal);
diffuse = diffuse * IN.SkinSilhouetteVec.x;
```

Edge specular color comes from our specular cube map, modulated by the specular intensity map that we got with the normal map (that is, in the alpha channel of `Skin-NormSideSpecMap`). We start building a cumulative result.

```
fixed4 sideSpec = normSideSpec.w * texCUBE(SpecularCubeMap,
                                           worldNormal);
fixed3 result = diffuse * IN.SkinSilhouetteVec.y + sideSpec;
```

Next, we retrieve the color of the environment *behind* Dawn, by indexing on `WorldEyeDir`, and we get the traditional reflection cube-map color. Add these, along with some artistic "fudge factoring," to our result.

```
fixed3 hilite = 0.7 * IN.SkinSilhouetteVec.x *
                IN.SkinSilhouetteVec.y *
                  texCUBE(HilightCubeMap, IN.WorldEyeDir);
fixed reflVect = IN.WorldEyeDir * nDotV - (worldNormal * 2.0x);
fixed4 reflColor = IN.SkinSilhouetteVec.w *
                     texCUBE(SpecularCubeMap, reflVect);
result += (reflColor.xyz * 0.02);
```

```
fixed hiLightAttenuator = tex2D(SpecularColorShiftMap,
                                IN.SkinUVST.xy).x;
result += (hilite * hiLightAttenuator);
```

Finally, we add a little extra silhouette information into the alpha channel of the final output, so that the "bloom" along Dawn's silhouette edges looks more natural when alpha blending.

```
fixed haze = reflColor.w * hiLightAttenuator;
return float4(result.xyz, haze);
```

3.6 Conclusion

Although many of the implementation details in the Dawn skin shaders may be too restrictive for many game engines, most of the concepts can be achieved using other means. The fundamentals of high dynamic range, subsurface scattering, rim lighting, and the like can also be computed from synthetic light sources or other scene information.

In many ways, it was difficult to work with Dawn being lit by the environment. More complex and more realistic lighting solutions often come at the expense of artistic control. In this instance, we wanted her goose bumps to be more visible, but the environment was diffuse enough that we had to unrealistically exaggerate her surface bump to compensate.

If we were to implement Dawn a second time, we would probably use a more hybrid approach to lighting, in which we would look up into the diffuse and specular map (given the smooth normal) and then use a primary "light direction" to compute the contribution of the bump map. This would give us more direct control over the look of the bump map and eliminate the need for the expensive matrix transpose performed in the vertex shader.

3.7 References

Debevec, Paul. 1998. "Rendering Synthetic Objects into Real Scenes: Bridging Traditional and Image-Based Graphics with Global Illumination and High Dynamic Range Photography." In *Proceedings of SIGGRAPH 98*, pp. 189–198.

Gritz, Larry, Tony Apodaca, Matt Pharr, Dan Goldman, Hayden Landis, Guido Quaroni, and Rob Bredow. 2002. "RenderMan in Production." Course 16, SIGGRAPH 2002.

McMillan, Leonard, and Gary Bishop. 1995. "Plenoptic Modeling: An Image-Based Rendering System." In *Proceedings of SIGGRAPH 1995*.

Stout, Bryan. 1996. "Smart Moves: Intelligent Pathfinding." *Game Developer*, October 1996. Available online at the Gamasutra Web site:
http://www.gamasutra.com/features/19970801/pathfinding.htm

Chapter 4

Animation in the "Dawn" Demo

Curtis Beeson
NVIDIA

4.1 Introduction

"Dawn" is a demonstration that was created by NVIDIA Corporation to introduce the GeForce FX product line and illustrate how a high-level language (such as HLSL or Cg) could be used to create a realistic human character. The vertex shaders deform a high-resolution mesh through indexed skinning and morph targets, and they provide setup for the lighting model used in the fragment shaders. The skin and wing fragment shaders offer both range and detail that could not have been achieved before the introduction of advanced programmable graphics hardware. See Figure 4-1.

This chapter discusses how programmable graphics hardware was used to accelerate the animation of the Dawn character in the demo.

4.2 Mesh Animation

Traditionally, mesh animation has been prohibitively expensive for complex meshes because it was performed on the CPU, which was already burdened with physical simulation, artificial intelligence, and other computations required by today's applications. Newer graphics hardware has replaced the traditional fixed-function pipeline with programmable vertex and fragment shaders, and it can now alleviate some of that burden from the CPU.

Figure 4-1. A Screen Capture of the Real-Time Dawn

Sometimes it is still necessary to perform such operations on the CPU. Many stencil-based shadow volume techniques must traverse the transformed mesh in order to find the silhouette edges, and the generation of the dynamic shadow frustum is often best done on the CPU (see Chapter 9, "Efficient Shadow Volume Rendering"). In scenes where the character is drawn multiple times per frame into shadow buffers, glow buffers, and other such temporary surfaces, it may be better to perform the deformations on the CPU if the application becomes vertex-limited. Deciding whether to perform mesh deformations on the CPU or on the GPU should be done on a per-application or even on a per-object basis.

The modeling, texturing, and animation of the Dawn character were done primarily in Alias Systems' Maya package. We therefore based our mesh animation methods on the tool set the software provides. We have since created a similar demo ("Dusk," used to launch the GeForce FX 5900) in discreet's 3ds max package, using the same techniques; these methods are common to a variety of modeling packages and not tied to any single workflow. The methods used in these two demos are (indexed) skinning, where vertices are influenced by a weighted array of matrices, and weighted morph targets, used to drive the emotions on Dawn's face.

4.3 Morph Targets

Using morph targets is a common way to represent complex mesh deformation, and the NVIDIA demo team has created a variety of demos using this technique. The "Zoltar" demo and the "Yeah! The Movie" demo (content provided by Spellcraft Studio) started with 30 mesh interpolants per second, then removed mesh keys based on an accumulated error scheme. This allowed us to reduce the file size and the memory footprint—up to two-thirds of the original keys could be removed with little to no visible artifacts. In this type of mesh interpolation, there are only two interpolants active at any given time, and they are animated sequentially.

Alternatively, morph targets can be used in parallel. Dawn is a standard example of how this approach can be useful. Beginning with a neutral head (27,000 triangles), our artist created 50 copies of that head and modeled them into an array of morph targets, as shown in Figure 4-2. Approximately 30 of those heads corresponded to emotions (such as happy, sad, thoughtful, and so on), and 20 more were modifiers (such as left eyebrow up, right eyebrow up, smirk, and so on). In this style of animation, the morph target weights will probably not add to 1, because you may have (0.8 * happy + 1.0 * ear_wiggle), for example—Dawn is a fairy, after all.

Although such complex emotional faces could have been made entirely of blends of more elemental modifiers, our artist found it more intuitive to model the face in the pose he desired, because it is hard to model an element such as an eyebrow creasing, without seeing how the eyes, cheeks, and mouth work together. This combination also helps with hardware register limitations, described later.

4.3.1 Morph Targets in a High-Level Language

Luckily, the implementation of morph targets in HLSL or Cg is simple. Assuming that vertexIn is our structure containing per-vertex data, applying morph targets in a linear or serial fashion is easy:

```
float4 position = (1.0f - interp) * vertexIn.prevPositionKey +
                  interp * vertexIn.nextPositionKey;
```

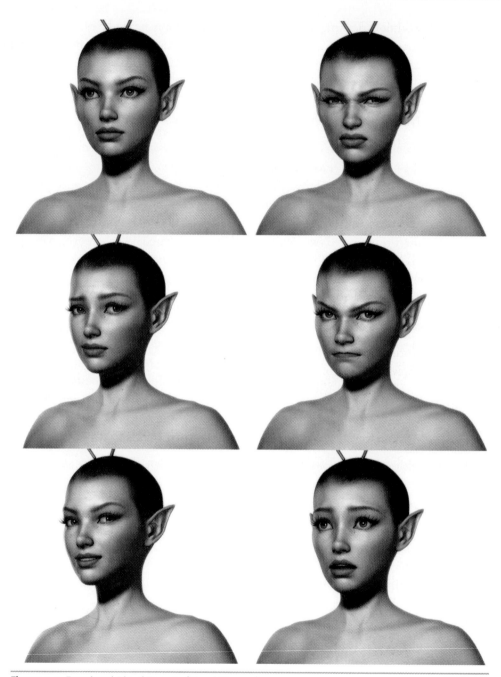

Figure 4-2. Emotional Blend Targets (Blend Shapes)

In this code, `interp` is a constant input parameter in the shader, but `prevPosition-Key` and `nextPositionKey` are the positions at the prior time and next time, respectively. When applying morph targets in parallel, we find the spatial difference between the morph target and the neutral pose, which results in a difference vector. We then weight that difference vector by a scalar. The result is that a weight of 1.0 will apply the per-vertex offsets to achieve that morph target, but each morph target can be applied separately. The application of each morph target is just a single "multiply-add" instruction:

```
// vertexIn.positionDiffN = position morph target N - neutralPosition
float4 position = neutralPosition;
position += weight0 * vertexIn.positionDiff0;
position += weight1 * vertexIn.positionDiff1;
position += weight2 * vertexIn.positionDiff2;
. . .
```

4.3.2 Morph Target Implementation

We wanted our morph targets to influence both the vertex position and the basis (that is, the normal, binormal, and tangent) so that they might influence the lighting performed in the fragment shader. At first it would seem that one would just execute the previous lines for position, normal, binormal, and tangent, but it is easy to run out of vertex input registers. When we wrote the "Dawn" and "Dusk" demos, the GPU could map a maximum of 16 per-vertex input attributes. The mesh must begin with the neutral position, normal, binormal, texture coordinate, bone weights, and bone indices (described later), leaving 10 inputs open for morph targets. We might have mapped the tangent as well, but we opted to take the cross product of the normal and binormal in order to save one extra input.

Because each difference vector takes one input, we might have 10 blend shapes that influence position, five blend shapes that influence position and normal, three position-normal-binormal blend shapes, or two position-normal-binormal-tangent blend shapes. We ultimately chose to have our vertex shader apply five blend shapes that modified the position and normal. The vertex shader would then orthonormalize the neutral tangent against the new normal (that is, subtract the collinear elements of the new normal from the neutral tangent and then normalize) and take the cross product for the binormal. Orthonormalization is a reasonable approximation for meshes that do not twist around the surface normal:

```
// assumes normal is the post-morph-target result
// normalize only needed if not performed in fragment shader
float3 tangent = vertexIn.neutralTangent - dot(vertexIn.neutralTangent,
                                                normal) * normal;
tangent = normalize(tangent);
```

Thus, we had a data set with 50 morph targets, but only five could be active (that is, with weight greater than 0) at any given time. We did not wish to burden the CPU with copying data into the mesh every time a different blend shape became active, so we allocated a mesh with vertex channels for neutralPosition, neutralNormal, neutralBinormal, textureCoord, and 50 * (positionDiff, NormalDiff). On a per-frame basis, we merely changed the names of the vertex input attributes so that those that should be active became the valid inputs and those that were inactive were ignored. For each frame, we would find those five position and normal pairs and map those into the vertex shader, allowing all other vertex data to go unused.

Note that the .w components of the positionDiff and normalDiff were not really storing any useful interpolants. We took advantage of this fact and stored a scalar self-occlusion term in the .w of the neutralNormal and the occlusion difference in each of the normal targets. When extracting the resulting normal, we just used the .xyz modifier to the register, which allowed us to compute a dynamic occlusion term that changed based on whether Dawn's eyes and mouth were open or closed, without any additional instructions. This provided for a soft shadow used in the lighting of her skin (as described in detail in Chapter 3, "Skin in the 'Dawn' Demo").

On the content-creation side, our animator had no difficulty remaining within the limit of five active blend shapes, because he primarily animated between three or so emotional faces and then added the elemental modifiers for complexity. We separated the head mesh from the rest of the body mesh because we did not want the added work of doing the math or storing the zero difference that, say, the happy face would apply to Dawn's elbow. The result remained seamless—despite the fact that the head was doing morph targets and skinning while the body was doing just skinning—because the outermost vertices of the face mesh were untouched by any of the emotional blend shapes. They were still modified by the skinning described next, but the weights were identical to the matching vertices in the body mesh. This ensured that no visible artifact resulted.

4.4 Skinning

Skinning is a method of mesh deformation in which each vertex of that mesh is assigned an array of matrices that act upon it along with weights (that should add up to 1.0) that describe how bound to that matrix the vertex should be. For example, vertices on the bicep may be acted upon only by the shoulder joint, but a vertex on the elbow may be 50 percent shoulder joint and 50 percent elbow joint, becoming 100 percent elbow joint for vertices beyond the curve of the elbow.

Preparing a mesh for skinning usually involves creating a neutral state for the mesh, called a *bind pose*. This pose keeps the arms and legs somewhat separated and avoids creases as much as possible, as shown in Figure 4-3. First, we create a transform hierarchy that matches this mesh, and then we assign matrix influences based on distance—usually with the help of animation tools, which can do this reasonably well. Almost always, the result must be massaged to handle problems around shoulders, elbows, hips,

Figure 4-3. Dawn's Bind Pose

and the like. This skeleton can then be animated through a variety of techniques. We used a combination of key-frame animation, inverse kinematics, and motion capture, as supported in our content-creation tool.

A skinned vertex is the weighted summation of that vertex being put through its active joints, or:

$$v' = \sum_{i \in bones} weight(v)[i] \times matrix[i] \times matrix[i]^{-1}_{bindpose} \times v_{bindpose}.$$

Conceptually, this equation takes the vertex from its neutral position into a weighted model space and back into world space for each matrix and then blends the results. The concatenated $matrix[i] \times matrix[i]^{-1}_{bindpose}$ matrices are stored as constant parameters, and the matrix indices and weights are passed as vertex properties. The application of four-bone skinning looks like this:

```
float4 skin(float4x4 bones[98],
            float4    boneWeights0,
            float4    boneIndices0)
{
   float4 result = boneWeights0.x * mul(bones[boneIndices.x], position);
   result = result + boneWeights0.y * mul(bones[boneIndices.y],
                                          position);
   result = result + boneWeights0.z * mul(bones[boneIndices.z],
                                          position);
   result = result + boneWeights0.w * mul(bones[boneIndices.w],
                                          position);

   return result;
}
```

In the "Dawn" demo, we drive a mesh of more than 180,000 triangles with a skeleton of 98 bones. We found that four matrices per vertex was more than enough to drive the body and head, so each vertex had to have four bone indices and four bone weights stored as vertex input attributes (the last two of the 16 xyzw vertex registers mentioned in Section 4.3.2). We sorted bone weights and bone indices so that we could rewrite the vertex shader to artificially truncate the number of bones acting on the vertex if we required higher vertex performance. Note that if you do this, you must also rescale the active bone weights so that they continue to add up to 1.

4.4.1 Accumulated Matrix Skinning

When skinning, one must apply the matrix and its bind pose inverse not only to the position, but also to the normal, binormal, and tangent for lighting to be correct. If your hierarchy cannot assume that scales are the same across *x*, *y*, and *z*, then you must apply the inverse transpose of this concatenated matrix. If scales are uniform, then the inverse is the transpose, so the matrix remains unchanged. Nonuniform scales create problems in a variety of areas, so our engine does not permit them.

If we call the `skin` function from the previous code, we must call `mul` for each matrix for each vertex property. In current hardware, multiplying a point by a matrix is implemented as four dot products and three adds, and vector-multiply is three dot products and two adds. Thus, four-bone skinning of position, normal, binormal, and tangent results in:

$$4 \times \Big(4 \text{ dots} + 3 \text{ adds} + 3 \times (3 \text{ dots} + 2 \text{ adds})\Big) = 52 \text{ dots} + 36 \text{ adds}$$
$$= 88 \text{ instructions.}$$

An unintuitive technique that creates the sum of the weighted matrices can be trivially implemented in HLSL or Cg as follows:

```
float4x4 accumulate_skin(float4x4 bones[98],
                         float4    boneWeights0,
                         float4    boneIndices0)
{
   float4x4 result = boneWeights0.x * bones[boneIndices0.x];
   result = result + boneWeights0.y * bones[boneIndices0.y];
   result = result + boneWeights0.z * bones[boneIndices0.z];
   result = result + boneWeights0.w * bones[boneIndices0.w];
   return result;
}
```

Although this technique does burn instructions to build the accumulated matrix (16 multiplies and 12 adds), it now takes only a single matrix multiply to skin a point or vector. Skinning the same properties as before costs:

$$
\begin{array}{ll}
16 \text{ muls} + 12 \text{ adds} & \textit{To build the matrix} \\
+\ 4 \text{ dots} + 3 \text{ adds} & \textit{For position} \\
+\ 3 \times (3 \text{ dots} + 2 \text{ adds}) & \\
\hline
\end{array}
$$
$$13 \text{ dots} + 16 \text{ muls} + 21 \text{ adds} = 50 \text{ instructions.}$$

4.5 Conclusion

It is almost always beneficial to offload mesh animation from the CPU and take advantage of the programmable vertex pipeline offered by modern graphics hardware. Having seen the implementation of skinning and morph targets using shaders, however, it is clear that the inner loops are quite easy to implement using Streaming SIMD Extensions (SSE) instructions and the like, and that in those few cases where it is desirable to remain on the CPU, these same techniques work well.

In the case of the "Dawn" demo, morph targets were used to drive only the expressions on the head. If we had had more time, we would have used morph targets all over the body to solve problems with simple skinning. Even a well-skinned mesh has the problem that elbows, knees, and other joints lose volume when rotated. This is because the mesh bends but the joint does not get "fatter" to compensate for the pressing of flesh against flesh. A morph target or other mesh deformation applied either before or after the skinning step could provide this soft, fleshy deformation and create a more realistic result. We have done some work on reproducing the variety of mesh deformers provided in digital content-creation tools, and we look forward to applying them in the future.

4.6 References

Alias Systems. Maya 5.0 Devkit. *<installation_directory>/devkit/animEngine/*

Alias Systems. Maya 5.0 Documentation.

Eberly, David H. 2001. *3D Game Engine Design*, pp. 356–358. Academic Press.

Gritz, Larry, Tony Apodaca, Matt Pharr, Dan Goldman, Hayden Landis, Guido Quaroni, and Rob Bredow. 2002. "RenderMan in Production." Course 16, SIGGRAPH 2002.

Hagland, Torgeir. 2000. "A Fast and Simple Skinning Technique." In *Game Programming Gems*, edited by Mark DeLoura. Charles River Media.

Chapter 5

Implementing Improved Perlin Noise

Ken Perlin
New York University

This chapter focuses on the decisions that I made in designing a new, improved version of my Noise function. I did this redesign for three reasons: (1) to make Noise more amenable to a gradual shift into hardware, (2) to improve on the Noise function's visual properties in some significant ways, and (3) to introduce a single, standard version that would return the same values across all hardware and software platforms.

The chapter is structured as follows: First, I describe the goals of the Noise function itself and briefly review the original implementation. Then I talk about specific choices I made in implementing improved Noise, to increase its quality and decrease visual artifacts. Finally, I talk about what is needed for gradual migration to hardware. The goal is to allow Noise to be implemented in progressively fewer instructions, as successive generations of GPUs follow a path to more powerful instructions.

5.1 The Noise Function

The purpose of the Noise function is to provide an efficiently implemented and repeatable, pseudo-random signal over R^3 (three-dimensional space) that is *band-limited* (most of its energy is concentrated near one spatial frequency) and visually *isotropic* (statistically rotation-invariant).

The general idea is to create something that gives the same effect as a completely random signal (that is, white noise) that has been run through a low-pass filter to blur out and thereby remove all high spatial frequencies. One example is the gradually rising and falling hills and valleys of sand dunes, as shown in Figure 5-1.

5.2 The Original Implementation

The initial implementation, first used in 1983 and first published in 1985 (Perlin 1985), defined Noise at any point (x, y, z) by using the following algorithm:

1. At each point in space (i, j, k) that has integer coordinates, assign a value of zero and a pseudo-random gradient that is hashed from (i, j, k).

2. Define the coordinates of (x, y, z) as an integer value plus a fractional remainder: $(x, y, z) = (i + u, j + v, k + w)$. Consider the eight corners of the unit cube surrounding this point: $(i, j, k), (i + 1, j, k), \ldots (i + 1, j + 1, k + 1)$.

Figure 5-1. Sand Dunes

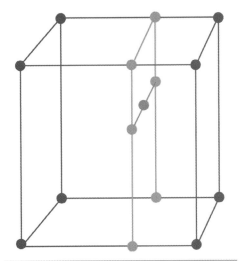

Figure 5-2. Steps Required to Interpolate a Value from Eight Samples in a Regular 3D Lattice

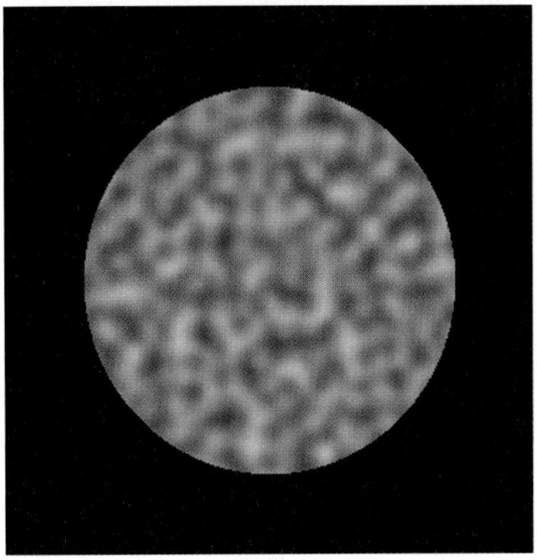

Figure 5-3. A Slice Through the Noise Function

3. Fit a Hermite spline through these eight points, and evaluate this spline at (x, y, z), using u, v, and w as interpolants. If we use a table lookup to predefine the Hermite cubic blending function $3t^2 - 2t^2$, then this interpolation requires only seven scalar linear interpolations: for example, four in x, followed by two in y, followed by one in z, as shown in Figure 5-2.

This approach worked reasonably well. A two-dimensional slice through the Noise function looks like Figure 5-3.

5.3 Deficiencies of the Original Implementation

Unfortunately, Noise had the following deficiencies:

- The choice of interpolating function in each dimension was $3t^2 - 2t^3$, which contains nonzero values in its second derivative. This can cause visual artifacts when the derivative of noise is taken, such as when doing bump mapping.

- The hashing of gradients from (i, j, k) produced a lookup into a pseudo-random set of 256 gradient vectors sown on a 3D sphere; irregularities in this distribution produce unwanted higher frequencies in the resulting Noise function. See Figure 5-4.

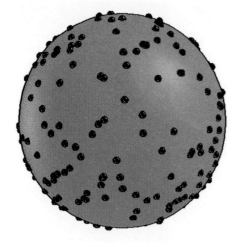

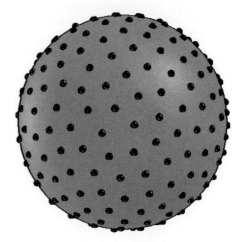

Figure 5-4. Irregular Distribution of Gradient Vectors

Figure 5-5. Regular Distribution of Gradient Vectors

In retrospect, I realize I should have applied a relaxation algorithm in the preprocessing step that chooses the pseudo-random gradient directions, repulsing these points away from each other around the sphere to form a more even, Poisson-like distribution, which would have reduced unwanted high spatial frequencies, giving a result like the one visualized in Figure 5-5.

Recently I realized that such a large number of different gradient directions is not even visually necessary. Rather, it is far more important to have an even statistical distribution of gradient directions, as opposed to many different gradient directions. This is consistent with perceptual research demonstrating that although human pre-attentive vision is highly sensitive to *statistical* anomalies in the orientation of texture features, our vision is relatively insensitive to the *granularity* of orientations, because our low-level vision system will convert a sufficiently dense set of discrete orientations into the equivalent continuous signal (Grill Spector et al. 1995). The human vision system performs this conversion at a very early stage, well below the threshold of conscious awareness.

Given a Noise implementation with a statistically even distribution of gradient directions, it is fairly straightforward to build procedural expressions that create complex-looking textures. For example, Figure 5-6 shows four successively more complex texture expressions built from Noise.

Moving clockwise from the top left, these expressions are:

Chapter 5   Implementing Improved Perlin Noise

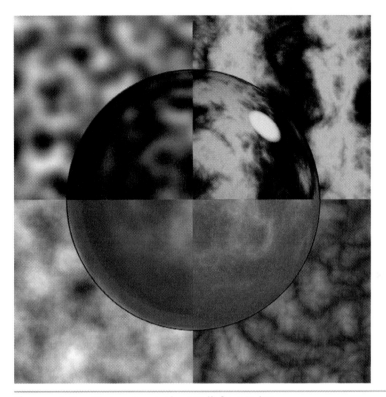

Figure 5-6. Four Texture Expressions Built from Noise

$$noise\left(x, y, z\right),$$

$$\sum \frac{noise\left(2^i x,\ 2^i y,\ 2^i z\right)}{2^i},$$

$$\sum \left| \frac{noise\left(2^i x,\ 2^i y,\ 2^i z\right)}{2^i} \right|,$$

$$\sin\left(x + \sum \left| \frac{noise\left(2^i x,\ 2^i y,\ 2^i z\right)}{2^i} \right| \right).$$

In each case, color splines have been applied as a postprocess to tint the results.

5.4 Improvements to Noise

The improvements to the Noise function are in two specific areas: the nature of the interpolant and the nature of the field of pseudo-random gradients.

As I discussed in Perlin 2002, the key to improving the interpolant is simply to remove second-order discontinuities. The original cubic interpolant $3t^2 - 2t^3$ was chosen because it has a derivative of zero both at $t = 0$ and at $t = 1$. Unfortunately, its second derivative is $6 - 12t$, which is not zero at either $t = 0$ or at $t = 1$. This causes artifacts to show up when Noise is used in bump mapping. Because the effect of lighting upon a bump-mapped surface varies with the derivative of the corresponding height function, second-derivative discontinuities are visible.

This problem was solved by switching to the fifth-degree interpolator: $6^5 - 15t^4 + 10t^3$, which has both first and second derivatives of zero at both $t = 0$ and $t = 1$.

The difference between these two interpolants can be seen in Figure 5-7. The green curve is the old cubic interpolant, which has second-order discontinuities at $t = 0$ and $t = 1$. The blue curve is the new fifth-order interpolant, which does not suffer from second-order discontinuities at $t = 0$ and $t = 1$.

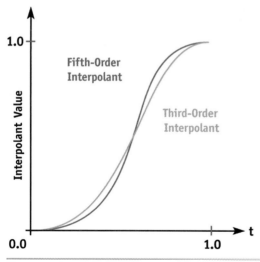

Figure 5-7. Interpolation Curves
The third-order curve is green, and the fifth-order curve is blue.

One nice thing about graphics accelerators is that you perform one-dimensional interpolations via a one-dimensional texture lookup table. When you take this approach, there is no extra cost in doing the higher-order interpolation. In practice, I have found that a texture table length of 256 is plenty, and that 16 bits of precision is sufficient. Even half-precision floating point (fp16), with its 10-bit mantissa, is sufficient.

Figure 5-8 shows two different renderings of a Noise-displaced superquadric. The one on the left uses the old cubic interpolant; the one on the right uses the newer, fifth-order interpolant. The visual improvement can be seen as a reduction in the 4×4-grid-like artifacts in the shape's front face.

The other improvement was to replace the 256 pseudo-random gradients with just 12 pseudo-random gradients, consisting of the edge centers of a cube centered at the origin: $(0, \pm 1, \pm 1)$, $(\pm 1, 0, \pm 1)$, and $(\pm 1, \pm 1, 0)$. This results in a much less "splotchy-looking" distribution, as can be seen in Figure 5-9's side-by-side comparison of a planar slice taken from implementations of Noise using the old and the new approach.

The reason for this improvement is that none of the 12 gradient directions is too near any others, so they will never bunch up too closely. It is this unwanted bunching up of adjacent gradients that causes the splotchy appearance in parts of the original Noise implementation.

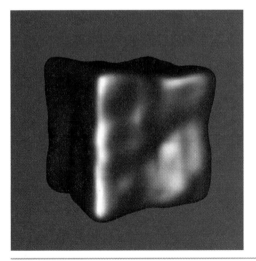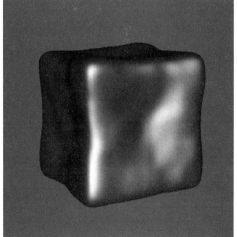

Figure 5-8. Noise-Displaced Superquadric
Renderings using the old interpolant (left) and the new one (right).

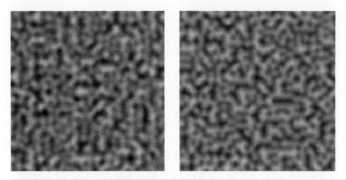

Figure 5-9. Improving Gradient Distribution
Old noise (left) and new, less splotchy noise (right).

Another nice thing about this approach is that it makes it possible to avoid many of the multiplies associated with evaluating the gradient function, because an inner product of (x, y, z) with, say, $(1, 1, 0)$ can be computed simply as $x + y$.

In order to make the process of hashing into this set of gradients compatible with the fastest possible hardware implementation, 16 gradients are actually defined, so that the hashing function can simply return a random 4-bit value. The extra four gradients simply repeat $(1, 1, 0)$, $(-1, 1, 0)$, $(0, -1, 1)$, and $(0, -1, -1)$.

5.5 How to Make Good Fake Noise in Pixel Shaders

It would be great to have some sort of reasonable volumetric noise primitive entirely in a pixel shader, but the straightforward implementation of this takes quite a few instructions. How can we use the capabilities of today's pixel shaders to implement some reasonable approximation of Noise in a very small number of instructions? Suppose we agree that we're willing to use piecewise trilinear rather than higher polynomial interpolation (because today's GPUs provide direct hardware acceleration of trilinear interpolation), and that we're willing to live with the small gradient discontinuities that result when you use trilinear interpolation.

One solution would be to place an entire volume of noise into a trilinear-interpolated texture. Unfortunately, this would be very space intensive. For example, a cube sampling noise from $(0, 0, 0)$ through $(72, 72, 72)$, containing three samples per linear unit distance plus one extra for the final endpoint, or $(3 \times 72) + 1$ samples in each direction, would require $217 \times 217 \times 217 = 10,218,313$ indexed locations, which is inconveniently large.

But the fact that today's GPUs can perform fast trilinear interpolation on reasonably small-size volumes can be exploited in a different way. For example, an $8 \times 8 \times 8$ volume sampled the same way requires $(3 \times 8) + 1$ samples in each direction, or only $25 \times 25 \times 25 = 15,625$ indexed locations. What I've been doing is to define noise through multiple references into such modest-size stored volumes.

So how do you get a 72^3 cube out of an 8^3 cube? The trick is to do it in two steps:

1. Fill the space with copies of an 8^3 sample that is a toroidal tiling. In other words, construct this sample so that it forms an endlessly repeating continuous pattern, with the top adjoining seamlessly to the bottom, the left to the right, and the back to the front. When these samples are stacked in space as cubic bricks, they will produce a continuous but repeating, space-filling texture.

2. Use this same sampled pattern, scaled up by a factor of nine, as a low-frequency pattern that varies this fine-scale brick tiling in such a way that the fine-scale pattern no longer appears to be repeating.

The details are as follows: Rather than define the values in this repeating tile as real numbers, define them as complex values. Note that this doubles the storage cost of the table (in this case, to 31,250 indexed locations). If we use a 16-bit quantity for each numeric scalar in the table, then the total required memory cost is $31,250 \times 2 \times 2$ bytes $= 125,000$ bytes to store the volume.

Evaluate both the low-frequency and the high-frequency noise texture. Then use the real component of the low-frequency texture as a rotational *phase shift* as follows: Let's say we have retrieved a complex value of (lo_r, lo_i) from the low-frequency texture and a complex value of (hi_r, hi_i) from the high-frequency texture. We use the low-frequency texture to rotate the complex value of the high-frequency texture by evaluating the expression:

$$hi_r \cos\left(2\pi lo_r\right) + hi_i \sin\left(2\pi lo_r\right).$$

The three images in Figure 5-10 show, in succession, (a) the real component of a planar slice through the high-frequency texture, (b) the real component of a planar slice through the low-frequency texture, and (c) the final noise texture obtained by combining them.

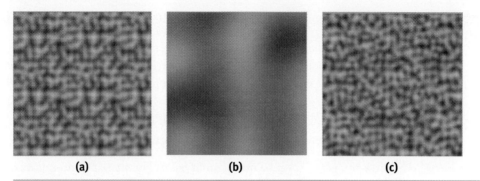

(a)   (b)   (c)

Figure 5-10. Combining High-Frequency and Low-Frequency Textures
(a) The real component of a planar slice through the high-frequency texture, (b) the real component of a planar slice through the low-frequency texture, and (c) the final noise texture obtained by combining them.

Notice that the visible tiling pattern on the leftmost image is no longer visible in the rightmost image.

5.6 Making Bumps Without Looking at Neighboring Vertices

Once you can implement Noise directly in the pixel shader, then you can implement bump mapping as follows:

1. Consider a point (x, y, z) and some function $F(x, y, z)$ that you've defined in your pixel shader through some combination of noise functions.

2. Choose some small value of ε and compute the following quantities:

$$
\begin{aligned}
F_0 &= F(x, y, z), \\
F_x &= F(x + \varepsilon, y, z), \\
F_y &= F(x, y + \varepsilon, z), \\
F_z &= F(x, y, z + \varepsilon).
\end{aligned}
$$

3. This allows a good approximation of the gradient (or derivative) vector of F at (x, y, z) by:

$$
dF = \left[\frac{F_x - F_0}{\varepsilon}, \frac{F_y - F_0}{\varepsilon}, \frac{F_z - F_0}{\varepsilon} \right].
$$

4. Subtract this gradient from your surface normal and then renormalize the result back to unit length:

$$N = normalize\left(N - dF\right).$$

Figure 5-11 shows the result of applying exactly this approach to three different procedural bump maps on a sphere: a simple *lumpy* pattern, an embossed *marble* pattern, and a fractal *crinkled* pattern.

Assuming that the model is a unit-radius sphere, the expressions that implement these bump patterns:

```
.03 * noise(x, y, z, 8);                        //LUMPY
.01 * stripes(x + 2 * turbulence(x, y, z, 1), 1.6);  //MARBLED
-.10 * turbulence(x, y, z, 1);                  //CRINKLED
```

are defined atop the following functions:

```
// STRIPES TEXTURE (GOOD FOR MAKING MARBLE)
double stripes(double x, double f) {
  double t = .5 + .5 * sin(f * 2*PI * x);
  return t * t - .5;
}


// TURBULENCE TEXTURE
double turbulence(double x, double y, double z, double f) {
  double t = -.5;
  for ( ; f <= W/12 ; f *= 2) // W = Image width in pixels
    t += abs(noise(x,y,z,f) / f);
  return t;
}
```

Figure 5-11. Bump Mapping a Sphere
Lumpy pattern (left), embossed marble (center), crinkled pattern (right).

5.7 Conclusion

Procedural texturing using volumetric noise is extremely useful in situations where you want to create an impression of natural-looking materials, without the necessity of creating an explicit texture image. Also, rather than trying to figure out how to map a texture image parametrically onto the surface of your shape, the volumetric nature of noise-based textures allows you simply to evaluate them at the (x, y, z) locations in your pixel shader. In this way, you are effectively carving your texture out of a solid material, which is often much more straightforward than trying to work out a reasonable undistorted parametric mapping.

Noise-based textures also allow you to work in a *resolution-independent* way: rather than the texture blurring out when you get nearer to an object, it can be kept crisp and detailed, as you add higher frequencies of noise to your texture-defining procedure.

As is always the case with procedural textures, you should try not to add very high frequencies that exceed the pixel sample rate. Such super-pixel frequencies do not add to the visual quality, and they result in unwanted speckling as the texture animates.

The key to being able to use noise-based textures efficiently on GPUs is the availability of an implementation of noise that really makes use of the enormous computational power of GPUs. Here we have outlined such an implementation, and shown several examples of how it can be used in your pixel shader to procedurally define bump maps.

These sorts of volumetric noise-based procedural textures have long been mainstays of feature films, where shaders do not require real-time performance, yet do require high fidelity to the visual appearance of natural materials. In fact, *all* special-effects films today make heavy use of noise-based procedural shaders. The convincing nature of such effects as the ocean waves in *A Perfect Storm* and the many surface textures and atmosphere effects in *The Lord of the Rings* trilogy, to take just two examples, is highly dependent on the extensive use of the noise function within pixel shaders written in languages such as Pixar's RenderMan. With a good implementation of the noise function available for real-time use in GPUs, I look forward to seeing some of the exciting visual ideas from feature films incorporated into the next generation of interactive entertainment on the desktop and the console.

5.8 References

Grill Spector, K., S. Edelman, and R. Malach. 1995. "Anatomical Origin and Computational Role of Diversity in the Response Properties of Cortical Neurons." In *Advances in Neural Information Processing Systems* 7, edited by G. Tesauro, D. S. Touretzky, and T. K. Leen. MIT Press.

Perlin, K. 1985. "An Image Synthesizer." *Computer Graphics* 19(3).

Perlin, K. 2002. "Improving Noise." *Computer Graphics* 35(3).

Chapter 6

Fire in the "Vulcan" Demo

Hubert Nguyen
NVIDIA

This chapter talks about the "Vulcan" demo that the NVIDIA demo team created for the launch of the GeForce FX 5900 Ultra. Inspired by the Balrog creature in *The Lord of the Rings* movies, our goal was to display a monster that would be the source of raging flames, as shown in Figure 6-1. The flames and smoke had to be massive and sometimes overwhelming. Our goal in writing this chapter is to share our experience of how we created the effect and to discuss possible enhancements. In the end, we hope that this exploration will help you to create more sophisticated fire effects in your own applications.

6.1 Creating Realistic Flames

When we started working on the demo, we first tried two solutions that looked promising: fully procedural flames and screen-space 2D distortion-based flames.

The fully procedural approach consumed very little memory, yet it created an appealing flame effect. To produce well-defined flames, we had to display thousands of particles, and processing all of those vertices and pixels put a heavy load on the CPU and the GPU. Figure 6-2 shows the effect.

The 2D distortion-based flames used a GPU-generated perturbation function that altered a flame shape to give it a realistic motion. The distortion involved making several render-to-texture passes and shifting 2D texture coordinates. Although it consumed

Figure 6-1. A Screen Capture from the "Vulcan" Demo

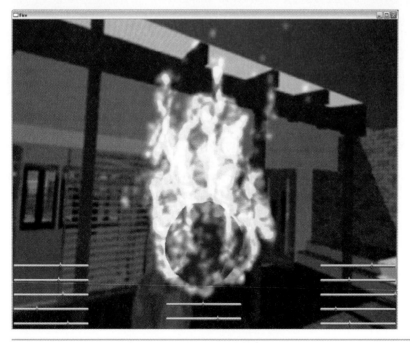

Figure 6-2. Five Thousand Particles Used to Create Fire

more memory than the particle system technique (because we had to allocate several render targets), the effect is perfect for creating candle-like flames. See Figure 6-3.

The screen-aligned nature of the effect made it sensitive to the camera view angle (constraints were needed for top and bottom views) and to motion in general (moving toward and away from the camera didn't work well in 2D sometimes). Integrating smoke was also a challenge.

Both procedural techniques have strong advantages, but they didn't meet our goal of creating a believable raging fire with smoke in a real-time, user-controllable environment. So we turned to video-textured sprites to make the fire more realistic. See Figure 6-4. Although full procedural and physically based flame generation is clearly the wave of the future, some cutting-edge movies (such as *The Lord of the Rings*) still use special effects composed of sprite-based flames.

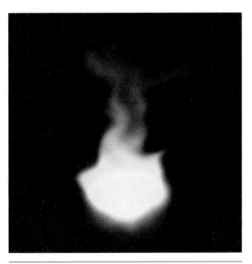 

Figure 6-3. A Flame Created Using 2D Flow   **Figure 6-4.** Three Video-Textured Fire Particles

6.2 Implementing Animated Sprites

In order to create the fire enveloping the Vulcan character, first we needed to decide where the fire was coming from. Using our modeling tool, we placed emitters on the character. Each emitter can be adjusted for size, density (that is, particles per second), texture, particle lifespan, and so on. This flexibility proved very useful, because it allowed us to tweak the fire's appearance to suit our needs. We could then spawn some particles and draw the flames, as shown in Figure 6-5.

6.2.1 Animating Flames and Smoke

Because the consumption of texture memory increased rapidly with the number of video textures we used, we had to limit ourselves to three animations: two for flames and one for smoke. At 64 frames each, 192 frames of animation were dedicated to fire and smoke, and 64 were allocated for other use, such as the flying animated spark in the demo. A 3D texture requires that the number of slices (or here, frames) be a power of two, so we used 256 frames. Had we wanted to add more, the minimum increase

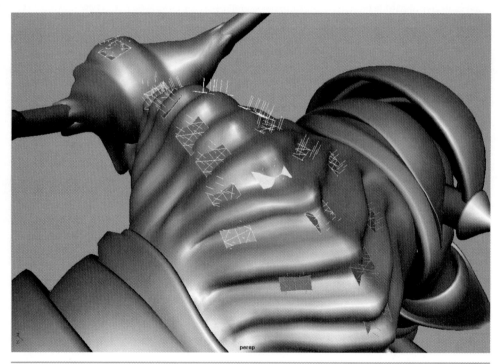

Figure 6-5. Spawning Flames
The fire is emitted from polygons placed on Vulcan. They are animated along with the polygons he comprises.

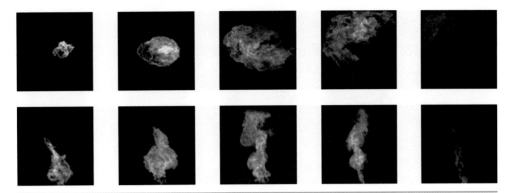

Figure 6-6. Video Footage Used to Create the Fire Effect
We used two separate video clips (top and bottom) to add variety to the final effect.

would have been to 512 frames—doubling the texture-memory footprint of this effect. See Figure 6-6.

Custom Smoke Generator

At first we thought about using video footage for the smoke as we did for the flames, but it's hard to find suitable footage of a single puff of smoke, with just the right lighting, color, and so on.

We ended up using a particle system to create a smoke generator, because the desired lighting could be achieved with various techniques, such as ray casting. We tweaked the lighting to fit the fire environment and, most important, we maintained control over the colors. We gave the smoke particles a rolling motion on the x axis so the smoke appeared to be folding into itself. This detail didn't cost anything, but it added a lot to the overall smoke effect. The result was a good integration of real fire footage and procedural smoke. See Figures 6-7 and 6-8.

Figure 6-7. Procedurally Generated Smoke
The smoke is generated procedurally and lit offline; then it is used as an animated texture.

Figure 6-8. Real-Time Smoke in the Demo

If we had used a simple smoke lighting algorithm, we might have been able to use the procedural smoke directly in the demo. However, lack of time prevented us from exploring this possibility, given that smoke lighting is a complex problem to solve.

6.2.2 Adding Variety to the Flames

Given the small number of animated frames that we could allocate to the effect, we expected that repetition of the same image in the animation could be a serious issue. There are simple ways to hide repetition and artificially add more variety. We started with a single animation, and it worked even better with two or more. In addition, we created particles with a random percentage of difference for a number of attributes: size, position, rate of decay, animation start frame, global transparency, and so on.

We also chose not to use hardware point sprites but instead generated our own quads. This technique allowed us to create custom texture coordinates to flip the animation on one or two axes. In the demo, we used horizontal and vertical flipping (along the u and v axes). This worked well, but arbitrary rotations would have been even better. See Figure 6-9.

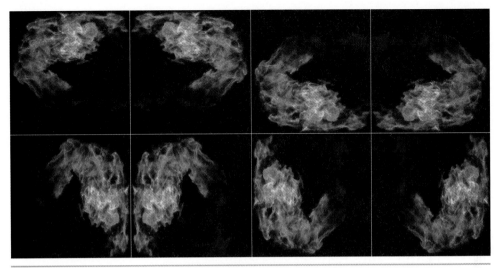

Figure 6-9. Variations Produced by Custom Texture Coordinates
Custom texture coordinates can provide more variations of a single animated frame. Arbitrary rotation would have added even more variations.

Because we had a second animation (taken from the video clips shown in Figure 6-6), we blended two kinds of sprites: A and B. Creating different percentages of A and B types added diversity to the flames and helped control the look of the effect. See Figure 6-10.

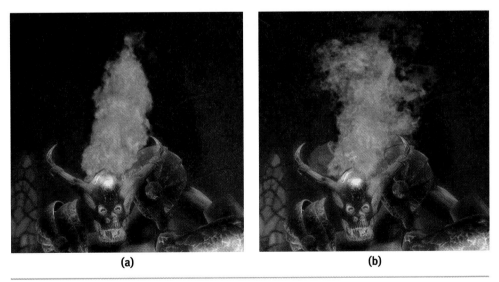

(a)   (b)

Figure 6-10. Improving Fire in the Demo
(a) Fire with less variety. (b) Fire with more variety.

6.2.3 Storing the Animation

We found it helpful to store the flames in a volume texture (also known as a 3D texture). Doing so resulted in interframe blending that compensated for the low number of animation frames. And it was convenient to handle because incrementing the z-texture coordinate "played" the animation. The whole animation appeared as a single texture to the application, which is great if the particles are sorted. Volume textures require that all sides (width, height, and depth) be a power of two. In our case, we used a compressed $256 \times 256 \times 256$ B8G8R8A8 texture, which is 16 MB. If you don't have much memory available (because you are running on a low-end card or on a console), you can try shrinking the volume; we reduced the volume size to $64 \times 64 \times 256$, and the results still looked great.

6.2.4 Blending Flames and Smoke

When we first started to implement the flames, like many game developers, we used *additive blending*, because it allows one to draw all the sprites independently (that is, in no particular order). Visually, additive blending is recognizable because it saturates color and thus removes most of the color control from the artists—whom we want to empower as much as possible. Saturation made the flames look cartoon-like, not realistic. Also, additive blending makes mixing flames and smoke even trickier—especially while rendering to the limited range and precision of an A8R8G8B8 target.

The switch to alpha blending solved those two issues, at the cost of sorting a few hundred particles per frame. The performance impact of sorting turned out to be negligible. See Figures 6-11 and 6-12.

6.3 Particle Motion

We expected the motion of the particles to involve nothing more than simple upward movement. However, getting the particle motion right required more attention than we had anticipated. Because the video texture contained most of the visual clues for the effect we wanted to create (that is, the fire), we used very few particles—a mere few hundred. Although using so few particles is great for geometric performance, it's a setback when the flame source is moving. There are not enough particles to fill the gap in the trailing flames, and particles that are sitting alone in the air ruin the effect.

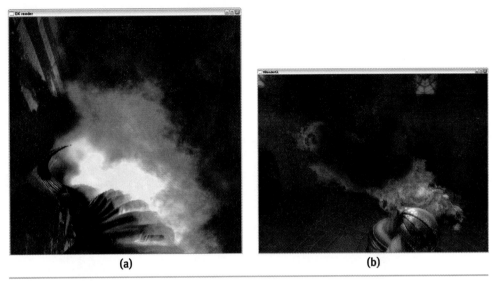

Figure 6-11. Mixing Fire and Smoke
(a) With additive blending, it's hard to combine fire and smoke. (b) Alpha blending enables the sorting of fire and smoke.

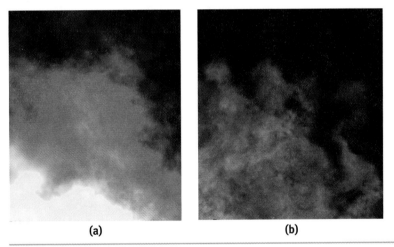

Figure 6-12. Controlling Color
(a) Additive blending saturates colors. (b) Alpha blending gives total color control.

What we wanted to see was a continuous stream of fire. To keep the continuity of the fire, we decided to bind the particles to their emitters by using weights. The principle is simple: When the particle is created, it is strongly bound to the emitter. If the emitter moves, the particle moves with it. As the particle ages, the influence of the emitter fades and the particle roams freely in the air. See Figure 6-13. This solution was enough to make the motion believable, with a minimal performance penalty.

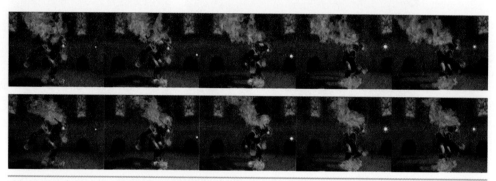

Figure 6-13. Weighting Particles for Believable Fire
Top: A few frames of fire, without using weighting. Notice that the flames are trailing too much and look unnatural. Bottom: The same frames, with weighting applied.

Finding a fluid dynamics solution for the smoke motion would have been preferable. When the character moved, he would update a fluid dynamics solution that in return would affect the smoke motion. We spent a lot of effort exploring this possibility. In the end, fluid dynamics, by itself, was effective and could be fast, if not applied over a large area. We planned to do the simulation in the character's root local space and have the fluid solution "follow" him. Unfortunately, the small number of particles and their large size prevented us from taking advantage of the subtle motion created by fluid dynamics. In future projects that have more (and smaller) particles, we will revisit this solution.

6.4 Performance

Performance was the primary concern from the start. Using large, video-textured billboards consumed an enormous amount of pixel-processing power. As shown in Figure 6-14, the average size of a sprite was big compared to the screen. Obviously, we tried to set up the blending to get the alpha-test rejection for zero-alpha pixels (GeForce FX hardware does this automatically), but we were still left with millions of frame-buffer blending and texture operations per frame, which we reduced through the following methods.

Figure 6-14. Sprite Size and Performance
Hundreds of big sprites can consume fill rate very quickly. Here, the depth complexity is significant.

6.4.1 Layer Composition

We found a solution by using layer composition. The flame source image was only 256×256, so we could afford to render it into a low-resolution buffer (a quarter of the screen resolution). This reduced the blending operations by a factor of four when we rendered the flames. See Figure 6-15.

The effect on the overall image quality was minimal, but the performance impact was huge. It was now possible to put the camera in the middle of the flames and yet have a good frame rate. See Figure 6-16.

6.4.2 Custom Sprites

As long as we were creating our own sprites, we decided that we might as well use them to enhance the performance. In the "Vulcan" demo, some particles were occupying down to one-third of the texture surface because of their square shape. In the end, it is wasteful to read all those unused texels, even if they're not blended to the frame buffer. Instead of doing square sprites, we could do rectangular sprites, which would be a better fit for some of the flames. Even better, we could do a pass that "analyzed" each frame, created the optimal rectangle to fit it, then added a 2D offset to center the sprite relative to the particle position. See Figure 6-17.

Figure 6-15. Using Layer Composition
The final composited image, with (inset, upper right) the low-resolution flames layer.

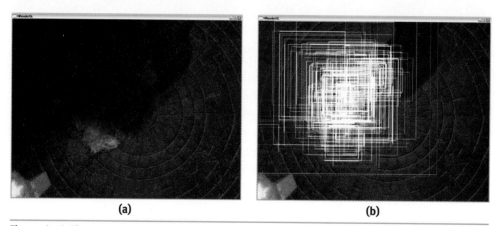

(a)　　　　　　　　　　　　　　(b)

Figure 6-16. The Worst-Case Scenario with Sprites
(a) The worst-case scenario when using sprites. (b) With compositing, the frame rate is barely affected.

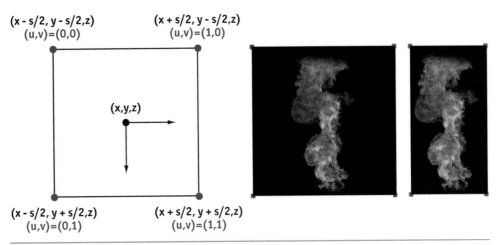

Figure 6-17. Generation Rules for DirectX 9 Point Sprites

6.5 Post-Rendering Effects

Using real-time compositing forced us to render the scene into a texture. We decided to turn this limitation into an advantage by adding post-rendering effects. We tried glow, film grain, and heat shimmer. Some effects didn't make it into the final demo because we preferred to shift pixel-processing power to other effects, such as the 2048×2048 shadow map. Conceptually, many 2D filters can be added as post-rendering effects at a linear cost, such as a color-correction matrix, as we did in our "Toys" demo.

Because we rendered the fire in a render target, we needed to z-test it against the character. Ideally we would have shared the depth buffer of the rendered scene with the fire rendering, but the render targets had different sizes, thus preventing depth-buffer sharing. As a fallback, we used a low-resolution model that we rendered into the depth buffer of the flames' render target. See Figure 6-18. It put a little bit of pressure on the vertex performance, but the savings in pixel processing justified it. In the end, only the glow effect is featured in the final demo, because it made the greatest visual contribution. See Figure 6-19.

6.5.1 Glow

We created glow by selectively adding a blurred version of the scene on top of the original one. The blur method was a two-pass box filter. In the first pass, we added an eight-pixel-wide blur on the x axis. Then we added an eight-pixel-wide blur on the y axis. We used the alpha channel of the blurred image to select which objects would be blurred.

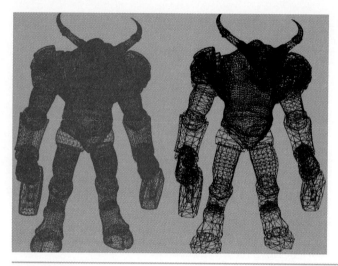

Figure 6-18.

Left: the high-resolution model. Right: the low-resolution mesh used for the fire z-test.

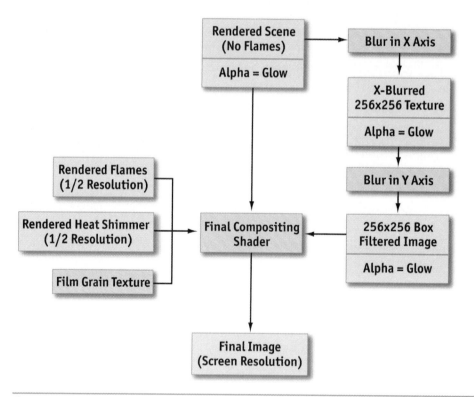

Figure 6-19. A Rendering Flowchart

See Figure 6-20, which illustrates the blurring and compositing process. Chapter 21 of this book, "Real-Time Glow," discusses this topic in much more detail.

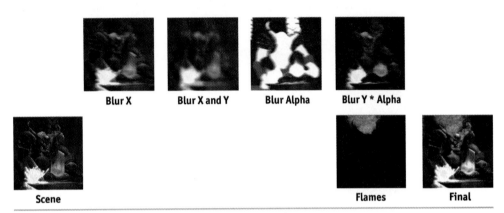

Figure 6-20. Images Computed During the Various Rendering Steps

6.5.2 Heat Shimmer

Although we had written all the code for heat shimmer, we decided in the end not to use it. The scene was too dark to make the effect interesting enough to spend the additional resources that would be needed.

Our heat shimmer was done in a straightforward way: We rendered a particle system of "heat" particles in a texture target. During the final compositing, we simply used the (red, green) values of each "heat render target" pixel as a (u, v) per-pixel 2D texture coordinates displacement during the texel fetch of the "rendered scene" texture target. That created a noise effect that looked like heat shimmer. See Figure 6-21.

Many game developers are using heat shimmering on a per-vertex basis, which also was a possibility for us. For example, it is possible to read from the same "heat render," and then use the values to perturb a tessellated 2D grid and deform the image. See Figure 6-22.

6.5.3 Grain

Grain is often used in the movie industry to give computer-generated effects the same grain as the film. In our demo, we used grain to "soften" the rendering, and it worked. However, we worried that the audience might not like the grain or, worse, think of it as "jaggies," so we removed it. The grain texture was simply created using the Photoshop Noise filter. See Figures 6-23 and 6-24.

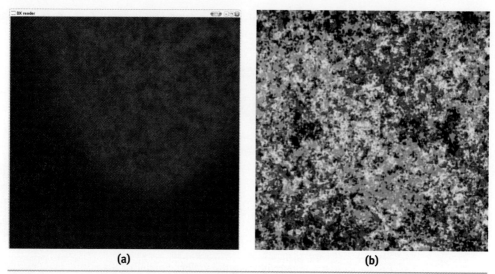

Figure 6-21. Heat Shimmer
(a) Heat particles rendered in a texture. (b) Heat shimmer noise texture.

Figure 6-22. Per-Pixel Heat Shimmer During Development

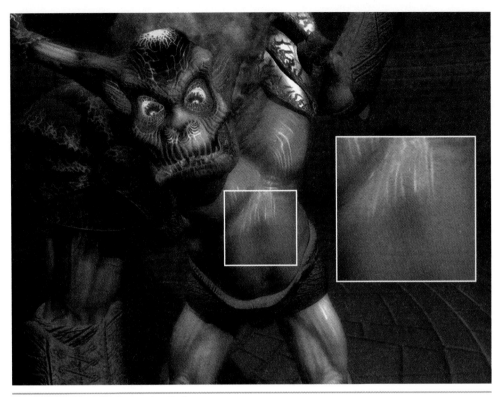

Figure 6-23. Zooming In on the Grain

Figure 6-24. The Texture Where the Grain Pattern Is Stored

6.5.4 The Final Program

Listing 6-1 shows the shader that brings together all the different layers to create the final image.

Listing 6-1. The Final Shader

```
struct v2fConnector {
  float2 tex1024x768   : TEXCOORD0;
  float2 colorTexGrain : TEXCOORD1;
  float2 tex256x192    : TEXCOORD2;
  float2 tex512x384    : TEXCOORD3;
  float2 texNormalized : TEXCOORD4;
};

struct f2fConnector {
  float4 COL;
};

f2fConnector main(v2fConnector v2f,
                  uniform texobjRECT renderedflames,  // "Flames"
                  uniform texobjRECT renderedscene,  // "Scene"
                  uniform texobj2D   grain,  // "Grain"
                  uniform texobjRECT heat,  // "Heat"
                  uniform texobjRECT blur)  // "BlurY", "Blur Alpha"
{
  f2fConnector f2f;

  // Fetch heat distortion offset
  half4 HeatDistort = f4texRECT(heat, v2f.tex512x384) *
                      float4(17, 23, 0, 1);

  // Fetch scene render using heat distortion
  half4 Scene = f4texRECT(renderedscene, v2f.tex1024x768 +
                          HeatDistort.xy);

  // Fetch blurred version of the scene
  half4 BlurredScene = f4texRECT(blur, v2f.tex256x192);

  // Fetch flames and smoke
  half4 FlamesSmoke = f4texRECT(renderedflames, v2f.tex512x384);

  // Extract bright parts from blurred scene
  half4 Glow = BlurredScene * BlurredScene.a + Scene;
```

Listing 6-1 (*continued*). The Final Shader

```
// Compute final color output
half4 Fcompoblur = lerp(Scene, BlurredScene, HeatDistort.a);
half4 Fcomposited = lerp(Fcompoblur, FlamesSmoke, FlamesSmoke.a);

f2f.COL = Fcomposited + Glow;

return f2f;
}
```

6.6 Conclusion

In the end, we were able to achieve our goal of displaying some fairly realistic fire. Using video-based footage proved to be a good solution. Even though this technique is fairly memory intensive, it is scalable enough to be used on GPUs that have a small amount of memory. Fire effects will always be needed in many games, and we hope that this chapter inspires you to produce more advanced fire effects in your own applications.

Chapter 7

Rendering Countless Blades of Waving Grass

Kurt Pelzer
Piranha Bytes

7.1 Introduction

To simulate an idyllic nature scene in a realistic fashion, besides detailed trees and bushes, as well as a complex water and sky dome simulation, we need a high-quality grass effect. We must be able to cover large areas of the terrain with it, without monopolizing the GPU. The grass should look naturally grown and should wave realistically in the wind.

In the past, a high-quality grass simulation would have been considered too complex for real-time applications. The Codecreatures Benchmark (published by Codecult in 2002) disproved this pessimistic assertion. See Figure 7-1. In this chapter, we describe a flexible, widely applicable grass simulation based on the grass effect shown in the benchmark. Additionally, a special version of our Codecreatures Benchmark application is included in this book's accompanying material, which offers an interactive demo mode.

7.2 Overview

First, we should realize that a detailed modeling of the individual blades of grass is not meaningful, because the number of polygons that would be required for larger meadows would be much too high. A scene with countless blades of polygonal grass would not be displayable in real time with the graphics hardware available today.

Figure 7-1. Screenshot of the Codecreatures Benchmark Application

So we have to build a simple and useful alternative that meets the following conditions:

- Many blades of grass must be represented by few polygons.
- Grass must appear dense from different lines of sight.

In the next section, we build grass objects that meet these conditions.

Additionally, we must be able to animate the grass realistically. In Section 7.4, we discuss three different animation methods.

7.3 Preparation of the Grass Objects

As we just mentioned, many blades of grass must be represented by few polygons. We start by solving this problem. Independent of the camera position and direction, the appearance should be like that of an open countryside. Fortunately, the solution is not too difficult. In Section 7.3.1, we start by combining several blades of grass and displaying them in one texture. But this is not enough: some polygons that use this texture must be combined in such a way that the individual polygons are not noticeable (see Section 7.3.2). When the viewer moves around, we add or remove grass objects in the distance by blending them in or out. This ensures that the complete grass effect will have robust visual quality.

7.3.1 Grass Texture

Now let us see how to build a texture for the task we have to solve. The required texture has to cluster several blades of grass; otherwise, it will have large transparent areas. We obtain this simply by drawing solid grass stems in a transparent alpha channel. In the color channel, we should use different shades of green and yellow to get a better differentiation of single blades. We may want to simulate blades of grass in good and bad conditions, to represent differences in age or ripeness, and even to distinguish front and back faces of the blades.

A concrete example of a grass texture is shown in Figure 7-2.

7.3.2 Grass Objects

This section explains how to combine some polygons, mapped with the grass texture built in the previous section, in a way that the simulated grass appears dense, and without highlighting individual polygons. The technique also guarantees that the individual polygons are not visible.

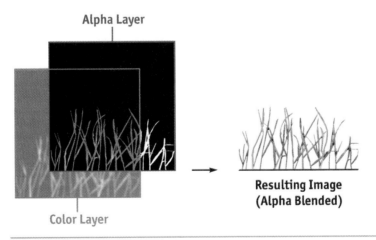

Figure 7-2. Schematic of a Grass Texture

Because the user can navigate freely through the scene, a construction similar to the one shown in Figure 7-3 would be insufficient to produce a convincing effect. A linear arrangement of the grass polygons would immediately make the structure recognizable if someone were to view the scene perpendicular relative to the direction of the polygons. Additionally, the grass would look very thin in this case. An arrangement like this one should be considered only with automatic camera navigation or unreachable, far-distant meadows.

To ensure good visual quality independent of the current line of sight, we have to cross the grass polygons. Using configurations that look like stars proves very worthwhile. Figure 7-4 presents two possible variants of "grass objects," consisting of three intersecting quads. We have to render the polygons with disabled back-face culling to achieve visibility on both sides. To attain proper illumination, we should orient the normal vectors of all vertices parallel to the polygons' vertical edges. This guarantees correct lighting for all grass objects situated on slopes, with no differences due to the brightness of the terrain.

If we set these grass objects quite close together in a large area, as shown in Figure 7-5, sort them back-to-front at runtime, use alpha blending, and enable z-testing/writing in the draw call, then the impression of a naturally and thickly grown meadow appears.

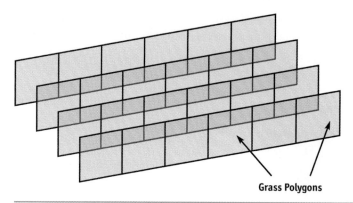

Grass Polygons

Figure 7-3. Linear Arrangement

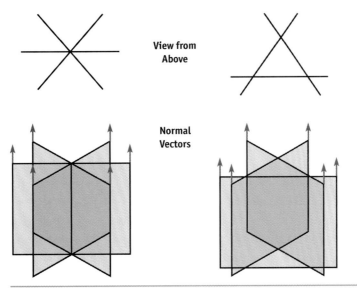

Figure 7-4. Grass Objects

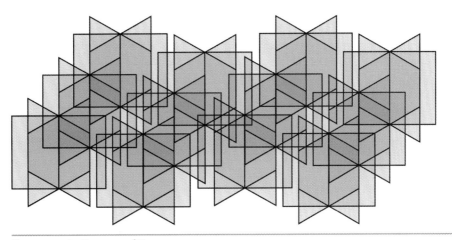

Figure 7-5. An Expanse of Grass

7.4 Animation

To continue with the next step, we want to realistically animate the grass of a complete meadow, built with "grass objects" like those presented in Figure 7-5. This section describes three different variants of animation. Each has its pros and cons. Section 7.4.1 presents the general idea of our animation methods. In Section 7.4.2, clusters of several grass objects standing close together are animated in the same way. In Section 7.4.3, each vertex gets its own translation vector. Finally, in Section 7.4.4, we try to find the golden mean: a different animation for each grass object.

7.4.1 The General Idea

In order to achieve a highly realistic animation, we are going to use a calculation based on trigonometric functions, especially sine and cosine. This calculation should take into account the position that has to be moved (whether it is a vertex or the center of an object or cluster) and the current time. Also, the direction and strength of the prevailing wind will be factors. Each of our techniques moves only the upper vertices of the grass objects. In a vertex shader it is easy to differentiate between these vertices and the lower ones by examining the texture coordinates. All upper vertices should have the same v coordinate for the grass texture: such as zero, or a value close to it. The framework in the vertex shader code, as shown in Listing 7-1, is the same in all three techniques; only the pure animation part differs. The animation code can be found in the following sections.

Listing 7-1. Framework in the Vertex Shader

```
//
// Equal Cg / HLSL framework in the vertex shaders
// for Sections 7.4.2, 7.4.3, and 7.4.4
//

struct VS_INPUT {
  float3 vPosition : POSITION;
  float3 vNormal   : NORMAL;
  float2 TexCoords : TEXCOORD0;

  // This member is needed in Section 7.4.4
  float3 vObjectPosition : TEXCOORD1;
};

struct VS_OUTPUT {
  float4 vPosition : POSITION;
  float4 vDiffuse  : COLOR;
  float2 TexCoords : TEXCOORD0;
};
```

Listing 7-1 (*continued*). Framework in the Vertex Shader

```
struct VS_TEMP {
  float3 vPosition;
  float3 vNormal;
};

float4x4 mWorldViewProjMatrix;
float4   vLight;
float    fObjectHeight;

VS_OUTPUT main(const VS_INPUT v)
{
  VS_OUTPUT out;
  VS_TEMP temp;

  // Animate the upper vertices and normals only
  if (v.TexCoords.y <= 0.1) {   // Or: if(v.TexCoords.y >= 0.9)
    // A N I M A T I O N  (to world space)
    // Insert the code for 7.4.2, 7.4.3, or 7.4.4
    . . .  // <- Code for our different animation methods
  }

  // Output stuff
  out.vPosition = mul(float4(temp.vPosition, 1),
                      mWorldViewProjMatrix);
  out.vDiffuse = dot(vLight, temp.vNormal);
  out.TexCoords = v.TexCoords;
  return out;
}
```

7.4.2 Animation per Cluster of Grass Objects

The following method was used in the Codecreatures Benchmark and produces a realistic look with gusting winds that constantly change strength and direction. Here, the shift of the upper polygon vertices happens uniformly for a group of nearby grass objects. To produce a natural-looking animation, we should select a cluster size that is not too large. See Figure 7-6.

The translation vector for the animation is computed by the CPU and is handed over to the vertex shader as a constant parameter. Using a more expensive algorithm on the CPU allows us to take advantage of a very complex wind simulation. Because we supply

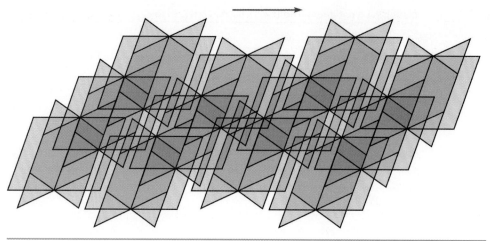

Figure 7-6. Animation per Cluster of Grass Objects

each cluster of grass objects with its own translation vector, we have to change this constant parameter for each cluster. So we have to interrupt the rendering of a complete meadow quite often and use a separate draw call for each cluster.

Pros

- Complex animation calculations are made through CPU-based algorithms.
- There are no distortions, because of the constant distance of the upper vertices of a polygon.

Cons

- Many draw calls are required to display a complete meadow.
- Clusters may be apparent due to synchronized animation of all vertices of a complete object cluster.

Algorithm

1. On the CPU, calculate the current translation vector for the next cluster using the position of the cluster's center.
2. Set the translation vector as a constant for the vertex shader.
3. Execute a draw call for the cluster.
4. In the vertex shader, add the translation vector to the positions of the upper vertices. See Listing 7-2.

Listing 7-2. Code for Animation per Cluster of Grass Objects

```
//
// Animation per Cluster of Grass Objects (7.4.2)
//

float3 vClusterTranslation; // Calculated on CPU

VS_OUTPUT main(const VS_INPUT v)
{
  . . .
  // A N I M A T I O N (to world space)
  // Here comes the code for 7.4.2
  temp.vPosition = v.vPosition + vClusterTranslation;
  temp.vNormal = normalize(v.vNormal * fObjectHeight +
                           vClusterTranslation);

  ...
}
```

7.4.3 Animation per Vertex

One of the main problems with the method discussed in Section 7.4.2 is poor performance because of the high number of draw calls, which individually render only a small number of polygons. It would be better if we could render a large area covered with grass by using a much lower number of draw calls. However, we have to relocate the complete animation computation into the vertex shader to be able to move each vertex separately, relative to its position. See Figure 7-7.

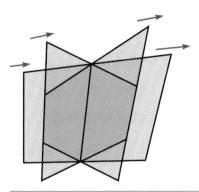

Figure 7-7. Animation per Vertex

Because the translations for each vertex are computed individually, the length of the edge between the upper vertices of the grass polygons is no longer constant, as shown in Figure 7-8. Therefore, visible distortions may appear because of the inconstant length and thickness of each blade of grass, but typically these artifacts will not be very noticeable.

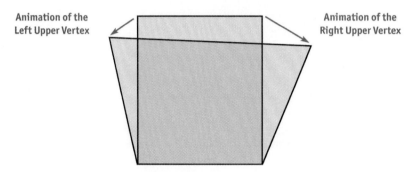

Animation of the Left Upper Vertex

Animation of the Right Upper Vertex

Figure 7-8. Texture Distortion

Additionally, the overall effect may seem more unnatural than in the previous method. Because the translation of all vertices in a nearby region is very similar, an absence of local chaos and a very homogeneous animation results. We are able to eliminate this disadvantage by using a pseudo-random function in the vertex shader to achieve more varied results.

Pros
- Only a few draw calls, perhaps even just one, are necessary to display a complete meadow.
- Varying the vertex position in the vertex shader allows for the continuity of a rippling wave of wind.
- The clusters are indistinguishable.

Cons
- Distortion appears, due to the variable distance of the upper vertices of a polygon.
- Animation may appear homogeneous due to a lack of local chaos.
- The complexity of the animation calculation is limited.

Algorithm

1. Set constants, such as time stamp and the basic strength and direction of the wind, for the vertex shader.

2. Execute one draw call for the complete meadow or large area of grass.

3. Use the vertex shader to calculate animation based on vertex position. See Listing 7-3.

Listing 7-3. Code for Animation per Vertex

```
//
// Animation per Vertex (7.4.3)
//

float   fTimeStamp;
float3  vWindDirection;
float   fWindStrength;

VS_OUTPUT main(const VS_INPUT v)
{
  . . .
  // A N I M A T I O N  (to world space)
  // Here comes the code for 7.4.3
  float3 vVertexTranslation = CalcTranslation(v.vPosition,
                                              fTimeStamp,
                                              vWindDirection,
                                              fWindStrength);
  temp.vPosition = v.vPosition + vVertexTranslation;
  temp.vNormal = normalize(v.vNormal * fObjectHeight +
                          vVertexTranslation);
  . . .
}
```

7.4.4 Animation per Grass Object

To increase the apparent visual complexity of the animation based on the methods presented in Sections 7.4.2 and 7.4.3, we combine an undistorted grass texture and a low number of draw calls with local chaos—and thereby gain the advantages of both methods. We are able to combine these methods because we do not compute the animation for each vertex based on its position; rather, we do it based on the center position of the grass object—each consisting of three intersecting quads (see Section 7.3.2).

Because neighboring grass objects now have different animations, we can represent the desired local chaos, as shown in Figure 7-9. Additionally, the constant animation for each grass object prevents the horizontal texture distortions.

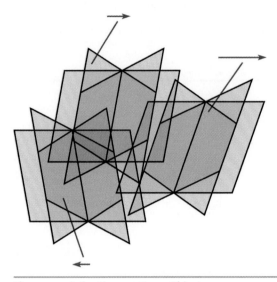

Figure 7-9. Animation per Grass Object

To make this possible, each vertex must know the center position of its object, either relative to its position or absolute in the world. The grass object position vector needed for this information must be in the vertex format (that is, stored in texture coordinates), because the vertex shader has to read this value.

Pros

- Only a few draw calls, perhaps even just one, are necessary to display a complete meadow.
- There are no distortions, because of the constant distance of the upper vertices of a polygon.
- Local variance creates a more natural look.

Cons

- Additional data is required in the vertex format, because each vertex also contains the center position value of its grass object.

- The complexity of the animation calculations is limited, in order to minimize shader cost.

Algorithm

1. Set constants, such as time stamp and the basic strength and direction of the wind, for the vertex shader.

2. Execute one draw call for the complete meadow or large area of grass.

3. In the vertex shader, compute animation based on the center position of the grass object. See Listing 7-4.

Listing 7-4. Code for Animation per Grass Object

```
//
// Animation per Grass Object (7.4.4)
//

float   fTimeStamp;
float3  vWindDirection;
float   fWindStrength;

VS_OUTPUT main(const VS_INPUT v)
{
  . . .
  // A N I M A T I O N  (to world space)
  // Here comes the code for 7.4.4
  float3 vObjectTranslation = CalcTranslation(v.vObjectPosition,
                                              fTimeStamp,
                                              vWindDirection,
                                              fWindStrength);
  temp.vPosition = v.vPosition + vObjectTranslation;
  temp.vNormal = normalize(v.vNormal * fObjectHeight +
                           vObjectTranslation);

  . . .
}
```

7.5 Conclusion

We have succeeded in building a realistic grass simulation that meets the three most important requirements:

- Extensive usability without overly stressing performance
- Natural appearance from all lines of sight
- Animation based on prevailing wind conditions (with three different variants)

A special version of the Codecreatures Benchmark application, offering an interactive demo mode as shown in Figure 7-10, can be found on the book's CD or Web site. In the application, you can navigate using a free camera and switch the render states. You are encouraged to examine this application and take a look behind the scenes!

Figure 7-10. Screenshot of the Codecreatures Benchmark

7.6 Further Reading

If you are interested in doing some more research on simulating animated grass, here are some resources that deal with this subject.

You can find articles that describe vertex shaders using a sine function to do the procedural animation of the grass geometry here:

NVIDIA Corporation. 2003. "Basic Profile Sample Shaders: Grass." In *The Cg Toolkit User's Manual.* Available online at
http://developer.nvidia.com/object/cg_users_manual.html

Isidoro, J., and D. Card. 2002. "Animated Grass with Pixel and Vertex Shaders." In *Direct3D ShaderX*, edited by W. F. Engel. Wordware Publishing.

Other demos presenting grass effects are available on the following two Web sites. These two demos also use vertex shaders to calculate the waving motions of the grass geometry:

NVIDIA Web site: **http://developer.nvidia.com/view.asp?IO=demo_grass**

ATI Web site: **http://www.ati.com/developer/Samples/Grass.html**

I would like to thank my colleagues at Piranha Bytes and Codecult who contributed to the Codecreatures Benchmark, especially Horst Dworczak (Lead Artist), who had the idea to build and animate the grass objects in the way presented in the Benchmark; and Oliver Hoeller (Lead Programmer), who helped to integrate the complete effect into the engine.

Chapter 8

Simulating Diffraction

Jos Stam
Alias Systems

8.1 What Is Diffraction?

Most surface reflection models in computer graphics ignore the wavelike effects of natural light. This is fine whenever the surface detail is much larger than the wavelength of light (roughly a micron). For surfaces with small-scale detail such as a compact disc, however, wave effects cannot be neglected. The small-scale surface detail causes the reflected waves to interfere with one another. This phenomenon is known as *diffraction.*

Diffraction causes the reflected light from these surfaces to exhibit many colorful patterns, as you can see in the subtle reflections from a compact disc. Other surfaces that exhibit diffraction are now common and are mass-produced to create funky wrapping paper, colorful toys, and fancy watermarks, for example.

In this chapter we show how to model diffraction effects on arbitrary surfaces in real time. This is possible thanks to the programmable hardware available on current graphics cards. In particular, we provide a complete implementation of our shader using the Cg programming language. Our shader is a simplified version of the more general model described in our SIGGRAPH 1999 paper (Stam 1999).

8.1.1 The Wave Theory of Light

At a fundamental level, light behaves as a wave. In fact, the ray theory of light used in computer graphics is an approximation of this wave theory. Waves appear in many physical theories of natural phenomena. This is not surprising, because Nature abounds with repeating patterns, both in space and in time.

The simple, one-dimensional wave in Figure 8-1 is completely described by its wavelength λ and amplitude A. The wavelength characterizes the oscillating pattern, while the amplitude determines the intensity of the wave. Visible light comprises a superposition of these waves, with wavelengths ranging from 0.5 microns (ultraviolet) to 1 micron (infrared). The color of a light source is determined by the distribution of amplitudes of the waves emanating from it. For example, a reddish light source is composed mainly of waves whose wavelengths peak in the 1-micron range, but sunlight has an equal distribution of waves across all wavelengths.

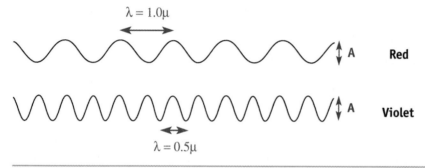

Figure 8-1. Light Waves Range from Ultraviolet to Infrared

8.1.2 The Physics of Diffraction

Our simple diffraction shader models the reflection of light from a surface commonly known as a *diffraction grating*. A diffraction grating is composed of a set of parallel, narrow reflecting bands separated by a distance d. Figure 8-2a shows a cross section of this surface.

A light wave emanating from a light source is usually approximated by a planar wave. A cross section of this wave is depicted by drawing the lines that correspond to the crests of the wave. Unlike a simple, one-dimensional wave, a planar wave requires a specified direction, in addition to its wavelength and amplitude. Figure 8-2a depicts a planar wave incident on our diffraction grating. Note that the spacing between the lines corre-

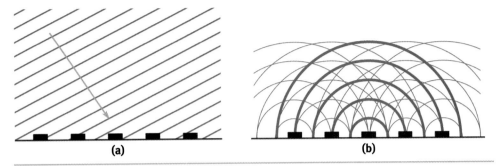

Figure 8-2. A Diffraction Grating
(a) A planar wave hits a diffraction grating and (b) generates spherical waves.

sponds to the wavelength λ. When this type of planar wave hits the diffraction grating, it generates a spherical wave at each band, as shown in Figure 8-2b. The wavelength of the spherical waves is the same as that of the incoming planar, and their crests are depicted similarly. The only difference is that the crests lie on concentric circles instead of parallel lines. The reflected wave at any receiving point away from the surface is equal to the sum of the spherical waves at that location.

The main difference between the wave theory and the usual ray theory is that the amplitudes do not simply add up. Waves interfere. We illustrate this phenomenon in Figure 8-3, where we show two extreme cases. In the first case (a), the two waves are "in phase" and the amplitudes add up, as in the ray theory. In the second case (b), the waves cancel each other, resulting in a wave of zero amplitude. These two cases illustrate that waves can interfere both positively and negatively. In general, the resulting

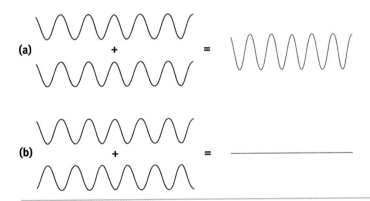

Figure 8-3. Wave Interference
(a) Two in-phase waves. (b) Two waves canceling each other.

wave lies somewhere in between these two extremes. The first case is, however, the one we are most interested in: When waves interfere in phase, they produce the maximum possible intensity, which eventually will be observed at the receiver.

We now explain in more detail the notion of waves being in phase. As is usual in this situation, we assume that the light source and the receiver are "far away" from the surface, as compared to the size of the surface detail. This is reasonable because the surface detail is a couple of microns wide, and we often observe a surface from a distance of 1 meter. That's six orders of magnitude in scale. In this case, we can assume that all the waves emanating from the surface and ending up at the receiver are parallel. Therefore, the waves reaching the receiver are exactly in phase when the paths from the light source to the receiver for different bands differ only by multiples of the wavelength λ. Let θ_1 be the angle of the direction of the incident planar wave and θ_2 be the angle to the receiver.

Then, from Figure 8-4 and using some basic trigonometry, we conclude that the waves are in phase whenever:

$$|u| d = n\lambda,$$

where n is an arbitrary positive integer and $u = \sin \theta_1 - \sin \theta_2$. This relation gives us exactly the wavelengths that interfere to give a maximum intensity at the receiver. These wavelengths are:

$$\lambda_n = \frac{|u| d}{n}.$$

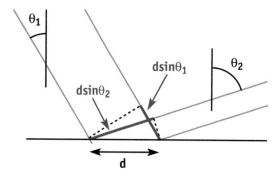

Figure 8-4. Angles Used for Computing the Difference in Phase Between Reflected Waves

Because n is arbitrary, this gives us an infinite number of wavelengths. However, only the wavelengths in the range [0.5, 1] microns correspond to visible light. So this gives us a range of possible values for n in terms of $|u|$ and the spacing d:

$$|u|d < n < 2|u|d.$$

Consequently, the color of the light at the receiver is equal to the sum of the colors of all waves having wavelengths given by the preceding formula.

What is the color corresponding to a given wavelength? As stated previously, the colors range from red to violet in a rainbow fashion. Although the exact color can be determined theoretically for a specific wavelength, we rely on a simple approximation instead. All that we require is a *rainbow map*, with colors ranging from violet to red, mimicking the rainbow. Let $C(\lambda) = (R(\lambda), G(\lambda), B(\lambda))$ be such a map, returning an RGB value for each wavelength λ in the interval [0.5, 1] microns. Then the color of the light reaching the observer is given by summing the colors $C(|u|d/n)$ for each valid n. Notice that when $u = 0$ (exact reflection), all wavelengths contribute to the reflection. We will deal with this case separately in the implementation of our shader.

8.2 Implementation

We now describe our implementation of the theory as a vertex program in Cg. Of course, we could have implemented it using a fragment program. Our implementation should work for any mesh, as long as a "tangent vector" is provided, plus the normal and position for each vertex. The tangent vectors supply the local direction of the narrow bands on the surface. For a compact disc, they are in the direction of the tracks, as shown in Figure 8-5.

The complete implementation of our vertex program is given in Listing 8-1.

Figure 8-5. Tangent Vectors for the Compact Disc

Listing 8-1. The Diffraction Shader Vertex Program

```
float3 blend3 (float3 x)
{
  float3 y = 1 - x * x;
  y = max(y, float3(0, 0, 0));
  return (y);
}

void vp_Diffraction (
  in float4 position : POSITION,
  in float3 normal    : NORMAL,
  in float3 tangent   : TEXCOORD0,
  out float4 position0 : POSITION,
  out float4 color0     : COLOR,
  uniform float4x4 ModelViewProjectionMatrix,
  uniform float4x4 ModelViewMatrix,
  uniform float4x4 ModelViewMatrixIT,
  uniform float r,
  uniform float d,
  uniform float4 hiliteColor,
  uniform float3 lightPosition,
  uniform float3 eyePosition
)
{
  float3 P = mul(ModelViewMatrix, position).xyz;
  float3 L = normalize(lightPosition - P);
  float3 V = normalize(eyePosition - P);
  float3 H = L + V;
  float3 N = mul((float3x3)ModelViewMatrixIT, normal);
  float3 T = mul((float3x3)ModelViewMatrixIT, tangent);
  float u = dot(T, H) * d;
  float w = dot(N, H);
  float e = r * u / w;
  float c = exp(-e * e);
  float4 anis = hiliteColor * float4(c.x, c.y, c.z, 1);

  if (u < 0) u = -u;

  float4 cdiff = float4(0, 0, 0, 1);
```

Listing 8-1 (*continued*). The Diffraction Shader Vertex Program

```
    for (int n = 1; n < 8; n++)
    {
        float y = 2 * u / n - 1;
        cdiff.xyz += blend3(float3(4 * (y - 0.75), 4 * (y - 0.5),
                                   4 * (y - 0.25)));
    }

    position0 = mul(ModelViewProjectionMatrix, position);

    color0 = cdiff + anis;
}
```

The code computes the colorful diffraction pattern and the main anisotropic highlight corresponding to the $u = 0$ case.

Let's first describe the computation of the diffraction pattern. From the halfway vector between the light source and the receiver (not normalized), we compute the u value by projecting it onto the local tangent vector. From this value and the spacing d, we then compute the wavelengths that interfere in phase. If we compute the wavelength correctly, we should first determine the range of n values that are valid, and then sum over the corresponding colors. However, currently the Cg compiler unrolls its for loops; therefore the size of the loop is limited by the allowable size of the vertex program. So we decided to use a fixed number of allowable n's in our implementation. The value we currently use is 8. In later versions of our shader, we might want to allow variable for loops, depending on $|u|$ and d, as explained in Section 8.1.2.

To determine the color corresponding to a given wavelength, we use a simple approximation of a rainbow map. Basically, the map should range from violet to red and produce most colors in the rainbow. We found that a simple blend of three identical bump functions (which peak in the blue, green, and red regions) worked well, as shown in Figure 8-6.

More precisely, our bump function is equal to:

$$bump(x) = |x| > 1 ? 0 : 1 - x \times x.$$

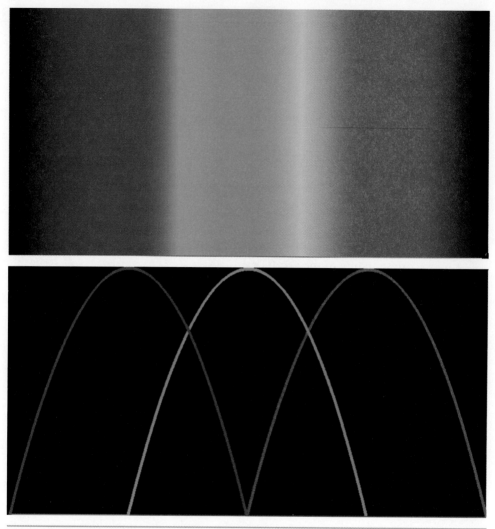

Figure 8-6. The Rainbow Color Map Used in the Shader

Then, using this function, we can define the RGB components of our rainbow map as:

$$R(\lambda) = bump\Big(C \times \big(y - 0.75\big)\Big),$$

$$G(\lambda) = bump\Big(C \times \big(y - 0.50\big)\Big),$$

$$B(\lambda) = bump\Big(C \times \big(y - 0.25\big)\Big),$$

where $y = 2\lambda - 1$ maps the wavelength to the [0, 1] micron range, and C is a shape parameter that controls the appearance of the rainbow map. In our implementation we found that $C = 4.0$ gave acceptable results. This is just one possible rainbow map. In fact, a better solution might be to use a one-dimensional texture map or a table lookup.

The case when $u = 0$ is dealt with using a simple anisotropic shader. Theoretically, this should just correspond to an infinitely thin white highlight. However, the irregularities in the bumps on each of the bands of the diffraction grating (on a compact disc, for example) cause a visible spread of the highlight. Therefore, we decided to model this contribution with a simple anisotropic shader by Greg Ward (Ward 1992). The spread of the highlight is modeled using a roughness parameter r and its color is given by the *hiliteColor* parameter. The resulting expression for this contribution is:

$$anis = hiliteColor \times \exp\left(-\left(ru/w\right)^2\right),$$

where w is the component of the halfway vector in the normal direction.

The final color is simply the sum of the colorful diffraction pattern and the anisotropic highlight.

8.3 Results

We wrote a program that uses the diffraction vertex shader to visualize the reflection from a compact disc. The compact disc is modeled as a set of thin quads. Of course, our shader is not restricted to the geometry of a compact disc: all that is required is that a tangent direction be provided for each vertex.

In addition, we added a thin transparent layer on the compact disc with a Fresnel-like reflection shader. This layer reflects the environment more strongly for glancing angles. Figure 8-7 shows three snapshots of our real-time demo, with the CD in three different positions. Figure 8-8 shows our diffraction shader applied to a surface where we have texture-mapped the principal direction of anisotropy.

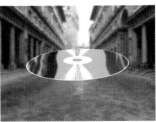

Figure 8-7. Three Snapshots of Our Compact Disc Real-Time Demo

Figure 8-8. Three Snapshots of a Surface with a Texture-Mapped Principal Direction of Anisotropy

8.4 Conclusion

We have shown how to implement a simple diffraction shader that demonstrates some of the wavelike features of natural light. Derivations for more complicated surface detail can be found in our SIGGRAPH 1999 paper (Stam 1999). Readers who are interested in learning more about the wave theory of light can consult the classic book *Principles of Optics* (Born and Wolf 1999), which we have found useful. Possible directions of future work might include more complicated surfaces than a simple diffraction grating. For example, it would be challenging to model the reflection from metallic paints, which consist of several scattering layers. The small pigments in these paints cause many visible wavelike effects. Developing such a model would have many applications in the manufacturing of new paints.

8.5 References

Born, Max, and Emil Wolf. 1999. *Principles of Optics: Electromagnetic Theory of Propagation, Interference and Diffraction to Light*, 7th ed. Cambridge University Press.

Stam, Jos, 1999. "Diffraction Shaders." In *Proceedings of SIGGRAPH 99*, pp. 101–110.

Ward, Greg. 1992. "Measuring and Modeling Anisotropic Reflection." In *Proceedings of SIGGRAPH 92*, pp. 265–272.

PART II
LIGHTING
AND SHADOWS

From surface shaders that determine how surface parameters and scene parameters are combined to produce color, to algorithms that organize scene objects in an efficient manner, the choice of a lighting and shadowing algorithm often has the single greatest impact on the design of your rendering engine. Choosing an algorithm influences more than just the look of your scenes: it affects the way content is authored and how complex and interactive your scenes can be. The chapters in this part of the book describe various algorithms for lighting and shadowing, along with techniques for making these algorithms more efficient and robust.

In **Chapter 9, "Effective Shadow Volume Rendering," Morgan McGuire** thoroughly covers the popular stencil shadow volume technique for rendering real-time shadows. Stencil shadow volumes, although often simple to implement initially, are notoriously difficult to make robust and fast. This chapter focuses on getting the corner cases right and reducing the geometry and fill-rate costs of the technique.

Fabio Pellacini and **Kiril Vidimce,** in **Chapter 10, "Cinematic Lighting,"** present a general lighting shader based on a shader used by Pixar Animation Studios but simplified for real-time lighting. This *uberlight* shader, as it is known, was written with the fundamental goal of giving control over as many lighting parameters as possible to the artist lighting the scene.

One of the most popular general real-time lighting algorithms today is shadow maps. A major issue that arises when using shadow maps is aliasing. In **Chapter 11, "Shadow Map Antialiasing," Mike Bunnell** and **Fabio Pellacini** describe how to reduce shadow map aliasing efficiently through percentage-closer filtering.

Chapter 12, "Omnidirectional Shadow Mapping" by **Philipp S. Gerasimov,** extends the shadow map idea to correctly handle omnidirectional (point) light sources. Implementation details, including fallbacks depending on hardware capabilities, are included.

Most shadows in real-time games are hard-edged and aliased, due to their being approximated as simple point lights without area. In the real world, all lights have nonzero area, and therefore all shadows have varying degrees of softness. In **Chapter 13, "Generating Soft Shadows Using Occlusion Interval Maps," Will Donnelly** and **Joe Demers** introduce a new technique for accurately rendering soft shadows in static scenes with lights that move along predetermined paths. This technique was used in the NVIDIA GeForce FX 5900 launch demo, "Last Chance Gas."

Simon Kozlov continues the antialiasing crusade in **Chapter 14, "Perspective Shadow Maps: Care and Feeding."** He presents new ideas on optimizing perspective shadow maps, a new kind of shadow map introduced by Stamminger and Drettakis at SIGGRAPH 2002. Perspective shadow maps strive to reduce or eliminate shadow map aliasing artifacts by maximizing shadow map texel density for objects that are projected to large pixel areas.

Finally, in **Chapter 15, "Managing Visibility for Per-Pixel Lighting," John O'Rorke** observes that techniques that increase visual complexity also tend to increase the number of batches being sent to the hardware—a crucial metric to minimize if you want to get the best performance out of modern GPUs. This chapter uses a number of visibility techniques to find an optimal set of batches to submit, resulting in large performance gains. The techniques have the nice side effect of reducing both CPU load and GPU load.

Cem Cebenoyan, NVIDIA

Chapter 9

Efficient Shadow Volume Rendering

Morgan McGuire
Brown University

9.1 Introduction

A security guard's shadow precedes him into a vault—enough advance warning to let the thief hide on the ceiling. Ready to pounce on an unwary space marine, the alien predator clings to a wall, concealed in the shadow of a nearby gun turret. Yellow and red shadows of ancient marbled gods flicker on the walls of a tomb when the knight's torch and the druid's staff illuminate the statues inside. These are just a few vivid examples of how real-time shadows are used today in gaming.

Real-time shadows are now required for new 3D games. Gamers are accustomed to the perceptual, strategic, and cinematic benefits of realistic lighting. Unlike other effects, shadows aren't rendered objects. Instead, they are areas of the screen that are darker than others because they receive less light during illumination calculations. The hard part of adding shadows to a rendering engine is finding those areas in real time. This chapter describes how to use *shadow volumes*, the shadowing method used in games such as id Software's *Doom 3*, to mark shadowed pixels in the stencil buffer. See Figure 9-1. Once each pixel is classified as shadowed or illuminated, it's simple to modify the pixel program responsible for lighting in order to zero out the illumination contribution at shadowed pixels.

Figure 9-1. A Scene from id Software's *Doom 3*
Doom 3 game image courtesy of id Software. Published by Activision.

9.1.1 Where to Use Shadow Volumes

The shadow volume technique creates sharp, per-pixel accurate shadows from point, spot, and directional lights. A single object can be lit by multiple lights, and the lights can have arbitrary colors and attenuation. The shadows are cast from triangle meshes onto whatever is in the depth buffer. This means that the objects *being shadowed* can be meshes, billboards, particle systems, or even prerendered scenes with depth buffers.

Compared to other algorithms, shadow volumes can handle many difficult-to-shadow scenes well. Figure 9-2 shows one such problematic scene. The only light source is a point light inside the jack-o'-lantern. The entire scene is in shadow except for the triangular patches of ground illuminated by light that shines out through the holes in the pumpkin. This is a hard case for several reasons. It inverts our usual assumption that most of the scene is lit and shadows are small—rarely do shadows enclose the entire scene. The lit areas are very large compared to the holes in the pumpkin that create

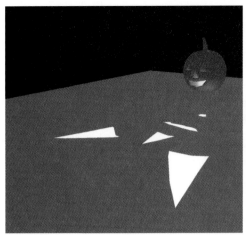

Figure 9-2. A Difficult Scene for Shadows: Light Inside a Jack-o'-Lantern
Right: The shadow volumes used to compute the image.

them. Although light shines out through only the front and the bottom, the light is omnidirectional and shadows must be considered from all angles. Finally, the shadow caster is more than close to the light source: it surrounds it.

Shadow volumes are not ideal for all scenes. The technique involves constructing a 3D volume that encloses all shadows cast by an object. This volume is constructed from the shadow caster's mesh; however, some shadow casters do not have a mesh that accurately represents their shape. Examples include a billboard, a particle system, or a mesh textured with an alpha matte (such as a tree leaf). These casters produce shadows based on their actual meshes, which do not match how the objects really appear. For example, a billboard smoke cloud casts a rectangular shadow.

Another problem object is a mesh containing edges that have only a single adjacent face, commonly known as a *crack*. In the real world, if you look into a crack, you see the inside of the object. Of course, in a rendering engine, you'll see through the object and out the other side because the inside is lined with back-facing polygons culled during rendering. This object is nonsensical as a shadow caster. From some angles, it casts a solid shadow; from other angles, light peeks through the hole and shines out the other side. Even worse, an optimization for the shadow volume breaks when using these objects, creating a large streak of darkness hanging in empty space, as shown in Figure 9-3.

Another potential limitation of the approach is that it requires that *everything* in a scene cast shadows. When a character's shadow is cast on a wall, it is also cast on everything

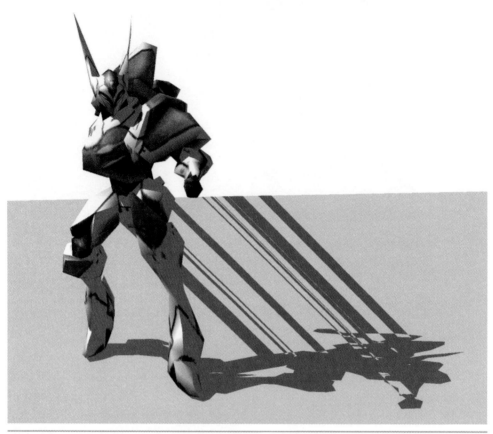

Figure 9-3. Cracks in a Model Let Shadows "Leak" Through the Air

behind the wall. The only reason the viewer doesn't see the shadow on the other side of the wall is that the wall casts its own shadow that overlaps it. If you cast shadows from characters but not from scene geometry, the shadows appear to go through solid objects.

The ideal scene for shadow volume performance is a top view, such as those found in many real-time strategy, sports, and above-ground adventure games. Such a scene is lit from a few downward-pointing directional lights, and the camera is above all the objects, looking down at the ground. The worst case for performance is a scene with multiple point lights in the middle of a large number of shadow-casting objects—such as a large party of torch-wielding adventurers in an underground room with pillars.

9.2 Program Structure

The shadow volume technique consists of two parts: constructing the volumes from silhouette edges and rendering them into the stencil buffer. These parts are repeated for each light source, and the resulting images are added together to create a final frame (a process called *multipass rendering*). The basic algorithm is easy to understand and implement, but it is slow for big scenes. To address this, a series of optimizations reduces the geometry-processing and fill-rate requirements.

We begin with a high-level view of the program structure. We follow up with a detailed discussion of each step, and then we look at several optimizations. Finally, we peek into the future by examining several research projects on shadow volumes.

9.2.1 Multipass Rendering

Mathematically, the illumination at a point is the sum of several terms. We see this in the Phong illumination equation for a single light, which is the sum of ambient, emissive (internal glow), diffuse, and specular components. A scene with multiple lights has a single ambient term and a single emissive term, but it has one diffuse term and one specular term for each light. When rendering *without* shadows, multiple lights can all be rendered in a single pass. This is typically done by enabling multiple hardware light sources or implementing a pixel shader with code for each light.

When rendering *with* shadows, the contribution from a given light is zero at some points because those points are shadowed. To account for this, the diffuse and specular contribution from each light is computed in a separate rendering pass. The final image is the sum of an initial pass that computes ambient and emissive illumination and the individual lighting passes. Because the initial pass writes depth values into the z-buffer, the additional passes have zero overdraw and can be substantially cheaper in terms of fill rate. Objects rendered in the additional passes are also good candidates for occlusion culling.

Although shadow volumes do not create the soft shadows cast by area sources, multiple passes can be exploited to create a similar effect by distributing multiple, dim spotlights over the surface of an area light. Unfortunately, for a complex scene having enough lights to make this look good, this method is too slow to be practical. (A new research technique, described in Assarsson et al. 2003, suggests a more efficient way of rendering soft shadows with shadow volumes.)

The individual lighting passes are combined using alpha blending. To do this, render the ambient/emissive pass to the back buffer with depth writing enabled and the blending function set to `glBlendFunc(GL_ONE, GL_ZERO)`. This initializes the depth buffer and creates the base illumination.

Then for the light passes, disable depth writing and change the blending function to `glBlendFunc(GL_ONE, GL_ONE)`. This blending mode adds newly rendered pixels to the ones already there. The pre-initialized depth buffer prevents overdraw. Also, be sure to set the depth test to `glDepthFunc(GL_LEQUAL)` to avoid z-fighting between subsequent passes.

With these settings, make one pass for each light source. Each pass clears the stencil buffer, marks shadowed areas in it, and then computes the illumination in nonshadowed areas and adds them to the frame buffer.

The overall structure of the rendering part of the program is shown in Figure 9-4.

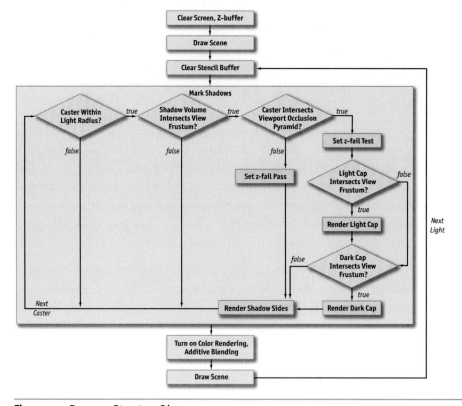

Figure 9-4. Program Structure Diagram

A simplified version of this procedure appears in Listing 9-1. The simplification is that the "mark shadows" step is reduced to the worst case, in which every one of the conditionals in the diagram returns *true*. After walking through the code in detail, we'll put the shorter paths back in as optimizations. The sections of code that will be changed by these optimizations are highlighted to make them easy to find later.

Listing 9-1. Program Structure Pseudocode

```
static const float black[] = {0.0f, 0.0f, 0.0f, 0.0f};

glPushAttrib(GL_ALL_ATTRIB_BITS);
setupCamera();

// -- Ambient + emissive pass --
// Clear depth and color buffers
glClear(GL_DEPTH_BUFFER_BIT | GL_COLOR_BUFFER_BIT);

glBlendFunc(GL_ONE, GL_ZERO); glEnable(GL_BLEND_FUNC);
glDepthMask(0xFF); glDepthFunc(GL_LEQUAL);
glEnable(GL_LIGHTING); glDisable(GL_LIGHT0);
glLightModelfv(LIGHT_MODEL_AMBIENT, globalAmbient);
drawScene();

// Light passes
glLightModelfv(LIGHT_MODEL_AMBIENT, black);
glEnable(GL_LIGHT0); glBlend(GL_ONE, GL_ZERO);
glDepthMask(0x00); glEnable(GL_LIGHT0); glEnable(GL_STENCIL_TEST);
glEnable(GL_STENCIL_TEST_TWO_SIDE_EXT);

for (int i = numLights - 1; i >= 0; --i) {
  // (The "XY" clipping optimizations set the scissor
  // region here.)

  //-- Mark shadows from all casters --
  // Clear stencil buffer and switch to stencil-only rendering
  glClear(GL_STENCIL_BUFFER_BIT); glColorMask(0, 0, 0, 0);
  glDisable(GL_LIGHTING); glStencilFunc(GL_ALWAYS, 0, ~0);
  glStencilMask(~0);

  loadVertexShader();
```

Listing 9-1 (*continued*). Program Structure Pseudocode

```
for (int c = 0; c < numCasters; ++c) {
    // (The "point and spot" optimization marks shadows
    // only for casters inside the light's range)
    setVertexParam("L", object->cframe.inv() * light[i]);
    object[c]->markShadows(light[i].direction);
}
unloadVertexShader();

//-- Add illumination -
// Configure lighting
configureLight(light[i]);

glEnable(GL_LIGHTING); glStencilFunc(GL_EQUAL, 0, ~0);
glActiveStencilFaceEXT(GL_FRONT);
glStencilOp(GL_KEEP, GL_KEEP, GL_KEEP);
glActiveStencilFaceEXT(GL_BACK);
glStencilOp(GL_KEEP, GL_KEEP, GL_KEEP);
glDepthFunc(GL_EQUAL); glColorMask(1, 1, 1, 1);
glCullFace(GL_BACK);

    // (The "point and spot" optimization adds illumination
    // only for objects inside the light's range)
    drawScene();
}

glPopAttrib();
```

9.2.2 Vertex Buffer Structure

The shadow of a mesh is cast by its silhouette. To quickly find the silhouette edges and extrude them into a shadow volume, meshes need more information than what's needed in a traditional rendering framework that uses only face triangles.

In our system, the vertex buffer for a mesh contains two copies of each vertex. Say there are n original vertices. Elements 0 through $n - 1$ of the vertex buffer contain typical vertices, of the form $(x, y, z, 1)$. Elements n through $2n - 1$ are copies of the first set but have the form $(x, y, z, 0)$. The first set can be used for normal rendering. Both sets will be used for shadow determination, where a vertex shader will transform the second set to infinity.

Objects also must have adjacency information and per-face normals. For every face, we need to know the three counterclockwise vertex indices and the surface normal. For every edge, we need the indices of the two adjacent faces and the indices of the two vertices. As mentioned previously, the model must be closed so it has no cracks. In terms of adjacency information, this means that every edge has exactly two adjacent faces that contain the same vertices but in opposite order. By convention, let the first face index of an edge be the one in which the edge vertices are traversed in order, and let the second index be the face in which the vertices are traversed in the opposite order. Note that there may be vertices in the model that are not in any edge or face. This is because it is a common practice when creating 3D models to collocate vertices with different texture coordinates. For adjacency information, we care only about the raw geometry and ignore the texture coordinates, normals, vertex colors, and so on that are stored with a model for rendering purposes.

9.2.3 Working at Infinity

Unlike other OpenGL programs you may have written, shadow volumes make extensive use of coordinates at infinity. Shadow volumes themselves consist of both finite geometry and geometry at infinity. The algorithm is implemented for point light sources, and directional lights are handled as point lights at infinity. The far clipping plane must be at infinity so that it will not cut off the infinite shadow volumes, and the perspective projection must be configured to take this into account.

OpenGL provides full support for working at infinity using homogeneous coordinates. This section reviews homogeneous vertices (for geometry and light sources) and shows how to configure an infinite-perspective matrix.

Finite homogeneous points are represented as $(x, y, z, 1)$; that is, the w component is equal to 1. This implicitly means the point at 3D position $(x/1, y/1, z/1)$. Perspective projection matrices use the w component to divide through by a nonunit value, creating vertices such as $(x, y, z, -z)$ that become $(x/-z, y/-z, -1)$ after the homogeneous divide. What happens when the w component is zero? We get a point that has the form $(x/0, y/0, z/0)$. This point is "at infinity." Of course, if we actually divided each component by 0 and computed the point, it would become (∞, ∞, ∞), which throws away important information—the direction in which the point went to infinity. The $(x, y, z, 0)$ representation uses $w = 0$ to flag the point as "at infinity" but retains the directional information (x, y, z).

Intuitively, a point at infinity acts as if it is very far away, regardless of the physical dimensions of the scene. Like stars in the night sky, points at infinity stay fixed as the viewer's position changes, but they rotate according to the viewer's orientation. OpenGL renders points with $w = 0$ correctly. Again like stars, they appear as if rendered on a sphere "at infinity" centered on the viewer. Note that for a point at infinity, only the *direction* (x, y, z) is important, not the magnitude of the individual components. It is not surprising that OpenGL therefore uses $w = 0$ to represent a directional light as a point light whose position is the vector to the light: a directional light is a point light that has been moved to infinity along a specific direction.

Throughout this chapter, we use $w = 0$ to represent points at infinity. We'll not only use point lights at infinity, but also extrude shadow volumes to infinity. In the previous section, we used $w = 0$ as a notation in the second half of the vertex buffer. This was because those vertices will be moved to infinity (they are the infinite end of the shadow volume). The vertex shader will move them relative to the light before they are actually transformed to infinity, however.

When rendering all of these objects at infinity, we can't have them clipped by the far plane. Therefore, we need to move the far clipping plane to infinity. This is done by computing the limit of the standard projection matrix as the far plane moves to infinity:

$$\lim_{Far \to \infty} \mathbf{P} = \mathbf{P}_{inf} = \begin{bmatrix} \dfrac{2 \times Near}{Right - Left} & 0 & \dfrac{Right + Left}{Right - Left} & 0 \\ 0 & \dfrac{2 \times Near}{Top - Bottom} & \dfrac{Top + Bottom}{Top - Bottom} & 0 \\ 0 & 0 & -1 & -2 \times Near \\ 0 & 0 & -1 & 0 \end{bmatrix}.$$

In code, this is a minor change to the way we compute the perspective projection matrix. Just create the projection matrix as shown in Listing 9-2 instead of using glFrustum.

Listing 9-2. An Infinite Projection Matrix in the Style of glFrustum

```
void perspectiveProjectionMatrix(double left,
                                 double right,
                                 double bottom,
                                 double top,
                                 double nearval,
                                 double farval)
{
    double x, y, a, b, c, d;
```

```
x = (2.0 * nearval) / (right - left);
y = (2.0 * nearval) / (top - bottom);
a = (right + left) / (right - left);
b = (top + bottom) / (top - bottom);

if ((float)farval >= (float)inf) {
  // Infinite view frustum
  c = -1.0;
  d = -2.0 * nearval;
} else {
    c = -(farval + nearval) / (farval - nearval);
    d = -(2.0 * farval * nearval) / (farval - nearval);
}

double m[] = {x, 0, 0, 0,
              0, y, 0, 0,
              a, b, c, -1,
              0, 0, d, 0};

glLoadMatrixd(m);
}
```

The Cg vertex shader from Listing 9-3 transforms points with $w = 1$ normally and sends points with $w = 0$ to infinity away from the light.

Listing 9-3. A Vertex Shader for Extruding $w = 0$ Vertices Away from the Light

```
VOut main(const float4x4 uniform in MVP,
          const float4 uniform in L,
          const VIn in vin)
{
  VOut vout;
  // (The "directional" optimization eliminates the vertex shader
  // by using different rendering loops for point and directional
  // lights.)
  vout.pos = MVP * (vin.pos.w == 0 ?
                    float4(vin.pos.xyz * L.w - L.xyz, 0) :
                    vin.posvin.pos);

  return vout;
}
```

The branch operator (?) can be replaced with a call to the `lerp` function on older graphics cards that don't support branching in vertex shaders. Note that multiplying the point position by `L.w` in the middle line makes the point's position irrelevant for a directional light. This is because the vector from the light to a point is independent of the point position for a directional light. In Listing 9-1, the call to `setVertexParam` sets the object-space light vector. The implementations of `loadVertexProgram`, `unloadVertexProgram`, and `setVertexParam` depend on the vertex shader runtime used.

9.3 Detailed Discussion

The goal of `markShadows` is to set the stencil buffer to zero for illuminated pixels and to a nonzero number for shadowed pixels. It does this by constructing a shadow volume—the geometry that bounds the shadow regions—and rendering it into the stencil buffer. Here we briefly look at the mathematical justification for this, and then we cover the implementation in detail.

9.3.1 The Math

Figure 9-5 shows a simple scene with a single point light (the light bulb icon), a shadow-casting box, a shadow-receiving ground plane, and a viewer on the left. The line in front of the viewer represents the image plane, which is important to the discussion in Section 9.5. The blue arrows represent light rays from the source (for clarity, only a few are shown). The ground plane is bright where the leftmost and rightmost rays strike it. The center rays hit the shadow caster instead and are blocked. The ground plane is dark (shadowed) underneath the caster where these rays are blocked. Somewhere between the outer and the inner rays in the diagram are critical lines, shown dashed. These lines mark the edges of the shadow. Note that they pass through the center of the light and the edges of the shadow caster. The diagram is 2D; in 3D, these are not lines but quadrilaterals. These lines are the sides of the shadow volume. Everything farther than the shadow caster and between them is shadowed. All other points are illuminated.

Figure 9-6 shows the shadow volume explicitly. The shadow volume has three pieces.

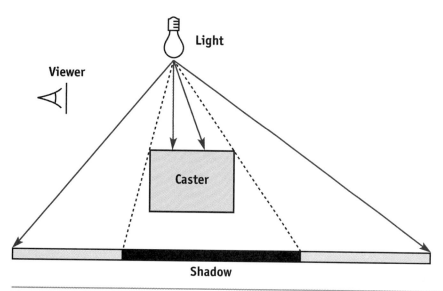

Figure 9-5. A Simple Scene

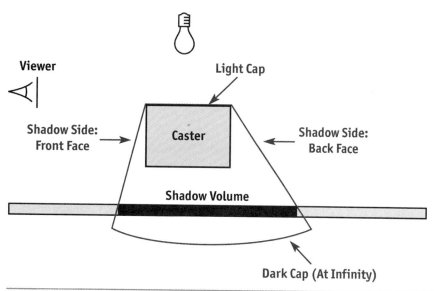

Figure 9-6. Shadow Volume for the Simple Scene

- The *sides* are constructed by extruding the edges of the caster away to infinity to form quads. Objects between the caster and the light should not be shadowed, so we have to close the volume on the top. Because an object casts the same shadow as its silhouette, we need to extrude only the silhouette edges. These are edges where, from the point of view of the light, one adjacent face is a back face ($\mathbf{N} \cdot \mathbf{L} < 0$) and one adjacent face is a front face ($\mathbf{N} \cdot \mathbf{L} > 0$).

- The *light cap* is the geometry that closes the volume on the side near the light. It is composed of the caster's light front-facing polygons (that is, polygons that are front faces from the light's point of view). Shadows extend infinitely away from the light, but mathematically we have to close the geometry at the back end to make it a volume.

- The *dark cap* is composed of the caster's light back-facing polygons (that is, polygons that are back faces from the light's point of view) expanded to infinity. In Figure 9-6, they are shown as a curve, because polygons at infinity can be thought of as lying on a very large sphere surrounding the entire scene.

Although the figures show a 2D diagram of a simple scene, keep in mind that the shadow volumes are in 3D and may have complicated geometry if the shadow caster has a complicated shape. For comparison, the geometry of real 3D shadow volumes is shown in Figures 9-2, 9-7, and 9-10. If there are multiple shadow casters (and there usually are), the shadow volume will have many separate parts. These parts might even overlap. None of this is a problem; the algorithm handles a triangle or a complete scene equally well without any special work on our part.

Here's a mathematical strategy for performing shadow determination using the shadow volume. When rendering, each pixel corresponds to a point in 3D space. We want to set the stencil buffer to a nonzero value (shadowed) at that pixel if the point is inside the shadow volume; otherwise, we'll set it to zero (illuminated). Call the point in question P. Consider intersections between the ray that starts at P and travels to infinity along the negative view vector, $-\mathbf{V}$, and the shadow volume. There are two kinds of intersections. An *entering* intersection occurs when the ray moves from outside the shadow volume to inside. Let $\mathbf{M}$ be the surface normal to the shadow face intersected. At an entering intersection, $\mathbf{M} \cdot \mathbf{V} > 0$. An *exiting* intersection occurs when the ray leaves a shadow volume and has $\mathbf{M} \cdot \mathbf{V} < 0$ (ignore glancing intersections where $\mathbf{M} \cdot \mathbf{V} = 0$). The key idea is to count the number of occurrences of each kind of intersection:

> **Point *P* is in shadow if and only if there were more entering intersections than exiting intersections along a ray to infinity.**

Rays that travel along the negative view vector lie within exactly one pixel under perspective projection. We exploit this fact to perform the intersection counts in hardware using the stencil buffer, which makes the method fast.

9.3.2 The Code

Here's how to implement our observations efficiently in hardware. Initialize the stencil buffer to zero and enable wrapping increment and decrement operations, if supported on the graphics card. (If wrapping is not supported, initialize all stencil values to 128 or some other value to avoid underflow.) Disable color rendering and render the shadow volume geometry to the stencil buffer. Because we're counting intersections with the ray that starts at each visible point and travels *away* from the viewer, set up the hardware to change the stencil value when the depth test *fails*. The stencil buffer is decremented for each front-face pixel that fails the depth test and incremented for each back-face pixel that fails the depth test.

Note that we disabled color rendering immediately before rendering shadow volumes, and we disabled depth writing a while ago, after the ambient illumination pass. Because both color and depth writing are disabled, rendering shadow volumes affects only the stencil buffer. Color writing must be disabled because we don't want to see the shadow volumes in the final image, just the shadows (which are based on the stencil counts). Depth writing needs to be disabled because we assumed that the depth values in the z-buffer represent the depths of visible surfaces (and not shadow volumes). Because depth writing is disabled, shadow faces do not interact with each other, and so the order in which they are rendered does not matter.

After rendering, the stencil value at a pixel will be zero if the same number of front and back faces were rendered, and the value will be nonzero if the counts differ. Entering intersections are always created by front faces, and exiting intersections are always created by back faces. The stencil count after rendering is therefore the number of entering intersections minus the number of exiting intersections—precisely the result we want for shadow determination.

9.3.3 The `markShadows` Method

The code for the `markShadows` method on the `Object` class is shown in Listing 9-4.

First, we take the light vector from world space to object space. For a point light or spotlight, this vector is the position $(x, y, z, 1)$. For a directional light, it has the form

Listing 9-4. The markShadows Method

```
// isBackface[f] = true if face f faces away from the light
std::vector<bool> backface;

void Object::markShadows(const Vector4& wsL)
{

    // (When the viewport is not shadowed by this object, this
    // section is changed by the "uncapping" optimization.)
    // Decrement on front faces; increment on back faces
    // (a.k.a. z-fail rendering)
    glActiveStencilFaceEXT(GL_FRONT);
    glStencilOp(GL_KEEP, GL_DECR_WRAP_EXT, GL_KEEP);
    glActiveStencilFaceEXT(GL_BACK);
    glStencilOp(GL_KEEP, GL_INCR_WRAP_EXT, GL_KEEP);
    glCullFace(GL_NONE);

    // (The "Z bounds" optimization sets the depth bounds here.)
    // Take light to object space and compute light back faces
    obj->findBackfaces(cframe.inv() * wsL);

    // Set up for vertex buffer rendering
    glVertexBuffer(vertexBuffer);

    renderShadowCaps();

    renderShadowSides();

    glVertexBuffer(NULL);
}
```

$(x, y, z, 0)$, where (x, y, z) is the vector *to* the light source. In general, a homogeneous vector with $w = 0$ can be thought of as a point on a sphere at infinity. A directional light is therefore the same as a point light at infinity.

With this object-space light vector, we compute the light front faces and light back faces. The facing directions are needed only temporarily and are stored in a global array. The (double-length) vertex buffer is then selected, and we render the shadow light and dark caps as triangles. Finally, the sides of the shadow volume are rendered as quads.

9.3.4 The findBackfaces Method

The findBackfaces method iterates over each face and computes $N \cdot L$, as shown in Listing 9-5.

Listing 9-5. The findBackfaces Method

```
void Object::findBackfaces(const Vector4& osL) // Object-space light
                                               // vector
{
  backface.resize(face.size());
  for (int f = 0; f < face.size(); ++f) {
    Vector3 L = L.xyz() - vertex[face[f].vertex[0]] * L.w;
    backface[f] = dot(face[f].normal, L) < 0;
  }
}
```

For a finite point light, the vector to the specific polygon is needed, so we subtract the position of one face vertex from the light position. For directional lights, the light direction is used unchanged. For performance, these cases can be handled in separate loops; they are combined in this example only for brevity. Note that none of the vectors needs to have unit length, because we're interested in only the sign of $N \cdot L$, not the magnitude.

If the model is animated, the face normals must be recomputed from the animated vertices for every frame. This precludes the use of matrix skinning or vertex blending in hardware, because the modified geometry would then not be available on the CPU. At the end of this chapter, we discuss some proposed techniques for combining shadow volumes with hardware vertex displacement.

9.3.5 Light and Dark Caps

Given the back face array, we can compute the caps and shadow volume sides. In each case, we will accumulate a list of vertex indices and then render the indices from the vertex buffer with glDrawElements. The indices are temporarily stored in another global array, called index.

The code for the light and dark caps is shown in Listing 9-6.

Listing 9-6. The `renderShadowCaps` Method

```cpp
// Indices into vertex buffer
std::vector<unsigned int>  index;

void Object::renderShadowCaps()
{
  // (The "Culling" optimization changes this method
  // to try to cull the light and dark caps separately.)
  index.resize(0);
  for (int f = face.size() - 1; f >= 0; --f) {
    if (backface[f]) {
      // Dark cap (same vertices but at infinity)
      for (int v = 0; v < 3; ++v) {
        index.pushBack(face[f].vertex[v] + n);
      }
    } else {
      // Light cap
      for (int v = 0; v < 3; ++v) {
        index.pushBack(face[f].vertex[v]);
      }
    }
  }

  glDrawElements(GL_TRIANGLES, index.size(),
              GL_UNSIGNED_INT, index.begin());
}
```

Light caps are simply polygons that face the light. To create dark caps, we take the light back faces and send them away from the light, to infinity. To do this, we render from the second set of vertices, which the vertex shader sends to infinity for us.

Figure 9-7 shows an animated *Quake 3* character standing on white ground lit by a white point light. The shadow volumes of the character are shown in yellow on the right side of the figure. Note that the shape of the dark cap, which is the part of the shadow volume far from the character, is the same as that of the character, but it is enlarged. The light cap is not visible because it is inside the character. The polygons stretching between the light and dark caps are the sides, which are constructed from silhouette edges.

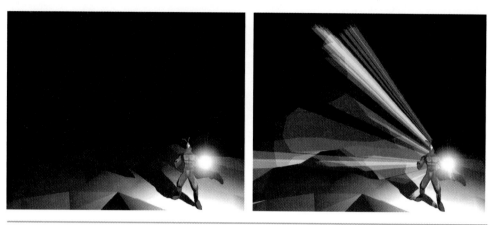

Figure 9-7. A Shadowed Character from *Quake 3*
Left: A single point light. Right: Visualization of shadow volumes.

9.3.6 Sides

The sides of the shadow volume are quadrilaterals between the first and second sets of vertices—that is, between the object and infinity. We iterate over the *edges* of the mesh. Recall that only those edges on the silhouette need be extruded into quads; the other edges do not affect the shadow volume.

A silhouette edge occurs where an object's light back face meets one of its light front faces. All of the information to make such a classification is available to us. The edges store the indices of the two adjacent faces, and the back-face array tells us which face indices correspond to light back faces. See Listing 9-7.

It is important to construct edge information for the mesh with consistent edge orientations, so that the resulting shadow-face quads have correct winding directions. On the shadow faces, the vertices must wind counterclockwise, so that the surface normal points out of the shadow volume. To ensure this, we use a convention in which the directed edge from vertex v0 = edge[e].vertex[0] to vertex v1 = edge[e].vertex[1] is counterclockwise in the mesh face with index edge[e].face[0] and clockwise (backward) in the mesh face with index edge[e].face[1].

The shadow quad must contain the edge directed in the same way as the back face. Therefore, if face edge[e].face[0] is a back face, the shadow face contains the edge from v0 to v1. Otherwise, it contains the edge from v1 to v0. Figure 9-8 shows the winding direction for the light front face and the shadow quad at an edge directed from v0 to v1.

Listing 9-7. The renderShadowSides Method

```
void Object::renderShadowSides()
{
  index.resize(0);

  for (int e = edges.size() - 1; e >= 0; --e) {
    if (backface[edge[e].face[0]] != backface[edge[e].face[1]]) {
      // This is a silhouette edge
      int v0, v1;
      if (backface[edge[e].face[0]]) {
        // Wind the same way as face 0
        v0 = edge[e].vertex[0];
        v1 = edge[e].vertex[1];
      } else {
        // Wind the same way as face 1
        v1 = edge[e].vertex[0];
        v0 = edge[e].vertex[1];
      }

      // (The "directional" optimization changes this code.)
      index.pushBack(v0);
      index.pushBack(v1);
      index.pushBack(v1 + n);
      index.pushBack(v0 + n);
    }
  }

  // (The "directional" optimization changes this to use
  // GL_TRIANGLES instead of GL_QUADS.)
  glDrawElements(GL_QUADS, index.size(),
                 GL_UNSIGNED_INT, index.begin());
}
```

We've now walked through the entire shadow-rendering procedure. We've built a system that classifies pixels as shadowed or unshadowed in the stencil buffer and then adds illumination to only the unshadowed pixels. This system can handle many different kinds of light sources and complex shadow-caster geometry. It can also interoperate with other shadow algorithms such as projective shadows and shadow maps. The program can be altered to add illumination only to those areas that pass *all* the shadow tests.

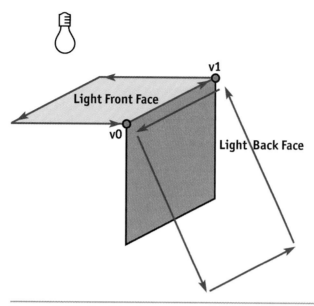

Figure 9-8. Winding Direction
The shadow-side face created by the silhouette edge from v_0 to v_1. Arrows show the counter-clockwise direction of vertex traversal in the front face and the shadow face.

By taking advantage of some common cases where the shadow volume algorithm is simplified, we can significantly speed up the process. The remainder of this chapter describes ways of speeding up shadow volume creation and rendering. In practice, the following methods can quadruple the speed of the base algorithm.

9.4 Debugging

To see if you are generating the shadow volumes correctly, temporarily enable color rendering and then draw shadow volumes with additive alpha blending. Turn on face culling and use one color for front faces and another for back faces. These shapes have other uses beyond debugging: you might want to render visible shadow volumes during gameplay for effects such as light rays passing through clouds or trees.

Remember that OpenGL requires the stencil *test* to be enabled, even if it is set to GL_ALWAYS_PASS, when using a stencil operation. Also, don't forget the stencil mask: glStencilMask(~0). If you forget either of these prerequisites, your write operations will be ignored.

Use assertions to check that every edge has exactly two adjacent faces. If you have cracks in a model, you'll get shadow streaks in the air like those we saw in Figure 9-3. Software modelers such as 3ds max have tools to fix cracks (called *welding vertices*) automatically—use them!

9.5 Geometry Optimizations

For clarity and simplicity, the base shadow-volume algorithm was described in the first half of the chapter in generic form, with directional lights, point lights, and spotlights treated the same. We used the mathematical trick L.xyz() – V * L.w in Listing 9-5 and a similar one in the vertex shader in Listing 9-3. These listings compute the light vector for both types of light with a single expression. We can improve performance by treating them separately in the vertex shader and throughout the process of generating shadow volumes. The shadow volume created by a directional light is simpler than that created by a point light, so this can turn into a big savings (at the expense of code complexity).

We can also improve geometry processing performance by using conservative bounding volumes to cull shadow geometry. This section describes these optimizations.

9.5.1 Directional Lights

For a directional light, the light vector is just L.xyz. Because the light vector is the same at all vertices, all vertices in the dark cap are at the same point, which is –L. This means there is no dark cap: the (parallel) sides of the shadow volume converge at infinity to a single point, and so the cap is unnecessary.

Because they converge to a point, the sides are triangles, not quads. The push statements in renderShadowSides (Listing 9-7) become:

```
index.pushBack(v0);
index.pushBack(v1);
index.pushBack(n);
```

These statements not only have fewer indices, but they are more friendly to the vertex cache. That's because the same vertex number *n* is transferred multiple times (we could transfer *any* one vertex with index greater than or equal to *n*, because they all transform to the same point). Alternatively, we could eliminate the vertex shader altogether and add one more vertex with index 2*n* that is set to the negative light vector before each shadow pass.

9.5.2 Point Lights and Spotlights

Point lights are typically attenuated by distance. After a certain distance, the light given off by a point light is negligible (when it drops below 1/255, we can't even see the result in an eight-bit frame buffer). Spotlights are attenuated by angle, and sometimes by distance. Outside the cone of the spotlight, they give no illumination.

If an object is outside the effective range of either kind of light source, it does not need to cast a shadow, because any object behind it is also outside the range. Detect this case by testing the bounding box of a shadow caster against the bounding sphere of a distance-attenuated light, or against the cone of an angularly attenuated light. When an object is outside the range, don't mark shadows for it. Likewise, no illumination pass is needed for objects outside the light's range.

9.5.3 Culling Shadow Volumes

Just as with regular geometry, the vertex-processing rate may be improved for shadow volumes by culling shadow geometry outside the view frustum. Note that the *caster* may be outside the view frustum and still cast a shadow on visible objects, so culling the caster and the shadow geometry are completely independent.

Cull the sides and cap separately. For each, approximate the shadow geometry with a geometric primitive and cull that primitive against the view frustum. The light cap can use the same bounds as the caster geometry, because the cap is inside the caster. The dark cap uses the same geometry, but sent to infinity away from the light source.

For example, say a bounding box is available for the caster. Transform each vertex, $\mathbf{v}$, of the bounding box to infinity using the equation $\mathbf{v}' = \mathbf{MV} * (\mathbf{v} * \mathbf{L}_w - \mathbf{L}_{xyz})$, where $\mathbf{L}$ is the object-space light vector and $\mathbf{MV}$ is the modelview matrix. Then test the transformed bounding box against the view frustum. If the box is culled, the dark cap can also be culled. The shadow volume sides are most easily bounded by a cylinder for directional lights and by a truncated cone for point lights.

Although any culling is helpful, culling the caps particularly speeds up vertex processing because caps have many more vertices than sides. For point lights, the dark cap is potentially huge; culling it can also save a lot of fill rate. This is the effect we see in cartoons when a kitten casts a lion's shadow by standing in front of a flashlight. This magnifying effect was illustrated in Figure 9-7, where the dark cap for the model is several times larger than the model itself.

9.5.4 Uncapped Performance

Even when the caps would otherwise be unculled, we can use another technique to remove the caps for a special case in which the viewport is unshadowed.

In the mathematical formulation, we used rays from a point to infinity *away* from the viewer. In the implementation, these rays were simulated by rendering polygons to the stencil buffer. We moved the far clipping plane to infinity and sent rays *away* from the viewer so that we wouldn't miss any intersections between the point and infinity because of clipping.

It's possible to count in the other direction. To count *away* from the viewer, increment or decrement the stencil buffer when the depth test *fails*. To count *toward* the viewer, increment or decrement when the depth test *passes*. When the viewport is not in a shadow volume, the number of intersections along a line segment from an unshadowed point *to* the image plane is zero. This is because the line had to pass through exactly the same number of entering and exiting intersections to get from an unshadowed point to an unshadowed viewport. If the point is shadowed, the number of intersections will be nonzero. Of course, we can count in this direction only if the viewport is not in a shadow itself; otherwise, the count will be off by the number of shadow volumes enclosing each viewport pixel. Figure 9-7 showed a case where this optimization can be used because the shadows, which stretch back into the scene, do not enclose the viewport. Figure 9-2 showed an example where it *cannot* be used, because the viewport is in the shadow cast by the pumpkin—in fact, *everything* in the scene is in shadow, except the triangles of ground plane, where light shines out of the eyes.

The advantage of counting toward the viewer is that we don't need to render the light and dark caps. The light cap will always fail the depth test, because it is inside the shadow caster, so there is no reason to render it. Because we're counting from visible points to the viewer, there is no way for the dark cap (which is at infinity) to create intersections, and so we don't need to render it, because it can't change the result.

This optimization requires two changes to the code:

1. We need to test whether the viewport is (conservatively) in a shadow volume. This test is performed separately for each shadow caster; we can choose our counting direction independently for each caster and still get a correct result.

2. If the viewport is not in a shadow volume, we need to reverse the increment/decrement sense of the stencil operations (for that caster only).

Figure 9-9 shows the *occlusion pyramid* of the viewport. The tip is at the light source (which is at infinity if it is a directional light), and the base is the viewport. If the bounding box of the shadow caster intersects this pyramid, the viewport may be shadowed and the optimization cannot be used. In that case, we must render with the normal depth-fail operations and draw both caps, if visible. If the bounding box does not intersect the pyramid, we can change the stencil operations.

The occlusion pyramid can be on either side of the viewport. If the shadow caster intersects the green pyramid, the "uncapped" optimization cannot be used.

For counting toward the viewer, set the stencil operations as follows:

```
// Increment on front faces, decrement
// on back faces (a.k.a. z-pass rendering)
glActiveStencilFaceEXT(GL_FRONT);
glStencilOp(GL_KEEP, GL_KEEP, GL_INCR_WRAP_EXT);
glActiveStencilFaceEXT(GL_BACK);
glStencilOp(GL_KEEP, GL_KEEP, GL_DECR_WRAP_EXT);
```

Because this is "uncapped" rendering, omit the code to render shadow volume caps entirely from this case.

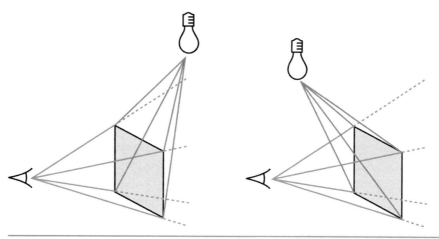

Figure 9-9. The Occlusion Pyramid
Extending from the viewport to the light source (which may be at infinity).

9.6 Fill-Rate Optimizations

Fill rate is the Achilles heel of shadow volumes. Shadow volumes cover many pixels and have a lot of overdraw. This is particularly troublesome for point lights, which create shadows that get *bigger* the farther they are from the caster. Fortunately, point lights also have great optimization potential, because their attenuation creates a range beyond which illumination is practically zero. We've already discussed not marking shadows for casters outside this range and not rendering illumination on objects outside the range. Now we'll look at three ways to reduce the fill rate required for casters *inside* the range: finite volumes, XY clipping, and z-bounds.

9.6.1 Finite Volumes

The range of a point light forms a sphere. Objects outside this sphere don't receive illumination, so there is no need to cast shadows beyond the sphere. Instead of extruding shadow volumes to infinity, we can extend them by the radius of the sphere and save the fill rate of rendering infinite polygons. This is a straightforward change to the vertex shader that can recoup significant fill rate. Because the dark cap is more likely to be on-screen under this method, it may increase the geometry processing because the dark cap is less likely to be culled.

An alternative is to still create polygons that stretch to infinity, but clip them to the light radius in 2D, as described in the next optimization.

9.6.2 XY Clipping

The range sphere projects to an ellipse on screen. Only pixels within that ellipse can be illuminated. We don't need to render shadow polygons or illumination outside of this ellipse. However, hardware supports a rectangular clipping region, not an elliptical one. We could compute the bounding box of the projected ellipse, but it is more convenient to use the 2D bounding box of the projected 3D bounding box surrounding the light range. Although the fixed-function pipeline supports only radial attenuation, artists can achieve more controlled effects by specifying an arbitrary attenuation function over the cubic volume about a light, as done in *Doom 3*. Attenuation can fall off arbitrarily within a box, so we just use that box as the light range. Clip the light's box to the view frustum. If it is not entirely clipped, project all vertices of the remaining polyhedron onto the viewport and bound them. That final 2D bound is used as the rectangular clipping region. Set the clipping region with the glScissor command:

```
glScissor(left, top, width, height);
glEnable(GL_SCISSOR_TEST);
```

Figure 9-10 shows a *Quake 3* character standing outside a building. This is the scene from Figure 9-7, but now the camera has moved backward. The single point light creates shadow volumes from the character and the building (shown in yellow), which would fill the screen were they not clipped to the effective bounds of the light. The scissor region is shown in the right half of the figure as a white box. The left half of the figure shows the visible scene, where the effect of clipping is not apparent because the light does not illuminate the distant parts of the building. For this scene, rendering only the shadow volume pixels within the scissor region cuts the fill-rate cost in half.

Figure 9-10. Clipping in *Quake 3*
Left: The final scene. Right: The shadow volumes (shown in yellow) are clipped to the scissor region (represented by the white box).

9.6.3 Z-Bounds

If the point at a given pixel is outside of the light range—because it is either closer to the viewer or farther from the viewer than the range bounds—that point cannot be illuminated, so we don't need to make a shadow-marking or illumination pass over that pixel. Restricting those passes to a specific depth range means that we pay fill rate for only those pixels actually affected by the light, which is potentially fewer pixels than those within the 2D bounds of the light.

The glDepthBoundsEXT function lets us set this behavior:

```
glEnable(GL_DEPTH_BOUNDS_TEST_EXT);
glDepthBoundsEXT(zMin, zMax);
```

This setting prevents rendering a pixel where the depth buffer *already* has a value outside the range [zMin, zMax]—that is, where the point visible at that pixel (rendered in the ambient pass) is outside the range. This is not the same as a clipping plane, which prevents rendering new pixels from polygons past a bound.

Figure 9-11 shows a viewer looking at an object illuminated from a point light. The caster's shadow projects downward toward the rugged ground slope. The bold green portion of the ground can't possibly be shadowed by the caster. The depth-bounds test saves the fill rate of rendering the orange parts of the shadow volume because the visible pixels behind them (the bold green ones) are outside the bounds. Notice that the shadow volume itself is inside the bounds, but this is irrelevant—the depth bound applies to the pixel rendered in the ambient pass, not to the shadow geometry.

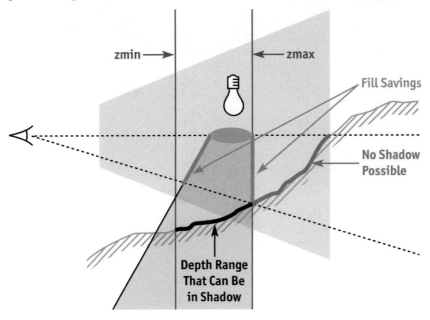

Figure 9-11. Depth Bounds

Note that the depth bounds are more restrictive than just the light range. It is the depth range defined by the intersection of the view frustum, the light range, and the shadow volume bounds. The arguments to the OpenGL function are post-projective camera-space values. If the geometry of the intersection is defined by a polyhedron whose vertices are stored in an array std::vector<Vector4> boundVert, the arguments are computed as:

```
float zMin = 1.0f;
float zMax = 0.0f;
```

```
for (int v = boundVertex.size() - 1; v >= 0; --v) {
    float z = 1.0f / (projectionMatrix * boundVert[v]).w;

    zMin = min(zMin, z);
    zMax = max(zMax, z);
}
```

9.7 Future Shadows

The current, highly optimized shadow volume method is the result of contributions from industry and academia over the past several decades. The basic method was introduced by Frank Crow at SIGGRAPH 1977 and has matured into the method described in this chapter. The history of shadow volumes and the individual contributions of several researchers and developers are summarized in technical reports available on the NVIDIA Developer Web site (Everitt and Kilgard 2002, McGuire et al. 2003). McGuire et al. 2003 gives a formal description and analysis of the method presented in this chapter.

Improving the performance of shadow volume generation through new optimizations continues to be an active research area. Silhouette determination has always been performed on the CPU, which is a major limitation. It precludes the use of matrix skinning or other deformations in the vertex shader and otherwise serializes rendering on CPU operations.

Several solutions have been proposed for performing silhouette determination directly on programmable graphics hardware. Michael McCool (2001) proposed a method for computing the caster silhouettes from a shadow map. Brabec and Seidel (2003) push geometry encoded as colors through the pixel processor, where they compute silhouettes. They then read back the frame buffer and use it as a vertex buffer for shadow rendering. John Hughes and I recently described how to find silhouettes and extrude them into shadow volume sides entirely in a vertex shader using a specially precomputed mesh (McGuire and Hughes 2003).

Getting good-looking, high-performance soft shadows from area light sources with shadow volumes is another open research topic. Ulf Assarsson and Tomas Akenine-Möller have worked on this problem for some time. Their most recent paper, with Michael Dougherty and Michael Mounier (Assarsson et al. 2003), describes how to construct explicit geometry for the interior and exterior edges of the penumbra (the soft-shadow region) and makes heavy use of programmable hardware.

Several people have proposed joining the individual silhouette edges into connected strips so that quad strips (for point lights) and triangle fans (for directional lights) can be used to render the shadow volume sides. Alex Vlachos and Drew Card (2002) have been working on another simplification idea: culling and clipping nested shadow volumes, because they won't affect the final result.

All of these methods are experimental and have yet to be refined and proven in an actual game engine. If you are interested in moving beyond the capabilities of the current shadow volume method, these are good starting points. Hopefully, future research and graphics hardware will improve and accelerate these methods.

9.8 References

Assarsson, U., M. Dougherty, M. Mounier, and T. Akenine-Möller. 2003. "An Optimized Soft Shadow Volume Algorithm with Real-Time Performance." In *Proceedings of the SIGGRAPH/Eurographics Workshop on Graphics Hardware 2003*.

Brabec, S., and H. Seidel. 2003. "Shadow Volumes on Programmable Graphics Hardware." Eurographics 2003 (Computer Graphics Forum).

Everitt, Cass, and Mark Kilgard. 2002. "Practical and Robust Stenciled Shadow Volumes for Hardware-Accelerated Rendering." NVIDIA Corporation. Available online at **http://developer.nvidia.com/object/robust_shadow_volumes.html**

McCool, Michael. 2001. "Shadow Volume Reconstruction from Depth Maps." *ACM Transactions on Graphics*, January 2001, pp. 1–25.

McGuire, Morgan, and John F. Hughes. 2003. "NPR on Programmable Hardware." To appear in *Proceedings of NPAR 2004*, June 7–9, Annecy, France.

McGuire, Morgan, John F. Hughes, Kevin Egan, Mark Kilgard, and Cass Everitt. 2003. "Fast, Practical and Robust Shadows." Available online at **http://developer.nvidia.com/object/fast_shadow_volumes.html**. An early version appeared as *Brown Univ. Tech. Report* CS03-19.

Vlachos, Alex, and Drew Card. 2002. "Computing Optimized Shadow Volumes." In *Game Programming Gems 3*, edited by Dante Treglia. Charles River Media.

Tekkaman Blade robot model by Michael Mellor (mellor@iaccess.com.au); Tick model by Carl Schell (carl@cschell.com). Both available for download at http:// www.polycount.com. Cathedral model by Sam Howell (sam@themightyradish.com), courtesy Sam Howell and Morgan McGuire. "The Tick" character is a trademark of New England Comics. Quake 2, Quake 3, and Doom 3 are trademarks of id Software.

Chapter 10

Cinematic Lighting

Fabio Pellacini
Pixar Animation Studios

Kiril Vidimce
Pixar Animation Studios

In this chapter, we present a simplified implementation of uberlight, a light shader that expresses the lighting model described by Ronen Barzel (1997, 1999). A superset of this model was developed over several years at Pixar Animation Studios and used for the production of animated movies such as the Walt Disney presentations of the Pixar Animation Studios films *Toy Story*, *A Bug's Life*, *Monsters, Inc.*, and *Finding Nemo*.

Our Cg implementation is based on Barzel's original approach and on the RenderMan Shading Language implementation written by Larry Gritz (Barzel 1999). Further details about this lighting approach and its uses in movie production can be found in Apodaca and Gritz 1999 and Birn 2000.

10.1 Introduction

Lighting is an important aspect of computer cinematography, in which lights and shadows are used to convey mood and support storytelling (Calahan 1999). Although realism remains an important aspect of computer-generated imagery, lighting directors constantly cheat the physics of light to support the artistic depiction of animated movies. Performing these tricks on a real-world set is a daunting task that often requires hours of setup.

Freed of the limitations of real physics, developers of computer cinematography have been devising lighting models that let artists illuminate scenes intuitively. The lighting model presented in this chapter is an adaptation of the model developed over the last decade at Pixar Animation Studios and used in the production of most of our movies. See Figures 10-1, 10-2, and 10-3.

Figure 10-1. Barn Lights in *Monsters, Inc.*
© *2001 Disney Enterprises, Inc./Pixar Animation Studios.*

Figure 10-2. Cookies Contribute to a Window Effect in *Monsters, Inc.*
© *2001 Disney Enterprises, Inc./Pixar Animation Studios.*

Figure 10-3. Lighting Conveys Mood in *Monsters, Inc.*
© *2001 Disney Enterprises, Inc./Pixar Animation Studios.*

10.2 A Direct Lighting Illumination Model

The shader we present in this chapter models only the shaping and controls of the light sources that illuminate the scene; it doesn't cover the intricacies of how to model the surface details and the light reflection behavior. (Some examples of interesting surface behaviors can be found in Apodaca and Gritz 1999.)

In general, the illumination model used in our movie production performs two kinds of operations, similar to the pseudocode shown here.

```
color illuminationModel()
{
  Compute the surface characteristic
  For each light {
    Evaluate the light source
    Compute the surface response
  }
}
```

First, we compute the surface shading information by performing various texture lookups, interpolating values over the mesh, and computing procedural patterns. Then we loop over each light source that illuminates the object and compute its contribution. We do this by evaluating first the light color and then the surface response to the illumination of each light.

In this chapter, we present a simple shader that computes the contribution of only one light for a plastic reflection model. Extending it to a more general solution for multiple lights and better-looking surfaces is left as an exercise for the reader.

Our lighting model provides artists with control over various aspects of illumination: selection, color, shaping, shadowing, and texturing.

10.2.1 Selection

Each object in the scene can selectively respond to each individual light. This powerful characteristic of our lighting model lets the artist turn off lights on objects when additional light is creating an undesired effect. It also lets artists add extra lights that create a desired effect in a specific location without affecting the rest of the scene.

10.2.2 Color

A light's most noticeable properties are the color and the intensity that describe its emission. Similar to the OpenGL fixed-function lighting, our implementation provides separate weights for the ambient, diffuse, and specular illumination effects that artists can separately tweak. One of the most important aspects of our lighting model is that these terms can be freely changed per-object, letting the artist light entire sets with a small number of lights.

10.2.3 Shaping

To control regions of a scene that are illuminated by a light, real-world cinematographers commonly employ spotlights and rectangular lights (known as barn doors) to shape the light distribution. Our lighting model generalizes on these concepts by providing two types of shaping:

- *Omni light*: This light specifies a near and far truncation distance (the light shines with full intensity inside each) and two adjustable, smooth drop-off zones around these edges.

- *Barn shaping*: Barn shaping is a generalized truncated pyramid whose cross section is a superellipse with adjustable soft edges. The width and height of each of the two superellipses can be controlled separately to allow a wider range of shapes. The use of a superelliptical cross section lets us continuously vary the shape of the light, from a circle to a square (and to even more exotic, star-like shapes). Furthermore, the pyramid can be freely sheared to allow window and doorway effects. Variations of the shape of the cross section of the pyramid are illustrated in Figures 10-4 and 10-5.

Figure 10-4. Barn Door Shapes
© 2003 Pixar Animation Studios.

Figure 10-5. Barn Door Edge Sizes
© 2003 Pixar Animation Studios.

10.2.4 Shadowing

Shadowing is an important aspect of our lighting model; shadows are probably the attributes that artists cheat most often. Shadows are tweaked not only for speed considerations, but also for the ability to control each little aspect of the shadow's look, which is so important in defining the overall mood of a movie. For example, compare the strong shadows in film noir movies with the almost invisible ones in musicals.

As for lighting intensity, artists decide which objects cast shadows and which ones receive them. Also, the lighting designer can cheat shadow positions by moving them in relationship to the light origin. For example, she can allow bright highlights in a character's eyes while making sure that the shadow does not cross the character's face.

Darkness

One of the biggest problems of a direct lighting model is that shadows tend to be too dark. This happens because most of the indirect illumination that naturally occurs in the environment is never computed. To mimic reality in our model, we've created lights that can be adjusted to change the density of shadows, by letting some light propagate through the objects in a scene. In our implementation, we use the diffuse contribution of the surface to color the shadow region. We believe this is better than using an ambient term, because our method lets us maintain those nice gradients that make the shadow believable. Later in the chapter, we elaborate on this topic.

Hue

The hue of a shadowed area in the real world is slightly different from that of a nearby unoccluded region—for example, notice the slight bluish tint of outdoor shadows on a bright, sunny day. To mimic this effect, we allow the artist to change the shadow color. Slight variations of the shadow hue can make the difference between a good-looking shadow and a fake-looking one. In practice, you should think of shadow casters "spraying" receivers with the shadow color, which is commonly black. See Figure 10-6 for images with different shadow colors.

Reflection

One important caveat concerns highlights. When computing the surface contribution in the shadow area, we use only the diffuse response to obtain those nice gradients seen

Figure 10-6. Variations in Shadow Colors
© 2003 Pixar Animation Studios.

in outdoor environments, but we don't want to see highlights in the shadow region, because we are cheating diffuse interreflections. To achieve this effect, we simply switch off the specular contribution in the shadow regions. This little adjustment is just one example of how light changes the reflection behavior of surfaces. Tweaks like these are used widely in movie production to achieve that specific look we hope viewers will love.

Shadow Maps

Of the various techniques used to implement shadows, we use shadow maps in our model, for their simplicity and flexibility—and because we use them often in our movies. Although the shader in this chapter is based on such an algorithm, we encourage the reader to experiment with other shadow algorithms. The important aspect of the shader is not how we decide if a pixel is in shadow, it's how we use this information.

Shadow Blurring

The most important aspect missing from our implementation is shadow blurring. Artists often adjust the softness of shadow edges in order to cheat area lights or simply to get the particular look that the director wants. Blurring shadow edges is particularly hard to do efficiently. Various techniques are available, but presenting them is outside the scope of this chapter.

10.2.5 Texturing

Finally, we added projective texture support to allow a wide variety of effects, such as slide projectors and fake shadows from off-screen objects. These tricks are known in the movie production world as *cookies*; they are also used in game production, but less often. While game developers use texture projection for shape, coloring, and shadowing effects, movie creators tend to use soft cookies to enrich visual details and to add special effects, such as off-camera shadow casters or strangely shaped lights.

10.2.6 Results

Figures 10-7 and 10-8 illustrate the use of the uberlight to illuminate the head of a character from Pixar's short film *Geri's Game*. The surface of the model is flat and plastic-like, and we don't apply any material-related textures on it. By using a simpler surface model for the object, we can better emphasize the various effects we can obtain by using just the light shader with different parameters. The proper combination of light and surface modeling brings this character to life, as in the original Pixar short.

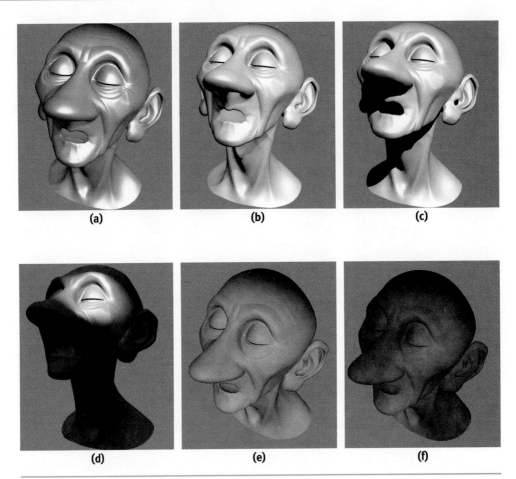

Figure 10-7. Lighting Geri

(a) Geri is lit by one light. (b) Changes to the light weightings modify the contrast of the specular highlights. (c) Changes to the shadow color strengthen the shadow. (d) Changes to the barn shape create a more dramatic pose. (e) Use of a soft texture cookie enriches the image. (f) Exaggerating the contrast of the projected cookie creates an alien-like effect.
© *1988 Pixar Animation Studios.*

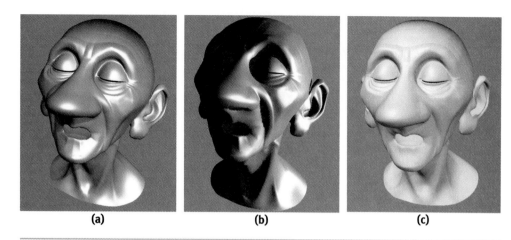

(a)   (b)   (c)

Figure 10-8. Lighting Styles
(a) Normal, (b) high-contrast film noir, and (c) soft look (obtained with two lights).
© *1988 Pixar Animation Studios.*

10.3 The Uberlight Shader

Listings 10-1 and 10-2 show the source code of the uberlight shader, based on the one by Larry Gritz in Barzel 1999.

Listing 10-1. The Vertex Program for an Uberlight-Like Shader

```
void uberlight_vp(
    varying float4 Pobject : POSITION,  // Vertex position in object space
    varying float3 Nobject : NORMAL,    // Vertex normal in object space
    varying float3 VertexColor : COLOR0, // Vertex color
    uniform float4x4 ModelViewProj,     // ModelViewProj matrix
    uniform float4x4 ObjectToWorld,     // ObjectToWorld matrix
    uniform float4x4 ObjectToWorldIT,   // Inverse transpose of the
                                        // ObjectToWorld matrix
    uniform float4x4 WorldToLight,      // Light space
    uniform float4x4 WorldToLightIT,    // Inverse transpose of light
                                        // space to transform normals
    uniform float4x4 WorldToShadowProj, // Light space concatenated with
                                        // the projection matrix used for
                                        // the shadow. This defines
                                        // shadow space.
```

```
  uniform float3 CameraPosInWorld,      // Camera position
                                        // in world space

  uniform float ShadowBias,             // Shadow bias
  out float4 HPosition : POSITION,      // Rasterizer position
  out float3 CameraPosInLight : TEXCOORD0, // Camera position
                                        // in light space

  out float3 Plight : TEXCOORD1,        // Interpolated position
                                        // in light space

  out float3 Nlight : TEXCOORD2,        // Interpolated normal
                                        // in light space

  out float4 ShadowUV : TEXCOORD3,      // Shadow UV
  out float3 Color : COLOR0)            // Surface color
{
  // Compute coordinates for the rasterizer
  HPosition = mul(ModelViewProj, Pobject);

  // Compute world space pos and normal
  float4 Pworld = mul(ObjectToWorld, Pobject);
  float3 Nworld = mul(ObjectToWorldIT, float4(Nobject, 0)).xyz;

  // Compute the position of the point in light space
  CameraPosInLight = mul(WorldToLight,
                          float4(CameraPosInWorld, 1)).xyz;
  Plight = mul(WorldToLight, Pworld).xyz;
  Nlight = mul(WorldToLightIT, float4(Nworld, 0)).xyz;

  // Compute the U-V for the shadow and texture projection
  float4 shadowProj = mul(WorldToShadowProj, Pworld);
  // Rescale x, y to the range 0..1
  ShadowUV.xy = 0.5 * (shadowProj.xy + shadowProj.ww);
  // When transforming z, remember to apply the bias
  ShadowUV.z = 0.5*(shadowProj.z + shadowProj.w - ShadowBias);
  ShadowUV.w = shadowProj.w;

  // Pass the color as is
  Color = VertexColor;
}
```

Listing 10-2. The Fragment Program for an Uberlight-Like Shader

```
// SHADER PARAMETERS =============================================
// Superellipse params
struct SuperellipseShapingParams {
  float width, height;
  float widthEdge, heightEdge;
  float round;
};

// Distance shaping params
struct DistanceShapingParams {
  float near, far;
  float nearEdge, farEdge;
};

// Light params
struct LightParams {
  float3 color;    // light color
  float3 weights;  // light weights (ambient, diffuse, specular)
};

struct SurfaceParams {
  float3 weights;    // surface weights (ambient, diffuse, specular)
  float  roughness;  // roughness
};

// BRDF/LIGHT INTERACTION =========================================
// Compute the light direction
float3 computeLightDir(float3 Plight)
{
  // Spot only
  return -normalize(Plight);
}

// Ambient contribution of lit
float ambient(float3 litResult)
{
  return litResult.x;
}
```

```
// Diffuse contribution of lit
float diffuse(float3 litResult)
{
  return litResult.y;
}

// Specular contribution of lit
float specular(float3 litResult)
{
  return litResult.z;
}

// SUPERELLIPSE ================================================================
float computeSuperellipseShaping(
  float3 Plight, // Point in light space
  bool barnShaping, // Barn shaping
  SuperellipseShapingParams params) // Superellipse shaping params
{
  if(!barnShaping) {
    return 1;
  } else {
    // Project the point onto the z == 1 plane
    float2 Pproj = Plight.xy/Plight.z;
    // Because we want to evaluate the superellipse
    // in the first quadrant, for simplicity, get the right values
    float a = params.width;
    float A = params.width + params.widthEdge;
    float b = params.height;
    float B = params.height + params.heightEdge;

    float2 pos = abs(Pproj);

    // Evaluate the superellipse in the first quadrant
    float exp1 = 2.0 / params.round;
    float exp2 = -params.round / 2.0;
    float inner = a * b * pow(pow(b * pos.x, exp1) +
                             pow(a * pos.y, exp1), exp2);
    float outer = A * B * pow(pow(B * pos.x, exp1) +
                             pow(A * pos.y, exp1), exp2);
    return 1 - smoothstep(inner, outer, 1);
  }
}
```

```
// DISTANCE SHAPING ================================================
float computeDistanceShaping(
  float3 Plight, // Point in light space
  bool barnShaping, // Barn shaping
  DistanceShapingParams params) // Distance shaping params
{
  float depth;
  if(barnShaping) {
    depth = -Plight.z;
  } else {
    depth = length(Plight.z);
    }

  return smoothstep(params.near - params.nearEdge, params.near, depth) *
                 (1 - smoothstep(params.far, params.far +
                                      params.farEdge, depth));
}

// MAIN ================================================================
float4 uberlight_fp(
  float3 CameraPosInLight : TEXCOORD0, // Camera position in light space
  float3 Plight : TEXCOORD1,    // Interpolated position in light space
  float3 Nlight : TEXCOORD2,    // Interpolated normal in light space
  float4 ShadowUV : TEXCOORD3,  // Shadow UV

  // SURFACE PROPERTIES -----------------------
  float3 SurfaceColor : COLOR0,   // Surface color
  uniform SurfaceParams Surface, // Other surface params
                                 // (weights, roughness)

  // LIGHT PROPERTIES -------------------------
  uniform LightParams Light, // Light properties

  // SHAPING -----------------------------------
  // Choose between barn shaping (superelliptic pyramid)
  // and omni shaping
  uniform bool BarnShaping,
  uniform SuperellipseShapingParams SuperellipseShaping, // Superellipse
                                                         // shaping
  uniform DistanceShapingParams DistanceShaping,         // Distance
                                                         // shaping
```

```
// DISTANCE FALLOFF ---------------------------
// COOKIES AND SHADOWS -----------------------
uniform sampler2D Shadow,      // Shadow texture
uniform float3 ShadowColor,    // Shadow color
uniform sampler2D Cookie,      // Cookie texture
uniform float CookieDensity)   // Cookie density
{
    // TRANSFORM VECTORS TO LIGHT SPACE ---------------------
    // Compute the normal in light space (normalize after vertex
    // interpolation)
    float3 N = normalize(Nlight);
    // Compute the light direction
    float3 L = computeLightDir(Plight);
    // Compute the view direction (vector from the point to the eye)
    float3 V = normalize(CameraPosInLight - Plight);
    // Compute the half-angle for the specular term
    float3 H = normalize(L + V);

    // COMPUTE THE TEXTURE PROJECTION - COOKIE
    float3 cookieColor = tex2Dproj(Cookie, ShadowUV).xyz;
    Light.color = lerp(Light.color, cookieColor, CookieDensity);

    // COMPUTE THE SHADOW EFFECT ----------------------------
    // Get the amount of shadow
    float shadow = tex2Dproj(Shadow, ShadowUV).x;
    // Modify the light color so that it blends with the shadow color
    // in the shadow areas
    float3 mixedLightColor = lerp(ShadowColor, Light.color, shadow);

    // COMPUTE THE ATTENUATION DUE TO SHAPING --------------
    float attenuation = 1;
    // Contribution from the superellipse shaping
    attenuation *= computeSuperellipseShaping(Plight,
                                              BarnShaping,
                                              SuperellipseShaping);
    // Contribution from the distance shaping
    attenuation *= computeDistanceShaping(Plight, BarnShaping,
                                          DistanceShaping);
```

```
// APPLY TO SURFACE --------------------------------------
// Here you should substitute other code for different
// surface reflection models. This code computes the lighting
// for a plastic-like surface.

// Lighting computation
float3 litResult = lit(dot(N, L), dot(N, H), Surface.roughness).xyz;

// Multiply by the surface and light weights
litResult *= Surface.weights * Light.weights;

// Compute the ambient, diffuse, and specular final colors.
// For the ambient term, use the color of the light as is
float3 ambientColor = Light.color * SurfaceColor * ambient(litResult);
// For the diffuse term, use the color of the light
// mixed with the color in the shadow
float3 diffuseColor = mixedLightColor * SurfaceColor *
                          diffuse(litResult);
// The specular color is simply the light color times the specular
// term, because we want to obtain white highlights regardless of the
// surface color. Our shadows won't be fully black, so we want to
// make sure that the highlights do not appear in shadow.
float3 specularColor = mixedLightColor * shadow *
                          specular(litResult);

// Compute the final diffuse color
float3 color = attenuation * (ambientColor + diffuseColor +
                          specularColor);

// Compute the diffuse color
return float4(color, 1);
}
```

10.4 Performance Concerns

10.4.1 Speed

We can easily speed up the uberlight shader by replacing certain analytic computations with texture lookups. The textures are generated by discretely sampling the functions of computations we want to avoid. As long as the textures have a high-enough resolution (potentially re-creating them based on the scene and camera parameters), the quality of the image can still be very good. Because of production and quality demands in the world of offline rendering, this kind of optimization is rarely performed.

10.4.2 Expense

The most expensive code in this shader is the computation of the light's shape-based attenuation. We can construct a texture map to evaluate the superelliptical shaping for a given set of barn parameters and then use the shadow texture coordinates to look up the barn map contribution in light space as a projective texture. The use of a barn map dramatically reduces the number of shader instructions. Plus, it can more than double the speed of shading (as measured on NVIDIA's Quadro FX 2000 board).

10.4.3 Optimization

When neither the camera nor the objects move in the scene, we can also optimize camera-dependent and scene-dependent shading components of the shader (such as the distance-based shaping). This is a typical usage scenario for a lighting artist who is modifying lighting parameters to light a frame in a given shot. When the artist replaces both the superellipse and the distance-based shaping with two texture lookups, the modified shader performs more than three times faster than the original one.

If you choose this approach to optimize your shaders, consider using a high-level language to create these maps on the fly. In our proprietary multipass interactive renderer, we define the creation of these maps as separate passes. Once created, the pass results are cached and constantly reused. Only when the parameters that affect these maps change are the passes marked as dirty, queued for reevaluation, and once again cached.

10.5 Conclusion

Our lighting model is a simple attempt to provide a comprehensive set of lighting controls that covers most effects used daily by lighting artists. Although our implementation covers a wide variety of effects, many more can be added (and are indeed added daily) to allow the artist more flexibility and expressiveness. Examples of such controls are found in Barzel 1999. Readers may extend our source code examples to cover these and other algorithms.

The lighting controls presented covered only part of the look for which the light source is responsible. When you are developing a full illumination model, be aware that the surface-reflection characteristic of a surface is also important; this property is what distinguishes the appearance of the materials in the scene.

10.6 References

Apodaca, Anthony A., and Larry Gritz, eds. 1999. *Advanced RenderMan: Creating CGI for Motion Pictures.* Morgan Kaufmann.

Barzel, Ronen. 1997. "Lighting Controls for Computer Cinematography." *Journal of Graphics Tools* 2(1), pp. 1–20. Available online at **http://www.acm.org/jgt/papers/Barzel97**

Barzel, Ronen. 1999. "Lighting Controls for Computer Cinematography." In *Advanced RenderMan*: *Creating CGI for Motion Pictures*, edited by Anthony A. Apodaca and Larry Gritz. Morgan Kaufmann. Code for the chapter was provided by Larry Gritz.

Birn, Jeremy. 2000. *Digital Lighting and Rendering.* New Riders Publishing.

Calahan, Sharon. 1999. "Storytelling through Lighting: A Computer Graphics Perspective." In *Advanced RenderMan*: *Creating CGI for Motion Pictures*, edited by Anthony A. Apodaca and Larry Gritz. Morgan Kaufmann.

Chapter 11

Shadow Map Antialiasing

Michael Bunnell
NVIDIA

Fabio Pellacini
Pixar Animation Studios

11.1 Introduction

Shadow mapping is the method of choice for creating shadows in high-end rendering for motion pictures and television. However, it has been problematic to use shadow mapping in real-time applications, such as video games, because of aliasing problems in the form of magnified *jaggies*. This chapter shows how to significantly reduce shadow map aliasing in a shader. It describes how to implement a simplified version of percentage-closer filtering that makes the most out of the GPU's shadow-mapping hardware to render soft-edged, antialiased shadows at real-time rates.

Shadow mapping involves projecting a shadow map on geometry and comparing the shadow map values with the light-view depth at each pixel. If the projection causes the shadow map to be magnified, aliasing in the form of large, unsightly jaggies will appear at shadow borders. Aliasing can usually be reduced by using higher-resolution shadow maps and increasing the shadow map resolution, using techniques such as *perspective shadow maps* (Stamminger and Drettakis 2002). However, using perspective shadow-mapping techniques and increasing shadow map resolution does not work when the light is traveling nearly parallel to the shadowed surface, because the magnification approaches infinity.

High-end rendering software solves the aliasing problem by using a technique called *percentage-closer filtering*.

11.2 Percentage-Closer Filtering

Unlike normal textures, shadow map textures cannot be prefiltered to remove aliasing. Instead, multiple shadow map comparisons are made per pixel and averaged together. This technique is called percentage-closer filtering (PCF) because it calculates the percentage of the surface that is closer to the light and, therefore, not in shadow.

The original PCF algorithm, described in Reeves et al. 1987, called for mapping *the region to be shaded* into shadow map space and sampling that region stochastically (that is, randomly). The algorithm was first implemented using the REYES rendering engine, so *the region to be shaded* meant a four-sided micropolygon. Figure 11-1 shows an example of that implementation.

In our implementation, we have changed the PCF algorithm slightly to make it easy and efficient to apply. Instead of calculating the region to be shaded in shadow map space, we simply use a 4×4-texel sample region everywhere. This region is large enough to significantly reduce aliasing, but not so large as to require huge numbers of samples or stochastic sampling techniques to achieve good results. Note that the sampling region is not aligned to texel boundaries. An aligned region would not achieve the antialiasing effect that we want.

Hardware shaders work on pixels, not on micropolygons, so matching the original implementation would involve transforming a four-sided polygon representing a screen pixel into shadow map space to calculate the sample region. Our implementation uses a

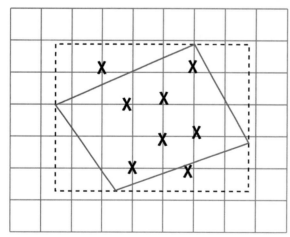

Figure 11-1. Percentage-Closer Filtering
The first implementation of percentage-closer filtering called for a micropolygon to be transformed to texture space to calculate the area to sample.

fixed-size sample region instead. A fixed-size region lets us skip a complicated transformation and allows us to calculate a precise shadow percentage instead of an approximate one using stochastic sampling. See Figure 11-2.

0	0	0	0	0	0	0	0	1
0	0	0	0	0	0	1	1	1
0	0	0	0	0	1	1	1	1
0	0	0	0	0	1	1	1	1
0	0	0	0	1	1	1	1	1
0	0	0	0	1	1	1	1	1
1	1	1	1	1	1	1	1	1

Figure 11-2. Sampling an Area of 4×4 Texels

11.3 A Brute-Force Implementation

NVIDIA GPUs have built-in percentage-closer filtering for shadow map sampling. The hardware does four depth compares and uses the fractional part of the texture coordinate to bilinearly interpolate the shadow value. The shadow result is the percentage that a texel-size sample area is in shadow. See Figure 11-3. A single texel-size sample region is not big enough to effectively remove aliasing, but the region can be increased to a 4×4 texel size by averaging 16 shadow compare values. The offsets for x and y are -1.5, -0.5, 0.5, and 1.5 for samples one texel unit apart.

0	0	0	1
0	0	1	1
1	1	1	1
1	1	1	1

Figure 11-3. Using the Hardware
Shadow map hardware samples a single texel-size area, resulting in a value of 0.75 in this case.

The following function can be used to do a projected texture map read with an offset given in texel units. The variable texmapscale is a `float2` containing 1/width and 1/height of the shadow map.

```
float3 offset_lookup(sampler2D map,
                     float4 loc,
                     float2 offset)
{
    return tex2Dproj(map, float4(loc.xy + offset * texmapscale * loc.w,
                                 loc.z, loc.w));
}
```

We can implement the 16-sample version in a fragment program as follows:

```
float sum = 0;
float x, y;

for (y = -1.5; y <= 1.5; y += 1.0)
   for (x = -1.5; x <= 1.5; x += 1.0)
      sum += offset_lookup(shadowmap, shadowCoord, float2(x, y));

shadowCoeff = sum / 16.0;
```

11.4 Using Fewer Samples

The performance of the brute-force method is better than one might expect. Many of the texture fetches are in the texture cache because they are guaranteed to be close to one another. However, if we change the sampling pattern per pixel, we can attain similar results with only four samples per pixel.

The four-sample technique produces results similar to those created by dithering black-and-white data to render a grayscale image. The sample region size remains the same, but we use only four of the 16 samples per pixel. The set of four samples varies depending on the screen location. Figure 11-4 shows the sampling pattern used in the four-sample version of the shader to pick four out of 16 possible sample locations per pixel.

0	3	0	3
2	1	2	1
0	3	0	3
2	1	2	1

Figure 11-4. The Sampling Pattern Used for the Four-Sample Version of the Shader

We can implement the four-sample version as follows:

```
offset = (float)(frac(position.xy * 0.5) > 0.25);  // mod
offset.y += offset.x;  // y ^= x in floating point
if (offset.y > 1.1)
  offset.y = 0;
shadowCoeff = (offset_lookup(shadowmap, sCoord, offset +
                      float2(-1.5, 0.5)) +
              offset_lookup(shadowmap, sCoord, offset +
                      float2(0.5, 0.5)) +
              offset_lookup(shadowmap, sCoord, offset +
                      float2(-1.5, -1.5)) +
              offset_lookup(shadowmap, sCoord, offset +
                      float2(0.5, -1.5)) ) * 0.25;
```

11.5 Why It Works

How can we antialias shadows with a fixed-size sample region even though texture projection can greatly magnify the shadow map? The answer is simple: When a texture is magnified, the texture map samples are close to each other for adjacent pixels. If the samples are close to each other and the sampled area is relatively large, then there can be only a very small difference between the shadow values, because the sample areas overlap a lot. Figure 11-5 shows how sample areas for adjacent pixels overlap when the shadow map is magnified.

The more the shadow map is magnified, the smaller the difference between adjacent pixels, and the smoother the transition between shadowed and unshadowed regions. The hardware calculates that shadow percentage with eight bits of precision, so even in the case of extreme magnification and high-contrast shadows, there will always be a smooth shadow transition without banding. If the shadow regions are very close to each other, the shadow value will differ only by the least significant bit for eight-bits-per-component output. This is illustrated in Figures 11-6, 11-7, and 11-8, which show shadows for a ninja model with 1, 4, and 16 samples, respectively. Figure 11-9 shows a magnification of the ninja's thumb shadow in each of the three cases. Notice the vastly improved shadow quality in the 16-sample case.

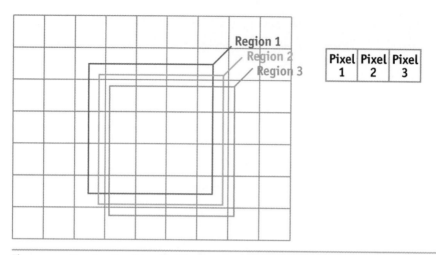

Figure 11-5. Overlapping Sampling Regions for Adjacent Pixels

Figure 11-6. Ninja Shadow with One Sample per Pixel
Ninja model by William "Proton" Vaughn.

Figure 11-7. Ninja Shadow with Four Dithered Samples per Pixel

Figure 11-8. Ninja Shadow with Sixteen Samples per Pixel

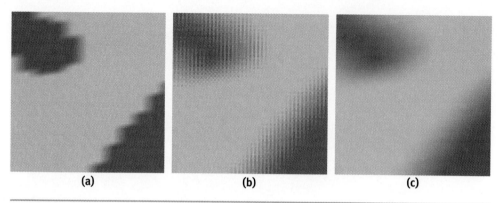

Figure 11-9. The Shadows Magnified

When the shadows of the ninja's thumb from Figures 11-6, 11-7, and 11-8 are magnified, the differences in quality become obvious: (a) the single-sample image, (b) the four-sample image, and (c) the sixteen-sample image.

11.6 Conclusion

Shadow mapping is a popular method for rendering shadows, but it suffers from aliasing artifacts. We can greatly reduce shadow map aliasing by averaging multiple shadow map values. If we take advantage of the GPU's shadow-mapping hardware and use clever sampling techniques, we can render soft-edged, antialiased shadows at high frame rates.

11.7 References

Fernando, Randima, and Mark Kilgard. 2003. *The Cg Tutorial.* Addison-Wesley. This introduction to the Cg language has a good section on shadow mapping.

Reeves, W. T., D. H. Salesin, and P. L. Cook. 1987. "Rendering Antialiased Shadows with Depth Maps." *Computer Graphics* 21(4) (Proceedings of SIGGRAPH 87).

Stamminger, Marc, and George Drettakis. 2002. "Perspective Shadow Maps." In *Proceedings of SIGGRAPH 2002*, pp. 557–562.

Chapter 12

Omnidirectional Shadow Mapping

Philipp S. Gerasimov
iXBT.com

12.1 Introduction

One of the most difficult problems in real-time computer graphics is generating high-quality shadows. Yet, the appearance of such shadows is one of the most important factors in achieving graphic realism. In computer-generated scenes, an object's shadow enhances our perception of the object and the relationship between objects. In computer games, shadows—along with lighting, music, and special effects—play a very important role in portraying a realistic game atmosphere. For example, shadows are a major part of the story line in id Software's *Doom 3*, one of the most technologically advanced games. Figures 12-1 and 12-2 show examples of shadows from our own demo, which is provided on the book's CD and Web site.

GPUs now allow us to create images previously available only in professional 3D offline-rendering programs. The geometry processors in modern GPUs can process millions of primitives per frame, letting us design complex worlds. With the advent of per-pixel shading, we can produce realistic materials using complex mathematical and physically based models of lighting.

Two popular methods are available for visualizing shadows in real-time computer graphics: stencil shadows and shadow mapping.

Figure 12-1. Screenshot of Our Demo, Showing a Light Source Flying Above a Character

Figure 12-2. A Close-Up of the Character in Our Demo

12.1.1 Stencil Shadows

The stencil shadows method, which is demonstrated in *Doom 3*, is used widely by game developers. It offers advantages such as the large number of GPUs that support it (the only essential hardware feature is support for an eight-bit stencil buffer), its independence from the type of light source, and the high quality of its generated shadows. However, the stencil shadows approach has some serious disadvantages: it's heavily dependent on CPU work, it can produce only hard shadows, it uses a large amount of fill rate (which means that even though a GPU may support the technique, it could run poorly), and it cannot be used with hardware-tessellated surfaces.

12.1.2 Shadow Mapping

The shadow-mapping algorithm came to computer graphics in 1978 when it was introduced by Lance Williams (Williams 1978). Today, this method is used in a multitude of Hollywood movies that contain computer graphics and special effects. Shadow mapping projects a special dynamically created texture on scene geometry to calculate shadows. It lets you render hard and soft shadows, as well as shadows from different types of light sources. Plus, it works with hardware-tessellated surfaces and with GPU-animated meshes (such as skinned meshes).

A number of GPU manufacturers, including NVIDIA, support shadow mapping directly in their hardware and promise to enhance this support in the future. The NVIDIA GeForce3, GeForce4 Ti, and all the GeForce FX (and more recent) GPUs support hardware shadow maps through both DirectX and OpenGL. (However, we do not use the native hardware shadow-mapping functionality in this chapter.) The possibilities offered by the NVIDIA CineFX architecture—including support for long fragment programs with true floating-point precision as well as floating-point texture formats—enable a new level of quality in shadow rendering.

12.2 The Shadow-Mapping Algorithm

12.2.1 Conditions

Shadow mapping lets us visualize shadows cast from different types of light sources, such as directional lights, point lights, and spotlights. The type of light source dictates the technology we need to use. This chapter focuses on visualizing shadows cast from point light sources. Point light sources are widely used in computer games, and the quality of shadows cast by objects illuminated by these lights is very important.

We also have these additional conditions:

- Cube maps, traditionally used in computer graphics to implement environment reflections, are the building blocks of our shadow-mapping algorithm.

- We focus our implementation on DirectX 9–compatible graphics hardware (for example, products in the GeForce FX family from NVIDIA, or the Radeon 9500 and more recent products from ATI).

- We use DirectX as the graphics API (but our algorithm works just as well in OpenGL).

- We take advantage of vertex and pixel shaders written in a high-level language.

- We use HLSL (but Cg is ideal for this task, too).

12.2.2 The Algorithm

There are two primary phases in using omnidirectional shadow maps: creating the shadow map and projecting it. In the *creation phase*, we render the squared distance from the light source of all objects that cast shadows into the shadow map texture (we'll see why the distance is squared a little later). In the *projection phase*, we render all the objects that receive shadows, and we compare the squared distance from the rendered pixel to the light source.

The following technique fills all six faces of a cube map, in all directions: $+x$, $-x$, $+y$, $-y$, $+z$, $-z$. The shadow maps can be either precalculated (for static scenes) or re-rendered every frame. We focus primarily on re-rendering the shadow map each frame for fully dynamic shadows. All objects cast a shadow, and receive a shadow, from each light source. And all objects self-shadow. We use a single shadow map for all light sources, creating an image with multipass rendering and performing one pass for each light source.

Listing 12-1 is an example of pseudocode for this algorithm.

Because we use a multipass algorithm (that is, making one pass for each light source), all objects must be composited into the frame buffer. To reduce overdraw and improve performance, we render a depth-only pass first. This standard technique ensures that all subsequent lighting passes occur only on visible pixels. Rendering to depth-only is very fast (many GeForce FX GPUs have double-speed "depth-only" rendering features), so it requires minimal overhead, even in low-overdraw situations. Transparent objects are not rendered in the depth-only pass, because transparent objects do not update the depth buffer. See Listing 12-2.

Listing 12-1. Pseudocode for the Omnidirectional Shadow-Mapping Algorithm

```
for (iLight = 0; iLight < NumberOfLights; iLight++) {
  // Fill the shadow map.
  for (iObject = 0; iObject < NumberOfObjects; iObject++) {
    RenderObjectToShadowMap(iLight, iObject);
  }

  // Lighting and shadow mapping.
  for (iObject = 0; iObject < NumberOfObjects; iObject++) {
    LightAndShadeObject (iLight, iObject);
  }
}
```

Listing 12-2. Depth-Only Rendering

```
// Clear color and depth buffers
ClearAllBuffers();

// Fill z-buffer
for (iObject = 0; iObject < NumberOfObjects; iObject++) {
  RenderObjectToZBufferOnly (iObject);
}
```

12.2.3 Texture Format

The type of texture format used is an important factor in this algorithm. We consider two formats: floating-point textures and integer 32-bit RGBA textures with packing/unpacking of the depth value into the color channels.

The *floating-point* texture format is ideal for shadow mapping because it allows for high-precision depth values. However, these textures are much slower than integer RGBA textures and are supported by only a limited number of GPUs. On the other hand, *integer 32-bit RGBA textures* are fast and are supported by most 3D hardware.

To conserve the high precision of calculation, however, we must pack depth values into the color channels of textures and unpack each value when performing the depth-compare for shadow mapping. We consider both methods and let you choose the one that's more convenient.

12.2.4 The Size of the Shadow Map

The size of the shadow map influences the shadow's quality and rendering speed. The size depends on the capabilities of the target hardware, the required quality, and the position of the shadow in relationship to the camera. Of course, a larger shadow map generally produces better results.

Because we use cube map textures, we have to keep in mind that we have six color surfaces and an additional z-buffer. For 32-bit textures and a 1024×1024 resolution, we'll need $4 \times (6 + 1) \times 1024 \times 1024$ bytes of video memory, or 28 MB! This highlights the importance of using a single shadow map for all light sources.

Section 12.3 examines each step of our algorithm.

12.2.5 The Range of Values for Geometry

To minimize rendering artifacts, we put all our geometry into a $-0.5 \ldots +0.5$ range (or $0..1$). This adds accuracy to our calculations, especially if we use 16-bit precision and integer textures. We can scale our geometry at load time or in the vertex shader, using vertex shader code such as this:

```
o.vPositionWorld = mul(vPosition, matWorld) *  fGeometryScale;
```

12.3 Implementation

12.3.1 System Requirements

These are our system requirements:

- Hardware that supports vertex shaders (vs.1.1+) and pixel shaders (ps.2.0+)
- Hardware capability for rendering into cube maps
- If using floating-point textures: support for a single-component floating-point cube-map texture format, such as D3DFMT_R16F or D3DFMT_R32F, with the D3DUSAGE_RENDERTARGET flag
- If using integer textures: support for the D3DFMT_A8R8G8B8 cube texture format, with the D3DUSAGE_RENDERTARGET flag

12.3.2 Resource Creation

We can create all the required objects and textures (the shadow map texture, the depth buffer, and the shaders) using several useful Direct3D library functions:

```
D3DXCreateCubeTexture()
D3DXCreateRenderToEnvMap()
D3DXCreateEffectFromFile()
```

12.3.3 Rendering Phase 1: Rendering into the Shadow Map

Next, we render into the shadow map. We'll render our objects into each face of the cube map from the point of view of the light source, following these requirements:

- The field of view must be 90 degrees.
- The view matrix for each face must be created properly. We can create these matrices from the up, down, east, west, north, and south vectors from the point of view of the light source.

The Vertex Shader

In the vertex shader, we write out the scaled world-space position of the vertex for the pixel shader. Or, we can write out the light direction and save one pixel shader instruction computing the world-space light vector.

The Pixel Shader

We can use either a floating-point texture or an integer texture.

- When we use floating-point textures, we write out the squared distance from the pixel to the light source, as in this pixel shader code:

```
return dot(vLight, vLight)
```

Why do we use squared distance? Because it's faster to compute—it's just a dot product, and no square root operation is necessary. We use squared distance when filling the shadow map, and we will use squared distance when accessing the shadow map in the base rendering pass. This saves pixel shader instructions twice. But using the squared distance can cause some precision problems, so we need to be careful when using it.

- When we use integer textures, we need to pack the squared distance value and write it into the color channel. How can we pack a floating-point number into an integer texture? Here are two ways:

1. ```
Out.r = SquaredDistance * 2^0
Out.g = SquaredDistance * 2^8
Out.b = SquaredDistance * 2^16
Out.a = SquaredDistance * 2^24
```

   ```
   float4 vPack = {1.0f, 256.0f, 65536.0, 16777216.0f};
   return vPack * dot(vLight, vLight);
   ```

2. ```
Out.r = floor(fDepth) / 256.0;
Out.g = frac(fDepth);
```

   ```
   float fDepth = dot(vLight, vLight);
   return float(floor(fDepth) / 256.0, frac(fDepth),
               frac(fDepth), frac(fDepth));
   ```

By writing `frac(fDepth)` into the green and alpha channels, we save this pixel shader instruction (otherwise, we need an additional instruction to fill these channels):

```
mov r2.gba, r0.g  // r0.g contains frac(fDepth)
```

Method 1 is computationally cheaper, but the second one gives you higher precision.

12.3.4 Rendering Phase 2: Base Rendering

The base rendering phase has two main parts:

1. Rendering objects only to the z-buffer (z-only pass), which requires these steps:

   a. Disabling rendering into the color channel

   b. Enabling rendering into the z-buffer

   c. Rendering all objects into the z-buffer (only)

2. Making a shading (lighting times shadow) pass for each light source

12.3.5 The Lighting Calculation

We need to calculate the lighting at each pixel from the light source, and we can use any lighting model (such as per-pixel Phong, Blinn, or Oren-Nayar).

12.3.6 The Shadow Calculation

Calculating the shadow requires these steps:

1. Calculate the squared distance from the current pixel to the light source.

2. Project the shadow map texture onto the current pixel.

3. Fetch the shadow map texture value at the current pixel.

4. Compare the calculated distance value with the fetched shadow map value to determine whether or not we're in shadow.

For floating-point textures, we just use the x component of the fetched texture sample.

Here is the pixel shader code:

```
float fDepth = fDistSquared - fDepthBias;
float3 vShadowSample = texCUBE(ShadowMapSampler, -vLight.xyz);
float fShadow = (fDepth - vShadowSample.x < 0.0f) ? 1.0f : 0.0f;
```

fDistSquared was computed previously in the pixel shader. For integer textures, we must unpack the value from the color channels of the fetched texture sample.

1. DepthValue = ShadowSample.r / 1 +
   ShadowSample.g / 256 +
   ShadowSample.b / 65536 +
   ShadowSample.a / 16777216

2. DepthValue = ShadowSample.r * 256 + ShadowSample.g

Here is the pixel shader code:

```
float fDepth = fDistSquared - fDepthBias;
float4 vShadowSample = texCUBE(ShadowMapSampler, -vLight.xyz);
float fShadow = (fDepth - dot(vShadowSample,
                        vUnpack) < 0.0f) ? 1.0f : 0.0f;
```

12.3.7 Tips and Tricks

1. There are a number of different ways you can compute depth bias:
   - fDistSquared - vShadowSample.x—artifacts are very possible.
   - (fDistSquared - DepthBias) - vShadowSample.x—the squared distance is not linear.
   - (fDistSquared * DepthBias) - vShadowSample.x—this method works best in practice.

2. Light direction: Move the light direction calculation into the vertex shader. The light direction is linear and can easily be calculated per vertex.

3. Opposite light direction: We need the opposite light direction for fetching from the shadow map. But the texld pixel shader instruction does not support the "negate"

modifier, so if we use `texCUBE(ShadowMapSampler, -vLight.xyz)`, we'll get an extra "add" instruction with every fetch. So, we can move this calculation into the vertex shader and interpolate `-vLight.xyz` instead of `vLight.xyz`.

4. Preprocessor directives with HLSL and Cg shaders: Use preprocessor directives for different options—such as floating-point/integer textures, hard/soft shadows, and full/half/fixed precision—to reduce the number of shaders you need to write.

5. Pixel shader precision: Use half precision for most shadow calculations. It's sufficient, and you will get extra speed on some hardware. If you see artifacts, however, use full precision.

12.3.8 Finalizing the Shading Pass (Lighting × Shadow)

The last step is to write the pixel color value based on the calculated lighting and shadowing. For each light source, we add the calculated lighting into the back buffer by repeating the shadow-writing and shading passes for all objects. When we finish processing all the light sources, we get a scene with dynamic lighting and shadowing.

12.4 Adding Soft Shadows

Looking at our scene, we notice that the shadows' edges are aliased and "hard." The level of aliasing depends on the size of the shadow map and the amount of magnification during projection. To reduce the appearance of these artifacts, we create a "softer" shadow by fetching multiple samples from the shadow map and averaging the results. Because real-world light sources are rarely perfect point sources, this action will also provide a more realistic shadow.

Listing 12-3 shows some sample code.

Listing 12-3. Making a Softer Shadow

```
float fShadow = 0;

for (int i = 0; i < 4; i++) {
  float3 vLightDirection = -vLight.xyz + vFilter[i];
  float4 vShadowSample = texCUBE(ShadowMapSampler, vLightDirection);
  fShadow += (fDepth - vShadowSample.x < 0.0f) ? 0.25f : 0.0f;
}
```

Note that we first compare the squared distances and *then* average the results of the comparison. This is called *percentage-closer filtering* and is the correct way to average multiple shadow map tests. (See Chapter 11 of this book, "Shadow Map Antialiasing," for a detailed discussion of this technique.)

We can save some pixel shader instructions when calculating `-vLight.xyz + vFilter[i]` values if we move it into the vertex shader.

If we choose different range values for `vFilter[i]`, we'll get different levels of softness for the shadow, ranging from a slight antialiasing effect to a very blurry shadow. The larger the filter kernel we define, the more samples we need to take to avoid banding artifacts. Obviously, taking more samples equals processing more instructions and more texture fetches, which can reduce performance in shader-bound situations. Although this technique can produce a "softer" look for the shadows, the shadows are of course not accurate soft shadows, because they do not take into account the relationships between occluders, receivers, and the size of the light source. (See Chapter 13, "Generating Soft Shadows Using Occlusion Interval Maps," for more on soft shadows.)

12.5 Conclusion

With the new capabilities of DirectX 9–class hardware, new algorithms for improving visual quality become possible and easier to implement. Using hardware shaders, we can create realistic, dynamic shadows from any number of point light sources, and we can even implement basic "soft" shadows.

With the current first-generation DirectX 9–class hardware, this algorithm is not quite fast enough to be practical (although it is definitely real time). That's because of the large number of renderings from the point of view of the light, and the long pixel shaders necessary for "soft" shadowing effects. But as always, much faster graphics hardware is right around the corner, and advances in performance will make these algorithms practical for implementation in real, shipping games.

12.6 References

Williams, Lance. 1978. "Casting Curved Shadows on Curved Surfaces." In *Proceedings of the 5th Annual Conference on Computer Graphics and Interactive Techniques*, pp. 270–274.

The author would like to thank Chris Wynn and John Spitzer of NVIDIA and Guennadi Riguer of ATI.

Chapter 13

Generating Soft Shadows Using Occlusion Interval Maps

William Donnelly
University of Waterloo

Joe Demers
NVIDIA

In this chapter we present a technique for rendering soft shadows that we call *occlusion interval mapping*. Occlusion interval maps were used to produce soft shadows in the NVIDIA GeForce FX 5900 demo "Last Chance Gas." See Figure 13-1. We call the technique occlusion interval mapping because it uses texture maps to store intervals that represent when the light source is visible and when it is occluded. In situations that satisfy the algorithm's requirements, occlusion interval mapping allows you to achieve impressive visual results at high frame rates.

13.1 The Gas Station

One of the goals of the GeForce FX 5900 demo "Last Chance Gas" was to create a scene with accurate outdoor lighting. One important aspect of outdoor lighting we wanted to capture is soft shadows from the Sun. Unlike the hard shadows produced by shadow maps or stencil shadow volumes, soft shadows have a *penumbra* region, which gives a smooth transition between shadowed and unshadowed regions. A correct penumbra makes for more realistic shadowing and gives the user a better sense of spatial relationships, making for a more realistic and immersive experience.

When we started writing the demo, we could not find any appropriate real-time soft shadow algorithm, even though a lot of research had been dedicated to the problem.

Figure 13-1. The "Last Chance Gas" Demo

Because the soft shadow problem is such a difficult one, we considered how we could simplify the problem to make it more feasible for real time.

Given that the gas station scene is static, we considered using a precomputed visibility technique such as *spherical harmonic lighting* (Sloan et al. 2002). Unfortunately for our purposes, spherical harmonic lighting assumes very low frequency lighting, and so it is not suitable for small area lights such as the Sun. We developed occlusion interval maps as a new precomputed visibility technique that would allow for real-time soft shadows from the Sun. Our method achieves this goal by reducing the problem to the case of a linear light source on a fixed trajectory.

The algorithm also bears some similarity to *horizon maps* (Max 1988). Unlike horizon maps, which cover the entire visible hemisphere, occlusion interval maps work only for lights along a single path on the visible hemisphere. Occlusion interval maps also can handle arbitrary geometry, not just height fields.

Occlusion interval maps are not meant to be a general solution to the soft shadow problem, but we found them useful for shadowing in a static outdoor environment. As with other precomputed visibility techniques, occlusion interval maps rely on an offline process to store all visibility information, and so they won't work for moving objects or arbitrary light sources.

13.2 The Algorithm

Suppose we have a light source such as the Sun that follows a fixed trajectory, and suppose that we want to precompute hard shadows for this light source. We can express the shadowing as a visibility function, which has a value of 0 when a point is in shadow and a value of 1 when it is illuminated. During rendering, this visibility function is computed, and the result is multiplied by a shading calculation to give the final color value.

The visibility function is a function of three variables: two spatial dimensions for the surface of the object and one dimension for time. Although we could store this function as a 3D texture, the memory requirements would be huge. Instead, because all the values of the visibility function are either 0 or 1, we can store the function using a method similar to run-length encoding. For each point, we find rising and falling edges in the time domain. These correspond to the times of day when the Sun appears and disappears, respectively. We define the "rise" vector as the vector of all rising edges, and the corresponding "fall" vector as the vector of all falling edges. See Figure 13-2.

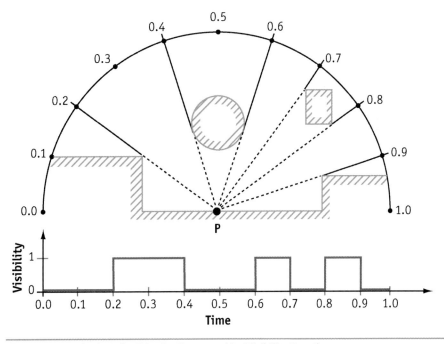

Figure 13-2. A Single Point **P** in the Scene and Its Visibility Function
*The rise vector for this point is **R** = (0.2, 0.6, 0.8), and the corresponding fall vector is*
F = (0.4, 0.7, 0.9).

We now have all we need for precomputed visibility of hard shadows; given a rise vector, a fall vector, and time of day, we can compute the visibility function to determine if the point is in shadow.

In order to turn this into a soft shadow algorithm, we extend the light source along its trajectory. Now instead of computing shadows from a point light source, we compute shadows from a linear light source. Imagine a time interval $[t - \frac{1}{2}dt, t + \frac{1}{2}dt]$. Over this time, the light source will sweep out a curve in space. If we take the average lighting over the time interval $[t - \frac{1}{2}dt, t + \frac{1}{2}dt]$, we will have computed the correct shadowing from the linear light source. This means that we can apply the same information used to render a hard shadow image to rendering a soft shadowed image. See Figure 13-3.

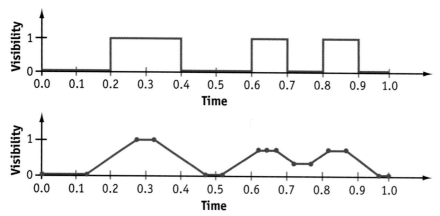

Figure 13-3. The Point Light Visibility Function and Corresponding Linear Light Visibility Function
The lower image is generated by blurring the upper image.

13.3 Creating the Maps

In order to generate occlusion interval maps, we have to compute the visibility function from every point on the light source trajectory to every pixel in the occlusion interval map. We do this by taking a sequence of evenly spaced points along the curve, tracing a ray from each occlusion interval map pixel to each of these points, and detecting the rising and falling edges of each visibility function. We store rising and falling edge values in eight bits; so 256 rays are enough to completely capture all of the intervals. To reduce the amount of information stored, we do not store rising and falling edges when a point's normal is facing away from the light source. Because back-facing pixels will be dark anyway, this decision will save space and have no effect on the rendered image.

Computing visibility functions can be done by any ray tracer with the right level of programmability. We computed all data for our scene using a custom shader in the mental ray software package. Computing these textures can be time-consuming, because you have to cast 256 rays for every pixel in the occlusion interval map. For the scene in "Last Chance Gas," it took several hours to compute the shadowing for the entire scene.

We store the rise vector and the fall vector in two sets of color textures, each texture having four channels. A "rise" texture stores the beginning of a light interval in each channel, and the matching "fall" texture stores the ends of the light intervals. It will become obvious why we divide the textures up like this when we describe the algorithm for rendering with occlusion interval maps.

To alleviate the extra memory requirements of storing the occlusion interval maps, we compute our maps at half the size of color textures, which reduces the storage requirements by a factor of four. The resolution of occlusion interval maps can be reduced because the softness of the shadows has a blurring effect that makes up for the lower resolution. In some cases, we found that we could even lower the resolution of the maps beyond half the color texture sizes without noticeable artifacts.

For parameterizing the objects, we use the objects' texture coordinates. Because the pixels of the occlusion interval map store information that depends on position, the objects' texture coordinates cannot overlap. For objects with tiled textures, this means computing a new set of unique texture coordinates.

13.4 Rendering

When rendering, we have to average the visibility function over an interval of parameter values. In mathematical terms, this means performing a convolution with a window function of width dt. The equation for this calculation is:

$$V_{LinearLight}(t) = \int_0^1 V_{PointLight}(u) W_{dt}(t - u) du,$$

where $V_{PointLight}$ is the visibility function and W_{dt} is a box filter of width dt, defined as $W_{dt}(t) = 1/dt$ for $-dt/2 < t < dt/2$, and $W_{dt}(t) = 0$ otherwise. Given a rise vector $\mathbf{R} = (R_1, R_2, \ldots, R_n)$ and a fall vector $\mathbf{F} = (F_1, F_2, \ldots, F_n)$, then we can express $V_{PointLight}$ as:

$$V_{PointLight}(t) = \sum_{i=1}^{n} B(R_i, F_i, t),$$

where $B(a, b, t)$ is the boxcar function, defined as $B(a, b, t) = 1$ for $a < t < b$ and $B(a, b, t) = 0$ otherwise. We can now evaluate $V_{LinearLight}$ as follows:

$$V_{LinearLight}(t) = \int_0^1 \sum_{i=1}^n B\left(R_i, F_i, u\right) W_{dt}\left(t - u\right) du$$

$$= \sum_{i=1}^n \int_0^1 B\left(R_i, F_i, u\right) W_{dt}\left(t - u\right) du$$

$$= \sum_{i=1}^n \int_{\max\left(t - \frac{1}{2}dt, \, R_i\right)}^{\min\left(t + \frac{1}{2}dt, \, F_i\right)} \frac{1}{dt} du$$

$$= \sum_{i=1}^n \frac{\max\left(0, \min\left(t + \frac{1}{2}dt, F_i\right) - \max\left(t - \frac{1}{2}dt, R_i\right)\right)}{dt}.$$

Using the preceding equation, we can easily calculate soft shadowing for a single rise/fall pair using just min, max, and subtraction. Fortunately, we optimize this even further. Because shader instructions operate on four-component vectors, four intervals can be done simultaneously at the same cost of doing a single interval. This is why we pack the rises and falls into separate textures. The final Cg code is shown in Listing 13-1.

Listing 13-1. Function for Computing Soft Shadows Using Occlusion Interval Maps

```
half softshadow(sampler2D riseTexture,
                sampler2D fallTexture,
                float2 texCoord,
                half intervalStart,
                half intervalEnd,
                half intervalInverseWidth)
{
  half4 rise = h4tex2D(riseTexture, texCoord);
  half4 fall = h4tex2D(fallTexture, texCoord);
  half4 minTerm = min(fall, intervalEnd);
  half4 maxTerm = max(rise, intervalStart);
  return dot(intervalInverseWidth, saturate(minTerm - maxTerm));
}
```

Note that `saturate(x)` is used in place of `max(0, x)`. The two operations will always be equivalent because the quantity being considered is the width of the visible light source interval, which is always less than 1. We choose to use `saturate(x)` over max(0, x) because it can be applied as an output modifier, saving an instruction. We used the 16-bit half data type and found it perfectly suited to our needs, because our calculations exceeded the range of fixed precision but did not require full 32-bit floating point.

The dot product on the last line of Listing 13-1 is not used for its usual geometric purpose; we use it to simultaneously divide by the light source width and add together the shadow values that are computed in parallel. We pass the values to the shader as intervalStart = t − 1/2dt, intervalEnd = t + 1/2dt, and intervalInverseWidth = 1/dt.

This shader compiles to only six assembly-code instructions for the GeForce FX: two texture lookups, a min, a max, a subtraction with a saturate modifier, and a dot product. The function computes up to four intervals' worth of shadows. If there are multiple rise and fall textures, we just call the function multiple times and add the results together.

13.5 Limitations

As previously discussed, the technique works only for static scenes with a single light traveling on a fixed trajectory. This means it would not work for shadowing on characters and other dynamic objects, but it is well suited for shadowing in static outdoor environments.

Because occlusion interval maps require all eight bits of precision per channel, texture compression will result in visual artifacts. Thus, texture compression has to be disabled, resulting in increased texture usage. This increase is offset by the lower resolution of the occlusion interval maps. The discontinuities in the occlusion interval maps mean that bilinear filtering produced artifacts as well. As a result, any kind of texture filtering must also be disabled on occlusion interval maps. This gives the shadows a blocky look. Once again, because of the smoothness of the shadowing, this effect is not as noticeable as it would be on detailed color textures.

Another visual artifact comes from the fact that the Sun is approximated by a linear light source. If you look closely at the shadow boundaries, you will see that shadows are smoother in the direction parallel to the light source path and harder in the perpendicular direction. Fortunately, this effect is subtle unless the light source is very large. For the range of widths we used, the effect is not very noticeable. Heidrich et al. (2000) also used linear lights to approximate area lights and noted that the shadowing from a linear light source looks very much like the shadowing from a true area light source. See Figure 13-4.

Figure 13-4. Lighting a Ladder
The ladder's shadow is blurred more vertically than horizontally. Even in this extreme case, the effect does not detract from the soft look of the shadows.

13.6 Conclusion

Rendering soft shadows in real time is an extremely difficult problem. Figures 13-5 and 13-6 show two examples of the subtleties involved. Precomputed visibility techniques produce soft shadows by imposing assumptions on the scene and on the light source. In the case of occlusion interval maps, we trade generality for performance to obtain a soft shadow algorithm that runs in real time on static scenes. Occlusion interval maps can act as a replacement for static light maps, allowing dynamic effects such as the variation of lighting from sunrise to sunset, as in "Last Chance Gas."

Figure 13-5. The Gas Station Entrance
Notice how the shadow on the gas station wall has a sharp boundary toward the upper left of the image, but it softens toward the lower right. This "hardening at contact" is an important property of real soft shadows that is correctly captured by occlusion interval maps.

Figure 13-6. Shadows on the Car's Tarp
The wooden boards above the tarp make for complex shadowing, which is the worst case for our algorithm. Because of these boards, the occlusion interval maps on the tarp had to be stored in five separate textures. For most objects in the scene, four textures were sufficient to capture all the shadows.

13.7 References

We also considered using the soft shadow volume technique presented by Assarsson et al., but we had too much geometry in our scene for a shadow volume technique to remain real-time.

Assarsson, Ulf, Michael Dougherty, Michael Mounier, and Tomas Akenine-Möller. 2003. "An Optimized Soft Shadow Volume Algorithm with Real-Time Performance." *Graphics Hardware*, pp. 33–40.

Heidrich, Wolfgang, Stefan Brabec, and Hans-Peter Seidel. 2000. "Soft Shadow Maps for Linear Lights." In *11th Eurographics Workshop on Rendering*, pp. 269–280.

Max, N. L. 1988. "Horizon Mapping: Shadows for Bump-Mapped Surfaces. *The Visual Computer* 4(2), pp. 109–117.

Sloan, Peter-Pike, Jan Kautz, and John Snyder. 2002. "Precomputed Radiance Transfer for Real-Time Rendering in Dynamic, Low-Frequency Lighting Environments." *ACM Transactions on Graphics 21*, pp. 527–536.

Chapter 14

Perspective Shadow Maps: Care and Feeding

Simon Kozlov
SoftLab-NSK

14.1 Introduction

Shadow generation has always been a big problem in real-time 3D graphics. Determining whether a point is in shadow is not a trivial operation for modern GPUs, particularly because GPUs work in terms of rasterizing polygons instead of ray tracing.

Today's shadows should be completely dynamic. Almost every object in the scene should cast and receive shadows, there should be self-shadowing, and every object should have soft shadows. Only two algorithms can satisfy these requirements: shadow volumes (or stencil shadows) and shadow mapping.

The difference between the algorithms for shadow volumes and shadow mapping comes down to *object space* versus *image space*:

- *Object-space shadow algorithms*, such as shadow volumes, work by creating a polygonal structure that represents the shadow occluders, which means that we always have pixel-accurate, but hard, shadows. This method cannot deal with objects that have no polygonal structure, such as alpha-test-modified geometry or displacement mapped geometry. Also, drawing shadow volumes requires a lot of fill rate, which makes it difficult to use them for every object in a dense scene, especially when there are multiple lights.

- *Image-space shadow algorithms* deal with any object modification (if we can render an object, we'll have shadows), but they suffer from aliasing. Aliasing often occurs in large scenes with wide or omnidirectional light sources. The problem is that the projection transform used in shadow mapping changes the screen size of the shadow map texels so that texels near the camera become very large. As a result, we have to use enormous shadow maps (four times the screen resolution or larger) to achieve good quality. Still, shadow maps are much faster than shadow volumes in complex scenes.

Perspective shadow maps (PSMs), presented at SIGGRAPH 2002 by Stamminger and Drettakis (2002), try to eliminate aliasing in shadow maps by using them in *post-projective space*, where all nearby objects become larger than farther ones. Unfortunately, it's difficult to use the original algorithm because it works well only in certain cases.

The most significant problems of the presented PSM algorithm are these three:

- To hold all potential shadow casters inside the virtual camera frustum, "virtual cameras" are used when the light source is behind the camera. This results in poor shadow quality.
- The shadow quality depends heavily on the light position in camera space.
- Biasing problems weren't discussed in the original paper. Bias is a problem with PSMs because the texel area is distributed in a nonuniform way, which means that bias cannot be a constant anymore and should depend on the texel position.

Each of these problems is discussed in the next section. This chapter focuses on directional lights (because they have bigger aliasing problems), but all the ideas and algorithms can easily be applied to other types of light source (details are provided, where appropriate). In addition, we discuss tricks for increasing the quality of the shadow map by filtering and blurring the picture.

In general, this chapter describes techniques and methods that can increase the effectiveness of using PSMs. However, most of these ideas still should be adapted to your particular needs.

14.2 Problems with the PSM Algorithm

14.2.1 Virtual Cameras

First, let's look at the essence of this problem. The usual projective transform moves objects behind the camera to the other side of the infinity plane in post-projective space. However, if the light source is behind the camera too, these objects are potential shadow casters and should be drawn into the shadow map.

In the perspective transform in Figure 14-1, the order of the points on the ray changes. The authors of the original PSM paper propose "virtually" sliding the view camera back to hold potential shadow casters in the viewing frustum, as shown in Figure 14-2, so that we can use PSMs the normal way.

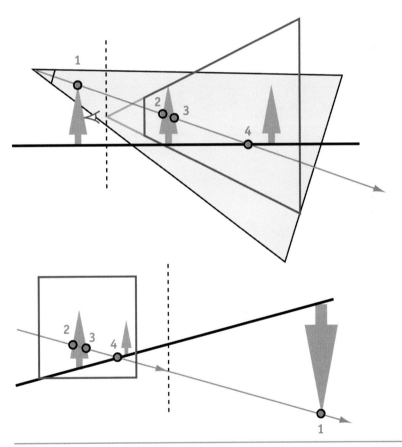

Figure 14-1. An Object Behind the Camera in Post-Projective Space
Adapted from Stamminger and Drettakis 2002.

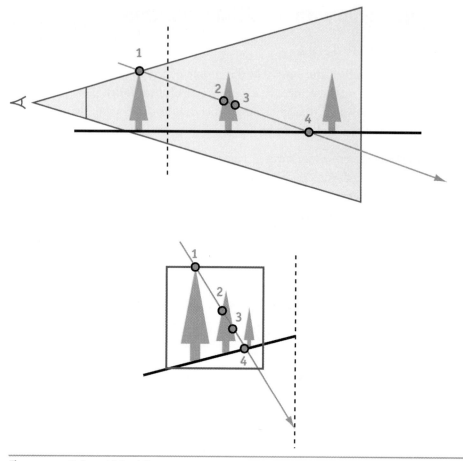

Figure 14-2. Using a Virtual Camera
Adapted from Stamminger and Drettakis 2002.

Virtual Camera Issues

In practice, however, using the virtual camera leads to poor shadow quality. The "virtual" shift greatly decreases the resolution of the effective shadow map, so that objects near the real camera become smaller, and we end up with a lot of unused space in the shadow map. In addition, we may have to move the camera back significantly for large shadow-casting objects behind the camera. Figure 14-3 shows how dramatically the quality changes, even with a small shift.

Another problem is minimizing the actual "slideback distance," which maximizes image quality. This requires us to analyze the scene, find potential shadow casters, and so on. Of course, we could use bounding volumes, scene hierarchical organizations, and simi-

Figure 14-3. The Effect of the Virtual Shift on Shadow Quality
Top: Without the Virtual Shift. Bottom: With the Virtual Shift.

lar techniques, but they would be a significant CPU hit. Moreover, we'll always have abrupt changes in shadow quality when an object stops being a potential shadow caster. In this case, the slideback distance instantly changes, causing the shadow quality to change suddenly as well.

A Solution for Virtual Camera Issues

We propose a solution to this virtual camera problem: Use a special projection transform for the light matrix. In fact, post-projective space allows some projection tricks that can't be done in the usual world space. It turns out that we can build a special projection matrix that can see "farther than infinity."

Let's look at a post-projective space formed by an original (nonvirtual) camera with a directional "inverse" light source and with objects behind the view camera, as shown in Figure 14-4.

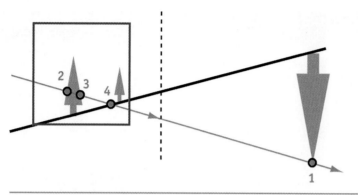

Figure 14-4. Post-Projective Space with an Inverse Light Source
Adapted from Stamminger and Drettakis 2002.

A drawback to this solution is that the ray should (but doesn't) come out from the light source, catch point 1, go to minus infinity, then pass on to plus infinity and return to the light source, capturing information at points 2, 3, and 4. Fortunately, there is a projection matrix that matches this "impossible" ray, where we can set the near plane to a negative value and the far plane to a positive value. See Figure 14-5.

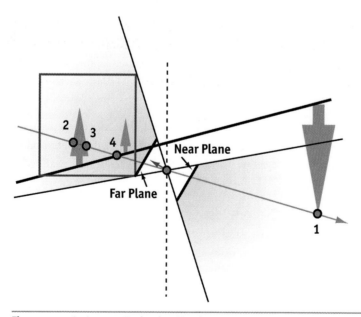

Figure 14-5. An Inverse Projection Matrix
The red arrow is the light camera direction.

In the simplest case,

$$\left|Z_n\right| = \left|Z_f\right| = a,$$

where a is small enough to fit the entire unit cube. Then we build this inverse projection as the usual projection matrix, as shown here, where matrices are written in a row-major style:

$$\begin{pmatrix} c & 0 & 0 & 0 \\ 0 & d & 0 & 0 \\ 0 & 0 & Q & 1 \\ 0 & 0 & -QZ_n & 0 \end{pmatrix} \rightarrow \begin{pmatrix} c & 0 & 0 & 0 \\ 0 & d & 0 & 0 \\ 0 & 0 & \frac{1}{2} & 1 \\ 0 & 0 & \frac{1}{2}a & 0 \end{pmatrix}, \text{ where}$$

$$Q = \frac{Z_f}{Z_f - Z_n} = \frac{a}{a - (-a)} = \frac{1}{2}.$$

So the formula for the resulting transformed z coordinates, which go into a shadow map, is:

$$Z_{psm} = Q \times \left(1 - \frac{Z_n}{Z}\right) = \frac{1}{2} \times \left(1 + \frac{a}{Z}\right).$$

$Z_{psm}(-a) = 0$, and if we keep decreasing the z value to minus infinity, Z_{psm} tends to ½. The same $Z_{psm} = $ ½ corresponds to plus infinity, and moving from plus infinity to the far plane increases Z_{psm} to 1 at the far plane. This is why the ray hits all points in the correct order and why there's no need to use "virtual slides" for creating post-projective space.

This trick works only in post-projective space because normally all points behind the infinity plane have $w < 0$, so they cannot be rasterized. But for another projection transformation caused by a light camera, these points are located behind the camera, so the w coordinate is inverted again and becomes positive.

By using this inverse projection matrix, we don't have to use virtual cameras. As a result, we get much better shadow quality without any CPU scene analysis and the associated artifacts.

The only drawback to the inverse projection matrix is that we need a better shadow map depth-value precision, because we use big z-value ranges. However, 24-bit fixed-point depth values are enough for reasonable cases.

Virtual cameras still could be useful, though, because the shadow quality depends on the location of the camera's near plane. The formula for post-projective z is:

$$Z_{pp} = Q\left(1 - \frac{Z_n}{Z_{world}}\right), \quad \text{where } Q = \frac{Z_f}{Z_f - Z_n}.$$

As we can see, Q is very close to 1 and doesn't change significantly as long as Z_n is much smaller than Z_f, which is typical. That's why the near and far planes have to be changed significantly to affect the Q value, which usually is not possible. At the same time, near-plane values highly influence the post-projective space. For example, for $Z_n = 1$ meter (m), the first meter in the world space after the near plane occupies half the unit cube in post-projective space. In this respect, if we change Z_n to 2 m, we will effectively double the z-value resolution and increase the shadow quality. That means that we should maximize the Z_n value by any means.

The perfect method, proposed in the original PSM article, is to read back the depth buffer, scan through each pixel, and find the maximum possible Z_n for each frame. Unfortunately, this method is quite expensive: it requires reading back a large amount of video memory, causes an additional CPU/GPU stall, and doesn't work well with swizzled and hierarchical depth buffers. So we should use another (perhaps less accurate) method to find a suitable near-plane value for PSM rendering.

Such other methods for finding a suitable near-plane value for PSM rendering could include various methods of CPU scene analysis:

- A method based on rough bounding-volume computations (briefly described later in "The Light Camera").
- A collision-detection system to estimate the distance to the closest object.
- Additional software scene rendering with low-polygon-count level-of-details, which could also be useful for occlusion culling.
- Sophisticated analysis based on particular features of scene structure for the specific application. For example, when dealing with scenarios using a fixed camera path, you could precompute the near-plane values for every frame.

These methods try to increase the actual near-plane value, but we could also increase the value "virtually." The idea is the same as with the old virtual cameras, but with one difference. When sliding the camera back, we *increase* the near-plane value so that the near-plane quads of the original and virtual cameras remain on the same plane. See Figure 14-6.

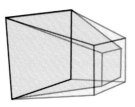
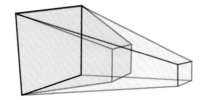

Proposed Virtual Camera   **Virtual Camera from Original Article**

Figure 14-6. Difference Between Virtual Cameras

When we slide the virtual camera back, we improve the z-values resolution. However, this makes the value distribution for *x* and *y* values worse for near objects, thus balancing shadow quality near and far from the camera. Because of the very irregular z-value distribution in post-projective space and the large influence of the near-plane value, this balance could not be achieved without this "virtual" slideback. The usual problem of shadows looking great near the camera but having poor quality on distant objects is the typical result of unbalanced shadow map texel area distribution.

14.2.2 The Light Camera

Another problem with PSMs is that the shadow quality relies on the relationship between the light and camera positions. With a vertical directional light, aliasing problems are completely removed, but when light is directed toward the camera and is close to head-on, there is significant shadow map aliasing.

We're trying to hold the entire unit cube in a single shadow map texture, so we have to make the light's field of view as large as necessary to fit the entire cube. This in turn means that the objects close to the near plane won't receive enough texture samples. See Figure 14-7.

The closer the light source is to the unit cube, the poorer the quality. As we know,

$$Z_\infty = Q = \frac{Z_f}{Z_f - Z_n},$$

so for large outdoor scenes that have $Z_n = 1$ and $Z_f = 4000$, $Q = 1.0002$, which means that the light source is extremely close to the unit cube. The Z_f/Z_n correlation is usually bigger than 50, which corresponds to $Q = 1.02$, which is close enough to create problems.

We'll always have problems fitting the entire unit cube into a single shadow map texture. Two solutions each tackle one part of the problem: *Unit cube clipping* targets the

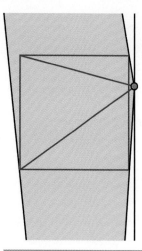

Figure 14-7. The Light Camera with a Low Light Angle

light camera only on the necessary part of the unit cube, and the *cube map* approach uses multiple textures to store depth information.

Unit Cube Clipping

This optimization relies on the fact that we need shadow map information only on actual objects, and the volume occupied by these objects is usually much smaller than the whole view frustum volume (especially close to the far plane). That's why if we tune the light camera to hold real objects only (not the entire unit cube), we'll receive better quality. Of course, we should tune the camera using a simplified scene structure, such as bounding volumes.

Cube clipping was mentioned in the original PSM article, but it took into account all objects in a scene, including shadow casters in the view frustum and potential shadow casters outside the frustum for constructing the virtual camera. Because we don't need virtual cameras anymore, we can focus the light camera on *shadow receivers only*, which is more efficient. See Figure 14-8. Still, we should choose near and far clip-plane values for the light camera in post-projective space to hold all shadow casters in the shadow map. But it doesn't influence shadow quality because it doesn't change the texel area distribution.

Because faraway parts of these bounding volumes contract greatly in post-projective space, the light camera's field of view doesn't become very large, even with light sources that are close to the rest of the scene.

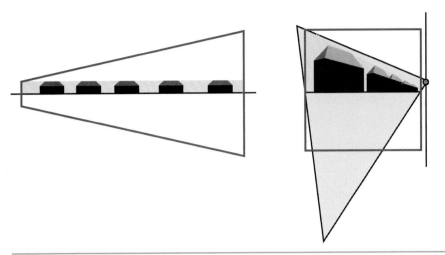

Figure 14-8. Focusing the Light Camera Based on the Bounding Volumes of Shadow Receivers
The bounding volume is shown in green.

In practice, we can use rough bounding volumes to retain sufficient quality—we just need to indicate generally which part of the scene we are interested in. In outdoor scenes, it's the approximate height of objects on the landscape; in indoor scenes, it's a bounding volume of the current room, and so on.

We'd like to formalize the algorithm of computing the light camera focused on shadow receivers in the scene after we build a set of bounding volumes roughly describing the scene. In fact, the light camera is given by position, direction, up vector, and projection parameters, most of which are predefined:

- We can't change the position: it's a light position in post-projective space and nothing else.
- In practice, the up vector doesn't change quality significantly, so we can choose anything reasonable.
- Projection parameters are entirely defined by the view matrix.

So the most interesting thing is choosing the light camera direction based on bounding volumes. The proposed algorithm is this:

1. Compute the vertex list of constructive solid geometry operation,

$$\bigcup_i \left(B_i \cap F_i \right),$$

where B_i is the ith bounding volume, F is the frustum for every shadow caster bounding volume that we see in the current frame, and all these operations are performed in a view camera space. Then transform all these vertices into post-projective space.

After this step, we have all the points that the light camera should "see." (By the way, we should find a good near-plane value based on these points, because reading back the depth buffer isn't a good solution.)

2. Find a light camera. As we already know, this means finding the best light camera direction, because all other parameters are easily computed for a given direction. We propose approximating the optimal direction by the axis of the minimal cone, centered in the light source and including all the points in the list. The algorithm that finds the optimal cone for a set of points works in linear time, and it is similar to an algorithm that finds the smallest bounding sphere for a set of points in linear time (Gartner 1999).

In this way, we could find an optimal light camera in linear time depending on the bounding volume number, which isn't very large because we need only rough information about the scene structure.

This algorithm is efficient for direct lights in large outdoor scenes. The shadow quality is almost independent of the light angle and slightly decreases if light is directed toward the camera. Figure 14-9 shows the difference between using unit cube clipping and not using it.

Using Cube Maps

Though cube clipping is efficient in some cases, other times it's difficult to use. For example, we might have a densely filled unit cube (which is common), or we may not want to use bounding volumes at all. Plus, cube clipping does not work with point lights.

A more general method is to use a cube map texture for shadow mapping. Most light sources become point lights in post-projective space, and it's natural to use cube maps for shadow mapping with point light sources. But in post-projective space, things change slightly and we should use cube maps differently because we need to store information about the unit cube only.

The proposed solution is to use unit cube faces that are back facing, with respect to the light, as platforms for cube-map-face textures.

For a direct light source in post-projective space, the cube map looks like Figure 14-10.

Figure 14-9. Unit Cube Clipping
Images produced using unit cube clipping (top) and not using it (bottom).

The number of used cube map faces (ranging from three to five) depends on the position of the light. We use the maximum number of faces when the light is close to the rest of the scene and directed toward the camera, so additional texture resources are necessary. For other types of light sources located outside the unit cube, the pictures will be similar.

For a point light located inside the unit cube, we should use all six cube map faces, but they're still focused on unit cube faces. See Figure 14-11.

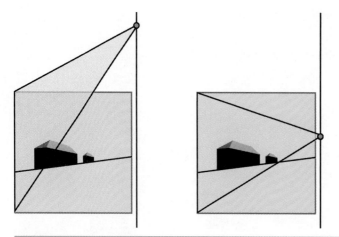

Figure 14-10. Using a Cube Map for Direct Lights

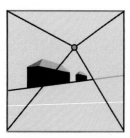

Figure 14-11. Using Cube Maps with a Point Light

We could say we form a "cube map with displaced center," which is similar to a normal cube map, but with a constant vector added to its texture coordinates. In other words, texture coordinates for cube maps are vertex positions in post-projective space shifted by the light source position:

$$\textit{Texture coordinates} = \textit{vertex position} - \textit{light position}$$

By choosing unit cube faces as the cube map platform, we distribute the texture area proportionally to the screen size and ensure that shadow quality doesn't depend on the light and camera positions. In fact, texel size in post-projective space is in a guaranteed range, so its projection on the screen depends only on the plane it's projected onto. This projection doesn't stretch texels much, so the texel size on the screen is within guaranteed bounds also.

Because the vertex and pixel shaders are relatively short when rendering the shadow map, what matters is the pure fill rate for the back buffer and the depth shadow map buffer. So there's almost no difference between drawing a single shadow map and drawing a cube map with the same total texture size (with good occlusion culling, though). The cube map approach has better quality with the same total texture size as a single texture. The difference is the cost of the render target switch and the additional instructions to compute cube map texture coordinates in the vertex and pixel shaders.

Let's see how to compute these texture coordinates. First, consider the picture shown in Figure 14-12. The blue square is our unit cube, P is the light source point, and V is the point for which we're generating texture coordinates. We render all six cube map faces in separate passes for the shadow map; the near plane for each pass is shown in green. They're forming another small cube, so $Z_1 = Z_n/Z_f$ is constant for every pass.

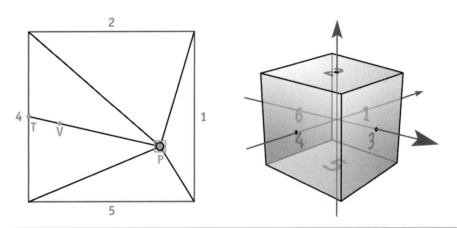

Figure 14-12. A Detailed Cube Map View in Post-Projective Space

Now we should compute texture coordinates and depth values to compare for the point V. This just means that we should move this point in the $(V - P)$ direction until we intersect the cube. Consider d_1, d_2, d_3, d_4, d_5, and d_6 (see the face numbers in Figure 14-12) as the distances from P to each cube map face.

The point on the cube we are looking for (which is also the cube map texture coordinate) is:

$$T = P + \frac{V - P}{a}, \quad \text{where}$$

$$a = \max\left(\frac{(V - P)_x}{d_1}, \frac{(V - P)_y}{d_2}, \frac{(V - P)_z}{d_3}, -\frac{(V - P)_x}{d_4}, -\frac{(V - P)_y}{d_5}, -\frac{(V - P)_z}{d_6}\right).$$

Compare the value in the texture against the result of the projective transform of the a value. Because we already divided it by the corresponding d value, thus effectively making $Z_f = 1$ and $Z_n = Z_1$, all we have to do is apply that projective transform. Note that in the case of the inverse camera projection from Section 14.2.1, $Z_n = -Z_1$, $Z_f = Z_1$.

$$Z_{out} = Q\left(1 - \frac{Z_n}{a}\right) = \frac{Z_f}{Z_f - Z_n}\left(1 - \frac{Z_n}{a}\right)$$

(All these calculations are made in OpenGL-like coordinates, where the unit cube is actually a unit cube. In Direct3D, the unit cube is half the size, because the z coordinate is in the $[0..1]$ range.)

Listing 14-1 is an example of how the shader code might look.

Listing 14-1. Shader Code for Computing Cube Map Texture Coordinates

```
// c[d1] = 1/d1, 1/d2, 1/d3, 0
// c[d2] = -1/d4, -1/d5, -1/d6, 0
// c[z] = Q, -Q * Zn, 0, 0
// c[P] = P
// r[V] = V
// cbmcoord - output cube map texture coordinates
// depth - depth to compare with shadow map values

//Per-vertex level
sub r[VP], r[V], c[P]
mul r1, r[VP], c[d1]
mul r2, r[VP], c[d2]

//Per-pixel level
max r3, r1, r2
max r3.x, r3.x, r3.y
max r3.x, r3.x, r3.z
rcp r3.w, r3.x
mad cbmcoord, r[VP], r3.w, c[P]

rcp r3.x, r3.w
mad depth, r3.x, c[z].x, c[z].y
```

Because depth textures cannot be cube maps, we could use color textures, packing depth values into the color channels. There are many ways to do this and many implementation-dependent tricks, but their description is out of the scope of this chapter.

Another possibility is to emulate this cube map approach with multitexturing, in which every cube map face becomes an independent texture (depth textures are great in this case). We form several texture coordinate sets in the vertex shader and multiply by the shadow results in the pixel shader. The tricky part is to manage these textures over the objects in the scene, because every object rarely needs all six faces.

14.2.3 Biasing

As we stated earlier, the constant bias that is typically used in uniform shadow maps cannot be used with PSMs because the z values and the texel area distributions vary greatly with different light positions and points in the scene.

If you plan to use depth textures, try z slope–scaled bias for biasing. It's often enough to fix the artifacts, especially when very distant objects don't fall within the camera. However, some cards do not support depth textures (in DirectX, depth textures are supported only by NVIDIA cards), and depth textures can't be a cube map. In these cases, you need a different, more general algorithm for calculating bias. Another difficulty is that it's hard to emulate and tweak z slope–scaled bias because it requires additional data—such as the vertex coordinates of the current triangle—passed into the pixel shader, plus some calculations, which isn't robust at all.

Anyway, let's see why we can't use constant bias anymore. Consider these two cases: the light source is near the unit cube, and the light source is far from the unit cube. See Figure 14-13.

The problem is that the Z_f/Z_n correlation, which determines the z-value distribution into a shadow map, varies a lot in these two cases. So the constant bias would mean a totally different actual bias in world and post-projective space: The constant bias tuned to the first light position won't be correct for the second light, and vice versa. Meanwhile, Z_f/Z_n changes a lot, because the light source could be close to the unit cube and could be distant (even at infinity), depending on the relative positions of the light and the camera in world space.

Even with a fixed light source position, sometimes we cannot find a suitable constant for the bias. The bias should depend on the point position—because the projective transform enlarges the near objects and shrinks the far ones—so the bias should be smaller near the camera and bigger for distant objects. Figure 14-14 shows the typical artifacts of using a constant bias in this situation.

In short, the proposed solution is to use biasing in world space (and not to analyze the results of the double-projection matrix) and then transform this world-space bias in

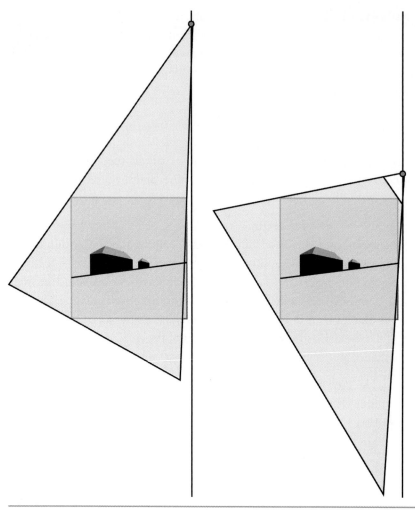

Figure 14-13. Light Close to and Far from the Unit Cube

post-projective space. The computed value depends on the double projection, and it's correct for any light and camera position. These operations could be done easily in a vertex shader. Furthermore, this world-space bias value should be scaled by texel size in world space to deal with artifacts caused by the distribution of nonuniform texel areas.

$$P_{biased} = \left(P_{orig} + L\left(a + bL_{texel}\right)\right)M,$$

where P_{orig} is the original point position, L is the light vector direction in world space, L_{texel} is the texel size in world space, M is the final shadow map matrix, and a and b are bias coefficients.

Figure 14-14. Artifacts with Constant Bias
Notice how some of the near-vertical surfaces (such as the wall at the far left and the bridge in the distance) are full of artifacts.

The texel size in world space could be approximately computed with simple matrix calculations. First, transform the point into shadow map space, and then shift this point by the texel size without changing depth. Next, transform it back into world space and square the length of the difference between this point and the original one. This gives us L_{texel}:

$$L_{texel} = \left| P_{orig} - \left(P_{orig} M + c \right) M^{-1} \right|^2, \text{ where}$$

$$c = \left(\frac{2}{S_x}, \frac{2}{S_y}, 0 \right),$$

and S_x and S_y are shadow map resolutions.

Obviously, we can build a single matrix that performs all the transformations (except multiplying the coordinates, of course):

$$L_{texel} = \left| P_{orig} M' \right|^2,$$

where M' includes transforming, shifting, transforming back, and subtracting.

This turns out to be a rather empirical solution, but it should still be tweaked for your particular needs. See Figure 14-15.

The vertex shader code that performs these calculations might look like Listing 14-2.

Listing 14-2. Calculating Bias in a Vertex Shader

```
def c0, a, b, 0 ,0

// Calculating Ltexel
dp4 r1.x, v0, c[LtexelMatrix_0]
dp4 r1.y, v0, c[LtexelMatrix_1]
dp4 r1.z, v0, c[LtexelMatrix_2]
dp4 r1.w, v0, c[LtexelMatrix_3]

// Transforming homogeneous coordinates
// (in fact, we often can skip this step)
rcp r1.w, r1.w
mul r1.xy, r1.w, r1.xy

// Now r1.x is an Ltexel
mad r1.x, r1.x, c0.x, c0.y

dp3 r1.x, r1, r1

// Move vertex in world space
mad r1, v0, c[Lightdir], r1.x

// Transform vertex into post-projective space
// (we need z and w only)
dp4 r[out].z, r1, c[M_2]
dp4 r[out].w, r1, c[M_3]
```

The r[out] register holds the result of the biasing: the depth value, and the corresponding w, that should be interpolated across the triangle. Note that this interpolation should be separate from the interpolation of texture coordinates (x, y, and the corresponding w), because these w coordinates are different. This biased value could be used when comparing with the shadow map value, or during the actual shadow map rendering (the shadow map holds biased values).

Figure 14-15. Bias Calculated in the Vertex Shader

14.3 Tricks for Better Shadow Maps

The advantage of shadow mapping over shadow volumes is the potential to create a color gradient between "shadowed" and "nonshadowed" samples, thus simulating soft shadows. This shadow "softness" doesn't depend on distance from the occluder, light source size, and so on, but it still works in world space. Blurring stencil shadows, on the other hand, is more difficult, although Assarsson et al. (2003) make significant progress.

This section covers methods of filtering and blurring shadow maps to create a fake shadow softness that has a constant range of blurring but still looks good.

14.3.1 Filtering

Most methods of shadow map filtering are based on the *percentage-closer filtering* (PCF) principle. The only difference among the methods is how the hardware lets us use it. NVIDIA depth textures perform PCF after comparison with the depth value; on other hardware, we have to take several samples from the nearest texels and average their results (for true PCF). In general, the depth texture filtering is more efficient than the manual PCF technique with four samples. (PCF needs about eight samples to produce comparable quality.) In addition, using depth texture filtering doesn't forbid PCF, so we can take several filtered samples to further increase shadow quality.

Using PCF with PSMs is no different from using it with standard shadow maps: samples from neighboring texels are used for filtering. On the GPU, this is achieved by shifting texture coordinates one texel in each direction. For a more detailed discussion of PCF, see Chapter 11, "Shadow Map Antialiasing."

The shader pseudocode for PCF with four samples looks like Listings 14-3 and 14-4.

These tricks improve shadow quality, but they do not hide serious aliasing problems. For example, if many screen pixels map to one shadow map texel, large stair-stepping

Listing 14-3. Vertex Shader Pseudocode for PCF

```
def c0, sample1x, sample1Y, 0, 0
def c1, sample2x, sample2Y, 0, 0
def c2, sample3x, sample3Y, 0, 0
def c3, sample4x, sample4Y, 0, 0
// The simplest case:
// def c0, 1 / shadowmapsizeX, 1 / shadowmapsizeY, 0, 0
// def c1, -1 / shadowmapsizeX, -1 / shadowmapsizeY, 0, 0
// def c2, -1 / shadowmapsizeX, 1/ shadowmapsizeY, 0, 0
// def c3, 1 / shadowmapsizeX, -1 / shadowmapsizeY, 0, 0

. . .

// Point - vertex position in light space
mad oT0, point.w, c0, point
mad oT1, point.w, c1, point
mad oT2, point.w, c2, point
mad oT3, point.w, c3, point
```

Listing 14-4. Pixel Shader Pseudocode for PCF

```
def c0, 0.25, 0.25, 0.25, 0.25
tex t0
tex t1
tex t2
tex t3

. . .

// After depth comparison
mul r0, t0, c0
mad r0, t1, c0, r0
mad r0, t2, c0, r0
mad r0, t3, c0, r0
```

artifacts will be visible, even if they are somewhat blurred. Figure 14-16 shows an aliased shadow without any filtering, and Figure 14-17 shows how PCF helps improve shadow quality but cannot completely remove aliasing artifacts.

14.3.2 Blurring

As we know from projective shadows, the best blurring results often come from rendering to a smaller resolution texture with a pixel shader blur, then feeding this resulting texture back through the blur pixel shader several times (known as *ping-pong rendering*). Shadow mapping and projective shadows are similar techniques, so why can't we use this method? The answer: because the shadow map isn't a black-and-white picture; it's a collection of depth values, and "blurring a depth map" doesn't make sense.

In fact, the proposal is to use the color part of the shadow map render (which comes almost for free) as projective texture for some objects. For example, assume that we have an outdoor landscape scene and we want a high-quality blurred shadow on the ground because ground shadows are the most noticeable.

Figure 14-16. Strong Aliasing

Figure 14-17. Filtered Aliasing

1. Before rendering the depth shadow map, clear the color buffer with 1. During the render, draw 0 into the color buffer for every object except the landscape; for the landscape, draw 1 in color. After the whole shadow map renders, we'll have 1 where the landscape is nonshadowed and 0 where it's shadowed. See Figure 14-18.

2. Blur the picture (the one in Figure 14-18) severely, using multiple passes with a simple blur pixel shader. For example, using a simple two-pass Gaussian blur gives good results. (You might want to adjust the blurring radius for distant objects.) After this step, we'll have a high-quality blurred texture, as shown in Figure 14-19.

3. While rendering the scene with shadows, render the landscape with the blurred texture instead of the shadow map, and render all other objects with the depth part of the shadow map. See Figure 14-20.

The difference in quality is dramatic.

Of course, we can use this method not only with landscapes, but also with any object that does not need self-shadowing (such as floors, walls, ground planes, and so on). Fortunately,

Figure 14-18. The Original Color Part for a Small Test Scene

Figure 14-19. The Blurred Color Part for a Small Test Scene

Figure 14-20. Applying Blurring to a Real Scene

in these areas shadows are most noticeable and aliasing problems are most evident. Because we have several color channels, we can blur shadows on several objects at the same time:

- Using depth textures, the color buffer is completely free, so we can use all four channels for four objects.
- For floating-point textures, one channel stores depth information, so we have three channels for blurring.
- For fixed-point textures, depth is usually stored in the red and green channels, so we have only two free channels.

This way we'll have nice blurred shadows on the ground, floor, walls, and so on while retaining all other shadows (blurred with PCF) on other objects (with proper self-shadowing).

14.4 Results

The screenshots in Figures 14-21, 14-22, 14-23, and 14-24 were captured on the NVIDIA GeForce4 Ti 4600 in 1600 × 1200 screen resolution, with 100,000 to 500,000 visible polygons. All objects receive and cast shadows with real-time frame rates (more than 30).

Figure 14-21.

Figure 14-22.

Figure 14-23.

Figure 14-24.

14.5 References

Assarsson, U., M. Dougherty, M. Mounier, and T. Akenine-Möller. 2003. "An Optimized Soft Shadow Volume Algorithm with Real-Time Performance." In *Proceedings of the SIGGRAPH/Eurographics Workshop on Graphics Hardware 2003*.

Gartner, Bernd. 1999. "Smallest Enclosing Balls: Fast and Robust in C++." Web page. **http://www.inf.ethz.ch/personal/gaertner/texts/own_work/esa99_final.pdf**

Stamminger, Marc, and George Drettakis. 2002. "Perspective Shadow Maps." In *Proceedings of ACM SIGGRAPH 2002*.

The author would like to thank Peter Popov for his many helpful and productive discussions.

Chapter 15

Managing Visibility for Per-Pixel Lighting

John O'Rorke
Monolith Productions

15.1 Visibility in a GPU Book?

This chapter looks at the role that visibility plays in efficiently rendering per-pixel lit scenes. We also consider how to use that visibility to minimize the number of batches that must be rendered, so that we can improve performance.

At first glance, you may think that visibility has no place in a book about the advanced use of graphics hardware. Yet, regardless of how many tricks and optimizations we use on the GPU, the fastest polygon will always be the one that isn't rendered. That means if we reduce the number of rendered batches, we can add more objects to a scene, or use more complex geometry and techniques for other objects.

Countless papers and presentations tout reducing the number of batches to the graphics card to prevent the application from becoming CPU-bound. To clarify terminology, in this chapter a *batch* is any set of polygons that is sent to the card without being broken up by a state change. For example, a single `DrawPrimitive` call in Direct3D represents one batch. Reducing batches has been important in the past and is even more significant with the latest GPUs. GPUs are processing batches faster and faster, meaning that polygons can be processed more quickly within a single batch. However, the rate at which batches can be sent to the GPU is increasing very slowly. Compounding this problem is the current trend of using per-pixel lighting, which substantially increases the number of batches required to render a scene.

15.2   Batches and Per-Pixel Lighting

The reason for the significant rise in the number of batches when using per-pixel lighting comes from the manner in which this technique is implemented. The algorithm renders an ambient pass to apply a global ambient term and to establish the depth buffer for the frame. Then for each light, two values must be determined: the shadowing term and the lighting contribution.

The shadowing term is often computed using extruded stencil volumes or shadow maps, both of which require at least one batch to be rendered per object. Once the shadowing term is determined, each object the light touches must be rendered again to apply the lighting contribution, with some objects being masked out appropriately when in shadow.

Many developers using per-pixel lighting have struggled to get scenes to batch and render efficiently. In effect, the number of batches required for this new technique multiplies the previous problem by the number of lights in the scene—making efficient rendering even more difficult to manage.

15.2.1   A Per-Pixel Example

To demonstrate how many batches could be required to render a per-pixel lit scene, let's examine a very simple scenario. We have a room, divided into eight separate batches because of the different materials in different parts of the room. In addition, there are three different models in the room, which are separated into two batches to allow for matrix-palette skinning. Placed within this room are three lights.

So now let's determine how many batches we need. For the ambient pass, which establishes the depth values of the scene and applies any ambient or emissive lighting, all batches are rendered once. That's 14 batches to start. Then for each light, all batches are rendered once for the shadow and once again for the actual lighting pass, to accumulate the lights into the frame buffer. In this simple scene, we are already up to 98 batches. We know that around 10,000 to 40,000 batches per second can be sent to the graphics hardware, consuming the full CPU time of a 1 GHz processor (Wloka 2003). If that CPU speed is our minimum specification and only 10 percent can be allocated to batch submission, then only 1,000 to 4,000 batches per second are possible! Thus, in this simple scene, batch submission alone will restrict our frame rate to a range of 10 to 40 frames a second. Realistic scenes require many more batches than this example, so lots of effort must be spent to bring the number of batches into a reasonable range.

The intent of this chapter is not to examine various visibility algorithms or implement a visibility system. (An excellent discussion of visibility algorithms can be found in Akenine-Möller and Haines 2002.) Instead, this chapter illustrates how to leverage existing visibility algorithms to suit the unique needs of per-pixel lighting, with the goal of minimizing the number of batches sent to the hardware.

15.2.2 Just How Many Batches, Anyway?

The following pseudocode illustrates the number of batches that must be rendered in a scene.

```
For each visible object
   For each pass in the ambient shader
      For each visible batch in the object
         Render batch
For each visible light
   For each visible shadow caster
      For each pass in the shadow shader
         For each shadow batch in the object
            Render batch
   For each lit visible object
      For each pass in the light shader
         For each visible batch in the object
            Render batch
```

As the pseudocode shows, some non-visibility-related optimizations can be performed to reduce the number of batches. The largest optimization is the number of passes required to render the batches for each lighting situation. The number of batches increases linearly with the number of passes, so we should minimize passes in CPU-bound games.

The pseudocode also shows different batches being used for the shadow rendering. Although extruded shadow volumes almost always use separate batches, shadow map implementations do so less frequently. Having different batches for normal and shadow rendering is beneficial because certain batch boundaries can often be removed when performing shadow rendering. For example, picture a mesh that has two different materials used on two distinct parts. The materials are visible only when we perform lighting operations, and they are irrelevant for the shadow operation. Therefore, during the preprocessing of a model, two collections of batches may result: one for use when rendering lighting and another for use when rendering shadows. Both the pass-reduction and the batch-reduction techniques are critical to reducing batch levels, but they are not enough by themselves. By using visibility testing, we can prune a significant number of the batches in a scene and achieve much greater performance.

15.3 Visibility As Sets

To understand how to use visibility to reduce the number of batches, we'll take a high-level look at the uses of visibility and define the operations in terms of set logic. Then we'll describe how to compute these sets. Visibility is considered not only for the viewer of a scene, but also for each light of a scene, because if a light cannot see an object, that object does not need to be rendered in the light's lighting pass.

15.3.1 The Visible Set

The first set to define is the visible set, which consists of all objects that are visible from the point of view of the camera. Nearly every rendering application can determine the visible set, which we refer to as V.

15.3.2 The Lights Set

In addition to finding out which objects are visible in the scene, we need to determine the set of lights in the visible set.

For each visible light, another visibility set must be created, this time from the point of view of the light. Let L denote the set of objects that are visible from the light. Most per-pixel lighting solutions apply one light at a time, simply accumulating the results in the frame buffer. As a result, there are often no dependencies between lights, and so only one light visible set needs to exist at a time for the current light being rendered. This technique avoids having to store all light sets in memory at once; however, this concept extends to rendering multiple lights in a single pass by simply accumulating the results into a single lighting set.

Now that we have defined visibility sets for the viewer and the lights, we can establish several sets that will reduce the number of objects drawn in rendering.

15.3.3 The Illumination Set

The first rule of determining the illumination set is that a lighting pass needs to occur only on the set of objects that exist in both sets V and L, or using set notation: $V \cap L$. This is because only those objects that the light can see need to be rendered again to provide the light contribution, and only those objects in the visible set are seen on the screen. This set of objects that will be rendered again in order to be illuminated is denoted as set I. If I is empty, we can skip rendering the light. This rule is typically fast and simple to apply, and it works well for quickly optimizing lights that are on the edge of the view frustum, have a very large radius, or are occluded within the frustum.

15.3.4 The Shadow Set

Now that the set of objects for the lighting pass has been reduced to a reasonable level, let's look at the set of objects for the shadow pass. The shadow set is more difficult to determine, and some balancing must be done between overall culling cost and the number of objects rendered.

A common initial mistake is to use set I for the shadow pass. However, as shown in Figure 15-1, sometimes an object outside the frustum can affect the final rendered image by projecting a shadow into the frustum. So we must generate a different set, called S, that is a subset of set L and includes all objects that cast a shadow into the visible region.

At this point, we have defined all the sets we need for rendering with per-pixel lighting. First set V is generated from the camera and rendered for the ambient pass. Next is the rendering of each light. For each light, set L is determined and from this, sets I and S are generated. Set S determines the shadowing term for the light, and then each object in set I is rendered to apply the lighting.

Now we discuss the details of efficiently generating each set.

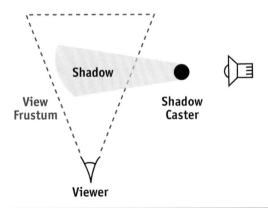

Figure 15-1. Objects Not in the Visible Set Can Influence the Rendered Scene

15.4 Generating Sets

Theory is great, but small details can make the difference between high stress and high frame rates. So in this section, we cover the fine points of generating each set introduced in the preceding section, with practical application in mind.

15.4.1 The Visible Set

The lights and the viewport each need to generate a visible set. But how tight should the visible set be? And how much processor time should be spent determining these sets? The answers depend on the type of application being developed. However, at the very minimum, the visibility determination algorithm should perform frustum-level culling and a fair amount of object-level occlusion. The reason for this requirement is simply a matter of scale. If a standard visible set contains ten objects in the frustum and 30 percent of the objects are occluded, three objects can be dropped.

Let's factor in the lights as well, because we will be using visibility for the lights in the scene. If each light has similar statistics for occlusion, then in realistic scenes we can avoid rendering dozens or even hundreds of objects per frame. So the level of occlusion within a frustum should be carefully considered when determining the visibility system for a per-pixel lighting renderer. From there, it is simply a balancing act to determine the best ratio of CPU time to occlusion.

15.4.2 The Lights Set

Determining this set is nearly identical to determining the visible set. However, point lights can cause problems for visibility algorithms that perform any sort of projection onto a plane. A point light has a full spherical field of view, so it cannot be mapped easily onto a plane, something that many visibility algorithms rely on. One solution to this problem is to place a cube around a light and then perform the visibility test once for each face of the cube, from the point of view of the light. This method can become very expensive, though, because it requires doing the visibility determination once for each of the six faces; care must be taken not to add the same object to the visible set multiple times if it is seen by multiple faces. As a general rule, examine the visibility system, and if it uses any form of projection onto a plane, consider switching to a visibility system that works without any projections, or implementing a separate visibility system exclusively for the point-light visibility queries.

15.4.3 The Illumination Set

Fast set operations are critical for efficiently determining the illumination set. There are two approaches to implementing the necessary set operations: (1) have sets that know which objects they contain and (2) have objects that know which sets they belong to.

The first approach uses sorted lists that contain references to all the objects within that set. The lists must be sorted to allow for determining intersections and unions in linear time through merging, but the sorting can be based on whatever criteria are appropriate. This implementation can be difficult to perform efficiently because it involves sorting, merging, and occasionally searching, but for some applications, it works well if these sets are already needed for other operations. Using this approach, determining the illumination set would simply be a matter of determining sets V and L and then finding the elements contained within both sets.

The second approach works particularly well for per-pixel lighting, where a fixed number of sets that the object belongs to can be stored as flags on the object. Then instead of building a set, we perform operations on the list of objects. To build the visible set, we find all the objects in view and flag them as belonging to the visible set. To determine the set L, we perform a similar process, but we flag the objects as being in the lighting group. Then set I is found simply by looking through the list of objects that the light can see and finding the objects that are also flagged as being in the visible set. The implementation of this second approach is much simpler than that of the first, but the flags do need to be reset after the operation is complete.

15.4.4 The Shadow Set

Shadow calculation is more difficult than the other operations because it involves operations on volumes extruded by a light. Often objects are represented with a bounding box or a bounding sphere that encompasses the visible geometry. The volume of space that the shadow of an object affects is determined by extruding each point of the primitive along the vector to the light, to the point where the distance to the light is equal to the radius of the light. Therefore, the shadow set must include all objects that, when extruded from the light up to the effective light radius, intersect the view frustum.

Shadows for Lights Inside a Frustum

Lights always project shadows away from the position of the light. Therefore, if a light is located within the view frustum, it is safe to discard from the shadow set any object that is outside the view frustum. This is because if a light is inside a convex volume and an object is outside the volume, the object will always be extruded away from the convex volume and therefore cannot intersect the frustum.

We need to use the set of all objects in the view frustum to determine which objects cast shadows, not the visible set V, which is only a subset of the objects in the view frustum. The set V may have occluded objects that are not directly visible but can still cast shadows into visible regions, as illustrated in Figure 15-2. Therefore, a new set, called set F, is defined for all objects in the view frustum without any occlusion. If the light is in the frustum, then the shadow set S is defined as the intersection of sets F and L.

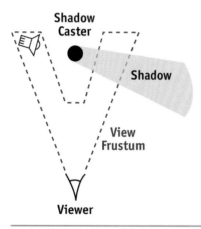

Figure 15-2. An Object Not in the Visible Set but in the Frustum, Casting Shadows

Shadows for Lights Outside a Frustum

Unfortunately, lights outside a frustum are not simple, because the light can project objects that are outside the view frustum into the view frustum. However, this occurs only within a certain region of space defined as the *convex hull* around the view frustum and the point of the light source (Everitt and Kilgard 2003). Once this convex hull is determined, detecting whether an object needs to cast a shadow is simply a matter of seeing if it overlaps this convex space.

The trick to this approach is to quickly determine the convex hull around the view frustum and the light position. This is a constrained case of adding a point to an already convex hull, so a simple solution can be used. The frustum begins as six planes defining a convex region of space, with the planes defining an inside half-space that includes the frustum and an outside half-space. Our goal is to create a volume that encloses the area

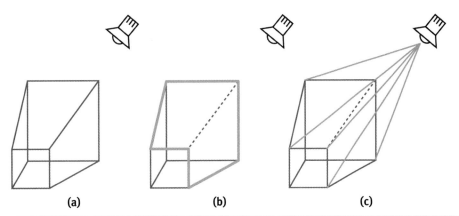

(a)   (b)   (c)

Figure 15-3. Creating the Convex Hull Around the Light and View Frustum
(a) The light is checked against each plane of the frustum. (b) Planes that contain the light position are added to the convex hull, and silhouette edges (shown in bold) are determined. (c) Planes are added for each silhouette edge and run through the edge and the light, forming the rest of the convex hull.

that would be covered if lines were connected from the light source to every point contained within the view frustum volume. Figure 15-3 illustrates the process.

The final convex hull will consist of any planes from the original view frustum where the light is contained within the inside half-space of the plane. In addition, it will consist of a plane for each silhouette edge that passes through the edge and the light. These silhouette edges are simply edges where the light is on the inside half-space of one of the touching planes, and in the outside half-space of the other plane. Both can be found simply and efficiently, but the view frustum will need some extra data in addition to just these planes. This data is a listing of:

- The edges in the view frustum
- The two points used by each edge in the view frustum
- An edge count that is used for detecting silhouette edges with respect to the light
- A mapping that indicates which edges each frustum plane partially defines
- A winding order for each edge with respect to each plane that touches the edge

For each plane of the view frustum, the position of the light is checked. If the light position is on the same side of the plane as the view frustum, that plane can be used directly in the convex hull. However, if the light position is on the opposite side of the view frustum, the plane must be discarded. At this point, the edge count of each edge that the plane affects must be incremented. Once this is done for all planes of the view frustum, there will be a listing of planes to use and a count for each edge in the view frustum.

The edge count serves the role of detecting the silhouette edge. If the count is zero, the light position was inside both defining planes, and there is no silhouette cast from that edge. If it is more than one, the light was outside both defining planes, and again there is no contributing silhouette edge. If an edge in the view frustum has a count of one, this indicates a silhouette edge from the perspective of the light, meaning that a plane must be generated that includes the light position and both points of the edge. The generation of this plane is where the winding order of the edges comes in. Whatever plane the light is outside of should store the winding order of the edge with that edge. The winding order should flag whether the edge is winding clockwise or counterclockwise with respect to the facing of the plane, and it is used to ensure that the resulting plane will be facing the correct direction. This is needed because two planes define the edge, and it is impossible to lay out all the edges so that the winding order is consistent with respect to all planes defining it.

The silhouette edge portion of the algorithm results in a frustum that extrudes from the point of view of the light and outlines the frustum with respect to the light. This volume would stretch on forever, but it is bound by the planes that contain the light in the inside half-space, effectively forming a cap and resulting in a convex hull around the frustum and the light.

This pseudocode can quickly generate the convex hull:

```
Initialize all edge counts to zero

For each plane
  If the light is on the inside
    Add the plane to the final plane list
  Else
    For each edge the plane partially defines
      Increment the edge count
      Store the winding for this edge

For each edge
  If the edge count is equal to one
    Add a plane that includes the edge and the light point,
      flipping the plane normal if the winding is reversed
```

15.5 Visibility for Fill Rate

Visibility can be used effectively to improve performance not only on the CPU, but also on the GPU. When we perform per-pixel lighting with stencil volumes, the fill rate consumed—by filling in stencil volumes or by rendering large objects multiple times—can quickly become a bottleneck. The best way to combat this bottleneck is to restrict the area that the card can render to by using a *scissor rectangle*. On the most recent NVIDIA cards, the scissor rectangle concept can be extended even further, to a depth test that acts like a z-scissor range and effectively emulates a scissor frustum in space.

To create a scissor rectangle, project the dimensions of the light onto the screen and restrict rendering to that region. However, on even medium-size lights, this method quickly loses most benefits because the light covers the majority of the screen. It becomes particularly inefficient in tight areas with large lights. In this situation, the lights do not affect a large portion of the screen; however, because of their radii, a naive implementation has a much larger scissor rectangle than necessary. Picture a ventilation shaft with a light that shines down most of the shaft. To illuminate this large area, the light must have a large radius, which leads to a large scissor rectangle—even though it is lighting only the shaft, which might be a small portion of the screen.

To ensure that the scissor rectangle is as tight as possible, we can use the sets that were outlined earlier. We already have the listing of objects that the light will influence when it is rendered. And we can determine the bounding rectangle of a primitive projected onto the screen. So we can find a very tight scissor rectangle by this method: Project each object that is affected by the light onto the screen, find the total bounding box of those objects, and perform an intersection with the projected bounding box for the light itself. It's best to use low-level primitives (such as bounding spheres or axis-aligned bounding boxes) for these projections because they can be costly and there's little benefit in increasing the tightness of the bounding primitives.

By performing these operations—even if a light has a huge radius—we create a scissor rectangle that is never larger than the area of the objects the light affects projected on the screen. This approach can dramatically reduce fill and greatly help keep frame rates consistent across scenes.

15.6 Practical Application

All the techniques mentioned in this chapter were implemented in an existing system and yielded significant performance improvements. The visibility solution was a portal visibility scheme, which allowed the use of the same visibility system for the viewer and the lights.

Table 15-1 shows the number of frames per second in a normalized form, as well as the number of batches required from various scenes, with different components enabled. For each scene, the frame rate is normalized and is shown when (a) no visibility is used; (b) visibility only for the camera is used; (c) visibility for lights and camera is used; (d) visibility for lights, camera, and shadow is used; and (e) scissor rectangles are added.

Table 15-1. The Effects of Different Visibility Techniques on Performance

Scene 1	Normalized Frame Rate	Batches
Frustum-based visibility	0.87	1171
Visibility occlusion	0.92	492
Lighting occlusion	0.99	468
Shadow occlusion	0.99	460
Scissor rectangle	1.00	460
Scene 2	Normalized Frame Rate	Batches
Frustum-based visibility	0.56	1414
Visibility occlusion	0.80	521
Lighting occlusion	0.98	438
Shadow occlusion	0.98	437
Scissor rectangle	1.00	437

As Table 15-1 affirms, the introduction of visibility into a scene can dramatically improve frame rate. Further testing of the scene showed that after a certain point, the application became fill-rate-limited, and performance improvements from the visibility were due to occlusion that resulted in fewer objects for the video card to rasterize.

15.7 Conclusion

The high number of batches and large amount of fill rate that per-pixel lighting requires means that we need to minimize the number of rendered objects and the area of the screen they affect. By using any standard visibility algorithm and the techniques illustrated in this chapter, we can substantially improve performance.

15.8 References

Akenine-Möller, Tomas, and Eric Haines. 2002. *Real-Time Rendering*, 2nd ed. A. K. Peters. See the discussion of visibility algorithms on pp. 345–389.

Everitt, Cass, and Mark J. Kilgard. 2003. "Optimized Stencil Shadow Volumes." Presentation at Game Developers Conference 2003. Available online at **http://developer.nvidia.com/docs/IO/8230/GDC2003_ShadowVolumes.pdf**

Wloka, Matthias. 2003. "Batch, Batch, Batch: What Does It Really Mean?" Presentation at Game Developers Conference 2003. Available online at **http://developer.nvidia.com/docs/IO/8230/BatchBatchBatch.pdf**

PART III
MATERIALS

My professional involvement in hardware-accelerated computer graphics began 15 years ago, and I am keenly aware of where our industry came from and how far we've evolved. In 1988, most workstation users would have considered themselves extremely fortunate to have a system with a hardware-accelerated z-buffer, not to mention something that supported even the most primitive form of lighting. On the other hand, once texture mapping and Phong lighting hardware acceleration appeared a couple of years later, what followed was more of an evolution in cost reduction and large-scale integration, not a functional revolution. In fact, up until one or two years ago, almost all games used at most a Phong lighting model, modulated with layers of textures.

Nevertheless, today we are seeing a virtual explosion of complex lighting and surface reflection models in real-time graphics research and in game demos, pushing the technological envelope. These techniques include high-dynamic-range environmental lighting and preconvolved diffuse maps, separable bidirectional reflectance distribution functions (BRDFs), and many techniques using depth and occlusion information to render more accurately all varieties of materials—transparent, translucent, or opaque. This part of the book covers a number of these techniques.

In **Chapter 16, "Real-Time Approximations to Subsurface Scattering," Simon Green** describes several different methods of approximating the look of translucent materials, such as skin and marble, using programmable graphics hardware.

Next, in **Chapter 17, "Ambient Occlusion," Matt Pharr** and **Simon Green** show how to combine the preprocessing of occlusion information of an object and its environment with an efficient real-time shader that takes these elements into account to create a realistically lit and shadowed object.

David McAllister presents an interesting approach to representing multiple complex materials by encoding separate BRDFs within a single texture map, in **Chapter 18, "Spatial BRDFs."** He then expands upon this notion to support discrete lights as well as environmental lighting.

In **Chapter 19, "Image-Based Lighting," Kevin Bjorke** breaks out of the standard cube-map environment and delves into a world with many more possibilities for realistic lighting effects. First he explores image-based lighting, including localized cube maps—the analogue of local lighting using image-based rendering—then he shows how to apply those critical final touches to the shading model, including realistic reflectance, shadows, and diffuse/ambient terms.

Finally, in **Chapter 20, "Texture Bombing," Steve Glanville** shows how texture bombing and related cellular techniques can add a visual richness to your shaders, amplifying the variability of your images and reducing the repetitive look of large textured regions. He concludes with an interesting exposition on developing Voronoi diagrams within a pixel shader, which could serve as the kernel of a broad spectrum of shaders depicting natural phenomena, including scales, bubbles, leaves, and skin.

John Spitzer, NVIDIA

Chapter 16

Real-Time Approximations to Subsurface Scattering

Simon Green
NVIDIA

Most shading models used in real-time graphics today consider the interaction of light only at the surface of an object. In the real world, however, many objects are slightly translucent: light enters their surface, is scattered around inside the material, and then exits the surface, potentially at a different point from where it entered.

Much research has been devoted to producing efficient and accurate models of subsurface light transport. Although completely physically accurate simulations of subsurface scattering are out of the reach of current graphics hardware, it is possible to approximate much of the visual appearance of this effect in real time. This chapter describes several methods of approximating the look of translucent materials, such as skin and marble, using programmable graphics hardware.

16.1 The Visual Effects of Subsurface Scattering

When trying to reproduce any visual effect, it is often useful to examine images of the effect and try to break down the visual appearance into its constituent parts.

Looking at photographs and rendered images of translucent objects, we notice several things. First, subsurface scattering tends to soften the overall effect of lighting. Light from one area tends to bleed into neighboring areas on the surface, and small surface details become less visible. The farther the light penetrates into the object, the more it is attenuated and diffused. With skin, scattering also tends to cause a slight color shift toward red where the surface transitions from being lit to being in shadow. This is caused by light entering the surface on the lit side, being scattered and absorbed by the blood and tissue beneath the skin, and then exiting on the shadowed side. The effect of scattering is most obvious where the skin is thin, such as around the nostrils and ears.

16.2 Simple Scattering Approximations

One simple trick that approximates scattering is *wrap lighting*. Normally, diffuse (Lambert) lighting contributes zero light when the surface normal is perpendicular to the light direction. Wrap lighting modifies the diffuse function so that the lighting wraps around the object beyond the point where it would normally become dark. This reduces the contrast of the diffuse lighting, which decreases the amount of ambient and fill lighting that is required. Wrap lighting is a crude approximation to the Oren-Nayar lighting model, which attempts to more accurately simulate rough matte surfaces (Nayar and Oren 1995).

The code shown here and the graph in Figure 16-1 illustrate how to change the diffuse lighting function to include the wrap effect. The value `wrap` is a floating-point number between 0 and 1 that controls how far the lighting will wrap around the object.

```
float diffuse = max(0, dot(L, N));
float wrap_diffuse = max(0, (dot(L, N) + wrap) / (1 + wrap));
```

To compute this efficiently in a fragment program, the function can be encoded in a texture, which is indexed by the dot product between the light vector and the normal. This texture can also be created to include a slight color shift toward red when the lighting approaches zero. This is a cheap way to simulate scattering for skin shaders. The same texture can also include the power function for specular lighting in the alpha channel. The FX code in Listing 16-1 demonstrates how to use this technique. See Figure 16-2 for examples.

$$y = (x + wrap)/(1 + wrap)$$

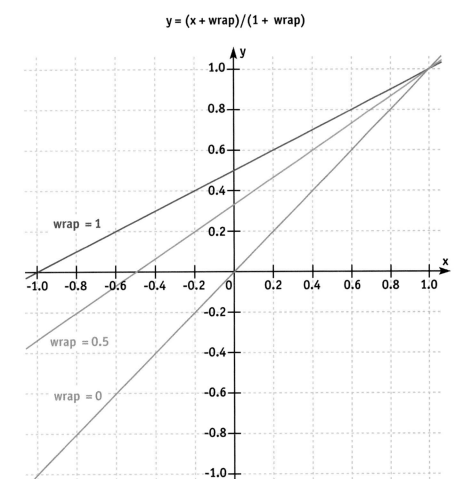

Figure 16-1. Graph of the Wrap Lighting Function

Listing 16-1. Excerpt from the Skin Shader Effect Incorporating Wrap Lighting

```
// Generate 2D lookup table for skin shading
float4 GenerateSkinLUT(float2 P : POSITION) : COLOR
{
    float wrap = 0.2;
    float scatterWidth = 0.3;
    float4 scatterColor = float4(0.15, 0.0, 0.0, 1.0);
    float shininess = 40.0;

    float NdotL = P.x * 2 - 1;   // remap from [0, 1] to [-1, 1]
```

```
    float NdotH = P.y * 2 - 1;

    float NdotL_wrap = (NdotL + wrap) / (1 + wrap); // wrap lighting
    float diffuse = max(NdotL_wrap, 0.0);

    // add color tint at transition from light to dark
    float scatter = smoothstep(0.0, scatterWidth, NdotL_wrap) *
                    smoothstep(scatterWidth * 2.0, scatterWidth,
                               NdotL_wrap);

    float specular = pow(NdotH, shininess);
    if (NdotL_wrap <= 0) specular = 0;
    float4 C;
    C.rgb = diffuse + scatter * scatterColor;
    C.a = specular;
    return C;
}


// Shade skin using lookup table
half3 ShadeSkin(sampler2D skinLUT,
                half3 N,
                half3 L,
                half3 H,
                half3 diffuseColor,
                half3 specularColor) : COLOR
{
    half2 s;
    s.x = dot(N, L);
    s.y = dot(N, H);
    half4 light = tex2D(skinLUT, s * 0.5 + 0.5);
    return diffuseColor * light.rgb + specularColor * light.a;
}
```

16.3 Simulating Absorption Using Depth Maps

One of the most important factors in simulating very translucent materials is absorption. The farther through the material light travels, the more it is scattered and absorbed. To simulate this effect, we need a measure of the distance light has traveled through the material.

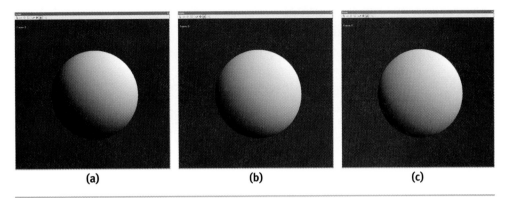

(a)   (b)   (c)

Figure 16-2. Applying Wrap Lighting to Spheres
Spheres lit (a) without wrap lighting, (b) with wrap lighting, and (c) with wrap lighting and color shift.

One method of estimating this distance is to use depth maps (Hery 2002). This technique is very similar to shadow mapping, and it is practical for real-time rendering. In the first pass, we render the scene from the point of view of the light, storing the distance from the light to a texture. This image is then projected back onto the scene using standard projective texture mapping. In the rendering pass, given a point to be shaded, we can look up into this texture to obtain the distance from the light at the point the ray entered the surface (d_i). By subtracting this value from the distance from the light to the point at which the ray exited the surface (d_o), we obtain an estimate of the distance the light has traveled through the object (s). See Figure 16-3.

The obvious problem with this technique is that it works only with convex objects: holes within the object are not accounted for correctly. In practice, this is not a big issue, but it may be possible to get around the problem using *depth peeling*, which removes layers of the object one by one (Everitt 2003).

You might be thinking that for static objects, it would be possible to paint or precalculate a map that represents the approximate thickness of the surface at each point. The advantage of using depth maps is they take into account the direction of the incoming light, and they also work for animating models (assuming that you regenerate the depth map each frame).

The programs in Listings 16-2 and 16-3 demonstrate how to render distance from the light to a texture. They assume the `modelView` and `modelViewProj` matrices have been set up by the application for the light view.

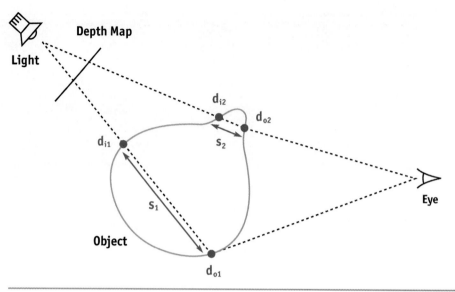

Figure 16-3. Calculating the Distance Light Has Traveled Through an Object Using a Depth Map

Listing 16-2. The Vertex Program for the Depth Pass

```
struct a2v {
  float4 pos    : POSITION;
  float3 normal : NORMAL;
};
struct v2f {
  float4 hpos : POSITION;
  float  dist : TEXCOORD0;  // distance from light
};

v2f main(a2v IN,
         uniform float4x4 modelViewProj,
         uniform float4x4 modelView,
         uniform float    grow)
{
  v2f OUT;
  float4 P = IN.pos;
  P.xyz += IN.normal * grow;  // scale vertex along normal
  OUT.hpos = mul(modelViewProj, P);
  OUT.dist = length(mul(modelView, IN.pos));
  return OUT;
}
```

Listing 16-3. The Fragment Program for the Depth Pass

```
float4 main(float dist : TEX0) : COLOR
{
  return dist;  // return distance
}
```

The fragment program extract in Listing 16-4 shows how to look up in the light distance texture to calculate depth. For flexibility, this code does the projection in the fragment program, but if you are taking only a few samples, it will be more efficient to calculate these transformations in the vertex program.

Listing 16-4. The Fragment Program Function for Calculating Penetration Depth Using Depth Map

```
// Given a point in object space, lookup into depth textures
// returns depth
float trace(float3 P,
            uniform float4x4  lightTexMatrix, // to light texture space
            uniform float4x4  lightMatrix,    // to light space
            uniform sampler2D lightDepthTex,
            )
{
  // transform point into light texture space
  float4 texCoord = mul(lightTexMatrix, float4(P, 1.0));

  // get distance from light at entry point
  float d_i = tex2Dproj(lightDepthTex, texCoord.xyw);

  // transform position to light space
  float4 Plight = mul(lightMatrix, float4(P, 1.0));

  // distance of this pixel from light (exit)
  float d_o = length(Plight);

  // calculate depth
  float s = d_o - d_i;
  return s;
}
```

Once we have a measure of the distance the light has traveled through the material, there are several ways we can use it. One simple way is to use it to index directly into an artist-created 1D texture that maps distance to color. The color should fall off exponentially with distance. By changing this color map, and combining the effect with other, more traditional lighting models, we can produce images of different materials, such as marble or jade.

```
float si = trace(IN.objCoord, lightTexMatrix, lightMatrix,
                 lightDepthTex);
return tex1D(scatterTex, si);
```

Alternatively, we can evaluate the exponential function directly:

```
return exp(-si * sigma_t) * lightColor;
```

The problem with this technique is that it does not simulate the way light is diffused as it passes through the object. When the light is behind the object, you will often clearly see features from the back side of the object showing through on the front. The solution to this is to take multiple samples at different points on the surface or to use a different diffusion approximation, as discussed in the next section.

16.3.1 Implementation Details

On GeForce FX hardware, when reading from a depth texture, only the most significant eight bits of the depth value are available. This is not sufficient precision. Instead, we can either use floating-point textures or use the pack and unpack instructions from the NVIDIA fragment program extension to store a 32-bit float value in a regular eight-bit RGBA texture. Floating-point textures do not currently support filtering, so block artifacts will sometimes be visible where the projected texture is magnified. If necessary, bilinear filtering can be performed in the shader, at some performance cost.

Another problem with projected depth maps is that artifacts often appear around the edges of the projection. These are similar to the self-shadowing artifacts seen with shadow mapping. They result mainly from the limited resolution of the texture map, which causes pixels from the background to be projected onto the edges of the object. The sample code avoids this problem by slightly scaling the object along the vertex normal during the depth-map pass.

For more accurate simulations, we may also need to know the normal, and potentially the surface color, at the point at which the light entered the object. We can achieve this by rendering additional passes that render the extra information to textures. We can look up in these textures in a similar way to the depth texture. On systems that support multiple render targets, it may be possible to collapse the depth, normal, and other passes into a single pass that outputs multiple values. See Figure 16-4.

Figure 16-4. Using a Depth Map to Approximate Scattering
Thin parts of the object transmit more light.

16.3.2 More Sophisticated Scattering Models

More sophisticated models attempt to accurately simulate the cumulative effects of scattering within the medium.

One model is the *single scattering approximation*, which assumes that light bounces only once within the material. By stepping along the refracted ray into the material, one can estimate how many photons would be scattered toward the camera. Phase functions are used to describe the distribution of directions in which light is scattered when it hits a particle. It is also important to take into account the Fresnel effect at the entry and exit points.

Another model, the *diffusion approximation*, simulates the effect of multiple scattering for highly scattering media, such as skin.

Unfortunately, these techniques are beyond the scope of this chapter.

Christophe Hery's chapter from the SIGGRAPH 2003 RenderMan course (Hery 2003) goes into the details of single and diffusion scattering for skin shaders.

16.4 Texture-Space Diffusion

As we noted earlier, one of the most obvious visual signs of subsurface scattering is a general blurring of the effects of lighting. In fact, 3D artists often emulate this phenomenon in screen space by performing Gaussian blurs of their renders in Adobe Photoshop and then adding a small amount of the blurred image back on top of the original. This "glow" technique softens the lighting and makes the images look less computer-generated.

It is possible to simulate diffusion in texture space (Borshukov and Lewis 2003). We can unwrap the mesh of the object with a vertex program that uses the UV texture coordinates as the screen position of the vertex. The program simply remaps the [0, 1] range of the texture coordinates to the [−1, 1] range of normalized device coordinates. We have to be careful that the object has a good UV mapping; that is, each point on the texture must map to only one point of the object, with no overlaps. By lighting this unwrapped mesh in the normal way, we obtain a 2D image representing the lighting of the object. We can then process this image and reapply it to the 3D model like a normal texture.

The vertex program in Listing 16-5 demonstrates how to render a model in UV space and perform diffuse lighting.

This technique is useful for other applications, because it decouples the shading complexity from the screen resolution: shading is performed only for each texel in the texture map, rather than for every pixel on the object. Many operations, such as convolutions, can be performed much more efficiently in image space than on a 3D surface. If the UV parameterization of the surface is relatively uniform, this is not a bad approximation, because points that are close in world space will map to points that are also close in texture space.

To simulate light diffusion in image space, we can simply blur the light map texture. We can take advantage of all the usual GPU image-processing tricks, such as using separable filters and exploiting bilinear filtering hardware. Rendering the lighting to a relatively low-resolution texture already provides a certain amount of blurring. Figure 16-5 shows an unwrapped head mesh and the results of blurring the light map texture.

Listing 16-5. A Vertex Program to Unwrap a Model and Perform Diffuse Lighting

```
struct a2v {
  float4 pos     : POSITION;
  float3 normal  : NORMAL;
  float2 texture : TEXCOORD0;
};

struct v2f {
  float4 hpos     : POSITION;
  float2 texcoord : TEXCOORD0;
  float4 col      : COLOR0;
};

v2f main(a2v IN,
         uniform float4x4 lightMatrix)
{
  v2f OUT;

  // convert texture coordinates to NDC position [-1, 1]
  OUT.hpos.xy = IN.texture * 2 - 1;
  OUT.hpos.z = 0.0;
  OUT.hpos.w = 1.0;

  // diffuse lighting
  float3 N = normalize(mul((float3x3) lightMatrix, IN.normal));
  float3 L = normalize(-mul(lightMatrix, IN.pos).xyz);
  float diffuse = max(dot(N, L), 0);
  OUT.col = diffuse;

  OUT.texcoord = IN.texture;
  return OUT;
}
```

A diffuse color map can also be included in the light map texture; then details from the color map will also be diffused. If shadows are included in the texture, the blurring process will result in soft shadows.

To simulate the fact that absorption and scattering are wavelength dependent, we can alter the filter weights separately for each color channel. The sample shader, shown in Listings 16-6 and 16-7, attempts to simulate skin. It takes seven texture samples with Gaussian weights. The width of the filter is greater for the red channel than for the green and blue channels, so that the red is diffused more than the other channels. The

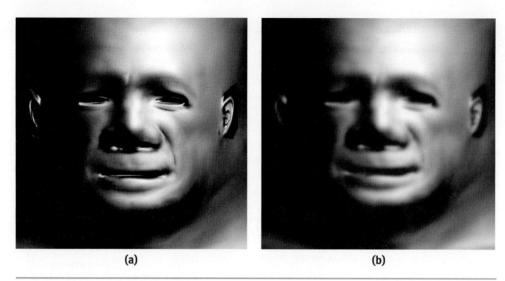

(a) (b)

Figure 16-5. Unwrapped Head Mesh
The mesh is shown (a) before and (b) after blurring the light map texture.

vertex program in Listing 16-6 calculates the sample positions for a blur in the *x* direction; the program for the *y* direction is almost identical. The samples are spaced two texels apart to take advantage of the bilinear filtering capability of the hardware.

Listing 16-6. The Vertex Program for Diffusion Blur

```
v2f main(float2 tex : TEXCOORD0)
{
  v2f OUT;
  // 7 samples, 2 texel spacing
  OUT.tex0 = tex + float2(-5.5, 0);
  OUT.tex1 = tex + float2(-3.5, 0);
  OUT.tex2 = tex + float2(-1.5, 0);
  OUT.tex3 = tex + float2(0, 0);
  OUT.tex4 = tex + float2(1.5, 0);
  OUT.tex5 = tex + float2(3.5, 0);
  OUT.tex6 = tex + float2(5.5, 0);
  return OUT;
}
```

Listing 16-7. The Fragment Program for Diffusion Blur

```
half4 main(v2fConnector v2f,
           uniform sampler2D lightTex
           ) : COLOR
{
  // weights to blur red channel more than green and blue
  const float4 weight[7] = {
    { 0.006, 0.0,  0.0,  0.0 },
    { 0.061, 0.0,  0.0,  0.0 },
    { 0.242, 0.25, 0.25, 0.0 },
    { 0.383, 0.5,  0.5,  0.0 },
    { 0.242, 0.25, 0.20, 0.0 },
    { 0.061, 0.0,  0.0,  0.0 },
    { 0.006, 0.0,  0.0,  0.0 },
  };

  half4 a;
  a  = tex2D(lightTex, v2f.tex0) * weight[0];
  a += tex2D(lightTex, v2f.tex1) * weight[1];
  a += tex2D(lightTex, v2f.tex2) * weight[2];
  a += tex2D(lightTex, v2f.tex3) * weight[3];
  a += tex2D(lightTex, v2f.tex4) * weight[4];
  a += tex2D(lightTex, v2f.tex5) * weight[5];
  a += tex2D(lightTex, v2f.tex6) * weight[6];
  return a;
}
```

To achieve a wider blur, you can either apply the blur shader several times or write a shader that takes more samples by calculating the sample positions in the fragment program. Figure 16-6 shows the blurred light map texture applied back onto the 3D head model.

The final shader blends the diffused lighting texture with the original high-resolution color map to obtain the final effect, as shown in Figure 16-7.

16.4.1 Possible Future Work

One possible extension to the depth map technique would be to render additional depth passes to account for denser objects within the object, such as bones within a body. The problem is that we are trying to account for volumetric effects using a surface-based representation. Volume rendering does not have this restriction, and it can produce

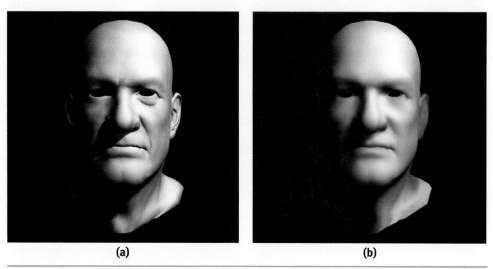

(a)   (b)

Figure 16-6. Texture-Space Diffusion on a Head Model
The model is shown with (a) the original and (b) the diffused light maps applied.

Figure 16-7. The Final Model, with Color Map

much more accurate renderings of objects whose density varies. For more on volume rendering, see Chapter 39 of this book, "Volume Rendering Techniques."

Another possible extension to this technique would be to provide several color maps, each representing the color of a different layer of skin. For example, you might provide one map for the surface color and another for the veins and capillaries underneath the skin.

Greg James (2003) describes a technique that handles arbitrary polygonal objects by first adding up the distances of all the back-facing surfaces and then subtracting the distances of all the front-facing surfaces. His application computes distances in screen space for volumetric fog effects, but it could be extended to more general situations.

An interesting area of future research is combining the depth-map and texture-space techniques to obtain the best of both worlds.

16.5 Conclusion

The effects of subsurface scattering are an important factor in producing convincing images of skin and other translucent materials. By using several different approximations, we have shown how to achieve much of the look of subsurface scattering today in real time. As graphics hardware becomes more powerful, increasingly accurate models of subsurface light transport will be possible.

We hope that the techniques described in this chapter will inspire you to improve the realism of real-time game characters. But remember, good shading can never help bad art!

16.6 References

Borshukov, George, and J. P. Lewis. 2003. "Realistic Human Face Rendering for 'The Matrix Reloaded.'" SIGGRAPH 2003. Available online at
http://www.virtualcinematography.org/

Everitt, Cass. 2003. "Order-Independent Transparency." Available online at
http://developer.nvidia.com/view.asp?IO=order_independent_transparency

Hery, Christophe. 2002. "On Shadow Buffers." Presentation available online at
http://www.renderman.org/RMR/Examples/srt2002/PrmanUserGroup2002.ppt

Hery, Christophe. 2003. "Implementing a Skin BSSRDF." RenderMan course notes, SIGGRAPH 2003. Available online at
http://www.renderman.org/RMR/Books/sig03.course09.pdf.gz

James, Greg. 2003. "Rendering Objects as Thick Volumes." In *ShaderX2: Shader Programming Tips & Tricks With DirectX 9*, edited by Wolfgang F. Engel. Wordware. More information available online at **http://www.shaderx2.com**

Jensen, Henrik Wann, Stephen R. Marschner, Marc Levoy, and Pat Hanrahan. 2001. "A Practical Model for Subsurface Light Transport." In *Proceedings of SIGGRAPH 2001*.

Nayar, S. K., and M. Oren. 1995. "Generalization of the Lambertian Model and Implications for Machine Vision." *International Journal of Computer Vision* 14, pp. 227–251.

Pharr, Matt. 2001. "Layer Media for Surface Shaders." Advanced RenderMan course notes, SIGGRAPH 2001. Available online at
http://www.renderman.org/RMR/Books/sig01.course48.pdf.gz

Statue model courtesy of De Espona Infographica (http://www.deespona.com). Head model courtesy of Steven Giesler (http://www.stevengiesler.com).

Chapter 17

Ambient Occlusion

Matt Pharr
NVIDIA

Simon Green
NVIDIA

The real-time computer graphics community has recently started to appreciate the increase in realism that comes from illuminating objects with complex light distributions from environment maps, rather than using a small number of simple light sources. In the real world, light arrives at surfaces from all directions, not from just a handful of directions to a point or directional light sources, and this noticeably affects their appearance. A variety of techniques have recently been developed to capture real-world illumination (such as on movie sets) and to use it to render objects as if they were illuminated by the light from the original environment, making it possible to more seamlessly merge computer graphics with real scenes. For completely synthetic scenes, these techniques can be applied to improve the realism of rendered images by rendering an environment map of the scene and using it to light characters and other objects inside the scene. Rather than using the map just for perfect specular reflection, these techniques use it to compute lighting for glossy and diffuse surfaces as well.

This chapter describes a simple technique for real-time environment lighting. It is limited to diffuse surfaces, but it is efficient enough for real-time use. Furthermore, this method accurately accounts for shadows due to geometry occluding the environment from the point being shaded. Although the shading values that this technique computes have a number of sources of possible errors compared to some of the more complex techniques recently described in research literature, the technique is relatively easy to implement. (To make it work, you don't have to understand and implement a spherical harmonics library!) The approach described here gives excellent results in many situations, and it runs interactively on modern hardware.

This method is based on a view-independent preprocess that computes occlusion information with a ray tracer and then uses this information at runtime to compute a fast approximation to diffuse shading in the environment. This technique was originally developed by Hayden Landis (2002) and colleagues at Industrial Light & Magic; it has been used on a number of ILM's productions (with a non-real-time renderer!).

17.1 Overview

The environment lighting technique we describe has been named *ambient occlusion* lighting. One way of thinking of the approach is as a "smart" ambient term that varies over the surface of the model according to how much of the external environment can be seen at each point. Alternatively, one can think of it as a diffuse term that supports a complex distribution of incident light efficiently. We will stick with the second interpretation in this chapter.

The basic idea behind this technique is that if we preprocess a model, computing how much of the external environment each point on it can see versus how much of the environment has been occluded by other parts of the model, then we can use that information at rendering time to compute the value of a diffuse shading term. The result is that the crevices of the model are realistically darkened, and the exposed parts of the model realistically receive more light and are thus brighter. The result looks substantially more realistic than if a standard shading model had been used.

This approach can be extended to use environment lighting as the source of illumination, where an environment map that represents incoming light from all directions is used to determine the color of light arriving at each point on the object. For this feature, in addition to recording how much of the environment is visible from points on the model, we also record from which direction most of the visible light is arriving. These two quantities, which effectively define a cone of unoccluded directions out into the scene, can be used together to do an extremely blurred lookup from the environment map to simulate the overall incoming illumination from a cone of directions of interest at a point being shaded.

17.2 The Preprocessing Step

Given an arbitrary model to be shaded, this technique needs to know two things at each point on the model: (1) the "accessibility" at the point—what fraction of the hemisphere above that point is unoccluded by other parts of the model; and (2) the average direction of unoccluded incident light. Figure 17-1 illustrates both of these ideas in 2D. Given a point P on the surface with normal N, here roughly two-thirds of the hemisphere above P is occluded by other geometry in the scene, while one-third is unoccluded. The average direction of incoming light is denoted by B, and it is somewhat to the right of the normal direction N. Loosely speaking, the average color of incident light at P could be found by averaging the incident light from the cone of unoccluded directions around the B vector.

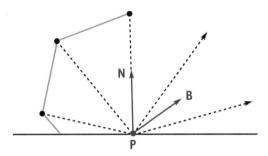

Figure 17-1. Computing Accessibility and an Average Direction

This B vector and the accessibility value, which are model dependent but not lighting dependent, can be computed offline in a preprocess with a ray tracer. For the examples in this chapter, the model we used was finely tessellated, so we computed these values at the center of each triangle and then stored values at each vertex that held the average of the values from the adjacent faces. We then passed these per-vertex values through the vertex shader so that they would be interpolated at each pixel for the fragment shader. Alternatively, we could have stored them in texture maps; this would have been preferable if the model had been more coarsely tessellated.

The pseudocode in Listing 17-1 shows our basic approach. At the center of each triangle, we generate a set of rays in the hemisphere centered about the surface normal. We trace each of these rays out into the scene, recording which of them intersect the model—indicating that we wouldn't receive light from the environment in that direction—and which are unoccluded. We compute the average direction of the unoccluded rays, which gives us an approximation to the average direction of incident light. (Of course, it's possible that the direction that we compute may in fact be occluded itself; we just ignore this issue.)

Listing 17-1. Basic Algorithm for Computing Ambient Occlusion Quantities

```
For each triangle {
  Compute center of triangle
  Generate set of rays over the hemisphere there
  Vector avgUnoccluded = Vector(0, 0, 0);
  int numUnoccluded = 0;
  For each ray {
    If (ray doesn't intersect anything) {
      avgUnoccluded += ray.direction;
      ++numUnoccluded;
    }
  }
  avgUnoccluded = normalize(avgUnoccluded);
  accessibility = numUnoccluded / numRays;
}
```

An easy way to generate these rays is with *rejection sampling*: randomly generate rays in the 3D cube from –1 to 1 in *x*, *y*, and *z*, and reject the ones that don't lie in the unit hemisphere about the normal. The directions that survive this test will have the desired distribution. This approach is shown in the pseudocode in Listing 17-2. More complex Monte Carlo sampling algorithms could also be used to ensure a better-distributed set of sample directions.

Listing 17-2. Algorithm for Computing Random Directions with Rejection Sampling

```
while (true) {
  x = RandomFloat(-1, 1); // random float between -1 and 1
  y = RandomFloat(-1, 1);
  z = RandomFloat(-1, 1);
  if (x * x + y * y + z * z > 1) continue; // ignore ones outside unit
                                            // sphere
  if (dot(Vector(x, y, z), N) < 0) continue; // ignore "down" dirs
  return normalize(Vector(x, y, z)); // success!
}
```

17.3 Hardware-Accelerated Occlusion

It is possible to accelerate the calculation of this occlusion information by using the graphics hardware instead of software ray tracing. Shadow maps provide a fast image-space method of determining whether a point is in shadow. (GeForce FX has special hardware support for rasterizing the depth-only images needed for shadow mapping at high speed.) Instead of shooting rays from each point on the surface, we can reverse the problem and surround the object with a large spherical array of shadow-mapped lights. The occlusion amount at a point on a surface is simply the average of the shadow contributions from each light. We can calculate this average using a floating-point accumulation buffer. For n lights, we render the scene n times, each time moving the shadow-casting light to a different position on the sphere. We accumulate these black-and-white images to form the final occlusion image. At the limit, this simulates a large area light covering the sky.

A large number of lights (128 to 1024) is required for good results, but the performance of modern graphics hardware means this technique can still be faster than ray tracing. The distribution of the lights on the sphere also affects the final quality. The most obvious method is to use polar coordinates, with lights distributed at evenly spaced longitudes and latitudes, but this tends to concentrate too many samples at the poles. Instead, you should use a uniform distribution on the sphere. If the object is standing on a ground plane, a full hemisphere of lights isn't necessary—a dome or a hemisphere can be used instead.

Another issue that can affect the quality of the final results is shadow-mapping artifacts. These often appear as streaking on the surface at the transition from lit to shadowed. This problem can be alleviated by multiplying the shadowing term by a function of the normal and the light direction that ensures that the side of the surface facing away from the light is always black.

One disadvantage of this method is that for each light, two passes are required: one to generate the shadow map and one to render the shadowed scene, plus the overhead needed to accumulate the image. For n lights, this means $2n$ passes are required. It may be faster to accumulate the effect of multiple shadow maps in a single pass. Since current hardware supports eight sets of texture coordinates, it is possible to accumulate eight shadows in the shader at once. This means that only $n + n/8$ renders of the scene would be required in total.

The approach can also be extended to produce the average unoccluded direction, or *bent normal*. We can use a shader to calculate the direction to the light multiplied by the shadow value, and then copy the result to the RGB output color. The occlusion information can be stored in the alpha channel. We accumulate these RGB normal values in the same way as the occlusion value, and then we normalize the final result to get the average unoccluded normal. Note that a half (16-bit) floating-point accumulation buffer may not have sufficient precision to represent the summation of these vectors accurately.

So far, the technique we have described generates occlusion images in camera space, but often we want to generate textures that store the occlusion information. If the objects we are using have unique texture coordinates (that is, the texture covers their entire surface without overlaps), this is relatively easy. We can unwrap the model with a vertex program that uses the UV texture coordinate as the screen-space position. The calculation proceeds as normal, but instead of rendering the object as normal, we are rendering the rectangular unwrapped mesh. Once this occlusion texture has been generated, it can be used in real-time rendering, as described in the rest of this chapter.

17.4 Rendering with Ambient Occlusion Maps

As an example, we applied this method to a complex model set on a plane. (There are no texture maps in this scene, so that we can see the effect of the method more clearly. Texturing is easily incorporated into this technique, however.) We used 512 rays per triangle to compute the accessibility values and average unoccluded directions for each of 150,000 triangles; the preprocess took approximately four minutes with a software ray tracer on an AMD Athlon 1800XP CPU. We then wrote this information out to disk in a file for use by our demo application. For comparison, Figure 17-2 shows an image of the model with a simple diffuse shading model light by a point light, with no shadows. Note the classic unrealistic computer graphics appearance and lack of shading complexity. For example, the underside of the creature and the inside of its far leg are both too bright.

In Figure 17-3, we shaded the model by setting the color to be the accessibility at each point, as computed by the ray-traced preprocess. Note that crevices under the legs of the model and points on its stomach are darker than exposed regions such as its back, which is almost fully exposed. The harsh transitions from light to dark in Figure 17-2 that were the result of the changing orientation of the surface normal with respect to the point light's position have been smoothed out, giving a realistic "overcast skylight" effect. There is a very soft shadow beneath the creature on the ground plane, the result of the creature's body reducing the amount of light arriving at the points beneath it.

Figure 17-2. Scene Shaded with the Simple Diffuse Shading Model
3D scan and representations by headus; design and clay sculpt by Martin Rezard.

Figure 17-3. Scene Shaded with Accessibility Information
Using the accessibility value to shade the model gives a more realistic look and includes the effects of self-shadowing. 3D scan and representations by headus; design and clay sculpt by Martin Rezard.

This shadow helps to ground the model, showing that it is in fact on the ground plane, rather than floating above it, as might be the case in Figure 17-2.

Best of all, shading with the accessibility value doesn't even require advanced programmable graphics hardware; it can be done with ancient graphics hardware, just by passing appropriate color values with each vertex of the model. As such, it can run at peak performance over a wide range of GPU architectures. If this model had a diffuse texture map, we'd just multiply the texture value by the accessibility for shading it.

17.4.1 Environment Lighting

If programmable graphics hardware is available, we can use the accessibility information in a more sophisticated way to generate more complex shading effects. Here, we compute an approximation of how the model would appear if it were inside a complex real-world environment, using captured illumination from an environment map of the scene. For this example, we used an environment map of Galileo's tomb, in Florence, shown in Figure 17-4.

This environment map has a different parameterization than the cube maps and sphere maps that are widely used now in interactive graphics. It is known as a *lat-long* map, for *latitude-longitude*, because the parameterization is similar to the latitudes and longitudes used to describe locations on Earth. It maps directions to points on the map using the spherical coordinate parameterization of a sphere, where θ ranges from 0 to π vertically and ϕ ranges from 0 to 2π horizontally, $x = \sin\theta\cos\phi$, $y = \sin\theta\sin\phi$, and $z = \cos\theta$. Given a direction (x, y, z), inverting these equations gives a (ϕ, θ) value, which is mapped to texture coordinates in the map by dividing it by $(2\pi, \pi)$. We used this type of

Figure 17-4. An Environment Map of Galileo's Tomb, in Latitude-Longitude Format
Courtesy of Paul Debevec.

environment map because it allows us to do extremely blurred lookups without artifacts; unfortunately, blurred cube-map lookups that span multiple faces of the cube are not handled correctly by current hardware.

The basic idea behind the program for shading with such an environment map is this: We would like to use the information that we have so far to compute a good approximation of how much light is arriving at the surface at the point being shaded. The two factors that affect this value are (1) which parts of the hemisphere above the point are unoccluded by geometry between the point and the environment map and (2) what is the incoming light along these directions. Figure 17-5 shows two cases of this scene. On the left, the point being shaded can see only a small fraction of the directions above it, denoted by the direction vector **B** and the circle indicating a cone of directions; accessibility here is very low. On the right, more light reaches the point, along a greater range of directions.

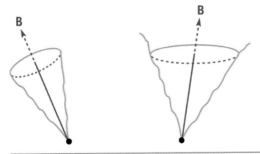

Figure 17-5. Approximating Different Amounts of Visibility
Left: Due to greater occlusion from nearby geometry, less illumination reaches this point. Right: A relatively large amount of light reaches this point along a wider cone of directions.

The accessibility value computed in the preprocess tells us what fraction of the hemisphere can see the environment map, and the average visible direction gives us an approximation of the direction around which to estimate the incoming light. Although this direction may point in a direction that is actually occluded (for example, if two separate regions of the hemisphere are unoccluded but the rest are occluded, the average direction may be between the two of them), it usually works well in practice.

The basic fragment shader we used is shown in Listing 17-3. The average direction of incoming light is passed in via the B variable, and the fraction of the hemisphere that was unoccluded is passed in via `accessibility`; the `envlatlong` sampler is bound to the environment map in Figure 17-4.

Listing 17-3. Fragment Shader for Shading with Accessibility Values and an Environment Map

```
half4 main(half3 B : TEXCOORD0,
           half accessibility : TEXCOORD1,
           uniform sampler2D envlatlong) : COLOR
{
    half2 uv = latlong(B);
    half2 blurx, blury;
    computeBlur(uv, accessibility, blurx, blury);
    half3 Cenv = tex2D(envlatlong, uv, blurx, blury).xyz;
    return half4(accessibility * Cenv, 1);
}
```

There are three main steps to the shader. First, we call the `latlong()` function shown in Listing 17-4 to compute the (*u*, *v*) texture coordinates in the latitude-longitude environment map. Second, the `computeBlur()` function, shown in Listing 17-5, determines the area of the map to blur over for the point that we are shading. Finally, we do the blurred environment map lookup via the variant of the `tex2D()` function that allows us to pass in derivatives. The derivatives specify the area of the map over which to do texture filtering, giving the average light color inside the cone. This is scaled by the accessibility value and returned. Thanks to mipmapping, computing blurred regions of large sections of the environment map can be done very efficiently in the graphics hardware.

Listing 17-4. The `latlong()` Function Definition

```
#define PI 3.1415926

half2 latlong(half3 v) {
    v = normalize(v);
    half theta = acos(v.z); // +z is up
    half phi = atan2(v.y, v.x) + PI;
    return half2(phi, theta) * half2(.1591549, .6366198);
}
```

For clarity, we have listed separately the two subroutines that the fragment shader uses. First is `latlong()`, which takes a 3D direction and finds the 2D texture position that the direction should map to for the latitude-longitude map. Because the hardware does not support latitude-longitude maps directly, we need to do this computation ourselves.

Listing 17-5. The `computeBlur()` Function Definition

```
void computeBlur(half2 uv,
                 half accessibility,
                 out half2 blurx,
                 out half2 blury)
{
  half width = sqrt(accessibility);
  blurx = half2(width, 0);
  blury = half2(0, width);
}
```

However, because inverse trigonometric functions are computationally expensive, in our implementation we stored `theta` and `phi` values in a 256×256 cube-map texture with signed eight-bit components and did a single cube-map lookup in place of the entire `latlong()` function. This modification saved approximately fifty fragment program instructions in the compiled result, with no loss in quality in the final image.

The only other tricky part of this shader is computing how much of the environment map to filter over. (Recall Figure 17-5, where the point on the left receives light from a smaller cone of directions than the point on the right does.) We make a very rough approximation of the area to filter over in the `computeBlur()` function; it just captures the first-order effect that increased accessibility should lead to an increased filter area.

The result of applying this shader to the model is shown in Figure 17-6. The shader compiles to approximately ten GPU instructions, and the scene renders at real-time rates on modern GPUs.

17.5 Conclusion

The environment lighting technique that we describe here employs many approximations, but it works well in practice and has proven itself in rendering for movie effects. The method separates the problem into a relatively expensive preprocess that computes just the right information needed to do fast shading at rendering time. The preprocess does not depend on the lighting environment map, so dynamic illumination from the scene can easily be used. Because a very blurred version of the scene's environment map is used, it doesn't necessarily need to be re-rendered for each frame. The visual appearance of objects shaded with this method is substantially more realistic than if standard graphics lighting models are used.

Figure 17-6. Scene Shaded with Accessibility Information and Illumination from an Environment Map
Shading the model using the bent normal and blurred illumination from the environment map is an efficient rough approximation to how the model would appear if it were actually in the surroundings captured in the environment map. 3D scan and representations by headus; design and clay sculpt by Martin Rezard.

Texture-mapped surfaces and standard light sources are easily incorporated into this method. Even better results can be had with a small number of standard point or directional lights to cast hard shadows, provide "key" lighting, and generate specular highlights.

While many applications of environment lighting have focused on the advantages of "high-dynamic-range" environment maps (that is, maps with floating-point texel values, thus encoding a wide range of intensities), this method works well even with standard eight-bit-per-channel texture maps. Because it simulates reflection only from diffuse surfaces—it averages illumination over many directions—it's less important to accurately represent bright light from a small set of directions, as is necessary for more glossy reflections.

We have not addressed animation in this chapter. As an animated character model changes from one pose to another, obviously the occlusion over the entire model changes. We believe that computing the occlusion information for a series of reference poses and interpolating between the results according to the character's pose would work well in practice, but we have not implemented this improvement here. However, NVIDIA's "Ogre" demo used this approach successfully. See Figure 17-7.

Figure 17-7. The Ogre Character
Shown with ambient occlusion (top) and full shading (bottom).
The Ogre character is courtesy of Spellcraft Studio.

17.6 Further Reading

This section describes alternative approaches to environment lighting in more general ways. In particular, ambient occlusion can be understood in the context of spherical harmonic lighting techniques; it is an extreme simplification that uses just the first spherical harmonic to represent reflection.

Landis, Hayden. 2002. "Production-Ready Global Illumination." Course 16 notes, SIG-GRAPH 2002. Available online at **http://www.renderman.org/RMR/Books/ sig02.course16.pdf.gz**. *Hayden Landis and others at ILM developed the ideas that we have described and implemented in Cg in this chapter. Hayden documented the approach in these notes, and a complete list of the inventors of this shading technique appears at the end.*

Zhukov, S., A. Iones, and G. Kronin. 1998. "An Ambient Light Illumination Model." In *Proceedings of Eurographics Rendering Workshop '98*, pp. 45–56. *Zhukov et al. described a similar "smart ambient" method based on a ray-traced preprocess in this article, though they didn't use it for environment lighting.*

Blinn, J. F., and Newell, M. E. 1976. "Texture and Reflection in Computer Generated Images." *Communications of the ACM* 19(10)(October 1976), pp. 542–547. *The idea of using environment maps for lighting specular objects was first described in this article.*

Miller, Gene S., and C. Robert Hoffman. 1984. "Illumination and Reflection Maps: Simulated Objects in Simulated and Real Environments." Course notes for Advanced Computer Graphics Animation, SIGGRAPH 84. *The application to lighting nonspecular objects was first described in these course notes.*

Debevec, Paul. 1998. "Rendering Synthetic Objects into Real Scenes: Bridging Traditional and Image-Based Graphics with Global Illumination and High Dynamic Range Photography." In *Proceedings of SIGGRAPH 98*, pp. 189–198. *Interest in environment lighting grew substantially after this paper appeared.*

Cohen, Michael, and Donald P. Greenberg. 1985. "The Hemi-Cube: A Radiosity Solution for Complex Environments." *This paper was the first to describe the hemi-cube algorithm for radiosity, another approach for the occlusion preprocess that would easily make use of graphics hardware for that step.*

A series of recent SIGGRAPH papers by Ramamoorthi and Hanrahan and by Sloan et al. has established key mathematical principles and algorithms based on spherical harmonics for fast environment lighting.

Chapter 18

Spatial BRDFs

David McAllister
NVIDIA

The spatial bidirectional reflectance distribution function (SBRDF) represents the reflectance of a surface at each different point, for each incoming and each outgoing angle. This function represents the appearance of the surface in a very general, detailed way. This chapter discusses a compact SBRDF representation as well as rendering approaches for SBRDFs illuminated by discrete lights or by environment maps.

18.1 What Is an SBRDF?

An SBRDF is a combination of texture mapping and the bidirectional reflectance distribution function (BRDF). A texture map stores reflectance, or other attributes, that vary spatially over a 2D surface. A BRDF stores reflectance at a single point on a surface as it varies over all incoming and outgoing angles. See Figure 18-1.

Real surfaces usually have significant variations, both spatially over the surface and angularly over all light and view directions. Thus, to represent most surfaces more realistically, we should combine BRDFs with texture mapping. This combination is the SBRDF. See McAllister 2002 for more details.

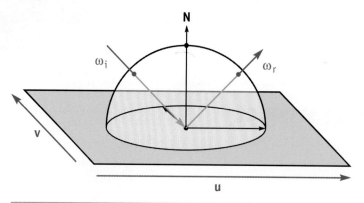

Figure 18-1. The SBRDF Domain

18.2 Details of the Representation

The most straightforward SBRDF representation is to store, at each texel of a texture map, all the parameters of that point's BRDF. Any BRDF representation could be used, but one that's compact and works well for hardware rendering is the Lafortune representation (Lafortune 1997). This representation consists of a sum of terms:

$$f_r(\omega_i \rightarrow \omega_r) = \rho_d + \sum_j \rho_{s,j} \cdot s_j(\omega_i, \omega_r),$$

where ρ_d is the diffuse reflectance. The terms in the summation are specular lobes. Each lobe j has an albedo (reflectance scaling factor), $\rho_{s,j}$, and a lobe shape, s_j. The incident and exitant directions are ω_i and ω_r. The lobe shape is defined as follows, similar to a standard Phong lobe:

$$s(\omega_i, \omega_r) = \left(\begin{bmatrix} \omega_{r,x} \\ \omega_{r,y} \\ \omega_{r,z} \end{bmatrix}^T \cdot \begin{bmatrix} C_x & & \\ & C_y & \\ & & C_z \end{bmatrix} \cdot \begin{bmatrix} \omega_{i,x} \\ \omega_{i,y} \\ \omega_{i,z} \end{bmatrix} \right)^n.$$

This equation can be thought of as a generalized dot product, in which the three terms are scaled arbitrarily:

$$s(\omega_i, \omega_r) = \left(C_x \omega_{i,x} \omega_{r,x} + C_y \omega_{i,y} \omega_{r,y} + C_z \omega_{i,z} \omega_{r,z} \right)^n.$$

See Figure 18-2.

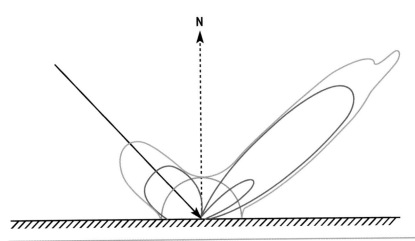

Figure 18-2. A BRDF (Green) Composed of Three Lobes (Blue) and a Diffuse Component (Orange)

The Lafortune representation is evaluated in local surface coordinates. The x axis and y axis are in the direction of anisotropy (the scratch or thread direction), and the z axis is the normal. Defining the matrix C as $C_x = -1$, $C_y = -1$, $C_z = 1$ causes ω_i to reflect about the normal, yielding a standard Phong lobe. But the C coefficients may take on other values to shear the specular lobe in ways that represent real surface-scattering behavior. The lobe's peak is in the direction $C \cdot \omega_i$. For isotropic BRDFs, $C_x = C_y$. For off-specular reflection, $|C_z| < |C_x|$, pulling the lobe toward the tangent plane. For retroreflection, $C_x > 0$ and $C_y > 0$. When C_x and C_y have opposite signs, a lobe forward-scatters light arriving parallel to the principal direction of anisotropy, but it back-scatters light arriving perpendicular to it, which models the behavior of threads and scratches.

The Lafortune representation's flexibility to aim and scale each scattering lobe is key to successfully using only a few lobes to approximate the BRDFs. This property also enables the glossy environment mapping technique described in Section 18.4. The Lafortune representation is well suited to the shape BRDFs typically have. It's compact and is capable of representing interesting BRDF properties, such as the increasing reflectance of Fresnel reflection, off-specular peaks, and retroreflection.

The ρ albedo values are RGB triples, but the C_x, C_y, C_z, and n values are shared between channels, totaling seven coefficients per specular lobe. One, two, or three specular terms are usually sufficient, depending on the nature of the surface and the quality-versus-speed tradeoff. With as few as ten coefficients (three diffuse plus seven specular), the SBRDF representation is only about three times larger than an RGB texture map, but it is dramatically more realistic.

The SBRDF data can be measured from real surfaces (McAllister 2002) or be painted by an artist using a custom-written paint program. The simplest painting approach is to use a palette of existing BRDFs and paint them into an SBRDF texture map. Palette entries can blend existing BRDFs, can be sampled from the SBRDF database (McAllister 2003), or can be defined using a dialog box to set the ρ, C_x, C_y, C_z, and n values.

18.3 Rendering Using Discrete Lights

The SBRDF is loaded into texture memory the same way for either rendering approach. The diffuse color, ρ_d, is stored in one texture map (with its alpha channel available for alpha kill or other use). For each lobe, ρ_s is stored in one texture map (with its alpha channel unused or used for the direction of anisotropy), and C_x, C_y, C_z, and n are stored in a second map. When using eight-bit texture maps, a scale and bias must be applied, because the useful range of C_x and C_y values is about -1.1 to 1.1. Scaling by 96, then biasing by 128, works well. Depending on the available memory bandwidth and fragment shader performance, it may be more efficient to store SBRDF data in floating-point textures rather than eight-bit texture, thus avoiding scaling and improving accuracy.

The Cg shader for illuminating SBRDF surfaces by standard point or directional lights is simple, as shown in Listing 18-1. It is similar to a shader for the standard Phong model and hardware lights. One difference is that all BRDF parameters, rather than just the diffuse color, are sampled from texture maps. Another is that the evaluation of the dot product occurs in local surface coordinates, so that its components can be scaled by C_x, C_y, and C_z. This requires that light vectors come from the vertex program in local surface coordinates. See Figure 18-3 for sample results.

Listing 18-1. An SBRDF Fragment Shader for Discrete Lights

```
#define NUM_LOBES 3
#define NUM_LIGHTS 2

// Store Cx, Cy, Cz on range -1.3333 .. 1.3333.
#define SCL (1.0 / (96.0 / 256.0))
#define BIAS (SCL / 2.0)
#define EXSCL 255.0 // Scale exponent to be on 0 .. 255.
```

Figure 18-3. Rendering with Discrete Lights

The white upholstery fabric, drapes, lamp, and plant leaves use measured SBRDFs. Notice how the fabric foreground shifts from dark to light, while the background shifts from light to dark. This is due to the different anisotropic BRDFs between the foreground and background.

Listing 18-1 (*continued*). An SBRDF Fragment Shader for Discrete Lights

```
// Rasterize the view vector and all the light vectors.
// Pass the light colors as uniform parameters.
struct fromrast
{
  float2 TexUV : TEXCOORD0; // Surface texcoords
  float3 EyeVec : TEXCOORD1; // Vector to eye (local space)
  float3 LightVec[NUM_LIGHTS] : TEXCOORD2; // Lights (local space)
};

float4 main(fromrast I,
            uniform sampler2D tex_dif,             // Diffuse
            uniform sampler2D tex_lshp[NUM_LOBES], // Lobe shape
            uniform sampler2D tex_lalb[NUM_LOBES], // Lobe albedo
            uniform float4 Expos,
            uniform float3 LightCol[NUM_LIGHTS]
            ) : COLOR
```

Listing 18-1 (*continued*). An SBRDF Fragment Shader for Discrete Lights

```
{
  // Load the BRDF parameters from the textures
  float4 lobe_shape[NUM_LOBES];
  float4 lobe_albedo[NUM_LOBES];

  for(float p = 0; p < NUM_LOBES; p++)
  {
    lobe_shape[p] = f4tex2D(tex_lshp[p], I.TexUV.xy) *
                        float4(SCL, SCL, SCL, EXSCL) -
                          float4(BIAS, BIAS, BIAS, 0.0);
    lobe_albedo[p] = f4tex2D(tex_lalb[p], I.TexUV.xy);
  }

  float4 dif_albedo = f4tex2D(tex_dif, I.TexUV.xy);

  // Vector to eye in local space.
  float3 toeye = normalize(I.EyeVec.xyz);

  // Accumulate exitant radiance off surface from each light
  float3 exrad = float3(0, 0, 0);

  for(int l = 0; l < NUM_LIGHTS; l++)
  {
    // Vector to light in local space.
    float3 tolight = normalize(I.LightVec[l].xyz);

    // Evaluate the SBRDF for this point and direction pair
    float3 refl = dif_albedo.xyz;

    for(float p = 0; p < NUM_LOBES; p++)
    {
      // Shear eye vector
      float3 Cwr_local = lobe_shape[p].xyz * toeye;
      float thedot = dot(Cwr_local, tolight);
      refl = refl + lit(thedot, thedot, lobe_shape[p].w).z *
              lobe_albedo[p].xyz;
    }

    // Irradiance for this light (incident radiance times NdotL).
    float NdotL = max(0, tolight.z);
    float3 irrad = LightCol[l] * NdotL;
```

Listing 18-1 (*continued*). An SBRDF Fragment Shader for Discrete Lights

```
        // Reflectance times irradiance is exitant radiance.
        exrad += refl * irrad;
    }

    float4 final_col = exrad.xyzz * Expos.xxxx; // Set HDR exposure.
    final_col.w = dif_albedo.w; // Put alpha from the map into pixel.

    return final_col;
}
```

18.3.1 Texture Sampling

C_x, C_y, C_z, and n are parameters of a nonlinear function, so applying bilinear or trilinear interpolation to these texture maps can cause sparkly artifacts. The simplest solution is to use point sampling for this map.

18.4 Rendering Using Environment Maps

Besides being illuminated with point or directional lights, SBRDFs can be illuminated with incident light from all directions by using environment maps. The key is to convolve the environment map with a portion of the BRDF before rendering. For most BRDF representations, this must be done separately for each different BRDF. But because one SBRDF might have a million different BRDFs, doing so would be impossible.

Instead, we simply convolve the environment map with Phong lobes that have a selection of different specular exponents—for example, $n = 0, 1, 4, 16, 64$, and 256. These maps can be stored in the various layers of a cube mipmap, with the $n = 0$ map at the coarsest mipmap level, and the $n = 256$ map at the finest mipmap level. The n value of the SBRDF texel then indicates the level of detail (LOD) value used to sample the appropriate mipmap level of the cube map.

An alternative representation of the set of convolved environment maps is a single 3D texture, with the s and t map dimensions mapping to a parabolic map (Heidrich and Seidel 1999) and the r dimension mapping to n.

18.4.1 The Math

The derivation begins by expressing the radiance of the pixel being shaded, $L(w_r)$, as separate diffuse and specular terms of the Lafortune BRDF:

$$L(w_r) = \rho_d \int_{\Omega_i} L_i(w_i)(\mathbf{N} \cdot w_i)\, dw_i + \sum_j \rho_{s,j} \int_{\Omega_i} s_j(w_i, w_r) L_i(w_i)(\mathbf{N} \cdot w_i)\, dw_i,$$

with Ω_i representing integration over the incident hemisphere. The incident radiance, $L_i(w_i)$, is stored in the environment map, which is indexed by the incident direction. The diffuse term can be easily encoded in an environment map indexed simply by $\mathbf{N}$:

$$D(\mathbf{N}) = \int_{\Omega_i} (\mathbf{N} \cdot w_i) L_i(w_i)\, dw_i.$$

$D(\mathbf{N})$ is independent of the BRDF, so it is precomputed once for all objects that are to reflect the environment map $L_i(w_i)$. The specular terms also take advantage of precomputed maps. Just as $\mathbf{N}$ indexes the preconvolved diffuse map, a function of the view direction indexes a preconvolved specular environment map:

$$p_j(w_r) = \begin{bmatrix} C_x & & \\ & C_y & \\ & & C_z \end{bmatrix} \cdot \begin{bmatrix} w_{r,x} \\ w_{r,y} \\ w_{r,z} \end{bmatrix}.$$

$p_j(w_r)$ is the peak vector of the lobe-shaped sampling kernel—the incident direction of maximum influence on the exitant radiance toward w_r due to lobe j. The equation is then:

$$L(w_r) = \rho_d D(\mathbf{N}) + \sum_j \rho_{s,j} \int_{\Omega_i} (p(w_r) \cdot w_i)^{n_j} L_i(w_i)(\mathbf{N} \cdot w_i)\, dw_i.$$

The environment map convolved with the specular lobe is:

$$S(w_p, n) = \int_{\Omega_i} \left(\frac{w_p}{\|w_p\|} \cdot w_i \right)^n L_i(w_i)\, dw_i.$$

This equation creates the convolved environment maps, given the original environment map. As mentioned, this map is parameterized both on the incident kernel peak direction w_p and on the exponent n. The pseudocode in Listing 18-2 represents a brute-force method of computing an environment map convolved with a Phong lobe of exponent n.

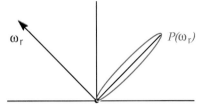

Figure 18-4. The Incident Lobe Peak for ω_r

Listing 18-2. Pseudocode for Convolving an Environment Map with a Phong Lobe

```
float3 S(float3 Wp, float n)
{
  float3 Sum = 0.xyz;
  float WgtSum = 0;

  for(int si = 0; si < 6; si++) {
    for(int yi = 0; yi < YMAX; yi++) {
      for(int xi = 0; xi < XMAX; xi++) {
        float3 Wi = VecFromCubeMap(xi, yi, si);
        float dp = dot(Wp, Wi);
        if(dp < 0) continue;

        float lobe_shape = pow(dp, n);
        float3 FN = FaceNormal(si);
        // Scale irradiance by length of cube vector to
        // compensate for irregular cube map distribution.
        float3 Irrad = Li(Wi) * dp / length2(Wi);

        Sum += Irrad * lobe_shape;
        WgtSum += lobe_shape; // Compute volume of lobe
      }
    }
  }
  return Sum / WgtSum;
}

// Convolve the cube map Li with a Phong lobe of exponent n
CubeMap PrecomputeEnvMap(float n)
{
  CubeMap Smap;
```

```
// Loop over all the pixels of the cube map
for(int s = 0; s < 6; s++) {
  for(int y = 0; y < YMAX; y++) {
    for(int x = 0; x < XMAX; x++) {
      float3 Wp = VecFromCubeMap(x, y, s);
      Smap(x, y, s) = S(Wp, n);
    }
  }
}
return Smap;
}
```

The final formulation used in hardware rendering is:

$$L\left(\omega_r\right) \approx \rho_d D\left(\mathbf{N}\right) + \sum_j \rho_{s,j} S\left(p\left(\omega_r\right), n_j\right) \left\| p\left(\omega_r\right)\right\|^{n_j} \left(\mathbf{N} \cdot p\left(\omega_r\right)\right).$$

The $\left\| p\left(\omega_r\right)\right\|^{n_j}$ factor arises because S is computed with a normalized ω_p, so the incident radiance must still be scaled by the magnitude of the lobe. This equation is only an approximation, because the irradiance falloff $\mathbf{N} \cdot \omega_i$ must be computed inside the integral over ω_i. But this can't be stored in an environment map, because it would then be parameterized by both $p(\omega_r)$ and $\mathbf{N}$. The proposed formulation instead weights all incident directions equally within the integral, but weights $S(\omega_p, n)$ by $\mathbf{N} \cdot p\left(\omega_r\right)$. This approximation has not presented a practical problem.

So with one environment map lookup and a few multiplies per lobe, we can render any number of independent BRDFs illuminated by the same set of arbitrary environment maps.

18.4.2 The Shader Code

Listing 18-3 shows the sample code for rendering with preconvolved environment maps. It calls the function f3texCUBE_RGBE_Conv (*env_tex, dir, n*), which samples the preconvolved environment map at the given direction with an LOD computed based on *n*. See Figure 18-5 for the result.

To compactly represent incident radiance values greater than 1.0, the RGBE representation can be used, with the decoding to float3 also performed within this function.

Listing 18-3. An SBRDF Fragment Shader for Environment Maps

```
#define NUM_LOBES 2

// Store Cx, Cy, Cz on range -1.3333 .. 1.3333.
#define SCL (1.0 / (96.0 / 256.0))
#define BIAS (SCL / 2.0)
#define EXSCL 255.0 // Scale exponent to be on 0 .. 255.

float3 ApplyLobe(float3 toeye,
                 float4 lobe_shape,
                 float3 lobe_albedo,
                 float3 Tan,
                 float3 BiN,
                 float3 Nrm,
                 uniform samplerCUBE tex_s)
{
  // Reflect the eye vector in local surface space to get p(wr)
  float3 Cwr_local = lobe_shape.xyz * toeye;

  // Transform lobe peak to world space before env. lookup
  float3 Cwr_world = ToWorld(Cwr_local, Tan, BiN, Nrm);

  // Sample the cube map at the lobe peak direction.
  float sharpness = lobe_shape.w; // This is n.
  float3 incrad = f3texCUBE_RGBE_Conv(tex_s, Cwr_world, sharpness);

  // (length^2)^(n*0.5) = length^n
  float lobelen = pow(dot(Cwr_world, Cwr_world), sharpness * 0.5);

  // Approximate the irradiance falloff at all points
  // by that of the peak dir.
  // This is N dot Cwr in local space.
  float3 irrad = incrad * (Cwr_local.z * lobelen);
  float3 radiance = irrad * lobe_albedo;

  return radiance;
}

struct fromrast
{
  float2 TexUV  : TEXCOORD0; // Surface texcoords
  float3 EyeVec : TEXCOORD1; // Vector to eye (local space)
                             // - needs normalization
```

Listing 18-3 (*continued*). An SBRDF Fragment Shader for Environment Maps

```
    float3 NrmVec : TEXCOORD2;  // Normal (world space)
                               // - needs normalization
    float3 TanVec : TEXCOORD3;  // Tangent (world space)
                               // - needs normalization
};

float4 main(fromrast I,
           uniform sampler2D tex_dif,    // Diffuse
           uniform sampler2D tex_lshp0,  // Lobe shape
           uniform sampler2D tex_lalb0,  // Lobe albedo
           uniform sampler2D tex_lshp1,  // Lobe shape
           uniform sampler2D tex_lalb1,  // Lobe albedo
           uniform samplerCUBE tex_envd, // Cube diffuse env map
           uniform samplerCUBE tex_envs, // Cube specular env map
           uniform float4 Expos) : COLOR
{
  // Preload all the BRDF parameters.
  float4 lobe_shape[NUM_LOBES];
  float4 lobe_albedo[NUM_LOBES];
  for(float p = 0; p < NUM_LOBES; p++)
  {
    lobe_shape[p] = f4tex2D(tex_lshp[p], I.TexUV.xy) *
                      float4(SCL, SCL, SCL, EXSCL) -
                        float4(BIAS, BIAS, BIAS, 0.0);
    lobe_albedo[p] = f4tex2D(tex_lalb[p], I.TexUV.xy);
  }

  float4 dif_albedo = f4tex2D(tex_dif, I.TexUV.xy);

  float3 Nrm = normalize(I.NrmVec.xyz);
  float3 Tan = normalize(I.TanVec.xyz);
  float3 BiN = cross(Nrm, Tan);

  // Vector to eye in local space.
  float3 toeye = normalize(I.EyeVec.xyz);

  // Accumulate exitant radiance off surface due to each lobe
  float3 exrad = float3(0, 0, 0);
  for(int l = 0; l < NUM_LOBES; l++)
    exrad += ApplyLobe(toeye, lobe_shape[l], lobe_albedo[l].xyz,
                       Tan, BiN, Nrm, tex_envs);
```

Listing 18-3 (*continued*). An SBRDF Fragment Shader for Environment Maps

```
    // Add the diffuse term. tex_envd contains the irradiance
    // for a surface with normal direction Nrm.
    float3 irrad = f3texCUBE_RGBE(tex_envd, Nrm);
    exrad = exrad + dif_albedo.xyz * irrad;

    float4 final_col = exrad.xyzz * Expos.xxxx; // Set HDR exposure.
    final_col.w = dif_albedo.w; // Put alpha from map into the pixel.

    return final_col;
}
```

Figure 18-5. Rendering with an Environment Map
An SBRDF made from measured blue paint and aluminum BRDFs with synthetic brush strokes and illuminated with a preconvolved environment map. This BRDF uses three lobes.

18.5 Conclusion

The performance of the discrete light shader is remarkably good considering the great generality of SBRDFs. It consists mainly of a dot product and a `lit()` computation for each lobe and for each light.

Likewise, the performance of the environment map shader is quite good considering that it allows every texel to have a completely different BRDF but still be illuminated by environment maps. The core of this shader is simply the environment map texture lookup, but unfortunately the computation of the lookup coordinates requires a matrix transform. For both shaders, much of the math can easily be performed at half precision with no visual differences.

For simplicity, I omitted spatially varying direction of anisotropy from this chapter. However, the details can be found in McAllister 2002, together with sample code for convolving environment maps, the vertex shaders corresponding to these fragment shaders, and more.

18.6 References

Heidrich, Wolfgang, and H.-P. Seidel. 1999. "Realistic, Hardware-Accelerated Shading and Lighting." In *Proceedings of SIGGRAPH 99*.

Lafortune, E. P. F., S.-C. Foo, et al. 1997. "Non-Linear Approximation of Reflectance Functions." In *Proceedings of SIGGRAPH 97*, pp. 117–126.

McAllister, David K. 2002. "A Generalized Surface Appearance Representation for Computer Graphics." Department of Computer Science, University of North Carolina, Chapel Hill. Available online at **http://www.cs.unc.edu/~davemc/Pubs.html**

McAllister, David K., and Anselmo A. Lastra. 2003. "The SBRDF Home Page." Web site. **http://www.cs.unc.edu/~davemc/SBRDF**

The author would like to thank Ben Cloward, who modeled and textured the hotel lobby scene and acquired the HDR radiance map of the hotel lobby, and Dr. Anselmo Lastra, who was the author's dissertation advisor and contributed to all aspects of the work.

Chapter 19

Image-Based Lighting

Kevin Bjorke
NVIDIA

Cube maps are typically used to create reflections from an environment that is considered to be infinitely far away. But with a small amount of shader math, we can place objects inside a reflection environment of a specific size and location, providing higher quality, image-based lighting (IBL).

19.1 Localizing Image-Based Lighting

Cube-mapped reflections are now a standard part of real-time graphics, and they are key to the appearance of many models. Yet one aspect of such reflections defies realism: the reflection from a cube map always appears as if it's infinitely far away. This limits the usefulness of cube maps for small, enclosed environments, unless we are willing to accept the expense of regenerating cube maps each time our models move relative to one another. See Figure 19-1.

When moving models through an interior environment, it would be useful to have a cube map that behaved as if it were only a short distance away—say, as big as the current room. As our model moved within that room, the reflections would scale appropriately bigger or smaller, according to the model's location in the room. Such an approach could be very powerful, grounding the viewer's sense of the solidity of our simulated set, especially in environments containing windows, video monitors, and other recognizable light sources. See Figure 19-2.

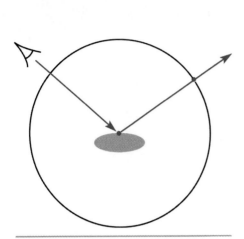

Figure 19-1. Typical "Infinite" Reflections
Simple reflection mapping grabs colors from a cube map that represents an infinitely distant sphere. Reflection vectors are consistent everywhere, relative only to the reflected direction.

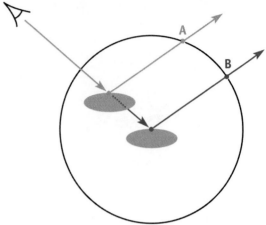

Figure 19-2. Localized Reflections
Choosing a center location and size for the reflection environment lets us create a greater illusion of locality. An infinitely distant map would sample the environment at point B, but a local reflection on the indicated finite sphere would sample at point A. The distortion creates the illusion of a local reflection.

Fortunately, such a localized reflection can be achieved with only a small amount of additional shader math. Developers of some recent games, in fact, have managed to replace a lot of their localized lighting with such an approach.

Let's look at Figure 19-3. We see a reflective object (a large gold mask) in a fairly typical reflection-mapped environment.

Now let's consider Figure 19-4, a different frame from the same short animation. The maps have not changed, but look at the differences in the reflection! The reflection of the window, which was previously small, is now large—and it lines up with the object. In fact, the mask slightly protrudes *through* the surface of the window, and the reflections of the texture-mapped window blinds line up precisely. Likewise, look for the reflected picture frame, now strongly evident in the new image.

At the same time, the green ceiling panels (this photographic cube map shows the lobby of an NVIDIA building), which were evident in the first frame, have now receded in the distance and cover only a small part of the reflection.

Figure 19-3. Reflective Object with Localized Reflection

Figure 19-4. Localized Reflection in a Different Location

This reflection can also be bump mapped, as shown in Figure 19-5 (only bump has been added). See the close-up of this same frame in Figure 19-6.

Figure 19-5. Bump Applied to Localized Reflection

Figure 19-6. Close-Up of Figure 19-5, Showing Reflection Alignment

Unshaded, the minimalism of the geometry is readily apparent in Figure 19-7.

The illustration in Figure 19-8 shows the complete simple scene. The large cube is our model of the room (the shading will be described later). The 3D transform of the room volume is passed to the shader on the reflective object, allowing us to create the correct distortions in the reflection directly in the pixel shader.

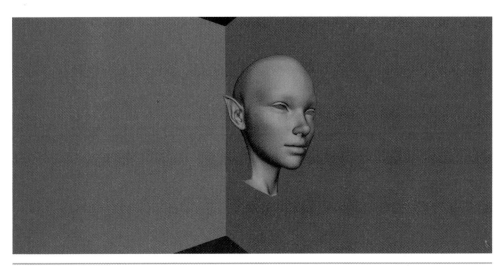

Figure 19-7. Flat-Shaded Geometry from the Sample Scene

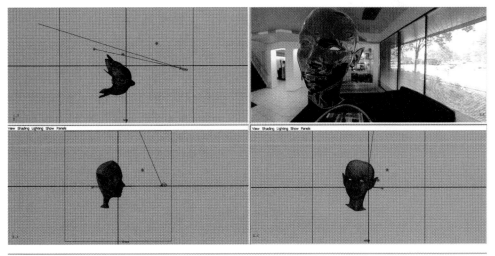

Figure 19-8. Top, Side, and Front Views Showing Camera, Reflective Object, and Simple "Room" Object

19.2 The Vertex Shader

To create a localized frame of reference for lighting, we need to create a new coordinate system. In addition to the standard coordinate spaces such as eye space and object space, we need to create *lighting space*—locations relative to the cube map itself. This new coordinate space will allow us to evaluate object locations relative to the finite dimensions of the cube map.

To simplify the math, we'll assume a fixed "radius" of 1.0 for our cube map—that is, a cube ranging from −1.0 to 1.0 in each dimension (the cube shape is really a convenience for the texturing hardware; we will project its angles against the sphere of all 3D direction vectors). This size makes it relatively easy for animators and lighting/level designers to pose the location and size of the cube map using 3ds max nulls, Maya `place3DTexture` nodes, or similar "dummy" objects.

In our example, we'll pass two `float4x4` transforms to the vertex shader: the matrix of the lighting space (relative to world coordinates) and its inverse transpose. Combined with the world and view transforms, we can express the surface coordinates in lighting space.

We'll pass per-vertex normal, tangent, and binormal data from the CPU application, so that we can also bump map the localized reflection.

```
// data from application vertex buffer
struct appdata {
    float3 Position : POSITION;
    float4 UV       : TEXCOORD0;
    float4 Normal   : NORMAL;
    float4 Tangent  : TEXCOORD1;
    float4 Binormal : TEXCOORD2;
};
```

The data we'll send to the pixel shader will contain values in both world and lighting coordinate systems.

```
// data passed from vertex shader to pixel shader
struct vertexOutput {
    float4 HPosition        : POSITION;
    float4 TexCoord         : TEXCOORD0;
    float3 LightingNormal   : TEXCOORD1;
    float3 LightingTangent  : TEXCOORD2;
```

```
    float3 LightingBinorm   : TEXCOORD3;
    float3 LightingEyeVec    : TEXCOORD4;
    float3 LightingPos       : TEXCOORD5;
};
```

Listing 19-1 shows the vertex shader.

Listing 19-1. Vertex Shader to Generate World-Space and Lighting-Space Coordinates

```
vertexOutput reflectVS(appdata IN,
                       uniform float4x4 WorldViewProjXf,
                       uniform float4x4 WorldITXf,
                       uniform float4x4 WorldXf,
                       uniform float4x4 ViewITXf,
                       uniform float4x4 LightingXf,
                       uniform float4x4 LightingITXf)
{
  vertexOutput OUT;
  OUT.TexCoord = IN.UV;
  float4 Po = float4(IN.Position.xyz,1.0); // pad to "float4"
  OUT.HPosition = mul(WorldViewProjXf, Po);
  float4 Pw = mul(WorldXf, Po); // world coordinates
  float3 WorldEyePos = ViewITXf [3].xyz;
  float4 LightingEyePos = mul(LightingXf, float4(WorldEyePos, 1.0));
  float4 Pu = mul(LightingXf, Pw);
  float4 Nw = mul(WorldITXf, IN.Normal);
  float4 Tw = mul(WorldITXf, IN.Tangent);
  float4 Bw = mul(WorldITXf, IN.Binormal);
  OUT.LightingEyeVec = (LightingEyePos - Pu).xyz;
  OUT.LightingNormal = mul(LightingITXf, Nw).xyz;
  OUT.LightingTangent = mul(LightingITXf, Tw).xyz;
  OUT.LightingBinorm = mul(LightingITXf, Bw).xyz;
  OUT.LightingPos = mul(LightingXf, Pw).xyz;
  return OUT;
}
```

In this example, the point and vector values are transformed twice: once into world space, and then from world space into lighting space. If your CPU application is willing to do a bit more work, you can also preconcatenate these matrices, and transform the position, normal, tangent, and binormal vectors with only one multiplication operator. The method shown is used in CgFX, where the "World" and "WorldIT" transforms are automatically tracked and supplied by the CgFX parser, while the lighting-space transforms are supplied by user-defined values (say, from a DCC application).

19.3 The Fragment Shader

Given the location of the shaded points and their shading vectors, relative to lighting space, the pixel portion is relatively straightforward. We look at the reflection vector expressed in lighting space, and starting from the surface location in lighting space, we intersect it with a sphere of radius = 1.0, centered at the origin of light space, by solving the quadratic equation of that sphere.

As a "safety precaution," we assign a default color of red (float4(1, 0, 0, 0)): if a point is shaded outside the sphere (so there can be no reflection), that point will appear red, making any error obvious during development. The fragment shader is shown in Listing 19-2.

Listing 19-2. Localized-Reflection Pixel Shader

```
float4 reflectPS(vertexOutput IN,
                uniform samplerCUBE EnvMap,
                uniform sampler2D NormalMap,
                uniform float4 SurfColor,
                uniform float Kr, // intensity of reflection
                uniform float KrMin, // typical: 0.05 * Kr
                uniform float FresExp, // typical: 5.0
                uniform float Bumpiness // amount of bump
                ) : COLOR
{
   float3 Nu = normalize(IN.LightingNormal);
   // for bump mapping, we will alter "Nu" to get "Nb"
   float3 Tu = normalize(IN.LightingTangent);
   float3 Bu = normalize(IN.LightingBinorm);
   float3 bumps = Bumpiness *
               (tex2D(NormalMap, IN.TexCoord.xy).xyz - (0.5).xxx);
   float3 Nb = Nu + (bumps.x * Tu + bumps.y * Bu);
   Nb = normalize(Nb); // expressed in user-coord space
   float3 Vu = normalize(IN.LightingEyeVec);
   float vdn = dot(Vu, Nb); // or "Nu" if unbumped - see text
   // "fres" attenuates the strength of the reflection
   //   according to Fresnel's law
   float fres = KrMin + (Kr - KrMin) * pow((1.0 - abs(vdn)), FresExp);
   float3 reflVect = normalize(reflect(Vu, Nb)); // yes, normalize
   // now we intersect "reflVect" with a sphere of radius 1.0
   float b = -2.0 * dot(reflVect, IN.LightingPos);
   float c = dot(IN.LightingPos, IN.LightingPos) - 1.0;
   float discrim = b * b - 4.0 * c;
```

Listing 19-2 (*continued*). Localized-Reflection Pixel Shader

```
  bool hasIntersects = false;
  float4 reflColor = float4(1, 0, 0, 0);
  if (discrim > 0) {
    // pick a small error value very close to zero as "epsilon"
    hasIntersects = ((abs(sqrt(discrim) - b) / 2.0) > 0.00001);
  }
  if (hasIntersects) {
    // determine where on the unit sphere reflVect intersects
    reflVect = nearT * reflVect - IN.LightingPos;
    // reflVect.y = -reflVect.y; // optional - see text
    // now use the new intersection location as the 3D direction
    reflColor = fres * texCUBE(EnvMap, reflVect);
  }
  float4 result = SurfColor * reflColor;
  return result;
}
```

19.3.1 Additional Shader Details

We supply a few additional optional terms, to enhance the shader's realism.

The first enhancement is for surface color: this is supplied for metal surfaces, because the reflections from metals will pick up the color of that metal. For dielectric materials such as plastic or water, you can eliminate this term or assign it as white.

The second set of terms provides Fresnel-style attenuation of the reflection. These terms can be eliminated for purely metallic surfaces, but they are crucial for realism on plastics and other dielectrics. The math here uses a power function: if user control over the Fresnel approximation isn't needed, the falloff can be encoded as a 1D texture and indexed against abs(vdn).

For some models, you may find it looks better to attenuate the Fresnel against the *un-bumped* normal: this can help suppress high-frequency "sparklies" along object edges. In that case, use Nu instead of Nb when calculating vdn.

For pure, smooth metals, the Fresnel attenuation is zero: just drop the calculation of fres and use Kr instead. But in the real world, few materials are truly pure; a slight drop in reflectivity is usually seen even on fairly clean metal surfaces, and the drop is pronounced on dirty surfaces. Likewise, dirty metal reflections will often tend toward less-saturated color than the "pure" metal. Use your best judgment, balancing your performance and complexity needs.

Try experimenting with the value of the `FresExp` exponent. See Figure 19-9. While Christophe Schlick (1994), the originator of this approximation, specified an exponent of 5.0, using lower values can create a more layered, or lacquered, appearance. An exponent of 4.0 can also be quickly calculated by two multiplies, rather than the potentially expensive `pow()` function.

The shader in Listing 19-2 can optionally flip the y portion of the reflection vector. This optional step was added to accommodate heterogeneous development environments where cube maps created for DirectX and OpenGL may be intermixed (the cube map specifications for these APIs differ in their handling of "up"). For example, a scene may be developed in Maya (OpenGL) for a game engine developed in DirectX.

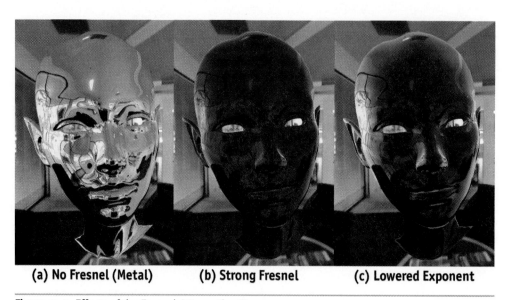

(a) No Fresnel (Metal)   (b) Strong Fresnel   (c) Lowered Exponent

Figure 19-9. Effects of the Fresnel-Attenuation Terms
(a) This image has no attenuation. (b) This image has typical nonmetallic attenuation, with a small `reflMin` *and a Fresnel exponent of 5.0. (c) This image has the exponent reduced to 2.0 for a "lacquered" look.*

19.4 Diffuse IBL

Cube maps can also be used to determine diffuse lighting. Programs such as Debevec's HDRShop can integrate the full Lambertian contributions from a cube-mapped lighting environment, so that the diffuse contribution can be looked up simply by passing the surface normal to this preconvolved cube map (as opposed to reflective lighting, where we would pass a reflection vector based on both the surface normal and the eye location).

Localizing the diffuse vector, unfortunately, provides a less satisfying result than localizing the reflections, because the diffuse-lighting map has encoded its notion of the point's "visible hemisphere." These integrations will be incorrect for values away from the center of the sphere. Depending on your application, these errors may be acceptable or not. For some cases, linearly interpolating between multiple diffuse maps may also provide a degree of localization. Such maps tend to have very low frequencies. This is a boon to use for simple lighting, because errors must be large before they are noticeable (if noticeable at all). Some applications, therefore, will be able to perform all lighting calculations simply by using diffuse and specular cube maps.

By combining diffuse and specular lighting into cube maps, you may find that some applications have no need of any additional lighting information.

19.5 Shadows

Using shadows with IBL complicates matters but does not preclude their use. Stencil shadow volume techniques can be applied here, as can shadow maps. In both cases, it may be wise to provide a small ambient-lighting term (applied in an additional pass when using stencil shadow volumes) to avoid objects disappearing entirely into darkness (unless that's what you want).

With image-based lighting, it's natural to ask: *Where does the shadow come from?* Shadows can function as powerful visual cues even if they are not perfectly "motivated." That is, the actual source of the shadow may not exactly correspond to the light source. In the case of IBL, this is almost certainly true: shadows from IBL would need to match a large number of potential light directions, often resulting in a very soft shadow. Yet techniques such as shadow mapping and stencil shadowing typically result in shadows with hard edges or only slight softening.

Fortunately, this is often not a problem if the directions of the shadow sources are chosen wisely. Viewers will often accept highly artificial shadows, because the spatial and graphical aspects of shadows are usually more important than as a means to "justify" the lighting (in fact, most television shows and movies tend to have very "unjustified" lighting). The best bet, when adding shadows to an arbitrary IBL scene, is to pick the direction in your cube map with the brightest area. Barring that, aim the shadow where you think it will provide the most graphic "snap" to the dimensionality of your models.

Shadows in animation are most crucial for connecting characters and models to their surroundings. The shadow of a character on the ground tells you if he is standing, running, or leaping in relationship to the ground surface. If his feet touch their shadow, he's on the ground (we call shadows drawn for this purpose *contact shadows*). If not, he's in the air.

This characteristic of shadowing, exploited for many years by cel animators, suggests that it may often be advantageous to worry *only* about the contact shadows in an IBL scene. If all we care about is the shadow of the character on the ground, then we can make the simplifying assumption when rendering that the shadow doesn't need to be evaluated for depth, only for color. This means we can just create a projected black-and-white or full-color shadow, potentially with blur, and just assume that it *always* hits objects that access that shadow map. This avoids depth comparisons and gives us a gain in effective texture bandwidth (because simple eight-bit textures can be used).

In such a scenario, characters' surfaces don't access their own shadow maps; that is, they don't self-shadow. Their lighting instead comes potentially exclusively from IBL. Game players will still see the character shadows on the environment, providing them with the primary benefit of shadows: a solid connection between the character and the 3D game environment.

19.6 Using Localized Cube Maps As Backgrounds

In the illustrations in this chapter, we can see the reflective object interacting with the background. Without the presence of the background, the effect might be nearly unnoticeable.

In many cases, we can make cube maps from 3D geometry and just apply the map(s) to the objects within that environment—while rendering the environment normally. Alternatively, as we've done in Figure 19-10, we can use the map *as* the environment, and project it onto simpler geometry.

Figure 19-10. Lines Showing the Edges of the Room Cube Object
The transform of this unit-size cube is used to calculate the reflection coordinate system and to color the background itself.

For the background cube, we also pass the same transform for the unit-cube room. In fact, for the demo scene, we simply pass the room shader its own transform. The simple geometry is just that—geometry—and doesn't need to have UV mapping coordinates or even surface normals.

As we can also see from Figure 19-10, using a simple cube in place of full scene geometry has definite limits! Note the "bent" ceiling on the left. Using proxy geometry in this way usually works best when the camera is near the center of the cube. Synthetic environments (as opposed to photographs, such as this one) can also benefit by lining up flat surfaces such as walls and ceilings exactly with the boundaries of the lighting space.

```
// data from application vertex buffer
struct appdataB {
  float3 Position : POSITION;
};
```

The vertex shader will pass a view vector and the usual required clip-space position.

```
// data passed from vertex shader to pixel shader
struct vertexOutputB {
  float4 HPosition : POSITION;
  float3 UserPos   : TEXCOORD0;
};
```

Listing 19-3 shows the vertex shader itself.

Listing 19-3. Vertex Shader for Background Cube Object

```
vertexOutput xfBoxVS(appdataB IN,
                        uniform float4x4 WorldViewProj,
                        uniform float4x4 WorldIT,
                        uniform float4x4 World,
                        uniform float4x4 ViewIT,
                        uniform float4x4 UserXf)
{
  vertexOutputB OUT;
  float4 Po = float4(IN.Position.xyz, 1.0);
  OUT.HPosition = mul(WorldViewProj, Po);
  float4 Pw = mul(World, Po);
  OUT.UserPos = mul(UserXf, Pw).xyz;
  return OUT;
}
```

The pixel shader just uses the fragment shader to derive a direct texture lookup into the cube map, along with an optional tint color. See Listing 19-4.

Listing 19-4. Pixel Shader for Background Cube Object

```
float4 xfBoxPS(vertexOutput IN,
              uniform samplerCUBE EnvMap,
              uniform float4 SurfColor) : COLOR
{
  float4 reflColor = SurfColor * texCUBE(EnvMap, -IN.UserPos);
  return reflColor;
}
```

This shader is designed specifically to work well when projected onto a (potentially distorted) cube. Using variations with other simple geometries, such as a sphere, a cylinder, or a flat backplane, is also straightforward.

19.7 Conclusion

Image-based lighting provides a complex yet inexpensive alternative to numerically intensive lighting calculations. Adding a little math to this texturing method can give us a much wider range of effects than "simple" IBL, providing a stronger sense of place to our 3D images.

19.8 Further Reading

Schlick, Christophe. 1994. "An Inexpensive BRDF Model for Physically-Based Rendering." *Computer Graphics Forum* 13(3), pp. 233–246. *This article presents the Fresnel equation approximation widely used throughout the graphics industry—so widely used, in fact, that some programmers mistakenly believe the approximation* is *the Fresnel equation.*

Paul Debevec provides a number of useful IBL tools and papers at **http://www.debevec.org**

Ramamoorthi, Ravi, and Pat Hanrahan. 2001. "An Efficient Representation for Irradiance Environment Maps." In *Proceedings of SIGGRAPH 2001. This article on diffuse convolution using spherical harmonics is available online at* **http://graphics.stanford.edu/papers/envmap**

Apodaca, Anthony A., and Larry Gritz, eds. 1999. *Advanced RenderMan: Creating CGI for Motion Pictures.* Morgan Kaufmann. *In this book, Larry Gritz describes a similar reflection algorithm using the RenderMan shading language.*

Chapter 20

Texture Bombing

R. Steven Glanville
NVIDIA

Textures are useful for adding visual detail to geometry, but they don't work as well when extended to cover large areas such as a field of flowers, or many similar objects such as a city full of buildings. Such uses require either a very large amount of texture data or repetition of the same pattern, resulting in an undesirable, regular look. *Texture bombing* is a procedural technique that places small images at irregular intervals to help reduce such pattern artifacts.

20.1 Texture Bombing 101

The basic idea behind texture bombing is to divide UV space into a regular grid of cells. We then place an image within each cell at a random location, using a noise or pseudo-random number function. The final result is the composite of these images over the background.

It's not very efficient to actually composite images in this manner, because we may have hundreds of images to combine. We may also want to compute the image procedurally, which is somewhat incompatible with compositing. We'll discuss both techniques in this chapter. To start, let's view things from a pixel's perspective and try to pare down the work. The first step is to find the cell containing the pixel. We need to compute each cell's coordinates in a way that lets us quickly locate neighbor cells, as you will see later on. We'll use these coordinates to access all of the cell's unique parameters, such as the image's location within that cell. Finally, we sample the image at its location within the cell and combine it with a default background color. We assume here that a sample is either 100 percent opaque or transparent, to simplify the compositing step.

It's not quite this simple, however. If a cell's image is located close to the edge of its cell, or if it is larger than a cell, it will cross into adjacent cells. Therefore, we need to consider neighboring cells' images as well. Large cell images would require that we sample many adjacent images. If we limit the image size to be no bigger than a cell, then we need to sample only nine cells: both side cells, those above and below, and the four cells at the corners. We can reduce the number of required samples to four by introducing a few minor restrictions on the images.

20.1.1 Finding the Cell

The cell's coordinates are computed simply, using a floor function of the pixel's UV parameters:

```
float2 scaledUV = UV * scale;
int2 cell = floor(scaledUV);
```

Note that the cell's coordinates are integral. Adjacent cells differ by 1 in either `cell.x` or `cell.y`. The `scale` factor allows us to vary the size as needed. Finding our location within the cell simply requires a subtraction:

```
float2 offset = scaledUV - cell;
```

20.1.2 Sampling the Image

Before we can sample the image, we need to determine its location. We use a two-dimensional texture filled with pseudo-random numbers for this task. The coordinates for the sample are derived from the cell's coordinates, scaled by small values.

```
float2 randomUV = cell * float2(0.037, 0.119);
fixed4 random = tex2D(randomTex, randomUV);
```

There's nothing magic about the scale factors used to compute `randomUV`. They map the integral cell name to somewhere within the random texture and should have the property of mapping nearby cells to uncorrelated values. Any value large enough to separate adjacent cells a distance of more than one texel should suffice.

We use the first two components of the texture for the image's location within the cell, which must be subtracted from the pixel's offset within the cell. If the alpha component of the image is not zero, then the image's color is used; otherwise, the original color is used.

```
fixed4 image = tex2D(imageTex, offset.xy - random.xy);
if (image.w > 0.0)
  color.xyz = image.xyz;
```

Putting this together into sample program texbomb_1.cg, and using the background and image patterns in Figure 20-1a and 20-1b, yields the result shown in Figure 20-1c. (All the sample programs shown in this chapter are included on the book's CD and are available on the book's Web site.)

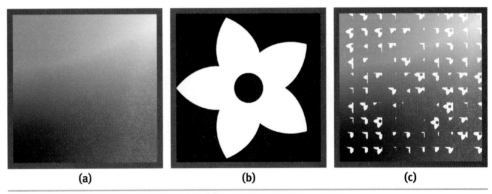

(a)   (b)   (c)

Figure 20-1. First Attempt at Texture Bombing
(a) The background and (b) flower pattern used in the examples, and (c) the output of
texbomb_1.cg.

It's not quite there. The images are clipped by the edges of the cell. The only time that the full image is visible is when its offset is zero. We also have to look for images in adjacent cells.

20.1.3 Adjacent Cells' Images

So far we've sampled only the current cell's image. We also need to check for overlapping images from adjacent cells. Because we've limited the image offset relative to a cell to be in the range 0 to 1, an image can overlap only those cells above and to the right of its home cell. Thus we need sample only four cells: the current cell plus those cells below and to the left of our cell. See Listing 20-1.

Listing 20-1. Extending the Sampling to Four Cells

```
for (i = -1; i <= 0; i++) {
  for (j = -1; j <= 0; j++) {
    float2 cell_t = cell + float2(i, j);
    float2 offset_t = offset - float2(i, j);
    randomUV = cell_t.xy * float2(0.037, 0.119);
    random = tex2D(randomTex, randomUV);
    image = tex2D(imageTex, offset_t - random.xy);
    if (image.w > 0.0)
      color = image;
  }
}
}
```

20.1.4 Image Priority

There's something not quite right. When two images overlap, the one to the upper right is always on top, because it was the last one tested. This might be acceptable for scales on a fish or shingles, but we'd generally like to avoid this effect. Introducing a priority for each cell, in which the highest priority image wins, solves this problem. We use the w component of the cell's random parameter for the priority and change the if test from Listing 20-1 to that shown in Listing 20-2.

Listing 20-2. Adding Image Priority

```
fixed priority = -1;
. . .
if (random.w > priority && image.w > 0.0) {
  color = image;
  priority = random.w;
}
```

Figure 20-2 shows an image from this revised program, called texbomb_2.cg.

20.1.5 Procedural Images

There is no reason that the image has to come from a texture. Procedural images work just as well. In Listing 20-3, we've replaced the image sample with a procedurally generated circle of radius 0.5.

Figure 20-2. The Output of `texbomb_2.cg`

Listing 20-3. Using a Procedurally Generated Circle

```
offset_t -= float2(0.5, 0.5) + (float2) random;
fixed radius2 = dot(offset_t, offset_t);
if (random.w > priority && radius2 < 0.25) {
  color = tex2D(randomTex, randomUV + float2(0.13, 0.4));
  priority = random.w;
}
```

A second sample of the random texture gives the circle's color, as shown in Figure 20-3, produced from the program `gem_proc_2.cg`.

Multiple Images per Cell

Using only one image per cell can lead to a regular-looking pattern, especially when the cells are small. There isn't enough variance to hide the grid nature of the computation, making the distribution look too regular. To counter this tendency, we can increase the number of images in each cell by simply adding a loop around the image sample and offsetting the coordinates used for looking up the random numbers. See Listing 20-4.

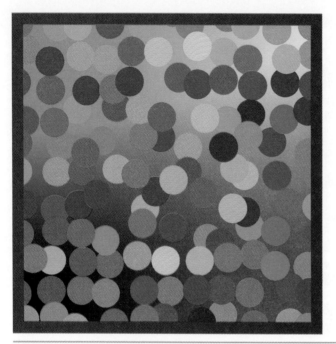

Figure 20-3. The Output of `gem_proc_2.cg`

Listing 20-4. Sampling Multiple Circles per Cell Reduces Grid-Like Patterns

```
randomUV = cell_t.xy * float2(0.037, 0.119);
for (k = 0; k < NUMBER_OF_SAMPLES; k++) {
  random = tex2D(randomTex, randomUV);
  randomUV += float2(0.03, 0.17);
  image = tex2D(imageTex, offset_t - random.xy);
  . . .
}
```

We offset the coordinates for each pass in the loop to prevent sampling the same value each time. See Figure 20-4.

We can also vary the number of images per cell by using another random value, or even by simply setting the initial priority to something higher than 0, such as 0.5. Then each image has a probability of 0.5 that it will be rejected. This variation further increases the apparent randomness of the result, as shown in Figure 20-5. Here the size of the cells has been reduced to show a larger number.

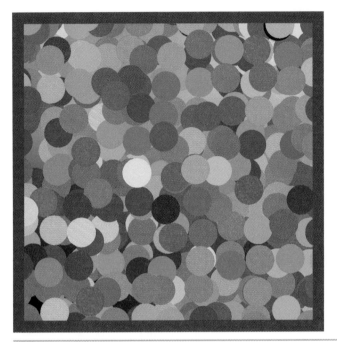

Figure 20-4. Sampling Three Circles per Cell

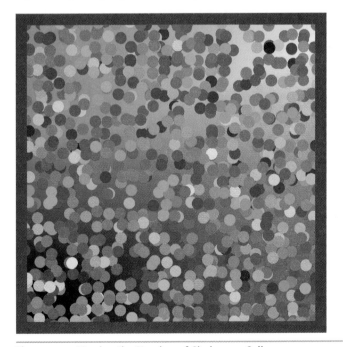

Figure 20-5. Varying the Number of Circles per Cell

20.1.6 Random Image Selection from Multiple Choices

Another dimension of variation can be added by selecting from one of multiple images for each choice. One way to do this is to tile the images into a single texture and use the z component of the random texture as an index into these images. It's simpler to arrange the images in a single horizontal row, as shown in Figure 20-6. The black area corresponds to the transparent region and has an alpha component of zero.

Figure 20-6. Storing Four Images in a Single Texture Map

Then all we need to do is change the image lookup call to select from one of four sub-images. Scaling the z component of the random vector and computing the floor yields an integer `index` of a random image. We need to clamp the x coordinate to prevent adjacent images from being sampled, add the value of `index`, and scale by 1/*number of images*.

```
float index = floor(random.z * NUM_IMAGES_PER_ROW);
float2 uv = offset_t.xy - random.xy;
uv.x = (saturate(uv.x) + index) / NUM_IMAGES_PER_ROW;
image = tex2D(imageTex, uv);
```

The result is shown in Figure 20-7. Note that the images need at least a two-pixel border separating them from the edges of their region, or else texture sampling will cause artifacts.

If ordinary mipmaps are used for a multiple-image texture, then a two-pixel border between images won't be sufficient. A sample near an image's edge taken from a higher-level map can blend with the adjacent image. You can reduce such problems by increasing the width of the border, or by constructing the mipmaps with a similar border at each level. You may also want to clamp the maximum mipmap level to avoid degenerate cases, or you can simply reduce the image size to zero.

Figure 20-7. Random Image Selection

20.2 Technical Considerations

There are a couple of implementation details that need discussing.

It is important to choose the right minification filter used for the random-number texture. When mipmapping is enabled, dependent texture reads such as those used to get the pseudo-random numbers generate a level of detail (LOD) based on the difference of the UV values in the current and adjacent pixels. Within a cell, `randomUV` is the same for all pixels. The difference is therefore zero and LOD 0 is sampled, yielding a (possibly bilinearly interpolated) value from the original random numbers. However, at the boundary between two cells, the value of `randomUV` changes abruptly. Thus, a higher mipmap level is used, and an artifact is introduced.

Specifying a minification filter of `LINEAR` or `NEAREST` for the random texture eliminates these artifacts, because they force all samples to LOD 0. It's better to use a `NEAREST` filter for static textures. A `LINEAR` filter reduces the variance of the random numbers and tends to keep the images closer to the center of their cells. But if you are animating the images' positions, then you will want to use `LINEAR` for smooth motion.

The wrap mode for the texture image should be set to CLAMP. Otherwise, we'll see ghost samples where we shouldn't. Alternatively, we can clamp the coordinates to the range [0..1]. Most GPUs have hardware to do this at no cost.

20.2.1 Efficiency Issues

Reducing execution time is always important for pixel shaders, and texture bombing is no exception. Dependent texture samples, repeated evaluation of the basic shading for multiple cells, and even multiple samples per cell combine to hinder performance. The resulting shaders can be hundreds of instructions in length.

For example, the complete daisy image from `texbomb_2.cg` shown earlier in Figure 20-2 requires eight texture samples and 44 math instructions. The first procedural image from `gem_proc_2.cg`, shown earlier in Figure 20-3, requires eight texture samples and 62 math instructions.

Some key optimizations can help performance considerably. When possible, move the final color texture sample out of the inner loop. Instead of sampling the texture multiple times, save the coordinates of the resulting sample in a variable and do one final sample at the end of the program. This works well for procedural shapes, such as circles, and for Voronoi-like regions, because the decision to use a particular color is not based on the value of that sample. (See Section 20.3.5 for more on Voronoi regions.) Unfortunately, this trick does not work for an image when you need the alpha component to determine if that value is transparent or not.

On GeForce FX hardware, use fixed and half-precision variables when possible. This allows more instructions to be executed per shader pass and reduces the number of registers needed to run a program. Unless you are rendering to a float frame buffer, colors fit well in less precision. Texture coordinates, however, normally should be stored in full float precision.

20.3 Advanced Features

Texture bombing can be extended in a variety of ways for an interesting range of effects.

20.3.1 Scaling and Rotating

One simple addition is to randomly scale or rotate each image for further variation. You must be careful to stay within the area sampled by the adjacent cells that the image can cover. For scaling, it's fairly obvious that you can only reduce the size, unless you are willing to test more than four cells per pixel.

Rotated images have similar limitations. The opaque part of the image should lie within a circle of diameter 1 centered in the cell. If it were to exceed this size into the corners, then these portions of the rotated image could extend farther than 0.5 cells width vertically or horizontally from their base cell. The four-cell sample algorithm would miss these parts as well.

20.3.2 Controlled Variable Density

Sometimes you want to control artistically the pattern of, say, leaves on the ground. Using a pseudo-random density doesn't handle this case well. Instead, you can use a specific density texture and paint the probability for a leaf to appear as you wish. This texture would be read as a normal UV-based sample, and that value would be used, as in the preceding example, to set the probability that a leaf appears.

20.3.3 Procedural 3D Bombing

Once you've decided to use procedural textures, there's really no reason to limit the cells to a 2D UV space. Why not extend the idea into 3D using the object-space coordinates of a pixel to derive the color? In Listing 20-5, we divide object space into unit cubes. We can still use a 2D pseudo-random texture, but we need to include the third dimension as a component in computing the sample's coordinates. Scaling the z coordinate and adding it to the x and y gives a good result.

Listing 20-5. Procedural 3D Bombing

```
for (i = -1; i <= 0; i++) {
  for (j = -1; j <= 0; j++) {
    for (k = -1; k <= 0; k++) {
      cell_t = cell + float3(i, j, k);
      offset_t = offset - float3(i, j, k);
      randomUV = cell_t.xy * float2(0.037, 0.119) +
                 cell_t.z * 0.003;
      . . .
    }
  }
}
```

You have to extend the number of cells sampled to three dimensions as well, for a total of eight samples. Three-dimensional texture bombing is inherently more expensive than 2D for this reason. The example in Figure 20-8 shows procedurally generated spheres. It uses a simple dot-product diffuse-lighting model to show the depth.

Figure 20-8. A Procedural 3D Texture with One Sphere per Cell

The full shader body is shown in Listing 20-6, for clarity.

Listing 20-6. The Procedural 3D Texture Program

```
priority = -1;
for (i = -1; i <= 0; i++) {
  for (j = -1; j <= 0; j++) {
    for (k = -1; k <= 0; k++) {
      cell_t = cell + float3(i, j, k);
      offset_t = offset - float3(i, j, k);
      randomUV = cell_t.xy * float2(0.037, 0.119) +
                 cell_t.z * 0.003;
      random = tex2D(randomTex, randomUV);
      offset_t3 = offset_t -(float3(0.5, 0.5, 0.5) +
                            (float3) random);
```

Listing 20-6 (*continued*). The Procedural 3D Texture Program

```
      radius2 = dot(offset_t3, offset_t3);
      if (random.w > priority && radius2 < 0.5) {
        color = tex2D(randomTex, randomUV + float2(0.13, 0.4));
        priority = random.w;
      }
    }
  }
}

float factor = dot(normal.xyz, float3(0.5, 0.75, -0.3)) * 0.7 + 0.3;
color.xyz = color.xyz * factor;
return color;
```

20.3.4 Time-Varying Textures

You can easily animate texture-bombed shaders. All that's required is varying one or more of the pseudo-random parameters based on time. If you sample the pseudo-random number texture with a bilinear filter, then many properties will animate fairly smoothly. However, you may sometimes notice the ramp-like nature of this filtering, especially for moving objects, because the human eye is good at detecting discontinuities in the direction of motion.

```
  random = tex2D(randomTex, randomUV * time * 0.0001);
```

In the code shown here, the value of time is expressed in seconds. The animation would go by too quickly if it were not scaled down by an appropriate factor. The scale factor depends on the rate of the animation and the size of the pseudo-random texture. If the texture used in the example is 1024 by 1024, then a new texel will be sampled approximately every 10 seconds:

$$rate\ of\ change = (scale\ factor \times time)\ /\ texture\ size.$$

20.3.5 Voronoi-Related Cellular Methods

An interesting variation on texture bombing is depicting Voronoi regions on a plane. See Steven Worley's 1996 SIGGRAPH paper for more information about this texturing technique. In a nutshell, given a plane and a set of points on that plane, a point's Voronoi region is the area in the plane that is closest to that particular point. You can see examples of Voronoi-like patterns in the shapes of cells on leaves or skin, cracks in dried mud, and to a certain extent in reptilian skin patterns, though these tend to be more regular. A typical view of Voronoi regions is shown in Figure 20-9.

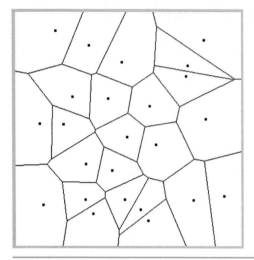

Figure 20-9. Sample Voronoi Regions

We can make these patterns with a small change to the basic texture-bombing code. Starting with the procedural circles' code shown earlier in Listing 20-3, we'll use the distance to a point as the priority, instead of the value in `random.w`, and we won't check to see if we're outside the radius of our circle. See Listing 20-7.

We use the square of the distance instead of the actual distance to avoid computing a square root. Each region is given a randomly assigned color. The result is shown in Figure 20-10a.

Listing 20-7. Computing Voronoi Regions

```
float priority = 999;
. . .
radius2 = dot(offset_t2, offset_t2);
if (radius2 < priority) {
  color = tex2D(randomTex, randomUV + float2(0.13, 0.4));
  priority = radius2;
}
```

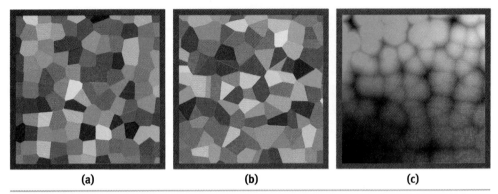

(a) **(b)** **(c)**

Figure 20-10. Voronoi Regions
Regions with (a) one point per cell and (b) three points per cell. (c) A web-like effect derived from (b).

Notice that the rectangular grid structure of the algorithm is fairly apparent in Figure 20-10a. By increasing the number of samples, we can reduce this regularity considerably. Figure 20-10b uses three samples per cell, with cells scaled by a factor of sqrt(3) to keep the average Voronoi region size the same.

On a technical note, the cells created by this algorithm aren't guaranteed to be Voronoi regions. The point in a neighboring cell, P_n, can be in the opposite corner from our sample, but the point in the cell past that, P_{n+1}, may be on the close edge, such that P_{n+1} is actually closer. However, we don't include the cell belonging to P_{n+1} in our computations. Practically speaking, this doesn't happen very often, and the regions are still useful. Increasing the number of samples per cell reduces the probability of this problem occurring.

You can create many interesting effects with these cells. Figure 20-10c has the same cell pattern as Figure 20-10b, but it uses the square of the distance from the closest point to modulate the background color.

20.4 Conclusion

Texture bombing and related cellular techniques can add visual richness to your shaders. Using a table of pseudo-random numbers stored in a texture, and a little programming, you can amplify the variability of an image or a set of images and reduce the repetitive look of large textured regions.

20.5 References

Apodaca, A. A., and L. Gritz. 2002. *Advanced RenderMan*, pp. 255–261. Morgan Kaufmann.

Ebert, D. S., F. K. Musgrave, D. Peachy, K. Perlin, and S. Worley. 2003. *Texturing and Modeling: A Procedural Approach*, 3rd ed., pp. 91–94. Morgan Kaufmann.

Lefebvre, S., and F. Neyret. 2003. "Pattern Based Procedural Textures." *ACM Symposium on Interactive 3D Graphics 2003*.

Schacter, B. J., and N. Ahuja. 1979. "Random Pattern Generation Processes." *Computer Graphics and Image Processing* 10, pp. 95–114.

Worley, Steven P. 1996. "A Cellular Texture Basis Function." In *Proceedings of SIGGRAPH 96*, pp. 291–294.

PART IV
IMAGE PROCESSING

When most people think of GPU power, they focus on purely 3D applications, yet the pictures we actually see on our monitors are 2D. Programmable pixel shaders provide personal computers with unprecedented image-processing power, extending our abilities for both 2D and 3D development.

Graphic designers and illustrators have long used complex controls in still-image photo-editing applications, but such programs can process only one picture at a time. The newest GPUs can perform these previously slow operations at interactive rates, allowing us to apply the full power of complex compositing and color-control applications not just to still images and layouts, but also to full-motion video and gameplay. Complex video coloring that previously required an entire suite of specialized equipment can now be done on a laptop PC.

Understanding color spaces is one aspect of image processing, whether we are mapping 2D images into new 2D images or rendering 3D scenes to the screen. Equally important is understanding how images of varying sizes and shapes can be filtered during manipulations to provide smooth, fast results. GPUs are capable of executing the same filtering algorithms as CPU-based image-processing tools, but they also can invoke new hardware-accelerated methods.

In **Chapter 21, "Real-Time Glow," Greg James** and **John O'Rorke** give us an example of how 3D gameplay can be enhanced with 2D image processing. By adding 2D lighting effects such as glows, they show how a little image processing can completely alter the feel and play-action of 3D imagery. Once you see how these results are accomplished, you may not be able to enjoy 3D imagery without them again.

In **Chapter 22, "Color Controls,"** I extend the discussion of image processing in games to the uses and methods of technical and artistic color control, for moving imagery into and out of unusual color spaces, as well as quickly adding polished color-tuning to any scene, 2D or 3D. The colors we see in print and on television today are almost universally color-controlled. Developers should be able to understand and use the same tools for their game engines.

In **Chapter 23, "Depth of Field: A Survey of Techniques," Joe Demers** writes about using GPU operations to create depth-of-field effects in real time. By following a few simple filtering rules, developers can simulate the complex effects of real-world camera focusing, film saturation, and more on 3D models.

Chapter 24, "High-Quality Filtering," generalizes image filtering and effects to images of arbitrary size, applying the notion of filter kernels and analytic calculation to the problem of 2D and 3D antialiasing. Significantly, we can see that some "classical" antialiasing and filtering problems are best solved on the GPU by using hardware accelerations not typically available to CPU-based approaches.

Matt Pharr describes an unusual application of texturing in 2D space in **Chapter 25, "Fast Filter-Width Estimates with Texture Maps."** By cleverly manipulating the results of texture operations, he's able to determine local partial derivatives of complex functions, even when using hardware profiles that don't provide direct hardware support for these operations.

In **Chapter 26, "The OpenEXR Image File Format," Florian Kainz, Rod Bogart,** and **Drew Hess** of Industrial Light & Magic (ILM) describe the OpenEXR standard, a new, high-dynamic-range image format that's quickly spreading through the top tiers of motion-picture computer imaging. OpenEXR is a key tool for developers looking to exploit the new world of image-based lighting, and the ILM team shows how they've adopted GPU processing speed to make OpenEXR a valuable day-to-day tool at ILM—not just for 3D work, but also for image acquisition, compositing, and playback—again, in real time.

Of course, to apply these techniques requires the developer to manage image-processing tasks. In **Chapter 27, "A Framework for Image Processing," Frank Jargstorff** presents a scheme for 2D image processing that's flexible and applicable to a variety of applications. The framework can even be extended to mix GPU and CPU operations in a way that's fairly transparent to developers of games, photo applications, and video applications alike.

Kevin Bjorke, NVIDIA

Chapter 21

Real-Time Glow

Greg James
NVIDIA

John O'Rorke
Monolith Productions

Glows and halos of light appear everywhere in the world, and they provide powerful visual cues about brightness and atmosphere. In viewing computer graphics, film, and print, the intensity of light reaching the eye is limited, so the only way to distinguish intense sources of light is by their surrounding glow and halos (Nakamae et al. 1990). These glows reproduce the visual effects of intense light and fool the observer into perceiving very bright sources. Even a subtle glow around an object gives the perception that it is brighter than an object with no glow. In everyday life, these glows and halos are caused by light scattering in the atmosphere or within our eyes (Spencer 1995). With modern graphics hardware, the effects can be reproduced with a few simple rendering operations. This allows us to fill real-time rendered scenes with bright, interesting objects that appear more realistic or more fantastic, and it is an elegant means to overcome the traditionally low-dynamic-range, flat look of real-time graphics.

Several games are now using various techniques to produce glows and halos of light. Among these are *Splinter Cell*, *Project Gotham Racing*, *Wreckless* (Kawase 2003), and *Halo 2*. Another notable and widespread use of glow can be seen in Pixar's film *Finding Nemo*, where glows convey the murkiness of seawater and help to set the mood for various scenes. This chapter focuses on a particular technique developed for the recently released *Tron 2.0* game, produced by Buena Vista Interactive and developed by Monolith Productions. The technique was designed to produce large-area glows over the entire screen, to be easily authored and controlled for a large set of game assets, and to

Figure 21-1. A *Tron 2.0* Cityscape With and Without Glow
Top: A scene with the glow effect. Bottom: The same scene without glow.
Courtesy of Buena Vista Interactive/Disney Productions.

be fast enough for a first-person shooter game running at more than 60 frames per second. The results are shown in Figures 21-1 and 21-2. Here, the effect conveys the vibrancy and electronic power of the *Tron 2.0* computer universe, though the technique can also be applied to create other effects, including depth of field, light scattering, edge detection, and image processing.

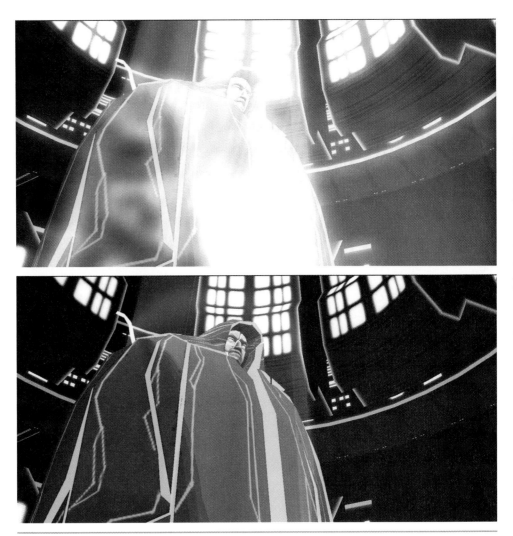

Figure 21-2. A *Tron 2.0* Character With and Without Glow
Top: Glow can enhance the importance of a character. Bottom: The character without glow is less captivating. Courtesy of Buena Vista Interactive/Disney Productions.

21.1 Overview of the Technique

There are several approaches to creating glow in a scene. For small point-like objects, a smooth, "glowy" texture can be applied to billboard geometry that follows the objects around the screen. In *Tron 2.0*, this is used for the Bit character. For large sources of glow or complex glowing shapes, it is best to post-process a 2D rendering of the scene in order to create the glow. This chapter focuses on the post-processing approach, whose steps are outlined in Figure 21-3.

First, the parts of a scene or model that glow have to be designated by some means that will allow them to be isolated and processed separately from the nonglowing parts. The scene is rendered normally, as it would be with no glow, but it is also rendered using the glow source information to create a texture map that is black everywhere except where the glow sources can be seen. An example of this rendered texture map is shown in Figure 21-3b. This rendered texture map can be used as an ordinary texture in later rendering. It is applied to simple geometry that causes it to be sampled many times at each pixel in a two-step image convolution operation, which blurs the glow source points out into the soft, broad-area glow pattern. Finally, the soft glow is applied on top of the ordinary rendering using additive alpha blending. In this way, the sources of glow are spread out into convincing auras of glow using hardware rendering and texture mapping.

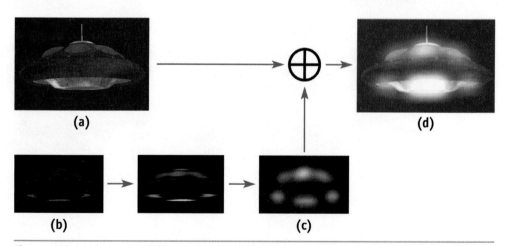

Figure 21-3. Rendering Steps for Creating Real-Time Glow
(a) The scene is rendered normally. (b) A rendering of glow sources is blurred to create (c) a glow texture, which is added to the ordinary scene to produce (d) the final glow effect.

Each of these steps can be done efficiently and quickly on a broad range of graphics hardware. The technique is best suited to hardware that supports Microsoft's Direct3D 8 Vertex and Pixel Shaders 1.1 or later, but a convenient fallback exists for hardware that supports only fixed-function Direct3D 7 rendering. For the older Direct3D 7–era hardware, which has lower fill-rate and texturing performance, the resolution of the render-target textures can be reduced to improve performance while not sacrificing much in terms of image quality. Because the blurred glow texture typically contains only low-frequency features, its resolution can be reduced with little loss in quality. In fact, as explained later, reducing the resolution of the texture render targets is a good way to create larger glows at no additional performance cost.

21.2 Rendering Glows: Step by Step

21.2.1 Specifying and Rendering the Sources of Glow

The first step in rendering glows is to specify which objects or parts of objects are the sources of glow. The color and brightness of these glow sources will translate directly into the color and brightness of the final glow, so this means we can easily control the look of the glow by varying the brightness of the glow sources. These sources could be whole pieces of geometry designated by some object property or flag, or the sources could be restricted to some small part of an object by using texture data. In the latter case, the texture data masks out the parts of an object that do not glow, turning them black in the glow source rendering. The remaining glow source areas can have any desired color and brightness. Using texture data is convenient and artist friendly, and it is our preferred approach.

The glow source mask could be contained in its own separate texture, but it is convenient to use the alpha channel of the ordinary diffuse color texture to hold the mask values. In this case, the texture RGB color is used to render the object normally without alpha blending. When rendering the glow sources, the RGB color is multiplied by the texture alpha channel. Where the alpha value is zero, there will be no source of glow, and as the alpha ramps up to full value, the intensity of the glow sources increases. Figure 21-4 illustrates the texture RGB and alpha channels used to designate sources of glow for a UFO. Additionally, per-vertex or per-object values can be multiplied into the glow source (RGB × alpha) value to animate the glow over time.

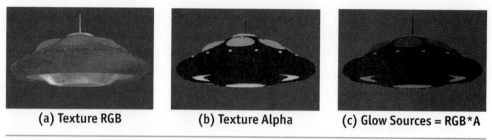

| (a) Texture RGB | (b) Texture Alpha | (c) Glow Sources = RGB*A |

Figure 21-4. Designating Glow Sources
The alpha channel of an object's texture can be used to specify glow sources and the glow source brightness.

Once the glow sources have been specified, they need to be written to an off-screen render-target texture that we can process to create the soft glow. This is a texture created with the Direct3D 9 D3DUSAGE_RENDERTARGET flag. There are two approaches for getting the glow sources into the texture render target: (1) the entire scene can be rendered to the texture using a method to render the glow sources in color and all non-glowing objects in black, or (2) the scene can be copied from the ordinary back buffer into the texture using the IDirect3DDevice9::StretchRect(..) function. Rendering the entire 3D scene again to the texture can be costly for complex scenes, and it requires an additional depth buffer dedicated to the texture render target, so the StretchRect(..) 2D image copy method is preferred. StretchRect(..) also allows us to resize and filter the back-buffer image in the process of copying it to the texture. This can be used to reduce the resolution and gain performance in processing the texture to create the glows.

For the StretchRect(..) method, the alpha value acting as the glow source mask can be rendered to the destination alpha value of the ordinary back buffer. This will have no effect on the ordinary scene, but in the StretchRect(..) operation it will be copied to the alpha channel of the texture. The alpha channel can then be multiplied by the RGB color to mask out scene objects and leave only the glow sources.

After this step, the glow source texture is blurred to create the soft look of glow. The blur operation smooths high-frequency or point-like features in the source texture, and the result has only broad, low-frequency features. Because of this, the glow and glow sources can be rendered at low resolution, and doing so will not reduce the quality. The glow can be created at one-third or one-quarter of the full-screen resolution in each axis, which will greatly improve the speed of rendering the effect.

Rendering the glow sources at low resolution does affect aliasing on the final glow. As the resolution of the glow source texture is reduced, aliasing of the glow source texture increases, and the source texels become more prone to flicker as objects move around the scene. A single texel of glow source may represent several pixels in the full-resolution image, and this single glow source texel is spread out into a large pattern of glow. This increases the effect of the aliasing, causing the glow to flicker and shimmer as objects move. The degree to which the resolution can be reduced depends on how much flicker is acceptable in the final image. This flickering can be decreased by improving the quality of filtering used when reducing resolution. For example, hardware-accelerated bilinear texture filtering can be used while down-sampling a high-resolution glow source image, and this will greatly diminish the flickering.

21.2.2 Blurring the Glow Sources

Blurring the glow sources spreads them out into a smooth, natural pattern of glow. The blurring is accomplished in hardware using a two-dimensional image-processing filter. The speed at which the glow effect can be created depends largely on how efficiently the blur can be performed. The time required to perform the blur depends on the size, in texels, of the filter used. As the blur filter increases in size to cover more texels, we have to read and write more texels in proportion to the area of the 2D blur. The area is proportional to the blur diameter squared, or d^2. Doubling the diameter of the glow would require processing four times the number of texels. For a blur shape covering 50×50 texels, we'd have to read 2,500 texels for every single pixel of glow that we create! This would make large-area glows very impractical, but fortunately, the nasty diameter-squared cost can be avoided by doing the blur in a two-step operation called a *separable convolution*. The separable convolution reduces the cost from d^2 to $2d$, so it will cost only 100 texel reads at each pixel to create a 50×50 glow. This calculation can be done quickly on modern graphics hardware.

21.2.3 Adapting the Separable Convolution

The technique of separable convolution was designed to save computation in certain special cases, namely, when the convolution kernel can be separated into the product of terms that are independent in each axis. In this case, a two-dimensional convolution of $n \times m$ elements can be reduced to two separate one-dimensional convolutions of n and m elements, respectively. This greatly reduces the computation cost of the convolution. Instead of calculating and summing $n \times m$ samples at each point, the convolution is reduced to a two-step process requiring only $n + m$ samples. First, an intermediate result

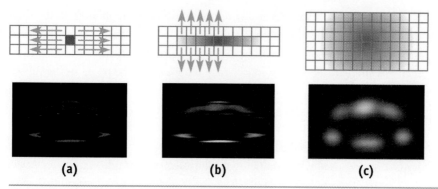

Figure 21-5. The Two-Step Separable Approach for Creating Blurs Efficiently
First, the glow source points in (a) are blurred in one axis to produce the temporary result in (b). This result is then blurred in the other axis to produce the final blur shown in (c).

image is created by sampling and summing n elements along one axis for each point in the result. Then, a neighborhood of m elements of the intermediate result is sampled along the other axis to create each point in the final result. The weighting factors for each of the n or m samples are the profiles of the convolution along each axis. The key concept, as far as we're concerned, is that the two-step approach can be used with any set of one-dimensional convolution profiles. Even though a particular 2D blur shape may not be mathematically separable, we can use two 1D profiles to approximate the shape. We can create a wide variety of 2D blur shapes by doing only the work of two 1D blurs.

In-depth information about separable convolutions can be found on the Web at OpenGL.org. For our purposes, the mathematical derivation might seem to restrict the shape of the blurs. This is because the derivation is typically based on only one or two separable functions, such as the two-dimensional Gaussian. Rather than work from the perspective of the derivation where a 2D profile is broken into two separate 1D profiles, we can instead specify any pair of 1D profiles we like. It doesn't matter what the shape of each profile is, as long as they produce some interesting 2D blur result. For the images shown here, we have used two Gaussian curves added together. One curve provides a smooth, broad base, and the other produces a bright spike in the center. Our Direct3D "Glow" demo (NVIDIA 2002) uses various other profiles. Among them is a periodic sawtooth profile that produces an interesting diffraction-like multiple-image effect. The demo and full source code are included on the book's CD and Web site.

21.2.4 Convolution on the GPU

To blur in one axis and then blur that blur in the other axis, we use render-to-texture operations on the GPU. The rendering fetches a local neighborhood of texels around each rendered pixel and applies the convolution kernel weights to the neighborhood samples. A convolution can be performed in a single rendering pass if the GPU can read all of the neighbors in one pass, or the result can be built up over several rendering passes using additive blending to accumulate a few neighbor samples at a time.

Rendering is driven by a simple piece of screen-aligned geometry. The geometry is a simple rectangle usually covering the entire render target and composed of two triangles. Each triangle's vertices have texture coordinates that determine the location at which texels are sampled from the source texture. The coordinates could also be computed in a vertex or pixel shader. If the coordinates are set to range from 0.0 to 1.0 across the render target, then rendering would copy the source texture into the destination. Each pixel rendered would read a texel from its own location in the source texture, resulting in an exact copy. Instead, the texture coordinates for each texture sampler can be offset from each other by one or more texels. In this case, each rendered pixel will sample a local area of neighbors from the source texture. The same pattern of neighbors will be sampled around each rendered pixel. This method is illustrated in Figure 21-6, and it provides a convenient way to perform convolution on the GPU. More information about the technique of neighbor sampling and image processing on the GPU can be found in James 2001 and on the Web at developer.nvidia.com and gpgpu.org.

To perform the blurring convolution operation on the graphics processor, the glow source texture is bound to one or more texture sampler units, and texture coordinates are computed to provide the desired pattern of neighbor sampling. The render target is set to a render-target texture that will hold the result of blurring along the first axis. Call this texture the *horizontal blur* texture. As each pixel is rendered, several texture samples (neighbor samples) are delivered to the pixel fragment processing hardware, where they are multiplied by the weight factors of the first 1D convolution kernel. Once the horizontal blur has been rendered using one or more passes of rendering to texture, the render target is switched to another texture render target that will hold the final blur. The horizontal blur texture is bound to the input texture samplers, and the texture coordinates and pixel shader weights for the second 1D convolution kernel (the *vertical blur*) are applied.

After the last blur operation, the glow is ready to be blended into the scene. The render target is switched back to the ordinary back buffer, and the glow texture is added to the scene by rendering a simple rectangle with additive alpha blending.

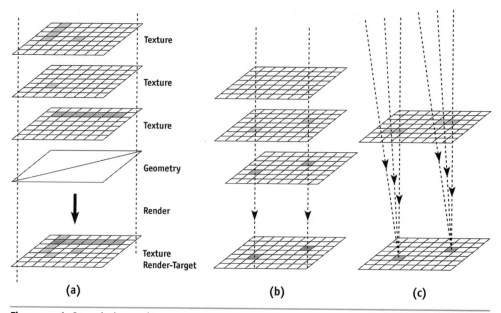

Figure 21-6. Convolution and Image Processing
(a) Rendering a simple rectangle geometry across the screen drives the processing of textures at each pixel. (b) By offsetting texture coordinates, each pixel rendered can sample a local area of neighbors. (c) The same neighbor-sampling pattern in (b) is shown with all samples coming from a single texture source.

21.3 Hardware-Specific Implementations

21.3.1 Direct3D 9

With Direct3D 9 ps.2.0–capable hardware, all of the neighbor samples can be read and convolved in a single, complex pixel shader pass. The neighbor-sampling texture coordinate offsets can be computed in a vertex shader program, but the vs.2.0 and ps.2.0 models support only eight iterated texture coordinates. Additional texture coordinates could be computed in the pixel shader, but this may or may not be faster than a multipass approach where only the eight hardware-iterated coordinates are used in each pass. Sample vs.2.0 and ps.2.0 shaders are shown in Listings 21-1 and 21-2. The vertex shader is designed to accept simple, full-screen coverage geometry with vertex coordinates in homogeneous clip space (screen space), where coordinates range from $(x, y) = ([-1, 1], [-1, 1])$ to cover the full screen. These shaders are used for both the horizontal and vertical blur steps, where only the input constant values change between steps. The constants specify the neighbor-sample placement and kernel weights.

Listing 21-1. Direct3D Vertex Shader to Set Texture Coordinates for Sampling Eight Neighbors

```
vs.2.0
dcl_position     v0
dcl_normal       v1
dcl_color        v2
dcl_texcoord     v3

mov oPos, v0 // output the vertex position in screen space

// Create neighbor-sampling texture coordinates by offsetting
// a single input texture coordinate according to several constants.
add oT0,   v3,  c0
add oT1,   v3,  c1
add oT2,   v3,  c2
add oT3,   v3,  c3
add oT4,   v3,  c4
add oT5,   v3,  c5
add oT6,   v3,  c6
add oT7,   v3,  c7
```

Listing 21-2. Direct3D Pixel Shader to Sum Eight Weighted Texture Samples

```
ps.2.0
// Take 8 neighbor samples, apply 8 conv. kernel weights to them
dcl t0.xyzw      // declare texture coords
dcl t1.xyzw
dcl t2.xyzw
dcl t3.xyzw
dcl t4.xyzw
dcl t5.xyzw
dcl t6.xyzw
dcl t7.xyzw
dcl_2d s0        // declare texture sampler
// Constants c0..c7 are the convolution kernel weights corresponding
// to each neighbor sample.
texld r0, t0, s0
texld r1, t1, s0
mul    r0, r0, c0
mad    r0, r1, c1, r0
texld r1, t2, s0
texld r2, t3, s0
mad    r0, r1, c2, r0
mad    r0, r2, c3, r0
```

```
texld r1, t4, s0
texld r2, t5, s0
mad   r0, r1, c4, r0
mad   r0, r2, c5, r0
texld r1, t6, s0
texld r2, t7, s0
mad   r0, r1, c6, r0
mad   r0, r2, c7, r0
mov oC0, r0
```

Note that in order to sample the texture at the exact texel centers, a texture coordinate offset of half the size of one texel must be added to the texture coordinates. This must be done for Direct3D but is not required for OpenGL, because the Direct3D convention is for coordinates to start from the texel corner, while the OpenGL convention is to start from the texel center. This is a simple adjustment to put into practice. For the vertex shader in Listing 21-1, it requires adding the half-texel offset to each of the constants c0 through c7. This should be done on the CPU.

21.3.2 Direct3D 8

With hardware that supports at most Direct3D 8 vertex and pixel shaders, we are limited to taking only four neighbor samples per pass. Although this limitation will require more rendering passes to build up a convolution of any given size, each pass can be performed very quickly, typically at a rate of several hundred passes per second for render-target textures containing a few hundred thousand texels (textures sized from 256×256 to 512×512). Sample vs.1.1 and ps.1.3 shaders are shown in Listings 21-3 and 21-4.

Listing 21-3. Direct3D Vertex Shader Program to Establish Neighbor Sampling

```
vs.1.1
dcl_position v0
dcl_texcoord v3
mov oPos, v0 // output the vertex position in screen space
// Create neighbor-sampling texture coordinates by offsetting
// a single input texture coordinate according to several constants.
add oT0,  v3, c0
add oT1,  v3, c1
add oT2,  v3, c2
add oT3,  v3, c3
```

Listing 21-4. Direct3D Pixel Shader Program to Sum Four Weighted Texture Samples

```
ps.1.3
tex t0     // sample 4 local neighbors
tex t1
tex t2
tex t3
// multiply each by kernel weight and output the sum
mul r0, t0, c0
mad r0, t1, c1, r0
mad r0, t2, c2, r0
mad r0, t3, c3, r0
```

21.3.3 Direct3D 7

Direct3D 7–class hardware lacks the convenient vertex and pixel shading capabilities of modern graphics hardware. It is also typically limited to only two texture samples per pass and will have a much lower fill rate. Still, the blurring convolution can be performed using several overlapping triangles of full-screen coverage geometry. Each pair of triangles, arranged to form a full-screen quad, has the same vertex positions but different vertex texture coordinates. For two-texture multisampling hardware, each quad carries two texture coordinates, and each coordinate is set to sample a different neighbor. Each quad's vertex color attributes are set to the kernel weight for the particular neighbor-sample location, and this vertex color is multiplied by the texture sample value using the fixed-function `SetTextureStageState(..)` API calls. A stack of these quads can be rendered with additive blending in a single `DrawPrimitive(..)` call to build up the convolution result.

21.4 Other Uses for Blur

Beyond the use discussed so far—simulating the perception of high-dynamic-range intensity values—this method of convolution and blurring can be used for a variety of other effects. It can be used to compute various degrees of focus for depth-of-field effects, where scene depth information may be used to control the degree of blur. It can be used to soften the edges of projected texture shadows or to accumulate results for percentage-closer filtering of depth shadow maps. A large-area convolution can be applied to an environment map to create an approximate irradiance map for more realistic scene lighting (Ramamoorthi and Hanrahan 2001). Many nonphotorealistic rendering techniques and other special effects can be done with large-area convolutions.

Among these are effects for frosted glass, lens flares that simulate diffraction, and approximations of subsurface scattering for rendering skin.

21.5 Adding the Effects to a Game Engine

Next, we focus on how the visual effects were used for Buena Vista Interactive's game, *Tron 2.0*, in which they played a significant role in the unique visual style of the game. Implementing these effects was surprisingly straightforward. However, some important issues had to be addressed before the effects could be robust enough for use throughout the wide range of situations in the game. Plus, some interesting effects and alternate uses for the glow were discovered during development.

21.5.1 Rendering Context

The first issue we addressed was how to render the source image that would be blurred to create the final screen glow. In *Tron 2.0*, there were two rendering pipelines: one for rendering the world geometry and one for rendering the models. Both rendering pipelines needed to be extended to support the concept of a rendering context, which allows the scene to be rendered in different ways for different purposes. Two rendering contexts were needed for *Tron 2.0*. One was *normal rendering*, which was used to handle the initial rendering of the scene without any screen glow. The second rendering context was *glow rendering*, which was used when rendering the source image for the glow.

The implementation of a rendering context varies widely among applications, but for illustrative purposes, we will describe how we created the model-rendering pipeline in *Tron 2.0*. The model rendering is based on a mesh and a collection of render states that indicate how the model should be rendered. These render states are stored as an external resource called a *render style*. To support the idea of contexts, this system was extended to allow artists to set up a table that would map any render style to a corresponding render style when rendering the glow. Through this mechanism, when rendering the scene normally, the original render style would be used, which would render the model as one would see it if the glow were disabled. Then when rendering the source image for the glow, it would instead use the render style that was found in the map that the artists had set up, which would render the glowing parts of the model. The artists found this system to be very flexible and easy to use, as it gave them control over which objects should glow and how each object should glow. Figure 21-7 shows the plain character model, the artist-created glow texture information, and the glow effect applied to the model.

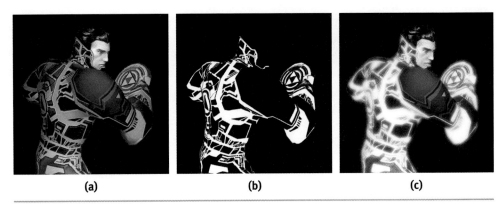

(a)   (b)   (c)

Figure 21-7. Jet, the Hero of *Tron 2.0*, With and Without Glow
(a) The 3D model is rendered with standard methods. (b) A rendering of the glow source texture, created by artists to specify the pattern and strength of glowing areas. (c) Applying glow to the ordinary rendering conveys the hero's power and intensity.
Courtesy of Buena Vista Interactive/Disney Productions.

21.5.2 Aliasing Issues

The problem of aliasing immediately appeared when we extended the glow effect from a simple test case to a full game scene. The *Tron* universe is characterized by strips of brightly colored geometry within the scene, almost like neon edging on the characters and their surroundings. In addition, most of the environments are vast, so these glowing strips of geometry range from very close to the camera to far off in the distance. We used a glow texture of 256×256 for *Tron 2.0* to allow for a fairly large blur with a minimal number of passes. The downside to this approach, though, was that this caused serious aliasing issues when rendering to the source image, and the aliasing became very apparent as the player moved or looked around.

To address this issue, we added support for artist-controlled fog that would be used only when rendering the source image for the screen glow. The fog would be enabled in large levels and set to black. Because of the additive blending of the screen glow, the black fog in the source image would result in distant objects contributing only faintly, if at all, to the final screen glow. Thus, the aliasing in the distance was made much less noticeable.

It isn't a perfect solution—for example, parts of the scene in the distance will not glow—but it is generally more acceptable visually than the aliasing artifacts are. In addition to avoiding aliasing, the fog was used in several places throughout the game in unanticipated ways to create extra atmosphere, such as that shown in Figure 21-8.

Figure 21-8. Using Fog with Screen Glow
Artists used a faint, white, screen-glow fog in this cinematic flashback to make the scene appear more dreamlike. Courtesy of Buena Vista Interactive/Disney Productions.

21.5.3 DirectX 7 Accuracy Issues

To fit the blend weight into a color component, the initial DirectX 7 implementation scaled it from the initial range of [0, 1] to an integer between 0 and 255. Most of these weights were very small, though, and thus not well spread over the full range. Consequently, the errors that occurred when converting to an integer resulted in a substantial visual difference between the DirectX 7 and 8 implementations. Even with rounding, the glow still appeared significantly different.

The solution? Perform the rounding, but first determine how much the resulting value differed from the actual value, and then apply the difference to the next weight calculated. For example, a weight of 0.13, when scaled by 255, is 33.15, which rounds to the integer value of 33. Therefore, the weight used for the color would be 33, and the left-over portion (the 0.15) would be added to the next weight to be rendered. As a result, the DirectX 7 and 8 implementations were visually almost identical.

21.5.4 The After-Image Effect

One effect didn't make it into *Tron 2.0* because it was discovered too late. It turns out that the previous frame's source texture can be added to the current frame's source texture, resulting in a very nice streaking of the glow as players move or look around. The technique is very simple to implement. It consists of an extra texture surface so the source image can be preserved for the following frame, and an additive blend that adds the previous source image to the current source image. This technique works by saving the image immediately before the blur is applied and then applying the blur. The saved image is added to the source image of the next frame, but it is dimmed slightly. As this process is repeated over a number of frames, it allows objects to fade out of the glow instead of instantly disappearing, which not only makes the effect more compelling, but also helps hide aliasing of the source image.

The degree of dimming applied to the previous frame before adding the frame to the current frame's glow source can be changed dynamically, resulting in a wide range of appearance. For example, by dimming the previous frame significantly, there will be very little after-image, and it will appear to users as only a brief burn-in of light in their retina, giving the look of a much brighter light. By dimming the previous frame less before adding it, the blurring and streaking becomes much more apparent and has the effect on the player of appearing drunk or near death.

One alternative does not require an additional buffer. We can use the previous frame's final screen-glow texture after the blur, which saves memory because the source image does not need to be preserved. However, this solution does have certain issues. If the previous frame's glow texture is too bright, it can bleed out of control when recursively added, continually blurring outward in each frame, eventually resulting in a fully white screen glow. To avoid this case, we have to be careful when setting up the blend weights and determining how much to dim the previous frame.

21.5.5 The Variable Ramping Effect

The screen glow must use a certain set of parameters—such as blending weights and fog—to create the final blur for a single frame. However, that doesn't mean the parameters can't change from frame to frame. In fact, by varying any of these parameters, you can achieve a variety of interesting effects. For example, in one of the levels of *Tron 2.0*, the player is inside a corrupted server that has a sickly green glow. To convey the unstable feeling, the blend weights of the blur were ramped from low to high to create a dull pulsing of the screen glow. See Figure 21-9.

Although not used in the game, other effects can be just as easily achieved. For example, by ramping the screen glow fog in and out, or changing the color of the fog, you can easily and efficiently make the atmosphere of a level feel as if it were constantly changing.

Figure 21-9. A Pulsing Screen Glow Creates a Sickly Feel
Courtesy of Buena Vista Interactive/Disney Productions.

21.6 Conclusion

Large blurs and convolutions can be computed efficiently in real time on a broad range of graphics hardware. The code for processing and creating these effects is easily encapsulated into a few C++ classes or a small library. These classes and sample code are available on NVIDIA's Developer Web site, developer.nvidia.com. The effect requires additional data to specify the brightness of glow sources, and this data can be incorporated into existing texture assets, namely the texture alpha channel. The effect offers intuitive controls for the brightness and shape of the glow. The ability to apply large-area convolutions to full-screen rendering is useful for a wide variety of effects. It is key to depicting bright objects in a scene and can greatly enhance the look and quality of real-time rendering.

Screen glow is one of the rare effects that are robust enough to be easily extended for use in nearly every situation, yet it is versatile enough to allow numerous additional effects to be created through it. The final effect is subtle but powerful, and well worth prototyping in any game.

21.7 References

Chiu, K., M. Herf, P. Shirley, S. Swamy, C. Wang, and K. Zimmerman. 1993. "Spatially Nonuniform Scaling Functions for High Contrast Images." *Graphics Interface '93*, pp. 245–253.

GPGPU Web site. 2003. **http://www.gpgpu.org**

James, Greg. 2001. "Operations for Hardware-Accelerated Procedural Texture Animation." In *Game Programming Gems 2*, edited by Mark DeLoura, pp. 497–509. Charles River Media.

Kawase, Masaki. 2003. Personal Web site. **http://www.daionet.gr.jp/~masa/column/2003-03-21.html**

Nakamae, Eihachiro, Kazufumi Kaneda, Takashi Okamoto, and Tomoyuki Nishita. 1990. "A Lighting Model Aiming at Drive Simulators." In *Proceedings of SIGGRAPH 90*, pp. 395–404.

NVIDIA Developer Web site. 2003. **http://developer.nvidia.com**

OpenGL.org Web site. 2003. "Advanced Graphics Programming Techniques Using OpenGL." Course notes, SIGGRAPH 99. Mathematics of separable convolution. **http://www.opengl.org/resources/tutorials/sig99/advanced99/notes/node235.html**

Ramamoorthi, Ravi, and Pat Hanrahan. 2001. "An Efficient Representation for Irradiance Environment Maps." In *Proceedings of SIGGRAPH 2001*, pp. 497–500. Available online at **http://graphics.stanford.edu/papers/envmap**

Spencer, Greg, Peter S. Shirley, Kurt Zimmerman, and Donald P. Greenberg. 1995. "Physically Based Glare Effects for Digital Images." In *Proceedings of SIGGRAPH 95*, pp. 325–334.

We offer tremendous thanks to the Developer Technology group at NVIDIA and to Monolith Productions for encouraging and assisting in the development of this technique and for transforming a simple tech demo into gorgeous visuals in the final shipping game.

Chapter 22

Color Controls

Kevin Bjorke
NVIDIA

Color correction is part of almost all print and film imaging applications. Color correction can be used to move color images from one color space to another (say, from Adobe RGB to sRGB); to stylize images (creating illusions such as faded film, cross-processing, or other stylistic variations); to combine art elements from different sources (such as matching color palettes between different video sources, or models made by different artists); or to give broad coherence and mood to entire parts of a game or scene without changing the underlying models and textures.

Most of the imagery we see on television, in magazines, and in movies has undergone very careful color correction and control. Understanding how the process works can help developers give real-time applications equivalent visual richness.

22.1 Introduction

In all forms of color correction, we want to change the color of individual pixels. Color corrections generally come in two flavors: per-channel corrections, which alter red, green, and blue components individually; and color-mixing operations, in which the value of each output channel may be an operation based on the red, green, and blue components simultaneously.

The mathematics of color corrections can be compactly and easily described in a shader. Just as important, they can be controlled effectively with common tools used widely by computer artists and programmers. In this chapter, we rely on Adobe Photoshop to let artists create control resources, which can then be applied in real time via pixel shaders.

22.2 Channel-Based Color Correction

Photoshop provides a number of channel-based correction tools. Features such as the Levels and the Curves tools are channel based. They offer a method to change the intensity of each individual channel in an image or all three channels as a single entity.

22.2.1 Levels

Figures 22-1 and 22-2 show a typical application of the Levels command in Photoshop (in this case, enhancing contrast and shifting the overall gamma). The artist can control the overall contrast, gamma, and dynamic range of the entire image, or she can manipulate those properties for each color channel independently.

For each channel, we can apply the following formula:

```
outPixel = (pow(((inPixel * 255.0) - inBlack) / (inWhite - inBlack),
                 inGamma) * (outWhite - outBlack) + outBlack) / 255.0;
```

Here, `inBlack`, `inGamma`, and `inWhite` are the "Input Levels" values, and `outBlack` and `outWhite` are the values marked in the "Output Levels" boxes in Figure 22-1. (For more on processing gamma values, see Chapter 26, "The OpenEXR Image File Format.")

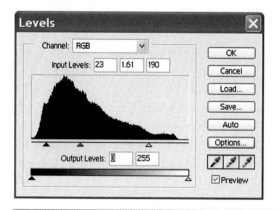

Figure 22-1. Adjusting Image Gamma and Overall Dynamic Range Using Photoshop Levels

| Original | After Levels Adjustment |

Figure 22-2. Before and After Levels Adjustments

Figure 22-2 shows the adjustment applied equally to all three color channels, but we can also adjust each channel individually.

For a production pipeline using a high-level shading language, an artist or art director could define the color correction by first opening a screen capture from the game or other image source in Photoshop, then applying the correction as a new layer in Photoshop. The writer of the shader could then open the image in Photoshop and copy the corrected values from the Levels dialog box and paste them as the inputs for the color-correction code.

In practice, the formula can often be simplified. The 1/255 intensity normalizations can be removed by predividing the terms used in Photoshop before passing them on to the shader. Default Levels values (such as 0–255 output values, or a gamma of 1.0) can simply be skipped.

If levels are applied to individual channels, the inputs can be defined as vector data, but results can only partially be calculated as vectors, unless the gamma terms for all channels match. If not, then three different pow() functions will be required.

22.2.2 Curves

Photoshop's Levels tool is useful because it is simple for the artist to understand and for the shader programmer to implement. Often, however, the artist may desire more precise control, or more unusual, nonlinear effects. The Curves tool in Photoshop provides more arbitrary remapping of the color channels; it is the color-correction tool of choice among many print and photographic professionals.

Using Curves, the input-output mapping of color channels can be defined by an arbitrary cubic spline or can be drawn freehand. This flexibility provides extreme generality, but it makes it difficult for coders to write a single algebraic expression to define the many possible relationships.

Figures 22-3 and 22-4 show a usage typical of an advertising imagery. A graphic designer or artist has processed an RGB image using a complex series of color curves in the Curves dialog box. In this case, curves have been applied in two ranks: the red, green, and blue curves are applied by Photoshop in *addition* to an overall curve applied to RGB equally.

The result, in this case, emulates the appearance of chemical *cross-processing*—specifically, the false-color appearance created by processing E6 film in C41 chemistry. Such manipulations have been popular in print, movies, and television for many years.

Although we could potentially duplicate the math performed by Photoshop, there is a much easier way to obtain results with a shader that exactly matches complex channel manipulations such as these. Because we know that there exist one-to-one mappings between the input values of each color channel and the final output values for the same channel, we can represent these mappings as a 1D map, which we can apply as a "dependent" texture.

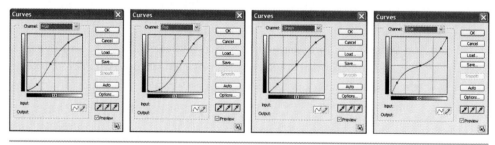

Figure 22-3. Photoshop Curves to Re-create a Cross-Processing Effect

| Original | After Curves Adjustment |

Figure 22-4. Fake Cross-Processing

For best results, a 1×256 texture map should be defined, although smaller maps can often be used effectively. Before creating the map, the artist must first define the color transformation, typically by applying adjustment layers to existing still images using the Curves tool in Photoshop. Once the adjustments are defined, they can be saved to disk as an Adobe ".acv" Curve file.

Now to make the texture:

1. Create a new 1×256-pixel RGB image in Photoshop.
2. Set the foreground and background colors to white and black, respectively.
3. Using the Gradient tool, apply a gradient ramp from the leftmost pixel to the rightmost pixel in the image, ranging from black on the left to white on the right. (Save this gradient as a reference: you may need it later.)
4. Now apply your saved ".acv" Curves file to the gradient file. If you have applied different adjustments to each color channel, the previously gray ramp will now show color banding. Figure 22-5 shows an example.
5. Save the new, colored ramp image in a form appropriate for texture mapping in your program (such as DDS or Targa formats).

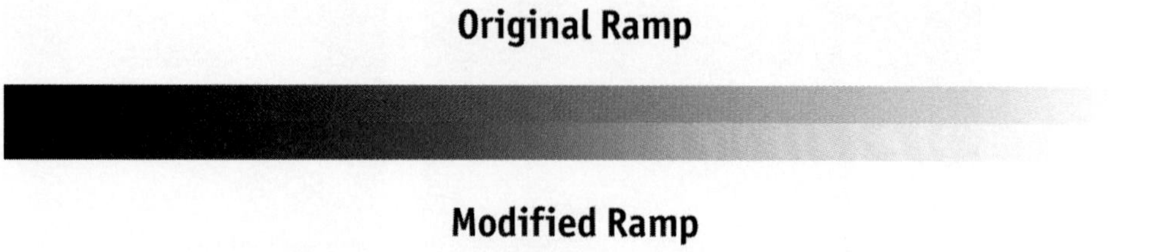

Original Ramp

Modified Ramp

Figure 22-5. Grayscale RGB and Modified RGB Ramps

We can now apply the following lines of shader code to the input color, using this correction texture map, to arbitrarily re-create any color alterations performed with the Curves tool (the same method can also be applied to Levels, if desired).

```
float3 InColor = tex2D(inSampler, IN.UV).xyz;
float3 OutColor;
OutColor.r = tex1D(ColorCorrMap, InColor.r).r;
OutColor.g = tex1D(ColorCorrMap, InColor.g).g;
OutColor.b = tex1D(ColorCorrMap, InColor.b).b;
```

In other words, we use the grayscale value of each original red, green, and blue pixel to determine where in the ramp texture we will look; then the ramp texture itself defines the remapping to the new colors defined by our complex Curves adjustment(s). See Figure 22-6.

22.3 Multichannel Color Correction and Conversion

Occasionally, we need to mix color channels together, such as when adjusting hue (that is, the rotation through 3D color space), when converting from one color space to another, or when converting from color to grayscale.

For generality, one can imagine extending the previous technique to three dimensions, providing a full mapping for any possible pixel into a large $256 \times 256 \times 256$ 3D map. Such a map size would demand too much memory for many modern-day graphics cards, but not all, and the code is astonishingly minimal:

```
float3 InColor = tex2D(inSampler, IN.UV).xyz;
float3 OutColor = tex3D(colorSpaceSampler, inColor);
```

As you can see, the code is simple. The only real-world limitation is the lack of common tools for creating such RGB-to-RGB 3D texture maps.

Figure 22-6. Channel-by-Channel Results of the Red, Green, and Blue Remappings

Fortunately, most color-space conversions are quite uniform and can be expressed efficiently as dot products and 3×3 matrix multiplications.

22.3.1 Grayscale Conversion

Consider the common conversion from RGB color to a grayscale. There are several approaches available: We can choose one color channel, or evenly blend all three channels, or mix the three RGB channels by varying weights to achieve a final grayscale result. The third choice, blending by weights, is generally accepted as the best, and it can be set to match the sensitivity of typical human eyesight.

We can express this blending with a dot product:

```
float grayscale = dot(float3(0.222, 0.707, 0.071), inColor);
```

The values (0.222, 0.707, 0.071) represent the relative scales for red, green, and blue, respectively. These numbers follow an international industrial color standard called ITU Rec 709 (there are actually a number of alternate formulations). Note that the components of the float3 vector used for this conversion sum to 1.0—this makes the conversion nominally "energy conserving," though in fact you can assign almost any values and get different interesting results, much as you can with the Photoshop Color Mixer tool.

In particular, a standardized conversion such as the one just described means that the brightness of pure colors may be limited—bright pure blues, for example, will never appear as more than a dark 7 percent gray. For artistic reasons, therefore, we may often want to vary the weights of our grayscale conversions, so that important colors aren't needlessly suppressed.

We can also use the results of such a grayscale conversion as a texture index to create alternative color mappings, using color-lookup textures similar to the one used in the previous section. Consider this mapping:

```
float grayscale = dot(float3(0.222, 0.707, 0.071), inColor);
// set the texture's edge-addressing to "clamp"
float3 OutColor = tex1D(ColorCorrMap, grayscale);
```

Using a grayscale-to-color-gradient mapping in this way permits us to create a wide variety of false-color and toned-print effects, both naturalistic (such as duotones or tritones) and highly stylized (such as robot vision or infrared "heat signatures" à la the movie *Predator*).

22.3.2 Color-Space Conversions

Converting between different color spaces can be done by calculating a different dot product for each resultant color channel—in other words, multiplying the input RGB values by a 3×3 matrix.

```
float3x3 conversionMatrix;

// plus some code to insert values into this matrix
. . .

float3 newColor = mul(conversionMatrix, inColor);
```

The code sample shows converting inColor to newColor according to the contents of conversionMatrix. Many conversion matrices are standardized: for example, the conversions from RGB colors to CIE colors, from video YIQ signals to RGB, or from color standards such as Adobe RGB to other standards such as sRGB. The "Color Space FAQ" (Bourgin 1994) is a good source of information on many standard conversions used in video. An excellent online source containing matrix values for most common industrial color spaces (such as those used in Photoshop color profiles) is Autiokari 2003. (Conversions from subsampled signals can also be assisted by texturing hardware—see Chapter 24 of this book, "High-Quality Filtering.")

Custom color conversions are also sometimes needed when doing 3D shading based on physical measurements from tools such as a *gonioreflectometer*. The color shifts may be needed to adjust between the color sensitivities of the original sensors and the output colors of a typical computer display. For maximum reproduction fidelity of the original, real-world BRDF of a given surface, this final adjustment can be crucial.

It's easy to experiment with rotations and scales of the 3D color cube using a DCC tool. For example, if you're using Cg, make a dummy 3D node and, using the appropriate Cg plug-in, attach the node's world-space matrix to a Cg shader such as this one:

```
float4 colorCubePS(vertexOutput IN,
                   sampler2D ColorTex,
                   float3x3  RGBxform) : COLOR
{
    float3 texColor = tex2D(ColorTex, IN.UV);
    float3 result = mul(RGBxform, texColor);
    return float4(result, 1.0);
}
```

The results are shown in Figure 22-7.

This technique allows you simply to grab the null object and scale or rotate it freely to try different effects. Besides the "psychedelic" aspects of random scaling and dragging, try the following settings for control over saturation, brightness, and color-wheel rotation:

- For brightness overall, scale around (0, 0, 0).

- For saturation, scale against the diagonal vector (1, 1, 1)—so that if the color cube were fully desaturated, it would simply degenerate to a line through the origin and (1, 1, 1).

- For rotating the color cube, rotate around that same diagonal-vector direction (1, 1, 1).

Figure 22-7. Color-Cube Transforms Previewed in a DCC Application
The large placard is shaded by a fragment program that transforms texture colors by the transform matrix of the color-cube object. Grabbing and scaling/rotating the color-cube object changes the color of the photograph, permitting easy interactive experimentation.

- For altering overall contrast, scale around any point in the color cube. Scaling around (0.5, 0.5, 0.5) will change the overall contrast relative to midgray; scaling around (1, 1, 1) will change the saturation against white. Desaturating to any other color is equally straightforward.

Any number of these operations can be concatenated, preferably in the CPU application, before being passed to the fragment shader.

22.4 References

Albers, Josef. 1987. *The Interaction of Color*, revised ed. Yale University Press.

Autiokari, Timo. 2003. "CIE_XYZ and CIE_xyY." Web site article.
    http://www.aim-dtp.net/aim/technology/cie_xyz/cie_xyz.htm

Bourgin, David. 1994. "Color Space FAQ." Web site page.
http://www.neuro.sfc.keio.ac.jp/~aly/polygon/info/color-space-faq.html

Fraser, Bruce. 2003. *Real World Color Management.* Peachpit Press.

Hummel, Rob. 2002. *American Cinematographer Manual*, 8th ed. American Society of Cinematographers.

Margulis, Dan. 2002. *Professional Photoshop*, 4th ed. Wiley.

Poynton, Charles. 2003. Web site. **http://www.poynton.com.** *Poynton's Web site contains a wealth of useful color-related digital information. Poynton contributed to many of the color standards now in use.*

Chapter 23

Depth of Field:
A Survey of Techniques

Joe Demers
NVIDIA

23.1 What Is Depth of Field?

Depth of field is the effect in which objects within some range of distances in a scene appear in focus, and objects nearer or farther than this range appear out of focus. Depth of field is frequently used in photography and cinematography to direct the viewer's attention within the scene, and to give a better sense of depth within a scene. In this chapter, I refer to the area beyond this focal range as the *background*, the area in front of this range as the *foreground*, and the area in focus as the *midground*.

The depth-of-field effect arises from the physical nature of lenses. A camera lens (or the lens in your eye) allows light to pass through to the film (or to your retina). In order for that light to converge to a single point on the film (or your retina), its source needs to be a certain distance away from the lens. The plane at this distance from the lens is called the *plane in focus*. Anything that's not at this exact distance projects to a region (instead of to a point) on the film. This region is known as the *circle of confusion* (CoC). The diameter of the CoC increases with the size of the lens and the distance from the plane in focus. Because there is a range of distances within which the CoC is smaller than the resolution of the film, photographers and cinematographers refer to this range as being *in focus*; anything outside of this range is called *out of focus*. See Figures 23-1 and 23-2.

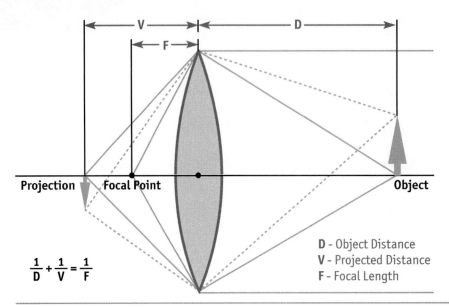

$$\frac{1}{D} + \frac{1}{V} = \frac{1}{F}$$

D - Object Distance
V - Projected Distance
F - Focal Length

Figure 23-1. A Thin Lens

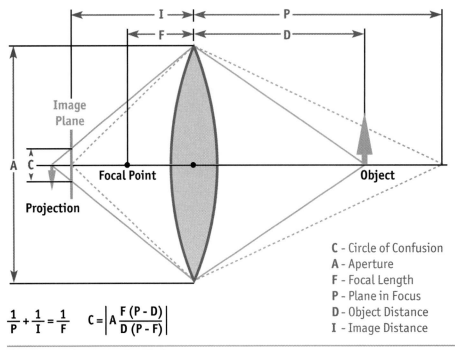

$$\frac{1}{P} + \frac{1}{I} = \frac{1}{F} \qquad C = \left| A \, \frac{F\,(P - D)}{D\,(P - F)} \right|$$

C - Circle of Confusion
A - Aperture
F - Focal Length
P - Plane in Focus
D - Object Distance
I - Image Distance

Figure 23-2. The Circle of Confusion

In computer graphics, we typically project onto our virtual film using an idealized pin-hole camera that has a lens of zero size, so there is only a single path for light to travel from the scene to the film. So to achieve the depth-of-field effect, we must approximate the blur that would otherwise happen with a real lens.

23.1.1 Calculating the Circle of Confusion

The circle of confusion for the world-space distance from the camera-object distance can be calculated from camera parameters:

```
CoC = abs(aperture * (focallength * (objectdistance - planeinfocus)) /
          (objectdistance * (planeinfocus - focallength)))
```

Object distance can be calculated from the z values in the z-buffer:

```
objectdistance = -zfar * znear / (z * (zfar - znear) - zfar)
```

The circle of confusion can alternatively be calculated from the z-buffer values, with the camera parameters lumped into scale and bias terms:

```
CoC = abs(z * CoCScale + CoCBias)
```

The scale and bias terms are calculated from the camera parameters:

```
CoCScale = (aperture * focallength * planeinfocus * (zfar - znear)) /
               ((planeinfocus - focallength) * znear * zfar)
CoCBias  = (aperture * focallength * (znear - planeinfocus)) /
               ((planeinfocus * focallength) * znear)
```

23.1.2 Major Techniques

This chapter reviews five main techniques that approximate the depth-of-field effect:

- Distributing traced rays across the surface of a (nonpinhole) lens (Cook et al. 1984)
- Rendering from multiple cameras—also called the accumulation-buffer technique (Haeberli and Akeley 1990)
- Rendering multiple layers (Scofield 1994)
- Forward-mapped z-buffer techniques (Potmesil and Chakravarty 1981)
- Reverse-mapped z-buffer techniques (Arce and Wloka 2002, Demers 2003)

We spend the most time on the z-buffer techniques, because the others are already well known and have ample coverage in computer graphics literature, and because z-buffer techniques are more amenable to rendering in real time on current graphics hardware.

23.2 Ray-Traced Depth of Field

One use of distributed ray tracing is to render accurate depth of field by casting rays from across the lens, rather than from a single point. With appropriate statistical distribution across the lens, you can achieve the most accurate depth-of-field renderings possible, because you are actually modeling the light transport for the camera and the scene. Although processing time is nowhere near real time, ray-tracing depth of field yields the best quality images. Even when fewer rays are used, the technique degrades nicely to noise, rather than more-objectionable artifacts such as banding or ghosting. It also accommodates effects such as motion blur and soft shadows better than other techniques, due to the ability to jitter samples in time and space independent of neighboring pixels. Figure 23-3 shows an example of this technique and illustrates how noise can occur when too few samples are used.

Figure 23-3. Ray-Traced Depth of Field

23.3 Accumulation-Buffer Depth of Field

The accumulation-buffer technique approximates the distributed ray-tracing approach using a traditional z-buffer, along with an auxiliary buffer called an accumulation buffer. An accumulation buffer is a higher precision color buffer that is typically used for accumulating multiple images in real-time rendering.

Whereas distributed ray tracing would cast rays through multiple locations through the lens into the scene, in this technique, we instead render the scene multiple times from different locations through the lens, and then we blend the results using the accumulation buffer. The more rendering passes blended, the better this technique looks, and the closer to "true" depth of field we can get. If too few passes are blended, then we begin to see ghosting, or copies of objects, in the most blurred regions: the extreme foreground and background. The number of passes required is proportional to the area of the circle of confusion, and so for scenes with nonsubtle depth-of-field effects, a prohibitively large number of passes can be required. A single pass per 4 pixels of the area of the largest CoC yields a typically acceptable depth-of-field effect with only barely visible artifacts, because this limits banding artifacts to, at most, 2×2 pixels. Thus, 50 passes are required for an 8-pixel-radius CoC containing roughly 200 pixels. However, a lower-quality rendering using a pass per nine samples (limiting banding to at most 3×3 pixels) with at most a 6-pixel-radius CoC requires only 12 passes. For integer-valued accumulation buffers, precision can quickly become an issue, yielding banding in the final image.

Figure 23-4 shows banding around the barrel of a toy tank, even with only slight amounts of depth of field in the image.

This is the only potentially real-time technique presented here that can yield "true" depth of field—rendering correct visibility and correct shading from a lens-aperture camera, as opposed to a pinhole camera. Unfortunately, the number of passes typically necessary for good results quickly brings this technique to non-real-time rates.

23.4 Layered Depth of Field

The layered depth-of-field technique is based upon a 2D approach (sometimes called 2½D for the use of layers) that can be performed for simple scenes in 2D paint and photo-editing packages. If objects can be sorted in layers that don't overlap in depth, each layer can be blurred based on some representative depth within its range. These layers can then be composited into a final image to give the impression of depth of field.

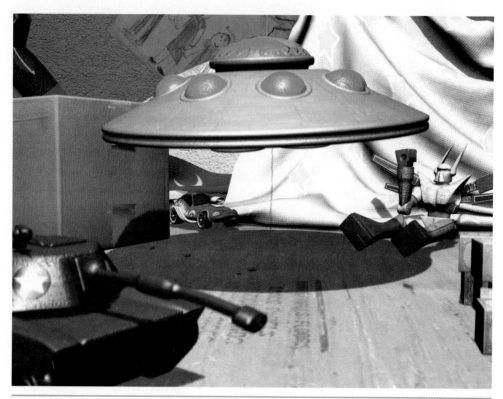

Figure 23-4. Accumulation-Buffer Depth of Field

23.4.1 Analysis

This technique is simple, and because each layer has a separate image of visible objects, visibility around the edges of objects is treated well. Although the shading is technically incorrect, this tends not to be a noticeable artifact for most scenes.

The downside is that because all pixels within a layer are blurred uniformly, objects that span large depth ranges, especially in the foreground, don't appear to have depth of field within them. Also, the amount of blur can change too quickly between objects that are in front of each other. This happens because their representative depths are based on some average depth of each, rather than the depths of the areas that are close to each other.

Last, many scenes can't be nicely partitioned this way, either because objects partially overlap each others' depth ranges or because objects just span the entire depth range, such as floors and walls. In theory, the scene could be split along planes of equal z, but

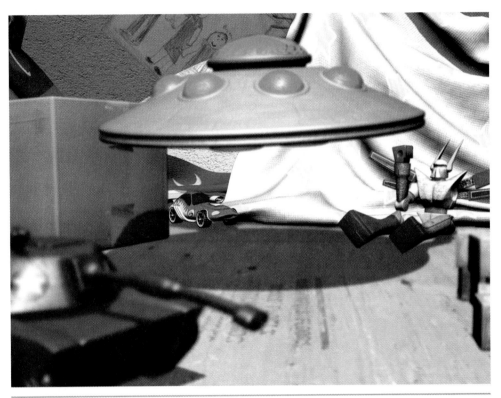

Figure 23-5. Layered Depth of Field

in practice, a couple of types of artifacts are difficult to overcome. The less-objectionable artifact is that an object split into multiple layers will be blurred differently on either side of that split, and so an artificial edge can become visible within the object. The worse artifact arises from potential errors of visibility due to the splitting along z. Because some objects are split, smaller objects behind them that shouldn't be visible can be blended into the layer. Figure 23-5 shows the constant blur artifact generated when simply rendering a layer for each object. This is especially noticeable in the floor, which is too sharp in the foreground and too blurry in the background.

Because of these artifacts, and the difficulty in resolving them in the general case, this technique tends to be used only in special cases where such problems can be fixed with ad hoc solutions.

23.5 Forward-Mapped Z-Buffer Depth of Field

Using forward mapping (that is, rendering sprites) to approximate depth of field allows for a depth-of-field effect that works for arbitrary scenes. This is the primary method used by post-processing packages to apply depth of field to rendered images and movies. Forward mapping in this case refers to the process of mapping source pixels onto the destination image, as opposed to reverse mapping, which identifies which source pixel needs to be mapped onto the destination image. The idea is to save both the color buffer and the depth buffer when rendering, and then use the depth buffer to determine the CoC for that pixel. The pixels are blended into the frame buffer as circles whose colors are the pixels' colors, whose diameter equals the CoC, and with alpha values inversely proportional to the circles' areas. Pixels blend into only those neighboring pixels farther from the camera than themselves, to avoid blurry pixels affecting sharp pixels in front of them. A final renormalizing pass is typically done to account for pixels whose final alphas don't sum to 1. This is necessary because pixels whose alpha is less than 1 also have colors that are artificially less than the weighted average of their contributors.

23.5.1 Analysis

Because this technique relies only on information from images rendered with a pinhole camera model, it uses incorrect visibility and shading in its calculations. So if a point light is animated passing behind an object, it will transition immediately from visible to not visible, rather than from fully visible, to visible from some parts of the lens, to not visible. For many applications, however, this technique is good enough, and the artifacts can be covered up with lens flares and other artistic patches.

Unfortunately, this technique doesn't map well to hardware, because it relies on rendering millions of sprites (the constant color circles) at typical screen resolutions. In software, special-purpose algorithms keep this reasonably efficient, but still nowhere near real time. Attempts have been made to use variants of these algorithms, by blending the translated source image multiple times with per-pixel weights based upon the CoC of the pixel and the distance translated. However, the same trade-offs apply here as for the layered depth-of-field effect. Although the passes are much simpler geometrically, even more passes are required: typically one per pixel of the largest CoC. Figure 23-6 shows an example of this technique, which worked rather well for this scene—no obvious artifacts are evident.

Figure 23-6. Forward-Mapped Z-Buffer Depth of Field

23.6 Reverse-Mapped Z-Buffer Depth of Field

The final technique is the reverse-mapped (that is, texture-mapped) z-buffer technique, which is similar in many ways to the forward-mapping technique. It also works off a color and depth image, but instead of rendering blended sprites onto the screen, this technique blurs the rendered scene by varying amounts per pixel, depending on the depth found in the z-buffer. Each pixel chooses a greater level of blurriness for a larger difference between its z value and the z value of the plane in focus. The ways in which this blurred version is generated and applied account for the main variants of this technique.

The simplest variant allows the hardware to create mipmaps of the scene texture and then performs a texture lookup, specifying the circle of confusion as the derivatives passed along to decide which mip level to read from. See Figures 23-7, 23-8, and 23-9. However, until the release of the GeForce FX and the Radeon 9700, graphics hardware couldn't choose which mip level of a texture to read per pixel.

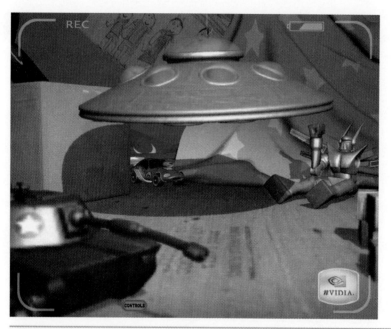

Figure 23-7. Reverse-Mapped Z-Buffer Depth of Field
The plane in focus is at the blanket in the background.

Figure 23-8. Reverse-Mapped Z-Buffer Depth of Field
The plane in focus is at the barrel of the tank in the foreground.

Figure 23-9. No Depth-of-Field Simulation

Earlier variants of this technique therefore used multiple blurred textures to approximate the blur introduced by depth of field. Some techniques used the same texture bound multiple times with different mip-level biases, and some explicitly created new blurred textures, often with better down-sampling filters (3×3 or 5×5 rather than 2×2). These variants would typically perform three lookups—the original scene, the quarter-sized ($\frac{1}{4} \times \frac{1}{4}$) texture, and the sixteenth-sized ($\frac{1}{16} \times \frac{1}{16}$) texture—and blend between them based upon the pixel's z value. Instead of letting the hardware generate mipmaps, it's also possible to render-to-texture to each mipmap with better filter kernels to get better-quality mipmaps. The hardware's mipmap generation is typically faster, however, so this becomes a bit of a quality/performance trade-off. Another interesting variant uses the hardware to generate a floating-point summed-area table for the color texture instead of mipmaps. Although the use of summed-area tables fixes the bilinear interpolation artifacts discussed later, this technique is quite a bit slower, and it actually isn't guaranteed to produce well-defined results.

Unfortunately, the technique used to build the summed-area table renders to the same texture it's reading from, rendering vertical lines to sum horizontally, and horizontal lines to sum vertically. Reading from the same texture being written isn't guaranteed to produce well-defined results using current graphics APIs (that is, the API allows the graphics driver to draw black, garbage, or something else rather than the expected result). It has been tested, and it does work on current hardware and drivers in OpenGL, but this could change with new hardware or a new version of the driver.

23.6.1 Analysis

Although this technique is in general significantly faster than other techniques, it has a variety of limitations. Some of these are minor and exist in many of the other techniques, but some are more objectionable and are unique to this technique alone.

Artifacts Due to Depth Discontinuities

The most objectionable artifact is caused by depth discontinuities in the depth image. Because only a single z value is read to determine how much to blur the image (that is, which mip level to choose), a foreground (blurry) object won't blur out over midground (sharp) objects. See Figure 23-10. One solution is to read multiple depth values, although unless you can read a variable number of depth values, you will have a halo effect of decreasing blur of fixed radius, which is nearly as objectionable as the depth discontinuity itself. Another solution is to read a blurred depth buffer, but this causes artifacts that are just as objectionable: blurring along edges of sharp objects and sharpening along edges of blurry objects. Extra blur can be added to the whole scene by uniformly biasing the calculated CoC. Adding a little extra blur when the focal plane moved too close (and not letting the focal plane move too close too often) helped hide this artifact fairly well in the GeForce FX launch demo, "Toys," from which the images in this chapter were taken.

Artifacts Due to Bilinear Interpolation

The magnification of the smaller mipmaps or blurred images results in bilinear interpolation artifacts. See Figure 23-11. This problem has some easier solutions, including using the summed-area tables approach, using the multiple blurred images approach with full-sized images (rather than down-sampling), or jittering the sampling position (potentially with multiple samples) proportional to the CoC in the mipmap approach. See Figure 23-12.

In the "Toys" demo, we used the jittered mipmap sample approach because it was the fastest. Although the jittering introduces artifacts of its own, the noise produced was preferable to the crawling, square, stair-stepping patterns of the non-jittered version, especially during animation.

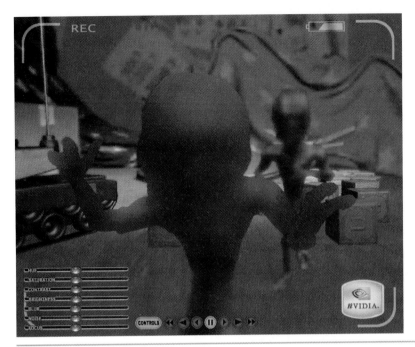

Figure 23-10. Depth Discontinuity Artifacts
The alien in the foreground, although blurry internally, has sharp edges and fails to blend out over nearby midground pixels.

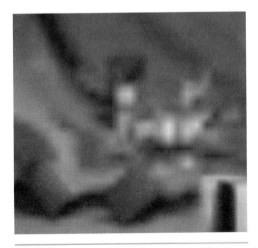

Figure 23-11. Magnification Artifacts with Trilinear Filtering

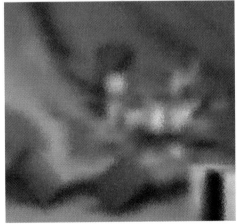

Figure 23-12. Noise Artifacts with Jittered Trilinear Filtering

Artifacts Due to Pixel Bleeding

The least objectionable artifact is pixel bleeding. Because the color image is blurred indiscriminately, areas in focus can incorrectly bleed into nearby areas out of focus. In a typical scene, this problem tends not to be very noticeable, but it's easy to build atypical situations where it becomes quite apparent. See Figure 23-13.

One solution is to render separate objects into layers, perform the reverse-mapped z-buffer depth-of-field technique on each separately, and then composite them together. This doesn't completely solve the problem. However, it resolves the common cases, because individual objects tend to have a similar color scheme internally, and they tend not to overlap themselves by large differences in depth. This can also reduce the effect of depth discontinuities if the clear depth for each layer is set to the farthest depth within the layer. Typically, if the layer's object is out of focus, this clear depth will also be out of focus, and so this object will blur out over objects behind it. There will generally be some discontinuity, but it will tend to be lessened by this technique. However, as in the layered depth-of-field technique, this layer sorting can be used only for certain scenes.

Figure 23-13. Pixel-Bleeding Artifacts
Pixel bleeding from the in-focus barrel to the out-of-focus table, yielding a halo effect around the barrel.

23.7 Conclusion

In this chapter, we've examined the major depth-of-field techniques, along with their benefits and problems. Unfortunately, no single depth-of-field algorithm meets everyone's quality and speed requirements. When correct shading is necessary but real-time processing isn't, the ray-traced or accumulation-buffer depth-of-field algorithms are the appropriate choices. When speed is of utmost importance, the layered or z-buffer depth-of-field algorithms are a better choice. For post-processing rendered scenes, the best quality is available through the splatting depth-of-field technique.

We've examined the z-buffer depth-of-field algorithm in detail, because there isn't a canonical paper in the literature, as there is for the other techniques, and because it's the one most likely to be useful for truly real-time applications. The pixel-bleeding artifact is the hardest to fix, but fortunately it is also the least objectionable. The bilinear interpolation artifacts are fairly easily solved, with some performance cost, by better filtering between mipmaps or textures. Last, the most objectionable artifacts due to depth discontinuities are only really solved by avoiding those cases in which they occur (that is, when the focal plane is far into the scene), which limits the utility of the algorithm for general purposes but is good enough for many real-time applications.

23.8 References

Arce, Tomas, and Matthias Wloka. 2002. "In-Game Special Effects and Lighting." Available online at
http://www.nvidia.com/object/gdc_in_game_special_effects.html

Cant, Richard, Nathan Chia, and David Al-Dabass. 2001 "New Anti-Aliasing and Depth of Field Techniques for Games." Available online at
http://ducati.doc.ntu.ac.uk/uksim/dad/webpagepapers/Game-18.pdf

Chen, Y. C. 1987. "Lens Effect on Synthetic Image Generation Based on Light Particle Theory." *The Visual Computer* 3(3).

Cook, R., T. Porter, and L. Carpenter. 1984. "Distributed Ray Tracing." In *Proceedings of the 11th Annual Conference on Computer Graphics and Interactive Techniques*.

Demers, Joe. 2003. "Depth of Field in the 'Toys' Demo." From "Ogres and Fairies: Secrets of the NVIDIA Demo Team," presented at GDC 2003. Available online at
http://developer.nvidia.com/docs/IO/8230/GDC2003_Demos.pdf

Dudkiewicz, K. 1994. "Real-Time Depth-of-Field Algorithm." In *Image Processing for Broadcast and Video Production: Proceedings of the European Workshop on Combined Real and Synthetic Image Processing for Broadcast and Video Production*, edited by Yakup Paker and Sylvia Wilbur, pp. 257–268. Springer-Verlag.

Green, Simon. 2003. "Summed Area Tables Using Graphics Hardware." Available online at **http://www.opengl.org/resources/tutorials/gdc2003/ GDC03_SummedAreaTables.ppt**

Haeberli, Paul, and Kurt Akeley. 1990. "The Accumulation Buffer: Hardware Support for High-Quality Rendering." *Computer Graphics* 24(4). Available online at **http://graphics.stanford.edu/courses/cs248-02/ haeberli-akeley-accumulation-buffer-sig90.pdf**

Krivánek, Jaroslav, Jiří Zára, and Kadi Bouatouch. 2003. "Fast Depth of Field Rendering with Surface Splatting." Presentation at Computer Graphics International 2003. Available online at **http://www.cgg.cvut.cz/~xkrivanj/papers/cgi2003/ 9-3_krivanek_j.pdf**

Mulder, Jurriaan, and Robert van Liere. 2000. "Fast Perception-Based Depth of Field Rendering." Available online at **http://www.cwi.nl/~robertl/papers/2000/vrst/paper.pdf**

Potmesil, Michael, and Indranil Chakravarty. 1981. "A Lens and Aperture Camera Model For Synthetic Image Generation." *Computer Graphics*.

Potmesil, Michael, and Indranil Chakravarty. 1982. "Synthetic Image Generation with a Lens and Aperture Camera Model." *ACM Transactions on Graphics*, April 1982.

Rokita, P. 1993. "Fast Generation of Depth of Field Effects in Computer Graphics." *Computers & Graphics* 17(5), pp. 593–595.

Scofield, Cary. 1994. "2½-D Depth of Field Simulation for Computer Animation." In *Graphics Gems III*, edited by David Kirk. Morgan Kaufmann.

Chapter 24

High-Quality Filtering

Kevin Bjorke
NVIDIA

GPU hardware can provide fast, filtered access to textures, but not for every texel format, and only with a few restrictive types of texture filtering. For many applications, building your own image-filtering method provides greater quality and flexibility. Understanding the quality and speed trade-offs between hardware and procedural filtering is crucial for these applications.

The same considerations used for filtering images apply also to 3D rendering, especially when models are textured: we are transforming 3D data (and potentially texture information) into a new 2D image. Understanding this transformation is key to drawing antialiased images.

Hybrid filtering approaches, which use hardware texture units alongside analytical shading, can offer an optimal middle path.

24.1 Quality vs. Speed

In some applications, quality filtering is crucial. Modern graphics hardware can deliver mipmapped texture access at very high speeds, but only by using a linear filtering method. Other filtering methods are available, and they are needed for some kinds of imaging applications.

When hardware filtering is unavailable, or when we need the utmost in image quality, we can use pixel-shading code to perform any arbitrary filter.

GPU shading programs are different from CPU shading programs in one key aspect: generally, the CPU is faster at math operations than texturing. In languages such as the RenderMan shading language, `texture()` is typically one of the most expensive operators. This is opposite to the situation in a GPU.

In GPU shading languages, texture operators such as `tex2D()` are typically among the fastest operators, because unlike CPU shaders, GPU shaders don't manage the surrounding graphics state or disk system. We can use this speed to gain a variety of useful elements for filtering, such as filter kernels and gamma-correction lookups.

24.1.1 Filter Kernels: Image-to-Image Conversions

The goal of image filtering is simple: given an input image A, we want to create a new image B. The transformation operation from source A to target B is the image filter. The most common transformations are image resizing, sharpening, color changes, and blurring.

In some cases (particularly in color transformations), every pixel in the new image B corresponds exactly to a pixel in image A. But for most other operations, we want to sample multiple pixels in image A and apply their values based on some user-defined function. The pattern of source pixels, and those pixels' relative contributions to the final pixel in image B, is called the *filter kernel*. The process of applying a kernel to the source image is called *convolution*: we convolve pixels in source A by a particular kernel to create the pixels in new image B.

In common imaging applications such as Adobe Photoshop, we can specify kernels as rectangular arrays or pixel contributions. Or we can let Photoshop calculate what kernels to use, in operations such as Sharpen and Blur, or when we resize the image.

If pixels within a kernel are simply averaged together, we call this pattern a *box filter*, because the pattern is a simple rectangle (all the pixels that fit in the box). Each sampled texel (that is, a pixel from a texture) is weighted equally. Box filters are easy to construct, fast to execute, and in fact are at the core of hardware-driven filtering in GPUs.

User-Defined Kernels

If we're okay using small kernels, we can pass the terms directly as parameters to the shader. The sample code in Listing 24-1 implements a 3×3 filter operation: the indexed texel and its neighbors are assigned weights W00 through W22, the weighted values are summed, and then they are renormalized against a precalculated Sum value. See Figure 24-1.

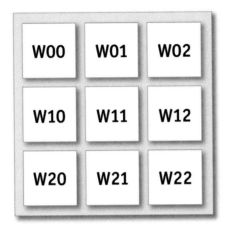

Figure 24-1. The Layout of Pixels for a 3×3 Kernel Centered at W11.
The resultant pixel will be the weighted sum of the surrounding texels, divided by the Sum value provided by the user.

Listing 24-1. Reading Nine Texels to Calculate a Weighted Sum

```
float4 convolve3x3PS(vertexOutput IN,
  uniform sampler2D ColorMap,
  uniform float W00, uniform float W01, uniform float W02,
  uniform float W10, uniform float W11, uniform float W12,
  uniform float W20, uniform float W21, uniform float W22,
  uniform float Sum,
  uniform float StepHoriz,
  uniform float StepVert) : COLOR
{
  float2 ox = float2(StepHoriz, 0.0);
  float2 oy = float2(0.0, StepVert);
  float2 PP = IN.UV.xy - oy;
  float4 C00 = tex2D(ColorMap, PP - ox);
  float4 C01 = tex2D(ColorMap, PP);
  float4 C02 = tex2D(ColorMap, PP + ox);
  PP = IN.UV.xy;
  float4 C10 = tex2D(ColorMap, PP - ox);
  float4 C11 = tex2D(ColorMap, PP);
  float4 C12 = tex2D(ColorMap, PP + ox);
```

```
    PP = IN.UV.xy + oy;
    float4 C20 = tex2D(ColorMap, PP - ox);
    float4 C21 = tex2D(ColorMap, PP);
    float4 C22 = tex2D(ColorMap, PP + ox);
    float4 Ci = C00 * W00;
    Ci += C01 * W01;
    Ci += C02 * W02;
    Ci += C10 * W10;
    Ci += C11 * W11;
    Ci += C12 * W12;
    Ci += C20 * W20;
    Ci += C21 * W21;
    Ci += C22 * W22;
    return (Ci/Sum);
}
```

The values `StepHoriz` and `StepVert` define the spacing between texels (pass $1/256$ for a 256×256 texture, and so on). The texture should not be mipmapped, because we want to read exact texels from the original data.

Depending on the hardware profile, such a shader may also be more efficient if the texture-lookup locations are precalculated in the vertex shader and simply passed as interpolators to the fragment shader, rather than calculating them explicitly in the fragment shader as shown here.

A Speedup for Grayscale Data

The shader in Listing 24-1 makes nine texture accesses and has to adjust its lookups accordingly. This means redundant accesses (hopefully cached by the GPU) between pixels, and a lot of small adds and multiplies. For grayscale-data textures, we can have the CPU do a little work for us in advance and then greatly accelerate the texture accesses.

Figure 24-2 shows a grayscale image and two "helper" images. A $4\times$ detail is also shown.

The first helper image is a copy of the first, but it has the red channel offset one texel to the left; the green, one texel to the right; the blue, one texel up; and the alpha (invisible on the printed page), one texel down.

The second helper image is offset similarly, but to the texel corners, rather than the immediate texel neighbors: so red is one texel left and up, green is one texel left and up, blue is one texel left and down, and so on.

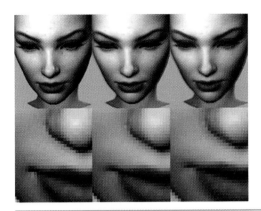

Figure 24-2. Grayscale Image Plus Two RGB "Helpers" with Offset Texel Data

By arranging the channels in this way, all four neighbors (or all four corners) can be accessed in *one* tex2D() call—and without having to adjust the texture indices. Our convolve shader now gets a lot shorter, as shown in Listing 24-2.

Listing 24-2. Nine Texel Accesses Reduced to Three

```
float4 convolve3x3GrayHPS(vertexOutput IN,
  uniform sampler2D GrayMap,
  uniform sampler2D NeighborMap,
  uniform sampler2D CornerMap,
  uniform float W00, uniform float W01, uniform float W02,
  uniform float W10, uniform float W11, uniform float W12,
  uniform float W20, uniform float W21, uniform float W22,
  uniform float Sum) : COLOR
{
  float gray = tex2D(GrayMap, IN.UV).x;
  float4 ntex = tex2D(NeighborMap, IN.UV);
  float4 ctex = tex2D(CornerMap, IN.UV);
  float Ci = ctex.x * W00;
  Ci += ntex.z * W01;
  Ci += ctex.y * W02;
  Ci += ntex.x * W10;
  Ci += gray * W11;
  Ci += ntex.y * W12;
  Ci += ctex.z * W20;
  Ci += ntex.w * W21;
  Ci += ctex.w * W22;

  return (Ci/Sum).xxxx;
}
```

We may be tempted to combine these multiply-add combinations into dot products, as in Listing 24-3.

Listing 24-3. As in Listing 24-2, Compactly Written Using Dot Products

```
float4 convolve3x3GrayHDPS(vertexOutput IN,
  uniform sampler2D GrayMap,
  uniform sampler2D NeighborMap,
  uniform sampler2D CornerMap,
  uniform float W00, uniform float W01, uniform float W02,
  uniform float W10, uniform float W11, uniform float W12,
  uniform float W20, uniform float W21, uniform float W22,
  uniform float Sum) : COLOR
{
  float gray = tex2D(GrayMap, IN.UV).x;
  float4 ntex = tex2D(NeighborMap, IN.UV);
  float4 ctex = tex2D(CornertMap, IN.UV);

  float Ci = gray + dot(ntex, float4(W10, W12, W01, W21)) +
             dot(ctex, float4(W00, W02, W20, W22));
  return (Ci/Sum).xxxx;
}
```

The result will be faster or slower, depending on the profile. The first shader takes 16 instructions in DirectX ps_2_0; the second uses 19 instructions, because of the many MOV operations required to construct the two `float4` terms.

If we preassemble those vectors in the CPU, however (they will be uniform for the entire image, after all), then we can reduce the function to 11 ps_2_0 instructions—one-third of the instructions from the original one-texture version. See Listing 24-4.

Listing 24-4. The Most Compact Form, Using Pre-Coalesced `float4` Weights

```
float4 convolve3x3GrayHDXPS(vertexOutput IN,
  uniform sampler2D GrayMap,
  uniform sampler2D NeighborMap,
  uniform sampler2D CornerMap,
  uniform float4 W10120121,
  uniform float4 W00022022,
  uniform float W11,
  uniform float Sum) : COLOR
```

```
{
    float gray = tex2D(GrayMap, IN.UV).x;
    float4 ntex = tex2D(NeighborMap, IN.UV);
    float4 ctex = tex2D(CornerMap, IN.UV);

    float Ci = W11 * gray + dot(ntex, W10120121) +
                    dot(ctex, W00022022);
    return (Ci/Sum).xxxx;
}
```

When the Kernel Is Constant

If the kernel won't change over the course of a shader's use, it's sometimes wise to plug the kernel values into the shader by hand, working through the values as constants, factoring out kernel values such as 0, 1, or –1 to reduce the number of instructions. That was the approach taken in the shader shown in Listing 24-5, which does edge detection, based on two constant 3×3 kernels. See the results shown in Figure 24-3.

Listing 24-5. Edge Detection Pixel Shader

```
float4 edgeDetectGPS(vertexOutput IN,
    uniform sampler2D TexMap,
    uniform float DeltaX,
    uniform float DeltaY,
    uniform float Threshold) : COLOR
{
    float2 ox = float2(DeltaX, 0.0);
    float2 oy = float2(0.0, DeltaY);
    float2 PP = IN.UV - oy;
    float g00 = tex2D(TexMap, PP - ox).x;
    float g01 = tex2D(TexMap, PP).x;
    float g02 = tex2D(TexMap, PP + ox).x;
    PP = IN.UV;
    float g10 = tex2D(TexMap, PP - ox).x;
    // float g11 = tex2D(TexMap, PP).x;
    float g12 = tex2D(TexMap, PP + ox).x;
    PP = IN.UV + oy;
    float g20 = tex2D(TexMap, PP - ox).x;
    float g21 = tex2D(TexMap, PP).x;
    float g22 = tex2D(TexMap, PP + ox).x;
```

Listing 24-5 (*continued*). Edge Detection Pixel Shader

```
float sx = g20 + g22 - g00 - g02 + 2 * (g21 - g01);
float sy = g22 + g02 - g00 - g20 + 2 * (g12 - g10);
float dist = (sx * sx + sy * sy);
float tSq = Threshold * Threshold; // could be done on CPU
float result = 1;
if (dist > tSq) { result = 0; }
return result.xxxx;
}
```

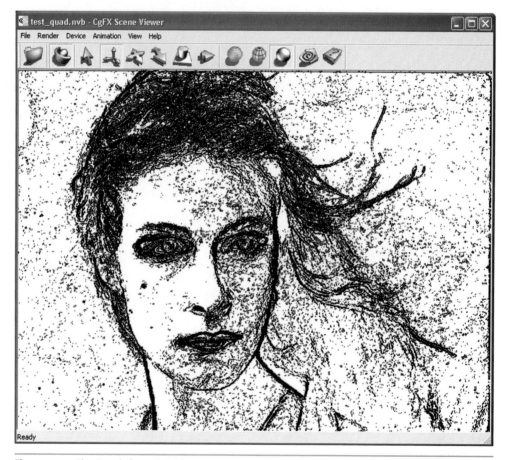

Figure 24-3. The Result from the Edge Detection Shader

By removing zero terms, we can drop several multiplications, adds, and even one of the texture fetches. This shader compiles to just under forty instructions.

If we have helper images as in the previous grayscale example, the instruction count drops by about half—and we can completely drop the original texture, as shown in Listing 24-6.

Listing 24-6. The Edge Detection Shader Written to Use Grayscale Helper Textures

```
float4 edgeDetectGXPS(vertexOutput IN,
  uniform sampler2D NeighborMap,
  uniform sampler2D CornerMap,
  uniform float Threshold) : COLOR
{
  float4 nm = tex2D(NeighborMap, IN.UV);
  float4 cm = tex2D(CornerMap, IN.UV);
  float sx = cm.z + cm.w - cm.x - cm.y + 2 * (nm.w - nm.x);
  float sy = cm.w + cm.y - cm.x - cm.z + 2 * (nm.z - nm.y);
  float tSq = Threshold * Threshold;
  float dist = (sx * sx + sy * sy);
  float result = 1;
  if (dist > tSq) { result = 0; }
  return result.xxxx;
}
```

A Bicubic Filter Kernel

The problem with box filtering is that the images it produces are often rather poor. When images are scaled down, edges will appear to lose contrast. When images are scaled up, they will look obviously "jaggy," because the rectangular shape of the box filter will reveal the rectangular shape of the pixels from image A.

By varying the relative importance of the source pixels, we can create better-looking resized images. A number of different filter patterns have been used, usually giving greater importance to pixels in A that lie near the center of the corresponding pixel in B.

A filter that's familiar to most users of imaging programs with "high-quality" resizing is commonly called the *cubic filter*; when applied in both *x* and *y* directions, we call the result *bicubic image filtering*. See Figure 24-4.

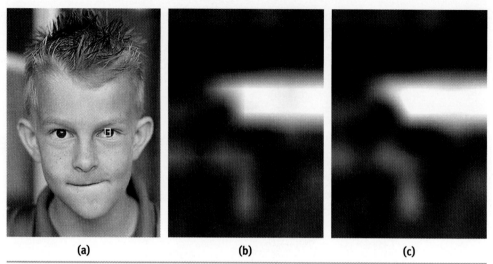

(a)   (b)   (c)

Figure 24-4. The Effects of Bilinear and Bicubic Filtering
(a) The original image; note the rectangle around one eye. (b) The rectangular sub-image area magnified 32 times with bilinear filtering. (c) The same area, magnified 32 times with bicubic filtering.

We can calculate a cubic kernel analytically. For example, to create a cubic sinc approximation filter, we would use the following rules:

$$(A + 2)x^3 - (A + 3)x^2 + 1.0, \quad 0 < x < 1$$
$$Ax^3 - 5Ax^2 + 8Ax - 4A, \quad 1 < x < 2$$
$$A = -0.75.$$

When graphed, these rules give us a shape like the one shown in Figure 24-5. The y value of this function shows the relative weight we should assign to texels that are distant from the center of a given texture coordinate. Texels more than two texels from that center are ignored, while texels at the center are given 100 percent weight. Note that for this particular filter, some weights may be *negative*: the result will give the re-sampled image a slight sharpening effect.

We could write a function to calculate a filter value for each sampled pixel. But since we don't need high-frequency precision inside the filter range, a lookup table will do nicely. We can just write these values into a small floating-point texture, which will provide us with adequate precision and quick lookup.

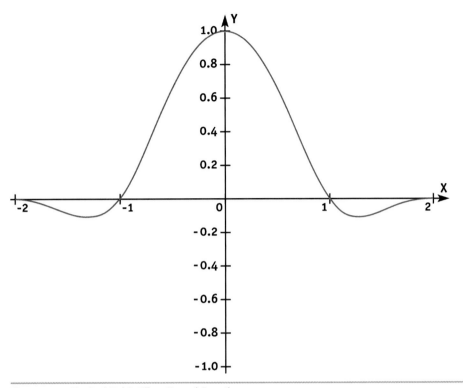

Figure 24-5. Typical Cubic Filter Kernel Function

The possible range of filter formulas that can be applied to different kinds of images is quite large, often depending as much on artistic assessment of the results as mathematical "correctness." A useful survey of common filter equations can be found at http://www.control.auc.dk/~awkr00/graphics/filtering/filtering.html.

Listing 24-7 shows the C++ code to generate such a filter-kernel texture for OpenGL, courtesy of Simon Green. This function uses a slightly different filter, called the Mitchell-Netravali.

A suggested size would be 256 elements: call `createWeightTexture(256, 0.5, 0.5)`.

Listing 24-8 is a short shader function that will return the filtered combination of four color values. Remember that floating-point textures always use the `samplerRECT` data type, so we use the `texRECT()` function for this small 1D texture with 256 elements and set the second index term to 0.

Listing 24-7. OpenGL C++ Code for Generating a Floating-Point Kernel Texture

```cpp
// Mitchell Netravali Reconstruction Filter
// B = 1,   C = 0    - cubic B-spline
// B = 1/3, C = 1/3 - recommended
// B = 0,   C = 1/2 - Catmull-Rom spline

float MitchellNetravali(float x, float B, float C)
{
  float ax = fabs(x);
  if (ax < 1) {
    return ((12 - 9 * B - 6 * C) * ax * ax * ax +
            (-18 + 12 * B + 6 * C) * ax * ax + (6 - 2 * B)) / 6;
  } else if ((ax >= 1) && (ax < 2)) {
      return ((-B - 6 * C) * ax * ax * ax +
              (6 * B + 30 * C) * ax * ax + (-12 * B - 48 * C) *
              ax + (8 * B + 24 * C)) / 6;
  } else {
      return 0;
  }
}


// Create a 1D float texture encoding weight for cubic filter
GLuint createWeightTexture(int size, float B, float C)
{
  float *img = new float[size * 4];
  float *ptr = img;
  for(int i = 0; i < size; i++) {
    float x = i / (float) (size - 1);
    *ptr++ = MitchellNetravali(x + 1, B, C);
    *ptr++ = MitchellNetravali(x, B, C);
    *ptr++ = MitchellNetravali(1 - x, B, C);
    *ptr++ = MitchellNetravali(2 - x, B, C);
  }
  GLuint texid;
  glGenTextures(1, &texid);
  GLenum target = GL_TEXTURE_RECTANGLE_NV;
  glBindTexture(target, texid);
  glTexParameteri(target, GL_TEXTURE_MAG_FILTER, GL_LINEAR);
  glTexParameteri(target, GL_TEXTURE_MIN_FILTER, GL_LINEAR);
  glTexParameteri(target, GL_TEXTURE_WRAP_S, GL_CLAMP_TO_EDGE);
  glTexParameteri(target, GL_TEXTURE_WRAP_T, GL_CLAMP_TO_EDGE);
```

```
    glPixelStorei(GL_UNPACK_ALIGNMENT, 1);
    glTexImage2D(target, 0, GL_FLOAT_RGBA_NV, size, 1, 0,
                GL_RGBA, GL_FLOAT, img);
    delete [] img;
    return texid;
}
```

Listing 24-8. Using the Kernel Texture as a Cg Function

```
float4 cubicFilter(uniform samplerRECT kernelTex,
                   float xValue,
                   float4 c0,
                   float4 c1,
                   float4 c2,
                   float4 c3)
{
  float4 h = texRECT(kernelTex, float2(xValue * 256.0, 0.0));
  float4 r = c0 * h.x;
  r += c1 * h.y;
  r += c2 * h.z;
  r += c3 * h.w;
  return r;
}
```

Listing 24-9 shows a bicubic filter that scans the four neighbors of any texel, then calls cubicFilter() on the columns of pixels surrounding our sample location, based on the fractional location of the filter, then once more to blend those four returned samples.

Listing 24-9. Filtering Four Texel Rows, Then Filtering the Results as a Column

```
float4 texRECT_bicubic(uniform samplerRECT tex,
                       uniform samplerRECT kernelTex,
                       float2 t)
{
  float2 f = frac(t);   // we want the sub-texel portion
  float4 t0 = cubicFilter(kernelTex, f.x,
                          texRECT(tex, t + float2(-1, -1)),
                          texRECT(tex, t + float2(0, -1)),
                          texRECT(tex, t + float2(1, -1)),
                          texRECT(tex, t + float2(2, -1)));
```

```
    float4 t1 = cubicFilter(kernelTex, f.x,
                            texRECT(tex, t + float2(-1, 0)),
                            texRECT(tex, t + float2(0, 0)),
                            texRECT(tex, t + float2(1, 0)),
                            texRECT(tex, t + float2(2, 0)));
    float4 t2 = cubicFilter(kernelTex, f.x,
                            texRECT(tex, t + float2(-1, 1)),
                            texRECT(tex, t + float2(0, 1)),
                            texRECT(tex, t + float2(1, 1)),
                            texRECT(tex, t + float2(2, 1)));
    float4 t3 = cubicFilter(kernelTex, f.x,
                            texRECT(tex, t + float2(-1, 2)),
                            texRECT(tex, t + float2(0, 2)),
                            texRECT(tex, t + float2(1, 2)),
                            texRECT(tex, t + float2(2, 2)));
    return cubicFilter(kernelTex, f.y, t0, t1, t2, t3);
}
```

We're calling `texRECT()` quite a bit here: we've asked the texturing system for sixteen separate samples from `tex` and five samples from `ftex`.

The method shown here permits the filter to be applied in a single pass, by filtering the local neighborhood four times along *x* and then the results filtered one time along *y*. Although this approach is workable and makes for a good textbook example, it is far from optimal. A more computationally efficient approach to uniform filtering of this sort can be found in *two-pass filtering,* where the *x* and *y* passes are used as separable functions. This technique is described in detail in Chapter 21 of this book, "Real-Time Glow."

Screen-Aligned Kernels

In the previous examples, we've applied a filter that "travels" with each texel: the kernel texture is aligned relative to the sample being generated.

Some kinds of images, particularly those generated by video and digital photo applications, can benefit from a similar method using "static kernels." These kernel textures can be used to decode or encode pixels into the formats used by digital capture and broadcast formats such as D1, YUV, GBGR, and related Bayer pattern sensors—even complex 2D patterns such as Sony RGBE.[1] In such cases, the relative weights of the texels are aligned to the *screen,* rather than to the sample.

---

1. Sony's RGBE acronym stands for *red, green, blue, emerald*—the four color filters used by some Sony sensors. This format is unrelated to the RGBE often used in high-dynamic-range imaging, which stands for *red, green, blue, exponent.*

Let's take the case of YCbCR "D1" 4:2:2 encoding. In a 4:2:2 image, the pixels are arranged as a single stream:

Y Cb Y Cr Y Cb Y Cr Y Cb…

So to decode this stream into RGB pixels, we need to apply a different weight to each of the neighboring pixels. While a number of slightly varying standards exist, we'll look at the most common one: ITU-R BT.601.

For a given Y value, we need to generate RGB from the Y and the neighboring Cb and Cr values. Typically, we'll interpolate these between neighbors on either side (linear interpolation is usually acceptable for most consumer applications), though along the edges of the frame we'll use only the immediate neighbors. We can cast these values as weights in a texture. Because of the special handling of the edge texels, we need the weight texture to be the same size as the entire screen. For most Y samples, the effective Cb or Cr values will be interpolated between the neighboring values on either side; but for Y values along the edge, we need to adjust the weight pattern to give full weight to the nearest Cb/Cr sample, while assigning zero weight to any "off-screen" texture lookups.

Given a composited (Y, Cb, Cr) pixel, the conversion will be:

```
#define MID (128.0/255.0)
#define VIDEO_BLACK (16.0/255.0)
float3 YUV = float3(1.164 * (Y - VIDEO_BLACK),(Cb - MID),(Cr - MID));
float3 RGB = float3((YUV.x + 1.596 * YUV.y),
                    (YUV.x - 0.813 * YUV.z - 0.392 * YUV.y),
                    (YUV.x + 2.017 * YUV.z));
```

This conversion also normalizes our RGB values to the range 0–1. By default, YUV data typically ranges from 16 to 235, rather than the 0–255 range usually used in RGB computer graphics. The values above video-white and below video-black are typically used for special video effects: for example, "superblack" is often used for video keying, in the absence of an alpha channel.

Video data usually needs gamma correction as well. Because the gamma is constant (2.2 for NTSC, 2.8 for PAL), this too can be performed quickly by a `tex1D()` lookup table.

24.2 Understanding GPU Derivatives

Complex filtering depends on knowing just how much of the texture (or shading) we need to filter. Modern GPUs such as the GeForce FX provide *partial derivative functions* to help us. For any value used in shading, we can ask the GPU: "How much does this value change from pixel to pixel, in either the screen-x or the screen-y direction?"

These functions are ddx() and ddy(). Although they are little used, they can be very helpful for filtering and antialiasing operations. These derivative functions provide us with the necessary information to perform procedural filtering or to adroitly modify the filtering inherent in most texture sampling.

For GPUs that do not directly support ddx() and ddy(), you can use the method outlined in Chapter 25 of this book, "Fast Filter-Width Estimates with Texture Maps."

The values returned by the GPU for ddx() and ddy() are numerically iterated values. That is, if you evaluate ddx(myVar), the GPU will give you the difference between the value of myVar at the current pixel and its value at the pixel next door. It's a straight linear difference, made efficient by the nature of GPU SIMD architectures (neighboring pixels will be calculated simultaneously). Of course, it should apply to values that interpolate across a polygon, passed from the vertex shader—the derivative of any uniform value will always be zero.

Because these derivatives are always linear, the second derivatives—for example, ddx(ddx(myVar))—will *always* be zero. If your shader contains some clever function whose higher-order derivatives could instead be accurately calculated analytically, use that formulation if the value is important (say, for scientific calculation or film-level rendering).

Once we know the amount of change in a given pixel, we're able to determine the appropriate filtering. For a texture, the correct filtering will be to integrate the texture not just at a given u-v coordinate, but across a quadrilateral-shaped window into that texture, whose texture coordinates will be ddx(UV) across and ddy(UV) in height. When we call functions such as tex2D(), this is in fact automatically calculated for us. Cg, for advanced profiles, allows us to optionally specify the size of the filter we want to apply. For example, by specifying:

```
float2 nilUV = float2(0, 0);
float4 pt = tex2D(myTextureSampler, IN.UV, nilUV, nilUV);
```

we can force the filter size to be zero—in effect, forcing the sampling of this texture always to use the "nearest-neighbor" method of filtering, regardless of the mode set by the API or the presence of mipmaps.

24.3 Analytical Antialiasing and Texturing

For shaders that use procedural texturing, knowing the size of the texture sample at each pixel is crucial for effective antialiasing.

To antialias a function, we need to integrate the function over that pixel. In the simplest case, we can just integrate exactly over the pixel boundaries and then take an average (this is known as *box filtering*). Alternate schemes may assign greater or lesser weights to areas in the pixel or to values from neighboring pixels (as we did in the blur example at the beginning of this chapter).

Consider the simple case of stripes. The stripe function could be expressed as all-on or all-off per pixel, but this would have jaggies, as in the function shown in Listing 24-10, which draws stripes perpendicular to an object's *x* coordinates. (`Balance` is a fractional number that defines the relationship of dark to light stripes: a default value of `0.5` means that both dark and light stripes have the same width.) We can use the `stripes` value to linearly interpolate between two colors.

Listing 24-10. Naive Stripe Function

```
float4 stripeJaggedPS(vertexOutput IN) : COLOR
{
  float strokeS = frac(IN.ObjPos.x / Scale);
  half stripes = 0.0;
  if (strokeS > Balance) stripes = 1.0;
  float4 dColor = lerp(SurfColor1, SurfColor2, stripes);
  return dColor;
}
```

Figure 24-6 shows the result. As you can see, the stripes have pronounced "jaggy" artifacts.

Instead, we can consider the integral of the stripe function over a pixel, and then divide by the area of that pixel to get an antialiased result.

The small graph in Figure 24-7 shows the stripe function and its integral along *x*. As you can see, the stripe goes on and off along *x*, while the integral—that is, the sum of the area covered by the stripe so far as *x* increases—rises steadily, then holds, then rises, then holds, then rises... for each successive stripe.

Figure 24-6. Naive Stripe As Applied to a Model

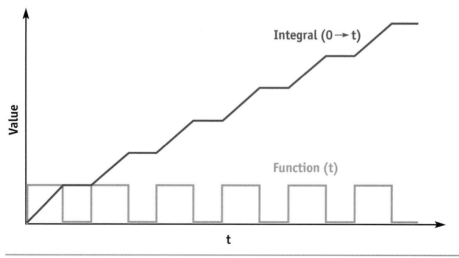

Figure 24-7. The Integral of the Stripe Function
Looking at the definite integral provides a way to think about the stripes cumulatively across a set of pixels.

So for any interval between values x0 and x1 along *x*, we can take the integral at x0, subtract it from the integral at x1, and know how many stripes we've crossed between x0 and x1. Dividing this by the width of the interval (x1 − x0) will give us an average distribution of stripe/nonstripe over the entire span. For an individual pixel, that statistical blend is exactly what we need.

Casting this solution as a shading function, we can antialias any value by estimating the change via ddx() and ddy(), as shown in Listing 24-11.

Listing 24-11. Stripe Function that Returns Grayscale Values Based on the Amount of Stripe Coverage

```
half stripe(float value, half balance, half invScale, float scale)
{
  half width = abs(ddx(value)) + abs(ddy(value));
  half w = width * invScale;
  half x0 = value/scale - (w / 2.0);
  half x1 = x0 + w;
  half edge = balance / scale;
  half i0 = (1.0 - edge) * floor(x0) + max(0.0, frac(x0) - edge);
  half i1 = (1.0 - edge) * floor(x1) + max(0.0, frac(x1) - edge);
  half strip = (i1 - i0) / w;
  strip = min(1.0, max(0.0, strip));
  return (strip);
}
```

We're making a simplifying assumption here, that the function varies in a roughly linear way. We've also separated scale and its reciprocal so we can scale the reciprocal to introduce oversampling, a user control allowing the result to be even fuzzier on demand.

With our stripe() function in hand, we can create another short pixel shader and apply it in EffectEdit. See Listing 24-12.

Listing 24-12. Simple Pixel Shader to Apply Our Filtered Stripe Function

```
float4 stripePS(vertexOutput IN) : COLOR
{
  half edge = Scale * Balance;
  half op = OverSample/Scale;
  half stripes = stripe(IN.ObjPos.x, edge, op, Scale);
  float4 dColor = lerp(SurfColor1, SurfColor2, stripes);
  return dColor;
}
```

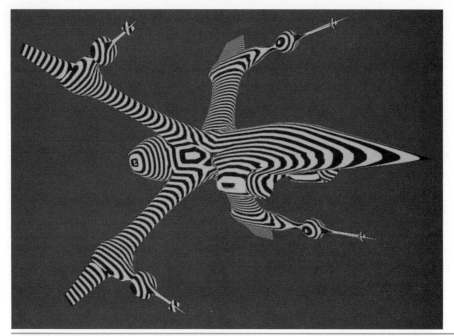

Figure 24-8. Filtered Stripe Applied to a Model

Figure 24-8 looks a lot better than Figure 24-6, but at a price: the first, jaggy version renders about twice as fast as this smooth version.

This also seems like a lot of work for a stripe. Can't we just use a black-and-white texture? Yes, in fact we can, as shown in Listing 24-13.

Listing 24-13. Using a Stripe Texture for Simple Striping

```
float4 stripeTexPS(vertexOutput IN) : COLOR
{
  half stripes = tex1D(stripe1DSampler,(IN.ObjPos.x / Scale)).x;
  float4 dColor = lerp(SurfColor1, SurfColor2, stripes);
  return dColor;
}
```

This version runs fastest of all—about three times as quickly as the procedurally antialiased version. As you can see in Figure 24-9, the resulting image seems to have lost its "balance" control, but this seems like a good trade-off for speed.

Figure 24-9. Simple Texture Applied to a Model

But what if we want to control the dark/light balance as part of the final appearance? We don't have to implement it as a user input. We can alter balance according to $(\mathbf{L} \cdot \mathbf{N})$ at each pixel to create an engraved-illustration look. See Listing 24-14.

Listing 24-14. Using Luminance to Control the Balance of the Stripe Function

```
float4 strokePS(vertexOutput IN) : COLOR
{
  float3 Nn = normalize(IN.WorldNormal);
  float strokeWeight = max(0.01, -dot(LightDir, Nn));
  half edge = Scale * strokeWeight;
  half op = OverSample / Scale;
  half stripes = stripe(IN.ObjPos.x, edge, op, Scale);
  float4 dColor = lerp(SurfColor1, SurfColor2, stripes);
  return dColor;
}
```

Figure 24-10 shows the image that results. This shader is slow again, even a little bit slower than our first analytic example. Fortunately, we can also speed up this function by applying a texture, based on the observation that we can "spread" our 1D black-and-white stripe texture over 2D, and then use our calculated "balance" value as a "V" index.

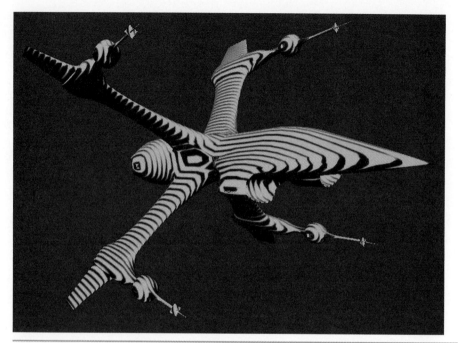

Figure 24-10. Light/Dark Balance Applied to a Model

Our stripe texture, then, will look like Figure 24-11. Such a texture can be generated within HLSL's .fx format by a procedure, as shown in Listing 24-15. The result is almost as fast as the `tex1D` stripe. See Listing 24-16.

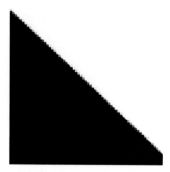

Figure 24-11. The Stripe Texture

Listing 24-15. HLSL .fx Instructions to Generate Variable Stripe Texture

```
#define TEX_SIZE 64

texture stripeTex <
  string function = "MakeStripe";
  int width = TEX_SIZE;
  int height = TEX_SIZE;
>;

sampler2D stripeSampler = sampler_state
{
  Texture = <stripeTex>;
  MinFilter = LINEAR;
  MagFilter = LINEAR;
  MipFilter = LINEAR;
  AddressU = CLAMP;
  AddressV = CLAMP;
};

float4 MakeStripe(float2 Pos : POSITION, float ps : PSIZE) : COLOR
{
  float v = 0;
  float nx = Pos.x + ps; // keep the last column full-on, always
  v = nx > Pos.y;
  return float4(v.xxxx);
}
```

Listing 24-16. Applying Variable Stripe Texture in a Pixel Shader

```
float4 strokeTexPS(vertexOutput IN) : COLOR
{
  float3 Nn = normalize(IN.WorldNormal);
  float strokeWeight = max(0.0, -dot(LightDir, Nn));
  float strokeS = (IN.ObjPos.x / Scale);
  float2 newST = float2(strokeS, strokeWeight);
  half stripes = tex2D(stripeSampler, newST).x;
  float4 dColor = lerp(SurfColor1, SurfColor2, stripes);
  return dColor;
}
```

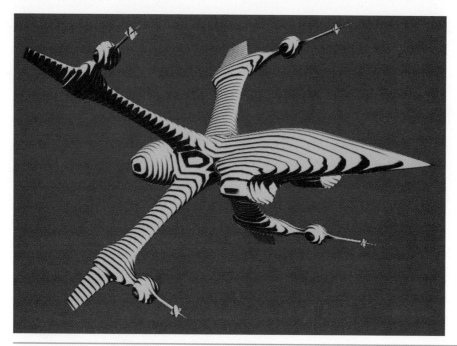

Figure 24-12. Variable Stripe Texture Applied to a Model

The textured version, shown in Figure 24-12, contains some small artifacts, which can be improved with higher resolution or with careful creation of the mip levels. Note that our HLSL texture-creation function `MakeStripe()` uses the optional `PSIZE` input. `PSIZE` will contain the width and height of the current texel relative to the texture as a whole. Its value will change depending on the mip level currently being calculated by `MakeStripe()`.

The speedup is evident in the size of the resultant shader: only 14 instructions for PS2.0, as opposed to 45 instructions for the analytic version.

The textured version has limited precision; in particular, if we get very close to the spaceship, the texels will start to appear clearly. The analytic version will *always* show a clean, smooth edge.

24.3.1 Interacting with Graphics API Antialiasing

The filtering methods we've described here ignore the application of antialiasing (AA) by the graphics API. Via the API, we can apply hardware AA to the entire frame: $2\times$, $4\times$, and so on. The API will sample the geometry within each pixel at multiple sub-pixel locations, according to its own hardware kernel. Such multiple-sample antialiasing can correct many problems, including some math functions that are otherwise intractable. However, for multisampling, the quality of polygon edges will improve but the quality of shading may *not* improve, because typically shaders are not reevaluated for each individual sample.

The downside of multisampled AA is that the surfaces must be sampled and evaluated multiple times, with a commensurate performance drop. A second downside, for some applications, may be that you simply don't know if AA has been turned on by the user or not. This presents a problem: How to balance quality and performance? Is procedural antialiasing a waste, if API AA is turned on, or is it crucial for maintaining quality if the user has turned AA off? The shader itself can't know the current AA settings. Instead, it's up to the CPU-side application to manage the API. In the end, you should probably test your program under the various sampling environments to choose the best balance—and try to control API-side AA from the application if it presents problems.

24.4 Conclusion

Pixel shading for image processing is one of the largely untapped areas of GPU usage. Not only can games and related entertainments gain from using GPU image processing, but many other imaging operations, such as image compositing, resizing, digital photography, even GUIs, can gain from having fast, high-quality imaging in their display pipelines.

The same values used in managing pixels for image processing can be used in 3D imaging for effective antialiasing and management of even complex nonphotorealistic shading algorithms.

24.5 References

Castleman, Kenneth R. 1996. *Digital Image Processing*. Prentice-Hall.

Madisetti, Vijay K., and Douglas B. Williams, eds. 1998. *The Digital Signal Processing Handbook*. CRC Press.

Poynton, Charles. 2003. Web site. **http://www.poynton.com**. *Charles Poynton's excellent Web site provides many useful references.*

Young, Ian T., Jan J. Gerbrands, and Lucas J. van Vliet. 1998. "Fundamentals of Image Processing." Available online at **http://www.ph.tn.tudelft.nl/DIPlib/docs/FIP2.2.pdf**

Chapter 25

Fast Filter-Width Estimates with Texture Maps

Matt Pharr
NVIDIA

This chapter describes a technique for computing an approximation to the derivative of arbitrary quantities in fragment programs. This technique loads special values into each level of a texture mipmap and uses the texture-mapping hardware in an unusual way to cause it to return the results of a derivative computation, giving an indication of how quickly the quantity is changing from pixel to pixel on the screen. Computing derivatives such as these is a critical operation to perform in shaders that compute procedural patterns, because it allows them to perform antialiasing on the patterns they generate by prefiltering them to remove detail that can't be represented by the pixel-sampling rate.

Cg's Standard Library provides ddx() and ddy() functions that compute the derivative of an arbitrary quantity with respect to the *x* and *y* pixels. In other words, given some arbitrary variable v, calling ddx(v) tells you approximately how much v will change between the current pixel and the next pixel in the *x* direction; the same is true for ddy(v) for the *y* direction. Unfortunately, some hardware profiles (for example, arbfp1) do not support these derivative computations, which makes it very difficult to write shaders that don't suffer from aliasing artifacts when using those profiles. This chapter gives a solution to this deficiency based on the texture-mapping functionality that those profiles do provide.

25.1 The Need for Derivatives in Shaders

Consider a simple procedural checkerboard function that returns a value of 0 or 1 based on the (u, v) texture coordinates at a point:

```
float checker(float2 uv)
{
    return (fmod(floor(uv.x) + floor(uv.y), 2) < 1) ? 0 : 1;
}
```

This function computes the integer components of the coordinates of the cell that the (u, v) point is in and alternates between returning 0 and 1 at adjacent cells. The result is the checkerboard pattern shown in Figure 25-1b. With programmable graphics hardware, it's no longer necessary to encode patterns like this in a texture map; the texture function can potentially be evaluated in a fragment program instead. (For a simple checkerboard, there's no real reason to do this procedurally, but in general, procedural texturing opens up a new level of flexibility in real-time rendering. In any case, the same antialiasing principles we will apply to the checkerboard apply for more complex procedural textures.)

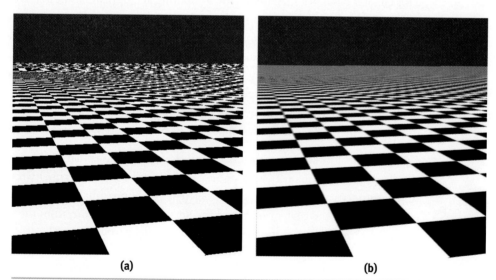

(a)   (b)

Figure 25-1. Procedural Checkerboard Texture, Without and With Antialiasing
(a) The procedural checkerboard texture has not been antialiased, so high-frequency detail at the horizon that can't be represented by the pixel sampling rate turns into aliasing artifacts.
(b) Excessively high frequencies were removed from the pattern, eliminating the aliasing artifacts. Computing accurate filter widths is crucial in order to do this.

One drawback of procedural textures is that the author of the shader needs to be careful to antialias the shader. Roughly speaking, this means that instead of computing the value of the procedural function at a single point, it is necessary to compute the average value of the function over an area. (Chapter 24, "High-Quality Filtering," discusses this topic in more depth.) Specifically, one needs to compute the average value of the function over the area between the current pixel and the adjacent pixels. If the fragment shader doesn't take care of this work, the image will be aliased, as is seen in Figure 25-1a. There, not only does the checkerboard break up into ugly patterns at the horizon, but the edges of the closer checkers have staircase artifacts as well. These errors look even worse when the viewer or the object is moving. (This aliasing is similar to the difference between using a point-sampling texture filtering mode when a texture map is minified instead of using trilinear filtering.)

To eliminate these errors, we need to compute the average color of the checkerboard over a small area on the screen around each pixel. The basic `filterwidth()` function shown below makes it easy to compute how quickly any value is changing from pixel to pixel, and thus the area over which the procedural texture needs to filter. When called with the `uv` coordinates in the `checker()` function shown earlier, the value it returns gives a single approximation of how much they will change between the current pixel and its neighbors. (Thus, it returns an *isotropic* filter width, as opposed to a more accurate *anisotropic* width, which may have a different extent along different directions.)

```
float filterwidth(float2 v)
{
  float2 fw = max(abs(ddx(v)), abs(ddy(v)));
  return max(fw.x, fw.y);
}
```

In particular, we can assume that if `uv` is the value of the texture coordinates at one pixel and `uv1` is the value at a neighbor, then their change is bounded by the filter width:

```
abs(uv.x - uv1.x) < filterwidth(uv)
abs(uv.y - uv1.y) < filterwidth(uv)
```

This should be true regardless of the geometry of the object being rendered or how `uv` was computed—it need not just be a value passed in from a vertex program, for instance. The `filterwidth()` function will generally overestimate the change in the value passed to it (leading to filtering over too large an area and an overblurred result), and it will try not to underestimate it (leading to filtering over too small an area and giving an aliased result). Graphics APIs such as OpenGL and Direct3D make this same trade-off when specifying texture-filtering behavior.

To compute the antialiased checkerboard, instead we would like to compute the average color over the 2D range of (u, v) coordinates from `uv - .5 * filterwidth(uv)` to `uv + .5 * filterwidth(uv)`. The code in Listing 25-1 implements this computation, which is effectively the integral of the function over the filter region divided by the size of the filter region. (The "Further Reading" section at the end of this chapter has pointers to additional information about how this method works.) An image rendered using this version of the `checker()` function is shown in Figure 25-1b. Note that both of the aliasing errors in the original checkerboard no longer appear in this image. The edges of the checks in the middle of the image are slightly overblurred, but this is a much less visually objectionable error.

Listing 25-1. Antialiased Checkerboard Function

```
float checker(float2 uv)
{
    float width = filterwidth(uv);
    float2 p0 = uv - .5 * width, p1 = uv + .5 * width;
    #define BUMPINT(x) \
            (floor((x)/2) + 2.f * max(((x)/2) - floor((x)/2) - .5f, 0.f))
    float2 i = (BUMPINT(p1) - BUMPINT(p0)) / width;
    return i.x * i.y + (1 - i.x) * (1 - i.y);
}
```

25.2 Computing Filter Width with Textures

Unfortunately, our `filterwidth()` function shown earlier will not compile on profiles that don't support the `ddx()` and `ddy()` functions. However, we can trick the texture-mapping hardware into computing essentially the same value that `filterwidth()` does. The key to this trick is the fact that texture-map lookups done with functions such as `tex2D()` automatically antialias the texture lookup, regardless of the texture coordinates that are passed in to them. For example, if you call `tex2D(map, float2(sin(u), tan(v)))`, even though the actual texture coordinates are changing in unusual ways from pixel to pixel, a properly filtered texture value will still be returned at each pixel. The hardware can determine the appropriate area of the texture to filter over for each individual lookup, based on the texture coordinates that are computed at adjacent pixels.

This feature of texture mapping can be used to compute the `filterwidth()` function without calling `ddx()` and `ddy()`. We will perform a texture lookup in a way that lets us deduce the area of the texture map that was filtered; this tells us the area of the procedural checkerboard texture we need to filter, as well. There are two components to our solution: (1) determining which mipmap level was chosen for a particular set of texture coordinates and then (2) using that knowledge to determine the filter width.

For the first part of the problem, consider a square texture with eight levels in its mipmap. There are 128×128 texels at the base level, 0, of the mipmap, 64×64 at the next level, and so on, up to the top level, 7, where there is a single texel. If we explicitly assign all values in each level of the mipmap so that level 0 has the value 0 in all of its texels, level 1 has the value 1, and so forth, then whenever we do a texture lookup with this texture, the value returned will tell us which mipmap level was actually chosen by the texture-mapping hardware for that particular lookup. In general, the texture-mapping hardware blends between two levels of the mipmap, so a fractional blend between values at two adjacent levels will be returned.

We will use this basic idea, but instead, let's encode the base-2 logarithm of the width of the texture map in texels at each level. Thus, the top level of the map has a value of 0 in its single texel, the level below it has a value of 1, the value below that has a value of 2, and so on. We will also scale this value up by 16, in order to cover more of the precision available in 8-bit-per-channel texture maps. Listing 25-2 shows the C++ source code for OpenGL that loads up a texture map in this manner.

Thus, when we do a texture lookup with this texture map in a Cg program, we can find out the base-2 logarithm of the width of the mipmap level used for texture filtering.

The key observation behind this technique is that mipmapped texture filtering will choose a mipmap level based on how quickly the given texture coordinates are changing from pixel to pixel, calculated so that the texels at the chosen mipmap level have about the same distance between them as the texture coordinates from adjacent pixels. In other words, if we can determine the texel spacing for the selected mipmap level, then we know approximately how much the texture coordinates are changing from pixel to pixel. Because we have stored the base-2 logarithm of the number of texels at

```
glTexParameteri(GL_TEXTURE_2D, GL_TEXTURE_MIN_FILTER,
                GL_NEAREST_MIPMAP_LINEAR);
glTexParameteri(GL_TEXTURE_2D, GL_TEXTURE_MAG_FILTER, GL_NEAREST);
glTexParameteri(GL_TEXTURE_2D, GL_TEXTURE_WRAP_S, GL_REPEAT);
glTexParameteri(GL_TEXTURE_2D, GL_TEXTURE_WRAP_T, GL_REPEAT);

#define LEVELS 10
#define RES (1 << (LEVELS - 1))
GLubyte *data = new GLubyte[RES * RES];
for (int level = 0; level < LEVELS; ++level) {
  int res = (1 << (LEVELS-1-level));
  int log2Width = LEVELS - 1 - level;
  for (int i = 0; i < res * res; ++i)
    data[i] = 16 * log2Width;
    glTexImage2D(GL_TEXTURE_2D, level, 1, res, res, 0,
                 GL_RED, GL_UNSIGNED_BYTE, data);
}
delete[] data;
```

each level of the mipmap, then the spacing between texels is just `1/exp2(logNum-Texels) == exp2(-logNumTexels)`. This is our desired filter width.

Thus, given a texture map initialized like the previous one bound to a `sampler2D` called `filterMap`, the Cg code in Listing 25-3 first finds the log-2 width of the mipmap level that would be used for filtering a texture lookup with the given texture coordinates. Note that the value returned by `tex2D()` will be between 0 and 1; the data values passed to `glTexImage2D()` above are effectively divided by 255 to put them in this range. Thus, we need to correct for both this scaling and the extra scaling by a factor of 16 that we did when filling in the mipmap levels to get the actual log-2 width in the Cg program.

Listing 25-3. Function to Compute Filter Widths Using Mipmaps from Listing 25-2

```
uniform sampler2D filterMap;

float filterwidth(float2 uv)
{
  float log2width = (255./16.) * tex2D(filterMap, uv).x;
  return exp2(-log2width);
}
```

Using this filter width function instead of the original gives a visually indistinguishable result. It compiles down to three fragment shader instructions, though in the context of a complete shader, we have not seen a measurable performance difference between the two.

25.3 Discussion

This approach can work well for computing filter width values in many situations. Its performance is nearly the same as the derivative-based approach for computing `filterwidth()`, though at a cost of using a texture unit and a megabyte or so of texture memory. Because the texture levels hold constant values, the textures used are potentially excellent candidates for compressed texture formats, which would reduce memory use and the GPU bandwidth needed at runtime.

The main drawback of this approach is that unlike the standard technique, this method may give incorrect results when the filter width value should be very large or very small. Consider a rapidly changing value, such that the filter width should have a value of 2. This technique will underestimate the filter width, because the top level of the mipmap would be chosen, and we are unable to differentiate from a quantity with a filter width of 1. Similarly, we may overestimate the filter width for a very slowly changing value: the most detailed level of the mipmap limits the smallest filter width it can compute, as well. If a general bound of the range of expected filter width values is known, however, this problem may not be very troublesome in practice. Alternatively, if we know that the filtered version of the procedural texture takes on a single average value for all filter widths beyond some point, we don't need to worry about that case.

We can work around these problems by detecting when we have a result from the top or bottom level of the mipmap (corresponding to texture mipmap level values of 0 and the number of mipmap levels minus 1, respectively). In that case, we can try another texture lookup with scaled texture coordinates, compute the filter width for those coordinates, and then rescale the filter width to compensate for the scaling of texture coordinates. The code in Listing 25-4 shows how this can be done for the case of underestimated filter widths resulting from going off the top of the mipmap pyramid. The analogous approach can be used to solve the problem of going off the bottom of the pyramid, as well.

Listing 25-4. Filter-Width Function That Is Less Prone to Under-Aliasing Filter Widths

```
float filterwidth(float2 uv)
{
  float log2width = (255./16.) * tex2D(filterMap, uv).x;
  if (log2width < .01) {
    log2width = (255./16.) * tex2D(filterMap, uv/512).x;
    return 512 * exp2(-log2width);
  } else
      return exp2(-log2width);
}
```

The scaling factor 512 used here was based on the fact that we loaded a ten-level mipmap in Listing 25-2. If more or fewer levels are available, we would need to adjust the scaling factor correspondingly.

25.4 Further Reading

Ebert, David S., F. Kenton Musgrave, Darwyn Peachey, Ken Perlin, and Steven Worley. 2003. *Texturing and Modeling: A Procedural Approach*. Morgan Kaufmann. *Chapter 2 of this book has an excellent introduction to issues related to antialiasing in procedural shaders.*

Apodaca, Anthony A., and Larry Gritz, eds. 1999. *Advanced RenderMan: Creating CGI for Motion Pictures*. Morgan Kaufmann. *This is another excellent resource for these issues.*

Williams, Lance. 1983. "Pyramidal Parametrics." In *Computer Graphics (Proceedings of SIGGRAPH 83)* 17(3), pp. 1–11. *Williams introduced mipmaps to the graphics world in this article.*

Fernando, Randima, Sebastian Fernandez, Kavita Bala, and Donald P. Greenberg. 2001. "Adaptive Shadow Maps." In *Proceedings of ACM SIGGRAPH 2001*, pp. 387–390. *This paper contains the first similar abuse of mipmapping that we are aware of; the authors used a comparable technique to determine the amount of magnification in shadow maps.*

Hadwiger, Markus, Helwig Hauser, Thomas Theußl, and Meister Eduard Gröller. 2003. "MIP-Mapping with Procedural and Texture-Based Magnification." Sketch presented at SIGGRAPH 2003. *More recently, the authors of this sketch used a similar technique to detect texture magnification in a fragment program in order to manually apply a bicubic filter, resulting in better images with magnified textures.*

Chapter 26

The OpenEXR Image File Format

Florian Kainz
Industrial Light & Magic

Rod Bogart
Industrial Light & Magic

Drew Hess
Industrial Light & Magic

Most images created on a GPU are fleeting and exist for only a fraction of a second. But occasionally you create one worth keeping. When you do, it's best to store it in an image file format that retains the high dynamic range possible in the NVIDIA `half` type and stores additional data channels, as well.

In this chapter, we describe the OpenEXR image file format, give examples of reading and writing GPU image buffers, and discuss issues associated with image display.

26.1 What Is OpenEXR?

OpenEXR is a high-dynamic-range image file format developed by Industrial Light & Magic (ILM) for use in computer imaging applications. The OpenEXR Web site, www.openexr.org, has full details on the image file format itself. This section summarizes some of the key features for storing high-dynamic-range images.

26.1.1 High-Dynamic-Range Images

Display devices for digital images, such as computer monitors and video projectors, usually have a dynamic range of about 500 to 1. This means the brightest pixel in an image is never more than 500 times brighter than the darkest pixel.

Most image file formats are designed to match a typical display's dynamic range: values stored in the pixels go from 0.0, representing "black," to 1.0, representing the display's maximum intensity, or "white." To keep image files small, pixel values are usually encoded as eight- or ten-bit integers (0–255 or 0–1023, respectively), which is just enough to match the display's accuracy.

As long as we only want to present images on a display, file formats with a dynamic range of 0 to 1 are adequate. There is no point in storing pixels that are brighter than the monitor's white, or in storing pixels with more accuracy than what the display can reproduce.

However, if we intend to process an image, or if we want to use an image as an environment map for 3D rendering, then it is desirable to have more information in the image file. Pixels should be stored with more accuracy than the typical eight or ten bits, and the range of possible pixel values should be essentially unlimited. File formats that allow storing pixel values outside the 0-to-1 range are called *high-dynamic-range* (HDR) formats. By performing image processing on HDR data and quantizing to fewer bits only for display, the best-quality image can be shown.

Here is a simple example that demonstrates why having a high dynamic range is desirable for image processing (other applications for HDR images are presented in Section 26.6).

Figure 26-1 shows a photograph of a scene with a rather high dynamic range. In the original scene, the flame of the oil lamp on the left was about 100,000 times brighter than the shadow under the small dish in the center.

The way the image was exposed caused some areas to be brighter than 1.0. On a computer monitor, those areas are clipped and displayed as white or as unnaturally saturated orange hues.

We might attempt to correct the white and orange areas by making the image darker. However, if the original image has been stored in a low-dynamic-range file format, for example, JPEG, darkening produces a rather ugly image. The areas around the flames become gray, as in Figure 26-2.

If the original image has been stored in an HDR file format such as OpenEXR, which preserves bright pixel values rather than clipping them at 1.0, then darkening produces an image that still looks natural. See Figure 26-3.

Figure 26-1. A Scene with a High Dynamic Range
Pixel values above 1.0 are clamped; very bright areas are discolored and lose detail.

Figure 26-2. Darker Version of Figure 26-1
Bright areas become gray, and details that were lost due to clamping cannot be recovered.

Figure 26-3. High-Dynamic-Range Version of Figure 26-1, Made Darker
Additional detail is revealed in bright areas, and colors look natural.

26.1.2 A "Half" Format

Early in 2003, ILM released a new HDR file format with 16-bit floating-point color-component values. Because the IEEE 754 floating-point specification does not define a 16-bit format, ILM created a `half` format that matches NVIDIA's 16-bit format. The `half` type provides an excellent storage structure for high-dynamic-range image content. This type is directly supported in the OpenEXR format.

The 16-bit, or "half-precision," floating-point format is modeled after the IEEE 754 single-precision and double-precision formats. A half-precision number consists of a sign bit, a 5-bit exponent, and a 10-bit mantissa. The smallest and largest possible exponent values are reserved for representing zero, denormalized numbers, infinities, and NaNs.

In OpenEXR's C++ implementation, numbers of type `half` generally behave like the built-in C++ floating-point types, `float` and `double`. The `half`, `float`, and `double` types can be mixed freely in arithmetic expressions. Here are a few examples:

```
half a (3.5);
float b (a + sqrt(a));
a += b;
b += a;
b = a + 7;
```

26.1.3 Range of Representable Values

The most obvious benefit of half is the range of values that can be represented with only 16 bits. We can store a maximum image value of 65504.0 and a minimum value of 5.96^{-8}. This is a dynamic range of a trillion to one. Any image requiring this range would be extremely rare, but images with a million-to-one range do occur, and thus they are comfortably represented with a half.

Photographers measure dynamic range in *stops*, where a single stop is a factor of 2. In an image with five stops of range, the brightest region is 32 times brighter than the darkest region. A range of one-million to one is 20 stops in photographic terms.

26.1.4 Color Resolution

The second, less obvious benefit of half is the color resolution. Each stop contains 1024 distinct values. This makes OpenEXR excellent for normal-dynamic-range images as well. In an eight-stop image that ranges from 1.0 down to 0.0039 (or 2^{-8}), the half format will provide 8192 values per channel, whereas an 8-bit, gamma 2.2 image will have only 235 values (21 through 255).

26.1.5 C++ Interface

To make writing and reading OpenEXR files easy, ILM designed the file format together with a C++ programming interface. OpenEXR provides three levels of access to the image files: (1) a general interface for writing and reading files with arbitrary sets of image channels; (2) a specialized interface for RGBA (red, green, blue, and alpha channels, or some subset of those); and (3) a C-callable version of the programming interface that supports reading and writing OpenEXR files from programs written in C.

The examples in this chapter use the RGBA C++ interface.

26.2 The OpenEXR File Structure

An OpenEXR file consists of two main parts: the header and the pixels.

26.2.1 The Header

The header is a list of attributes that describe the pixels. An attribute is a named data item of an arbitrary type. In order for OpenEXR files written by one program to be read by other programs, certain required attributes must be present in all OpenEXR file headers. These attributes are presented in Table 26-1.

In addition to the required attributes, a program can include optional attributes in the file's header. Often it is necessary to annotate images with additional data that's appropriate for a particular application, such as computational history, color profile information, or camera position and view direction. These data can be packaged as extra attributes in the image file's header.

Table 26-1. Required Attributes in OpenEXR Headers

Name	Description
displayWindow	The image's resolution[1]
dataWindow	Crop and offset
pixelAspectRatio	Width divided by the height of a pixel when the image is displayed with the correct aspect ratio
channels	Description of the image channels stored in the file
compression	The compression method applied to the pixel data of all channels in the file
lineOrder	The order in which the scan lines are stored in the file (increasing y or decreasing y)
screenWindowWidth, screenWindowCenter	The perspective projection that produced the image

1. See the OpenEXR Web site, www.openexr.org, for details.

26.2.2 The Pixels

The pixels of an image are stored as separate channels. With the general library interface, you can write RGBA and as many additional channels as necessary. Each channel can have a different data type, so the RGBA data can be half (16 bits), while a z-depth channel can be written as float (32 bits).

26.3　OpenEXR Data Compression

OpenEXR offers three different data compression methods, each of which has differing trade-offs in speed versus compression ratio. All three compression schemes, as listed in Table 26-2, are lossless; compressing and uncompressing does not alter the pixel data.

Optionally, the pixels can be stored in uncompressed form. If stored on a fast file system, uncompressed files can be written and read significantly faster than compressed files.

Table 26-2. OpenEXR Supported Compression Options

Name	Description
PIZ	A wavelet transform is applied to the pixel data, and the result is Huffman-encoded. This scheme tends to provide the best compression ratio for photographic images. Files are compressed and decompressed at about the same speed. For photographic images with film grain, the files are reduced to between 35 and 55 percent of their uncompressed size.
ZIP	Differences between horizontally adjacent pixels are compressed using the open-source zlib library. ZIP decompression is faster than PIZ decompression, but ZIP compression is significantly slower. Compressed photographic images are often 45 to 55 percent of their uncompressed size.
RLE	Run-length encoding of differences between horizontally adjacent pixels. This method is fast, and it works well for images with large flat areas. However, for photographic images, the compressed file size is usually 60 to 75 percent of the uncompressed size.

26.4　Using OpenEXR

The electronic materials accompanying this book contain the full source code for a simple image-playback program, along with the associated Cg shader code.

This section provides excerpts of the code to demonstrate reading an OpenEXR image file, displaying the image buffer with OpenGL, performing a simple compositing operation, and writing the result to an OpenEXR file.

26.4.1　Reading and Displaying an OpenEXR Image

The simple code in Listing 26-1 reads an OpenEXR file into an internal image buffer. Note that the OpenEXR library makes use of exceptions, so errors such as "file not found" are handled in a catch block. There is no need to explicitly close the file because it is closed by the C++ destructor for the `RgbaInputFile` object.

Listing 26-1. Reading an OpenEXR Image File

```
Imf::Rgba * pixelBuffer;

try
{
    Imf::RgbaInputFile in(fileName);

    Imath::Box2i win = in.dataWindow();

    Imath::V2i dim(win.max.x - win.min.x + 1,
                  win.max.y - win.min.y + 1);

    pixelBuffer = new Imf::Rgba[dim.x * dim.y];

    int dx = win.min.x;
    int dy = win.min.y;

    in.setFrameBuffer(pixelBuffer - dx - dy * dim.x, 1, dim.x);
    in.readPixels(win.min.y, win.max.y);
}
catch(Iex::BaseExc & e)
{
    std::cerr << e.what() << std::endl;

    //
    // Handle exception.
    //
}
```

Once the buffer is filled, the code segment in Listing 26-2 binds the image to a texture for display with a Cg fragment shader (see Section 26.5 for more details). The full program invokes this display code to play back multiple frames.

Listing 26-2. Binding an Image to a Texture

```
GLenum target = GL_TEXTURE_RECTANGLE_NV;

glGenTextures(2, imageTexture);
glBindTexture(target, imageTexture);
```

Listing 26-2 (*continued*). Binding an Image to a Texture

```
glTexParameteri(target, GL_TEXTURE_MIN_FILTER, GL_NEAREST);
glTexParameteri(target, GL_TEXTURE_MAG_FILTER, GL_NEAREST);
glTexParameteri(target, GL_TEXTURE_WRAP_S, GL_CLAMP_TO_EDGE);
glTexParameteri(target, GL_TEXTURE_WRAP_T, GL_CLAMP_TO_EDGE);

glPixelStorei(GL_UNPACK_ALIGNMENT, 1);

glTexImage2D(target, 0, GL_FLOAT_RGBA16_NV, dim.x, dim.y, 0,
             GL_RGBA, GL_HALF_FLOAT_NV, pixelBuffer);

glActiveTextureARB(GL_TEXTURE0_ARB);
glBindTexture(target, imageTexture);

glBegin(GL_QUADS);
glTexCoord2f(0.0,   0.0);   glVertex2f(0.0,   0.0);
glTexCoord2f(dim.x, 0.0);   glVertex2f(dim.x, 0.0);
glTexCoord2f(dim.x, dim.y); glVertex2f(dim.x, dim.y);
glTexCoord2f(0.0,   dim.y); glVertex2f(0.0,   dim.y);
glEnd();
```

26.4.2 Rendering and Writing an OpenEXR Image

Images rendered by the GPU can be saved in OpenEXR files. Often, we want to create a foreground image and a background image and combine them later. The example in Listing 26-3 uses a pbuffer to do a simple compositing operation, and then it writes the result to an OpenEXR file. In the code fragment, we read the two input images (which are already open) into the allocated image buffers, and then we call a compositing routine and write the result.

Listing 26-3. Compositing Two Images and Writing an OpenEXR File

```
//
// Read A and B.
//

Imath::V2i dim(dataWinA.max.x - dataWinA.min.x + 1,
               dataWinA.max.y - dataWinA.min.y + 1);
int dx = dataWinA.min.x;
int dy = dataWinA.min.y;
```

```
Imf::Array<Imf::Rgba> imgA(dim.x * dim.y);
Imf::Array<Imf::Rgba> imgB(dim.x * dim.y);

inA.setFrameBuffer(imgA - dx - dy * dim.x, 1, dim.x);
inA.readPixels(dataWinA.min.y, dataWinA.max.y);

inB.setFrameBuffer(imgB - dx - dy * dim.x, 1, dim.x);
inB.readPixels(dataWinB.min.y, dataWinB.max.y);

//
// Do the comp, overwrite image B with the result.
//

Comp::over(dim, imgA, imgB, imgB);

//
// Write comp'ed image.
//
Imf::RgbaOutputFile outC(outputFilename.c_str(),
                         dpyWinA, dataWinA, Imf::WRITE_RGBA);

outC.setFrameBuffer(imgB - dx - dy * dim.x, 1, dim.x);
outC.writePixels(dim.y);
```

The call to Comp::over is implemented simply as a call to the routine shown in Listing 26-4 (Comp::comp) with the name of a Cg shader that performs an over operation. Full details of over and various other compositing operators are found in Porter and Duff 1984. The GlFloatPbuffer class (which is provided in the accompanying materials) hides the mechanics of creating and deleting a floating-point pbuffer. Note that we can get half data from the pbuffer with glReadPixels without loss of precision and without clamping.

Listings 26-5 through 26-7 are the Cg shaders for the over operation and for in and out operations, respectively.

Listing 26-4. Compositing into a Pbuffer

```cpp
void
Comp::comp(const Imath::V2i & dim,
           const Imf::Rgba * imageA,
           const Imf::Rgba * imageB,
           Imf::Rgba * imageC,
           const char * cgProgramName)
{
  GlFloatPbuffer pbuffer(dim);

  pbuffer.activate();

  //
  // Set up default ortho view.
  //
  glLoadIdentity();
  glViewport(0, 0, dim.x, dim.y);
  glOrtho(0, dim.x, dim.y, 0, -1, 1);

  //
  // Create input textures.
  //
  GLuint inTex[2];
  glGenTextures(2, inTex);

  GLenum target = GL_TEXTURE_RECTANGLE_NV;

  glActiveTextureARB(GL_TEXTURE0_ARB);
  glBindTexture(target, inTex[0]);

  glTexParameteri(target, GL_TEXTURE_MIN_FILTER, GL_NEAREST);
  glTexParameteri(target, GL_TEXTURE_MAG_FILTER, GL_NEAREST);
  glTexParameteri(target, GL_TEXTURE_WRAP_S, GL_CLAMP_TO_EDGE);
  glTexParameteri(target, GL_TEXTURE_WRAP_T, GL_CLAMP_TO_EDGE);

  glPixelStorei(GL_UNPACK_ALIGNMENT, 1);

  glTexImage2D(target, 0, GL_FLOAT_RGBA16_NV, dim.x, dim.y, 0,
               GL_RGBA, GL_HALF_FLOAT_NV, imageA);
```

Listing 26-4 (*continued*). Compositing into a Pbuffer

```
glActiveTextureARB(GL_TEXTURE1_ARB);
glBindTexture(target, inTex[1]);

glTexParameteri(target, GL_TEXTURE_MIN_FILTER, GL_NEAREST);
glTexParameteri(target, GL_TEXTURE_MAG_FILTER, GL_NEAREST);
glTexParameteri(target, GL_TEXTURE_WRAP_S, GL_CLAMP_TO_EDGE);
glTexParameteri(target, GL_TEXTURE_WRAP_T, GL_CLAMP_TO_EDGE);

glPixelStorei(GL_UNPACK_ALIGNMENT, 1);

glTexImage2D(target, 0, GL_FLOAT_RGBA16_NV, dim.x, dim.y, 0,
             GL_RGBA, GL_HALF_FLOAT_NV, imageB);

//
// Compile the Cg program and load it.
//

cgSetErrorCallback(cgErrorCallback);

CGcontext cgcontext = cgCreateContext();
CGprogram cgprog = cgCreateProgramFromFile(cgcontext, CG_SOURCE,
                                           cgProgramName,
                                           CG_PROFILE_FP30, 0, 0);
cgGLLoadProgram(cgprog);
cgGLBindProgram(cgprog);
cgGLEnableProfile(CG_PROFILE_FP30);

//
// Render to pbuffer.
//

glEnable(GL_FRAGMENT_PROGRAM_NV);
glBegin(GL_QUADS);
glTexCoord2f(0.0,   0.0);   glVertex2f(0.0,   0.0);
glTexCoord2f(dim.x, 0.0);   glVertex2f(dim.x, 0.0);
glTexCoord2f(dim.x, dim.y); glVertex2f(dim.x, dim.y);
glTexCoord2f(0.0,   dim.y); glVertex2f(0.0,   dim.y);
glEnd();
glDisable(GL_FRAGMENT_PROGRAM_NV);
```

Listing 26-4 (*continued*). Compositing into a Pbuffer

```
  //
  // Read pixels out of pbuffer.
  //

  glReadPixels(0, 0, dim.x, dim.y, GL_RGBA,
               GL_HALF_FLOAT_NV, imageC);

  checkGlErrors();

  pbuffer.deactivate();
}
```

Listing 26-5. Cg Shader for an "Over" Operation

```
void
over(float2 wpos    : WPOS,
     out half4 c    : COLOR,
     uniform float2 dim,
     uniform samplerRECT A,
     uniform samplerRECT B)
{
  half4 a = texRECT(A, wpos.xy);
  half4 b = texRECT(B, wpos.xy);

  c = a +(1 - a.a) * b;
}
```

Listing 26-6. Cg Shader for an "In" Operation

```
void
in(float2 wpos    : WPOS,
   out half4 c    : COLOR,
   uniform float2 dim,
   uniform samplerRECT A,
   uniform samplerRECT B)
{
  half4 a = texRECT(A, wpos.xy);
  half4 b = texRECT(B, wpos.xy);

  c = b.a * a;
}
```

Listing 26-7. Cg Shader for an "Out" Operation

```
void
out(float2 wpos    : WPOS,
    out half4 c    : COLOR,
    uniform float2 dim,
    uniform samplerRECT A,
    uniform samplerRECT B)
{
  half4 a = texRECT(A, wpos.xy);
  half4 b = texRECT(B, wpos.xy);

  c = (1 - b.a) * a;
}
```

26.5 Linear Pixel Values

We prefer to store linear images in OpenEXR files. The word *linear* has different meanings to different people—for us, an image is in linear color space if the values in the image are proportional to the relative scene luminances represented. When we double the number, we double the light. To make a scene half as bright—that is, make it a stop darker—we divide each image value by two. As we'll describe later, this has implications for how images should be displayed.

Most image-processing algorithms assume linear images. The standard compositing operation over performs a linear blend of the foreground and the background based on an alpha channel. When the alpha is truly a coverage mask, it indicates the percentage of light that should leak through from the background. This works correctly when the images represent linear amounts of light. In addition to image processing, antialiasing is best done in linear space (Blinn 2002).

Software rendering is usually performed in linear space as well. With higher-quality rendering available in the GPU, it is correct to do the hardware rendering in linear space. When the image is viewed, it must be gamma-corrected. Although *gamma* also has many meanings in the graphics community, we are referring here to correcting for the *monitor gamma*. Monitors used for image display have circuits that cause the monitor's light output to have a power-law relationship to the frame buffer value. Because we assume that OpenEXR images are linear, we tell the display program the gamma of the monitor so the program can apply the inverse gamma to the image for display.

A typical monitor has a gamma of 2.2. You can measure this with a light meter (preferably a high-quality one). If you don't have a light meter, see the method described in Berger 2003. When you display a white value of 1.0, the meter may display a value such as 92 nit (1 nit equals 1 candela per square meter). For a second data point, we display a gray patch. (We don't use a black patch because a black region will have suspect light readings; also, we're about to do some log math, which is undefined at zero.)

Let's assume the 0.5 gray value gives a luminance of 20 nit. Remember, this value of 0.5 is the digital value in the frame buffer, with no other processing downstream before the digital-to-analog converters. The monitor's output luminance, $L(v)$, as a function of the input value, v, is:

$$L(v) = L_m \cdot v^\gamma,$$

where v is in the range from 0.0 to 1.0 and L_m is the monitor's maximum output luminance. From this we can derive gamma (γ) as:

$$L(1.0) = L_m \cdot 1.0^\gamma = L_m = 92 \text{ nit}$$

$$L(0.5) = L_m \cdot 0.5^\gamma = 92 \text{ nit} \cdot 0.5^\gamma = 20 \text{ nit}$$

$$\frac{20 \text{ nit}}{92 \text{ nit}} = 0.5^\gamma$$

$$\gamma = \log_{0.5} \frac{20}{92} \approx 2.2.$$

To apply gamma correction to the linear image data, we simply raise the image value to the power of 1 over the monitor gamma. We demonstrate this in the simple fragment shader in Listing 26-8.

Listing 26-8. Gamma-Correcting an Image for Display

```
struct Out
{
  half4 color : COLOR;
};

Out
main(float2 texCoord : TEXCOORD0,
     uniform samplerRECT image,
     uniform float gamma)
{
  half4 pixel = h4texRECT(image, texCoord);
```

Listing 26-8 (*continued*). Gamma-Correcting an Image for Display

```
    Out output;
    output.color = pow(pixel, gamma);
    return output;
}
```

The playback program lets the user change the exposure of the image. The image is linear before gamma correction, so we just multiply by a constant and pass the result to the power function. See Listing 26-9.

Listing 26-9. Adjusting an Image's Exposure

```
Out
main(float2 texCoord : TEXCOORD0,
      uniform samplerRECT image,
      uniform float gamma,
      uniform float expMult)
{
    half4 pixel = h4texRECT(image, texCoord);
    pixel.rgb *= expMult;
    Out output;
    output.color = pow(pixel, gamma);
    return output;
}
```

Finally, the image may need some overall color correction to look right. The reasons for this may be aesthetic, or it may be that the image is intended to look as if it were shown on a different display device. For example, if you want your image on the monitor to look like film, you can perform a simulation of the film behavior just before gamma correction. Often, digital image designers have to use lighting tricks to achieve the right look. Instead, we prefer to do our lighting and rendering in linear space and simulate the behavior of film at display time. In the basic example shown in Listing 26-10, we provide a three-channel lookup table that contains a simple S-shaped film simulation curve.

This shader uses a trick to do the lookup function. The `samplerRECT` types that are used as lookup tables store a `half` for each possible input `half`. The simplest encoding of this is a sampler rect with dimensions 1×66536. Because of limitations in current GPUs, this rect is too large. So instead, we fold the lookup table into a 256×256 texture, which we index using the `pack_2half` and `unpack_4ubyte` Cg Standard

Listing 26-10. Using a Lookup Table to Simulate the Look of Photographic Film

```
half
lookup(samplerRECT lut, half h)
{
    float f = pack_2half(h.xx);
    half4 bytes = unpack_4ubyte(f);
    return h1texRECT(lut, bytes.xy * 256.0);
}

Out
main(float2 texCoord : TEXCOORD0,
     uniform samplerRECT image,
     uniform samplerRECT lutR,
     uniform samplerRECT lutG,
     uniform samplerRECT lutB,
     uniform float gamma,
     uniform float expMult)
{
    half4 c = h4texRECT(image, texCoord) * expMult;
    c.r = lookup(lutR, c.r);
    c.g = lookup(lutG, c.g);
    c.b = lookup(lutB, c.b);
    Out output;
    output.color = pow(c, gamma);
    return output;
}
```

Library functions. These take the given `half` input value and split it into two indices for the 256×256 lookups.

Fully commented versions of these routines are provided, along with the OpenGL code for binding the various textures and displaying the image, on the book's CD and Web site.

26.6 Creating and Using HDR Images

HDR images can be created synthetically on the GPU or in software. They can also be captured from the real world. High-dynamic-range cameras do exist. For example, Spheron's SpheroCam captures 26-stop dynamic-range panoramas. With a regular camera, you can take multiple exposures and construct a single HDR image using software such as Greg Ward's PhotoSphere or Paul Debevec's HDRShop.

Lighting can be done in 3D scenes with a global illumination model using high-dynamic-range images rather than individual light sources. In Debevec 1998, synthetic objects are rendered with Radiance software. In Ng et al. 2003, realistic rendering of diffuse surfaces, including shadows, is done in real time on NVIDIA hardware. Both methods use environment maps instead of light sources; the maps must have a wide enough dynamic range to represent the brightest regions in the environment (for example, the Sun) without clipping.

Image processing also benefits from a wider dynamic range. For example, depth-of-field blurring spreads individual pixels over large areas. When an individual pixel is very bright, spreading it out should result in many reasonably bright pixels. But if a bright pixel, for example a specular highlight, has been clamped to zero-to-one before blurring, the blurred highlight is unnaturally dim. A similar effect can be seen with motion blur. Even performing a simple color correction can require high-dynamic-range data, as seen in Section 26.1.1.

In Figure 26-4a, we have a high-dynamic-range image of an automobile engine. The highlights range much higher than 1.0. For Figure 26-4b, we first converted the image to a low-dynamic-range file format, which clamped the pixels to zero-to-one. Then we applied a depth-of-field blur. In Figure 26-4c, we blurred the full range of data read from the OpenEXR file.

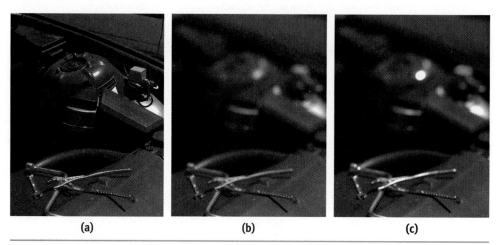

(a)   (b)   (c)

Figure 26-4. Blurring an Image with Very Bright Highlights
(a) The original HDR image; specular highlights are brighter than 1.0. (b) Image (a) was clamped to zero-to-one by storing it in a low-dynamic-range file, and then it was blurred. Blurred highlights are unnaturally dark. (c) Image (a) was blurred without clamping. Blurred highlights remain bright.

In previous sections, we assumed that values above 1.0 are clamped when an HDR image is displayed. This can work reasonably well, and in fact, it was the method used for printing the figures in this chapter. However, it is often possible to do better. Several effective techniques for reducing the dynamic range without significantly altering the subjective appearance of the image, known as *tone mapping*, have been published in recent years—for example, Fattal et al. 2002 and Durand and Dorsey 2002. Alternatively, future displays may show HDR imagery directly. For example, Seetzen et al. 2003 describes a prototype HDR display with a dynamic range of 120,000 to 1.

26.7 Conclusion

OpenEXR was originally released for GNU/Linux and Irix, and through the efforts of the open-source community, it was ported to Mac OS X and Windows. The OpenEXR library has been proven in the visual effects production environment of Industrial Light & Magic.

In addition to NVIDIA, a growing number of vendors support the OpenEXR format in their software applications. For more information, visit the OpenEXR Web site at www.openexr.org.

26.8 References

Berger, Robert W. 2003. "Why Do Images Appear Darker on Some Displays?" Article on Web site. **http://www.bberger.net/rwb/gamma.html**

Blinn, Jim. 2002. *Jim Blinn's Corner: Notation, Notation, Notation*, pp. 133–146. Morgan Kaufmann.

Debevec, Paul. 1998. "Rendering Synthetic Objects into Real Scenes." In *Computer Graphics (Proceedings of SIGGRAPH 98)*, pp. 189–198.

Durand, Frédo, and Julie Dorsey. 2002. "Fast Bilateral Filtering for the Display of High-Dynamic-Range Images." In *Computer Graphics (Proceedings of SIGGRAPH 2002)*, pp. 257–266.

Fattal, Raanan, Dani Lischinski, and Michael Werman. 2002. "Gradient Domain High Dynamic Range Compression." In *Computer Graphics (Proceedings of SIGGRAPH 2002)*, pp. 249–256.

Ng, Ren, Ravi Ramamoorthi, and Pat Hanrahan. 2003. "All-Frequency Shadows Using Non-linear Wavelet Lighting Approximation." In *Computer Graphics (Proceedings of SIGGRAPH 2003)*, pp. 376–381.

Porter, Thomas, and Tom Duff. 1984. "Compositing Digital Images." In *Computer Graphics* 18(3) *(Proceedings of SIGGRAPH 84)*, pp. 253–259.

Seetzen, H., W. Stürzlinger, A. Vorozcovs, H. Wilson, I. Ashdown, G. Ward, and L. Whitehead. 2003. "High Dynamic Range Display System." Emerging technologies demonstration at SIGGRAPH 2003.

Chapter 27

A Framework for Image Processing

Frank Jargstorff
NVIDIA

In this chapter, we introduce a C++ framework for image processing on the GPU. Using this framework, a programmer can easily define image filters and link filters to form filter graphs. Most of the classes in the framework act simply as handles to structures living on the graphics board, so that the actual processing of the image is almost completely performed by the GPU. The framework is based on the OpenGL API and uses the Cg programming language to implement image-processing algorithms. However, the ideas represented in this chapter apply similarly to Microsoft's DirectX API and the HLSL programming language. Our hope is that the framework will be useful to readers who are designing similar image-processing systems, either as a working foundation or as an analysis of the issues that must be resolved along the way.

27.1 Introduction

The framework we present is valuable for two reasons. First, there is the increasingly flexible programming paradigm for vertex and fragment shaders supported by recent GPUs such as the GeForce FX family. Second, today's GPUs are so powerful that they surpass the CPU's performance in many signal-processing-like applications.

Organizing image filters using filter graphs is especially practical for video processing, where a long sequence of images is processed using the same configuration of filters (for example, Microsoft's DirectShow is a filter-graph-based, real-time video-processing library). See Figure 27-1. Filter graphs are also useful in batch-processing scenarios, such as compositing movie-quality frames or processing large sets of images for Web publications (for example, Apple's Shake compositor or Adobe's ImageReady).

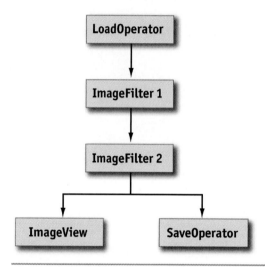

Figure 27-1. A Filter Graph

GPUs are programmed through traditional 3D APIs such as Direct3D and OpenGL. These APIs are fairly low level and were originally designed to implement 3D applications. Implementing GPU image processing directly in these APIs would be an awkward task. A framework acting as an isolation layer and specifically designed for image processing would drastically simplify the implementation of image processing on the GPU. To be simple to program, the framework should encapsulate all recurring tasks and should strive to shield the programmer from the underlying graphics API as much as possible. In the following sections, we describe a basic version of such a framework. The framework functions as an example and tries to address the most important design and implementation aspects. It does not address, however, many of the more complicated schemes necessary in an industrial-strength library, such as dividing images into tiles to process arbitrarily large images.

27.2 Framework Design

Filter networks deal with two kinds of objects:

- Data objects that flow through the network. In our case, the data flowing are images.
- Operators that act on the data. Operators come in different flavors. Some operators produce output images without absorbing input images (for example, an operator that loads an image from disk). These operators act as sources in the network, so they are called *source operators*. Other operators consume an input image without producing an output image (for example, operators that display an image on the screen). Because these operators act as data sinks, we refer to them as *sink operators*. See Figure 27-2.

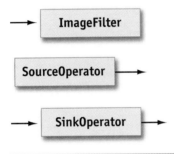

Figure 27-2. A SinkOperator, a SourceOperator, and an ImageFilter

For a C++ implementation, this poses two problems. For one, it is considered good design for an object that creates objects to be responsible for also deleting those objects (Meyers 1997). Because the operators creating and deleting images are usually not the same, we need some kind of automatic memory management for the Image class.

Images are fairly simple data structures that don't contain references, especially not to themselves. Thus, simple reference counting suffices as memory-management strategy.

A second issue is how the pipeline should be updated. That is, what is the mechanism that makes data percolate through the graph? The two options are to push data down the graph or pull data from the result nodes, which in turn pull the necessary data from their inputs. Because of the common use of a model-view-controller pattern (Gamma et al. 1995) for applications, we decided to implement updating by pulling.

27.2.1 Operators and Filters

The basic operators described in the previous section map directly to abstract base classes in the framework's design.

The `SourceOperator` base class consists of two purely virtual functions:

```
virtual bool dirty() = 0;
virtual Image image() = 0;
```

The `image()` method returns the operator's output image. The `dirty` method determines if the most recently returned image is still valid.

The `SinkOperator` base class contains only a single virtual function and a protected reference to a `SourceOperator`.

```
virtual void setSourceOperator(SourceOperator * pSourceOperator);

protected:
   SourceOperator * _pSourceOperator;
```

The sink operator retrieves its input images from the source operator pointed to by `_pSourceOperator`. The `setSourceOperator()` method sets this reference.

The `ImageFilter` class is derived from both `SourceOperator` and `SinkOperator`, as shown in Figure 27-3.

`ImageFilter` overloads both the `image()` and the `dirty()` methods with default implementations for all filters derived from it.

- The `image()` method retrieves the input image from the input operator and draws a rectangle exactly covering the entire output image. The drawing code for the rectangle sets up Cg vertex and fragment programs and uses the input operator's image as a texture. The fragment program determines how the texture is rendered to the output image. Thus, different image filters can be implemented by simply using different Cg fragment programs.

- The `dirty()` method recursively queries the `dirty()` methods of all operators upstream. If it finds that its image filter depends on a dirty operator's output, it will return `true`. An operator becomes dirty when any of its parameters is changed. Note: It is the responsibility of the implementer of an operator or filter to make sure that the dirty flag is set correctly.

The `image()` method implements everything necessary to set up and execute fragment and vertex programs. It uses a `ShaderManager` class to retrieve shared Cg re-

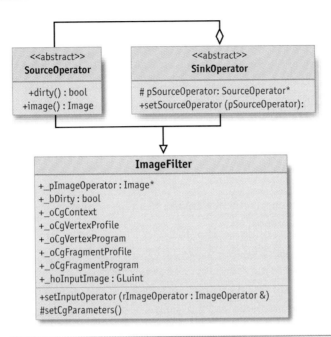

Figure 27-3. The `ImageFilter` Class Diagram

sources. Most of the necessary and tedious Cg plumbing is encapsulated in the image method. All the implementer of a new filter class has to do is set up the actual fragment shader for his or her filter in the class's constructor.

27.2.2 Image Data

The `Image` class functions as a container for our image data. Therefore, it must support two basic functions: retrieving the image data and drawing new image data into the image. Because the `Image` class is a mere handle to the actual image residing on the graphics board, support for these functions will be high level (as opposed to low-level accesses such as setting and retrieving color values of single pixels).

This high-level interface to the image data consists simply of the following three methods:

```
GLuint textureID() const;
void renderBegin();
void renderEnd();
```

These methods allow the programmer to retrieve an OpenGL texture handle pointing to a texture containing the image data.

The render methods make the image the current OpenGL render context, so that any OpenGL draw commands issued between these two commands will draw directly into the image. Using several OpenGL extensions, it is possible to implement this interface so that the image data never gets copied around when the image is drawn to and used as a texture repeatedly, nor does it ever leave the graphics card's memory.

Beyond this, the `Image` class has the usual methods for querying image size and resizing the image:

```
int width() const;
int height() const;
void setSize(int nWidth, int nHeight);
```

We found in the beginning of this section that the `Image` class must implement automatic memory management via reference counting. In fact, the `Image` class is a proxy (Gamma et al. 1995) for a class called `Buffer`, which implements the actual functionality. See Figure 27-4. `Buffer` objects may be referenced only through `Image` objects. Each `Buffer` has a reference counter. The `Image` objects' constructor, destructor, copy constructor, and assignment operator all manipulate the reference count of the `Buffer` objects they point to. When the last `Image` referencing a `Buffer` is destructed, the `Buffer` object's reference count drops to zero, indicating that the `Buffer` should be destroyed also.

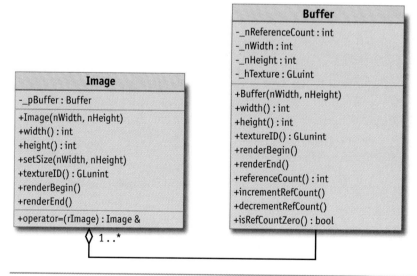

Figure 27-4. `Image` and `Buffer` Class Diagrams

27.2.3 Missing Pieces

We now have our data type and a handful of abstract classes to describe filter graphs. But to implement a real app, we need concrete means for image input and output. A simple application would load an image from disk, maybe apply a filter, and display the results on the screen. To do that, we need an operator to load images from disk and a display operator that renders an image to the screen.

The LoadOperator is obviously a data source and thus derived from the Source-Operator class. The load operator takes two parameters: a file name (including the path) and a file-type identifier. The operator reads the data from the file and creates an Image instance from it. The operator returns this image on every invocation of its image() method. The operator reloads a new image from the disk only when the file name or type is changed. See Figure 27-5.

The ImageView class displays the processed images. The class is also responsible for allowing the user to resize the image (that is, zooming in and out) and move it around in the viewport (panning). Because the view only consumes processed images but doesn't produce any output for the pipeline, it is derived from the SinkOperator class.

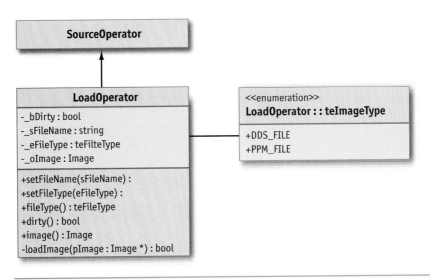

Figure 27-5. The LoadOperator Class Diagram

The methods supporting this class are the following:

```
int   imagePositionX() const;
int   imagePositionY() const;
void  setImagePosition(int nX, int nY);
float zoomFactor() const;
void  setZoomFactor(float nZoomFactor);
```

These setters and getters for position and zoom factor are self-explanatory.

More interesting are the following two methods:

```
void center();
void changeZoomFactor(float nPercent);
```

The `center()` method centers the current image within the viewport. The `change-ZoomFactor(nPercent)` method allows the programmer to incrementally change the zoom factor by a certain percentage. This is convenient because it allows resizing based on the current size without having to query for this information.

To correctly display the image even when the user changes the application's window size, `ImageView` needs to update the viewport transformation. This is achieved through a simple function that communicates any changes of the viewport size to the `ImageView`. The programmer of the application needs to ensure that the application informs the viewer class of any viewport changes.

```
void reshape(int nViewportWidth, int nViewportHeight);
```

The mechanism to display the viewport is implemented by the following two methods:

```
void display();
void update();
```

The `display()` method simply renders the image currently stored in the view. Pipeline processing is not triggered by an invocation of `display()`. The image stored in the view is updated using the `update()` method. This method simply retrieves a new image from the pipeline. See Figure 27-6.

27.3 Implementation

Processing an image is fairly simple and straightforward. The filter renders a screen-aligned quad into an invisible pixel buffer. The screen-aligned quad has the input image bound as a texture. For each rendered pixel, a Cg fragment program is executed, which does the

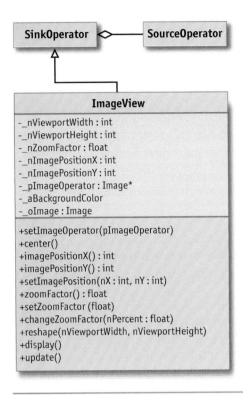

Figure 27-6. The ImageView Class Diagram

actual image processing. Because the quad is rendered using the input image as a texture, the Cg program can access the pixels in the input image though simple texture reads.

This is why implementing new image filters is so simple. It consists of writing a new Cg fragment program and some C++ code to provide the Cg program with the necessary (uniform) parameters.

All of the magic that makes sure the image isn't copied unnecessarily or moved between system memory and the graphics card is hidden in the implementation of the Image class.

The basic mechanism is to render the processed image into an invisible buffer. Once the rendering is finished and the image is ready to be processed by the next filter in the pipeline, the invisible buffer's content needs to be bound as a texture for the next rendering path.

27.3.1 The `Image` Class

This mechanism of rendering into an invisible buffer and using this buffer as a texture can be implemented in OpenGL using two ARB extensions: `WGL_ARB_pbuffer` and `WGL_ARB_render_texture`.

Pixel buffers (or *pbuffers*, created using the `WGL_ARB_pbuffer` extension) are such invisible buffers for OpenGL. Pixel buffers allow you to do everything that can be done with visible frame buffers. Now that we can render into an invisible buffer that resides on the graphics board, we need to find a way to use this buffer as a texture. That is exactly what the render-to-texture extension (`WGL_ARB_render_texture`) allows us to do.

To make things more fun, we decided to support *non-power-of-two* (NPOT) textures, because typical video and image resolutions are not powers of two. OpenGL supports NPOT textures through the `NV_texture_rectangle` extension.

Modern GPUs increasingly support floating-point data and arithmetic for color values. Floating-point numbers have great advantages over fixed-point numbers for color representation. In linear color space, the uneven distribution of floating-point numbers along the number scale matches that of the human perceptual system. Floating-point numbers are very dense around zero and have increasingly bigger steps between successive values for bigger values. Similarly, our perceptual system can distinguish small intensity variations at low intensities and gets increasingly less sensitive at high intensities. When floating-point arithmetic is used for image processing, one can also avoid clamping values to a 0-to-1 range for any intermediate steps in the process. Only for the very last step is it necessary to "normalize" the dynamic range to a fixed interval. In the easiest case, this is a simple affine mapping. But elaborate tone-mapping schemes do exist, which segment the image based on local intensities and map each segment differently. Such algorithms usually try to avoid dark areas in the image being mapped to black, and bright areas being mapped to white, respectively.

NVIDIA hardware supports two types of floating-point numbers: `float` (IEEE 32-bit floating point) and `half`. For the implementation of this framework, we decided to use the `half` data type for color representation. The advantages of `half` over `float` are these:

- There is a good trade-off between speed and accuracy.
- The `half` data type has a smaller memory footprint than the 32-bit `float`.

- The OpenEXR image format uses the same 16-bit floating-point numbers as NVIDIA's hardware. This allows us to load and save high-dynamic-range images in a standard format without any quality loss. (See Chapter 26 of this book, "The OpenEXR Image File Format," for a full discussion of this resource.)

To create 16-bit pbuffers, we need to use yet another OpenGL extension: `WGL_ARB_pixel_format`. This extension allows querying pixel formats for pixel buffers based on the tasks for which the buffer will be used (see sample code below).

So, once the WGL extensions are initialized (see DVD or NVIDIA SDK for sample code), we can write constructors and destructors for the `Buffer` class. See Listing 27-1.

Listing 27-1. Code Setting Up OpenGL Texture Properties and Filtering

```
Buffer::Buffer(int nWidth,
               int nHeight): _nReferenceCount(0),
                             _nWidth(nWidth),
                             _nHeight(nHeight)
{
  // Set up the texture properties
  glGenTextures(1, &_hTexture);
  glBindTexture(GL_TEXTURE_RECTANGLE_NV, _hTexture);
  glTexParameteri(GL_TEXTURE_RECTANGLE_NV, GL_TEXTURE_MAG_FILTER,
                  GL_NEAREST);
  glTexParameteri(GL_TEXTURE_RECTANGLE_NV, GL_TEXTURE_MIN_FILTER,
                  GL_NEAREST);
  glTexParameteri(GL_TEXTURE_RECTANGLE_NV, GL_TEXTURE_WRAP_S,
                  GL_CLAMP_TO_EDGE);
  glTexParameteri(GL_TEXTURE_RECTANGLE_NV, GL_TEXTURE_WRAP_T,
                  GL_CLAMP_TO_EDGE);
```

Listing 27-1 sets the properties for the texture to which we will bind the buffer. Notice that at the time of this writing, floating-point textures don't support any filtering except GL_NEAREST.

Because pixel buffers need their own device and render contexts, we save the current contexts now:

```
_hOldDC = wglGetCurrentDC();
_hOldRenderContext = wglGetCurrentContext();
```

Now we have to query for a suitable pixel format, as shown in Listing 27-2.

Listing 27-2. Pixel-Format Selection Code

```
int aIntegerAttributes[15] = {
  WGL_DRAW_TO_PBUFFER_ARB, GL_TRUE,
  WGL_BIND_TO_TEXTURE_RECTANGLE_FLOAT_RGBA_NV, GL_TRUE,
  WGL_FLOAT_COMPONENTS_NV, GL_TRUE,
  WGL_RED_BITS_ARB, 16,
  WGL_GREEN_BITS_ARB, 16,
  WGL_BLUE_BITS_ARB, 16,
  WGL_ALPHA_BITS_ARB, 16,
  0 };

float aFloatAttributes[2] = {0.0f, 0.0f};

int nPixelFormat;
unsigned int nPixelFormats;

if (0 == wglChoosePixelFormatARB(
  _hOldDC,
  aIntegerAttributes,
  aFloatAttributes,
  1, &nPixelFormat, &nPixelFormats))
{
  std::cerr << "Error: Couldn't find a suitable pixel format."
            << std::endl;
  exit(1);
}
```

As you can see, the call to `wglChoosePixelFormatARB()` requires quite a bit of preparation. The most interesting part of all this is the list of properties the pixel format must support. This property list is specified in the form of an array. The content of the array follows a simple parameter-value-pair pattern. The array has to be zero-terminated.

The `wglChoosePixelFormatARB()` method can return a complete array of values, but we've decided to request only a single value, specified by setting the fourth parameter to 1. The `nPixelFormat` variable receives our return value; the `nPixelFormats` variable receives the total number of pixel formats supported by the hardware that would fit our requirements. Because we need only one format to fit the bill, we discard this information.

The code in Listing 27-3 creates the actual buffer. The buffer attributes are given to the create function in an array. These attributes tell the creation method how the buffer will be used. `gnFormatRGBA` contains the pixel-format number. We found this number using the `ARB_pixel_format` extension.

Listing 27-3. Pbuffer Creation Code

```
int aPBufferAttributes[7] = { WGL_TEXTURE_TARGET_ARB,
                              WGL_TEXTURE_RECTANGLE_NV,
                              WGL_TEXTURE_FORMAT_ARB,
                              WGL_TEXTURE_FLOAT_RGBA_NV,
                              WGL_PBUFFER_LARGEST_ARB,
                              0, 0 };
_hPBuffer = wglCreatePbufferARB(_hOldDC, nPixelFormat,
                               _nWidth,
                               _nHeight,
                               aPBufferAttributes);
```

Now is also the time to store the pbuffer's device and render contexts. The `wglShareLists()` command tells OpenGL that the application and the buffer share resources (such as textures, and so on):

```
_hDC = wglGetPbufferDCARB(_hPBuffer);
_hRenderContext = wglCreateContext(_hDC);
wglShareLists(_hOldRenderContext, _hRenderContext);
```

As a last step, we bind the buffer to a texture. The buffer's default mode is to be bound to a texture. Only when we want to render to it do we unbind it:

```
wglMakeCurrent(_hDC, _hRenderContext);
glBindTexture(GL_TEXTURE_RECTANGLE_NV, _hTexture);
wglBindTexImageARB(_hPBuffer, WGL_FRONT_LEFT_ARB);
wglMakeCurrent(_hOldDC, _hOldRenderContext);
}
```

The destructor releases all the resources:

```
Buffer::~Buffer()
{
  wglReleasePbufferDCARB(_hPBuffer, _hDC);
  wglDestroyPbufferARB(_hPBuffer);
  wglDeleteContext(_hRenderContext);
}
```

With this in place, switching the buffer into render mode and back into texture mode is really simple, as shown in Listing 27-4.

Listing 27-4. Switching Active Pbuffers and Binding Textures Rolled into an Easy-to-Use Begin/End Render Mechanism

```
void Buffer::renderBegin()
{
  glBindTexture(GL_TEXTURE_RECTANGLE_NV, _hTexture);
  wglReleaseTexImageARB(_hPBuffer, WGL_FRONT_LEFT_ARB);
  wglMakeCurrent(_hDC, _hRenderContext);
}

void Buffer::renderEnd()
{
  glBindTexture(GL_TEXTURE_RECTANGLE_NV, _hTexture);
  wglBindTexImageARB(_hPBuffer, WGL_FRONT_LEFT_ARB);
  wglMakeCurrent(_hOldDC, _hOldRenderContext);
}
```

27.3.2 The `ImageFilter` Class

As we mentioned previously, we implement the image processing by rendering a screen-aligned quad into our pbuffer. Because the actual image processing is done by a Cg program, we can implement the `ImageFilter` class's `image()` method right away, using the following trick. We define a purely virtual function, `cgFragment-Program()`, which when overloaded by a derived class returns a handle to the fragment program. The `image()` method binds this program to render the screen-aligned quad. Concrete image filters derived from the `ImageFilter` base class just have to overload the method and make it return the fragment program that they want to use to process the image.

The following is a simplified version of the `image()` method:

```
Image oOutputImage;
Image oInputImage = _pSourceOperator->image();

oOutputImage.setSize(oInputImage.width(), oInputImage.height());
```

First, we create objects for the output image and retrieve the input image from the filter's input operator. Then we specify that the output image has the same size as the input image. (This means that, for example, a resize filter could not reuse this implementation.) See Listing 27-5. The call to `renderBegin()` prepares our image (that is, our pbuffer) for rendering. The code that follows sets up the rendering pipeline for simple rendering of our screen-aligned quad.

Listing 27-5. Setting Up the Viewport and Projection for Processing an Image

```
oOutputImage.renderBegin();
{
  glViewport(0, 0,
             (GLsizei) oOutputImage.width(),
             (GLsizei) oOutputImage.height());

  glMatrixMode(GL_PROJECTION);
  glLoadIdentity();
  gluOrtho2D(0, oOutputImage.width(), 0, oOutputImage.height());
  glMatrixMode(GL_MODELVIEW);
  glLoadIdentity();
```

We then tell the Cg runtime to use a very simple vertex shader. The shader and profile are retrieved from the ShaderManager class, as shown in the following code snippet. All the vertex shader does is transform vertex coordinates according to the model-view matrix and pass the texture coordinates to the fragment shader.

```
cgGLEnableProfile(ShaderManager::gVertexIdentityProfile);
cgGLBindProgram(ShaderManager::gVertexIdentityShader);
```

Now we tell the Cg runtime which fragment program to use:

```
cgGLEnableProfile(cgFragmentProfile());
cgGLBindProgram(cgFragmentProgram());
```

Then the runtime retrieves the OpenGL texture ID from the input image and makes it the texture that the fragment program renders:

```
cgGLSetTextureParameter(_hoInputImage, oInputImage.textureID());
cgGLEnableTextureParameter(_hoInputImage);
```

What follows is another purely virtual function of the ImageFilter class. It should be used in derived classes to set additional parameters of the fragment program:

```
setCgParameters();
```

Then we simply draw a screen-aligned quad, as in the following code. One note about the texture coordinates: Although texture coordinates are usually in the range [0, 1], NV_texture_rectangle textures expect their texture coordinates to be in pixels.

```
glBegin(GL_QUADS);
  glTexCoord2f(0.0f,   0.0f);      glVertex2f(   0.0f, 0.0f);
  glTexCoord2f(nWidth, 0.0f);      glVertex2f(nWidth, 0.0f);
  glTexCoord2f(nWidth, nHeight);   glVertex2f(nWidth, nHeight);
```

```
    glTexCoord2f(0.0f,   nHeight);  glVertex2f(  0.0f, nHeight);
    glEnd();
```

Finally, we conclude the rendering and return the output image:

```
}
oOutputImage.renderEnd();

return oOutputImage;
}
```

27.3.3 Implementing a Filter

Implementing a new filter derived from the general `ImageFilter` class involves the following tasks:

1. Adding the filter's parameters. This involves defining the necessary member variables, setter methods, and getter methods. Because each parameter also needs to be passed to the Cg fragment program, it is convenient to have members representing the Cg parameters.

2. Implementing the Cg fragment program. Code to load this program should be added to the filter's constructor.

3. Overloading the `setCgParameters()` method. This method passes the parameter values stored in the filter's data members to the Cg program whenever it gets invoked.

The sample code in the following discussion comes from a simple filter implementing Gaussian blur. A Gaussian blur filter convolves the image with a filter kernel with a two-dimensional Gaussian bell curve. To avoid unbearably slow processing speeds, we limit the maximum filter-kernel size to 7×7 filters.

Filter Parameters

Blurriness is specified in terms of `sigma`, the Gaussian's standard deviation. `sigma` is the distance from the Gaussian's center to the point where the Gaussian has dropped to 50 percent of its center value. The actual filter has to be changed whenever `sigma` changes, so we've decided to calculate the actual filter kernel on the CPU. Therefore, we also have to store the kernel as a `float` array. The complete class definition for `GaussFilter` appears in Listing 27-6.

Listing 27-6. Class Declaration for a Gaussian Filter

```
class GaussFilter: public ImageFilter
{
  public:
    // Construction and destruction
    GaussFilter();
    virtual ~GaussFilter() { ; }

    // Set/Get sigma
    float sigma() const;
    void setSigma(float nSigma);

  protected:
    virtual void setCgParameters();
    void recalculateKernel(float nSigma);

  private:
    float _nSigma;          // Standard deviation
    float _aKernel[49];     // The filter kernel

    CGparameter _hmModelView;
    CGparameter _hKernel;
};
```

Deriving a new filter class obviously involves very little overhead. Except for _hmModelView, everything directly relates to the Gaussian filter. The Cg parameter for the model-view matrix is required by the vertex program to transform vertices correctly.

The Fragment Program

The Cg program for the Gauss filter simply evaluates the convolution of the filter kernel with the pixels in the original image. So, for every pixel, it multiplies all pixels covered by the filter kernel with the corresponding value in the filter kernel, and then it sums all these values to form the new pixel's color.[1] The program appears in Listing 27-7.

---

1. This is the simplest but also a very inefficient way to implement a Gaussian filter. The Gaussian filter, like many other simple filter kernels, falls into the group of *separable* filters. That is, they are 2D filter kernels that can be rewritten as the product of two 1D filters. This trick turns the convolution problem from an $O(n^2)$ into an $O(2n)$ problem, which in almost all cases results in a faster implementation. For more information on convolution and separable filters, see Chapter 21 of this book, "Real-Time Glow."

Listing 27-7. The Fragment Program for the Gaussian Filter

```
void gauss(in float2 vUV  : TEXCOORD0,
           out half4 vOut : COLOR,
           const uniform samplerRECT oImage,
           const uniform half aKernel[N])
{
  half4 vSum;
  int i, j, k;

  vOut = half4(0, 0, 0, 0);
  k = 0;
  for (i = -RAD; i <= RAD; i++)
    for (j = -RAD; j <= RAD; j++)
    {
      vSum += texRECT(oImage, vUV + half2(i, j)) * aKernel[k];
      k++;
    }
  vOut = vSum;
}
```

The constants N and RAD are used for better readability. In our case, they are defined as follows:

```
#define RAD 3 // Filter kernel radius
#define N   49 // Number of elements in the filter kernel
```

The code to set up the Cg programs and their parameters in the filter's default constructor is shown in Listing 27-8.

Setting the Cg Parameters

As previously mentioned, the code providing the Cg program with its data on invocation goes into the setCgParameters() method that needs to be overloaded by every class derived from ImageFilter.

```
void GaussFilter::setCgParameters()
{
  cgGLSetParameterArray1f(_hKernel, 0, 0, &(_aKernel[0]));
  cgGLSetStateMatrixParameter(_hmModelView,
                              CG_GL_MODELVIEW_PROJECTION_MATRIX,
                              CG_GL_MATRIX_IDENTITY);
}
```

Listing 27-8. Implementation of the GaussFilter Constructor

```
GaussFilter::GaussFilter(): _nSigma(1.0f)
{
   _oCgVertexProgram = cgCreateProgramFromFile(_oCgContext, CG_SOURCE,
      "VertexIdentity.cg", _oCgVertexProfile, "vertexIdentity", 0);
   cgGLLoadProgram(_oCgVertexProgram);

   _oCgFragmentProgram = cgCreateProgramFromFile(_oCgContext,
      CG_SOURCE, "Gauss.cg", _oCgFragmentProfile, "gauss", 0);
   cgGLLoadProgram(_oCgFragmentProgram);

   _hmModelView = cgGetNamedParameter(_oCgVertexProgram,
                                      "mModelView");

   setSigma(_nSigma);
}
```

Well, that's it—we're done with our first image filter. In Figure 27-7, you can see the effect of applying this filter to an image.

27.4 A Sample Application

To demonstrate the usefulness of our framework, we created a simple demo application. The application implements a filter that simulates night vision. When the human eye adapts to dark environments—and must rely on *scotopic vision,* or vision under reduced illumination—we lose most of our ability to see color. Scenes appear blurred and shaded in blue. Moviemakers exploit this behavior of the human visual system by using blue filters to shoot night scenes in bright daylight. Based on an article by William B. Thompson et al. (2002), we implemented an advanced version of this "Hollywood Night."

The post-processing algorithm proposed in Thompson et al. 2002 first converts the color image into a shades-of-blue image. Next, this image is blurred, which simulates the eye's reduced resolution in dark environments. Then an edge-sharpening filter is applied to the image. According to the article, this procedure resembles the image processing our brain applies to the blurry images our visual system delivers in darkness.

We implemented the color-conversion procedure in one operator, called Night-Filter. The complete scotopic vision filter (ScotopicFilter) is a composite filter: it implements a small subpipeline within itself. See Figure 27-8.

Figure 27-7. Applying a Gauss Filter
Top: The original input image. Bottom: The same image with a Gauss filter applied.

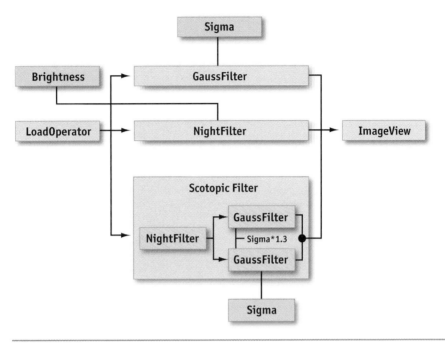

Figure 27-8. The Scotopic Filter Pipeline

The complete demo application allows processing an input image with a Gauss filter, the night-vision filter, and the scotopic filter. This is implemented by setting up the three "pipelines" and, depending on user choice, plugging the pipeline into the view operator.

In Figure 27-9, you can see the effect of the scotopic filter applied to an image.

The demo application is part of the NVIDIA Developer SDK and is available on this book's CD and Web site.

27.5 Performance and Limitations

So far in this chapter, we've avoided addressing some issues that are critical for the adoption of technologies into real-world applications: such issues include performance and hardware limitations (such as maximum texture size, limited video memory, and more). Graphics hardware continues to evolve at a pace that makes it almost impossible to discuss these issues in absolute numbers. Today's hardware limits will likely be gone tomorrow.

When designing algorithms that utilize the GPU, one should generally keep a couple of things in mind: A GPU is a highly specialized second processor. Writing code for multiprocessor systems is naturally more complex than writing ordinary code. GPUs

Figure 27-9. The Scotopic Filter Applied to the Photograph from Figure 27-7.
Top: The parameters are tweaked to produce a realistic night-scene look. Bottom: The filter is applied with a different set of parameters, which yield a more "artistic" effect.

are primarily designed to render 3D scenes. Thus, only those solutions that fit the hardware's primary purpose will benefit maximally.

Many image-processing problems map well to today's GPUs, and tenfold accelerations have been measured (Colantoni et al. 2003). Other problems that don't match very well can still profit from offloading some of the workload to the GPU. For best performance, algorithms should aim to saturate both processors—the CPU and the GPU—with workload.

Implementers of image-processing algorithms have faced hardware limitations in the past, most notably memory limitations and limited cache sizes. These problems were usually overcome by designing specific solutions. Many of these solutions have remained useful even after the original restriction was lifted (for example, virtual memory management) because of their better performance. We believe that GPU programming will develop in a similar manner.

27.6 Conclusion

The image-processing framework described in this chapter demonstrates that the processing power of modern 3D graphics hardware can be utilized for 2D image-processing tasks. The way our framework was designed and implemented shows that current (primarily 3D-oriented) graphics APIs support a clean and straightforward implementation.

The remaining limitations with respect to current hardware can be overcome with smart engineering. Future hardware and APIs will further improve performance and simplify the programming task.

27.7 References

Colantoni, Philippe, Nabil Boukala, and Jerome Da Rugna. 2003. "Fast and Accurate Color Image Processing Using 3D Graphics Cards." In *Proceedings of Vision, Modeling, and Visualization 2003*.

Gamma, E., R. Helm, R. Johnson, and J. Vlissides. 1995. *Design Patterns: Elements of Reusable Object-Oriented Software*. Addison-Wesley.

Meyers, Scott. 1997. *Effective C++: 50 Specific Ways to Improve Your Programs and Designs*. Addison-Wesley.

Thompson, William B., Peter Shirley, and James A. Ferwerda. 2002. "A Spatial Post-Processing Algorithm for Images of Night Scenes." *Journal of Graphics Tools* 7(1), pp. 1–12.

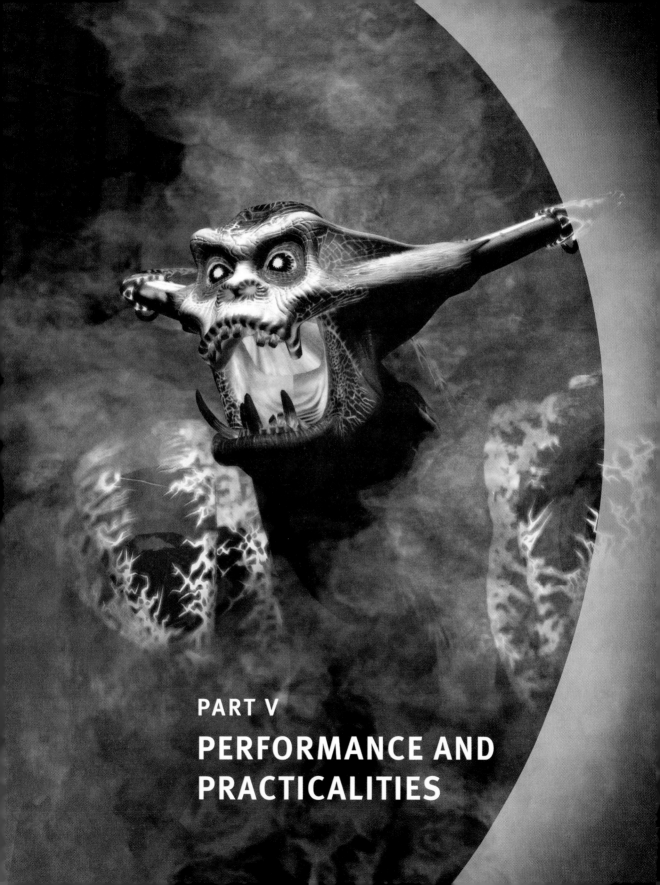

PART V
PERFORMANCE AND PRACTICALITIES

As GPUs become more complex, incorporating the GPU efficiently into your application can become challenging. This part of the book offers several perspectives on shader management and integration, as well as an overview of the graphics performance characteristics that shape integration decisions.

In **Chapter 28, "Graphics Pipeline Performance," Cem Cebenoyan** gives an overview of the modern graphics pipeline, including the programmable pipelines that give rise to many of the techniques discussed in this book. In this chapter, he describes a process to test for bottlenecks in the GPU pipeline, and he offers potential remedies for several bottlenecks.

Dean Sekulic of Croteam discusses the powerful but often-misused *occlusion query* feature in **Chapter 29, "Efficient Occlusion Culling."** Occlusion queries allow the GPU to return the amount of pixels that an object would represent on screen. If the object represents no pixels, due to z or stencil tests, it can be skipped. But because of the decoupled nature of the CPU and the GPU, an occlusion query can't be issued like a single-threaded function call, or else one would lose most or all of the performance benefit. Instead, Dean discusses several methods of ensuring that the results of the GPU occlusion query can be applied quickly and efficiently.

In **Chapter 30, "The Design of FX Composer," Christopher Maughan** discusses a powerful shader-authoring tool. FX Composer 1.0 provides a full IDE for shader authors, as well as an artist-tweakable GUI to adjust shader attributes. Chris describes design aspects of the tool, offering insight into cutting-edge shader integration.

Chapter 31, "Using FX Composer," also by **Christopher Maughan**, delves into the details of FX Composer usage, including shader authoring, setting up simple scenes, and applying shaders to objects. This chapter provides a good introduction to both shader authoring and tool usage.

In **Chapter 32, "An Introduction to Shader Interfaces," Matt Pharr** describes shader objects, which can simplify the integration of shaders into applications via the concept of *shader interfaces*. By specifying shader fragments as objects, with well-defined interfaces, you can efficiently combine these fragments at runtime automatically, improving both flexibility and performance.

In **Chapter 33, "Converting Production RenderMan Shaders to Real Time," Stephen Marshall** of Sony Pictures Imageworks tells how RenderMan-style off-line shaders can be modified and leveraged in a GPU-aware production pipeline. Offline shaders are written with CPU advantages and limitations in mind; only by rethinking shaders in terms of modern GPUs can the maximum speed benefits be realized.

Cinema 4D is another modern, shader-capable authoring tool. **Jörn Loviscach**, in **Chapter 34, "Integrating Hardware Shading into Cinema 4D,"** discusses how he integrated GPU shaders to emulate the existing CPU shading pipeline as closely as possible. Jörn offers a compelling example of how to seamlessly add GPU capability to a more traditional, existing workflow.

Although GPUs get more flexible and powerful each year, it will likely be quite a while before all content-creation rendering tasks can be handled on the graphics card. In **Chapter 35, "Leveraging High-Quality Software Rendering Effects in Real-Time Applications," Alexandre Jean Claude** and **Marc Stevens** discuss how they leveraged the GPU shader horsepower while still retaining the flexibility of a mature, existing software rendering and modeling pipeline.

Finally, **John O'Rorke**'s chapter on shader integration, **Chapter 36, "Integrating Shaders into Applications,"** focuses on the DirectX .fx file format and how it can be used. John demonstrates how to use .fx file features such as semantics and annotations, which enable simpler shader integration. He concludes with several ideas for customizing and extending .fx files, including shader inheritance.

Sim Dietrich, NVIDIA

Chapter 28

Graphics Pipeline Performance

Cem Cebenoyan
NVIDIA

28.1 Overview

Over the past few years, the hardware-accelerated rendering pipeline has rapidly increased in complexity, bringing with it increasingly intricate and potentially confusing performance characteristics. Improving performance used to mean simply reducing the CPU cycles of the inner loops in your renderer; now it has become a cycle of determining bottlenecks and systematically attacking them. This loop of *identification* and *optimization* is fundamental to tuning a heterogeneous multiprocessor system; the driving idea is that a pipeline, by definition, is only as fast as its slowest stage. Thus, while premature and unfocused optimization in a single-processor system can lead to only minimal performance gains, in a multiprocessor system such optimization very often leads to *zero* gains.

Working hard on graphics optimization and seeing zero performance improvement is no fun. The goal of this chapter is to keep you from doing exactly that.

28.1.1 The Pipeline

The pipeline, at the very highest level, can be broken into two parts: the CPU and the GPU. Although CPU optimization is a critical part of optimizing your application, it

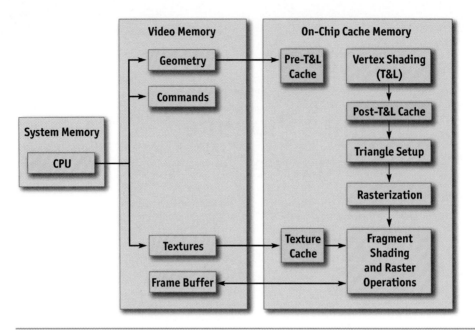

Figure 28-1. The Graphics Pipeline

will not be the focus of this chapter, because much of this optimization has little to do with the graphics pipeline.

Figure 28-1 shows that within the GPU, there are a number of functional units operating in parallel, which essentially act as separate special-purpose processors, and a number of spots where a bottleneck can occur. These include vertex and index fetching, vertex shading (transform and lighting, or T&L), fragment shading, and raster operations (ROP).

28.1.2 Methodology

Optimization without proper bottleneck identification is the cause of much wasted development effort, and so we formalize the process into the following fundamental identification and optimization loop:

1. **Identify the bottleneck.** For each stage in the pipeline, vary either its workload or its computational ability (that is, clock speed). If performance varies, you've found a bottleneck.

2. **Optimize.** Given the bottlenecked stage, reduce its workload until performance stops improving or until you achieve your desired level of performance.

3. **Repeat.** Do steps 1 and 2 again until the desired performance level is reached.

28.2 Locating the Bottleneck

Locating the bottleneck is half the battle in optimization, because it enables you to make intelligent decisions about focusing your actual optimization efforts. Figure 28-2 shows a flow chart depicting the series of steps required to locate the precise bottleneck in your application. Note that we start at the back end of the pipeline, with the frame-buffer operations (also called raster operations) and end at the CPU. Note also that while any single primitive (usually a triangle), by definition, has a single bottleneck, over the course of a frame the bottleneck most likely changes. Thus, modifying the workload on more than one stage in the pipeline often influences performance. For example, a low-polygon skybox is often bound by fragment shading or frame-buffer access; a skinned mesh that maps to only a few pixels on screen is often bound by CPU or vertex processing. For this reason, it frequently helps to vary workloads on an object-by-object, or material-by-material, basis.

For each pipeline stage, we also mention the GPU clock to which it's tied (that is, core or memory). This information is useful in conjunction with tools such as PowerStrip (EnTech Taiwan 2003), which allows you to reduce the relevant clock speed and observe performance changes in your application.

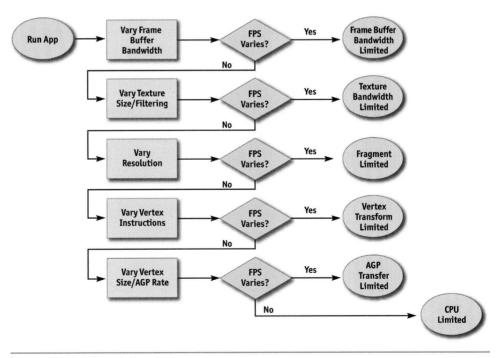

Figure 28-2. Bottleneck Flowchart

28.2.1 Raster Operations

The very back end of the pipeline, raster operations (often called the ROP), is responsible for reading and writing depth and stencil, doing the depth and stencil comparisons, reading and writing color, and doing alpha blending and testing. As you can see, much of the ROP workload taxes the available frame-buffer bandwidth.

The best way to test if your application is frame-buffer-bandwidth bound is to vary the bit depths of the color or the depth buffers, or both. If reducing your bit depth from 32-bit to 16-bit significantly improves your performance, then you are definitely frame-buffer-bandwidth bound.

Frame-buffer bandwidth is a function of GPU memory clock, so modifying memory clocks is another technique for helping to identify this bottleneck.

28.2.2 Texture Bandwidth

Texture bandwidth is consumed any time a texture fetch request goes out to memory. Although modern GPUs have texture caches designed to minimize extraneous memory requests, they obviously still occur and consume a fair amount of memory bandwidth.

Modifying texture formats can be trickier than modifying frame-buffer formats as we did when inspecting the ROP; instead, we recommend changing the effective texture size by using a large amount of positive mipmap level-of-detail (LOD) bias. This makes texture fetches access very coarse levels of the mipmap pyramid, which effectively reduces the texture size. If this modification causes performance to improve significantly, you are bound by texture bandwidth.

Texture bandwidth is also a function of GPU memory clock.

28.2.3 Fragment Shading

Fragment shading refers to the actual cost of generating a fragment, with associated color and depth values. This is the cost of running the "pixel shader" or "fragment shader." Note that fragment shading and frame-buffer bandwidth are often lumped together under the heading *fill rate*, because both are a function of screen resolution. However, they are two distinct stages in the pipeline, and being able to tell the difference between the two is critical to effective optimization.

Before the advent of highly programmable fragment-processing GPUs, it was rare to be bound by fragment shading. It was often frame-buffer bandwidth that caused the inevitable correlation between screen resolution and performance. This pendulum is now starting to swing toward fragment shading, however, as the newfound flexibility enables developers to spend oodles of cycles making fancy pixels.

The first step in determining if fragment shading is the bottleneck is simply to change the resolution. Because we've already ruled out frame-buffer bandwidth by trying different frame-buffer bit depths, if adjusting resolution causes performance to change, the culprit is most likely fragment shading. A supplementary approach would be to modify the length of your fragment programs and see if this influences performance. But be careful not to add instructions that can easily be optimized away by a clever device driver.

Fragment-shading speed is a function of the GPU core clock.

28.2.4 Vertex Processing

The vertex transformation stage of the rendering pipeline is responsible for taking an input set of vertex attributes (such as model-space positions, vertex normals, texture coordinates, and so on) and producing a set of attributes suitable for clipping and rasterization (such as homogeneous clip-space position, vertex lighting results, texture coordinates, and more). Naturally, performance in this stage is a function of the work done per vertex, along with the number of vertices being processed.

With programmable transformations, determining if vertex processing is your bottleneck is a simple matter of changing the length of your vertex program. If performance changes, you are vertex-processing bound. If you're adding instructions, be careful to add ones that actually do meaningful work; otherwise, the instructions may be optimized away by the compiler or the driver. For example, no-ops that refer to constant registers (such as adding a constant register that has a value of zero) often cannot be optimized away because the driver usually doesn't know the value of a constant at program-compile time.

If you're using fixed-function transformations, it's a little trickier. Try modifying the load by changing vertex work such as specular lighting or texture-coordinate generation state.

Vertex processing speed is a function of the GPU core clock.

28.2.5 Vertex and Index Transfer

Vertices and indices are fetched by the GPU as the first step in the GPU part of the pipeline. The performance of vertex and index fetching can vary depending on where the actual vertices and indices are placed. They are usually either in system memory—which means they will be transferred to the GPU over a bus such as AGP or PCI Express—or in local frame-buffer memory. Often, on PC platforms especially, this decision is left up to the device driver instead of the application, although modern graphics APIs allow applications to provide usage hints to help the driver choose the correct memory type.

Determining if vertex or index fetching is a bottleneck in your application entails modifying the vertex format size.

Vertex and index fetching performance is a function of the AGP/PCI Express rate if the data is placed in system memory; it's a function of the memory clock if data is placed in local frame-buffer memory.

If none of these tests influences your performance significantly, you are primarily CPU bound. You may verify this fact by underclocking your CPU: if performance varies proportionally, you are CPU bound.

28.3 Optimization

Now that we have identified the bottleneck, we must optimize that particular stage to improve application performance. The following tips are categorized by offending stage.

28.3.1 Optimizing on the CPU

Many applications are CPU bound—sometimes for good reason, such as complex physics or AI, and sometimes because of poor batching or resource management. If you've found that your application is CPU bound, try the following suggestions to reduce CPU work in the rendering pipeline.

Reduce Resource Locking

Anytime you perform a synchronous operation that demands access to a GPU resource, there is the potential to massively stall the GPU pipeline, which costs both CPU and GPU cycles. CPU cycles are wasted because the CPU must sit and spin in a loop, waiting for the (very deep) GPU pipeline to idle and return the requested resource. GPU cycles are then wasted as the pipeline sits idle and has to refill.

This locking can occur anytime you

- Lock or read from a surface you were previously rendering to
- Write to a surface the GPU is reading from, such as a texture or a vertex buffer

In general, you should avoid accessing a resource the GPU is using during rendering.

Maximize Batch Size

We can also call this tip "Minimize the Number of Batches." A *batch* is a group of primitives rendered with a single API rendering call (for example, `DrawIndexed-Primitive` in DirectX 9). The *size* of a batch is the number of primitives it contains. As a wise man once said, "Batch, Batch, Batch!" (Wloka 2003). Every API function call to draw geometry has an associated CPU cost, so maximizing the number of triangles submitted with every draw call will minimize the CPU work done for a given number of triangles rendered.

Some tips to maximize the size of your batches:

- **If using triangle strips, use degenerate triangles to stitch together disjoint strips.** This will enable you to send multiple strips, provided that they share material, in a single draw call.

- **Use texture pages.** Batches are frequently broken when different objects use different textures. By arranging many textures into a single 2D texture and setting your texture coordinates appropriately, you can send geometry that uses multiple textures in a single draw call. Note that this technique can have issues with mipmapping and antialiasing. One technique that sidesteps many of these issues is to pack individual 2D textures into each face of a cube map.

- **Use GPU shader branching to increase batch size.** Modern GPUs have flexible vertex- and fragment-processing pipelines that allow for branching inside the shader. For example, if two batches are separate because one requires a four-bone skinning vertex shader and the other requires a two-bone skinning vertex shader, you could instead write a vertex shader that loops over the number of bones required, accumulating blending weights, and then breaks out of the loop when the weights sum to one. This way, the two batches could be combined into one. On architectures that don't support shader branching, similar functionality can be implemented, at the cost of shader cycles, by using a four-bone vertex shader on everything and simply zeroing out the bone weights on vertices that have fewer than four bone influences.

- **Use the vertex shader constant memory as a lookup table of matrices.** Often batches get broken when many small objects share all material properties but differ only in matrix state (for example, a forest of similar trees, or a particle system). In these cases, you can load *n* of the differing matrices into the vertex shader constant memory and store indices into the constant memory in the vertex format for each object. Then you would use this index to look up into the constant memory in the vertex shader and use the correct transformation matrix, thus rendering *n* objects at once.

- **Defer decisions as far down in the pipeline as possible.** It's faster to use the alpha channel of your texture as a gloss factor, rather than break the batch to set a pixel shader constant for glossiness. Similarly, putting shading data in your textures and vertices can allow for larger batch submissions.

28.3.2 Reducing the Cost of Vertex Transfer

Vertex transfer is rarely the bottleneck in an application, but it's certainly not impossible for it to happen. If the transfer of vertices or, less likely, indices is the bottleneck in your application, try the following:

- **Use the fewest possible bytes in your vertex format.** Don't use floats for everything if bytes would suffice (for colors, for example).

- **Generate potentially derivable vertex attributes inside the vertex program instead of storing them inside the input vertex format.** For example, there's often no need to store a tangent, binormal, and normal: given any two, the third can be derived using a simple cross product in the vertex program. This technique trades vertex-processing speed for vertex transfer rate.

- **Use 16-bit indices instead of 32-bit indices.** 16-bit indices are cheaper to fetch, are cheaper to move around, and take less memory.

- **Access vertex data in a relatively sequential manner.** Modern GPUs cache memory accesses when fetching vertices. As in any memory hierarchy, spatial locality of reference helps maximize hits in the cache, thus reducing bandwidth requirements.

28.3.3 Optimizing Vertex Processing

Vertex processing is rarely the bottleneck on modern GPUs, but it may occur, depending on your usage patterns and target hardware.

Try these suggestions if you're finding that vertex processing is the bottleneck in your application:

- **Optimize for the post-T&L vertex cache.** Modern GPUs have a small first-in, first-out (FIFO) cache that stores the result of the most recently transformed vertices; a hit in this cache saves all transform and lighting work, along with all work done earlier in the pipeline. To take advantage of this cache, you must use indexed primitives, and you must order your vertices to maximize locality of reference over the mesh. There are tools available—including D3DX and NVTriStrip (NVIDIA 2003)—that can help you with this task.

- **Reduce the number of vertices processed.** This is rarely the fundamental issue, but using a simple level-of-detail scheme, such as a set of static LODs, certainly helps reduce vertex-processing load.

- **Use vertex-processing LOD.** Along with using LODs for the number of vertices processed, try LODing the vertex computations themselves. For example, it is likely unnecessary to do full four-bone skinning on distant characters, and you can probably get away with cheaper approximations for the lighting. If your material is multi-passed, reducing the number of passes for lower LODs in the distance will also reduce vertex-processing cost.

- **Pull out per-object computations onto the CPU.** Often, a calculation that changes once per object or per frame is done in the vertex shader for convenience. For example, transforming a directional light vector to eye space is sometimes done in the vertex shader, although the result of the computation changes only once per frame.

- **Use the correct coordinate space.** Frequently, choice of coordinate space affects the number of instructions required to compute a value in the vertex program. For example, when doing vertex lighting, if your vertex normals are stored in object space and the light vector is stored in eye space, then you will have to transform one of the two vectors in the vertex shader. If the light vector was instead transformed into object space once per object on the CPU, no per-vertex transformation would be necessary, saving GPU vertex instructions.

- **Use vertex branching to "early-out" of computations.** If you are looping over a number of lights in the vertex shader and doing normal, low-dynamic-range, [0..1] lighting, you can check for saturation to 1—or if you're facing away from the light—and then break out of further computations. A similar optimization can occur with skinning, where you can break when your weights sum to 1 (and therefore all subsequent weights would be 0). Note that this depends on how the GPU implements vertex branching, and it isn't guaranteed to improve performance on all architectures.

28.3.4 Speeding Up Fragment Shading

If you're using long and complex fragment shaders, it is often likely that you're fragment-shading bound. If so, try these suggestions:

- **Render depth first.** Rendering a depth-only (no-color) pass before rendering your primary shading passes can dramatically boost performance, especially in scenes with high depth complexity, by reducing the amount of fragment shading and frame-buffer memory access that needs to be performed. To get the full benefits of a depth-only pass, it's not sufficient to just disable color writes to the frame buffer; you should also disable all shading on fragments, even shading that affects depth as well as color (such as alpha test).

- **Help early-z optimizations throw away fragment processing.** Modern GPUs have silicon designed to avoid shading occluded fragments, but these optimizations rely on knowledge of the scene up to the current point; they can be improved dramatically by rendering in a roughly front-to-back order. Also, laying down depth first (see the previous tip) in a separate pass can help substantially speed up subsequent passes (where all the expensive shading is done) by effectively reducing their shaded-depth complexity to 1.

- **Store complex functions in textures.** Textures can be enormously useful as lookup tables, and their results are filtered for free. The canonical example here is a normalization cube map, which allows you to normalize an arbitrary vector at high precision for the cost of a single texture lookup.

- **Move per-fragment work to the vertex shader.** Just as per-object work in the vertex shader should be moved to the CPU instead, per-vertex computations (along with computations that can be correctly linearly interpolated in screen space) should be moved to the vertex shader. Common examples include computing vectors and transforming vectors between coordinate systems.

- **Use the lowest precision necessary.** APIs such as DirectX 9 allow you to specify precision hints in fragment shader code for quantities or calculations that can work with reduced precision. Many GPUs can take advantage of these hints to reduce internal precision and improve performance.

- **Avoid excessive normalization.** A common mistake is to get "normalization-happy": normalizing every single vector every step of the way when performing a calculation. Recognize which transformations preserve length (such as transformations by an orthonormal basis) and which computations do not depend on vector length (such as cube-map lookups).

- **Consider using fragment shader level of detail.** Although it offers less bang for the buck than vertex LOD (simply because objects in the distance naturally LOD themselves with respect to pixel processing, due to perspective), reducing the complexity of the shaders in the distance, and decreasing the number of passes over a surface, can lessen the fragment-processing workload.

- **Disable trilinear filtering where unnecessary.** Trilinear filtering, even when not consuming extra texture bandwidth, costs extra cycles to compute in the fragment shader on most modern GPU architectures. On textures where mip-level transitions are not readily discernible, turn trilinear filtering off to save fill rate.

- **Use the simplest shader type possible.** In both Direct3D and OpenGL, there are a number of different ways to shade fragments. For example, in Direct3D 9, you can specify fragment shading using, in order of increasing complexity and power, texture-stage states, pixel shaders version 1.x (ps.1.1 – ps.1.4), pixel shaders version 2.x., or pixel shaders version 3.0. In general, you should use the simplest shader type that allows you to create the intended effect. The simpler shader types offer a number of implicit assumptions that often allow them to be compiled to faster native pixel-processing code by the GPU driver. A nice side effect is that these shaders would then work on a broader range of hardware.

28.3.5 Reducing Texture Bandwidth

If you've found that you're memory-bandwidth bound, but mostly when fetching from textures, consider these optimizations:

- **Reduce the size of your textures.** Consider your target resolution and texture coordinates. Do your users ever get to see your highest mip level? If not, consider scaling back the size of your textures. This can be especially helpful if overloaded frame-buffer memory has forced texturing to occur from nonlocal memory (such as system memory, over the AGP or PCI Express bus). The NVPerfHUD tool (NVIDIA 2003) can help diagnose this problem, as it shows the amount of memory allocated by the driver in various heaps.

- **Compress all color textures.** All textures that are used just as decals or detail textures should be compressed, using DXT1, DXT3, or DXT5, depending on the specific texture's alpha needs. This step will reduce memory usage, reduce texture bandwidth requirements, and improve texture cache efficiency.

- **Avoid expensive texture formats if not necessary.** Large texture formats, such as 64-bit or 128-bit floating-point formats, obviously cost much more bandwidth to fetch from. Use these only as necessary.

- **Always use mipmapping on any surface that may be minified.** In addition to improving quality by reducing texture aliasing, mipmapping improves texture cache utilization by localizing texture-memory access patterns for minified textures. If you find that mipmapping on certain surfaces makes them look blurry, avoid the temptation to disable mipmapping or add a large negative LOD bias. Prefer anisotropic filtering instead and adjust the level of anisotropy per batch as appropriate.

28.3.6 Optimizing Frame-Buffer Bandwidth

The final stage in the pipeline, ROP, interfaces directly with the frame-buffer memory and is the single largest consumer of frame-buffer bandwidth. For this reason, if bandwidth is an issue in your application, it can often be traced to the ROP. Here's how to optimize for frame-buffer bandwidth:

- **Render depth first.** This step reduces not only fragment-shading cost (see the previous section), but also frame-buffer bandwidth cost.

- **Reduce alpha blending.** Note that alpha blending, with a destination-blending factor set to anything other than 0, requires both a read and a write to the frame buffer, thus potentially consuming double the bandwidth. Reserve alpha blending for only those situations that require it, and be wary of high levels of alpha-blended depth complexity.

- **Turn off depth writes when possible.** Writing depth is an additional consumer of bandwidth, and it should be disabled in multipass rendering (where the final depth is already in the depth buffer); when rendering alpha-blended effects, such as particles; and when rendering objects into shadow maps (in fact, for rendering into color-based shadow maps, you can turn off depth reads as well).

- **Avoid extraneous color-buffer clears.** If every pixel is guaranteed to be overwritten in the frame buffer by your application, then avoid clearing color, because it costs precious bandwidth. Note, however, that you should clear the depth and stencil buffers whenever you can, because many early-z optimizations rely on the deterministic contents of a cleared depth buffer.

- **Render roughly front to back.** In addition to the fragment-shading advantages mentioned in the previous section, there are similar benefits for frame-buffer bandwidth. Early-z hardware optimizations can discard extraneous frame-buffer reads and writes.

In fact, even older hardware, which lacks these optimizations, will benefit from this step, because more fragments will fail the depth test, resulting in fewer color and depth writes to the frame buffer.

- **Optimize skybox rendering.** Skyboxes are often frame-buffer-bandwidth bound, but you must decide how to optimize them: (1) render them last, reading (but *not* writing) depth, and allow the early-z optimizations along with regular depth buffering to save bandwidth; or (2) render the skybox first, and disable all depth reads and writes. Which option will save you more bandwidth is a function of the target hardware and how much of the skybox is visible in the final frame. If a large portion of the skybox is obscured, the first technique will likely be better; otherwise, the second one may save more bandwidth.

- **Use floating-point frame buffers only when necessary.** These formats obviously consume much more bandwidth than smaller, integer formats. The same applies for multiple render targets.

- **Use a 16-bit depth buffer when possible.** Depth transactions are a huge consumer of bandwidth, so using 16-bit instead of 32-bit can be a giant win, and 16-bit is often enough for small-scale, indoor scenes that don't require stencil. A 16-bit depth buffer is also often enough for render-to-texture effects that require depth, such as dynamic cube maps.

- **Use 16-bit color when possible.** This advice is especially applicable to render-to-texture effects, because many of these, such as dynamic cube maps and projected-color shadow maps, work just fine in 16-bit color.

28.4 Conclusion

As power and programmability increase in modern GPUs, so does the complexity of extracting every bit of performance out of the machine. Whether your goal is to improve the performance of a slow application or to look for areas where you can improve image quality "for free," a deep understanding of the inner workings of the graphics pipeline is required. As the GPU pipeline continues to evolve, the fundamental ideas of optimization will still apply: first identify the bottleneck, by varying the load or the computational power of each unit; then systematically attack those bottlenecks, using your understanding of how each pipeline unit behaves.

28.5 References

EnTech Taiwan. 2003. Web site. **http://www.entechtaiwan.com.** *Information on the PowerStrip package is available here.*

NVIDIA. 2003. Developer Web site. **http://developer.nvidia.com.** *On this site, you can find tools that will help you with performance tuning.*

Wloka, Matthias. 2003. "Batch, Batch, Batch: What Does It Really Mean?" Presentation at Game Developers Conference 2003. Available online at **http://developer.nvidia.com/docs/IO/8230/BatchBatchBatch.pdf**

Specific information can be found at the following Web addresses.
D3DX: Available in the Microsoft DirectX 9 SDK. See **http://msdn.microsoft.com/directx**

NVTriStrip: **http://developer.nvidia.com/object/nvtristrip_library.html**

NVPerfHUD: **http://developer.nvidia.com**

Chapter 29

Efficient Occlusion Culling

Dean Sekulic
Croteam

29.1 What Is Occlusion Culling?

Most graphics algorithms show us how to render something quickly, or how to make it look nice. Some techniques favor performance, while others aim for quality, but the challenge is how to strike a balance between the two.

Occlusion culling increases rendering performance simply by not rendering geometry that is outside the view frustum or hidden by objects closer to the camera. Two common types of occlusion culling are *occlusion query* and *early-z rejection*.

This chapter examines the occlusion query and how to use it properly, including two examples proving how efficient occlusion culling can be. Because one of the examples relies heavily on the usage of bounding boxes, these will also be covered, just to make things more understandable.

29.1.1 Occlusion Query

Starting with the GeForce3 GPU, all NVIDIA GPUs (and many from other vendors) have included the occlusion query feature, which lets us avoid rendering occluded objects. By skipping the entire rendering process for an occluded object, we can reduce the rendering load on the GPU.

29.1.2 Early-Z Rejection

Also supported in most GPUs since the GeForce3 is early-z rejection. In the rasterizer stage of the rendering process, early-z compares the depth value of a fragment to be rendered against the value currently stored in the z-buffer. If the fragment is not visible (because the depth test failed), rejection occurs without fetching the texture for the fragment or executing the fragment program. The result: memory bandwidth is saved at the per-fragment level.

There's a big difference between occlusion query and early-z rejection. Occlusion query rejects polygons at the geometry level, whereas early-z occurs at the rasterization level. Plus, culling geometry through occlusion query requires more control from the application.

Both approaches require a programmer to sort the objects from front to back. Note, however, that because the depth buffer and the stencil buffer are often stored together, using the stencil buffer may reduce early-z performance. (Also, early-z rejection tends to require more caveats, but these are not directly related to the subject of this chapter.) For early-z rejection, the programmer's work is done, and the GPU takes care of the rest.

But for occlusion query, there's still a long way to go. . . .

29.2 How Does Occlusion Query Work?

In OpenGL, the ARB_occlusion_query extension (which is based on NVIDIA's NV_occlusion_query extension, a much-improved form of Hewlett-Packard's original HP_occlusion_test extension) implements the occlusion query idea on the GPU and fetches the query results. (See NVIDIA 2003 for more.) Microsoft has incorporated the same functionality in DirectX 9. (See Microsoft 2003 for more.)

An occlusion query is fundamentally simple. The GPU tells us how many pixels should have ended up visible on-screen. These pixels successfully passed various tests at the end of the pipeline—such as the frustum visibility test, the scissor test, the alpha test, the stencil test, and the depth test. Not an easy ride!

Here is how the process works:

1. Create a query.
2. Disable rendering to screen (set the color mask of all channels to False).
3. Disable writing to depth buffer (just test against, but don't update, the depth buffer).

4. Issue query begin (which resets the counter of visible pixels).

5. "Render" the object's bounding box (it'll only do depth testing; pixels that pass depth testing will not be rendered on-screen because rendering and depth writing were disabled).

6. End query (stop counting visible pixels).

7. Enable rendering to screen.

8. Enable depth writing (if required).

9. Get query result (the number of "visible" pixels).

10. If the number of visible pixels is greater than 0 (or some threshold),

    a. Render the complete object.

These steps allow us to substitute a geometrically complex object with a simple bounding box. This bounding box will determine whether we need to render the object itself. If the object's bounding box ends up occluded by other on-screen polygons, we can avoid the object entirely.

The catch? Be very careful not to update the color or depth buffer when testing the object's bounding box—that's why we disabled color and depth writing.

In the sections that follow, we begin with a naive attempt at using occlusion queries and proceed to refine our approach into a robust, real-world implementation.

29.3 Beginning to Use Occlusion Queries

The real problem is the GPU pipeline flush. Normally the CPU and GPU work in parallel: When the CPU issues a command to the GPU (for example, "render some triangles"), it doesn't wait for the GPU to finish. Instead, the CPU's driver feeds the commands and triangles to the GPU command queue, which lets the CPU continue with other tasks. When the GPU is ready to process the stored commands, the triangles are rendered on screen.

However, the rendering process differs for occlusion queries. The GPU needs to tell the CPU how many pixels were drawn on-screen, which means it must render them first. The problem? The CPU must *wait* until the GPU finishes rendering triangles used for the occlusion query—and not only those triangles, but all triangles given to the GPU before the occlusion test.

This is not good. Trying to "save" the GPU from rendering the occluded object doesn't speed up the rendering process. The truth is that even when most tested objects are occluded, rendering is *much* slower because the CPU and GPU no longer work in parallel.

It's clear that the naive approach isn't going to work very well. So, the real question is...

29.3.1 How to Use Occlusion Queries Properly

The good news is that both OpenGL and DirectX 9 support multiple outstanding queries. This means we can start several counters to count visible pixels and then query the counters later.

So now, the algorithm changes to the following:

1. Create *n* queries.
2. Disable rendering to screen.
3. Disable writing to depth buffer.
4. For each of *n* queries,
    a. Issue query begin.
    b. "Render" the object's bounding box.
    c. End query.
(End of query loop)
5. Enable rendering to screen.
6. Enable depth writing (if required).
7. For each of *n* queries,
    a. Get the query result.
    b. If the number of visible pixels is greater than 0,
        i. Render the complete object.
(End of query loop)

Although this approach is much better than the original one, it still won't give enough time to the GPU to actually render all the geometry that the CPU has fed to it, which means that stall has not been completely eliminated.

And there's another issue...

29.3.2 Occluders vs. Occludees

The problem with the basic approach is that bounding boxes cannot write to the depth buffer, because there are some really weird cases when one bounding box completely occludes another bounding box, but the object inside the occluder's bounding box doesn't in fact occlude the object inside the occludee's bounding box, as shown in Figure 29-1.

So, some scene geometry needs to be rendered in front, without occlusion culling. This geometry will act as an occluder, so it should be something that ends up being large on screen. (A tall wall or a big building is a good example.) After these objects have been rendered, occlusion query for smaller objects can begin.

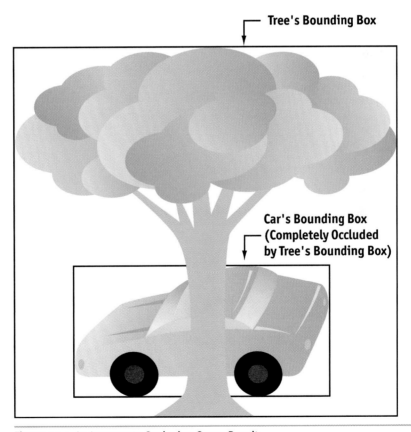

Figure 29-1. An Inaccurate Occlusion Query Result

However, all this tends to complicate things a bit, and it makes occlusion culling less effective (even a big object itself can sometimes be completely occluded). Therefore, we need a different approach.

29.4 One Step Further

To be on the safe side and to make sure that the GPU has rendered everything we've asked, we'll do something really radical: We'll check the occlusion query in the *next* frame!

The game loop now looks something like this (for the sake of simplicity, we show just one query):

1. Create the query.
2. Game loop:
   a. Do AI.
   b. Do physics.
   c. Rendering:
      i. Check the query result from the previous frame.
      ii. Issue query begin:
         (1) If the object was visible in the last frame:
            (a) Enable rendering to screen.
            (b) Enable or disable writing to depth buffer (depends on whether the object is translucent or opaque).
            (c) Render the object itself.
         (2) If the object wasn't visible in the last frame:
            (a) Disable rendering to screen.
            (b) Disable writing to depth buffer.
            (c) "Render" the object's bounding box.
      (End query)
      (Repeat for every object in scene.)
   d. Swap buffers.
(End of game loop)

It's not important to check frequently whether the object is still visible, so let's safely assume that any object that was visible in the previous frame remains visible in the current frame. However, there is a drawback to this approach: geometry that is no longer visible can be shipped to the GPU. In addition, we can add another optimization: checking the invisibility of an object every few frames. This way, we'll have fewer outstanding occlusion queries at any given time. But testing of occluded (invisible) objects needs to be done in every frame! We cannot assume that the object is still occluded in the current frame because this might introduce excessive "rendering" errors (that is, objects appearing out of thin air).

All in all, the problem of lagging one frame behind and culling the visible objects ("what you see is not exactly what you get") is not that serious. Not seeing an object in one frame is not that important if you see it in the next one, especially when the frame rate exceeds 30 frames per second. It's just a little "now you don't see me, now you do" syndrome, so this popping-in shouldn't be that noticeable.

Sometimes even testing the next frame induces a stall, because some drivers let the GPU render two or three frames behind by actually queuing the `SwapBuffers` request. This could be an issue, but the performance loss is normally less than 10 percent, which is acceptable, considering the speed-up that occlusion queries offer.

As you may already have noticed, testing the occlusion of an object that was visible in the last frame is done on the object itself, while testing the occlusion of an object that was previously invisible is done on the object's *bounding box*. Apart from being just an optimization (no need to render both the object and its bounding box!), this method is essential to determining which objects are potential occluders and which are occludees.

29.4.1 Sorting Things Out

This advanced approach automatically eliminates the need to actually separate potential occluders from occludees (as stated in Section 29.3.2), because every object that has been rendered as visible acts as an occluder just by being written to the depth buffer. Therefore, we don't need to have the occluders (objects without occlusion testing) rendered before the occludees. However, to help the algorithm a bit, we need to sort the objects by distance.

Once we have all the objects that need to be rendered in the current scene (that is, the ones that passed frustum culling), we need to separate them into two groups: opaque objects and translucent objects. Because we can see through translucent objects (and they cannot be written to the depth buffer!), these can act only as occludees and not occluders. On the other hand, opaque objects can be both occluders and occludees, which means that they should be sorted from front to back and rendered before translucent objects. After that, translucent objects are sorted back to front and rendered on-screen as well.

This approach nicely exploits the occlusion query feature, because potential occluders are rendered first, which makes many other objects potential occludees, and the rendering of those can be culled by occlusion tests. Once all opaque objects are rendered, they automatically begin to act as potential occluders of all translucent objects.

29.4.2 A Small Caveat

Sometimes, from certain viewpoints, an object is occluded but its bounding box is visible. This occurs when the bounding box is much bigger than the object. When this happens, the object will be rendered in every other frame: the bounding box will have a "visible" result, and so the object will need to be rendered in the next frame. However, the object rendered in the next frame will have an "invisible" result, which means we'll need to render the bounding box in the next frame, and so on. Although our method might introduce a little variation in frame rate, it's a good optimization because both the objects and the bounding boxes don't have to be drawn each frame.

29.5 A Word About Bounding Boxes

Bounding boxes, which can be static or animated, are often *much* larger than the objects they contain, so it's worth considering a few optimizations for them.

29.5.1 Static Objects

For a static object, the bounding box is usually not much larger than the object. However, in the classic example of the pyramid, we might want to use more than one box to efficiently represent its extents, as shown in Figure 29-2.

One has to be careful when using these sub-bounding boxes, because testing them can introduce more overhead than testing just one big bounding box. Of course, this all depends on how complex the object's geometry is. The pyramid case is just an example to make things more obvious, because it certainly isn't optimal to use several bounding boxes to represent five polygons of a pyramid.

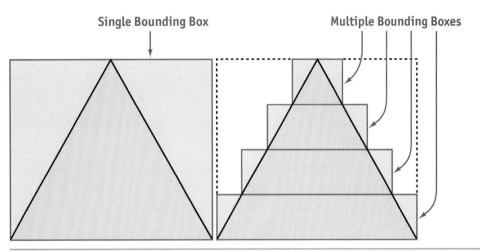

Single Bounding Box　　　　　　　**Multiple Bounding Boxes**

Figure 29-2. Bounding Boxes for a Pyramid (Cross Section)

29.5.2 Animated Objects

Animated objects are more complex. What's a good way to calculate the bounding box of an animated object? There are many approaches; here are a few.

1. **Calculate the bounding box for each frame of each animation.**
   This can get complex and CPU-intensive, especially if the object's skeletal animation system is incorporated into the GPU vertex shader. The overhead introduced by animating this object with the CPU (to calculate its bounding box) can be much higher than rendering the object.

2. **Store one bounding box for all frames of each animation.**
   This is the simplest and fastest approach. However, results can be inaccurate because the bounding box can be significantly larger than the object, indicating that the object is visible when it's actually occluded.

   We can reduce the bounding box a bit by animating an object "in place"—in other words, translating the object via animation routine instead of in animation itself. For example, if we shoot an enemy, he'll fly through the air and land a couple of meters away. If we use an animation to transport the enemy through the air, we'll end up with a huge bounding box. On the other hand, if we animate the enemy's flight in one place (not translating him), we'll have a small bounding box and can do actual translation through animation code when the animation triggers. See Figure 29-3.

3. Store one bounding box for each animation.

This is the best solution, but it introduces a small problem: when blending several animations, we'll need to calculate the union of bounding boxes for each animation. Not a big deal, considering the effort we save because the bounding box of one animation is often much smaller than the bounding box of all animations.

The best approach is to combine the second and third methods and see which is optimal for a particular object.

In some cases, if we need to render multiple passes for an object and the first pass is fairly simple, we can use that first pass (instead of a bounding box) for testing visibility. However, we still need to be careful about the number of polygons in that single pass; remember, it's geometry throughput we're trying to spare.

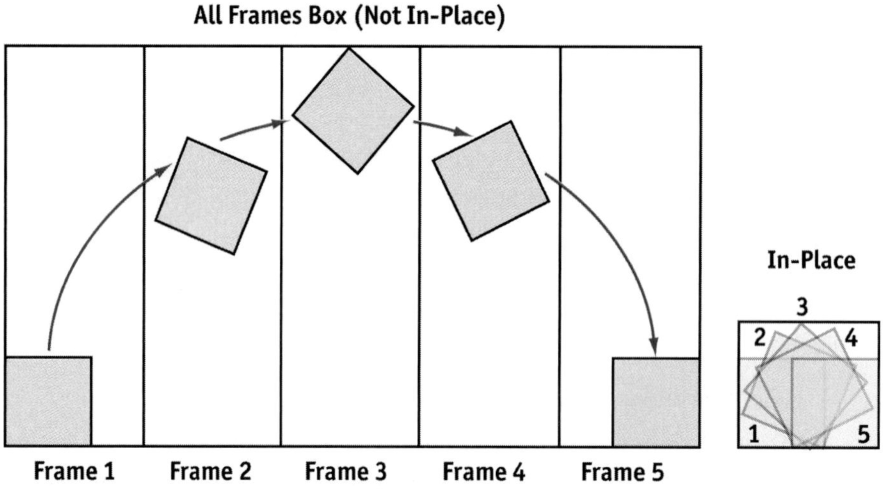

Figure 29-3. Per-Frame Bounding Boxes vs. In-Place Bounding Boxes

29.6 Other Issues

29.6.1 CPU Overhead Too High

We need to account for the CPU overhead incurred when we send rendering requests to the GPU. If an object is easy to render, then it may be cheaper to simply render it than to draw the bounding box and perform the occlusion test. For example, rendering 12 triangles (a bounding box) and rendering around 200 triangles (or more!) takes almost the same time on today's GPUs. The CPU is the one that takes most of the time just by preparing the objects for rendering.

However, testing the object's bounding box is sometimes a must, no matter how many polygons the actual object has. What if the rendered object has a very complex pixel shader and occupies a notable portion of the screen? In such a case, even though the bounding box has more pixels to be drawn, the pixels can be rendered much faster (especially because they are rendered only to the depth buffer!) than an object itself, which would tax the GPU with many operations per pixel.

29.6.2 Rendering at High Resolutions

Applications can become fill-rate limited when we render at high resolutions but with simple pixel shaders. Rendering the whole bounding box could require many more pixels than rendering only the object inside the box; the GPU would need to do more work at the per-pixel level.

The rule of thumb is that objects that are not fill-rate bound (that is, objects that don't use complex fragment programs, many texture layers, and so on) should not be tested for occlusion at higher resolutions. This is because there are more pixels to fill at a higher resolution, so it's likely the GPU will spend more time rendering the object's bounding box than the object itself. Keep in mind that if the object is occluded, the early-z rejection will do its work at the per-pixel level, so processing complex fragment programs will be avoided.

The fill-rate problem can get even worse, because sometimes a bounding box needs to be rendered from both sides, with front-facing and back-facing polygons! The catch is that when you test an object that is very close to the view origin, the viewer ends up *inside* the bounding box. That's why we need to render back faces also; otherwise, because of back-face culling, no pixels will be drawn on-screen, and we'll get a false result. To be safe, skip occlusion testing for models that are too near the viewer; it can really do more harm than good, and an object that close is definitely visible.

29.6.3 Fast Depth-Writing Performance

But it's not all bad news. When only depth testing or stencil writing is taking place, some new GPUs (such as the GeForce FX family) use a higher-performance rendering path. In the past, hardware didn't benefit much when the color buffer was switched off during testing for the visibility of a bounding box, because the circuits for color and depth value output were in the same pipeline. Now, however, on newer hardware, if the color-buffer output is switched off, the pipelines are used for depth testing and the bounding box testing is faster.

29.6.4 Frustum Culling

Even though occlusion testing can cull pixels that are out of the view frustum, it is not advisable to use it for doing frustum culling. Rendering the bounding box of an object can induce more overhead than simply testing that bounding box against frustum clip planes with the conventional approach on the CPU. Moreover, some bounding boxes can be easily replaced with bounding spheres, which make CPU-style frustum testing even faster.

One approach is first to test the bounding sphere against the frustum. If the sphere ends up completely inside, we go ahead and render the whole object (with occlusion culling, of course). If the sphere is completely outside the view frustum, this is a trivial rejection case, so we just proceed to the next object. However, if the sphere intersects the frustum (that is, intersects one or more clipping planes, to be more precise), we have to check whether the bounding box of the object has one dimension that is much larger than the other two. If that's the case, it means that the bounding sphere is much bigger than the object itself! Then it's best to also test the bounding box against the view frustum, because it might end up being culled. A good example is a tall pillar, as shown in Figure 29-4.

29.7 A Little Reminder

Keep in mind that occlusion culling works best when objects have lots of polygons. An occlusion query won't accomplish much for objects of, say, 300 triangles, even if there are hundreds of them on-screen. Speed might improve moderately, but it depends on the CPU load and the speed ratio between the CPU and the GPU. A fast GPU, coupled with a slow CPU, makes an application CPU-bound, and occlusion testing won't help much.

On the other hand, if there are a lot of polygons per model (more than 1,000 is a good start), occlusion culling shows all its glory. Speed-ups can be more than double (depending on the scene, of course), plus it's almost free. And rendering is not noticeably slower—even if *all* the tested objects end up visible!

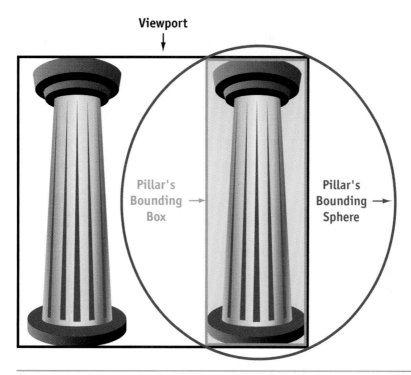

Figure 29-4. A Bounding Box Represents an Object More Closely Than a Bounding Sphere

29.8 An Application: Lens Flares

Another useful application of the occlusion query technique is rendering lens flares. See Figures 29-5 and 29-6. Lens flares are great effects that help add realism to games, but it's easy to end up knee-deep in problems trying to render them accurately.

The catch is that lens flares aren't just nice light-halos around light sources: they are a camera's lens effect, which means they *cannot* be partially occluded by objects in a scene. Therefore, a lens flare is either completely visible or completely invisible, so lens flares must be overlaid on the previously rendered scene.

Rendering a lens flare isn't such a big deal: you need to render only one rectangle, properly filled with a nifty lens-flare glow or ring texture. However, the problem arises when it comes to determining the lens flare's visibility. In theory, it doesn't sound too bad, because "all" you need to do is render the whole scene and then check the depth value of each light source that holds a lens flare against the depth value stored in the depth buffer. If the light source's depth value is closer to the viewer, the flare is visible.

Figure 29-5. A Lens Flare from *Serious Sam: The Second Encounter*

Figure 29-6. Another Lens Flare from *Serious Sam: The Second Encounter*

Unfortunately, checking the depth-buffer value requires reading from the depth buffer—and that's not very GPU-friendly. Another option is not to check the depth-buffer value but instead to cast a ray from each light source to the viewer. If the ray reaches the viewer, the lens flare is visible. Even this sounds relatively simple, but problems arise when you need to do a ray cast through a polygon that holds alpha-tested texture (for example, the leaves of a tree). Because alpha testing rejects pixels at places where the texture has an alpha-channel value lower than some threshold (usually 0.5), the texture will write the depth buffer only at certain places. To emulate this accurately with a ray cast, we would have to do a complete texture mapping in the CPU, which is a painfully slow operation.

So how *do* we efficiently test visibility for lens flares?

29.8.1 Rendering Lens Flares the Old Way

Without using occlusion queries, we definitely need access to the depth buffer to determine visibility. But reading from the depth buffer will inevitably induce a stall in the graphics pipeline, because the GPU needs to render all polygons in its queue to generate the correct depth-buffer image. To make things more difficult, the Direct3D API doesn't actually allow reading from the depth buffer in the first place (well, it does in some rare occasions, but that's completely unusable in practice). There's a way to get around this limitation, but it's really a weird workaround, and it's beyond the scope of this chapter. Well—looks like we ended up in a tight spot here.

OpenGL makes it easy to read from the depth buffer, so there's an opportunity for us to get around this GPU stall. We can batch all the readings from the depth buffer to the end of the frame, even *after* the actual rendering of the lens flares. This will make the lens flares' visibility result lag one frame behind, but that's perfectly acceptable in the context. Unfortunately, even though this optimization brings some speed improvements, it isn't much, and we'll have to get more radical. Again.

We can check depth-buffer values *after* the `SwapBuffers` call and right before the beginning of rendering the next frame. This will buy us some time, because the GPU might actually finish rendering the last frame, during which time the CPU will still be occupied with calculating AI and similar work for the current frame. So, the algorithm for rendering one frame looks something like this:

1. Do AI, physics, and collision detection.
2. Do other stuff, apart from rendering.

3. Read the lens flares' depth values (these are from the last frame).

4. Clear the depth buffer.

5. Do the rendering.

6. Render the lens flares.

7. Swap buffers.

Even though this approach would eliminate a fair amount of GPU stall, there are still some problems. The overhead of a GPU stall depends on the ratio of GPU and CPU speeds. Ironically, this actually means that the cost of a stall is greater on faster GPUs. Another issue is even more serious: no one guarantees that the depth-buffer content will be intact after the `SwapBuffers` call! On all of today's GPUs, the depth-buffer content will survive the `SwapBuffers` call, but you can't count on that much, because things can change. To make matters worse, multisample antialiasing approaches can produce some nasty side effects when it comes to depth-buffer content after swap. Basically, this is a risky approach, which should be implemented only as a last resort.

Summing it all up: we definitely need occlusion query to come to the rescue!

29.8.2 Rendering Lens Flares the New Way

You can probably see where we're headed by now. We can use the occlusion query feature to test the visibility of a lens flare by "rendering" one pixel (with the depth test enabled, but with depth writes and color writes disabled) at the screen location and depth of the lens flare's light source. Next, we check to see how many pixels passed the occlusion test. If one pixel passed, the lens flare is visible. To minimize the effect of GPU stalls, we issue the occlusion query in this frame and read its result in the next one.

Why stop here? Due to its large performance hit, direct depth reading didn't give us much space to experiment, so reading multiple pixels per lens flare was out of the question. But with an occlusion query, we can find out how much of a lens flare is actually visible. Instead of checking only one pixel to get a yes-or-no answer, we can render a block of pixels (say, 16×16) and see what fraction of them actually got rendered. We can then use this fraction to modulate the lens flare's brightness. Now we can have smoother flares, and we don't have to bother with special fade-in and fade-out routines that prevent the lens flare from suddenly popping in and out of visibility. The number of pixels to test can easily be determined from the lens flare's size on-screen or the distance of the lens flare source from the viewer, or both.

This is nice ground for experimentation, but one thing is sure: the result will look great and won't hurt the GPU much at all.

29.9 Conclusion

At first sight, occlusion query looks like a really powerful tool—and it definitely is. However, like any other tool, it requires a certain degree of skill and knowledge to use effectively. You need to be able to recognize the situations in which it can be helpful.

In this chapter, we gave just two examples of how to use this technique efficiently. Of course, you don't have to stop here: there are many more things you can do with it. For example, occlusion query can be used for determining geometric level of detail based on the number of pixels occupied by an object. Or you can even use it in a visible-surface-determination algorithm.

Like any other technique, occlusion query will evolve. In the beginning, it will be used for rather simple tasks. But over time, we expect programmers to find amazing new applications for it as various obstacles are removed. With a little luck, this chapter has helped you to get started. Now the real exploration is up to you.

29.10 References

Maughan, Chris. 2001. "Texture Masking for Faster Lens Flare." In *Game Programming Gems 2*, edited by Mark DeLoura, pp. 474–480. Charles River Media.

Microsoft. 2003. Web site. **http://msdn.microsoft.com/directx/default.asp**

NVIDIA. 2003. Web site.
http://developer.nvidia.com/view.asp?IO=nvidia_opengl_specs

Chapter 30

The Design of FX Composer

Christopher Maughan
NVIDIA

FX Composer is a tool designed to help developers and artists create Direct3D effects. These effects are stored in .fx files, which contain complete information on how to apply a shader to a given 3D model. FX Composer is essentially an IDE, with a look and feel that is similar to Microsoft's Visual Studio .NET application. In developing FX Composer, we wanted to enable people to interactively edit effects in a friendly environment, and we wanted to build a solid foundation for future expansion into areas such as shader debugging and profiling.

This chapter describes the design of the FX Composer tool and explains the reasons behind the decisions we made along the way. By discussing the problems we faced and the approaches we took to fix them, we hope to give you insight into the complexities of developing a large Direct3D application. Note: The Direct3D 9 SDK help documentation and other supporting materials cover .fx files in detail and explain how to use them in 3D applications. For that reason, this chapter does not explore the specifics of using .fx files.

30.1 Tools Development

The primary job of a tools developer is to give end users an application they can use in a productive way. Thus, the design and evolution of a tool can be quite different from that of a typical game, where the main focus usually is developing a fast engine with a fixed feature set. Tools development is interesting because it allows the tools developer to engineer software without that restrictive mantra "must run at x FPS." In a tool program, functionality and stability take precedence over speed of execution. As such, the primary focus of FX Composer development was to create a useful tool that could be extended to keep up with future Direct3D API changes, with a clean, public interface for future expansion.

30.2 Initial Features and Target Audience

When we began the FX Composer project, these were our major design goals:

1. A familiar IDE, with a similar look and feel to .NET.
2. An extensible engine.
3. A stable environment for creating .fx files and visualizing the results.

The target audience for FX Composer is software developers and technical artists who have some level of programming knowledge. With that in mind, the tool would need to combine .fx file-editing capabilities and a user interface for editing shader properties. To facilitate this functionality, the .NET-like IDE would allow users to add features that could be docked conveniently into window panels and then hidden when necessary. At the outset, the following application features were planned:

- A Materials panel to display multiple .fx files, rendered on a 3D object.
- A Textures panel showing render targets as well as material textures.
- An Editor window with the usual features: undo/redo, bookmarks, syntax highlighting, and so on.
- A Render window showing simple scenes with effects applied.

What follows is a description of the FX Composer application and engine as they stand at the time of writing.

30.3 Object Design

FX Composer is built almost entirely of interfaces and objects. The model very closely follows the principles of Microsoft's COM specification, with a core runtime implementing the object creation and registration features. Such an interface-based approach has several advantages, and it makes for a very clean design, as we show later. One key result of our design is a clean plug-in model, which pervades the entire FX Composer application. Almost every component in the application is a plug-in, enabling easy integration of new features and externally authored extensions.

A simplified interface from the SDK is shown in Listing 30-1.

Listing 30-1. A Sample Interface

```
class INVImportScene : public INVObject
{
public:
  virtual bool ImportScene(INVScenePtr& pScene,
                            const char* pszFileName) = 0;
  virtual bool GetFileExtension(unsigned int i,
                                 const char** pszName,
                                 const char** pszExtension) const = 0;
  virtual unsigned int GetNumFileExtensions() const = 0;
};
```

Any objects in the system that wish to implement INVImportScene can do so by inheriting the pure abstract base class and implementing the methods. All engine interfaces are pure abstract, and all inherit from the base interface, INVObject. INVObject has three methods familiar to any COM programmer: AddRef, Release, and QueryInterface. These enable lifetime control through reference counting, and they allow any instantiated object in the system to be asked if it implements a particular interface. Thus, any object in the system must at a minimum implement the INVObject interface, so that it can always be queried for pointers to other interfaces, and reference-counted.

A typical engine object, implementing the INVImportScene interface, would do so as shown in Listing 30-2.

The additional function CreateNVObject is typically declared using a macro, and it is called by the runtime to create a new instance of this object and return a pointer to the requested interface, if supported.

All plug-ins—in our case, dynamic link libraries (DLLs), are required to export two functions: RegisterNVObjects and UnRegisterNVObjects. At startup, the runtime will load the plug-ins and ask them to register each object type that can be created. As with COM, each object and each interface have globally unique identifiers (GUIDs).

Listing 30-2. The `XFileImporter` Object

```
class XFileImporter : public INVImportScene
{
public:
  // Implement INVImportScene methods
  . . .

  // Declare INVObject (addref/release/queryinterface)
  . . .

  // A static creation function
  static bool CreateNVObject(INVCreatorPtr,
                             NVGUID& Interface,
                             void** ppObject);
};
```

Essentially, every object in the FX Composer framework is a plug-in—from complex objects such as file importers to simple ones such as string containers. Loadable DLLs contain any number of such objects, each implementing any number of interfaces. Additionally, all objects have human-readable strings and an optional *category*, which groups together objects of a particular type, enabling them to be found easily. An *object factory* implementing the `INVCreator` interface is declared once for each object type; it can be used to manufacture registered objects as needed. The FX Composer system is an example of a *pluggable class factory*.

Here is an example. All the shapes you can create in FX Composer are in the category `geopipeobject_shape`. The following code shows how FX Composer finds the list of shape plug-ins available:

```
INVCreatorArrayPtr pCreators = GetSYSInterface()->
                   GetCreatorsInCategory("geopipeobject_shape");
```

The call to `GetSYSInterface` is global and can be done anywhere to return a pointer to the `nv_sys` runtime. The returned array of object creators can then be used to create shapes for display in the materials and rendering viewports. It would therefore be a fairly simple process to create a plug-in object capable of generating a unique shape, and making it available for immediate use inside FX Composer. Further, this shape can be saved to the project file and reloaded with all of its associated parameters.

Discussion of the technical implementation of these components is beyond the scope of this chapter, but it boils down to a few simple macros that declare the objects and their interfaces. We took the useful parts of the COM specification and avoided the more complex features, such as aggregation and component registration through the registry. To simplify usage further, we used smart pointers to remove the necessity of calling `AddRef/Release`, and to make interface querying automatic. For example, the following code fragment checks to see if a scene importer object supports the `INVProperties` interface:

```
INVSceneImporterPtr pImporter = GetImporter();
INVPropertiesPtr pProps = pImporter;
if (pProps)
{
   . . .
}
```

The assignment from the importer pointer to the properties pointer will call an implicit `QueryInterface` on the importer object, and it will return a valid pointer if successful. All additional references are cleaned up by the reference-counting properties of the smart pointer (signified by the `Ptr` suffix on the interface name). Every interface in FX Composer is declared with an equivalent smart pointer, and they are rarely referenced without one.

30.3.1 Benefits of the Interface Approach

Not everyone favors an interface-based/COM approach. For FX Composer, it has turned out to be a great feature, one that has made the underlying implementation clean and easy. Using interface-based programming, we have managed to expose FX Composer objects in a very accessible fashion, making extensions and new features easy to add.

The following are some of the advantages of our approach.

Object Querying

In FX Composer, any object can support any interface, giving great extensibility. A good example of this is the IDE's Properties panel. When a material is selected, an "object selection" message arrives, which contains an `INVObjectPtr`. The Properties panel can now cast it to an `INVPropertiesPtr`, and if successful, it can walk through a list of property values using this standard interface and enable them to be edited in the GUI. This works for any object that chooses to expose its properties to the system. For example, when we added the shape plug-ins, it was a trivial matter to have them expose their dimensions, tessellation, and so on. When these shapes are loaded and selected, the Properties panel allows the user to change their values. For this reason, many objects in the FX Composer system support the properties interface, and they give useful information in the user interface as a result.

This feature has paid off time and again. When we added the ability to save the scene to an XML file, it was simple to have serialized objects support an `INVXMLStreamable` interface that could be used to stream the object out to an XML-formatted file. When we wanted to clone an object, we added an `INVClone` interface, giving objects control over how they were duplicated.

Future ideas for interfaces include an `INVScript` interface, enabling system objects to expose their scripting functions.

Object Lifetime

Because all components are reference-counted and smart pointers typically point to them, we have had very few memory leaks—they usually end up in pieces of external code. Of course, there are disadvantages to reference counting: there is always a fixed overhead in passing around interface pointers; it can sometimes be difficult to make an object go away when you want it to; and circular references can often be an issue—such as when two objects hold references to each other. When we came across these issues, we worked around them by making "weak" pointers on occasion—that is, holding pointers to objects that were not "smart" and did not have a reference. This approach does feel a little like a workaround, but in practice, it is not often needed. The additional overhead was not a consideration for this tool, as mentioned earlier.

Plug-In Management

Plug-ins in FX Composer essentially come for free with the object model we are using. Each object registers itself with the system and can be used by any interested party at a later time. Creating a new plug-in is as simple as declaring a new interface, assigning an associated category, and writing simple code to load the objects in that category and use them. The core runtime takes care of tracking objects, and in fact it always has an internal list of every instantiated object in the system, as well as all the loaded plug-in modules. This can be a useful debug feature, because it's possible to analyze the runtime system at any time. An additional debugging dialog in FX Composer presents a tree view of the current system objects, which has been used on many occasions to analyze behavior and track down bugs.

Our approach has one drawback: it does require a little understanding to use it well, especially if a developer is not familiar with this kind of programming. To make this adjustment process easier, we added several macros to make the creation of objects and interfaces as simple as possible; we also included a heavily documented sample plug-in.

Connection Parameters

Right from the start, we decided that FX Composer should handle the animation of scenes, skinned characters, and parameters in materials. To that end, we designed a connection parameter type, closely matched to D3DX effect parameter types, with full support for animation. The result is that just about any parameter in FX Composer can be animated with time keys and interpolators of various types, to generate intermediate values between two separate keys. For example, it's possible to apply an effect to a skinned mesh and then animate a value such as "bump height" in the effect. The character will animate, and the effect will change in real time. Connection parameters have several additional properties, such as semantics, annotations, and names, just as in .fx files, making them a useful generic holder for any item of data in an object.

The connection parameters FX Composer supports have been useful in several ways:

- Our Properties window can query any object for a list of parameters and display them in a sensible way. As long as an object supports the INVProperties interface, it can enable its parameters to be edited through a common Property Sheet window. This gives the user a consistent look and feel when editing objects of different types, such as materials, shapes, lights, cameras, and others.

- The project file streaming code can trivially save or restore connection parameters, making serialization for most objects a simple process.

- Connection parameters can be compared for type, semantic, name, annotation, and more. This is particularly useful when mapping one list of connection parameters to another, which can often happen. One typical scenario occurs when a reloaded project file contains a reference to an .fx effect that has been modified. In such a case, we want to maintain as much of the saved data as possible but work with the new .fx file. We achieve this result by mapping from the old list of parameters to the new one. When a conflict arises, the user is then prompted to resolve it. Another mapping scenario takes place when trying to match material parameters to objects in a scene in a sensible way, such as hooking up a light to a material position parameter.

Message Senders and Receivers

With a complex system such as the FX Composer engine, good communication between different components is essential. We took a two-pronged approach to this problem. At first, we developed a global message-broadcasting system that allowed any object to send messages to all interested parties in a "fire-and-forget" fashion. The NewScene message is a good example of this, where many components may wish to know that a new scene has been created.

This scheme worked well at first, but it quickly became bloated due to the generic nature of the broadcast. To enhance the system, an additional messaging protocol was developed that enabled a close link between two interested parties. In the system, any object can implement the INVMessageReceiver interface, and any object can implement the INVMessageSender interface. Interested parties can then register themselves with objects and find out about events they wish to know. The usual issues with such a scheme come up, and it is essential to carefully maintain both ends of the communication link. Care must be taken so that the participants do not get out of sync and find themselves with references to objects that either no longer exist or no longer matter to them. The message sender/receiver system is an example of the "Publish/Subscribe" pattern described in the book *Design Patterns* (Gamma et al. 1995).

30.4 File Format

We decided that FX Composer needed its own file format in order to save and restore the current scene, the material palette, the file paths, and optionally the current media set. This file would hold the entire workspace and allow the user to package textures, .fx files, and other items into one file—a bonus for our Developer Relations group, who often want to send self-contained examples to developers. The file extension of this workspace format is ".fxcomposer".

The first file format we considered was one consisting entirely of XML data, but this was rejected due to the large amount of binary data in a given scene; such data does not encode well into XML. Instead, we implemented a hybrid approach that offered the best of both worlds. The FX Composer project file is a compound format, in which all the data is actually stored inside a single .zip file (albeit with the .fxcomposer extension). The .zip file contains an XML scene description with some references to external binary data, in the form of offsets into a binary chunk. The binary chunk is also encoded in the same .zip file. To further simplify the design, objects in the system can support an XML streaming interface, and they are capable of writing out their data in XML format. The interface they use to do this also allows them to add data to the zipped binary file, returning an offset for later retrieval. Saving the entire workspace is simply a matter of walking the object hierarchy and building the XML for each object. Reloading is almost as simple: each object reloads itself based on the XML data. As a further abstraction, each element in the XML has an `ObjectID`, which can be retrieved from the end of the file. In this way, FX Composer can check ahead of time that the necessary plug-ins are loaded and that it can support the objects being streamed from the workspace file. This step protects against such problems as saving out a scene containing a "teapot shape" plug-in, for example, and trying to reload it on a version of FX Composer without that plug-in installed. In such a case, the program can inform the user that a plug-in is missing and then try to load the rest of the scene.

An interesting side effect of the new file format is its efficiency. Because common data is compressed into a binary chunk without the interleaved scene data, the file sizes have turned out to be quite compact, resulting in storage requirements smaller than the original mesh file when compressed. This compactness is impressive, given that the .fxcomposer file contains not only the mesh, but also the materials in the palette. In the case of an imported .x file, the gains are the greatest when compared to our internally developed .nvb file format, and the saved file actually includes more mesh data in the form of tangent and binormal vectors.

Table 30-1 shows example file sizes in bytes, for an .nvb and an .x imported file, saved as .fxcomposer files. The savings shown represent the percentage savings over the original file in compressed form (.zip file). Note that the compressed original files would not usually be stored on the user's hard drive, so the savings in this case would be greater.

Table 30-1. File Sizes Compared

File Name	File Size	Original File Size	Original File Size, Compressed	Savings
Gooch_alien.fxcomposer	906,486	1,561,000 (.nvb)	968,696	62,210 (6%)
Tiny.fxcomposer	211,819	1,533,978 (.x)	338,252	126,433 (62%)

We have also done some experimentation with XSLT transforms. This declarative language enables the display of XML files by transforming the data into a human-readable Web page. In the future, this will enable us to make our project files self-describing, by packaging the .xslt file with the .fxcomposer project. Adding an XML schema is another interesting option, which would enable validation of our XML format, again enclosed within the compound .zip file.

30.5 User Interface

Typically, a tools project involves a great deal of user-interface work. Such work can be tedious and, if not done well, can often lead to incomplete tools with difficult-to-use interfaces. The outcome often depends on the windows-programming experience of the developer. We knew at the start that FX Composer would need a complex UI, and we wanted to support floating and docking windows to save space and to give users a familiar development environment.

We considered writing our own MFC code, but such a complex task requires a dedicated project of its own. Another possibility was to write an extension to VC.NET, but we weren't absolutely sure that the different requirements of a real-time 3D app would be met by the .NET IDE—and we would have had to climb a steep learning curve just to answer that preliminary question.

In the end, BCGSoft (www.bcgsoft.com) came to our rescue with its BCGControlBar Professional MFC extension library. This robust component implements many of the features found in advanced IDEs such as Visual Studio .NET. It can handle floating and docking windows, and as a bonus, it comes with an editor supporting bookmarks, undo/redo, and even IntelliSense. So far, we've been really pleased with the results. BCGControlBar is so big, in fact, that we have not turned on all the available features in the toolkit—we want to contain the complexity until we need it. For example, the SDK supports a fully customizable menu and hot-key layout, which users can modify to create a look and feel that suits them, just as in .NET.

A side effect of using such a complex toolkit, aside from the additional application complexity, is the testing burden. With so many windows arranged in different ways—and with each one potentially open, closed, or hidden at any time, including at application startup—a thorough testing methodology is needed to ensure that all combinations of layout will work. We are approaching this problem in several ways, through quality assurance, manual application modification to uncover potential problems, and automated tests. One plan we wish to implement is a unit-testing framework, at the object level. With a simple interface, such as `INVUnitTest`, it should be possible to have components of the system run automated tests in a clean way. FX Composer can then periodically test all the objects in the system for integrity on debug builds, or in response to a key press.

30.6 Direct3D Graphics Implementation

FX Composer is essentially a graphics application and, with its multiple device windows, a fairly complex one. It is also responsible for managing a list of .fx files and all associated media. At any one time on the current system, up to four Direct3D devices may be employed: the Media panel, the Textures panel, the Render panel, and the Shader Perf bar—a feature that enables the disassembly of .fx files and the display of profiling information for NVIDIA GPUs.

30.6.1 Device Windows

Understanding the need to simplify the implementation of the separate components, we decided to use unique Direct3D devices for each panel in the application. Although this approach may seem resource hungry, it does allow users to "tear off" any single panel in the application and run it full screen on a second monitor, for example. It also makes it easy to run the reference rasterizer alongside hardware-accelerated device windows, for validation of effects or for shaders not supported on current hardware.

The cost of separate devices shows up in the Materials and Render window panels. These two windows might contain duplicates of textures from shared materials. For example, loading the DiffTex.fx file into the Materials panel will load the texture onto the Materials panel device. If that material is then applied to a mesh in the scene, the texture will also be instantiated on the Render window. On top of this, the texture will be created in the Textures panel if the material is selected. It may also appear in the Shader Perf panel when it loads the material to analyze the effect—though it is not strictly necessary to load the texture to do this, or to hold on to the material for any length of time. The Shader Perf panel and the Textures panel show only one material at a time, so this is not a major problem.

The Materials panel and the Render panel are therefore the main places where resources are potentially duplicated—in particular, textures. In practice, this has not been a problem, and it would take a rather large scene for it to become an issue. In addition, most textures, except for render targets, are managed; they are not necessarily instantiated on the device until they are used, and they can be paged out if necessary. In the future, we may investigate sharing textures across devices—Direct3D allows you to do this—or enabling a device to be shared across windows. This would add a certain level of inflexibility and complication to the design, which we currently see as unnecessary—especially because FX Composer is intended for developers and artists running development machines with reasonably modern hardware, containing plenty of video memory.

30.6.2 Direct3D Effects

FX Composer's main work is managing .fx files. D3DX provides a rich API for working with .fx files, which FX Composer uses to good effect. The key concept in D3DX is the ability to load an effect in two steps. Although that is not the only way to do it, FX Composer takes this approach.

First, FX Composer creates a material. We think of a material as an instantiation of an .fx file and associated parameters unique to that material. At any one time, we may have several materials created from the same .fx file, each of which has a different set of connection parameters. For example, assume that we have two different cartoon materials, both referencing a file named cartoon.fx. Each material may have a different color in the diffuse parameter of the .fx file, to give a different look to a cartoon character. This mimics the way an artist works in a typical CAD package, first selecting a material type, then tweaking the parameters to get the right look. The material at this point has no connection to any particular Direct3D device, and no matter how many windows reference it, there is only one object representing a material.

30.6.3 `ID3DXEffectCompiler`

Once we have the material, we load the .fx file using the `ID3DXEffectCompiler` interface. This enables us to compile the effect file and check it for errors without instantiating the effect on a device. The effect compiler creates a compact representation of the effect, which can be used later to create a device-specific effect. But there is a catch here: because we want one set of material parameters for the effect, we must store a collection of connection parameters for the .fx file. This becomes our master set of parameters, which all parts of the engine modify. We must do this because once we have added the effect to a particular device, a new set of parameters will be created for that device, and we need to map from our current set to the device set.

To simplify the rendering of material on a device, we added an API to our material interface, called `ApplyToDevice`. This API is called just before a material is used on a device window. If at that time the material has not been used on the window, the material will use the compiled effect from the `ID3DXEffectCompiler` and create an effect for the device. At this point, D3DX will convert the compact effect representation to an `ID3DXEffect` interface, which we can use to render the effect. Because we previously compiled the .fx file, this step is effectively faster than going straight to an `ID3DXEffect` from a .fx file; it also means that we compile once, no matter how many windows are rendering the effect.

30.6.4 `ID3DXEffect`

We now have a device-specific interface, with several additional APIs. Here we can look at the effect as it applies to the current device and check that it can render with the capabilities of that device. FX Composer will render the object in blue wireframe if the device capabilities required by the effect are not available; if the previous compile step failed, the result will be red wireframe. D3DX effects are split up into techniques, each of which may have different resource requirements. For this reason, we also keep a list of possible techniques for the current device, so that we can present them in the user interface and potentially pick a different one if the current selection is not available.

30.7 Scene Management

FX Composer contains its own scene graph, which is implemented in a fairly straight-forward way. Additional importers enable files in the .nvb and .x file formats to be imported into the scene graph; in the future, we will likely offer more formats, depending on developer demand. The scene is essentially a "node soup," containing geometry, cameras, lights, and so on. Connecting the nodes are transform links, which enable the traversal of the scene graph. The system is flexible enough that in the future we could traverse the nodes in different ways, depending on need. For example, we might want to walk the scene from the point of view of a light, front to back. The current scene graph does not preclude this, because nodes and links are separate entities.

Nodes and node links also have the standard animated connection parameters, so they can be animated at different key frames, enabling scene animation effects, skinning, camera pans, and more.

30.7.1 Geometry Pipes

D3DX effects completely specify the interface from the application to the vertex shader input through semantics. Using an API called `D3DXGetShaderInputSemantics`, it is possible to find out the vertex buffer layout that an effect requires. Given this, it seemed appropriate that FX Composer could handle complex geometry streams and map them to the current .fx file. To facilitate doing so, FX Composer implements the concept of a *geometry pipe* node. A geometry pipe node consists of a number of geometry pipe objects, each of which can modify a *geometry pipe bundle*. The bundle is a collection of geometry data, with one stream object for each data type. A typical bundle might contain a position stream, a normal stream, and a texture coordinate stream. As the geometry flows up the pipeline, geometry pipe objects can modify the bundle by adding data, modifying it, or removing it. The resulting bundle at the top of the pipeline is then converted to a Direct3D vertex buffer, which can be made to match the effect file being used on that geometry pipe. To assist in the brokering between the geometry bundle and the .fx file input format, the geometry bundle streams have semantic and usage indices.

This approach allows plug-ins to be created to satisfy the current effect's usage scenario. For example, it should be possible to create a plug-in that adds "fins" to a fur shader. The author of the plug-in might also add a geometry stream to the bundle to indicate the presence of a fin, or a stream of triangles to render it.

A special kind of geometry pipe plug-in is always placed at the bottom of the stack. This plug-in is either a "shape" or a "mesh." It is the starting point for the geometry bundle before it flows up the stack. Shape plug-ins are very compact, containing simple information about how to build the shape. Mesh plug-ins are typically created by importers from the preloaded geometry data, though there is nothing to stop a plug-in author from creating a procedural mesh object, for example.

Skinning

One common problem with .fx files is how to handle skinning. FX Composer takes one of three approaches:

1. If the current geometry bundle contains bones and weights but the assigned .fx file does not take them as inputs, FX Composer will pre-skin the data on the host before passing it to the effect.

2. If the current .fx file has bone weights but the current geometry stream does not, FX Composer will set the bone weights to 1 and supply the current transform in the bone matrix palette—hence ensuring that a nonskinned character works on a skinned effect.

3. If the current .fx file contains bone weights and the model also has the same number of bone weights, FX Composer will send the data directly to the effect, assuming that the current hardware is capable of handling the bone palette size.

30.8 Conclusion

With FX Composer, we hope to have built a tool that developers can use to create great effects for their apps. We have strived to design an application that will grow with future APIs and GPUs, and enable us to continue to offer a useful tool. The plug-in features will give developers the power to integrate their workflow with FX Composer and get their assets into it in a simple way.

We hope that this chapter has given you insight into our approach to writing this complex Direct3D tool and inspired some interesting approaches to implementations using .fx files. Direct3D effects provide powerful effect-authoring features, and tools such as FX Composer should help encourage their widespread use in 3D applications. With its rich IDE for building effects and its solid framework for future developer tools, we believe that FX Composer has achieved its goals.

30.9 References

Gamma, E., R. Helm, R. Johnson, and J. Vlissides. 1995. *Design Patterns*. Addison-Wesley.

Rogerson, Dale. 1997. *Inside COM*. Microsoft Press.

Tennison, Jeni. 2002. *Beginning XSLT*. Wrox Press.

Wyke, R. Allen, Sultan Rehman, and Brad Leupen. 2002. *XML Programming*. Microsoft Press.

Chapter 31

Using FX Composer

Christopher Maughan
NVIDIA

This chapter gives a basic introduction to FX Composer, which is included on this book's CD (and can also be found on the book's Web site). FX Composer enables you to create advanced shading effects using .fx files, which are text descriptions of the Direct3D graphics API state and which can be loaded by any Direct3D application using the D3DX effects framework. Effect files contain rendering state, texture state, vertex and pixel shaders, and parameters. FX Composer can be used to create these files and display them on imported models. Additional tools are available to make development with .fx files as productive as possible.

31.1 Getting Started

We recommend that you install the "2003 Summer Update" release of DirectX 9 to enable all the supplied .fx files to run. The FX Composer installer will install everything else that is needed, including many sample media files, which will be located in the "MEDIA" directory, beneath the main FX Composer install location. For best results, use a current graphics card supporting DirectX 9. Figure 31-1 shows FX Composer running with a loaded model and with materials applied.

FX Composer has been designed from the ground up to be a useful shader development tool. The design is as flexible as possible, while offering several advanced features

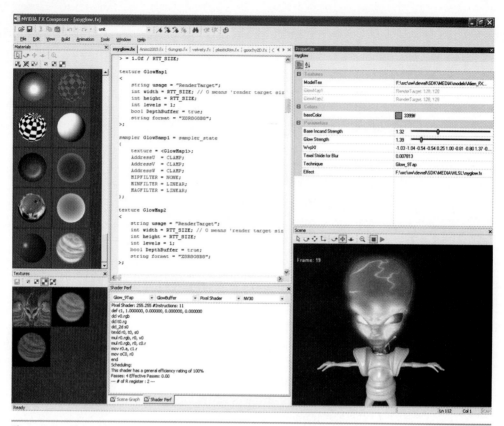

Figure 31-1. The Main FX Composer IDE

to enhance productivity. You can use FX Composer to view shader examples and projects, to develop your collection of .fx files, or to analyze and improve the performance of your shader libraries through the advanced chip profiling features. We hope that FX Composer will become a valuable part of your tool chain, and we have tried to ensure that the application is as extensible as possible, to match your needs. If you need to do more than simply create shaders, if you have special needs for geometry data, or if you want to use FX Composer to import your application data format, doing so won't be a problem. We intend to offer a full SDK to enable the creation of plug-ins that will have full access to all the features of the FX Composer engine. In fact, many functions of FX Composer, such as the scene importers, are themselves plug-ins.

What follows is a brief overview of the FX Composer IDE, version 1. We describe each component separately, to introduce all the program's features in a modular way. This kind of overview will help you get a feel for the capabilities of each component, before you dive in and start using FX Composer to build effects. At the end of the chapter, we load a simple project to show how the pieces hang together. Additionally, FX Composer ships with a full user guide for more in-depth information on usage.

31.1.1 The Materials Panel

Here you can load .fx files and preview them before applying them to parts of the scene. In fact, you may want to use the Materials panel, shown in Figure 31-2, as *the* shader development window: with the ability to change material sizes, it's a quick way to view your effects without applying them directly to scenes. Thus, the Materials panel is effectively a palette of materials. Each material represents an instance of an effect file,

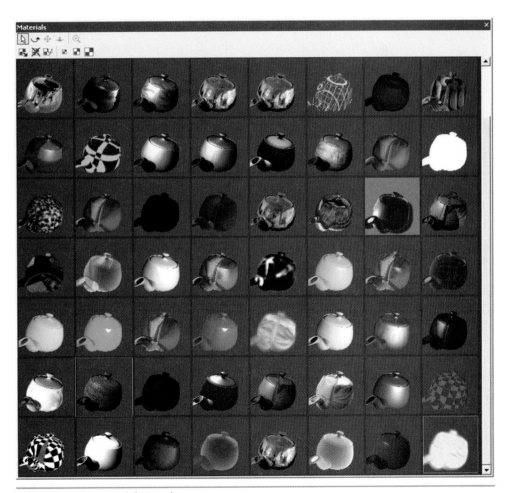

Figure 31-2. The Materials Panel

with a unique set of parameters. Multiple materials may refer to the same .fx file, but with different parameters; in this way, you can load multiple materials of the same type but modify their colors and textures to suit the model in the scene.

Initially, the Materials panel contains just one simple material: a basic lighting example. Note that you can select the material, rotate it, change its size, and more. Each material is really a miniature 3D view, giving a feel for the effect in a real situation. This may seem a little unusual at first, because many CAD applications show only static, 2D versions of materials; but effects often depend on lighting changes and bump maps, so our 3D versions make material viewing much easier.

To choose different preview shapes for the material objects, right-click on the material and select Objects on the pop-up menu. Currently, objects such as teapots, spheres, and cubes can be created. Anyone can write a shape plug-in, and the FX Composer engine can support any type of geometry here. Removing materials and creating new ones is easy; once a new material has been created, its assigned effect file can be changed from the Properties panel. A faster way to create a material, though, is to load it directly from an .fx file, by choosing File...Open Material.

Some materials may be displayed in red wireframe or in blue wireframe. These are special display modes: red indicates an invalid effect file, and blue indicates an effect that won't run on the graphics device. These display modes make it easy to click on broken materials and bring them up in the Editor for repair.

When a material is selected, a red outline appears around its preview in the Materials panel. When part of the current scene is selected, a blue outline appears around any materials associated with that part. In this way, it is easy to find materials in the panel from objects in the scene.

31.1.2 The Scene Graph Panel

The Scene Graph panel, shown in Figure 31-3, gives access to the current scene in a tree representation. Here you can see what objects are in the scene, view their properties, and select them. Most objects in FX Composer can be selected from the Scene Graph panel, and it is often a useful way to find objects in complex scenes. Using this panel and the Properties panel, you can manipulate any object in the scene. For example, in the scene represented by the Scene Graph panel shown in Figure 31-3, there is a single default spotlight. Navigating down the Scene Graph tree, you find the light object and then change its properties by right-clicking on it and choosing Properties. The

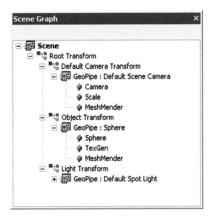

Figure 31-3. The Scene Graph Panel

Properties panel now shows the light's information, and you can change the light's color or any of its other parameters.

Figure 31-3 also shows several GeoPipe objects. A GeoPipe is the node in FX Composer that holds geometry. You can see from the expanded GeoPipe in the figure that it contains the objects that build the geometry data for this node. The first item in the sphere's GeoPipe is the Sphere plug-in, which adds polygons to the pipeline to make up a sphere shape. Right-clicking and selecting the plug-in causes the Properties panel to display editable properties, such as the number of rings and the radius. These properties can be edited to alter the sphere. Another pipeline object is a MeshMender. This object is placed here to generate tangent-space vectors from the sphere. In a GeoPipe, data flows down the pipe until it reaches the end, where it is rendered. There are currently no editable parameters for the MeshMender. GeoPipes are built by importer plug-ins and by FX Composer in response to created shapes. They may contain various stages. Using the FX Composer SDK planned for the future, additional pipeline objects can be created.

31.1.3 The Editor Window

The Editor, shown in Figure 31-4, is used to modify and create .fx effect files. Syntax highlighting shows keywords in different colors, making the source for the shader easier to read. IntelliSense is built in for Direct3D device state, resulting in suggestions for keywords being presented while you edit the .fx file. For example, if you type the Direct3D render state fillmode into an .fx file, the Editor would suggest the following three options:

```
technique Glow_9Tap
{
    pass GlowBuffer <
        string rendertarget = "GlowMap1";
        float cleardepth = 1.0f;
        dword clearcolor = 0x0;
    > {
        cullmode = none;
        ZEnable = true;
        VertexShader = compile vs_1_1 VS();
        PixelShader  = compile ps_2_0 PS_BlurBuffer();
    }

    pass BlurGlowBuffer_Horz <
        string rendertarget = "GlowMap2";
        string geometry = "fullscreenquad";
    > {
        cullmode = none;
        ZEnable = false;
        fillmode=incorrect;
        VertexShader = compile vs_2_0 VS_Quad_Horizontal_9tap();
        PixelShader  = compile ps_2_0 PS_Blur_Horizontal_9tap();
    }
    pass BlurGlowBuffer_Vert <
        string rendertarget = "GlowMap1";
        string geometry = "fullscreenquad";
    > {
        cullmode = none;
        ZEnable = false;
        VertexShader = compile vs_2_0 VS_Quad_Vertical_9tap();
        PixelShader  = compile ps_2_0 PS_Blur_Vertical_9tap();
    }
    pass ModelRender
    {
        ZEnable = true;
        VertexShader = compile vs_1_1 VS();
        PixelShader  = compile ps_2_0 PS_Model();
    }
    pass GlowPass <
        string geometry = "fullscreenquad";
    > {
```

Figure 31-4. The Editor Window

- Solid
- Wireframe
- Point

These equate to D3DFILL_SOLID, D3DFILL_WIREFRAME, and D3DFILL_POINT, and they are set into the render state D3DRS_FILLMODE.

Bookmarks, Find, and Undo/Redo also feature in the Editor. Undo/Redo remembers all edits and allows you to undo all the way back to the point where you started editing the file. Bookmarks offer a quick way to jump to a key point in the shader, and using the Find box on the toolbar is an easy way to search for text strings in the current file.

Tabs along the top of the window allow fast switching between multiple .fx files. Selecting a new material in the Materials panel will automatically bring up the associated .fx file in the Editor. Any modifications you make to the file will update all the associated materials when you press the Compile button on the toolbar. All information about the build process is output to the Log and Tasks panels; you can click on errors in the Tasks panel to automatically highlight their file and location in the Editor. This makes it easy to target and fix syntax errors.

31.1.4 The Shader Perf Panel

It can often be useful to see the generated pixel and vertex shader assembly code from a given effect file. The Shader Perf panel, shown in Figure 31-5, displays the currently selected material shaders. Four drop-down boxes are provided. The first selects the technique to be interrogated, the second the pass, and the third the vertex or pixel shader for that pass. Once you are looking at a pixel shader, you can view scheduling information using the fourth drop-down box. Here you can see how the shader will perform on any of the supported GPU profiles. A list of chip-specific information is appended to the shader, and a summary of the efficiency is presented. In this way, it is possible to adjust the .fx file in question for optimum performance. Figure 31-5 shows an effect file being scheduled on the GeForce FX 5900 chip.

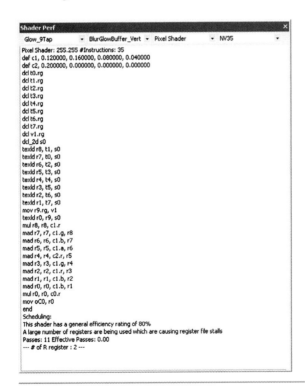

Figure 31-5. The Shader Perf Panel

In the future, we will add support for new devices on the Shader Perf panel, extending the usefulness of this tool for judging the performance of your shader code on all NVIDIA chips.

31.1.5 The Properties Panel

FX Composer's Properties panel, shown in Figure 31-6, enables users to tweak various parameters with an artist-friendly interface. When a material is selected, the Properties panel will show a list of parameters for the associated .fx file. These can be modified to change the look of an effect, perhaps by editing a color or a floating-point value. Figure 31-6 shows the properties for a material called "check3d". The Properties panel knows that the values should be displayed as colors because the author of the .fx file specified that the `UIType` of the parameters is `color`. The colors have human-readable names in the panel because the author also added annotations to indicate each color's `UIName`. These and other markup details for .fx files are covered in the FX Composer user guide.

Note in Figure 31-6 that a small icon is attached to the `lightPos` property. Clicking on the icon brings up the Parameter dialog, shown in Figure 31-7, which lets you connect objects in the scene to properties. The dialog is available because of the annotation

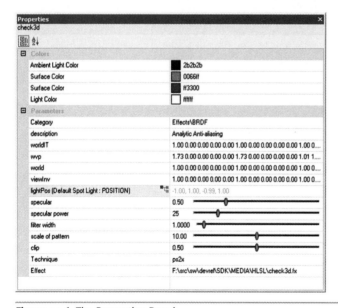

Figure 31-6. The Properties Panel

UIOBJECT = POINTLIGHT, supplied in the .fx file for this parameter. The Parameter dialog, shown in Figure 31-7, enables you to switch light options and gives detailed information about how the calculation for this parameter value is done, depending on the option selected. The current value is also displayed. We can see from the dialog that the light position is currently being calculated using a light called "Default Spot Light" inside the scene. You can also use this dialog to "disconnect" parameters from the scene and edit them manually.

In addition to the properties of materials, the Properties panel will display the properties of objects: if an object such as a sphere is selected, the panel will enable changes to the dimensions and tessellation of the sphere. As you edit the properties of the sphere, you can see it change size in the main display window. Similarly, selecting a texture will give information about that texture, but in general, textures cannot currently be modified from the Properties panel—they are set up from the effect file annotations. In addition to modifying values in the shader, you can also assign components of the current scene to properties in the panel. You might want to do this when you have a light, for example, where you need the shader to contain the current light position at all times.

The Properties panel is thus a context-dependent editor of FX Composer parameters; it is capable of editing color values, numbers, vectors, and matrices. For vectors and matrices, the Properties panel offers sliders and editors; other controls appear depending on the requirements of the edited property. Note that not all properties can be edited; those

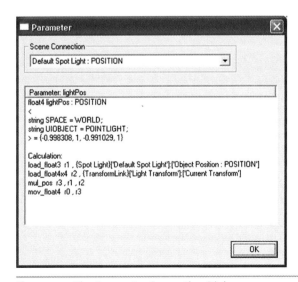

Figure 31-7. The Parameter Connection Dialog

that cannot be edited are displayed in gray. The typical workflow in FX Composer involves selecting something to modify and then using the Properties panel to change it. Values are always modified at the current key frame, and they are interpolated across the scene's other key frames, if appropriate. The Properties panel is the key component for modifying information in FX Composer, and it is always live: when objects in the scene are moved, corresponding values in the panel change simultaneously.

31.1.6   The Scene Panel

The Scene panel contains the geometry and applied materials for the current scene. In this window, you can select sections of imported models and apply materials to them. The initial scene is a simple sphere with a single light source; the light is positioned at the top left. Controls are provided for adjusting the entire scene and individual objects. All these options are available in the right-click pop-up menu.

Figure 31-8 shows a sample Scene panel. Note that the bounds of geometry objects are shown in blue, the bounds of the scene are shown in red, and the selected shape is indicated by the small white markers. Additionally, we have turned on the "Show Transform" option, to enable visualization of object translations. In this scene, it results in a line from the center of the world to the light in the top left corner. In a scene with a skinned character, the lines represent bone translations.

FX Composer supports simple shape plug-ins, enabling users to supply their own objects for display in simple test scenes; these objects can also be used in the Materials panel. The right mouse button always offers a quick way to build a scene from such shapes, allowing users quickly to test a shader on different types of geometry. Geometry data can also be imported using the supplied .x file and .nvb file import plug-ins. Developers can add their own import plug-ins for custom scene formats. The scene in Figure 31-8 was imported from an .nvb file.

Using the buttons at the top of the Scene window, users can manipulate the scene. There are buttons for camera movements (Pan/Dolly/Rotate) and object movements (Translate/Scale/Rotate), for selected objects in the scene. If the scene contains animation data, the Play button on the toolbar enables playback, and a counter in the window shows the current key frame of the running animation. To see the properties of individual scene objects, right-clicking on them and choosing Properties will often bring up useful controls in the Properties panel. Even the background of the scene has its own properties, enabling you to see scene extents and to modify options such as background colors. The right-click menu also enables you to select and delete scene

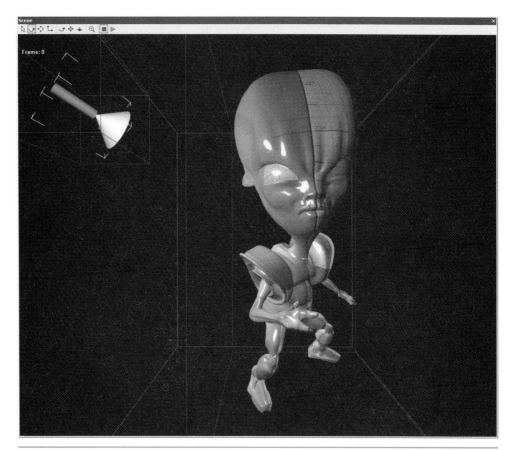

Figure 31-8. The Scene Panel

items, as well as create objects such as point, spot, and directional lights, which can be connected to materials in the scene using the Properties panel.

31.1.7 The Textures Panel

When a material is selected, the Textures panel displays all the textures associated with that material. They may be textures loaded from files, procedurally generated textures from functions inside .fx files, or render targets. A render target example, with material from the glow.fx file, is shown in Figure 31-9. When loaded into the Materials panel and selected, the "blur" textures can be seen in the textures panel. Rotating the glow material in the Materials panel will then show the blur textures being updated in real time. Thus, you can easily see the texture that an effect is generating and debug the algorithm, if necessary. Clicking on the Save icon on the Textures panel toolbar saves a

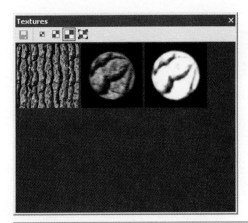

Figure 31-9. The Textures Panel

texture as a .dds file in the texture's native format. This feature enables you to create textures from effect file shaders. Other buttons on the toolbar change the viewing size of the texture, including "actual size," which can be large but is useful for checking pixel accuracy.

31.1.8 The Tasks Panel

The Tasks panel (which is hidden beneath the Log panel at startup) contains a list of current errors and warnings. See Figure 31-10. Errors can result from incorrect edits to .fx files and failure to load resources such as textures, for example. Warnings provide more-general guidance and may indicate, for example, that an effect cannot be used because the current graphics hardware cannot support it, or that suspicious syntax has been found in an .fx file, such as unrecognized semantics or annotations that could be typing errors.

When an error displayed in the Tasks panel results from a shader compilation problem, you can select the error with the mouse, and the FX Composer Editor will automatically load the appropriate .fx file and highlight the error in red. The first error in an .fx file after a compilation will automatically be highlighted in the Tasks panel for you.

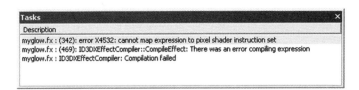

Figure 31-10. The Tasks Panel

31.1.9 The Log Panel

Details of informational events, such as project and material loading, are presented in the Log panel, as shown in Figure 31-11. Here you can track the progress of builds, the loading of models such as imported .x files, and information on what FX Composer is currently doing.

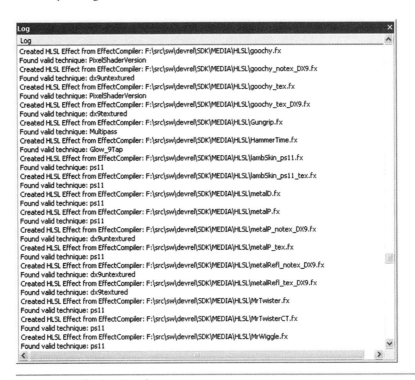

Figure 31-11. The Log Panel

31.2 Sample Project

Now that you are familiar with the basic panels and windows in FX Composer, try loading a sample project. Sample media are located under the FX Composer directory, in a folder called "MEDIA". Beneath MEDIA, you will find an "fxcomposer" directory containing sample projects. FX Composer project files have the .fxcomposer extension and contain geometry, materials, textures, and other elements—in other words, everything needed to load a scene into the application and view it with materials applied.

FX Composer ships with a sample project called "alien_gooch.fxcomposer". Choose File…Load Project to load it. A section of the loaded FX Composer application window is shown in Figure 31-12.

Here we can see that the alien has an effect with a default yellow material, with a per-pixel specular highlight. In the Materials panel, we have selected the material and, using the Properties panel, changed the color to green. We have also played the animation as far as frame 10, and the alien is busy skulking across the floor.

To apply a different material to the alien, we can right-click on the Materials panel (or use the File menu) to open a new material. Once the material is open, we select the alien to apply the new effect and double-click our new material to apply it. Additional models can be imported independent of the .fxcomposer files, using the Import Scene

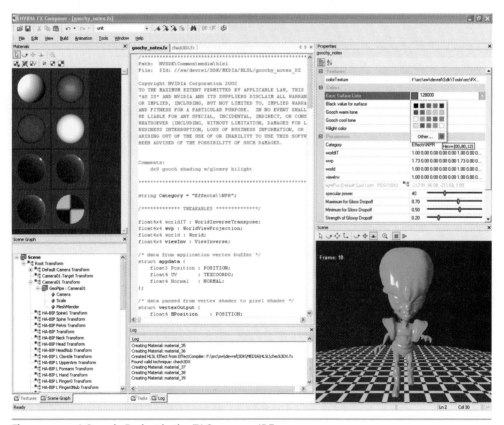

Figure 31-12. A Sample Project in the FX Composer IDE

command on the File menu. Currently, FX Composer can import .x and .nvb files. Once your scene is ready to send to another FX Composer user, you can choose File…Save Project to save the workspace exactly as you have it set up. Reloading this workspace will bring back the scene exactly as you last saved it.

31.3 Conclusion

This chapter was written using the first release of FX Composer, which is included on the book's CD (and available at the book's Web site). FX Composer is a growing application, and it is designed to satisfy the requirements for a powerful shader IDE. As they become available, updates will be posted at http://www.fxcomposer.com. To request a feature in FX Composer or to report a bug, please send e-mail to fxcomposer@nvidia.com.

We hope you enjoy using FX Composer!

Chapter 32

An Introduction to Shader Interfaces

Matt Pharr
NVIDIA

The release of Cg 1.2 introduced an important new feature to the Cg programming language called *shader interfaces*. Shader interfaces provide functionality similar to Java or C# interface classes and C++ abstract base classes: they allow code to be written that makes calls to abstract interfaces, without knowing what the particular implementation of the interface will be. The user must provide objects that implement the interfaces used in the program to the Cg runtime, which then handles putting together the final shader code to run on the hardware.

Unlike object-oriented languages that provide this kind of mechanism for abstraction for developing large software systems, the motivation for adding this feature to Cg was to make it easy to construct shaders at runtime out of multiple pieces of source code. By allowing applications to build shaders by composing the effect of modular pieces that implement well-defined bits of functionality, shader interfaces give the application greater flexibility in creating shading effects and help hide limitations of hardware profiles with no reduction in the quality or efficiency of the final compiled code that runs on the GPU.

For example, consider writing a fragment program that needs to compute a shaded color for a surface while supporting a variety of different types of light source: point light, spotlight, complex projective light source with shadow map and procedurally defined distance attenuation function, and so on. A very inefficient approach would be to pass a "light type" parameter into the program and have a series of `if` tests to determine which light-source model to use. Alternatively, the preprocessor could be used, and the application could use `#ifdef` guards so that it could manually compile a specialized version of the program, depending on which light-source model was actually being used. This approach is somewhat unwieldy, and it doesn't scale elegantly to multiple lights—especially if the number of lights is unknown ahead of time as well.

Shader interfaces provide a type-safe solution to this kind of problem. They do so in a way that reduces the burden on the programmer without compromising performance. The developer can write generic shaders, with large chunks of the functionality expressed in terms of shader object interfaces (such as a basic "light source" interface). As new specific implementations of these interfaces are developed, old shaders can use them without needing to be rewritten. Applications that use this feature would no longer need to implement string-concatenation routines to synthesize Cg source code on the fly to solve this problem—avoiding an approach that is both error prone and unwieldy.

In this chapter, we describe the basic syntax for shader interfaces and how they are used with the Cg compiler and runtime. To give a sense of possible applications for shader interfaces, we then show three examples of how they can be used in Cg: (1) to choose between two methods of vector normalization, (2) to support variable numbers of lights in shaders, and (3) to describe materials and texture in a general, hierarchical manner.

Two other new features in Cg 1.2 complement shader interfaces, improving both the flexibility and the efficiency of shaders. The first, unsized arrays, allows the programmer to declare and use arrays without a fixed size. The array size must be provided to the Cg runtime before the program can be executed. This feature is particularly handy for writing shaders that use a variable number of light parameter sets, skinning matrices, and so on. The second feature is the ability to flag shader parameters as constant values; the compiler can use the knowledge that a particular parameter is constant to substantially improve how well it optimizes the code. For example, an `if` test based on only constant parameters can be fully evaluated at compile time, and the compiler can either discard all the code inside the block after the `if` or run it unconditionally, depending on the test's value.

32.1 The Basics of Shader Interfaces

We start with a simple example based on a fragment program that uses shader interfaces to choose between two different methods of normalizing vectors: one based on a cube-map texture lookup and one based on computing the normalized vector numerically. The application might want to choose between these two vector normalization methods at runtime for maximum performance, depending on the capabilities of the graphics hardware available. This is a simple example, but it helps convey some of the key ideas behind shader interfaces.

First, we need to describe a generic interface for vector normalization. The keyword `interface` introduces a new interface, which must be named with a valid identifier. The methods provided by the interface are then declared between the braces, and the declaration of the interface is terminated by a semicolon.

```
interface Normalizer {
  float3 nrm(float3 v);
};
```

Multiple methods can be declared inside the interface, and the usual function-overloading rules apply. For example, we could have also declared a `half3 nrm(half3)` function as well, and the appropriate one would be chosen based on the type of the vector passed into it.

Given this declaration, we can write a Cg program that takes an instance of the `Normalizer` interface as a parameter. Listing 32-1 shows a very simple fragment program that computes a diffuse lighting term from a single point light. The `nrm()` function in the `Normalizer` interface is called twice: once to normalize the light vector from the light position to the point being shaded, and once to normalize the interpolated normal from the vertex shader.

By using a shader object interface, it was possible to write this shader based on *some* `Normalizer` implementation being bound to `normalizer`, but without knowing how normalization would actually be done at runtime.

We next need to define an implementation or two of the interface. First is `StdNormalizer`, which normalizes the vector using the `normalize()` Cg Standard Library routine, which divides the vector's components by its length. We define a new structure and indicate that it implements the `Normalizer` interface by following the structure name with a colon and the name of the interface that it provides. Having promised to implement the interface, the structure must define implementations of all of the functions

Listing 32-1. Simple Fragment Program Using a Shader Interface to Hide the Details of the Vector Normalization Technique

```
float4 main(float3 Pworld : TEXCOORD0,
            float3 Nworld : TEXCOORD1,
            float3 Kd      : COLOR0,
            uniform float3 Plight,
            uniform Normalizer normalizer) : COLOR
{
    float3 L = normalizer.nrm(Plight - Pworld);
    float3 C = Kd * max(0, dot(L, normalizer.nrm(Nworld)));
    return float4(C, 1);
}
```

declared in the interface. As in Java and C#, the implementations of the methods must be defined inside the structure definition.

```
struct StdNormalizer : Normalize {
    float3 nrm(float3 v) { return normalize(v); }
};
```

We might also define a shader object that normalizes vectors using a cube-map texture, where the faces of the texture have been initialized so that they hold the normalized vector for their corresponding direction. In the next snippet, CubeNormalizer declares a samplerCUBE parameter inside its structure to hold this cube map, and its implementation of nrm() uses it in the usual manner.

```
struct CubeNormalizer : Normalize {
    samplerCUBE normCube;
    float3 nrm(float3 v) { return texCUBE(normCube, v).xyz; }
};
```

Given a program that has interface parameters like normalizer in the preceding code, we need to use the Cg runtime to specify a particular implementation of the interface before the program can execute. We first need to tell the runtime not to immediately try to compile the program we give it when we call cgCreateProgram() or cgCreateProgramFromFile(), as it does by default. Otherwise, the compilation will fail, because the interface hasn't yet been bound to a specific implementation. The cgSetAutoCompile() routine controls this behavior; here we will set it to not compile the program until we tell it to do so explicitly. (There are other settings available for cgSetAutoCompile() that will automatically recompile the program as needed, though possibly at a cost of excess recompilations.)

```
cgSetAutoCompile(context, CG_COMPILE_MANUAL);
CGprogram prog = cgCreateProgramFromFile(context, CG_SOURCE,
                    "frag.cg", profile, NULL, NULL);
```

The `CGprogram` handle returned by `cgCreateProgramFromFile()` can't yet be loaded into the GPU; we need to connect an instance of a `StdNormalizer` structure to the `normalizer` parameter of the program first. Fortunately, the runtime allows us to create an instance of a `StdNormalizer` structure purely through Cg runtime API calls. We turn the string type name "StdNormalizer" into a `CGtype` value with the `cgGetNamedUserType()` call, and then we use `cgCreateParameter()` with that type to create a `StdNormalizer` instance out of thin air.

```
CGtype nrmType = cgGetNamedUserType(prog, "StdNormalizer");
CGparameter stdNorm = cgCreateParameter(context, nrmType);
```

If `StdNormalizer` had parameters inside the structure, we could now initialize them with the `cgSetParameter*()` routines or profile-specific parameter-setting routines, including those for binding texture units to samplers, although we don't need to worry about that for `StdNormalizer`. (We would need to bind an appropriate cube-map texture to the `CubeNormalizer` structure's `normCube` parameter, however.)

Having created the instance of the `StdNormalizer`, all that's left is to get a parameter handle for the interface from the `main()` routine's parameter list and to connect the `StdNormalizer` that we just created to it.

```
CGparameter normIface = cgGetNamedParameter(prog, "normalizer");
cgConnectParameter(stdNorm, normIface);
```

We now have a fully specified program, with no interface parameters without bound implementations. We wrap up by manually compiling the program. After doing this, we can use the program in the normal fashion, loading it on the GPU and using it for rendering.

```
cgCompileProgram(prog);
```

If we later want to swap in a different `Normalizer` implementation for this instance of the program, we just call `cgConnectParameter()` again to connect the new parameter and recompile the new program. Furthermore, if we had multiple programs in the same `CGcontext`, they could all share the same single instance of the `StdNormalizer`, by connecting it to multiple parameters with multiple calls to `cgConnectParameter()`—it wouldn't be necessary to create multiple instances of the `StdNormalizer`.

32.2 A Flexible Description of Lights

A more interesting application of shader interfaces is to use them to handle the problem of writing a Cg program that supports an arbitrary type of light source. In conjunction with another new feature of Cg 1.2, unsized arrays, shader interfaces provide a clean solution to the general problem of writing a program that supports an arbitrary number of light sources, where each light source may be a totally different type of light.

Previously, one solution to this problem was to render the scene once per light source, adding together the results of each pass to compute the final image. This is an inefficient approach, because it requires running vertex programs multiple times, and because it leads to unnecessary repeated computation in the fragment programs each time through. It is also unwieldy, because adding a new type of light means having to write a new instance of every one of the existing surface shaders for the new light model. With shader interfaces, if we have a variety of different types of surface reflection models implemented using the same light-source interface, then adding a new type of light doesn't require any source code modification to the already-existing shaders.

A basic, generic interface that provides a good abstraction for the behavior of diverse types of light sources passes the point being shaded P to the light source. The light source in turn is responsible for initializing a variable L, which gives the direction of incoming light at P, and returning the amount of light arriving at P. Figure 32-1 shows the basic setting for computing illumination from a light in this manner.

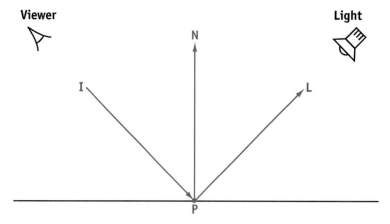

Figure 32-1. Basic Setting for Lighting Computation
Light arrives at the point P along the direction L; the surface normal is N, and the incident direction from the viewer is I.

```
interface Light {
    float3 illuminate(float3 P, out float3 L);
};
```

Given this interface, we might define a simple shadow-mapped spotlight that implements the interface. This spotlight holds a `sampler2D` for its shadow map and uses a cube-map texture to describe the angular distribution of light. The 3D position of the light and its color round out the light's definition. For this example, we assume that the light's position and the position of the point being shaded are already expressed in the same coordinate system, so that we don't have to worry about transforming them to a common coordinate system.

The implementation of this light is quite straightforward; the light direction L is easily computed using the light's position, and the amount of light arriving at P is the product of the light's color, the visibility factor from the shadow-map lookup, and the texture lookup for the spotlight's intensity in the direction to the point receiving light. See Listing 32-2.

Listing 32-2. The `SpotLight` Light Source, Defined As the Implementation of the `Light` Interface

```
struct SpotLight : Light {
    sampler2D shadow;
    samplerCUBE distribution;
    float3 Plight, Clight;
    float3 illuminate(float3 P, out float3 L) {
        L = normalize(Plight - P);
        return Clight * tex2D(shadow, P).xxx *
                texCUBE(distribution, L).xyz;
    }
};
```

One can easily implement a wide variety of light types with this interface: point lights, directional lights, lights that project a texture into the scene, lights with linear or distance-squared fall-off, lights with fall-off defined by a 1D texture map, and many others.

In the fragment program in Listing 32-3, the Cg code loops over all of the lights that are illuminating the surface, calls the `illuminate()` function of each one, and then accumulates a sum of basic diffuse shading terms for each light. Cg's new unsized array feature lets us declare an array of indeterminate length by using the `[]` syntax for the array length after the array name, `lights`. We will shortly see how the Cg runtime can be used to set the number of elements in an unsized array at runtime before the shader finally executes. Note also that there is a `length` member for arrays that gives the number of elements in them; this lets us write a loop over all of the items in an unsized array, even on profiles that don't natively support a variable number of loop iterations.

Listing 32-3. Fragment Shader That Takes an Arbitrary Number of `Light` Interface Parameters

```
float4 main(float3 Pworld  : TEXCOORD0,
            float3 Nworld  : TEXCOORD1,
            float2 uv      : TEXCOORD2,
            uniform sampler2D diffuse,
            uniform Light lights[]) : COLOR
{
  float3 C = float3(0, 0, 0);
  Nworld = normalize(Nworld);
  float3 Kd = tex2D(diffuse, uv).xyz;
  for (int i = 0; i < lights.length; ++i) {
    float3 L, Cl;
    Cl = lights[i].illuminate(Pworld, L);
    C += Kd * Cl * max(0, dot(Nworld, L));
  }
  return float4(C, 1);
}
```

Before this shader can be used in a program, two things must be done using the Cg runtime. First, the final length of the unsized `lights[]` array must be set, and second, each of the interface instances in the array must be bound to an instance of a structure that implements the `Light` interface. For the first problem, the Cg runtime has a routine to set the length of an unsized array:

```
void cgSetArraySize(CGparameter param, int size);
```

The second problem is solved as in the previous example, by calling `cgCreatePara-meter()` to create individual instances of lights and `cgConnectParameter()` to connect the instances to entries in the array of light interfaces for each of the lights in the array. As in that example, the same light-source instance can be shared by multiple programs in the same Cg context.

Because we have used shader interfaces and unsized arrays for this shader, we can write a shader that works with any implementation of the `Light` interface, and we can easily write a shader that doesn't need to have a hard-coded number of light sources bound to it. We have been able to write a very flexible Cg program in a clean way, and without needing to pay an efficiency penalty at runtime. Final GPU instructions are generated for the program only after the particular number of lights and their individual types have been set, so there is no performance price to pay for using the shader object and unsized array features.

Note that if we had instead solved this problem by re-rendering the scene once per light, then we'd have had to renormalize `Nworld` and redo the texture lookup for `Kd` for each pass. If the fragment program did more complex texturing operations than the simple ones here, the performance cost would be correspondingly worse.

32.3 Material Trees

Our final example shows how the composition of interfaces leads to interesting ways of describing materials. One of the most successful approaches to describing complex materials and texture in graphics has been to decompose them into trees or networks, where a collection of nodes is hooked up to compute a complex shading model through the actions of individual nodes that perform simpler operations. (Maya's HyperShade and 3ds max's material editor are two well-known examples of this approach.) Not only is this a convenient way to describe complex materials in content-creation applications, but it's also an elegant way to structure material and texture libraries in applications, allowing them great flexibility in constructing surface descriptions at runtime. Before shader interfaces were added to Cg, there wasn't a clean way to express materials described in this manner in Cg programs.

In this section, we show how shader interfaces make it possible to cleanly map this method of material description to Cg. Here, we make the distinction between a *material*, which represents the full procedural description of how a surface reacts to light, and *texture*, which represents a function that computes some value at a point that a material uses to account for variation in surface properties over a surface.

First, we need to define a material interface. A material has the responsibility of computing the color of reflected light at the given point, accounting for the material properties and illumination from the light sources. It needs information about the local geometry of the surface (at a minimum, the point being shaded `P`, the surface normal at that position `N`, and the texture coordinates `uv`), as well as the incident viewing direction `I` and information about the lights illuminating that point. Note that we are passing an unsized array of `Light` interfaces, `lights[]`, into the `color()` method of the material interface.

```
interface Material {
   float3 color(float3 P, float3 N, float3 I, float2 uv,
              Light lights[]);
};
```

A fragment program that uses a `Material` to compute shading is trivial; we just need a little bit of glue code that passes the right interpolated parameters into the material and returns the result as the color of the fragment, as shown in Listing 32-4.

Listing 32-4. Fragment Shader That Delegates Almost All of Its Computation to a `Material` Interface Implementation

```
float4 main(float3 Pworld : TEXCOORD0,
            float3 Nworld : TEXCOORD1,
            float3 Iworld : TEXCOORD2,
            float2 uv     : TEXCOORD3,
            uniform Light lights[],
            uniform Material material) : COLOR
{
   Nworld = normalize(Nworld);
   float3 C = material.color(Pworld, Nworld, Iworld, uv, lights);
   return float4(C, 1);
}
```

We might first implement a basic `DiffuseMaterial` that abstracts out the information about where diffuse color Kd comes from. So that we don't have to have different `DiffuseMaterial` objects for surfaces with a constant Kd, a Kd defined by a texture map, a Kd defined by a procedural checkerboard function, and so on, we define a `Texture` interface to hide the details of how such possibly varying color values are computed.

```
interface Texture {
   float3 eval(float3 P, float3 N, float3 uv);
};
```

Now the `DiffuseMaterial` just calls the interface's `eval()` function and then does the usual diffuse-reflection computation, as shown in Listing 32-5.

By designing the material in this manner, we make it easy to use the `DiffuseMaterial` with any kind of `Texture` that we might develop in the future, without needing

Listing 32-5. Diffuse Shading Model, Expressed As the Implementation of the Generic `Material` Interface—*An instance of the* `Texture` *interface is used to compute the diffuse reflection coefficient at the shading point.*

```
struct DiffuseMaterial : Material {
  Texture diffuse;
  float3 color(float3 P, float3 N, float3 I, float2 uv,
              Light lights[]) {
    float3 Kd = diffuse.eval(P, N, uv);
    float3 C = float3(0, 0, 0);
    for (float i = 0; i < lights.length; ++i) {
      float3 L;
      float3 Cl = lights[i].illuminate(P, L);
      C += Kd * max(0, dot(N, L));
    }
    return C;
  }
};
```

to modify its source code. As we assemble a large collection of different `Material` implementations (such as materials that implement complex BRDF models), this orthogonality becomes progressively more important.

To connect this `DiffuseMaterial` to the `material` parameter of `main()` in Listing 32-4, we need first to create an instance of the `DiffuseMaterial` structure and then to connect an instance of an implementation of the `Texture` interface to its `diffuse` parameter. We can then connect the `DiffuseMaterial` to the `material` parameter of `main()`.

A natural implementation of a `Texture` to have available is an `ImageTexture` that returns a color from a `sampler2D`.

```
struct ImageTexture : Texture {
  sampler2D map;
  float3 eval(float3 P, float3 N, float3 uv) {
    return tex2D(map, uv).xyz;
  }
};
```

For convenience, we might also want a texture that always returns a constant color. This would allow us always to use the general `DiffuseMaterial` without needing a separate `Material` implementation for when the color was constant. Fortunately, there is no runtime performance penalty for organizing the code in this way.

```
struct ConstantTexture : Texture {
  float3 C;
  float3 eval(float3 P, float3 N, float3 uv) { return C; }
};
```

Even more interesting, we can define a Texture implementation that itself uses Texture interfaces to do its work. In the following code snippet, a BlendTexture blends between two Textures according to a blend amount specified by a third Texture. Of course, each of the three Textures here could be a completely different type: one might look up a value from a 2D image map, one might always return a constant value, and the third might compute a value procedurally.

```
struct BlendTexture : Texture {
  Texture map1, map2, amt;
  float3 eval(float3 P, float3 N, float3 uv) {
    return lerp(map1.eval(P, N, uv), map2.eval(P, N, uv),
             amt.eval(P, N, uv));
  }
};
```

Shader interfaces allow us to implement the BlendTexture in a generic fashion, without needing to know ahead of time which particular types of Texture will be used for any particular instance of a BlendTexture. As with initializing the Texture interface parameter in the DiffuseMaterial, we need to connect instances of structures that implement the Texture interface to map1, map2, and amt using the Cg runtime. It's easy to extend the types of textures available in a system by just implementing new Texture types and extending the application to create them and connect them to interface parameters as appropriate. No preexisting types need to be modified.

Having begun writing implementations of interfaces that themselves hold interfaces, we can apply this idea in many other ways. For example, we can implement a Material that applies a fog atmospheric model to any other Material, as we've done in Listing 32-6.

Thus, we don't need to add support for fog to all of our materials. We can do it just once with the FogMaterial and connect a FogMaterial instance to the parameter to our program's main() function, with the FogMaterial's base instance variable set to our original unfogged material.

Listing 32-6. `Material` That Modifies the Value Returned by Another `Material`, Blending in a Fog Term

```
struct FogMaterial : Material {
  Material base;
  float3 fogAtten, fogColor;
  float3 color(float3 P, float3 N, float3 I, float2 uv,
               Light lights[]) {
    float3 C = base.color(P, N, I, uv, lights);
    float fogFactor = exp(-P.z * fogAtten);
    return lerp(C, fogColor, fogFactor);
  }
};
```

32.4 Conclusion

Shader interfaces and unsized arrays don't make it possible to write any program in Cg that couldn't be written before they were added to the language. However, by making it easier for applications to build shaders out of pieces of code at runtime, they make it substantially easier to implement a number of classic approaches to procedural shading. They provide this functionality in an efficient manner that has no performance penalty on the GPU; the only cost is some runtime and compiler overhead at compile time.

This chapter has described a few examples of this functionality. An application might demand a more complex light-source interface—for example, including a way to express the ideas of a light source that contributes only to diffuse reflection and doesn't cast specular highlights, as described in Barzel 1997. An application might require a more complex texture interface, with information about the surface's partial derivatives at the point being shaded. Many generalizations could be added to improve the interfaces we have used in the examples here.

For example, the `Texture` interface could be generalized to abstract out the decision about where texture coordinates come from by adding an interface that describes texture-coordinate generation (such as spherical mapping, cylindrical mapping, and so on). A texture-coordinate transformation implementation of this interface could transform the generated texture coordinates with a matrix, via a procedure or a texture-map lookup, for example.

Many useful `Material` interfaces could also be implemented, such as a double-sided material that chooses between two other materials, depending on which side of the surface is seen; or a blend material that blends between two materials according to a `Texture` or Fresnel reflection term. It would also likely be useful to be able to express bump mapping in a generic way with these interfaces.

The Cg 1.2 User's Manual has extensive information about the language syntax for shader interfaces and unsized arrays, as well as a description of the new Cg runtime calls that were added for these features.

32.5 References

Barzel, Ronen. 1997. "Lighting Controls for Computer Cinematography." *Journal of Graphics Tools* 2(1), pp. 1–20. *This article describes a complex light-source model with many useful parameters.*

Cook, Robert. 1984. "Shade Trees." *Computer Graphics (Proceedings of SIGGRAPH 84)* 18(3), pp. 223–231. *This paper was the first to present the idea of hierarchical description of shading models with a tree of shading nodes.*

Chapter 33

Converting Production RenderMan Shaders to Real-Time

Stephen Marshall
Sony Pictures Imageworks

33.1 Introduction

Since the late 1980s, visual effects houses have used shading languages to generate convincing images for the motion picture industry. Although these shading languages are extremely powerful, the complexity they need in order to produce innovative images often leads to long rendering times. Additionally, with the demand for bigger and better effects, the complexity of these shaders increases.

If the rendering time takes hours per frame, it is critical to be able to visualize incremental changes in the least amount of time. Consequently, visual effects houses are considering real-time gaming techniques for optimized visualization. In particular, the recent advances of graphics hardware technology and the development of hardware shading languages have offered a recognizable mapping between real-time and production effects.

This chapter demonstrates that it is possible to convert a Pixar RenderMan surface shader into a hardware shader. The hardware shading language used is Cg. Using Cg does not limit the scope of the chapter, because the Cg compiler can generate many different forms of shader instructions, including OpenGL `ARB_fragment` program-compliant code. See NVIDIA 2002 for details. The concepts we present are applicable to other shading languages as well.

You can find each listing mentioned in this chapter on the book's CD or Web site, in the appropriate subdirectory. For example, Listing 33-1, which contains the fur shader for *Stuart Little*, is in the listing1 subdirectory for Chapter 33.

33.1.1 Conversion by Example

The RenderMan fur shader from the movie *Stuart Little* is used throughout this chapter as an example of converting a RenderMan shader to a Cg program (see Berney and Redd 2000 for a description of the fur shader). The topics covered are the following:

- Frequency-independent issues, particularly handling multiple light sources
- A comparison of vertex and fragment programs, with close attention paid to hardware-specific optimizations (which are necessary for good performance)
- An analysis of the results, which covers the differences between the original Cg shaders and their optimizations, as well as the differences between the Cg and RenderMan results

33.2 Lights

As of this writing, lights and the way they are handled are arguably the largest deviation from the RenderMan specification when writing Cg code. That's because these RenderMan constructs have no equivalent mapping. This section covers light sources and light source shaders.

33.2.1 Light Sources

In RenderMan, light sources are iterated over by the illuminance statement. The illuminance statement lets the surface shader gather samples over all light sources in a scene, at the point being shaded. Extra information, beyond the light color and the light direction vector, can be exchanged between the surface and the light through message passing. More information on this topic can be found in Upstill 1990.

The single illuminance statement in the RenderMan fur shader code is:

```
// RenderMan illuminance statement
illuminance (P, norm_hair, radians(illum_width))
```

This statement indicates that the following code will be executed for all lights in the scene that satisfy the illuminance condition. Unfortunately, there is no equivalent statement in Cg. The number of lights in the scene must be known before a shader can be written. Also, each light might have a grouping of similar parameters, but with different values. For example, if all lights in the scene are simple directionals, each light in the parameter list needs at least a light direction vector. If there are ten lights in the scene, the parameter list might look like this:

```
// Example Cg shader parameter list
Output cgProgram(Input In,
                 uniform float3 lightDir[10],
                 . . . , // Other program parameters
```

It's possible to loop over the ten lights, but the process is inflexible. The Cg program must be modified if more than ten light sources are needed.

An alternate approach is to execute the program in a multipass fashion. If all the lights have similar parameters, only the current light's parameters are bound to the current render state. The result of the pass is then added into the frame buffer. So it is not necessary to specify the number of lights in the scene for the Cg program. Now it is left to the application to manage this information. This has the nice side effect of simplifying the parameter list of the Cg program to:

```
// Example Cg shader parameter list with multipass in mind
Output cgProgram(Input In,
                 uniform float3 lightDir,
                 . . . , // Other program parameters
```

Note that although this resolves the need for rewriting the Cg program, there is a necessary performance hit from running multiple passes of our program. As the number of lights in the scene increases, expect a significant decrease in application performance if the Cg program is complex.

33.2.2 Light Source Shaders

Likewise, there is no equivalent Cg statement for the concept of the RenderMan light source shader. A similar assumption can be made for light source shaders as was made for light sources—that all lights in the scene share the same shader.

This may seem like a serious limitation for production use. However, it's common to have a main light source shader that encapsulates all usable light parameters. A single Cg function can be written to implement the common complex lighting equation. More information on implementation of this topic can be found in Barzel 1997 and Gritz 1998.

33.2.3 Additional Lighting Parameters

A complex light source shader can potentially add many parameters to the Cg program. The shader preprocessor can manage this complexity—as well as help with readability—by defining multiple light shader parameter lists. The following two lists are defined and used to simplify the program's parameter list:

```
// uber_light parameter list
#define DEFINE_UBER_LIGHT_PARAMS        \
  uniform float3 lightColor,            \
  uniform float  lightIntensity,        \
  uniform float  lightConeInner,        \
  uniform float  lightConeOuter,        \
  uniform float  lightConeRoundness, \
  . . .

// uber_light parameters
#define UBER_LIGHT_PARAMS              \
  lightColor,                         \
  lightIntensity,                     \
  lightConeInner,                     \
  lightConeOuter,                     \
  lightConeRoundness,                 \
  . . .
```

The Cg shader entry point can then be simplified to:

```
// Example Cg shader parameter list with multipass in mind
Output cgProgram(Input In,
                 DEFINE_UBER_LIGHT_PARAMS,
                 . . . , // Other program parameters
```

The call to the light source implementation in the `cgProgram` block might look like this:

```
// Example Cg shader parameter list with multipass in mind
 float3 lightColor = uber_light(UBER_LIGHT_PARAMS,
                                . . . , // Other parameters
```

Finally, the message-passing facilities in RenderMan must be replaced. This is trivial because the shader is aware of the parameter values for the current light source. These parameter values are encapsulated in the previous parameter list definitions of the Cg program.

33.3 The Vertex Program vs. the Fragment Program

Writing Cg programs (instead of RenderMan shaders) involves different concepts of computation frequency. The execution rate of a shader in RenderMan is governed by the `ShadingRate` parameter (Apodaca and Gritz 2000). This parameter is a floating-point value that specifies the area (in pixels) that a shading sample can represent.

In contrast, the rate that shading occurs in the GPU is defined by the type of program in use. For example, all operations for a vertex program are performed on vertex data passed to the GPU from the API (OpenGL, Microsoft DirectX, and so on). However, all operations of a fragment program are executed on primitives that directly relate to a pixel in the final image.

In hardware, vertex and fragment programs do not necessarily have the same capabilities. In many cases, these programs must work together to supply the same functionality that a single RenderMan surface shader provides. A vertex program overrides the transformation and lighting portion of the graphics pipeline. Consequently, at least a homogeneous clip-space position for the input vertex must be provided. Thus, the transformation portion of the pipeline must be produced manually by passing the modelview projection matrix to the program, transforming the incoming vertex, and assigning the new vertex position to the output vertex-position register. This differs from RenderMan because in RenderMan, it's not necessary to worry about the output of the shader, except for the final color.

In contrast, a fragment program overrides the multitexturing portion of the graphics pipeline, so any texture operation must be performed manually. The result of executing a fragment program is the color for the fragment and possibly a new depth. This new color must be bound to the output color register.

Cg is a hardware-independent language. It is only through hardware profiles that the compiler is made aware of the platform for which it is building. More details on hardware limitations can be found in Appendix B of NVIDIA 2002. The reader is encouraged to read and understand these details before writing hardware shaders.

33.4 Using Vertex and Fragment Programs

As mentioned earlier, it is often necessary to write a vertex and a fragment program to achieve the same functionality of a RenderMan shader. For our fur example, a vertex program prepares the rasterization process, and the shading calculations are implemented in the fragment program. Listing 33-2 shows an initial implementation of a vertex program set up to seed the rasterizer for the fragment program.

The vertex program processes two types of data. The first are attribute values generated in the vertex program. For example, the light direction (L) and the eye direction (V), which are needed by the fragment shader, depend on the position of the input vertex. Because of this dependency, these values are computed in the vertex program at runtime.

Additional per-vertex data can be passed through the vertex shader to the fragment shader as data streams. These attributes are passed and assigned directly to the outputs of the vertex program without further processing. For our fur example, these attributes are the normalized hair tangents (T), a hair parameter value (v), and a surface normal (nSN). This is similar to assigning extra primitive variables to geometry in RenderMan. The difference between RenderMan and the vertex program is that values can be generated through an interpolation scheme in RenderMan (for example, by interpolating data specified at the control points of a NURBS surface). The vertex program merely receives uninterpolated data passed in from the application.

The interpolation of data for the GPU occurs before the fragment program, in the rasterization phase. The user has no control over how the intermediate fragment values are computed. Values passed through the standard graphics pipeline are linearly interpolated across a scanline. This indicates that the sample rate of the input geometry will affect the final quality of the image.

The final component is the fragment program itself, where most of the shading calculations are performed. Listing 33-3 shows the Cg fragment program, which is almost identical to the original RenderMan shader. The initial conversion is very tractable because Cg provides many of the same standard library functions as RenderMan. The only important differences are the interactions with the vertex program, the different names for the program types, and the introduction of the saturate, dot, and cross functions. The saturate function is a minimal-cost function that should be used when clamping a value between 0 and 1. The dot and cross functions are used to replace the . and ^ operators in the RenderMan shading language.

33.5 Optimization Techniques on the Fragment Program

The implementation of the current fragment program may seem adequate; however, it will run slowly. This may seem disappointing at first, but remember that the GPU is not a typical processor. Although converting the fur shader was trivial, the architecture of the hardware was not taken into account. The GPU is composed of two processors: the vertex processor and the fragment processor. It is preferable to do as much computation as possible in the vertex processor, which is only executed on each vertex, because there will generally be far fewer vertices in the model than fragments in the final image. The vertex processing may be complemented by some amount of high-quality processing in the fragment program, because the fragment programs execute on all generated fragments—visible and not visible. Also, computations that do not change over the course of interaction should be moved into the application level; it's wasteful to recompute them each time the vertex or fragment program executes.

It is also important to consider the vectorized nature of the GPU. In general, the GPU can perform a set of four arithmetic instructions in the same time it can perform a set of one, two, or three. The shader source code should be organized to help the compiler recognize and optimize for these cases. Finally, because texture-map lookups on the GPU are extremely efficient, 1D, 2D, and 3D textures can be used as lookup tables for complex functions of one, two, or three variables, respectively.

The goal is to reduce the size of the fragment program. In general, the shorter the program, the faster the execution. If the fp30 profile is used, the compiled size of our original fragment program is 104 instructions. A reduction in size and a gain in efficiency can be achieved if the user has a more in-depth understanding of the hardware.

33.5.1 Moving Code to the Application Level

In the first part of the fragment program, it is clear the code does not change if the view or light changes:

```
// Fragment Program lines
float3 S = cross(IN.nSN, IN.T);
float3 N_hair = cross(IN.T, S);

float l = saturate(dot(IN.nSN, IN.T));
float3 hairNorm = normalize((l * IN.nSN) + ((1.0f - l) * N_hair));
```

This part can therefore be moved into the application level, where the new attribute, hairNorm, will be passed to the vertex program.

33.5.2 Moving Code to the Vertex Program

The next set of dot-product calculations cannot be moved into the application level because the L and V vectors depend on the light and eye positions, respectively:

```
float T_Dot_nL = saturate(dot(IN.T, IN.L));
float T_Dot_nV = saturate(dot(IN.T, IN.V));
```

This set of calculations may, however, be moved into the vertex program because the vectors are generally changing slowly along the fragments generated from a single segment of the curve. In general, the higher the sampling rate along the curve, the less error will be introduced due to this interpolation.

We can estimate the amount of potential error from this interpolation in a rigorous manner. Because the dot product is equal to the cosine of the angle between two normalized vectors, using the analysis of Crenshaw 2000, the error function for a single-valued cosine function is:

$$e_{max} = \cos\left(x_1 + \frac{\Delta x}{2}\right) - \frac{1}{2}\left[\cos(x_1) + \cos(x_1 + \Delta x)\right]. \tag{1}$$

Assuming that the maximum error occurs at the point of highest curvature, x_1 and x_2 are placed about $\cos(0)$. Then:

$$x_1 = -\frac{\Delta x}{2},$$

$$x_2 = \frac{\Delta x}{2}. \tag{2}$$

Therefore:

$$e_{max} = 1 - \frac{1}{2}\left[\cos\left(-\frac{\Delta x}{2}\right) + \cos\left(\frac{\Delta x}{2}\right)\right]. \tag{3}$$

Using the trigonometric identity:

$$\cos(a + b) + \cos(a - b) = 2\cos(a)\cos(b), \tag{4}$$

where for this example $a = 0$ and $b = \Delta x/2$, Equation 1 becomes:

$$e_{max} = 1 - \cos\left(\frac{\Delta x}{2}\right). \tag{5}$$

Assuming that Δx is small enough, the cosine term of Equation 5 can be approximated by the first two terms of an infinite-series expansion of the cosine function, giving:

$$E = \frac{\Delta x^2}{8}. \tag{6}$$

As expected, Equation 6 shows that the largest errors occur where the sample rate is low. In particular, the tangent values need to be almost the same value from sample to sample. This means that the application must ensure that the hair is sampled higher in areas of higher curvature. If this assumption can be made, then the dot products, shown below, can be moved into the vertex program.

```
float2 dots = float2(saturate(dot(IN.T, IN.L)),
                     saturate(dot(IN.T, IN.V)));
```

33.5.3 Optimizing Through Texture Lookups

The Kajiya-Kay hair-shading model includes terms based on a complex function of two variables, `T_Dot_nL` and `T_Dot_e`.

```
float Alpha = acos(T_Dot_nL);
float Beta = acos(T_Dot_e);
float Kajiya = T_Dot_nL * T_Dot_e + sin(Alpha) * sin(Beta);
```

A more detailed derivation can be found in Kajiya and Kay 1989.

This set seems an ideal candidate for a texture lookup. A floating-point texture can be generated for this application. The texture function can then be sampled between 0 and 1 in both independent variables.

An analysis similar to the one in the previous section can be used to determine a sample rate and appropriate texture size for our function lookup; however, this is overly complicated. Instead, a separate program can be written that uses a simple fragment program to compute the difference between a texture lookup of the function and a full computation of the Kajiya-Kay terms. This difference can be displayed as a color for the final fragment. An appropriate texture size that minimizes error can be chosen by simple visual comparison, as shown in Figure 33-1.

The Kajiya-Kay terms of the texture can now be found through this lookup:

```
float2 Kajiya = texRECT(kajiyaTexture, IN.dots);
```

Note that the dot products computed in the vertex program in Section 33.5.2 are used as the texture lookup parameters. Also, note that the `texRECT()` function is used for texture lookup. As a result, the texture lookup must be done in an unnormalized texture space. This is accomplished by multiplying the texture-lookup parameters (the dot products in the vertex program) by the size of the Kajiya-Kay texture.

Figure 33-1. Difference Image Between Texture Lookup and Full Computation
Axes represent dot products between 0 and 1. Blue region indicates error less than 0.0001f; green region indicates error less than 0.01f.

33.5.4 Optimizing for Vectorization

The following power functions compute the specular component of the shading term:

```
float3 Cspec = (spec.x * lightColor * pow(Kajiya, iroughness.x)) +
                   (spec.y * lightColor * pow(Kajiya, iroughness.y));
```

This function can be reordered to take advantage of the vector form of multiplication. In particular, the result of the power functions can be multiplied with the spec components in parallel:

```
float2 powVal = spec * pow(Kajiya, iroughness);
float3 Cspec = lightColor * powVal.x + lightColor * powVal.y;
```

33.5.5 Final Optimizations

The diffuse component calculation of the shading term is performed in the function fnc_diffuselgt, defined at the top of Listing 33-3. This function also uses a dot product between the light direction and the hair normal. From the dot-product analysis in Section 33.5.2, we know that this function can be moved into the vertex program. The resulting varying attribute passed to the fragment program is called dComp.

The Kd multiplication and the final_c computation (minus the darkening term) can be moved to the vertex program to increase performance. Kd must be multiplied by the diffuse component that was moved earlier into the vertex program. The intermediate hair-color value is stored in the varying attribute hairCol. The vertex program code now looks like this:

```
OUT.hairCol = ((1.0 - IN.v) * rootColor) + (IN.v * tipColor);
OUT.dComp = saturate(dot(lDir, IN.hairNorm)) * Kd;
```

Finally, looking at the complete fragment color:

```
OUT.col.xyz = saturate((Kd * Cdiff + staticAmbient) * final_c +
                       (In.v * Kspec * Cspec * specularColor));
```

The IN.v * Kspec calculation can be moved into the vertex program, and the specular value can be stored in the varying attribute specColor to produce:

```
OUT.col.xyz = saturate((Cdiff + staticAmbient) * final_c +
                       (In.specColor * Cspec * specularColor));
```

Note that no conditional statements were used to eliminate unnecessary computations. Unfortunately, current GPUs do not support conditional code natively in the fragment program. Therefore, both the if and the else clauses of a conditional are computed, regardless of the result of the conditional. There is no performance benefit (and there might even be a slowdown from conditionals), so the computation should be calculated using the more complex version.

33.6 Results and Conclusions

This application was run on an Intel Pentium 4 with a 2.8 GHz Xeon processor and tested on Linux with an NVIDIA Quadro FX 2000 and an NVIDIA Quadro 4 980. The Cg version 1.1.0003 compiler was used to generate 27,488 b-spline curves with ten uniformly sampled points.

Although the conversion from the RenderMan shader to a fragment program was straightforward, the initial performance was disappointing. However, through the various optimization techniques discussed in this chapter, the fragment program size was reduced from 104 instructions to 42. This significantly increased the performance.

Some concessions were made on the quality of the image because of the optimization. However, these differences turned out to be unnoticeable in practice.

Figures 33-2 and 33-3 show the original and optimized versions of the fragment program, respectively, and Figure 33-4 shows the difference between the two images produced by the two versions. Notice that the difference is negligible.

Also of interest is the difference between the renderings produced by the fragment program and those produced by RenderMan. Using the same curve geometry, Figure 33-5 was rendered in 20 seconds with Pixar's PRMan. Although the image of the fragment program is slightly different from the RenderMan image, all the important highlights and color changes of the RenderMan image are produced in the correct locations of the fragment program image. It should be easy to see that the hardware version gives a reasonable approximation to the PRMan rendering in a fraction of the time.

Production-quality characters often have millions of hairs. Even after culling, there are still hundreds of thousands of hairs to shade. The optimized fragment program becomes too slow for this type of character, so a complete fur shader was implemented in a vertex program, as shown in Listing 33-4. The results can be seen in Figure 33-6. Although this approach is less accurate than the fragment program, the performance gain is significant.

Figure 33-2. The Result of the Original Fragment Program

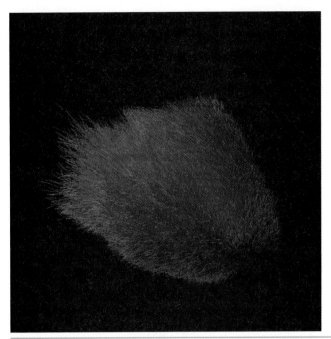

Figure 33-3. The Result of the Optimized Fragment Program

Figure 33-4. The Difference Between the Original and Optimized Images
Differences enhanced to show detail.

Figure 33-5. The Result of the PRMan Rendering

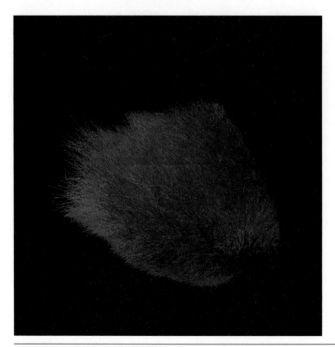

Figure 33-6. The Result of the Fur Shader Vertex Program

Note that if shader writers apply hand optimizations, the fragment program is very different from the original RenderMan surface shader. If it becomes necessary to modify the original RenderMan shader code, it might not be obvious to identify which section of code to modify in the hardware shader to make the equivalent change. This means that writers must be very knowledgeable in how RenderMan works, as well as how hardware shaders work.

No mention of RenderMan *shadeops* has been made in this chapter. A shadeop is a user-defined function written in C or C++ that adds functionality to the standard library of RenderMan. This takes the form of a shared library created by a user, which is dynamically loaded at runtime by the RenderMan renderer. The issue? Current GPUs do not allow this type of programmability. The texture-lookup method described in Section 33.5.3 can possibly replace this if the shadeop's parameter list can be simplified.

33.7 References

Apodaca, A., and L. Gritz. 2000. *Advanced RenderMan: Creating CGI for Motion Pictures.* Morgan Kaufmann.

Barzel, Ronen. 1997. "Lighting Controls for Computer Cinematography." *Journal of Graphics Tools* 2(1), pp. 1–20.

Berney, J., and J. Redd. 2000. "Stuart Little: A Tale of Fur, Costumes, Performance, and Integration: Breathing Real Life Into a Digital Character." SIGGRAPH 2000 Course 14.

Crenshaw, J. 2000. *Math Toolkit for Real-Time Programming.* CMP Books.

Gritz, L. 1998. "uberlight.sl". Available online at the RenderMan Repository: **http://www.renderman.org/RMR/Shaders/BMRTShaders/uberlight.sl**

Kajiya, J., and T. Kay. 1989. "Rendering Fur with Three Dimensional Textures." *ACM Computer Graphics (SIGGRAPH 89)* 23(3), pp. 271–280.

NVIDIA Corporation. 2002. *Cg Toolkit User's Manual: A Developer's Guide to Programmable Graphics.* Available online at **http://developer.nvidia.com**

Upstill, S. 1990. *The RenderMan Companion: A Programmer's Guide to Realistic Computer Graphics.* Addison-Wesley.

This work was supported by Sony Pictures Imageworks. I would also like to thank Murilo Coutinho, Maria Giannakouros, and Hiro Miyoshi for their many thoughtful comments and contributions.

Chapter 34

Integrating Hardware Shading into Cinema 4D

Jörn Loviscach
Hochschule Bremen

Most 3D graphics design software uses graphics hardware to accelerate the interactive previews shown during construction. Given the tremendous computing power of current 3D chips, there are many interesting problems to solve in terms of how this hardware can be leveraged for high-quality rendering. The goal is both to accelerate offline rendering and to provide interactive display at higher quality, thus offering better feedback to the designer. This chapter outlines how the CgFX toolkit has been used to bring these capabilities to Maxon Cinema 4D and discusses the problems that had to be solved in doing so. The approaches used can easily be generalized to similar 3D graphics design software.

34.1 Introduction

To investigate hardware-based rendering, it is not necessary to develop new 3D graphics design software from scratch. Rather, one can augment an off-the-shelf product with such functions, emulating the built-in final renderer by graphics hardware. This chapter describes the implementation of this approach as a plug-in for Maxon Cinema 4D called C4Dfx. Most of this development did not depend on our choice of host software; instead, we focused on shader programming, geometry computation, and object orientation. Thus, our techniques can readily be applied to many other 3D graphics solutions that still lack support for programmable hardware shading.

Cinema 4D offers a modeling, animation, and rendering environment, which is functionally comparable to Alias Maya and discreet 3ds max. However, Cinema 4D's support for the special features of current graphics hardware has been quite restricted up to now. Given its expandability via plug-ins, this software represents a good test case of how to apply CgFX.

Cinema 4D's preview window, shown in the upper left of Figure 34-1, uses standard OpenGL rendering, based on Gouraud interpolation. The hardware-accelerated renderer C4Dfx (in the upper right of the figure) shows smooth, Phong-interpolated highlights, bump maps, shadows, and environment maps. Apart from the soft shadows, the quality of this rendering is nearly comparable to that of Cinema 4D's offline renderer (shown in the lower left of the figure).

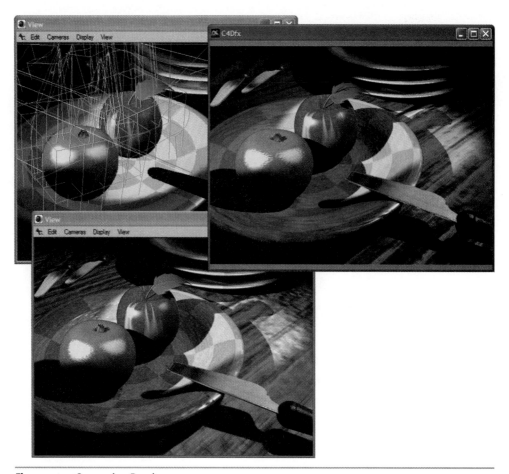

Figure 34-1. Comparing Renderers

The plug-in for hardware-accelerated rendering offers a display updated at near-interactive rates as well as an offline renderer, which generates .avi files. Although the plug-in does not exactly re-create the results of the Cinema 4D offline renderer, its fast and quite accurate preview is helpful. The results of the plug-in's offline renderer may be used for fast previsualization or even as the final result.

The plug-in is built on OpenGL and the CgFX toolkit. The surface materials of the 3D software are transparently emulated by CgFX shaders, including such effects as bump maps, environment maps, and shadows. One may also load CgFX shaders from .fx files. In this case, a graphical user interface is generated on the fly, letting the designer control a shader's tweakable parameters. This approach makes it possible to use the growing number of .fx shaders not only for game development but also as regular materials for high-quality rendering. They may also cast shadows onto objects carrying the emulated Cinema 4D material. Figure 34-2 shows this result for seven of the .fx shaders included in the NVIDIA CgFX plug-in for Maya. The figure also shows that various types of 3D objects can be treated in the same manner.

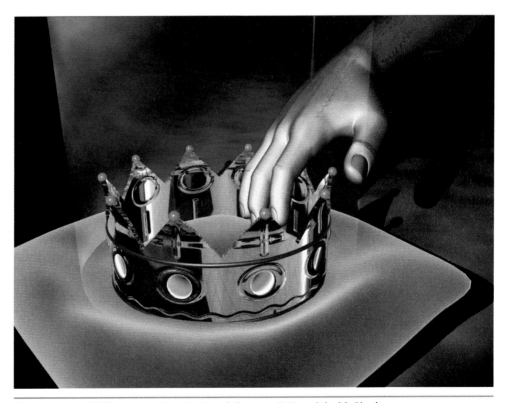

Figure 34-2. CgFX Shaders and an Emulated Cinema 4D Material with Shadows

34.2 Connecting Cinema 4D to CgFX

One minor hurdle occurs when one tries to use Win32, OpenGL, and CgFX calls together with Cinema 4D's C++ API: the corresponding header files conflict and cannot be included together due to type redefinitions. This problem is solved cleanly by introducing wrapper functions and classes. They encapsulate the employed functions and classes of the API.

For third-party programmers, Cinema 4D allows only limited access to its windows. To gain full control over device contexts, the plug-in builds its own Win32 threads. Its high-quality preview and its offline renderer operate concurrently with Cinema 4D; they use off-screen buffers and deliver their results via bitmaps to Cinema 4D's dialog boxes for display. This design allows, for instance, switching between different antialiasing (multisampling) modes on the fly. Furthermore, if the user resizes one of the windows, only the displayed bitmaps are rescaled, which leads to immediate visual feedback. This is not possible when re-rendering the scene on a resize event.

Thanks to multithreading, the user can work in the construction windows without waiting for the interactive or the offline renderer to finish. However, this concurrent operation means that the plug-in has to receive a cloned copy of the scene. Otherwise, the plug-in might try, for instance, to access objects that the user has just deleted.

The plug-in uses the CgFX framework to build shaders and render scenes with them. Each time the interactive renderer is invoked for a frame or the offline renderer is invoked for a frame sequence, for all materials, instances of ICgFXEffect are built either from .fx files or by emulating the standard Cinema 4D material (more on that below). During rendering, the corresponding ICgFXEffect is invoked for each object. Each render pass of the CgFX framework calls an OpenGL indexed vertex array. This includes normal and (multi)texture coordinate arrays.

These arrays are prepared as follows. While Cinema 4D works with spline surfaces, metaballs and so on, the Hierarchy class of its API makes it easy for the plug-in developer to traverse the scene data structures and collect tessellated and deformed versions of all objects, together with their global transformation matrices. The vertex and polygon structures can immediately be used in OpenGL as an indexed vertex array of quadrilaterals. Note that Cinema 4D does not support arbitrary polygons, but only quadrilaterals and triangles; the latter are treated as degenerated quadrilaterals.

In addition to the spatial coordinates, typical .fx shaders require lots of additional data per vertex: normal vector, tangent vector, binormal vector, and u-v texture coordinates.

The latter are immediately accessible if we require that the object be a built-in parametric type (such as a sphere or a mannequin) or require that the user assign u-v coordinates to the object.

Through the adjacency information offered by Cinema 4D, one can easily determine face normals and, by averaging the face normal vectors around a vertex, vertex normal vectors. To compute tangent and binormal vectors at a vertex, vectors pointing in the u and v directions of the texture coordinates are needed. This would be easy for spline-based objects: just take partial derivatives. However, here we have to deal with geometry that has been tessellated or was polyhedral from the very beginning. Under these circumstances, the u and v directions are not well defined. They may, for instance, be inferred for each vertex by considering the u and v coordinates of the vertex itself and those of its surrounding neighbors, trying to find a best linear approximation.

This works as follows: From the position x_i and the texture coordinates u_i, v_i of the vertex i adjacent to vertex 0, compute the auxiliary quantities a, b, c, $\mathbf{d}$, and $\mathbf{e}$ (vectors in boldface):

$$a = \sum_{i=1}^{n}(u_i - u_0)^2, \quad b = \sum_{i=1}^{n}(u_i - u_0)(v_i - v_0), \quad c = \sum_{i=1}^{n}(v_i - v_0)^2,$$

$$\mathbf{d} = \sum_{i=1}^{n}(u_i - u_0)(\mathbf{x}_i - \mathbf{x}_0), \quad \mathbf{e} = \sum_{i=1}^{n}(v_i - v_0)(\mathbf{x}_i - \mathbf{x}_0).$$

From these, determine non-normalized vectors $\mathbf{u}$, $\mathbf{v}$ in the u and v directions, possibly not yet orthogonal to the normal $\mathbf{n}$ at the central vertex 0:

$$\mathbf{u} = c\mathbf{d} - b\mathbf{e}, \quad \mathbf{v} = a\mathbf{e} - b\mathbf{d}.$$

To construct an orthogonal frame (normal, tangent, binormal), compute the tangential component of $\mathbf{u}$:

$$\mathbf{u}_t = \mathbf{u} - (\mathbf{u} \cdot \mathbf{n})\mathbf{n},$$

and use the following triplet of vectors: $\mathbf{n}$, $\mathbf{u}_t^0$, $\mathbf{n} \times \mathbf{u}_t^0$, where $\mathbf{u}_t^0$ denotes normalization of $\mathbf{u}_t$ and $\times$ denotes the vector product. For normal maps generated from bump maps, the tangent and binormal vectors may be replaced by $\mathbf{u}_t^0$ and $\mathbf{v}_t^0$ or by the vectors $(\mathbf{v} \times \mathbf{n})^0$ and $(\mathbf{n} \times \mathbf{u})^0$, which resemble the original form of bump mapping more closely and work better for u-v coordinates that are not locally orthogonal. For other choices, see Kilgard 2000.

34.3 Shader and Parameter Management

Thanks to the CgFX toolkit, it is easy to load an .fx file and use it as a shader, as described above. However, there still remains some work concerning its parameters: the user needs access to the tweakable ones, including their animation, and the untweakable ones have to be computed from the scene.

To handle .fx files, the plug-in adds a proprietary material type to Cinema 4D that can be attached to objects as usual. An instance of this material stores the name of the .fx file and the values and animations of its tweakable parameters. When the user reloads an .fx file or selects a new one, the plug-in uses an instance of `ICgFXEffect` to load and parse the file.

For each parameter, a special object is built, which manages the GUI of the parameter, its value, and so on. This object belongs to a subclass of a newly defined C++ base class called `ParamWrapper`; subclasses of this base class are used for the different types of parameters, such as color triplet or texture file name. Each `ParamWrapper` subclass contains virtual methods that are called to do the following:

- Build and initialize a GUI if this parameter type is tweakable

- Retrieve animated values from a GUI

- Allocate resources and initialize settings when starting to render a frame (such as loading a texture)

- Allocate resources and initialize settings when starting to render an object (for instance, hand its world matrix to CgFX)

- Release resources after an object has been rendered

- Release resources after a frame has been rendered

Furthermore, each `ParamWrapper` subclass can be asked to try to instantiate itself for a given parameter of an `ICgFXEffect`. The constructor then reads the parameter's type and annotations and reports if it was successful. On parsing an .fx file, the plug-in calls this method for each parameter until a fitting subclass is found. This approach makes it possible to encapsulate all knowledge about a parameter type inside the corresponding subclass.

Through the subclasses, some of the tweakable parameters receive special GUI elements offered by Cinema 4D. For textures, names of .dds files are stored. Positions and directions are linked to the position or the z axis of other objects, preferably light sources; these can be dragged to and dropped onto an input field of the GUI. The untweakable and hence GUI-less matrix parameters receive special treatment. The world matrix is delivered by the API as a by-product on traversing the scene. The view and projection matrices are computed from the camera settings. The products of these matrices, perhaps inverted or transposed, are computed if the shader requires them.

For convenience, the plug-in offers to open the .fx file in a user-specified editor. Upon reloading an edited .fx file, existing parameter values are conserved if they are the correct type and in the allowed range. If the CgFX toolkit reports an error upon loading an .fx file, this file is opened in the editor with the cursor placed on the error's line. All messages about errors, as well as problems such as unknown parameter types, are written to the text console of Cinema 4D.

34.4 Emulating the Offline Renderer

Instead of loading .fx files, the user may simply use standard Cinema 4D surface materials. The plug-in converts these internally and transparently to memory-based .fx shaders, fitting well into the process described for external shader files. The plug-in employs string streams to build the internal .fx shaders.

A Cinema 4D material can contain bitmap files, movie files, or procedural shaders as maps. The plug-in reads these pixel by pixel in a user-selectable resolution (typically 256×256 texels) and builds corresponding textures. Three types of maps are converted: diffuse maps, bump maps, and environment maps. The latter are used with spherical mapping in the ray tracer; the plug-in computes cube maps from them in order to optimize resolution. The bump maps are grayscale height fields. For these, a normal map is formed from horizontal and vertical pixelwise differences of the bump map, scaled by its size to compensate for steeper gradients at smaller resolutions.

For shadow generation, we relied on a shadow map method similar to the one used in Everitt et al. 2002. In contrast to a hardware-accelerated shadow-volume algorithm (Everitt and Kilgard 2002), it may later quite easily be extended to treat objects deformed by displacement maps or vertex shaders.

For each cone light in the scene tagged as shadow casting, a depth map of user-controllable size is generated (typically 256×256 texels). To this end, all objects of the scene, regardless of the surface material they carry, are rendered into an off-screen buffer without textures and shaders. This requires traversing the scene as in the final rendering described earlier, although no texture coordinates nor normal, tangent, or binormal vectors are computed during this pass. In fact, the rendering of the shadow maps does not use CgFX at all. To use an off-screen buffer as a depth-map texture, it is built with the OpenGL extension `WGL_NV_render_depth_texture`.

Another texture is used to store Cinema 4D's proprietary shape of specular highlights. It involves several transcendental functions, such as power and arc cosine. This complex relationship is precomputed per frame as a 1D texture of 1024 texels.

To allow an unlimited number of lights, one possibility is to use a single render pass for each light, possibly adding another pass for self-illumination. However, this causes a large amount of recomputation, such as for normalization of interpolated vectors. Joining several passes comes at a price, however. Because current graphics cards support only a fixed number of textures, the number of light sources that can cast shadows is strictly limited.

The vertex shader part of the generated CgFX shaders is quite simple:

1. The position is transformed to normalized screen coordinates using the `WorldViewProjection` matrix.
2. Tangent and binormal vectors are transformed to world coordinates through the `World` matrix.
3. To preserve orthogonality, the normal vector is transformed to world coordinates through the inverse transposed `World` matrix.
4. The position in world coordinates is computed using the `World` matrix.
5. Finally, a unit vector from the viewer's position (which can be read off from the inverse transposed `View` matrix) to the vertex is determined in world coordinates.

Listing 34-1 shows the pixel shader generated when there is one cone light with shadow. When there are more light sources, parameters such as `depthSampler1` are added and the block between the braces { . . . } is repeated accordingly. The listing's initial part is standard; the computations done per light source deserve some explanation, however. `Ld` is the world-space vector from the vertex to the light source. `baseCol` sums the contribution of the light source: first the diffuse, and then the specular part. The latter reads the precomputed highlight shape using `specShadeSampler`. If the reflected ray points away from the viewer, the texture coordinate for `specShadeSampler` becomes negative and is clamped to zero, where the texture is zero, too.

```
pixelOutput mainPS(vertexOutput IN,
                    uniform sampler2D diffuseSampler,
                    uniform sampler1D specShapeSampler,
                    uniform sampler2D normalSampler,
                    uniform samplerCUBE enviSampler,
                    uniform sampler2D depthSampler0,
                    uniform float4 lumiCol,
                    uniform float4 diffCol,
                    uniform float bumpHeight,
                    uniform float4 enviCol,
                    uniform float4 specCol,
                    uniform float4 lightPos0,
                    uniform float4 lightCol0,
                    uniform float4 lightParams0,
                    uniform float4 lightUp0,
                    uniform float4 lightDir0,
                    uniform float4 lightSide0)
{
  pixelOutput OUT;
  float3 Vn = normalize(IN.view);
  float3 Nn = normalize(IN.norm);
  float3 tangn = normalize(IN.tang);
  float3 binormn = normalize(IN.binorm);
  float3 bumps = bumpHeight *
                  (tex2D(normalSampler, IN.uv.xy).xyz *
                   2.0 - float3(1.0, 1.0, 2.0));
  float3 Nb = normalize(bumps.x * tangn +
                        bumps.y * binormn +
                        (1.0 + bumps.z) * Nn);
  float3 env = texCUBE(enviSampler, reflect(Vn, Nb)).rgb;
  float3 colorSum = lumiCol.rgb + env * enviCol.rgb;
  float3 baseDiffCol = diffCol.rgb +
                        tex2D(diffuseSampler, IN.uv.xy).rgb;
  {
    float3 Ld = lightPos0.xyz - IN.wPos;
    float3 Ln = normalize(Ld);
    float3 baseCol = max(0.0, dot(Ln, Nb)) * baseDiffCol;
    float spec = tex1D(specShapeSampler,
                       dot(Vn, reflect(Ln, Nb))).r;
    baseCol += specCol.rgb * spec;
```

```
    float3 L1 = (Ln / dot(Ln, lightDir0.xyz) -
                lightDir0.xyz) * lightParams0.z;
    float shadowFactor = max(lightParams0.x,
                             smoothstep(1.0, lightParams0.w,
                                        length(L1)));
    float d = dot(Ld, lightDir0.xyz);
    float z = 10.1010101 / d + 1.01010101;
    float2 depthUV = float2(0.5, 0.5) + 0.5 *
                     float2(dot(L1, lightSide0.xyz),
                            dot(L1, lightUp0.xyz));
    shadowFactor *= max(lightParams0.y,
                        tex2Dproj(depthSampler0,
                                  float4(depthUV.x,
                                         depthUV.y, z -
                                         0.00005, 1.0)).x);
    colorSum +=shadowFactor * baseCol * lightCol0.rgb;
  }
  OUT.col = colorSum;
  return OUT;
}
```

The remaining computations deal with the soft cone and the shadow, combined into the variable shadowFactor. L1 measures how far away the vertex is from the light's optical axis; this vector has length 1 if the vertex is exactly on the rim of the cone, as shown in Figure 34-3. To this end, lightParams0.z has to be set to the inverse of the tangent of the half aperture angle of the cone. To create a soft cone, lightParams0.w is set to the quotient of the tangent of the half aperture angle of the inner, fully lighted part of the cone divided by the former tangent. From this, the smoothstep function creates a soft transition. lightParams0.x is set to 1.0 for omni lights and 0.0 for cone lights, so that only the latter are restricted to a cone.

To generate shadowing, d measures the z coordinate of the vertex in the coordinate frame of the light source. This is then converted to the depth coordinate used in the depth map and afterward is compared to the actual value found in that map. Note that for tex2Dproj to work, the texture has to be defined with glTexParameteri(GL_TEXTURE_2D, GL_TEXTURE_COMPARE_SGIX, GL_TRUE).

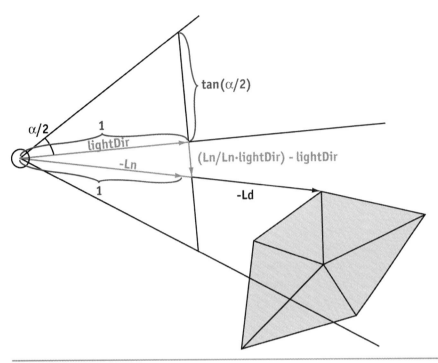

Figure 34-3. The Geometry of a Cone Light

34.5 Results and Performance

Figure 34-1 showed that the rendered images can withstand comparison with the original offline renderer. Complex features such as transparency and reflection effects are still missing, but they may be added in a later version—for instance, through environment maps rendered on the fly and layered rendering (Everitt 2001). Further possible improvements include soft shadows (Hasenfratz et al. 2003), physically based lighting models, and indirect illumination (Kautz 2003).

Of course, the main question is what speed the hardware-accelerated solution offers. In terms of raw megapixels per second, the graphics card can asymptotically outperform the offline renderer by nearly a factor of nine. This can be seen from the growth of render time with frame size in Figure 34-4. However, as Figure 34-4 also shows, compiling CgFX shaders on the fly and, in particular, building OpenGL textures from Cinema 4D texture maps and procedural shaders leads to some startup costs before any frame is rendered. Thus, the hardware-accelerated solution excels only for large frame sizes and frame sequences, but not for single frames. To improve on this result, an intelligent

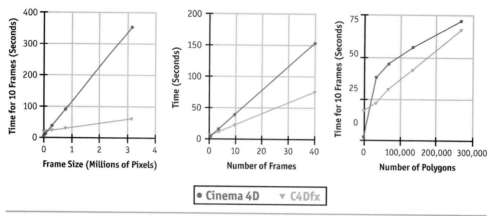

Figure 34-4. Comparing Benchmark Results

approach concerning the textures is needed. The textures need to be conserved as long as possible, rather than rebuilt each frame. This requires an automatic, in-depth examination of the animation.

The benchmarks performed use a base scene of approximately 33,000 polygons, almost all quadrilaterals, and an animation of 10 frames at 640×480 pixels (0.31 million pixels) with no antialiasing. The system used was a Pentium 4 PC at 2.5 GHz with a GeForce FX 5900, running Cinema 4D release 8.207. In each part of Figure 34-4, one of three parameters is varied: frame size, sequence length, and complexity.

With growing geometric complexity of the scene, the offline renderer of Cinema 4D obviously profits from some optimization techniques. The hardware-accelerated solution needs a similar improvement. Easiest to implement would be view-frustum culling and hardware-based occlusion culling on a per-object basis.

34.6 Lessons Learned

The CgFX toolkit makes it feasible to add both hardware-accelerated, high-quality displays and hardware-accelerated, offline renderers to existing software. The solution presented here fits into roughly 150 KB of C++ source code.

CgFX allows programmers to address a wide range of graphics cards from different vendors via a set of techniques defined in an .fx file. However, for optimum performance, it is a good idea to carefully count in advance how many parameters and textures will be needed simultaneously. Even the latest graphics cards may deliver only limited power in this respect.

Chapter 34   Integrating Hardware Shading into Cinema 4D

Shaders usually form only a tiny part of a program. The remainder of the software tends to become quite specific in its demands for hardware. The project presented here started out with the large range of hardware compatibility offered by CgFX itself. But adding any slightly advanced feature, such as rendering into an off-screen buffer, multi-sampling, or shadow generation, cuts down the target range. Some OpenGL extensions may be missing or different on some graphics cards, or their implementation may even contain serious bugs.

Our plug-in functions only on Windows, despite the fact that Cinema 4D is available for both Windows and Mac OS. The unavailability of CgFX on platforms other than Windows (at the time of development) accounts for only part of the problem. A cross-platform API such as Cinema 4D's may hide many of the differences in the handling of windows, events, and threads. However, this design conflicts with the goal of providing enough functionality and granting enough access to the underlying structures to fully support complex OpenGL-based software.

Users of graphics design software may create arbitrarily complex scenes, but they still expect a decent response time from the software. During the development of the C4Dfx plug-in, we learned how crucial it is to understand and plan for the elaborate interworkings of threads and how data and events are shared and transmitted between them.

Another area requiring profound design consideration from the very beginning turned out to be the management of textures and shaders. Creating textures, loading them to the graphics card, and compiling shaders needs to be avoided at nearly all cost, as the benchmarks show. This restriction demands a highly intelligent design. Of course, such a design is difficult to implement as an add-on to existing software.

Real-time shaders can closely emulate many functions that usually are still being computed on the CPU. For instance, the soft rims of the light cones and the specular highlights of the plug-in described here look identical to those of the software renderer. But such a perfect reproduction requires access to the original algorithms or extensive reverse engineering. Even standard features such as bump mapping can be implemented in dozens of ways, all of which yield slightly different results. How do you form the tangent and the binormal? How do you mix the bumped normal vector with the original one, depending on the bump strength parameter? How do you compute the normal map from the bump map? Do you use the original, possibly non-power-of-two, bump-map image or some mipmap level? In this respect and many others, Cg has presented itself as an ideal tool for experimenting with computer graphics algorithms.

34.7 References

Everitt, C. 2001. "Order-Independent Transparency." Available online at **http://developer.nvidia.com/view.asp?IO=order_independent_transparency**

Everitt, C., and M. J. Kilgard. 2002. "Practical and Robust Stenciled Shadow Volumes for Hardware-Accelerated Rendering." Available online at **http://developer.nvidia.com/object/robust_shadow_volumes.html**

Everitt, C., A. Rege, and C. Cebenoyan. 2002. "Hardware Shadow Mapping." Available online at **http://developer.nvidia.com**

Hasenfratz, J.-M., M. Lapierre, N. Holzschuch, and F. X. Sillion. 2003. "A Survey of Real-time Soft Shadow Algorithms." *Eurographics 2003 State of the Art Reports*, pp. 1–20.

Kautz, J. 2003. "Hardware Lighting and Shading." *Eurographics 2003 State of the Art Reports*, pp. 33–57.

Kilgard, M. J. 2000. "A Practical and Robust Bump-Mapping Technique for Today's GPUs." Available online at **http://developer.nvidia.com**

Maxon. Cinema4D. **http://www.maxon.net**

## Chapter 35

Leveraging High-Quality Software Rendering Effects in Real-Time Applications

Alexandre Jean Claude
Softimage

Marc Stevens
Softimage

35.1 Introduction

Today's graphics hardware is capable of computing complex vertex and pixel-shading programs that can display advanced real-time effects. These effects require not only a vertex or pixel-shading program, but also the rich input data used by these programs to drive high-quality output. Examples of this rich input data are vertex attributes (such as normals and tangents), texture coordinates, and texture maps (such as diffuse maps, normal maps, and reflection maps). The methods and tools that generate components for the hardware-rendering process range from those created by hand to those using integrated and automated solutions.

High-quality input is important. As the demand for high-quality rendered output from hardware increases, so does the demand on the digital artist to produce it. Today's digital artists need tools that let them efficiently produce this output in an environment that facilitates continuous iteration on the results.

It's best to generate that input from high-end modeling and animation systems, rather than exporting to another tool that is specialized for real time. Current tools that generate attribute maps for sophisticated real-time shading effects are packaged as standalone programs. This forces a costly conversion process that can sometimes lose key pieces of data between the 3D scene data of the main DCC tool and the standalone programs. An integrated workflow helps artists visualize the effects of the different operations in the final shading program and easily iterate on the results.

Existing high-end rendering solutions, such as mental images' mental ray and Pixar's RenderMan, were developed over many years and have a rich set of capabilities. These renderers excel at generating high precision and highly detailed, photorealistic images. Developing solutions to produce this visual information from scratch involves rewriting a lot of code already implemented by most high-end rendering solutions. Examples of some of the advantages are support of arbitrary networks of shading nodes rendered into a single map that are used as a diffuse map, micro-polygons generated by a renderer's tessellation algorithm for displacement maps baked into normal maps, or the effects of global illumination models baked into maps.

This chapter discusses the process, its use in practice, potential pitfalls, and how to work around them.

35.2 The Content Pipeline for Hardware Rendering

The pipeline for creating content suitable for hardware rendering often constrains the artist into working within the limitations of the target engine. The artist usually works with a budget of limited textures and triangles. The common workflow is to start building content with the engine limitation in mind. Although this workflow is terrific for generating optimal content for hardware rendering, it reduces the artist's freedom to use all the available tools to produce outstanding content. On the other hand, working with high-quality content and trying to reduce it to something that works within the hardware renderer's limitations is daunting and does not always produce good results.

Our approach lets artists work with all the available tools to produce high-quality content and to bring its details onto a hardware-rendering-ready version of the content. A diagram of the pipeline is shown in Figure 35-1. It works like this:

- The artist creates high-quality objects and shading effects using the DCC tool and the high-end software renderer's shading capabilities. This content is not used directly in hardware rendering, but it will be used as source material for generating the components for hardware rendering.

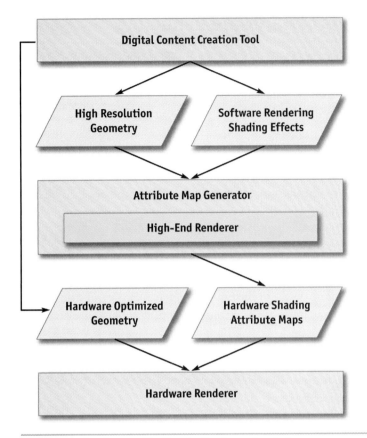

Figure 35-1. The Content Pipeline for Hardware Rendering

- The artist creates a hardware-rendering-ready version of the original high-quality content. At this point, the artist creates only skeleton data, which is later updated by automated tools to contain the high-quality details. For example, the artist creates a lower-resolution object that has roughly the same shape as the original content and then lets the tools bake the attribute maps for the hardware renderer.

The tools use high-quality geometry and shading effects and compile the necessary attributes to apply onto the low-resolution version of the object. The result is that the final hardware rendering looks as close as possible to the high-quality content. By relying on a software-renderer solution, the tools can use all the features of the software renderer and then bake the result onto the final attribute maps. The rest of the chapter breaks down the process in detail.

35.3 Components of Hardware Rendering

We now have a good overview of the content pipeline for hardware rendering. In this section, we go into more detail about the specifications of the different components used in hardware shading effects. The components fall into two categories: geometric data and attribute maps.

35.3.1 Geometric Data

Geometric data is composed of the polygon mesh structure and its vertex attributes. This data is used by the hardware rasterizer to generate the pixels to be displayed. In the hardware-rendering pipeline, vertex data is processed by the vertex shader; each triangle is rasterized into fragments; and then the fragments are fed to the pixel shader, which displays them.

The mesh structure consists of triangles that are combined and sent through the hardware graphics pipeline. Users of the DCC tool generate the polygon meshes, and then the DCC converts the polygons into triangles and, optionally, creates triangle strips.

The u-v texture coordinates are important attributes of the vertex; they contain mapping information about how to sample the texture image over the surface. They also are used in several algorithms that generate tangents. Later we show how tangents are generated from the u-v texture coordinates.

Normals, tangents, and binormals are essential if the normal map is expressed in tangent space. The normals, tangents, and binormals define the basis of each vertex. Most current authoring tools support only normal editing. Later we show how to generate tangents and binormals using the surface normals and u-v coordinates.

35.3.2 Attribute Maps

Attribute maps are essentially texture maps sampled by the hardware pipeline rasterizer. Texture maps have a greater density than geometry used to create details on the surface of an object without increasing the geometric density. For example, we use texture maps to add color details to a polygon mesh.

Normal maps store normals at each texel. Each normal component (x, y, and z) is encoded in the pixel components of the texture (red, green, and blue). Because normals are of unit length, each component has a range of -1 to 1. Red, green, and blue have the range 0 to 1. Normals are encoded with an offset of 0.5 per component and a scaling of 0.5 per component. Normal maps can be optionally expressed in model space or in tangent space, as shown in Figures 35-2 and 35-3, respectively.

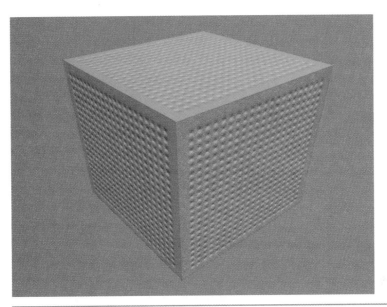

Figure 35-2. A Normal Map in Model Space
Each face of the cube has a very different normal map because the normals are expressed in model space and are pointing to different directions.

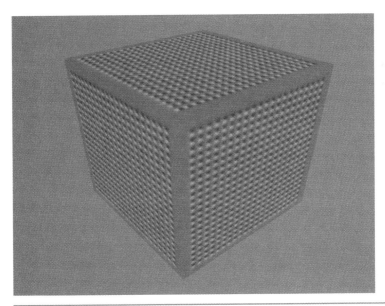

Figure 35-3. A Normal Map in Tangent Space
Each face of the cube has a similar normal map because the normals are expressed in tangent space and are pointing to the same direction regardless of the face orientation.

Normal maps in model space generally require less computation at runtime than normal maps in tangent space. However, each map is unique to the object and cannot be shared or reused on another object. Normal maps in tangent space require more vertex operations, but on the other hand, they can be tiled and reused on other objects.

Diffuse maps, as shown in Figure 35-4, are used as standard color texture maps. They are encoded as regular red, green, blue, and alpha components and represent the color at the surface of the object.

Figure 35-4. A Diffuse Map for a Surface

Reflection maps are also used as standard color texture maps. They are also encoded as regular red, green, blue, and alpha components and represent the color of the environment that is reflected by the object.

Every day new techniques for achieving advanced real-time shading effects are being explored and discovered. Other types of maps are used in hardware pixel shaders to achieve these effects:

- Procedural textures (such as noise, marble, and wood)
- Environment-based lighting
- Nonphotorealistic rendering

The technique described in this chapter for generating attribute maps can be extended and applied to these shading effects.

35.4 Generating the Components

Now that we have the specifications for the components required by the hardware renderer, we need to generate them. The artist generates some components; automated tools create others.

Ideally, the component generation step is open and flexible enough to cover the range of algorithms people use when creating vertex attributes and attribute maps. Automating the process as much as possible without sacrificing flexibility is the goal. Tangent creation often demands the most flexibility, in specifying how tangents are formed.

Normal maps are generated in the reference frame that is the most suitable for the application. However, "normal maps in tangent space" is the most popular technique, because it allows reuse of the normal map on other objects. The maps should be generated from an object with a much higher vertex density and applied to an object with a lower density. This technique allows artists to freely model highly detailed objects and bake the details of these objects onto a normal map that applies to the low-resolution model.

The technique that generates the map consists of these steps:

1. Compute the normal at the surface of the high-resolution objects in model space, using the texture coordinate parameterization of the low-resolution object.

2. Apply that normal map on the low-resolution object.

3. Compute the tangents of the low-resolution object.

4. Use the normal map in model space, plus the tangents of the low-resolution object, to compute the normal map in tangent space.

The workflow allows artists to bake arbitrary numbers of high-resolution objects, which contain arbitrary shading effects, into simple texture maps.

35.4.1 Creating the Geometry

On the geometry side, the artist creates the object with the DCC tool. However, some vertex attributes are very difficult to build by hand, so the artist usually uses a set of helper tools to create them.

35.4.2 Rendering to Textures and Vertices

To generate attribute maps, we need a tool that can render the software renderer's shading effects into texture maps using the parameterization of the target object. The same effects are also to be baked into vertex attributes.

Rendering to a texture uses an existing texture coordinate parameterization, coupled with a target texture map. For each texel of the texture, the algorithm finds the coordinates at the surface of the object. The software renderer fires a ray and sample attributes at the coordinates. By rendering to vertices, we sample these attributes at each vertex position, instead of at each texel position.

Rendering to a texture and to vertices generates only surface color attributes, so we need to find a way to render custom attributes, such as tangents and normals. The solution is to create a custom software shader that renders the surface tangents and normals into surface colors. Because hardware-programmable shading ultimately works with four-component registers, any custom attribute can be encoded as an RGBA value, either in vertex colors or in texture maps.

Figure 35-5 is an example of an object rendered with normals set into surface colors.

We can create u-v coordinates by using a texture coordinate editor. There are also solutions that automatically unfold geometry and create a texture coordinate set that is good enough to use in the hardware pipeline.

These are the main criteria for the u-v coordinates:

- The u-v coordinates should have a good general u and v flow (good flow is characterized by minimizing any discontinuities between successive u or v values). This is critical for tools that generate tangents based on u-v coordinates. Most tangent-generation algorithms use the u and v flows of a given texture coordinate parameterization to orient the tangents at the surface of the objects.

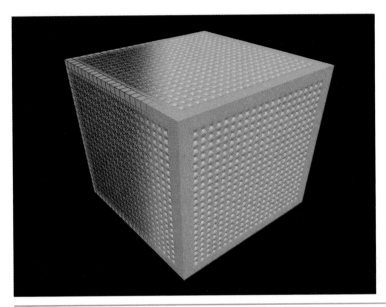

Figure 35-5. Object Normals Rendered by mental ray
A wireframe display has been blended with the resulting colors to show the complexity of the geometry.

- The u-v coordinate sets should have minimal *islands*, which are groups of connected triangles in u-v space; islands introduce texture-map discontinuity. These discontinuities can cause problems when the algorithm samples texels on edges that border discontinuities. This problem can be circumvented by spilling or averaging texel values, but in general, we recommend avoiding discontinuities.

Creating normals is usually part of the object modeling process. However, tangents and binormals are easily derived from u-v coordinates and the normal vectors. In our test case, we compute the binormal vector inside the vertex program by using the normal and tangent provided by the application. Tangents have to be accessible to users of the DCC tools because they may want to override the computation. We accomplish this by storing the tangents in the vertex color attributes, because the vertex color is not used in the bump-mapping test case.

The resulting vertex format to be passed to the vertex program is shown in Listing 35-1.

The binormal is computed using a cross product between the normal and the tangents.

Listing 35-1.

```
struct app2vertex
{
    float4 position : POSITION;
    float4 normal   : NORMAL;
    float4 tangent  : COLOR0;
    float4 uv0      : TEXCOORD0;
    float4 uv1      : TEXCOORD1;
    float4 uv2      : TEXCOORD2;
    float4 uv3      : TEXCOORD3;
};
```

To compute the tangents in our test case, we use a custom mental ray shader that temporarily overrides the current object's shading and displays the tangents as vertex colors, as shown in Figure 35-6. Rendering to vertices does its magic to evaluate the mental ray shader and puts the results in vertex colors.

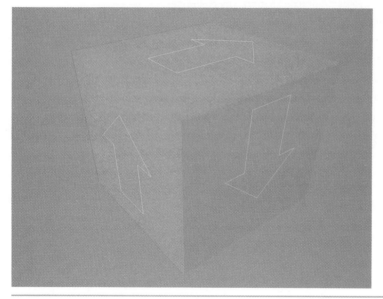

Figure 35-6. Tangents Rendered by mental ray and Set As Vertex Colors
The arrows illustrate the flow of tangents. In this case, the left front face and the top face are flowing seamlessly, and the right front face is flowing in a different direction.

The tangents could also be recomputed using a plug-in or a script that writes the tangent's results into the color property of the vertex.

The process for creating the texture maps required by the hardware version of the bump-map effect should be as automated as possible. The goal is to bake the complex geometry details and shading effects into the final low-resolution object. The high- and low-resolution models need not have any correlation in their u-v mapping or topology.

Generating normal maps is done in two passes. The first pass computes the normals at the surface of the high-resolution objects in model space by using the texture coordinate parameterization of the low-resolution object.

The technique we use in our test case for the first pass is as follows:

1. The high-resolution objects are temporarily shaded, using a mental ray shader that renders normals as colors.
2. The low-resolution object is rendered completely transparent, so its own geometry is not taken into account when rendering the details of the high-resolution objects.
3. Rendering to a texture is invoked, and the high-resolution objects' details are rendered into the normal map in model space, using the low-resolution object's texture coordinate parameterization.

The geometric details of the high-resolution objects are rendered into the normal map. The cool thing is that geometric operations performed by the software renderer, such as displacement maps and geometry shaders, are taken into account. The possibility exists to "bake" procedural geometries, such as hair or particles, with this method.

The second pass uses the previously computed tangents on the low-resolution object, plus the normal map in model space, to create the normal map in tangent space.

The technique we use for the second pass is as follows:

1. Make all objects, except low-resolution objects, temporarily invisible.
2. On the surface of the low-resolution object, sample the normal map in model space.
3. On the surface of the low-resolution object, sample the tangent by using the vertex color property.
4. Using the normal and the tangent, compute the binormal to create the new referential of the sampled normal.
5. Transform the sampled normal from model space to tangent space.

Generating the diffuse map is similar. In our case, an issue arises when we compute this map. Because the software renderer might execute a network of arbitrary material shaders, it is impossible to extract the different terms of the lighting equation and return the diffuse color without any lighting on it. But we can trick the renderer by providing even lighting across the surface of the objects. This trick allows the diffuse color to show up evenly, regardless of the light setup of the scene or the surface normal.

The following steps are performed to do this:

1. Ambient and specular contributions are temporarily disabled on high-resolution objects. This ensures that we get a pure diffuse map.

2. Lights in the scenes are temporarily disabled, and a light rig is put in place to evenly light the high-resolution objects.

3. The low-resolution object is rendered completely transparent, so that its own geometry is not taken into account when rendering the details of the high-resolution objects.

4. Rendering to a texture is invoked. The high-resolution objects' details are rendered into the normal map in model space, using the low-resolution object texture coordinate parameterization.

Even though our light rig setup allows us to sample the diffuse color without too much of the lighting contribution, we still get some lighting artifacts. These artifacts can be corrected using color-correction tools.

During rendering of the diffuse map pass, the shading effects that affect the diffuse color of the objects are taken into account. Artists can use procedural effects such as marble, wood, or noise textures, which are automatically baked into the surface map.

When the environment is static, we can use environment maps to simulate reflective materials. In this case, we can effectively take advantage of the high-end rendering software to generate high-quality environment maps that can even take advanced rendering effects, such as global illumination and final gathering, into account. The two most common environment maps are cubic maps and spherical maps.

For cubic maps, the rendering must be set up to fit on the bounding cube of the object and render the environment on that cube. For each face of the cube, we render the reflected image from the point of view of the reflective object. The maps generated are then used in a hardware reflection-map shader in the graphics pipeline.

For spherical maps, the camera field of view must be set up to render a hemisphere covering the part of the object that faces the viewpoint, which is then used in the hardware graphics pipeline as a spherical map for an environment shader.

This method bakes the entire advanced rendering functionally such as global illumination models and caustics using software renderers, into the resulting texture map.

35.5 Test Case and Results

To illustrate the technique documented in this chapter, we present a real-life test case and then comment on the results.

The high-resolution model we are using for the test case has 440 distinct polygon meshes and a little over 260,000 triangles. See Figures 35-7 and 35-8. The model has different types of material attached to each section of the character. The armor plates are made of a reflective, Phong-type material; the fabric on the arms is made of a nonreflective, Lambert-type material.

The low-resolution model is composed of a single mesh and just under 4,000 triangles, as shown in Figure 35-9. Two types of real-time shaders will be attached to this model: (1) the real-time equivalent of a reflective bump map, which will be used for the armor; and (2) a simple nonspecular bump map, which will be used for the fabric on the arms.

The high-resolution and low-resolution models have very different topologies. The high-resolution model itself has no texture coordinates, and it does not result from texture maps. All the details on the high-resolution model have been modeled as polygonal meshes. On the other hand, the low-resolution model relies entirely on texture maps to get to the result. In this case, we use two different maps: a normal map in tangent space and a diffuse map for the illumination color. The final real-time shading takes these maps as input and produces the final image, shown in Figure 35-10.

Notice that small details on the armor, as well as the cloth quilting, actually do not exist as geometry. The GPU surface FX plug-in bakes these details into the normal maps used for the bump-map real-time effect from the high-resolution model. The same normal map is also used for doing reflection bump mapping, so the surface details appear to be distorting the reflection map.

Figure 35-7. Wireframe View of the High-Resolution Model
This model will be used as a source for generating attribute maps for real-time output.

Figure 35-8. Final Rendering of the High-Resolution Model
The final rendering was done with mental ray.

Figure 35-9. Wireframe View of the Low-Resolution Model
Real-time shading techniques will be applied to this model to approximate the look of the original, high-resolution model.

Figure 35-10. Real-Time Shading View of the Low-Resolution Model
Real-time shading techniques make this model look like the original, high-resolution model. Final rendering was done using Cg shaders.

Looking closely at the generated maps, we can see that the intermediate normal map in object space, shown in Figure 35-11, contains all the surface details of the high-resolution model. The surface of the high-resolution model is projected into the u-v space of the low-resolution model.

The normal map in tangent space, shown in Figure 35-12, is derived from the normal map in object space and the tangents of the low-resolution model.

Figure 35-13 shows the surface map that is used as the color component of the real-time effect. We can see that we have obtained good results in extracting the color from the original model as seen in Figure 35-8.

Figure 35-14 compares the software-rendered and hardware-rendered models. The result is very close to the original. However, several conditions are required for the system to generate good attribute maps. The first requirement is that the u-v space used by the low-resolution model must be adequate: it should be nonoverlapping and have minimal discontinuities. The second requirement is that the shape of the high-resolution model must resemble that of the low-resolution model. The shapes do not need a topological correlation, but the forms of both models should be similar. This requirement allows the

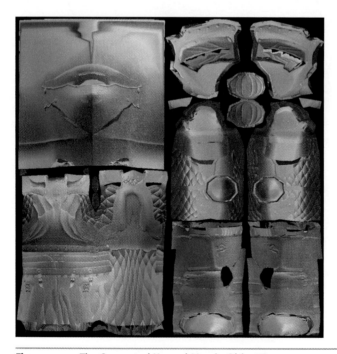

Figure 35-11. The Generated Normal Map in Object Space

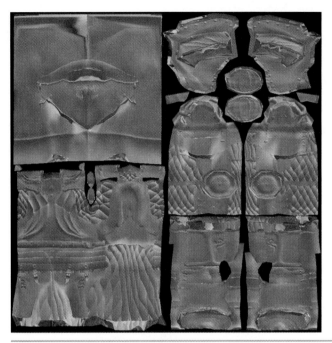

Figure 35-12. The Generated Normal Map in Tangent Space

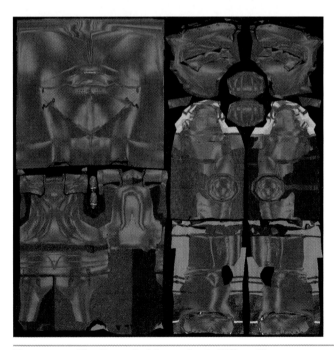

Figure 35-13. The Generated Approximate Diffuse Map

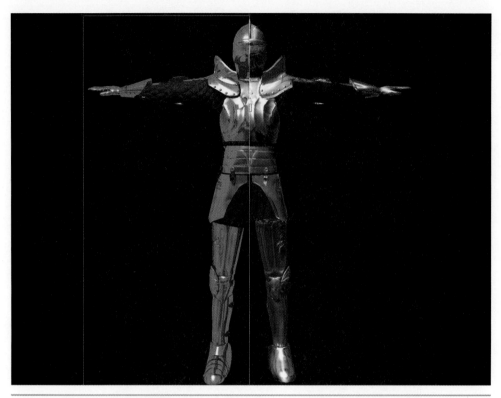

Figure 35-14. Comparing Renderers
A side-by-side comparison of the software-rendered, high-resolution model (on the left) and the hardware-rendered, low-resolution model (on the right). Note that the arms and legs do not have the same colors. The right arm and left leg are red, and the left arm and right leg are black on the original source material.

generation of attribute maps to minimize errors when projecting the attributes of the high-resolution model onto the low-resolution model. In this test case, the artist manually edited the u-v coordinates to maximize the usage of the texture map on the surface of the model. In terms of shape delta, we found that the maximum projected distance from the high-resolution model and the low-resolution model should be relatively small.

35.6 Conclusion

High-end software rendering tools offer a robust and flexible pipeline for generating simple attribute maps such as diffuse and normal maps. The workflow we've described demonstrates how an artist's creativity can be enhanced by using an arbitrary set of high-resolution models with an arbitrary set of shader networks to generate attribute data used in the hardware-rendering pipeline and how the artist can easily iterate on the results achieved in the process.

The tools for baking down information from high-resolution models and complex shaders to usable hardware-rendering components need to be automated, keeping technical details away from the artist. Finally, if the tool set is flexible, it can be adapted to generate other types of attribute maps and to work with different hardware-rendering techniques.

The technique does need some improvements. The generation of the surface map (shown in Figure 35-13) still exhibits some shading artifacts, which require correcting with image-editing software. In the future, we will consider using a different technique to get rid of these shading artifacts. Also, rendering speed will almost always be an issue, simply because it is the bottleneck of the iterative process.

35.7 References

AVID Corporation. "Leveraging the Power of the GPU with SOFTIMAGE XSI." Available online at **http://www.softimage.com**

AVID Corporation. *XSI User Manual.*

Driemeyer, Thomas, ed. 2001. *Rendering with Mental Ray*, 2nd ed. Springer.

Driemeyer, Thomas, and Rolf Herken, eds. 2003. *Programming Mental Ray*, 2nd ed. Springer.

Fernando, Randima, and Mark J. Kilgard. 2003. *The Cg Tutorial.* Addison-Wesley.

Kilgard, M. J. 2000. "A Practical and Robust Bump-Mapping Technique for Today's GPUs." Available online at **http://developer.nvidia.com**

Microsoft Corporation. *DirectX 8.0 Programmer's Reference.* Available online at **http://msdn.microsoft.com/directx**

NVIDIA Corporation. 2002. *Cg Toolkit User's Manual: A Developer's Guide to Programmable Graphics.* Available online at **http://developer.nvidia.com**

Chapter 36

Integrating Shaders into Applications

John O'Rorke
Monolith Productions

36.1 Introduction

This chapter addresses the issues associated with adding support for shaders into an application to improve its flexibility and ease its maintenance. This chapter does not cover individual APIs for dealing with shaders or shader languages. Instead, it takes a high-level view of the communication layer needed between the application and the shader to create a flexible and powerful, data-driven renderer. The motivation for this chapter is simple: When designing a shader-driven renderer, I found plenty of documentation for authoring shaders and for using the associated APIs. But nothing discussed what an application needs to provide to enable robust handling of different shaders. Many articles discussed how one can get variable names and annotations from an effect, but they never mentioned how an application should use that information to provide the necessary data to the shaders. A fair amount of work must be put into an application for it to support shaders in a flexible manner. This chapter attempts to identify each of these areas and provide suggestions for an efficient and powerful solution.

The techniques for managing shaders described here have come from trial-and-error personal experience, discussions with other engineers, and analysis of other applications that perform similar tasks. They are designed to act as the glue between an application's technical design and the selected shader API.

36.2 About Shaders

Let's examine the role of shaders before we integrate them into an application. The purpose of the shader is to specify a way to render a collection of geometry. If taken to the appropriate scale, shaders let us treat the rendering state as a resource. This is amazingly powerful, because it allows the renderer of an application to be almost entirely resource driven.

In the past, only external resource files were able to control aspects of rendering, such as textures and meshes. But now, with shaders, even the setup of the device that renders the actual geometry can be treated as an external resource. This technique has long benefited the film industry (with languages such as the RenderMan Shading Language), and it has dramatically increased the flexibility of real-time rendering. This shader-driven approach allows for more variety in rendering a scene because it doesn't require adding custom code to the application. Plus, it lets us easily add and maintain many more methods of rendering and allow for rapid prototyping of new effects and optimizations. In the future, as better tools are developed, this capability may even give complete control of the rendering to artists.

36.2.1 Shader Languages

Already there is a wide variety of real-time shader languages, and more languages are bound to appear in the future. These shader languages can be grouped into two categories: individual programs and *effect files*.

Individual Programs

The individual-program approach consists of a collection of files, each of which implements either a vertex shader or a pixel shader for a single pass of rendering. Examples are the Cg programming language and standard vertex and pixel shader files. In addition, many custom implementations of shader languages fall into this category, because of the simplicity of the implementation. However, a downside to this approach is that it becomes difficult to construct and manage a large number of complex effects in this manner, because each pass typically requires two source files: one for the vertex unit and another for the pixel unit.

The major problem with this approach, though, is that because other device states—such as fill mode or cull mode—are not tied to an individual vertex or pixel shader program, it is difficult to control this state using individual files. Picture an object that renders two passes: the first pass is a solid Gouraud fill, and the second pass is a flat wireframe color. This simple process requires up to four individual shaders: two for the vertex units and two for the pixel units. It also requires logic in the application to change the fill-mode state of the device to wireframe on the second rendering pass when using these shaders.

As you can see, it would be nice if all the programs for a particular rendering style could be neatly bundled into a single shader resource that could control the entire device state. This is where effect files come into play.

Effect Files: Why Use Them?

The most prevalent implementations of effect files are Microsoft's effect framework (Microsoft 2003) and NVIDIA's CgFX (NVIDIA 2003), which is a superset of the Microsoft effect framework. The effect-file approach allows individual pixel and vertex programs to be placed into a single file. These vertex and pixel shaders can then be grouped into passes and techniques. By introducing these concepts of techniques and passes, the effect files allow the device state to be specified per pass, thus resulting in a more manageable, more resource-driven, and ultimately more powerful approach over a collection of various vertex and pixel shader files. Listing 36-1 is an example of an effect file.

Listing 36-1. A Sample Effect File

```
// Our vertex format
struct SVertex {
  float3 Position : POSITION;
  float4 Color    : COLOR0;
} ShaderVertex;

// Scene parameters
float4x4 CameraTrans : WorldViewProjection;

// Material parameters
float4 FillColor : MaterialParam <string desc = "object color">;

//Selected rendering technique
struct SVSOut {
  float4 Position : POSITION;
  float4 Color    : COLOR0;
};
```

Listing 36-1 (*continued*). A Sample Effect File

```
SVSOut Selected_VS(MaterialVertex IN) {
  SVSOut OUT;
  OUT.Position = mul(CameraTrans, float4(IN.Pos, 1.0f));
  OUT.Color = FillColor * IN.Color;
  return OUT;
}

struct SPSOut {
  float4 Color : COLOR;
};

SPSOut Selected_PS(SVSOut IN) {
  SPSOut OUT;
  OUT.Color = IN.Color;
  return OUT;
}

technique Selected
{
  pass p0
  {
    CullMode = CCW;
    BlendEnable = false;

    VertexShader = compile vs_1_1 Selected_VS();
    PixelShader = compile ps_1_1 Selected_PS();
  }
}
```

Throughout the remainder of this chapter, we will examine techniques for incorporating effect files into applications based upon the standards established by Microsoft and NVIDIA. The reason for using effect files in this chapter is that every feature that effect files provide—from coordinating which shaders must be used for each pass, to setting up the device state—needs to be supported in any robust shader system that is to be integrated into an application.

From personal experience, I recommend using these effect systems rather than trying to create a custom implementation. Used appropriately, they can be very efficient, very simple to work with, much faster for authoring shaders, and less prone to error. The APIs for using these shader languages are also very easy to work with, and they significantly reduce development time. In addition, using an external implementation helps future-proof your application, because it helps insulate the application from underlying platform-specific APIs. However, using an existing API may not be an option on certain platforms at present, so in these cases a custom approach must be implemented. Even in such a case, if a custom-made system is needed, effect-file standards should be carefully studied as a model foundation of a robust and flexible shader system.

36.3 The Anatomy of an Effect File

This section analyzes the parts of the effect file we will be using, and it examines each component that is relevant to communication between a shader and an application that we will be using later. It does not address the full syntax of the effect file format but simply identifies the relevant components.

Again, even systems not using the effect format can, and should, try to include equivalent constructs to allow integration into their applications.

36.3.1 Variables

Variables in an effect file serve the same role as variables in any other programming language. Each has a unique name and an associated value, and each can be one of many different types, including strings, structures, and multidimensional arrays. All variables in the global scope can be enumerated by the application and have their values read or written by the application. These global variables are the primary method of conveying data to shaders, such as which texture should be applied or what the current camera transform is.

An application can determine not only the values of global parameters, but also the type of each variable, so that the application can ensure type safety when writing data out to, or reading data in from, the shader. Global variables in an effect file have an associated tag—called a *semantic*—that is not found in other languages. A semantic is an additional textual symbol; this symbol can be associated with the variable to be queried by the application. The semantic can be used by the application for any purpose, but it often specifies how a variable is to be used or what data the variable needs. The following is an example of a variable with a semantic called `LightRadius`, which can then be read in by an application at runtime:

```
float Radius = 1.0 : LightRadius;
```

36.3.2 Structures

Effect file structures are similar to C-style structures. They contain a collection of variables that will be instantiated once per instance of the structure. Each entry in the structure can contain a semantic as well, much like global parameters. Structures cannot be accessed directly by the application, however. Information about a structure must be gathered through an instance of the structure. So if a definition of a structure is important to an application, a variable instance of the structure must be defined within the shader, and that variable is then examined by the application.

36.3.3 Passes

A pass represents the device state for a single rendering pass of a shader. This includes the associated vertex and pixel pipeline setup. Each pass can have a unique name associated with it and can be accessed by the application. The pass serves as the atomic rendering unit. It is ultimately the source of the device state, and if an object is to be rendered, there must be an active pass to indicate how it is to be rendered.

36.3.4 Techniques

Rendering in a certain style often requires multiple passes, which therefore requires some means of grouping passes. This is the role played by the technique. A technique is a named wrapper for a collection of passes and serves as the atomic unit for device validation. This means that when the effect API checks for support on a device, each pass within a technique is checked to see if it can operate on the device. If any pass is not supported by the device, the entire technique is considered unsupported on the device. For this reason of validation, passes cannot exist outside a technique. At runtime, techniques also provide support for iterating through each contained pass and accessing information about each pass.

36.3.5 Annotations

Annotations are user data attached to the techniques, passes, and global variables of an effect file. Annotations let the shader author provide additional data that can be exported from the shader; they take the form *type name = value;*. The application can then query any technique, pass, or parameter for its annotations. At runtime, each annotation can be queried for its name, type, and value. These annotations are constant and can only be viewed by the applications as read-only. The following code is an example of annotation:

```
float Alpha = 1.0 <string Description = "Opacity of the object";>;
```

36.4 Types of Shader Data

We have identified the primitives that can be used for communication between the shader and the application, but we have not yet described the information that needs to be communicated. This section identifies the information itself; techniques for communicating the information to and from the shader will be discussed later. Figure 36-1 is a diagram that gives a high-level view of how the data interoperates between the application and the shader.

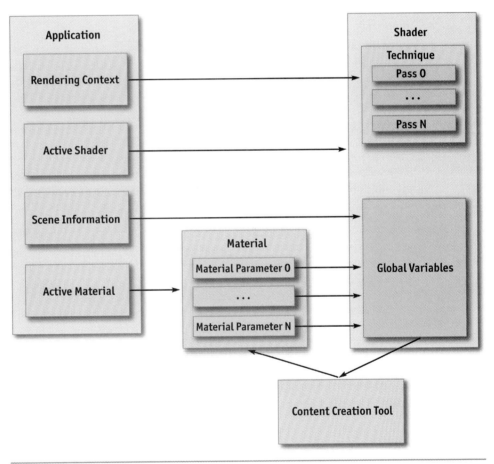

Figure 36-1. Communication Flow Between a Shader and an Application

36.4.1　Scene Information

The first set of data that must be communicated from the application to the shader is the scene information. The scene information contains any rendering state that is required for rendering a shader, effectively acting as a contract between the application and the shader. The shader must know that it can rely on the application to provide certain information through specific variables in order to perform its tasks. Without this scene information, the shader operates in a vacuum and cannot perform even the simplest operation.

Examples of scene information are object-space-to-clip-space transformations, skeletal transforms, camera positions, the current object color, and any other data the application maintains that would be relevant to shaders. This data is one-way, going from the application to the shader, and must be updated in the shader each time the scene information changes.

36.4.2　Materials

The scene information covers application-generated information, but it does not include a critical collection of data that lets the shaders be customized. This data includes any aspect of the shader that is parameterized to allow control by artists. Examples are textures that will be used by the shader, the specular power of a surface, or the speed of a panning texture. The communication of material data is more bidirectional than the scene information. This is because the shader defines the variables that can be supplied by the material, which must be read out by some application or tool. Then the material defines the values for the variables, which must be passed in to the shader.

Materials often fit into the content-creation and rendering pipeline in the following manner: A tool will examine a shader and determine which values should be provided to the shader as material parameters. Then it will allow a content creator to specify these parameters. At rendering time, when a material becomes active, it will fill in all the values that the artist entered into the shader. This flow allows for shaders that have unique and varied data, which can be directly and easily controlled by content creators.

36.4.3　Renderer Context

So far, all the information that has been passed to the shader has come from variables. However, sometimes the shader needs to perform tasks that cannot be data driven. To address this issue, the concept of a *context* is introduced.

The context allows the shader to apply different types of rendering for different situations. Picture an application that has a large collection of shaders in a scene. Each shader has a distinctive look and renders in a particular manner. However, the application needs an effect to play on any object the user selects, but it still must let each shader have its unique look. Therefore, the shader must have a concept of context, which in this case would be one of two states: "selected" or "unselected." The shader can then perform completely different rendering techniques, based on the current context.

36.4.4 Vertex Data

Another form of data the shader requires is, of course, the vertex data itself. Different shaders might require vastly different information, so a shader must be able to indicate which vertex components it needs. For example, a bump-mapping shader may require a full tangent space per vertex and one texture coordinate set, whereas another shader may require only a position, normal, and two texture-coordinate sets. If each shader can indicate which components it requires, the application can then generate only the necessary vertex components, which saves bandwidth and memory.

36.5 Communicating with the Shader

Now that we have identified the data that needs to be sent to and from the shader, as well as the facilities available for this communication, we now examine the process of setting up an application to allow shader support.

36.5.1 Scene Information

The first issue is how to send the scene information to the shader. A shader can't do anything if it doesn't have the correct transforms and other necessary data. This data will be passed to the shader through global variables because it's the only communication method available to the shader for providing values from the application. The trick is finding the variables in the shader that are expected to contain the desired scene information.

Use the Variable Name

The most straightforward approach to determine which variables should hold the scene information is to simply use the name and type of the global variables. For example, the application could enumerate the global variables within the shader, and when it finds a variable named `CameraTransform` that is a 4×4 matrix, it installs the camera transform matrix into that variable.

This approach forces consistency across all shaders, because the naming of variables must be consistent across all shaders used by the application for it to work properly. For a large shader library, this method is useful if different people work on or maintain the library.

Use Semantics or Annotations

A more flexible approach is to use the semantics or annotations associated with the global variables. For example, inside annotations could be a key/value pair similar to `string Usage = "CameraTransform"`. Or the variable could have a specific semantic indicating the usage. This usage value could be read to determine the value that should be loaded into the variable at runtime.

This approach is more flexible because it lets shader authors name the variables whatever they like, as long as they correctly indicate the usage. The semantic approach is used by FX Composer, developed by NVIDIA. (See Chapter 31, "Using FX Composer.") The following sample variable declaration uses semantics that work with FX Composer and receive the camera transformation at runtime:

```
float4x4 wvp : WorldViewProjection;
```

Optimizing Scene Communication

Resolving the mapping of a variable to its value can be costly because it can involve iterating through a large number of variables and performing numerous string operations. So, this mapping should be performed only once, when the shader is created. All current effect APIs support handles that allow direct access to variables, techniques, passes, and even annotations. However, these handles are not transferable between shaders, so a single handle cannot be created that refers to a specific variable across all shaders. Instead, a handle must be created for each variable in each shader. A simple implementation of this caching mechanism is to create a handle table per shader, where each entry in the table refers to a specific variable. Then, when a value in the scene information changes, the table of the active shader can be indexed directly, based on what variable is being set to find the appropriate handle, which can then be used to communicate the new data to the shader. In addition, when the active shader changes, all scene information has to be set up in the new shader. This can be done by running through the handle table and providing the scene data for each value of scene information.

36.5.2 Material Parameters

Like scene information parameters, material parameters are communicated to the shader; however, unlike scene information, this data typically comes from a material resource that has been set up by content creators. Therefore, a mechanism must exist to map this data from a resource into the global variables of a shader. For material parameters, using the name is not a very good solution, because the material parameters can vary widely across shaders and are often relevant to only a single shader.

Instead, annotations or a semantic indicating a material parameter can be used. Then any variable with a specific annotation or semantic set would be treated as a material parameter, allowing a value to be specified in the material.

Annotations can be adapted for many other purposes for material parameters. A string annotation can provide a description for tools to provide help for the parameter. Or a default value can be specified if no value exists. The information needed in the annotation depends on the functionality the application is intended to support, but generally it is best to have at least a default value and a description for each variable. The following example shows how a material parameter could be set up with semantics indicating that it is a material parameter; annotations provide information that can be used by either a material creation tool or the application at runtime.

```
float Specular = 4.0 : MaterialParam <
    float Default = 4.0;
    string Desc = "Specular power of the surface";
    float Min = 2.0;
    float Max = 8.0;>;
```

36.5.3 Vertex Format

There are many different ways to determine what vertex data is needed by a particular shader. The first method is to name variables specifically to indicate different vertex components. For example, there could be a collection of predefined variable names, such as `Vertex_Normal`, `Vertex_Position`, and so on. Each shader would be checked to determine which variables it contains, and for each one, the appropriate vertex information would be included in any vertices the shader renders.

A more elegant approach is to create a structure that contains an entry for each vertex element that is needed. The names of these variables, or their associated semantics, can then be used to determine the necessary vertex components. This is probably the most intuitive method, because the concept of vertex data maps well to a structure, and most shaders use a structure of some sort to represent the incoming vertex data already. The one caveat is that structures cannot be examined directly; therefore, an instance of that structure must be defined. Here is an example:

```
struct SVertex
{
    float3 vPosition : Position;
    float3 vNormal   : Normal;
};
SVertex VertexDecl;
```

Some other possibilities for specifying the necessary vertex data: have a string variable that contains a delimited list of components that can be parsed, or have a single variable and specify the components using annotations.

Using one of these methods, we can determine the information that needs to be provided for each vertex in any geometry the shader will be rendering. This data can be used at preprocessing time if the shader that will be bound to the geometry is known at that time, which allows us to generate and pack only those vertex components the shader needs. This approach can significantly reduce the amount of memory needed to store geometry for most shaders, while still allowing for shaders that require complex vertex information. However, if the shader is not known at preprocessing time, we need to use a vertex format that includes all possible vertex data. Or else we need runtime support for generating vertex information, neither of which are optimal solutions.

36.5.4 Context

The concept of a context maps directly to a technique. For each context the application requires, we need to place a corresponding technique in the shader. Let's use the original context example of an application that needs each shader to render in a different style when the object is selected. Inside the shader could be two different techniques: Selected and Unselected. When it's time for the object to be rendered, the appropriate technique is activated based on the state of the object, and then the object rendering proceeds using that technique. This allows each shader to implement an appropriate style of rendering for any context the application needs. Plus, it lets the application ensure that the shader can change the manner in which it operates to function appropriately for any situation needed. To make this work, though, a contract between the shader and the renderer must exist. It would function much like scene variables, in which the renderer calls each context in a specific situation to render in a certain manner, and in return, the shader is expected to work properly in each situation. However, this contract between the shaders and the renderer depends on each application, which makes this context-binding method very application-specific as well.

36.5.5 Techniques vs. Passes for Context

An argument can be made that passes, instead of techniques, should be used to represent context within a shader. The reason? Techniques are validated as a whole; therefore, they avoid a situation where one context may validate correctly while another context fails. This could cause objects to be visible in one context but invisible in another.

Using passes for contexts adds work and reduces clarity somewhat, but it can be implemented easily by using a naming convention for the pass name. The naming convention would indicate the context name and the pass number. The following code is an example of a technique that holds two contexts, with the Selected context requiring two passes:

```
technique SomeShader
{
   pass Selected_0 { . . . }
   pass Selected_1 { . . . }
   pass Unselected_0 { . . . }
}
```

Then, when the application loads a shader, a valid technique would be found for the current device and the passes would be parsed. Parsing determines which passes need to be rendered, and in what order, when a certain context is used. This approach makes it easier to add support for fallbacks within the same shader file. We recommend this approach when supporting a wide range of hardware.

36.6 Extending the Effect File Format

We can integrate a full shader system into an application and create a very powerful and flexible renderer by using the approaches discussed in this chapter. However, we can add a few more extensions to the application and shaders to make shader development and management much easier.

36.6.1 Supporting the Preprocessor

An application that provides preprocessor support for shaders is invaluable. All current effect APIs allow support for the preprocessor if the application includes certain hooks for the include directive. These hooks let applications implement their own file system, and it's usually simple to add support for the hooks. An important consideration is the current working directory, which is defined as relative to the file that is currently being compiled.

Once preprocessor support is added to the application, a full utility library of standard definitions and functions can quickly be created. This helps reduce the size and complexity of individual shaders. For example, we can create a shader file that contains utility functions for skinning models. This file could be included in any shader requiring skinning, thus reducing the size of each shader and the amount of code that must be duplicated between shaders.

36.6.2 Supporting Shader Variations

With careful setup, the preprocessor can allow the same shader to be used for both rigid and skinned objects. The only difference between skinned and rigid meshes is the manner in which any geometry-related data—including the position and the tangent space of the vertex—is obtained. Therefore, with rigid meshes, the geometry data is used as specified in the vertex, but in skinned meshes, it must undergo a skinning process before the vertex data is used. Therefore, all accesses to the geometry information can be hidden behind code that can be conditionally compiled either to perform skinning of the vertex data or simply to return the vertex data as stored.

Also, bone weights data (and possibly bone indices data) is needed. This can be added using a macro that expands to nothing for rigid shaders and expands to the appropriate definitions needed for declaring the vertex data in skeletal shaders. If this is done, only a single shader needs to be developed. Compiling this shader with a different set of preprocessor definitions can change it to support either skinned meshes or rigid meshes, as shown in Listing 36-2.

Listing 36-2. Using the Preprocessor to Support Skeletal Shader Variations

```
#ifdef SKELETAL
    //Used in the vertex struct to indicate the weights of the vertex
    #define DECLARE_SKELETAL_WEIGHTS float4 Weights : BLENDWEIGHT
    //Used anywhere that point data is accessed from a vertex
    #define SKIN_POINT(Point, Vert) SkinPoint(Point, Vert.Weights)
    //Used anywhere that vector data is accessed from a vertex
    #define SKIN_VECTOR(Vector, Vert) SkinVector(Vector, Vert.Weights)
#else
    //We aren't supporting skeletal animation
    #define DECLARE_SKELETAL_WEIGHTS
    #define SKIN_POINT(Point, Vert) (Point)
    #define SKIN_VECTOR(Vector, Vert) (Vector)
#endif
```

A similar approach can be taken with the number of lights being rendered. A macro can define the number of lights supported, and the shader can simply iterate through to the number specified by the macro. This allows for getting numerous light variations from only a single shader source file.

36.6.3 Adding Shader Inheritance

Another useful extension is the concept of inheritance. The idea is that if a shader cannot be properly validated, or if a cheaper shader needs to be used, a fallback shader can be substituted for the specified shader. This can be implemented at a global level with a string parameter that indicates the shader file to which the shader will fall back. It can also be implemented at a per-technique level, by specifying a fallback shader using the appropriate annotations. However, if a shader uses inheritance, the material parameters and vertex declarations must be determined as the union of all shaders from which the shader derives, in addition to its data, because it is not known in advance when the fallback shader may need to be used.

Implementation of inheritance is usually simple, and it dramatically improves hardware scalability and performance. In the future, this will be increasingly important, due to the inevitable wide range of hardware capabilities in the marketplace.

36.7 Conclusion

A fair amount of work goes into developing a communication layer that supports shaders. However, if you follow these guidelines, the task is straightforward and results in an amazingly flexible and powerful renderer.

Shaders are the future of real-time rendering. By integrating shaders into the rendering pipeline now, you'll allow applications to take the next step forward in power and flexibility. Doing so will not only allow the applications to be more competitive, but also simplify development of the renderer and accommodate a wide variety of effects.

36.8 References

Microsoft Corporation. 2003. "Effect Reference." MSDN Online.
http://msdn.microsoft.com/library/default.asp?url=/library/en-us/directx9_c/directx/graphics/reference/EffectFileReference/EffectFileReference.asp

NVIDIA Corporation. 2003. "CgFX Overview." Available online at
http://developer.nvidia.com/object/cg_users_manual.html

PART VI
BEYOND TRIANGLES

Graphics processors are no longer used just for processing graphics. The advent of graphics processing units (GPUs) that are fully programmable and support floating-point mathematical operations has enabled them to be used for many types of more general-purpose computation as well. Indeed, today's researchers are using GPUs in ways never imagined by their original designers.

This part of the book describes a number of nontraditional applications of GPUs, from simulating physics to rendering stereoscopic images. Although some of these applications may not be widely used on today's hardware, they offer an insight into how graphics processors might be used in the future.

Chapter 37, "A Toolkit for Computation on GPUs" by **Ian Buck** and **Tim Purcell**, provides an introduction to general-purpose computing on the GPU, and it describes a number of programming primitives that can be used to implement general algorithms on the GPU. Even if you didn't know that your GPU can be programmed to sort and search arrays, this chapter will show you how.

Chapter 38, "Fast Fluid Dynamics Simulation on the GPU" by **Mark J. Harris**, describes in detail how to implement a physically accurate fluid simulation that executes entirely on the GPU. Modeling physics is an inherently parallel problem and therefore well suited to the parallel-processing ability of the GPU. As graphics hardware becomes faster, more parallel, and more flexible, we will see more and more types of physical simulation migrating to the GPU. The final output of many physics simulations is graphics, so it makes sense to keep the computation close to the display.

This part also includes two chapters on volume rendering. In 1991, Jim Kajiya famously predicted, "In ten years, all rendering will be volume rendering." Although this prediction has not come true, volume rendering definitely still has advantages for visualizing data that cannot be described as polygonal geometry. As texture memory becomes cheaper and shading power increases, volume rendering will become more widespread. **Chapter 39, "Volume Rendering Techniques"** by **Milan Ikits, Joe Kniss, Aaron Lefohn**, and **Charles Hansen**, provides a nice overview of volume rendering. **Chapter 40, "Applying Real-Time Shading to 3D Ultrasound Visualization"** by **Thilaka Sumanaweera,** describes some of the practical issues that arise when using volume rendering to render ultrasound data.

Chapter 41, "Real-Time Stereograms" by **Fabio Policarpo,** explains how to use the GPU to generate single-image random-dot stereograms (SIRDs). These images are interesting because they prove that the human visual system can infer depth purely from matching features in stereo images, even in the absence of all other depth cues such as texture and perspective. When Bela Julesz invented random-dot stereograms in the 1960s, he probably never imagined that it would be possible to produce stereograms of a dynamic 3D scene in real time.

Finally, in **Chapter 42, "Deformers," Eugene d'Eon** generalizes the concept of animation by encompassing several techniques into what he calls "deformers." Using this definition, he then develops a standard method for obtaining a vertex normal using a Jacobian matrix, hence removing the necessity of using finite differences to derive the gradient vectors.

This part will give you a feel for applications of the GPU outside the normal realm of video games, and we hope it will inspire you to find your own ways to use and abuse the hardware.

Simon Green, NVIDIA

Chapter 37

A Toolkit for Computation on GPUs

Ian Buck
Stanford University

Tim Purcell
Stanford University

Traditionally the GPU has been a rendering coprocessor or, as the name implies, a graphics processing unit to the host PC. Many of the chapters in this book demonstrate how to render cool effects really fast using the GPU. But who says that the GPU is limited just to rendering? The research community has clearly demonstrated how non-graphics-related computing can be performed on the GPU, with more than a dozen papers published in the SIGGRAPH and Graphics Hardware conferences. This chapter discusses some basic approaches for performing general computation on the GPU and demonstrates how to implement some fundamental algorithms needed for many GPU-based applications.

37.1 Computing with the GPU

Why would you want to use a GPU for general computation? First: performance. Modern GPUs perform floating-point calculations much faster than today's CPUs. For example, a 3 GHz Pentium 4 can theoretically issue around 6 billion floating-point multiplies per second (6 gigaflops). However, a fragment program running on the NVIDIA GeForce FX 5900 Ultra achieves over 20 billion multiplies per second,[1] roughly equivalent to a 10 GHz Pentium 4. Combine this computational performance

---

1. Twenty billion multiplies per second is an observed result obtained by executing a fragment shader consisting solely of 1000 `MULR R0, R0, R0` instructions over 262,144 pixels 100 times and then timing the results.

with the increased memory bandwidth available on the GPU—25.3 GB/sec peak compared to the Pentium 4's 5.96 GB/sec peak—and it's clear why the GPU outperforms the CPU.[2]

The second reason is load balancing. If the CPU limits the application performance, leaving the GPU with idle cycles, we can offload work to the GPU with an overall speedup in our application.

Finally, looking toward the future, GPUs are on a much faster performance growth curve than CPUs. The Pentium 4 performance over the two years leading up to June 2003 increased from 4 gigaflops to 6.3 gigaflops, or 0.65 gigaflops per year. NVIDIA GPUs, however, over only a six-month period ending with the release of the GeForce FX 5900 Ultra, increased from 8 gigaflops to 20 gigaflops, a rate of 24 gigaflops per year. In other words, GPUs have passed CPUs in performance and will continue to outpace CPUs in the future.

37.1.1 The Programming Model

As you are probably aware, there's a big difference between programming GPUs versus CPUs. We can't just change a few compiler flags and recompile. The reason is that the programming models are slightly different.

The main distinction is that the GPU is not a serial processor, but a *stream* processor. A serial processor, also known as a von Neumann architecture (von Neumann 1945), executes instructions sequentially, updating memory as it goes. A stream processor works in a slightly different manner—by executing a function (such as a fragment program) on a set of input records (fragments), producing a set of output records (shaded pixels) in parallel. Stream processors typically refer to this function as a *kernel* and to the set of records as a *stream*. Data is streamed into the processor, operated on via a kernel function, and output to memory, as shown in Figure 37-1. Each element passed into the processor is processed independently, without any dependencies between elements. This permits the architecture to execute the program in parallel without the need to expose the parallel units or any parallel constructs to the programmer.

---

2. GeForce FX 5900 Ultra Memory System:
     256-bit DDR @ 425 MHz = $425 \times 2 \times 32$ bytes = 25.3 GB/sec
  Pentium 4 Front Side Bus:
     64-bit QDR @ 200 MHz = $200 \times 4 \times 8$ bytes = 5.96 GB/sec
  1 GB = 2^{30} bytes; 1 MHz = 10^6 Hz

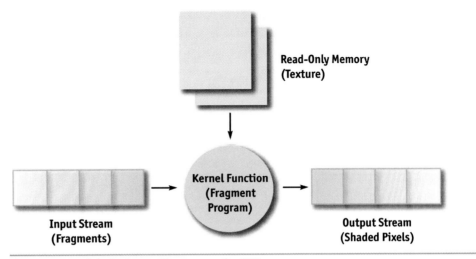

Figure 37-1. Model of a Stream Program on the GPU

As we describe in this chapter, however, these functions and records don't have to be pixels and shaders; they can just as well be arbitrary data, such as mesh points and physics equations. For example, let's say we want to implement a simple particle simulation and let the GPU perform most of the physics operations. Using floating-point textures and pixel buffers (pbuffers), we store the particle positions, velocities, and orientations. A fragment program performs the necessary calculations to compute the new position of a single particle. To compute the new position of all the particles, we simply render a large quad, where the number of fragments in the quad equals the number of particles, as shown in Figure 37-2. The texture coordinates for the quad indicate to the fragment program which stored particle it needs to process. The result stored in the pbuffer contains the new position values.

Our example of a particle system demonstrates an obvious but useful application of the GPU for general-purpose computing. The operation of updating the positions of the particles can be generalized to the process of applying a function to an array of data. This operation—also called a *map* in functional programming languages—can be used for a variety of applications. Simon Green (2003) illustrated how to simulate cloth on the GPU using the same technique as our particle simulator.

37.1.2 Parallel Programming

There are some constraints on what can be mapped to the GPU. The most important is that the function must be parallelizable. Because fragment programs cannot share

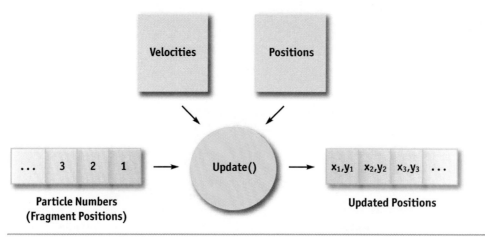

Figure 37-2. Example of a Particle System

writable memory between different fragments, the calculations executed on each particle, mesh point, or whatever, must be computed *independently* of each other. Just as we cannot access the computed result of a neighboring fragment when shading, the function applied to the stream data must observe the same rule. Fortunately, most physical simulations for graphics are naturally parallel, as in the example of our particle system. Each particle does not need to know the newly computed position of its neighbor to update itself.

Using the GPU for general computation poses other challenges, which will be covered later, but the most important consideration in mapping computation to the GPU, or to most stream processors, is mandatory parallelism.

37.1.3 Advanced GPU Programming

Our simple particle system example is interesting, but what if we want to compute something more complex on the GPU? Not all applications can be implemented with a simple *map* operation.

The rest of this chapter describes a few basic tools you can use to implement more advanced algorithms on the GPU, with its parallel programming environment. "Reduce" provides a method to compute a single value from a set of data. "Sort and Search" provides mechanisms to build and use data structures on the GPU. Using these operations, we can perform many general-purpose computing operations that were once left to the CPU.

37.2 Reduce

In general, GPU shaders apply a function to a set of data to produce a set of results, such as applying a fragment program to shade pixels or applying a vertex shader to vertices. In either case, we pass in a set of values and get back a set of results. But what if we want only a *single* result from a set of values? For example, consider the problem of tone mapping. We render a high-dynamic-range scene using floating-point pbuffers and need to display the scene in the frame buffer, which has limited precision. One straightforward approach is to map the largest floating-point value to white and scale the rest of the values accordingly.

How do we get the largest value? We could read back the entire scene and let the CPU perform the computation. However, if we have to do this for every frame, the readback can seriously impede our frame rate. A better solution is to use the GPU to compute the largest value from all the pixels in the scene. In other words, use the GPU to *reduce* the set of floating-point pixels to a single result, the largest value.

In general, a reduction is any operation that computes a single result from a set of data. Examples include min/max, average, sum, product, or any other user-defined function. This section explains how you can use the GPU to compute reductions in just a few passes.

37.2.1 Parallel Reductions

Consider our tone-mapping example. Current graphics hardware lacks built-in features that could provide us the largest floating-point value in a pbuffer. However, we can use the programmable fragment pipeline to do a partial reduction, which will decrease the number of pixels we need to reduce.

The fragment program in Listing 37-1 outputs the largest value of four floating-point values.

Using this program, we can reduce the number of pixels by four, keeping only the larger-valued pixels. Here's how: (1) Bind the image buffer to the texture unit corresponding to the variable img and render a quad one-fourth the size of the image size (each dimension divided by two). (2) Set the texture coordinates so that each fragment of the quad corresponds to a different 2×2 rectangle in the texture. The rendered quad is one-fourth the size of the original image, keeping only the larger values. We can repeat this algorithm with the new image until we have a single floating-point value that can be read back to the CPU, as shown in Figure 37-3.

Listing 37-1. Performing a Partial Reduction

```
float main(float2 texcoord   :  TEXCOORD0,
    uniform samplerRECT img)  :  COLOR
{
    float a, b, c, d;
    a = f1texRECT(img, texcoord);
    b = f1texRECT(img, texcoord + float2(0, 1));
    c = f1texRECT(img, texcoord + float2(1, 0));
    d = f1texRECT(img, texcoord + float2(1, 1));
    return max(max(a, b), max(c, d));
}
```

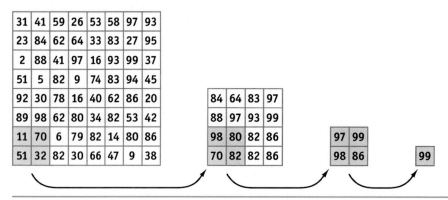

Figure 37-3. Max Reduction Performed with Multiple Passes

Performance

To perform a large reduction of a 1024×1024 image requires only ten passes, with each pass one-fourth the size of the previous pass. In general, $O(\log n)$ passes are required for performing a reduction of n^2 elements. We don't necessarily need to go all the way down to one pixel for the readback. In some cases, it may be faster to read back a small square and let the CPU do the final reductions. We can also increase the number of reductions performed within the fragment program, doing more than just one reduction per pass, decreasing the total number of passes required.

37.2.2 Reduce Tidbits

Although our example is specific to tone mapping, the basic algorithm can be applied anywhere you need to do a reduction, assuming it fits within the constraints of the hardware. Obviously, we need to be able to write the reduction as a fragment program, so we are limited by the number of instructions and the size of outputs. If the GPU supports only a single four-component float output (that is, the fragment color), we cannot implement a reduction operation for a 4×4 matrix multiply (at least, not easily) that requires four four-component float outputs from the shader. Also, the situation can be more complex if the amount of data we are reducing is not a power of two in either dimension.

37.3 Sort and Search

Suppose we want to add collision detection to our particle system example for the GPU. Writing the fragment program to perform a particle-particle interaction is relatively easy. However, as more and more particles are added to the system, interacting every particle with every other particle quickly becomes expensive. The total number of passes is proportional to the number of particles in the system *squared*. To make matters worse, distant particles have little or no effect on a given particle. All the time spent computing interactions between distant pairs of particles is wasted frame time because these particles don't collide.

A better idea is to compute only those interactions with neighboring particles that are likely to produce collisions. One way to do this is to organize particles into a spatial data structure like a uniform grid. Neighboring particles reside in the same grid cell or group of grid cells. This method can reduce the number of particle-collision tests from n^2 to a *constant*, based on the number of particles that fit into a grid cell and on the number of grid cells to be searched.

This section describes the two algorithms required for constructing the uniform-grid data structure for our particle system simulation: *sort* and *search*. We implement sorting as a small multipass shader, and we implement searching in a single rendering pass.

37.3.1 Bitonic Merge Sort

Sorting is a classic algorithmic problem that has inspired many different sorting algorithms. Unfortunately, most sorting algorithms are not well suited for a GPU implementation. *Bitonic merge sort* (Batcher 1968) is a classic parallel sorting algorithm that fits well within the constrained programming environment of the GPU.

The first step in building the uniform grid for our particle system is to sort the data into grid cells. The grid cell location for a particle is determined by dividing the scene's bounding box into cubes (grid cells). Each particle center belongs to exactly one grid cell. We can number the grid cells and then order the particles by ascending grid cell number.

Algorithm

Bitonic merge sort allows an array of n processors to sort n elements in $O(\log^2 n)$ steps: $\log n$ steps of up to $\log n$ stages each. Each stage performs n comparisons and swaps in parallel.

A bitonic merge sort running over an eight-element data set is shown in Figure 37-4. The arrows indicate the two elements to compare (located at the head and tail of each arrow) and the direction to swap them such that we end up with the smallest element at the tail. For example, at stage 1, step 1, we compare 4 and 8 and swap their locations since the smaller element (4) needs to be at the tail of the arrow.

Bitonic merge sort works by repeatedly grouping two sorted sequences to make a bitonic sequence, and then sorting that sequence to form a single sorted list. Recall that a bitonic sequence is one that either monotonically increases and then decreases, or decreases and then increases. Using Figure 37-4 as an example, we can see that at the end of step 1, the initial sequence has been sorted into four sublists: (3, 7), (8, 4), (2, 6), and (5, 1). These four sublists actually make up two bitonic sequences: (3, 7, 8, 4) and (2, 6, 5, 1). These two sequences get sorted in step 2. The two resulting sorted lists form the single bitonic sequence (3, 4, 7, 8, 6, 5, 2, 1). This sequence is sorted in step 3, resulting in the final sorted list.

GPU Implementation

Bitonic merge sort (and binary search, described later) requires a helper function, convert1dto2d, which simply changes 1D array addresses into 2D texture coordinates. Its implementation is straightforward, as shown in Listing 37-2.

Listing 37-2. The Bitonic Merge Sort Helper Function

```
float2 convert1dto2d(float coord1d, float width)
{
  float2 coord2d;
  coord2d.y = coord1d/width;
  coord2d.x = floor(frac(coord2d.y) * width);
  coord2d.y = floor(coord2d.y);
  return coord2d;
}
```

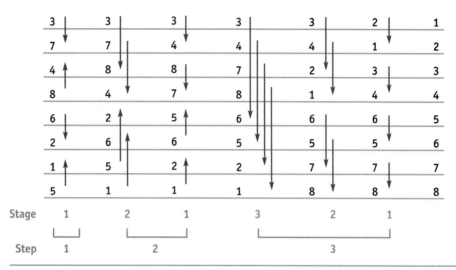

Figure 37-4. Bitonic Merge Sort over Eight Elements
This sort requires three steps of up to three stages each.

Bitonic merge sort is implemented as a multipass shader. Cg code for bitonic merge sort is shown in Listing 37-3. An optimized implementation can be found on the book's CD and Web site.

The data we are sorting is stored in texture memory. Each rendering pass corresponds to a parallel comparison stage. The fragment program computes which two elements need to be compared based on the current step (`stepno`) and stage (`stage`) of the sort. The min or max value of the comparison is written out, again depending on the current stage and step of the sort. The newly generated texture is used as input to the next comparison stage. An n-element sort requires exactly $(\log n \times (\log n + 1)) \div 2$ rendering passes.

Performance

Sorting just over a million elements (stored in a 1024×1024 texture) requires 210 rendering passes. Even the fastest graphics cards today are hard pressed to render 210 passes over a megapixel region in real time. However, sorting a smaller number of elements requires far fewer passes over a much smaller region. A data set of 4,096 elements can be sorted in only 20 milliseconds. Good CPU-based sorting routines have $O(n \log n)$ runtime asymptotics, meaning they will often be able to sort faster than the GPU. However, if the sorted data needs to live in GPU memory, the transfer time to and from the host can negate this advantage.

Listing 37-3. Bitonic Merge Sort

```
float BitonicSort(float2 elem2d : WPOS,
                  uniform float offset,    // offset = 2^(stage - 1)
                  uniform float pbufwidth,
                  uniform float stageno,   // stageno = 2^stage
                  uniform float stepno,    // stepno = 2^step
                  uniform samplerRECT sortedlist) : COLOR
{
  elem2d = floor(elem2d);
  float elem1d = elem2d.y * pbufwidth + elem2d.x;

  half csign = (fmod(elem1d, stageno) < offset) ? 1 : -1;
  half cdir  = (fmod(floor(elem1d/stepno), 2) == 0) ? 1 : -1;

  float adr1d = csign * offset + elem1d;
  float2 adr2d = convert1dto2d(adr1d, pbufwidth);

  float val0 = f1texRECT(sortedlist, elem2d);
  float val1 = f1texRECT(sortedlist, adr2d);

  float cmin = (val0 < val1) ? val0 : val1;
  float cmax = (val0 > val1) ? val0 : val1;

  return (csign == cdir) ? cmin : cmax;
}
```

37.3.2 Binary Search

Search is another classic algorithm. As mentioned during our discussion of sort, most of the algorithms for search do not work in the limited programming environment of the GPU. However, *binary search* is one of the most common searching algorithms, and it maps nicely onto the GPU.

With a sorted list of particles, we have almost all the data to complete our uniform-grid data structure. Although the sorted list has the particles ordered by grid cell, we have no indication of where the sublist of particles for one grid cell ends and the next list begins. We perform several sequential binary searches in parallel over our list of sorted particles to build the uniform grid. Each grid cell initiates a search for itself in the sorted list. The search returns the starting location of the particle list for every grid cell.

Algorithm

Binary search works only on a sorted list of elements. The algorithm works by looking at the middle element of a list and deciding which half of the list to examine further. This test is applied to each subsequent sublist until the sublist is of length 1. At this point, we need a final "correction" comparison to determine whether to increment the position if the value at the final position is not equal to our search value. This is an artifact of searching for the first instance of a given element, as illustrated in Figure 37-5. The algorithm requires $O(\log n)$ comparisons.

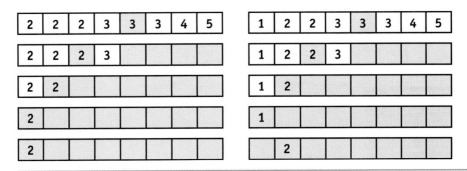

Figure 37-5. Two Binary Searches over Eight Elements for the Value 2
The need for a final correction step can be seen in the right half of the figure, where the first element in the array is a 1 instead of a 2.

GPU Implementation

Binary search easily maps to a single-pass fragment program. The list of elements to be searched is stored in texture memory. A single fragment executes the entire binary search in one execution of the fragment program. The fragment program is a simple unrolled loop that iterates exactly $\log n + 1$ times through the list. The program boils down to a sequence of dependent texture lookups. The final returned value will be either the cell searched for or the next cell's starting location. See Listing 37-4.

The Search routine, shown in Listing 37-5, simply performs the dependent texture fetch, then computes and returns the position to be examined next.

Listing 37-4. Bitonic Search

```
float BinarySearch(float2 elem2d : WPOS,
                   uniform float stride,
                   uniform float pbufwidth,
                   uniform float sortbufwidth,
                   uniform samplerRECT sortlist) : COLOR
{
  elem2d = floor(elem2d);
  float elem1d = elem2d.y * pbufwidth + elem2d.x;
  float curpos = stride;

  //loop over (LOGN - 1) search passes
  for(int i = 0; i < LOGN - 1; i++){
    stride = floor(stride * 0.5);
    curpos = Search(curpos, elem1d, stride,
                    sortlist, sortbufwidth);
  }

  //log nth pass
  curpos = Search(curpos, elem1d, 1.0, sortlist, sortbufwidth);

  //cleanup pass
  curpos = SearchFinal(curpos, elem1d, 1.0, sortlist, sortbufwidth);

  return curpos;
}
```

Listing 37-5. The Search Routine

```
float Search(float curpos,
             float elem,
             float stride,
             uniform samplerRECT data,
             float texw)
{
  float2 adr2d = convert1dto2d(curpos, texw);
  float val = f1texRECT(data, adr2d);
  float dir = (elem <= val) ? -1.0 : 1.0;
  return dir * stride + curpos;
}
```

Recall that after finishing the search, a final "correction" comparison is needed to possibly increment the final location. The code for `SearchFinal` is identical to the code for `Search`, except for one line:

```
float dir = (elem <= val) ? 0.0 : 1.0;
```

Performance

Binary search is very efficient. Unlike reduce and sort, search can often be performed in a single rendering pass. A search for a single element out of more than one million sorted elements (stored in a 1024×1024 texture) requires less than a millisecond. Building a grid data structure and performing several searches in parallel consumes only a few milliseconds.

37.4 Challenges

There are some challenges that come with using current GPUs for computation—namely, limited outputs and slow readback.

37.4.1 Limited Outputs

One difficulty is the number of outputs available in the fragment program. The number of outputs supported by today's GPUs can vary from a single four-component floating-point output to four or more such outputs with the latest hardware. A limited number of outputs can restrict what we can compute in a pass. For example, if we are implementing a ray tracer where each incoming ray may produce multiple output rays (reflection, transmission, and shadow), we can easily be limited by the number of outputs supported by the GPU. This drawback should diminish as GPU technology evolves.

37.4.2 Slow Readback

Readback can be one of the biggest limitations for computation on the GPU. After computing the new particle positions, our application could use the CPU to do some challenging operation, such as collision detection with scene objects. To do this, we would read the values back from graphics card memory with the appropriate API commands. However, this requires that all of our data be sent over the AGP connection, and although modern GPUs support fast 8× AGP transfers, the readback path is only

$1\times$ AGP.[3] This slow transfer could wipe out any performance benefit obtained by off-loading the physics calculation to the GPU. Avoiding this readback penalty provides motivation to put as much of the computation as possible on the GPU. Upcoming PCI Express–compatible motherboards should alleviate this constraint.

37.4.3 GPU vs. CPU

As we've seen in this chapter, many traditional algorithms that excel on the CPU may not map well to the GPU stream programming model. The mandatory parallelism enforced by the stream programming model, in addition to some of the constraints mentioned in this section, can force us to rethink how we solve certain problems. In some cases, the GPU is not the platform of choice for implementing an algorithm. Additionally, programming support tools such as debuggers and profilers are much more readily available on the CPU. However, we expect that many new and exciting algorithms will continue to be written for the GPU, as people learn to map their algorithms onto the stream programming model. The "Further Reading" section of this chapter includes references to some of the exciting things people are implementing on GPUs. These programs include ray tracing, photon mapping, fluid-flow solvers, cloth simulation, and global illumination calculations. Also, we expect the GPU to continue to evolve to more fully support general-purpose computation—including programmer support and tools commonly found for CPU programming.

37.5 Conclusion

This chapter demonstrates that the GPU can do quite a bit more than just render shaded pixels. We've shown four useful operations—*map*, *reduce*, *sort*, and *search*—and provided examples of how they can be used. As GPU performance continues to grow at a rapid pace, it's likely that using the GPU for general-purpose computation will become commonplace.

---

3. The readback limit results from how the AGP specification was originally defined and is a constraint set by all AGP2.0 motherboards, not by the graphics card.

37.6 Further Reading

Note: www.gpgpu.org has links to several recent results and is a great repository of information for general-purpose computing on the GPU.

Batcher, Kenneth E. 1968. "Sorting Networks and Their Applications." *Proceedings of AFIPS Spring Joint Computer Conference* 32, pp. 307–314.

Bolz, Jeff, Ian Farmer, Eitan Grinspun, and Peter Schröder. 2003. "Sparse Matrix Solvers on the GPU: Conjugate Gradients and Multigrid." *ACM Transactions on Graphics* 22(3), pp. 917–924.

Carr, Nathan A., Jesse D. Hall, and John C. Hart. 2002. "The Ray Engine." *Proceedings of the SIGGRAPH/Eurographics Workshop on Graphics Hardware 2002,* pp. 37–46.

Carr, Nathan A., Jesse D. Hall, and John C. Hart. 2003. "GPU Algorithms for Radiosity and Subsurface Scattering." *Proceedings of the SIGGRAPH/Eurographics Workshop on Graphics Hardware 2003*, pp. 51–59.

Goodnight, Nolan, Rui Wang, Cliff Woolley, and Greg Humphreys. 2003. "Interactive Time-Dependent Tone Mapping Using Programmable Graphics Hardware." *Eurographics Symposium on Rendering: 14th Eurographics Workshop on Rendering,* pp. 26–37.

Goodnight, Nolan, Cliff Woolley, Gregory Lewin, David Luebke, and Greg Humphreys. 2003. "A Multigrid Solver for Boundary Value Problems Using Programmable Graphics Hardware." *Proceedings of the SIGGRAPH/Eurographics Workshop on Graphics Hardware 2003*, pp. 102–111.

Green, Simon. 2003. "Stupid OpenGL Shader Tricks." Presentation at Game Developers Conference 2003. Available online at **http://developer.nvidia.com/docs/IO/8230/GDC2003_OpenGLShaderTricks.pdf**

Harris, Mark J., Greg Coombe, Thorsten Scheuermann, and Anselmo Lastra. 2002. "Physically-based Visual Simulation on Graphics Hardware." *Proceedings of the SIGGRAPH/Eurographics Workshop on Graphics Hardware 2002*, pp. 109–118.

Harris, Mark J., William Baxter III, Thorsten Scheuermann, and Anselmo Lastra. 2003. "Simulation of Cloud Dynamics on Graphics Hardware." *Proceedings of the SIGGRAPH/Eurographics Workshop on Graphics Hardware 2003*, pp. 92–101.

Hillesland, Karl E., Sergey Molinov, and Radek Grzeszczuk. "Nonlinear Optimization Framework for Image-Based Modeling on Programmable Graphics Hardware." *ACM Transactions on Graphics* 22(3), pp. 925–934.

Krüger, Jens, and Rüdiger Westermann. 2003. "Linear Algebra Operators for GPU Implementation of Numerical Algorithms." *ACM Transactions on Graphics* 22(3), pp. 908–916.

Ma, Vincent C. H., and Michael D. McCool. 2002. "Low Latency Photon Mapping Using Block Hashing." *Proceedings of the SIGGRAPH/Eurographics Workshop on Graphics Hardware 2002,* pp. 89–99.

Moreland, Kenneth, and Edward Angel. 2003. "The FFT on a GPU." *Proceedings of the SIGGRAPH/Eurographics Workshop on Graphics Hardware 2003*, pp. 112–120.

Purcell, Timothy J., Ian Buck, William R. Mark, and Pat Hanrahan. 2002. "Ray Tracing on Programmable Graphics Hardware." *ACM Transactions on Graphics* 21(3), pp. 703–712.

Purcell, Timothy J., Craig Donner, Mike Cammarano, Henrik Wann Jensen, and Pat Hanrahan. 2003. "Photon Mapping on Programmable Graphics Hardware." *Proceedings of the SIGGRAPH/Eurographics Workshop on Graphics Hardware 2003*, pp. 41–50.

Sen, Pradeep, Michael Cammarano, and Pat Hanrahan. 2003. "Shadow Silhouette Maps." *ACM Transactions on Graphics* 22(3), pp. 521–526.

von Neumann, John. 1945. "First Draft of a Report on the EDVAC." Moore School of Electrical Engineering, University of Pennsylvania, Philadelphia. W-670-ORD-4926.

Chapter 38

Fast Fluid Dynamics Simulation on the GPU

Mark J. Harris
University of North Carolina at Chapel Hill

This chapter describes a method for fast, stable fluid simulation that runs entirely on the GPU. It introduces fluid dynamics and the associated mathematics, and it describes in detail the techniques to perform the simulation on the GPU. After reading this chapter, you should have a basic understanding of fluid dynamics and know how to simulate fluids using the GPU. The source code accompanying this book demonstrates the techniques described in this chapter.

38.1 Introduction

Fluids are everywhere: water passing between riverbanks, smoke curling from a glowing cigarette, steam rushing from a teapot, water vapor forming into clouds, and paint being mixed in a can. Underlying all of them is the flow of fluids. All are phenomena that we would like to portray realistically in interactive graphics applications. Figure 38-1 shows examples of fluids simulated using the source code provided with this book.

Fluid simulation is a useful building block that is the basis for simulating a variety of natural phenomena. Because of the large amount of parallelism in graphics hardware, the simulation we describe runs significantly faster on the GPU than on the CPU. Using an NVIDIA GeForce FX, we have achieved a speedup of up to six times over an equivalent CPU simulation.

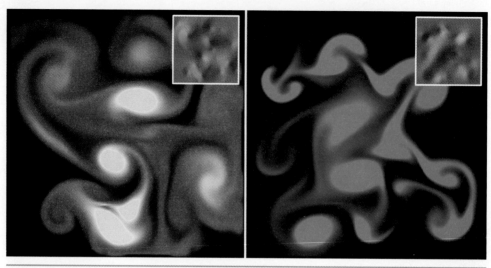

Figure 38-1. Colored "Dye" Carried by a Swirling Fluid
Insets: The velocity field of each fluid. Velocities in the x and y directions are stored in the red and green color channels, respectively.

38.1.1 Our Goal

Our goal is to assist you in learning a powerful tool, not just to teach you a new trick. Fluid dynamics is such a useful component of more complex simulations that treating it as a black box would be a mistake. Without understanding the basic physics and mathematics of fluids, using and extending the algorithms we present would be very difficult. For this reason, we did not skimp on the mathematics here. As a result, this chapter contains many potentially daunting equations. Wherever possible, we provide clear explanations and draw connections between the math and its implementation.

38.1.2 Our Assumptions

The reader is expected to have at least a college-level calculus background, including a basic grasp of differential equations. An understanding of vector calculus principles is helpful, but not required (we will review what we need). Also, experience with finite difference approximations of derivatives is useful. If you have ever implemented any sort of physical simulation, such as projectile motion or rigid body dynamics, many of the concepts we use will be familiar.

38.1.3 Our Approach

The techniques we describe are based on the "stable fluids" method of Stam 1999. However, while Stam's simulations used a CPU implementation, we choose to implement ours on graphics hardware because GPUs are well suited to the type of computations required by fluid simulation. The simulation we describe is performed on a grid of cells. Programmable GPUs are optimized for performing computations on pixels, which we can consider to be a grid of cells. GPUs achieve high performance through parallelism: they are capable of processing multiple vertices and pixels simultaneously. They are also optimized to perform multiple texture lookups per cycle. Because our simulation grids are stored in textures, this speed and parallelism is just what we need.

This chapter cannot teach you everything about fluid dynamics. The scope of the simulation concepts that we can cover here is necessarily limited. We restrict ourselves to simulation of a continuous volume of fluid on a two-dimensional rectangular domain. Also, we do not simulate *free surface* boundaries between fluids, such as the interface between sloshing water and air. There are many extensions to these basic techniques. We mention a few of these at the end of the chapter, and we provide pointers to further reading about them.

We use consistent mathematical notation throughout the chapter. In equations, *italics* are used for variables that represent scalar quantities, such as pressure, p. **Boldface** is used to represent vector quantities, such as velocity, $\mathbf{u}$. All vectors in this chapter are assumed to be two-dimensional.

Section 38.2 provides a mathematical background, including a discussion of the equations that govern fluid flow and a review of basic vector calculus concepts and notation. It then discusses the approach to solving the equations. Section 38.3 describes implementation of the fluid simulation on the GPU. Section 38.4 describes some applications of the simulation, Section 38.5 presents extensions, and Section 38.6 concludes the chapter.

38.2 Mathematical Background

To simulate the behavior of a fluid, we must have a mathematical representation of the state of the fluid at any given time. The most important quantity to represent is the velocity of the fluid, because velocity determines how the fluid moves itself and the things that are in it. The fluid's velocity varies in both time and space, so we represent it as a *vector field*.

A vector field is a mapping of a vector-valued function onto a parameterized space, such as a Cartesian grid. (Other spatial parameterizations are possible, but for purposes of this chapter we assume a two-dimensional Cartesian grid.) The velocity vector field of our fluid is defined such that for every position $\mathbf{x} = (x, y)$, there is an associated velocity at time t, $\mathbf{u}(\mathbf{x}, t) = (u(\mathbf{x}, t), v(\mathbf{x}, t), w(\mathbf{x}, t))$, as shown in Figure 38-2.

The key to fluid simulation is to take steps in time and, at each time step, correctly determine the current velocity field. We can do this by solving a set of equations that describes the evolution of the velocity field over time, under a variety of forces. Once we have the velocity field, we can do interesting things with it, such as using it to move objects, smoke densities, and other quantities that can be displayed in our application.

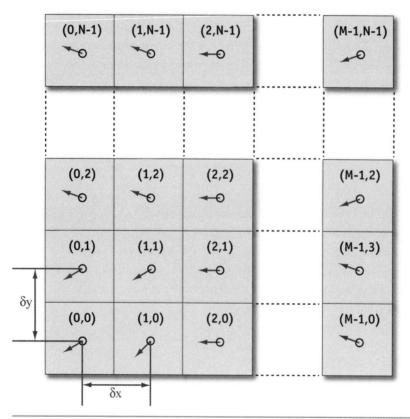

Figure 38-2. The Fluid Velocity Grid
The state of the fluid simulation is represented on an M×N grid like the one shown here. The arrows represent velocity.

38.2.1 The Navier-Stokes Equations for Incompressible Flow

In physics it's common to make simplifying assumptions when modeling complex phenomena. Fluid simulation is no exception. We assume an *incompressible, homogeneous* fluid.

A fluid is incompressible if the volume of any subregion of the fluid is constant over time. A fluid is homogeneous if its density, ρ, is constant in space. The combination of incompressibility and homogeneity means that density is constant in both time and space. These assumptions are common in fluid dynamics, and they do not decrease the applicability of the resulting mathematics to the simulation of real fluids, such as water and air.

We simulate fluid dynamics on a regular Cartesian grid with spatial coordinates $\mathbf{x} = (x, y)$ and time variable t. The fluid is represented by its velocity field $\mathbf{u}(\mathbf{x}, t)$, as described earlier, and a scalar pressure field $p(\mathbf{x}, t)$. These fields vary in both space and time. If the velocity and pressure are known for the initial time $t = 0$, then the state of the fluid over time can be described by the *Navier-Stokes equations for incompressible flow*:

$$\frac{\partial \mathbf{u}}{\partial t} = -\left(\mathbf{u} \cdot \nabla\right)\mathbf{u} - \frac{1}{\rho}\nabla p + \nu\nabla^2\mathbf{u} + \mathbf{F}, \tag{1}$$

$$\nabla \cdot \mathbf{u} = 0, \tag{2}$$

where ρ is the (constant) fluid density, ν is the kinematic viscosity, and $\mathbf{F} = (f_x, f_y)$ represents any external forces that act on the fluid. Notice that Equation 1 is actually two equations, because $\mathbf{u}$ is a vector quantity:

$$\frac{\partial u}{\partial t} = -\left(\mathbf{u} \cdot \nabla\right)u - \frac{1}{\rho}\nabla p + \nu\nabla^2 u + f_x,$$

$$\frac{\partial v}{\partial t} = -\left(\mathbf{u} \cdot \nabla\right)v - \frac{1}{\rho}\nabla p + \nu\nabla^2 v + f_y.$$

Thus, we have three unknowns (u, v, and p) and three equations.

The Navier-Stokes equations may initially seem daunting, but like many complex concepts, we can better understand them by breaking them into simple pieces. Don't worry if the individual mathematical operations in the equations don't make sense yet. First, we will try to understand the different factors influencing the fluid flow. The four terms on the right-hand side of Equation 1 are accelerations. We'll look at them each in turn.

38.2.2 Terms in the Navier-Stokes Equations

Advection

The velocity of a fluid causes the fluid to transport objects, densities, and other quantities along with the flow. Imagine squirting dye into a moving fluid. The dye is transported, or *advected*, along the fluid's velocity field. In fact, the velocity of a fluid carries *itself* along just as it carries the dye. The first term on the right-hand side of Equation 1 represents this *self-advection* of the velocity field and is called the advection term.

Pressure

Because the molecules of a fluid can move around each other, they tend to "squish" and "slosh." When force is applied to a fluid, it does not instantly propagate through the entire volume. Instead, the molecules close to the force push on those farther away, and pressure builds up. Because pressure is force per unit area, any pressure in the fluid naturally leads to acceleration. (Think of Newton's second law, $\mathbf{F} = m\mathbf{a}$.) The second term, called the *pressure term*, represents this acceleration.

Diffusion

From experience with real fluids, you know that some fluids are "thicker" than others. For example, molasses and maple syrup flow slowly, but rubbing alcohol flows quickly. We say that thick fluids have a high *viscosity*. Viscosity is a measure of how resistive a fluid is to flow. This resistance results in diffusion of the momentum (and therefore velocity), so we call the third term the diffusion term.

External Forces

The fourth term encapsulates acceleration due to external forces applied to the fluid. These forces may be either *local forces* or *body forces*. Local forces are applied to a specific region of the fluid—for example, the force of a fan blowing air. Body forces, such as the force of gravity, apply evenly to the entire fluid.

We will return to the Navier-Stokes equations after a quick review of vector calculus. For a detailed derivation and more details, we recommend Chorin and Marsden 1993 and Griebel et al. 1998.

38.2.3 A Brief Review of Vector Calculus

Equations 1 and 2 contain three different uses of the symbol ∇ (often pronounced "del"), which is also known as the *nabla* operator. The three applications of nabla are the gradient, the divergence, and the Laplacian operators, as shown in Table 38-1. The

Table 38-1. Vector Calculus Operators Used in Fluid Simulation

Operator	Definition	Finite Difference Form	
Gradient	$\nabla p = \left(\dfrac{\partial p}{\partial x}, \dfrac{\partial p}{\partial y} \right)$	$\dfrac{p_{i+1,j} - p_{i-1,j}}{2\delta x}$,	$\dfrac{p_{i,j+1} - p_{i,j-1}}{2\delta y}$
Divergence	$\nabla \cdot \mathbf{u} = \dfrac{\partial u}{\partial x} + \dfrac{\partial v}{\partial y}$	$\dfrac{u_{i+1,j} - u_{i-1,j}}{2\delta x} +$	$\dfrac{v_{i,j+1} - v_{i,j-1}}{2\delta y}$
Laplacian	$\nabla^2 p = \dfrac{\partial^2 p}{\partial x^2} + \dfrac{\partial^2 p}{\partial y^2}$	$\dfrac{p_{i+1,j} - 2p_{i,j} + p_{i-1,j}}{(\delta x)^2} +$	$\dfrac{p_{i,j+1} - 2p_{i,j} + p_{i,j-1}}{(\delta y)^2}$

subscripts i and j used in the expressions in the table refer to discrete locations on a Cartesian grid, and δx and δy are the grid spacing in the x and y dimensions, respectively (see Figure 38-2).

The gradient of a scalar field is a vector of partial derivatives of the scalar field. Divergence, which appears in Equation 2, has an important physical significance. It is the rate at which "density" exits a given region of space. In the Navier-Stokes equations, it is applied to the velocity of the flow, and it measures the net change in velocity across a surface surrounding a small piece of the fluid. Equation 2, the *continuity equation*, enforces the incompressibility assumption by ensuring that the fluid always has zero divergence. The dot product in the divergence operator results in a sum of partial derivatives (rather than a vector, as with the gradient operator). This means that the divergence operator can be applied only to a vector field, such as the velocity, $\mathbf{u} = (u, v)$.

Notice that the gradient of a scalar field is a vector field, and the divergence of a vector field is a scalar field. If the divergence operator is applied to the result of the gradient operator, the result is the *Laplacian* operator $\nabla \cdot \nabla = \nabla^2$. If the grid cells are square (that is, if $\delta x = \delta y$, which we assume for the remainder of this chapter), the Laplacian simplifies to:

$$\nabla^2 p = \frac{p_{i+1,j} + p_{i-1,j} + p_{i,j+1} + p_{i,j-1} - 4p_{i,j}}{(\delta x)^2}. \qquad (3)$$

The Laplacian operator appears commonly in physics, most notably in the form of diffusion equations, such as the heat equation. Equations of the form $\nabla^2 x = b$ are known as *Poisson equations*. The case where $b = 0$ is *Laplace's equation*, which is the origin of the Laplacian operator. In Equation 2, the Laplacian is applied to a vector field. This is a notational simplification: the operator is applied separately to each scalar component of the vector field.

38.2.4 Solving the Navier-Stokes Equations

The Navier-Stokes equations can be solved analytically for only a few simple physical configurations. However, it is possible to use numerical integration techniques to solve them incrementally. Because we are interested in watching the evolution of the flow over time, an incremental numerical solution suits our needs.

As with any algorithm, we must divide the solution of the Navier-Stokes equations into simple steps. The method we use is based on the *stable fluids* technique described in Stam 1999. In this section we describe the mathematics of each of these steps, and in Section 38.3 we describe their implementation using the Cg language on the GPU.

First we need to transform the equations into a form that is more amenable to numerical solution. Recall that the Navier-Stokes equations are three equations that we can solve for the quantities u, v, and p. However, it is not obvious how to solve them. The following section describes a transformation that leads to a straightforward algorithm.

The Helmholtz-Hodge Decomposition

Basic vector calculus tells us that any vector $\mathbf{v}$ can be decomposed into a set of basis vector components whose sum is $\mathbf{v}$. For example, we commonly represent vectors on a Cartesian grid as a pair of distances along the grid axes: $\mathbf{v} = (x, y)$. The same vector can be written $\mathbf{v} = x\hat{\mathbf{i}} + y\hat{\mathbf{j}}$, where $\hat{\mathbf{i}}$ and $\hat{\mathbf{j}}$ are unit basis vectors aligned to the axes of the grid.

In the same way that we can decompose a vector into a sum of vectors, we can also decompose a vector field into a sum of vector fields. Let D be the region in space, or in our case the plane, on which our fluid is defined. Let this region have a smooth (that is, differentiable) boundary, ∂D, with normal direction $\mathbf{n}$. We can use the following theorem, as stated in Chorin and Marsden 1993.

> **Helmholtz-Hodge Decomposition Theorem**
> A vector field $\mathbf{w}$ on D can be uniquely decomposed in the form:
>
> $$\mathbf{w} = \mathbf{u} + \nabla p, \tag{7}$$
>
> where $\mathbf{u}$ has zero divergence and is parallel to ∂D; that is, $\mathbf{u} \cdot \mathbf{n} = 0$ on ∂D.

We use the theorem without proof. For details and a proof of this theorem, refer to Section 1.3 of Chorin and Marsden 1993.

This theorem states that any vector field can be decomposed into the sum of two other vector fields: a divergence-free vector field, and the gradient of a scalar field. It also says that the divergence-free field goes to zero at the boundary. It is a powerful tool, leading us to two useful realizations.

First Realization

Solving the Navier-Stokes equations involves three computations to update the velocity at each time step: advection, diffusion, and force application. The result is a new velocity field, $\mathbf{w}$, with *nonzero* divergence. But the continuity equation requires that we end each time step with a divergence-free velocity. Fortunately, the Helmholtz-Hodge Decomposition Theorem tells us that the divergence of the velocity can be corrected by subtracting the gradient of the resulting pressure field:

$$\mathbf{u} = \mathbf{w} - \nabla p. \tag{8}$$

Second Realization

The theorem also leads to a method for computing the pressure field. If we apply the divergence operator to both sides of Equation 7, we obtain:

$$\nabla \cdot \mathbf{w} = \nabla \cdot \left(\mathbf{u} + \nabla p \right) = \nabla \cdot \mathbf{u} + \nabla^2 p. \tag{9}$$

But since Equation 2 enforces that $\nabla \cdot \mathbf{u} = 0$, this simplifies to:

$$\nabla^2 p = \nabla \cdot \mathbf{w}, \tag{10}$$

which is a Poisson equation (see Section 38.2.3) for the pressure of the fluid, sometimes called the *Poisson-pressure equation*. This means that after we arrive at our divergent velocity, $\mathbf{w}$, we can solve Equation 10 for p, and then use $\mathbf{w}$ and p to compute the new divergence-free field, $\mathbf{u}$, using Equation 8. We'll return to this later.

Now we need a way to compute $\mathbf{w}$. To do this, let's return to our comparison of vectors and vector fields. From the definition of the dot product, we know that we can find the projection of a vector $\mathbf{r}$ onto a unit vector $\hat{\mathbf{s}}$ by computing the dot product of $\mathbf{r}$ and $\hat{\mathbf{s}}$. The dot product is a projection operator for vectors that maps a vector $\mathbf{r}$ onto its component in the direction of $\hat{\mathbf{s}}$. We can use the Helmholtz-Hodge Decomposition Theorem to define a projection operator, $\mathbb{P}$, that projects a vector field $\mathbf{w}$ onto its divergence-free component, $\mathbf{u}$. If we apply $\mathbb{P}$ to Equation 7, we get:

$$\mathbb{P}\mathbf{w} = \mathbb{P}\mathbf{u} + \mathbb{P}\left(\nabla p\right).$$

But by the definition of $\mathbb{P}$, $\mathbb{P}\mathbf{w} = \mathbb{P}\mathbf{u} = \mathbf{u}$. Therefore, $\mathbb{P}(\nabla p) = 0$. Now let's use these ideas to simplify the Navier-Stokes equations.

First, we apply our projection operator to both sides of Equation 1:

$$\mathbb{P}\frac{\partial \mathbf{u}}{\partial t} = \mathbb{P}\left(-\left(\mathbf{u} \cdot \nabla\right)\mathbf{u} - \frac{1}{\rho}\nabla p + \nu\nabla^2\mathbf{u} + \mathbf{F}\right).$$

Because $\mathbf{u}$ is divergence-free, so is the derivative on the left-hand side, so $\mathbb{P}(\partial\mathbf{u}/\partial t) = \partial\mathbf{u}/\partial t$. Also, $\mathbb{P}(\nabla p) = 0$, so the pressure term drops out. We're left with the following equation:

$$\frac{\partial \mathbf{u}}{\partial t} = \mathbb{P}\left(-\left(\mathbf{u} \cdot \nabla\right)\mathbf{u} + \nu\nabla^2\mathbf{u} + \mathbf{F}\right). \tag{11}$$

The great thing about this equation is that it symbolically encapsulates our entire algorithm for simulating fluid flow. We first compute what's inside the parentheses on the right-hand side. From left to right, we compute the advection, diffusion, and force terms. Application of these three steps results in a divergent velocity field, $\mathbf{w}$, to which we apply our projection operator to get a new divergence-free field, $\mathbf{u}$. To do so, we solve Equation 10 for p, and then subtract the gradient of p from $\mathbf{w}$, as in Equation 8.

In a typical implementation, the various components are not computed and added together, as in Equation 11. Instead, the solution is found via composition of transformations on the state; in other words, each component is a step that takes a field as input, and produces a new field as output. We can define an operator $\mathbb{S}$ that is equivalent to the solution of Equation 11 over a single time step. The operator is defined as the composition of operators for advection ($\mathbb{A}$), diffusion ($\mathbb{D}$), force application ($\mathbb{F}$), and projection ($\mathbb{P}$):

$$\mathbb{S} = \mathbb{P} \circ \mathbb{F} \circ \mathbb{D} \circ \mathbb{A}. \tag{12}$$

Thus, a step of the simulation algorithm can be expressed $\mathbb{S}(\mathbf{u}) = \mathbb{P} \circ \mathbb{F} \circ \mathbb{D} \circ \mathbb{A}(\mathbf{u})$. The operators are applied right to left; first advection, followed by diffusion, force application, and projection. Note that time is omitted here for clarity, but in practice, the time step must be used in the computation of each operator. Now let's look more closely at the advection and diffusion steps, and then approach the solution of Poisson equations.

Advection

Advection is the process by which a fluid's velocity transports itself and other quantities in the fluid. To compute the advection of a quantity, we must update the quantity at each grid point. Because we are computing how a quantity moves along the velocity field, it helps to imagine that each grid cell is represented by a particle. A first attempt at computing the result of advection might be to update the grid as we would update a particle system. Just move the position, $\mathbf{r}$, of each particle forward along the velocity field the distance it would travel in time δt:

$$\mathbf{r}(t + \delta t) = \mathbf{r}(t) + \mathbf{u}(t)\delta t.$$

You might recognize this as Euler's method; it is a simple method for explicit (or forward) integration of ordinary differential equations. (There are more accurate methods, such as the midpoint method and the Runge-Kutta methods.)

There are two problems with this approach: The first is that simulations that use explicit methods for advection are unstable for large time steps, and they can "blow up" if the magnitude of $\mathbf{u}(t)\delta t$ is greater than the size of a single grid cell. The second problem is specific to GPU implementation. We implement our simulation in fragment programs, which cannot change the locations of the fragments they are writing. This forward-integration method requires the ability to "move" the particles, so it cannot be implemented on current GPUs.

The solution is to invert the problem and use an implicit method (Stam 1999). Rather than advecting quantities by computing where a particle moves over the current time step, we trace the trajectory of the particle from each grid cell back in time to its former position, and we copy the quantities at that position to the starting grid cell. To update a quantity q (this could be velocity, density, temperature, or any quantity carried by the fluid), we use the following equation:

$$q(\mathbf{x}, t + \delta t) = q(\mathbf{x} - \mathbf{u}(\mathbf{x}, t)\delta t, t). \tag{13}$$

Not only can we easily implement this method on the GPU, but as Stam showed, it is stable for arbitrary time steps and velocities. Figure 38-3 depicts the advection computation at the cell marked with a double circle. Tracing the velocity field back in time leads to the green ×. The four grid values nearest the green × (connected by a green square in the figure) are bilinearly interpolated, and the result is written to the starting grid cell.

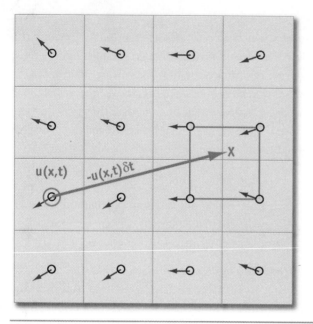

Figure 38-3. Computing Fluid Advection
The implicit advection step traces backward through the velocity field to determine how quantities are carried forward.

Viscous Diffusion

As explained earlier, viscous fluids have a certain resistance to flow, which results in diffusion (or dissipation) of velocity. A partial differential equation for viscous diffusion is:

$$\frac{\partial \mathbf{u}}{\partial t} = \nu \nabla^2 \mathbf{u}. \tag{14}$$

As in advection, we have a choice of how to solve this equation. An obvious approach is to formulate an explicit, discrete form in order to develop a simple algorithm:

$$\mathbf{u}\left(\mathbf{x}, t + \delta t\right) = \mathbf{u}\left(\mathbf{x}, t\right) + \nu \delta t \nabla^2 \mathbf{u}\left(\mathbf{x}, t\right).$$

In this equation, ∇^2 is the discrete form of the Laplacian operator, Equation 3. Like the explicit Euler method for computing advection, this method is unstable for large values of δt and ν. We follow Stam's lead again and use an implicit formulation of Equation 14:

$$\left(\mathbf{I} - \nu \delta t \nabla^2\right) \mathbf{u}\left(\mathbf{x}, t + \delta t\right) = \mathbf{u}\left(\mathbf{x}, t\right), \tag{15}$$

where $\mathbf{I}$ is the identity matrix. This formulation is stable for arbitrary time steps and viscosities. This equation is a (somewhat disguised) Poisson equation for velocity. Remember that our use of the Helmholtz-Hodge decomposition results in a Poisson equation for pressure. These equations can be solved using an iterative relaxation technique.

Solution of Poisson Equations

We need to solve two Poisson equations: the Poisson-pressure equation and the viscous diffusion equation. Poisson equations are common in physics and well understood. We use an iterative solution technique that starts with an approximate solution and improves it every iteration.

The Poisson equation is a matrix equation of the form $\mathbf{Ax} = \mathbf{b}$, where $\mathbf{x}$ is the vector of values for which we are solving (p or $\mathbf{u}$ in our case), $\mathbf{b}$ is a vector of constants, and $\mathbf{A}$ is a matrix. In our case, $\mathbf{A}$ is implicitly represented in the Laplacian operator ∇^2, so it need not be explicitly stored as a matrix. The iterative solution technique we use starts with an initial "guess" for the solution, $\mathbf{x}^{(0)}$, and each step k produces an improved solution, $\mathbf{x}^{(k)}$. The superscript notation indicates the iteration number. The simplest iterative technique is called Jacobi iteration. A derivation of Jacobi iteration for general matrix equations can be found in Golub and Van Loan 1996.

More sophisticated methods, such as conjugate gradient and multigrid methods, converge faster, but we use Jacobi iteration because of its simplicity and easy implementation. For details and examples of more sophisticated solvers, see Bolz et al. 2003, Goodnight et al. 2003, and Krüger and Westermann 2003.

Equations 10 and 15 appear different, but both can be discretized using Equation 3 and rewritten in the form:

$$x_{i,j}^{(k+1)} = \frac{x_{i-1,j}^{(k)} + x_{i+1,j}^{(k)} + x_{i,j-1}^{(k)} + x_{i,j+1}^{(k)} + \alpha b_{i,j}}{\beta}, \tag{16}$$

where α and β are constants. The values of x, b, α, and β are different for the two equations. In the Poisson-pressure equation, x represents p, b represents $\nabla \cdot \mathbf{w}$, $\alpha = -(\delta x)^2$, and $\beta = 4$.[1] For the viscous diffusion equation, both x and b represent $\mathbf{u}$, $\alpha = (\delta x)^2 / \nu \delta t$, and $\beta = 4 + \alpha$.

We formulate the equations this way because it lets us use the same code to solve either equation. To solve the equations, we simply run a number of iterations in which we

---

1. Note that the solution of this equation is actually $p\delta t$, not p. This is not a problem, because the pressure is used only to compute the gradient in the projection step. Because δt is constant over the grid, it does not affect the gradient.

apply Equation 16 at every grid cell, using the results of the previous iteration as input to the next ($\mathbf{x}^{(k+1)}$ becomes $\mathbf{x}^{(k)}$). Because Jacobi iteration converges slowly, we need to execute many iterations. Fortunately, Jacobi iterations are cheap to execute on the GPU, so we can run many iterations in a very short time.

Initial and Boundary Conditions

Any differential equation problem defined on a finite domain requires *boundary conditions* in order to be well posed. The boundary conditions determine how we compute values at the edges of the simulation domain. Also, to compute the evolution of the flow over time, we must know how it started—in other words, its *initial conditions*. For our fluid simulation, we assume the fluid initially has zero velocity and zero pressure everywhere. Boundary conditions require a bit more discussion.

During each time step, we solve equations for two quantities—velocity and pressure—and we need boundary conditions for both. Because our fluid is simulated on a rectangular grid, we assume that it is a fluid in a box and cannot flow through the sides of the box. For velocity, we use the *no-slip* condition, which specifies that velocity goes to zero at the boundaries. The correct solution of the Poisson-pressure equation requires *pure Neumann* boundary conditions: $\partial p / \partial \mathbf{n} = 0$. This means that at a boundary, the rate of change of pressure in the direction normal to the boundary is zero. We revisit boundary conditions at the end of Section 38.3.

38.3 Implementation

Now that we understand the problem and the basics of solving it, we can move forward with the implementation. A good place to start is to lay out some pseudocode for the algorithm. The algorithm is the same every time step, so this pseudocode represents a single time step. The variables u and p hold the velocity and pressure field data.

```
// Apply the first 3 operators in Equation 12.
u = advect(u);
u = diffuse(u);
u = addForces(u);
// Now apply the projection operator to the result.
p = computePressure(u);
u = subtractPressureGradient(u, p);
```

In practice, temporary storage is needed, because most of these operations cannot be performed in place. For example, the advection step in the pseudocode is more accurately written as:

```
uTemp = advect(u);
swap(u, uTemp);
```

This pseudocode contains no implementation-specific details. In fact, the same pseudocode describes CPU and GPU implementations equally well. Our goal is to perform all the steps on the GPU. Computation of this sort on the GPU may be unfamiliar to some readers, so we will draw some analogies between operations in a typical CPU fluid simulation and their counterparts on the GPU.

38.3.1 CPU–GPU Analogies

Fundamental to any computer are its memory and processing models, so any application must consider data representation and computation. Let's touch on the differences between CPUs and GPUs with regard to both of these.

Textures = Arrays

Our simulation represents data on a two-dimensional grid. The natural representation for this grid on the CPU is an array. The analog of an array on the GPU is a texture. Although textures are not as flexible as arrays, their flexibility is improving as graphics hardware evolves. Textures on current GPUs support all the basic operations necessary to implement a fluid simulation. Because textures usually have three or four color channels, they provide a natural data structure for vector data types with two to four components. Alternatively, multiple scalar fields can be stored in a single texture. The most basic operation is an array (or memory) read, which is accomplished by using a texture lookup. Thus, the GPU analog of an array offset is a texture coordinate. We need at least two textures to represent the state of the fluid: one for velocity and one for pressure. In order to visualize the flow, we maintain an additional texture that contains a quantity carried by the fluid. We can think of this as "ink." Figure 38-4 shows examples of these textures, as well as an additional texture for vorticity, described in Section 38.5.1.

Loop Bodies = Fragment Programs

A CPU implementation of the simulation performs the steps in the algorithm by looping, using a pair of nested loops to iterate over each cell in the grid. At each cell, the same computation is performed. GPUs do not have the capability to perform this inner loop over each texel in a texture. However, the fragment pipeline is designed to perform

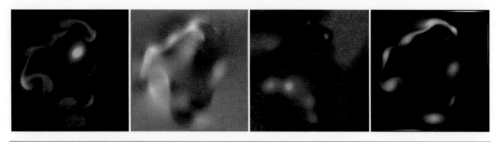

Figure 38-4. The State Fields of a Fluid Simulation, Stored in Textures
From left to right, the fields are "ink," velocity (scaled and biased into the range [0, 1], so zero velocity is gray), pressure (blue represents low pressure, red represents high pressure), and vorticity (yellow represents counter-clockwise rotation, blue represents clockwise rotation).

identical computations at each fragment. To the programmer, it appears as if there is a processor for each fragment, and that all fragments are updated simultaneously. In the parlance of parallel programming, this model is known as single instruction, multiple data (SIMD) computation. Thus, the GPU analog of computation inside nested loops over an array is a fragment program applied in SIMD fashion to each fragment.

Feedback = Texture Update

In Section 38.2.4, we described how we use Jacobi iteration to solve Poisson equations. This type of iterative method uses the result of an iteration as input for the next iteration. This *feedback* is common in numerical methods. In a CPU implementation, one typically does not even consider feedback, because it is trivially implemented using variables and arrays that can be both read and written. On the GPU, though, the output of fragment processors is always written to the frame buffer. Think of the frame buffer as a two-dimensional array that cannot be directly read. There are two ways to get the contents of the frame buffer into a texture that can be read:

- *Copy to texture* (CTT) copies from the frame buffer to a texture.

- *Render to texture* (RTT) uses a texture as the frame buffer so the GPU can write directly to it.

CTT and RTT function equally well, but have a performance trade-off. For the sake of generality we do not assume the use of either and refer to the process of writing to a texture as a *texture update*.

Earlier we mentioned that, in practice, each of the five steps in the algorithm updates a temporary grid and then performs a swap. RTT requires the use of two textures to implement feedback, because the results of rendering to a texture while it is bound for reading are undefined. The swap in this case is merely a swap of texture IDs. The performance cost of RTT is therefore constant. CTT, on the other hand, requires only one texture. The frame buffer acts as a temporary grid, and a swap is performed by copying the data from the frame buffer to the texture. The performance cost of this copy is proportional to the texture size.

38.3.2 Slab Operations

We break down the steps of our simulation into what we call *slab operations* (*slabop*, for short).[2] Each slabop consists of processing one or more (often all) fragments in the frame buffer—usually with a fragment program active—followed by a texture update. Fragment processing is driven by rendering geometric primitives. For this application, the geometry we render is simple: just quad and line primitives.

There are two types of fragments to process in any slab operation: interior fragments and boundary fragments. Our 2D grid reserves a single-cell perimeter to store and compute boundary conditions. Typically, a different computation is performed on the interior and at the boundaries. To update the interior fragments, we render a quadrilateral that covers all but a one-pixel border on the perimeter of the frame buffer. We render four line primitives to update the boundary cells. We apply separate fragment programs to interior and border fragments. See Figure 38-5.

38.3.3 Implementation in Fragment Programs

Now that we know the steps of our algorithm, our data representation, and how to perform a slab operation, we can write the fragment programs that perform computations at each cell.

Advection

The fragment program implementation of advection shown in Listing 38-1 follows nearly exactly from Equation 13, repeated here:

$$q(\mathbf{x}, t + \delta t) = q(\mathbf{x} - \mathbf{u}(\mathbf{x}, t)\delta t, t). \tag{13}$$

There is one slight difference. Because texture coordinates are not in the same units as our simulation domain (the texture coordinates are in the range $[0, N]$, where N is the grid resolution), we must scale the velocity into grid space. This is reflected in Cg code with the multiplication of the local velocity by the parameter rdx, which represents the

---

2. We call them slab operations because GPU simulation in 3D requires us to break the 3D grid down into a stack of 2D "slabs," because the frame buffer is limited to two dimensions.

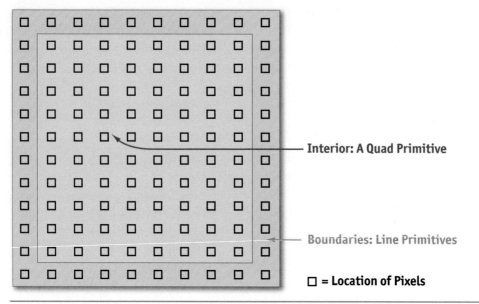

Interior: A Quad Primitive

Boundaries: Line Primitives

□ = Location of Pixels

Figure 38-5. Primitives Used to Update the Interior and Boundaries of the Grid
Updating a grid involves rendering a quad for the interior and lines for the boundaries. Separate fragment programs are applied to interior and border fragments.

reciprocal of the grid scale δx. The texture wrap mode must be set to CLAMP_TO_EDGE so that back-tracing outside the range $[0, N]$ will be clamped to the boundary texels. The boundary conditions described later correctly update these texels so that this situation operates correctly.

Listing 38-1. Advection Fragment Program

```
void advect(float2 coords   : WPOS,     // grid coordinates
            out float4 xNew : COLOR,    // advected qty
            uniform float timestep,
            uniform float rdx,          // 1 / grid scale
            uniform samplerRECT u,      // input velocity
            uniform samplerRECT x)      // qty to advect
{
    // follow the velocity field "back in time"
    float2 pos = coords - timestep * rdx * f2texRECT(u, coords);

    // interpolate and write to the output fragment
    xNew = f4texRECTbilerp(x, pos);
}
```

In this code, the parameter u is the velocity field texture, and x is the field that is to be advected. This could be the velocity or another quantity, such as dye concentration. The function f4texRECTbilerp() is a utility to perform bilinear interpolation of the four texels closest to the texture coordinates passed to it. Because current GPUs do not support automatic bilinear interpolation in floating-point textures, we must implement it with this type of code.

Viscous Diffusion

With the description of the Jacobi iteration technique given in Section 38.2.4, writing a Jacobi iteration fragment program is simple, as shown in Listing 38-2.

Listing 38-2. The Jacobi Iteration Fragment Program Used to Solve Poisson Equations

```
void jacobi(half2 coords   : WPOS,    // grid coordinates
            out half4 xNew : COLOR,   // result
            uniform half alpha,
            uniform half rBeta,       // reciprocal beta
            uniform samplerRECT x,    // x vector (Ax = b)
            uniform samplerRECT b)    // b vector (Ax = b)
{
  // left, right, bottom, and top x samples
  half4 xL = h4texRECT(x, coords - half2(1, 0));
  half4 xR = h4texRECT(x, coords + half2(1, 0));
  half4 xB = h4texRECT(x, coords - half2(0, 1));
  half4 xT = h4texRECT(x, coords + half2(0, 1));

  // b sample, from center
  half4 bC = h4texRECT(b, coords);

  // evaluate Jacobi iteration
  xNew = (xL + xR + xB + xT + alpha * bC) * rBeta;
}
```

Notice that the rBeta parameter is the reciprocal of β from Equation 16. To solve the diffusion equation, we set alpha to $(\delta x)^2/\nu\delta t$, rBeta to $1/(4 + (\delta x)^2/\nu\delta t)$, and the x and b parameters to the velocity texture. We then run a number of iterations (usually 20 to 50, but more can be used to reduce the error).

Force Application

The simplest step in our algorithm is computing the acceleration caused by external forces. In the demonstration application found in the accompanying materials, you can apply an impulse to the fluid by clicking and dragging with the mouse. To implement this, we draw a spot into the velocity texture at the position of the click. The color of the spot encodes the direction and magnitude of the impulse: the red channel contains the magnitude in x, and the green channel contains the magnitude in y. The spot is actually a two-dimensional Gaussian "splat."

We use a fragment program to check each fragment's distance from the impulse position. Then we add the quantity $\mathbf{c}$ to the color:

$$\mathbf{c} = \mathbf{F}\delta t \exp\left[\frac{\left(x - x_p\right)^2 + \left(y - y_p\right)^2}{r}\right].$$

Here, $\mathbf{F}$ is the force computed from the direction and length of the mouse drag, r is the desired impulse radius, and (x, y) and (x_p, y_p) are the fragment position and impulse (click) position in window coordinates, respectively.

Projection

In the beginning of this section, we learned that the projection step is divided into two operations: solving the Poisson-pressure equation for p, and subtracting the gradient of p from the intermediate velocity field. This requires three fragment programs: the aforementioned Jacobi iteration program, a program to compute the divergence of the intermediate velocity field, and a program to subtract the gradient of p from the intermediate velocity field.

The divergence program shown in Listing 38-3 takes the intermediate velocity field as parameter w and one-half of the reciprocal of the grid scale as parameter halfrdx, and it computes the divergence according to the finite difference formula given in Table 38-1, on page 643.

The divergence is written to a temporary texture, which is then used as input to the b parameter of the Jacobi iteration program. The x parameter of the Jacobi program is set to the pressure texture, which is first cleared to all zero values (in other words, we are using zero as our initial guess for the pressure field). The alpha and rBeta parameters are set to $-(\delta x)^2$ and ¼, respectively.

To achieve good convergence on the solution, we typically use 40 to 80 Jacobi iterations. Changing the number of Jacobi iterations will affect the accuracy of the simulation. It is not a good idea to go below 20 iterations, because the error is noticeable. Using more iterations results in more detailed vortices and more overall accuracy, but it requires more computation time. After the Jacobi iterations are finished, we bind the

Listing 38-3. The Divergence Fragment Program

```
void divergence(half2 coords  : WPOS,      // grid coordinates
                out half4 div : COLOR,     // divergence
                uniform half halfrdx,      // 0.5 / gridscale
                uniform samplerRECT w)     // vector field
{
  half4 wL = h4texRECT(w, coords - half2(1, 0));
  half4 wR = h4texRECT(w, coords + half2(1, 0));
  half4 wB = h4texRECT(w, coords - half2(0, 1));
  half4 wT = h4texRECT(w, coords + half2(0, 1));

  div = halfrdx * ((wR.x - wL.x) + (wT.y - wB.y));
}
```

pressure field texture to the parameter p in the following program, which computes the gradient of *p* according to the definition in Table 38-1 and subtracts it from the intermediate velocity field texture in parameter w. See Listing 38-4.

Listing 38-4. The Gradient Subtraction Fragment Program

```
void gradient(half2 coords   : WPOS,       // grid coordinates
              out half4 uNew : COLOR,      // new velocity
              uniform half halfrdx,        // 0.5 / gridscale
              uniform samplerRECT p,       // pressure
              uniform samplerRECT w)       // velocity
{
  half pL = h1texRECT(p, coords - half2(1, 0));
  half pR = h1texRECT(p, coords + half2(1, 0));
  half pB = h1texRECT(p, coords - half2(0, 1));
  half pT = h1texRECT(p, coords + half2(0, 1));

  uNew = h4texRECT(w, coords);
  uNew.xy -= halfrdx * half2(pR - pL, pT - pB);
}
```

Boundary Conditions

In Section 38.2.4, we determined that our "fluid in a box" requires no-slip (zero) velocity boundary conditions and pure Neumann pressure boundary conditions. In Section 38.3.2 we learned that we can implement boundary conditions by reserving the one-pixel perimeter of our grid for storing boundary values. We update these values by drawing line primitives over the border, using a fragment program that sets the values appropriately.

First we should look at how our grid discretization affects the computation of boundary conditions. The no-slip condition dictates that velocity equals zero on the boundaries, and the pure Neumann pressure condition requires the normal pressure derivative to be zero at the boundaries. The boundary is defined to lie on the edge between the boundary cell and its nearest interior cell, but grid values are defined at cell centers. Therefore, we must compute boundary values such that the average of the two cells adjacent to any edge satisfies the boundary condition.

For the velocity boundary on the left side, for example, we have:

$$\frac{\mathbf{u}_{0,j} + \mathbf{u}_{1,j}}{2} = 0, \quad \text{for } j \in [0, N], \tag{17}$$

where N is the grid resolution. In order to satisfy this equation, we must set $\mathbf{u}_{0,j}$ equal to $-\mathbf{u}_{1,j}$. The pressure equation works out similarly. Using the forward difference approximation of the derivative, we get:

$$\frac{p_{1,j} - p_{0,j}}{\delta x} = 0. \tag{18}$$

On solving this equation for $p_{0,j}$, we see that we need to set each pressure boundary value to the value just inside the boundary.

We can use a simple fragment program for both the pressure and the velocity boundaries, as shown in Listing 38-5.

Listing 38-5. The Boundary Condition Fragment Program

```
void boundary(half2 coords : WPOS,      // grid coordinates
              half2 offset : TEX1,      // boundary offset
              out half4 bv : COLOR,     // output value
              uniform half scale,       // scale parameter
              uniform samplerRECT x)    // state field
{
   bv = scale * h4texRECT(x, coords + offset);
}
```

Figure 38-6 demonstrates how this program works. The x parameter represents the texture (velocity or pressure field) from which we read interior values. The offset parameter contains the correct offset to the interior cells adjacent to the current boundary. The coords parameter contains the position in texture coordinates of the fragment being processed, so adding offset to it addresses a neighboring texel. At each

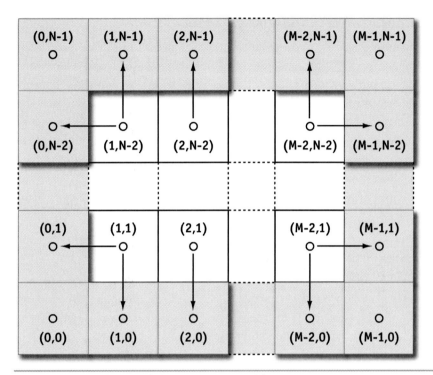

Figure 38-6. Boundary Conditions on an M × N Grid
The arrows indicate how offsets are used to copy values from just inside the boundaries to the boundary cells.

boundary, we set `offset` to adjust our texture coordinates to the texel just inside the boundary. For the left boundary, we set it to (1, 0), so that it addresses the texel just to the right; for the bottom boundary, we use (0, 1); and so on. The `scale` parameter can be used to scale the value we copy to the boundary. For velocity boundaries, `scale` is set to −1, and for pressure it is set to 1, so that we correctly implement Equations 17 and 18, respectively.

38.4 Applications

In this section we explore a variety of applications of the GPU simulation techniques discussed in this chapter.

38.4.1 Simulating Liquids and Gases

The most direct use of the simulation techniques is to simulate a continuous volume of a liquid or gas. As it stands, the simulation represents only the velocity of the fluid, which is not very interesting. It is more interesting if we put something else in the fluid. The demonstration application does this by maintaining an additional scalar field. This field represents the concentration of dye carried by the fluid. (Because it is an RGB texture, it is really three scalar fields: one for each of three dye colors.) Quantities like this are known as *passive scalars* because they are only carried along by the fluid; they do not affect how it flows.

If d is the concentration of dye, then the evolution of the dye field is governed by the following equation:

$$\frac{\partial d}{\partial t} = -(\mathbf{u} \cdot \nabla)d. \tag{19}$$

To simulate how the dye is carried by the fluid, we apply the advection operator to the scalar field, just as we do for the velocity. If we also want to account for the diffusion of the dye in the fluid, we add a diffusion term:

$$\frac{\partial d}{\partial t} = -(\mathbf{u} \cdot \nabla)d + \gamma \nabla^2 d + S, \tag{20}$$

where γ is the coefficient of the diffusion of dye in water (or whatever liquid we assume the fluid is). To implement dye diffusion, we use Jacobi iteration, just as we did for viscous diffusion of velocity. Note that the demonstration application does not actually perform diffusion of the dye, because numerical error in the advection term causes it to diffuse anyway. We added another term to Equation 20, S. This term represents any sources of dye. The application implements this term by adding dye anywhere we click.

38.4.2 Buoyancy and Convection

Temperature is an important factor in the flow of many fluids. Convection currents are caused by the changes in density associated with temperature changes. These currents affect our weather, our oceans and lakes, and even our coffee. To simulate these effects, we need to add buoyancy to our simulation.

The simplest way to incorporate buoyancy is to add a new scalar field for temperature, T, to the simulation. We can then insert an additional buoyancy operator that adds force where the local temperature is higher than a given ambient temperature, T_0:

$$f_{buoy} = \sigma\left(T - T_0\right)\hat{\mathbf{j}}. \qquad (21)$$

In this equation, $\hat{\mathbf{j}}$ is the vertical direction and σ is a constant scale factor. This force can be implemented in a simple fragment program that evaluates Equation 21 at each fragment, scales the result by the time step, and adds it to the current velocity.

Smoke and Clouds

We now have almost everything we need to simulate smoke. What we have presented so far is similar to the smoke simulation technique introduced by Fedkiw et al. 2001. In addition to calculating the velocity and pressure fields, a smoke simulation must maintain scalar fields for smoke density, d, and temperature, T. The smoke density is advected by the velocity field, just like the dye we described earlier. The buoyant force is modified to account for the gravitational pull on dense smoke:

$$f_{buoy} = \left(-\kappa d + \sigma\left(T - T_0\right)\right)\hat{\mathbf{j}}, \qquad (22)$$

where κ is a constant mass scale factor.

By adding a source of smoke density and temperature (possibly representing a smoke-stack or the tip of a cigarette) at a given location on the grid, we simulate smoke. The paper by Fedkiw et al. describes two other differences from our basic simulation. They use a staggered grid to improve accuracy, and they add a vorticity confinement force to increase the amount of swirling motion in the smoke. Both extensions are discussed in the next section.

As demonstrated in Harris et al. 2003, a more complex simulation can be used to simulate clouds on the GPU. A sequence of stills from a 2D GPU cloud simulation is shown in Figure 38-7. The cloud simulator combines fluid simulation with a thermo-dynamic simulation (including buoyancy), as well as a simulation of water condensation and evaporation. A 128×128 cloud simulation runs at over 80 iterations per second on an NVIDIA GeForce FX 5950 Ultra GPU.

38.5 Extensions

The fluid simulation presented in this chapter is a building block that can serve as the basis for more complex simulations. There are many ways to extend this basic simulation. To get you started, we describe some useful extensions.

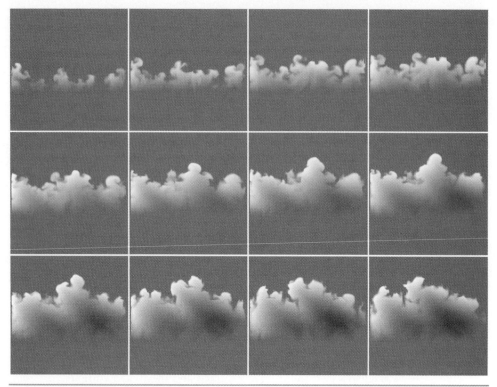

Figure 38-7. Cloud Simulation
A sequence of frames (20 iterations apart) from a two-dimensional cloud simulation running on a GPU.

38.5.1 Vorticity Confinement

The motion of smoke, air and other low-viscosity fluids typically contains rotational flows at a variety of scales. This rotational flow is *vorticity*. As Fedkiw et al. explained, numerical dissipation caused by simulation on a coarse grid damps out these interesting features (Fedkiw et al. 2001). Therefore, they used *vorticity confinement* to restore these fine-scale motions. Vorticity confinement works by first computing the vorticity, $\omega = \nabla \times \mathbf{u}$. From the vorticity we compute a normalized vorticity vector field:

$$\Psi = \frac{\eta}{|\eta|}.$$

Here, $\eta = \nabla |\omega|$. The vectors in this vector field point from areas of lower vorticity to areas of higher vorticity. From these vectors we compute a force that can be used to restore an approximation of the dissipated vorticity:

$$\mathbf{f}_{vc} = \varepsilon \left(\mathbf{\Psi} \times \boldsymbol{\omega} \right) \delta x.$$

Here ε is a user-controlled scale parameter. The "curl" operator, $\nabla \times$, can be derived using the definitions of the gradient and the cross-product operator. The accompanying source code implements vorticity confinement.

38.5.2 Three Dimensions

All the simulations presented in this chapter are two-dimensional. There is nothing preventing us from extending them to 3D. The equations remain essentially the same, but we must extend them to incorporate a 3D velocity, $\mathbf{u} = (u, v, w)$. The fragment programs must be rewritten to account for this; samples from four neighbors in two dimensions become samples from six neighbors in three dimensions.

The biggest change is in how the vector and scalar fields are represented. One option is to use 3D textures. This is a problem on hardware that does not support 3D floating-point textures. In this situation, we can tile the slabs of a 3D texture in a grid stored in a 2D texture (for example, a $32 \times 32 \times 32$ grid would tile onto a 256×128 2D texture, with eight tiles in one dimension and four in the other). This technique, called *flat 3D textures,* is presented in detail in Harris et al. 2003.

38.5.3 Staggered Grid

In our simulation we represent velocity, pressure, and any other quantities at cell centers. This is just one way to discretize the continuous domain on which we represent our fluid. This approach is known as a *collocated,* or *cell-centered,* discretization. Another way is to use a *staggered grid.* In a staggered grid, we represent scalar quantities (such as pressure) at cell centers and vector quantities (such as velocity) at the boundaries between cells. Specifically, on a two-dimensional grid, we represent the horizontal velocity, u, at the right edge of each cell and the vertical velocity, v, at the top edge of each cell. The staggered grid discretization increases the accuracy of many calculations. It can also reduce numerical oscillations that may arise when forces such as buoyancy are applied on a cell-centered grid. Details of the implementation of fluid simulation on a staggered grid can be found in Griebel et al. 1998.

38.5.4 Arbitrary Boundaries

So far we have assumed that our fluid exists in a rectangular box with flat, solid sides. If boundaries of arbitrary shape and location are important, you need to extend the simulation.

Incorporating arbitrary boundaries requires applying the boundary conditions (discussed in Section 38.3.3) at arbitrary locations. This means that at each cell, we must determine in which direction the boundaries lie in order to compute the correct boundary values. This simulation requires more decisions to be made at each cell, leading to a slower and more complicated simulation. However, many interesting effects can be created this way, such as smoke flowing around obstacles. Moving boundaries can even be incorporated, as in Fedkiw et al. 2001. We refer you to that paper as well as Griebel et al. 1998 for implementation details.

38.5.5 Free Surface Flow

Another assumption we made is that our fluid is continuous—the only boundaries we represent are the solid boundaries of the box. So we cannot simulate things like the ocean surface, where there is an interface between the water and air. This type of interface is called a *free surface*. Extending our simulation to incorporate a free surface requires tracking the location of the surface as it moves through cells. Methods for implementing free surface flow can be found in Griebel et al. 1998.

38.6 Conclusion

The power and programmability now available in GPUs enables fast simulation of a wide variety of phenomena. Underlying many of these phenomena is the dynamics of fluid motion.

After reading this chapter, you should have a fundamental understanding of the mathematics and technology you need to implement basic fluid simulations on the GPU. From these initial ideas you can experiment with your own simulation concepts and incorporate fluid simulation into graphics applications. We hope these techniques become powerful new tools in your repertoire.

38.7 References

Bolz, J., I. Farmer, E. Grinspun, and P. Schröder. 2003. "Sparse Matrix Solvers on the GPU: Conjugate Gradients and Multigrid." In *Proceedings of SIGGRAPH 2003*.

Chorin, A.J., and J.E. Marsden. 1993. *A Mathematical Introduction to Fluid Mechanics*. 3rd ed. Springer.

Fedkiw, R., J. Stam, and H.W. Jensen. 2001. "Visual Simulation of Smoke." In *Proceedings of SIGGRAPH 2001*.

Golub, G.H., and C.F. Van Loan. 1996. *Matrix Computations*. 3rd ed. The Johns Hopkins University Press.

Goodnight, N., C. Woolley, G. Lewin, D. Luebke, and G. Humphreys. 2003. "A Multigrid Solver for Boundary Value Problems Using Programmable Graphics Hardware." In *Proceedings of the SIGGRAPH/Eurographics Workshop on Graphics Hardware 2003*.

Griebel, M., T. Dornseifer, and T. Neunhoeffer. 1998. *Numerical Simulation in Fluid Dynamics: A Practical Introduction*. Society for Industrial and Applied Mathematics.

Harris, M.J., W.V. Baxter, T. Scheuermann, and A. Lastra. 2003. "Simulation of Cloud Dynamics on Graphics Hardware." In *Proceedings of the SIGGRAPH/Eurographics Workshop on Graphics Hardware 2003*.

Krüger, J., and R. Westermann. 2003. "Linear Algebra Operators for GPU Implementation of Numerical Algorithms." In *Proceedings of SIGGRAPH 2003*.

Stam, J. 1999. "Stable Fluids." In *Proceedings of SIGGRAPH 1999*.

Chapter 39

Volume Rendering Techniques

Milan Ikits
University of Utah

Joe Kniss
University of Utah

Aaron Lefohn
University of California, Davis

Charles Hansen
University of Utah

This chapter presents texture-based volume rendering techniques that are used for visualizing three-dimensional data sets and for creating high-quality special effects.

39.1 Introduction

Many visual effects are volumetric in nature. Fluids, clouds, fire, smoke, fog, and dust are difficult to model with geometric primitives. Volumetric models are better suited for creating such effects. These models assume that light is emitted, absorbed, and scattered by a large number of particles in the volume. See Figure 39-1 for two examples.

In addition to modeling and rendering volumetric phenomena, volume rendering is essential to scientific and engineering applications that require visualization of three-dimensional data sets. Examples include visualization of data acquired by medical imaging devices or resulting from computational fluid dynamics simulations. Users of interactive volume rendering applications rely on the performance of modern graphics accelerators for efficient data exploration and feature discovery.

This chapter describes volume rendering techniques that exploit the flexible programming model and 3D texturing capabilities of modern GPUs. Although it is possible to

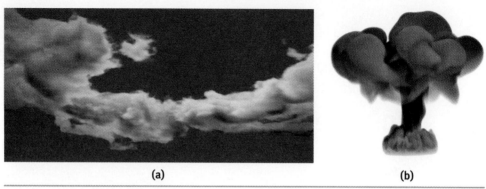

(a)   (b)

Figure 39-1. Volumetric Effects
(a) Cumulus clouds and (b) fire simulation.

implement other popular volume rendering algorithms on the GPU, such as ray casting (Roettger et al. 2003, Krüger and Westermann 2003), this chapter describes texture-based volume rendering only. Texture-based techniques are easily combined with polygonal algorithms, require only a few render passes, and offer a great level of interactivity without sacrificing the quality of rendering.

Section 39.2 introduces the terminology and explains the process of direct volume rendering. Section 39.3 describes the components of a typical texture-based volume rendering application, and illustrates it with a simple example. Section 39.4 provides additional implementation details, which expand the capabilities of the basic volume renderer. Section 39.5 describes advanced techniques for incorporating more realistic lighting effects and adding procedural details to the rendering. Section 39.6 concludes with a summary of relevant performance considerations.

39.2 Volume Rendering

Direct volume rendering methods generate images of a 3D volumetric data set without explicitly extracting geometric surfaces from the data (Levoy 1988). These techniques use an *optical model* to map data values to *optical properties*, such as color and opacity (Max 1995). During rendering, optical properties are accumulated along each viewing ray to form an image of the data (see Figure 39-2).

Although the data set is interpreted as a continuous function in space, for practical purposes it is represented by a uniform 3D array of samples. In graphics memory, volume data is stored as a stack of 2D texture slices or as a single 3D texture object. The term *voxel* denotes an individual "volume element," similar to the terms *pixel* for "picture element" and *texel* for "texture element." Each voxel corresponds to a location in data space and has one or more data values associated with it. Values at intermediate locations are obtained by interpolating data at neighboring volume elements. This process is known as *reconstruction* and plays an important role in volume rendering and processing applications.

In essence, the role of the optical model is to describe how particles in the volume interact with light. For example, the most commonly used model assumes that the volume consists of particles that simultaneously emit and absorb light. More complex models incorporate local illumination and volumetric shadows, and they account for light scattering effects. Optical parameters are specified by the data values directly, or they are computed from applying one or more *transfer functions* to the data. The goal of the transfer function in visualization applications is to emphasize or *classify* features of interest in the data. Typically, transfer functions are implemented by *texture lookup tables*, though simple functions can also be computed in the fragment shader. For example, Figure 39-2 illustrates the use of a transfer function to extract material boundaries from a CT scan of a tooth.

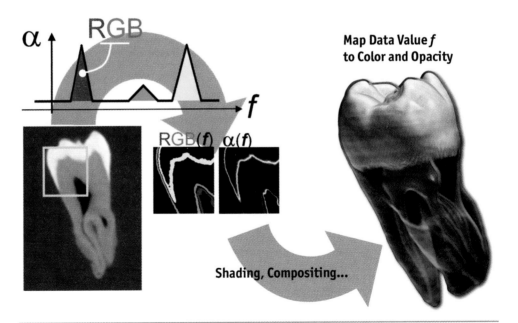

Figure 39-2. The Process of Volume Rendering
The transfer function maps data values to color and opacity, which are then modified by shading and composited along the viewing direction. (Thanks to Gordon Kindlmann for help with rendering the tooth.)

Images are created by sampling the volume along all viewing rays and accumulating the resulting optical properties, as shown in Figure 39-3. For the emission-absorption model, the accumulated color and opacity are computed according to Equation 1, where C_i and A_i are the color and opacity assigned by the transfer function to the data value at sample i.

$$C = \sum_{i=1}^{n} C_i \prod_{j=1}^{i-1} \left(1 - A_j\right)$$

$$A = 1 - \prod_{j=1}^{n} \left(1 - A_j\right)$$

(1)

Discrete Volume Rendering Equations

Opacity A_i approximates the absorption, and opacity-weighted color C_i approximates the emission and the absorption along the ray segment between samples i and $i + 1$. For the color component, the product in the sum represents the amount by which the light emitted at sample i is attenuated before reaching the eye. This formula is efficiently evaluated by sorting the samples along the viewing ray and computing the accumulated color C and opacity A iteratively. Section 39.4 describes how the *compositing* step can be performed via alpha blending. Because Equation 1 is a numerical approximation to the continuous optical model, the *sampling rate s*, which is inversely proportional to the distance between the samples *l*, greatly influences the accuracy of approximation and the quality of rendering.

Texture-based volume rendering techniques perform the sampling and compositing steps by rendering a set of 2D geometric primitives inside the volume, as shown in Figure 39-3. Each primitive is assigned texture coordinates for sampling the volume texture. The *proxy geometry* is rasterized and blended into the frame buffer in back-to-front or front-to-back order. In the fragment shading stage, the interpolated texture coordinates are used for a data texture lookup. Next, the interpolated data values act as texture coordinates for a *dependent lookup* into the transfer function textures. Illumination techniques may modify the resulting color before it is sent to the compositing stage of the pipeline.

39.3 Texture-Based Volume Rendering

In general, as shown in Figure 39-4, texture-based volume rendering algorithms can be divided into three stages: (1) Initialize, (2) Update, and (3) Draw. The Initialize stage is

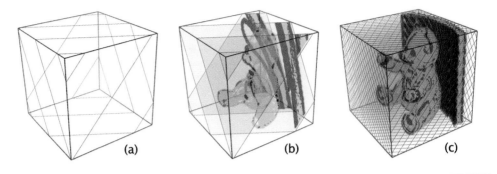

(a)   (b)   (c)

Figure 39-3. Volume Sampling and Compositing
(a) The data set is sampled by rendering proxy polygons perpendicular to the viewing direction. (b) The transfer function assigns color and opacity to the scalar data values at the sampling locations. (c) The assigned color and opacity are accumulated along the viewing direction, resulting in an image of the data.

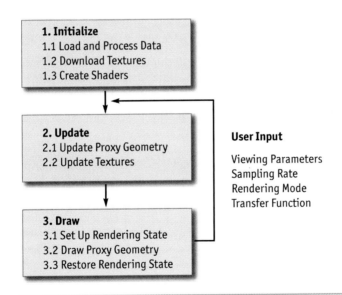

1. Initialize
1.1 Load and Process Data
1.2 Download Textures
1.3 Create Shaders

2. Update
2.1 Update Proxy Geometry
2.2 Update Textures

3. Draw
3.1 Set Up Rendering State
3.2 Draw Proxy Geometry
3.3 Restore Rendering State

User Input

Viewing Parameters
Sampling Rate
Rendering Mode
Transfer Function

Figure 39-4. The Steps of a Typical Texture-Based Volume Rendering Implementation

usually performed only once. The Update and Draw stages are executed whenever the application receives user input—for example, when viewing or rendering parameters change.

At the beginning of the application, data volumes are loaded into CPU memory. In certain cases, the data sets also need to be processed before packing and downloading them to texture memory. For example, one may choose to compute gradients or down-sample the data at this stage. Some of the data processing operations can also be done outside the application. Transfer function lookup tables and fragment shaders are typically created in the Initialize stage of the application.

After initialization and every time viewing parameters change, the proxy geometry is computed and stored in vertex arrays. When the data set is stored as a 3D texture object, the proxy geometry consists of a set of polygons, slicing through the volume perpendicular to the viewing direction (see Section 39.4.2). Slice polygons are computed by first intersecting the slicing planes with the edges of the volume bounding box and then sorting the resulting vertices in a clockwise or counterclockwise direction around their center. For each vertex, the corresponding 3D texture coordinate is calculated on the CPU, in a vertex program, or via automatic texture-coordinate generation.

When a data set is stored as a set of 2D texture slices, the proxy polygons are simply rectangles aligned with the slices. Despite being faster, this approach has several disadvantages. First, it requires three times more memory, because the data slices need to be replicated along each principal direction. Data replication can be avoided with some performance overhead by reconstructing slices on the fly (Lefohn et al. 2004). Second, the sampling rate depends on the resolution of the volume. This problem can be solved by adding intermediate slices and performing trilinear interpolation with a fragment shader (Rezk-Salama et al. 2000). Third, the sampling distance changes with the viewpoint, resulting in intensity variations as the camera moves and image-popping artifacts when switching from one set of slices to another (Kniss et al. 2002b).

During the Update stage, textures are refreshed if the rendering mode or the transfer function parameters change. Also, opacity correction of the transfer function textures is performed if the sampling rate has changed (see Equation 3).

Before the slice polygons are drawn in sorted order, the rendering state needs to be set up appropriately. This step typically includes disabling lighting and culling, and setting up alpha blending. To blend in opaque geometry, depth testing has to be enabled, and writing to the depth buffer has to be disabled. Volume and transfer function textures have to be bound to texture units, which the fragment shader uses for input. At this point, shader input parameters are specified, and vertex arrays are set up for rendering. Finally, after the slices are drawn in sorted order, the rendering state is restored, so that the algorithm does not affect the display of other objects in the scene.

39.3.1 A Simple Example

The following example is intended as a starting point for understanding the implementation details of texture-based volume rendering. In this example, the transfer function is fixed, the data set represents the opacity directly, and the emissive color is set to constant gray. In addition, the viewing direction points along the z axis of the data coordinate frame; therefore, the proxy geometry consists of rectangles in the x-y plane placed uniformly along the z axis. The algorithm consists of the steps shown in Algorithm 39-1.

Algorithm 39-1. The Steps of the Simple Volume Rendering Application

1. Create and download the data set as a 3D alpha texture.

2. Load the fragment program shown in Listing 39-1.

3. Load the modelview and projection matrices.

4. Enable alpha blending using 1 for the source fragment and (1 – source alpha) for the destination fragment.

5. Disable lighting and depth testing (there is no opaque geometry in this example).

6. Bind the data texture to texture unit 0.

7. Enable and bind the fragment program and specify its input.

8. Draw textured quads along the z axis.
   The x-y vertex coordinates are (–1, –1), (1, –1), (1, 1), (–1, 1).
   The corresponding x-y texture coordinates are (0, 0), (1, 0), (1, 1), (0, 1).
   The z vertex and texture coordinates increase uniformly from –1 to 1 and 0 to 1, respectively.

Listing 39-1. The Fragment Program for the Simple Volume Renderer

```
void main(uniform float3 emissiveColor,
          uniform sampler3D dataTex,
          float3 texCoord : TEXCOORD0,
          float4 color : COLOR)
{
  float a = tex3D(texCoord, dataTex);  // Read 3D data texture
  color = a * emissiveColor;           // Multiply color by opacity
}
```

Figure 39-5 shows the image generated by the simple volume renderer. The following sections demonstrate how to make each stage of the example more general and useful for a variety of tasks.

Figure 39-5. Output of the Simple Volume Renderer Using a Voxelized Model of a Familiar Object

39.4 Implementation Details

This section presents an overview of the components commonly used in texture-based volume rendering applications. The goal is to provide enough details to make it easier to understand typical implementations of volume renderers that utilize current-generation consumer graphics hardware, such as the GeForce FX family of cards.

39.4.1 Data Representation and Processing

Volumetric data sets come in a variety of sizes and types. For volume rendering, data is stored in memory in a suitable format, so it can be easily downloaded to graphics memory as textures. Usually, the volume is stored in a single 3D array. Depending on the kind of proxy geometry used, either a single 3D texture object or one to three sets of 2D texture slices are created. The developer also has to choose which available texture formats to use for rendering. For example, power-of-two-size textures are typically used to maximize rendering performance. Frequently, the data set is not in the right format and not the right size, and it may not fit into the available texture memory on the GPU. In simple implementations, data processing is performed in a separate step outside the renderer. In more complex scenarios, data processing becomes an integral part of the application, such as when data values are generated on the fly or when images are created directly from raw data.

To change the size of a data set, one can resample it into a coarser or a finer grid, or pad it at the boundaries. Padding is accomplished by placing the data into a larger volume and filling the empty regions with values. Resampling requires probing the volume (that is, computing interpolated data values at a location from voxel neighbors). Although the commonly used trilinear interpolation technique is easy to implement, it is not always the best choice for resampling, because it can introduce visual artifacts. If the quality of resampling is crucial for the application, more complex interpolation functions are required, such as piecewise cubic polynomials. Fortunately, such operations are easily performed with the help of publicly available toolkits. For example, the Teem toolkit includes a great variety of data-processing tools accessible directly from the command line, exposing the functionality of the underlying libraries without having to write any code (Kindlmann 2003). Examples of using Teem for volume data processing are included on the book's CD and Web site. Advanced data processing can also be performed on the GPU, for example, to create high-quality images (Hadwiger et al. 2001).

Local illumination techniques and multidimensional transfer functions use gradient information during rendering. Most implementations use central differences to obtain the gradient vector at each voxel. The method of central differences approximates the gradient as the difference of data values of two voxel neighbors along a coordinate axis, divided by the physical distance. For example, the following formula computes the x component of the gradient vector at voxel location $\vec{P}_{(i,\,j,\,k)}$:

$$g_x\left(\vec{P}_{(i,\,j,\,k)}\right) = \frac{v\left(\vec{P}_{(i+1,\,j,\,k)}\right) - v\left(\vec{P}_{(i-1,\,j,\,k)}\right)}{2h}, \qquad (2)$$

Gradient Computation Using Central Differences

where h is the distance between the voxels along the x axis. To obtain the gradient at data boundaries, the volume is padded by repeating boundary values. Visual artifacts caused by central differences are similar to those resulting from resampling with trilinear interpolation. If visual quality is of concern, more complex derivative functions are needed, such as the ones that Teem provides. Depending on the texture format used, the computed gradients may need to be quantized, scaled, and biased to fit into the available range of values.

Transfer functions emphasize regions in the volume by assigning color and opacity to data values. Histograms are useful for analyzing which ranges of values are important in the data. In general, histograms show the distribution of data values and other related data measures. A 1D histogram is created by dividing up the value range into a number of bins. Each bin contains the number of voxels within the lower and upper bounds assigned to the bin. By examining the histogram, one can see which values are frequent in the data. Histograms, however, do not show the spatial distribution of the samples in the volume.

The output of the data-processing step is a set of textures that are downloaded to the GPU in a later stage. It is sometimes more efficient to combine several textures into a single texture. For example, to reduce the cost of texture lookup and interpolation, the value and normalized gradient textures are usually stored and used together in a single RGBA texture.

39.4.2 Proxy Geometry

During the rendering stage, images of the volume are created by drawing the proxy geometry in sorted order. When the data set is stored in a 3D texture, view-aligned planes are used for slicing the bounding box, resulting in a set of polygons for sampling the volume. Algorithm 39-2 computes the proxy geometry in view space by using the modelview matrix for transforming vertices between the object and view coordinate systems. Proxy polygons are tessellated into triangles, and the resulting vertices are stored in a vertex array for more efficient rendering.

Figure 39-6 illustrates Algorithm 39-2 with two slice polygons. The first polygon contains three vertices, the second is composed of six vertices and is tessellated into six triangles.

There are several ways to generate texture coordinates for the polygon vertices. For example, texture coordinates can be computed on the CPU in step 3(c) of Algorithm 39-2 from the computed vertex positions and the volume bounding box. In this case the coordinates are sent down to GPU memory in a separate vertex array or interleaved with the vertex data. There are different methods for computing the texture coordinates on the GPU, including automatic texture coordinate generation, the texture matrix, or with a vertex program.

Advanced algorithms, such as the one described in Section 39.5, may use a different slicing axis than the viewing direction. In this case, the algorithm works the same way, but the modelview matrix needs to be modified accordingly.

Algorithm 39-2. View-Aligned Slicing for Volume Rendering

1. Transform the volume bounding box vertices into view coordinates using the model-view matrix.

2. Find the minimum and maximum *z* coordinates of the transformed vertices. Compute the number of sampling planes used between these two values using equidistant spacing from the view origin. The sampling distance is computed from the voxel size and current sampling rate.

3. For each plane in front-to-back or back-to-front order:

   a. Test for intersections with the edges of the bounding box. Add each intersection point to a temporary vertex list. Up to six intersections are generated, so the maximum size of the list is fixed.

   b. Compute the center of the proxy polygon by averaging the intersection points. Sort the polygon vertices clockwise or counterclockwise by projecting them onto the *x-y* plane and computing their angle around the center, with the first vertex or the *x* axis as the reference. Note that to avoid trigonometric computations, the tangent of the angle and the sign of the coordinates, combined into a single scalar value called the *pseudo-angle*, can be used for sorting the vertices (Moret and Shapiro 1991).

   c. Tessellate the proxy polygon into triangles and add the resulting vertices to the output vertex array. The slice polygon can be tessellated into a triangle strip or a triangle fan using the center. Depending on the rendering algorithm, the vertices may need to be transformed back to object space during this step.

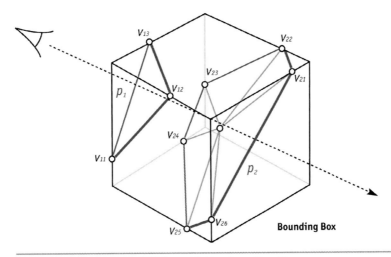

Figure 39-6. View-Aligned Slicing with Two Sampling Planes

39.4.3 Rendering

Transfer Functions

The role of the transfer function is to emphasize features in the data by mapping values and other data measures to optical properties. The simplest and most widely used transfer functions are one dimensional, and they map the range of data values to color and opacity. Typically, these transfer functions are implemented with 1D texture lookup tables. When the lookup table is built, color and opacity are usually assigned separately by the transfer function. For correct rendering, the color components need to be multiplied by the opacity, because the color approximates both the emission and the absorption within a ray segment (*opacity-weighted color*)(Wittenbrink et al. 1998).

Listing 39-2. The Fragment Program for 1D Transfer Function Dependent Textures

```
void main(uniform sampler3D dataTex,
          uniform sampler1D tfTex,
          float3 texCoord : TEXCOORD0,
          float4 color : COLOR)
{
  float v = tex3d(texCoord, dataTex);  // Read 3D data texture and
  color = tex1d(v, tfTex);             // transfer function texture
}
```

Using data value as the only measure for controlling the assignment of color and opacity may limit the effectiveness of classifying features in the data. Incorporating other data measures into the transfer function, such as gradient magnitude, allows for finer control and more sophisticated visualization (Kindlmann and Durkin 1998, Kindlmann 1999). For example, see Figure 39-7 for an illustration of the difference between using one- and two-dimensional transfer functions based on the data value and the gradient magnitude.

Transfer function design is a difficult iterative procedure that requires significant insight into the underlying data set. Some information is provided by the histogram of data values, indicating which ranges of values should be emphasized. The user interface is an important component of the interactive design procedure. Typically, the interface consists of a 1D curve editor for specifying transfer functions via a set of control points. Another approach is to use direct manipulation widgets for painting directly into the transfer function texture (Kniss et al. 2002a). The lower portions of the images in Figure 39-7 illustrate the latter technique. The widgets provide a view of the joint distribution of data values, represented by the horizontal axis, and gradient magnitudes, represented

Figure 39-7. The Difference Between 1D and 2D Transfer Functions
Two-dimensional transfer functions based on value and gradient magnitude (b, d) are used to separate different features in the data, which would not be possible with one-dimensional functions (a, c).

by the vertical axis. Arches within the value and gradient magnitude distribution indicate the presence of material boundaries. A set of brushes is provided for painting into the 2D transfer function dependent texture, which assigns the resulting color and opacity to voxels with the corresponding ranges of data values and gradient magnitudes.

The assigned opacity also depends on the sampling rate. For example, when using fewer slices, the opacity has to be scaled up, so that the overall intensity of the image remains the same. Equation 3 is used for correcting the transfer function opacity whenever the user changes the sampling rate s from the reference sampling rate s_0:

$$A = 1 - \left(1 - A_0\right)^{s_0/s} \tag{3}$$

Formula for Opacity Correction

To control the quality and speed of rendering, users typically change the maximum number of slices, or the relative sampling rate s/s_0, via the user interface.

Illumination

Illumination models are used for improving the visual appearance of objects. Simple models locally approximate the light intensity reflected from the surface of an object. The most common approximation is the *Blinn-Phong model*, which computes the reflected intensity as a function of local surface normal $\vec{n}$, the direction $\vec{l}$, and intensity I_L of the point light source, and ambient, diffuse, specular, and shininess coefficients k_a, k_d, k_s, and n:

$$I = k_a + I_L k_d \left(\vec{l} \cdot \vec{n} \right) + I_L k_s \left(\vec{h} \cdot \vec{n} \right)^n \qquad (4)$$

The Blinn-Phong Model for Local Illumination

The computed intensity is used to modulate the color components from the transfer function. Typically, Equation 4 is evaluated in the fragment shader, requiring per-pixel normal information. In volume rendering applications, the normalized gradient vector is used as the surface normal. Unfortunately, the gradient is not well defined in homogeneous regions of the volume. For volume rendering, the Blinn-Phong model is frequently modified, so that only those regions with high gradient magnitudes are shaded (Kniss et al. 2002b).

Local illumination ignores indirect light contributions, shadows, and other global effects, as illustrated by Figure 39-8. Section 39.5 describes how to incorporate simple global illumination models into the rendering model for creating high-quality volumetric effects.

(a)   (b)

Figure 39-8. Comparison of Simple and Complex Lighting Effects
(a) Using the Blinn-Phong model in volume rendering. (b) Simple lighting models do not capture important global effects, such as self-shadows and translucency.

Compositing

To efficiently evaluate the volume rendering equation (Equation 1), samples are sorted in back-to-front order, and the accumulated color and opacity are computed iteratively. A single step of the compositing process is known as the *Over operator*:

$$\hat{C}_i = C_i + \left(1 - A_i\right)\hat{C}_{i+1},$$

$$\hat{A}_i = A_i + \left(1 - A_i\right)\hat{A}_{i+1},$$

(5)

Back-to-Front Compositing Equations

where C_i and A_i are the color and opacity obtained from the fragment shading stage for segment i along the viewing ray, and $\hat{C}_i$ is the accumulated color from the back of the volume. If samples are sorted in front-to-back order, the *Under operator* is used:

$$\hat{C}_i = \left(1 - \hat{A}_{i-1}\right)C_i + \hat{C}_{i-1},$$

$$\hat{A}_i = \left(1 - \hat{A}_{i-1}\right)A_i + \hat{A}_{i-1},$$

(6)

Front-to-Back Compositing Equations

where $\hat{C}_i$ and $\hat{A}_i$ are the accumulated color and opacity from the front of the volume.

The compositing equations (Equations 5 and 6) are easily implemented with hardware alpha blending. For the Over operator, the source blending factor is set to 1 and the destination blending factor is set to (1 – source alpha). For the Under operator, the source blending factor is set to (1 – destination alpha) and the destination factor is set to 1. Alternatively, if the hardware allows for reading and writing the same buffer, compositing can be performed in the fragment shading stage by projecting the proxy polygon vertices onto the viewport rectangle (see Section 39.5).

To blend opaque geometry into the volume, the geometry needs to be drawn before the volume, because the depth test will cull proxy fragments that are inside objects. The Under operator requires drawing the geometry and the volume into separate color buffers that are composited at the end. In this case, the depth values from the geometry pass are used for culling fragments in the volume rendering pass.

39.5 Advanced Techniques

This section describes techniques for improving the quality of rendering and creating volumetric special effects.

39.5.1 Volumetric Lighting

The local illumination model presented in the previous section adds important visual cues to the rendering. Such a simple model is unrealistic, however, because it assumes that light arrives at a sample without interacting with the rest of the volume. Furthermore, this kind of lighting assumes a surface-based model, which is inappropriate for volumetric materials. One way to incorporate complex lighting effects, such as volumetric shadows, is to precompute a shadow volume for storing the amount of light arriving at each sample after being attenuated by the intervening material. During rendering, the interpolated values from this volumetric shadow map are multiplied by colors from the transfer function. But in addition to using extra memory, volumetric shadow maps result in visual artifacts such as blurry shadows and dark images.

A better alternative is to use a pixel buffer to accumulate the amount of light attenuated from the light's point of view (Kniss et al. 2003). To do this efficiently, the slicing axis is set halfway between the view and the light directions, as shown in Figure 39-9a. This allows the same slice to be rendered from both the eye and the light points of view. The amount of light arriving at a particular slice is equal to 1 minus the accumulated opacity of the previously rendered slices. Each slice is first rendered from the eye's point of view, using the results of the previous pass rendered from the light's point of view, which are used to modulate the brightness of samples in the current slice. The same slice is then rendered from the light's point of view to calculate the intensity of the light arriving at the next slice. Algorithm 39-3 uses two buffers: one for the eye and one for the light. Figure 39-10 shows the setup described in Algorithm 39-3.

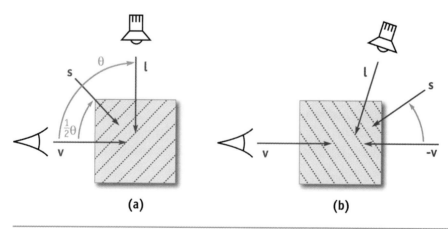

(a)   (b)

Figure 39-9. Half-Angle Slicing for Incremental Lighting Computations

Algorithm 39-3. Two-Pass Volume Rendering with Shadows

1. Clear the eye buffer and initialize the light buffer to the light color C_L. A texture map can be used to initialize the light buffer for creating special effects, such as spotlights.

2. Compute the proxy geometry in object space using Algorithm 39-1. When the dot product of the light and the view directions is positive, set the slice direction to halfway between the light and the view directions, as shown in Figure 39-9a. In this case, the volume is rendered front to back for the eye using the Under operator (see Section 39.4.3). When the dot product is negative, slice along the vector halfway between the light and the inverted view directions, and render the volume back to front for the eye using the Over operator (see Figure 39-9b). In both cases, render the volume front to back for the light using the Over operator.

3. For each slice:

   a. Pass 1: Render and blend the slice into the eye buffer.

      i. Project the slice vertices to the light buffer using the light's modelview and projection matrices. Convert the resulting vertex positions to 2D texture coordinates based on the size of the light's viewport and the light buffer.

      ii. Bind the light buffer as a texture to an available texture unit and use the texture coordinates computed in step 3(a)(i). Recall that a set of 3D texture coordinates is also needed for the data texture lookup.

      iii. In the fragment shader, evaluate the transfer function for reflective color C and opacity A. Next, multiply C by the color from the light buffer C_L, and blend C and A into the eye buffer using the appropriate operator for the current slice direction.

   b. Pass 2: Render and blend the slice into the light buffer using the Over operator. In the fragment shader, evaluate the transfer function for the alpha component and set the fragment color to 0.

Volumetric shadows greatly improve the realism of rendered scenes, as shown in Figure 39-11. Note that as the angle between the observer and the light directions changes, the slice distance needs to be adjusted to maintain a constant sampling rate. If the desired sampling distance along the observer view direction is d_v and the angle between the observer and the light view directions is θ, the slice spacing d_s is given by Equation 7:

$$d_s = \cos\left(\theta/2\right) d_v \qquad (7)$$

Relationship Between Slice Spacing and Sampling Distance Used for Half-Angle Slicing

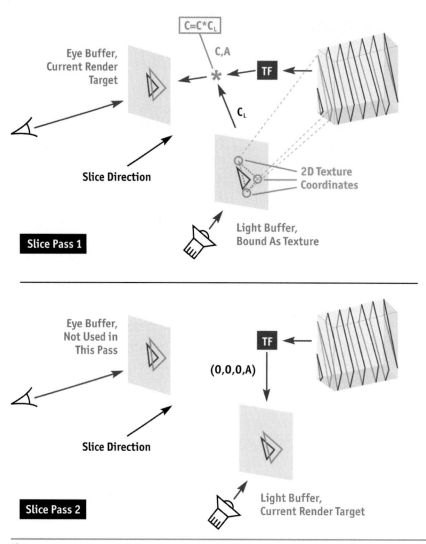

Figure 39-10. Two-Pass Volumetric Shadow Setup

Unfortunately, Algorithm 39-3 still produces dark and unrealistic images, because it ignores contributions from light scattering within the volume. Scattering effects can be fully captured through physically based volume lighting models, which are too complex for interactive rendering. It is possible, however, to extend Algorithm 39-3 to approximate certain scattering phenomena. One such phenomenon is *translucency*, which is the result of light propagating into and scattering throughout a material. While general scattering computations consider the incoming light from all directions, for translu-

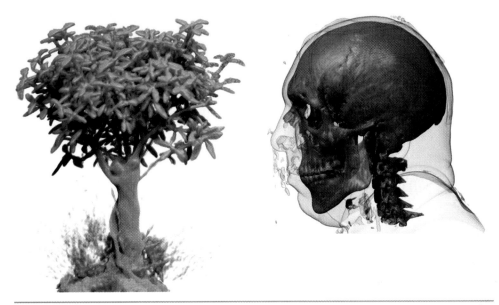

Figure 39-11. Examples of Volume Rendering with Shadows

cency it is sufficient to include the incoming light within a cone in the direction of the light source only, as shown in Figure 39-12. The result of this simplification is that the indirect scattering contribution at a particular sample depends on a local neighborhood of samples computed in the previous iteration of Algorithm 39-3. Thus, translucency effects are possible to incorporate by propagating and blurring indirect lighting components from slice to slice in the volume.

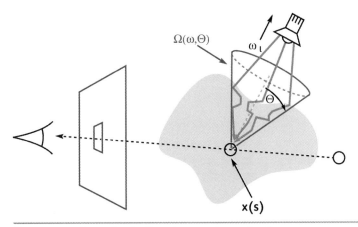

Figure 39-12. Setup for the Translucency Approximation

To incorporate translucency into Algorithm 39-3, first add indirect attenuation parameters A_i. These parameters are alpha values for each of the RGB color channels, as opposed to the single alpha value A used in Algorithm 39-3. Second, instead of initializing the light buffer with the light color C_L, use $1 - C_L$. Third, in step 3(a)(iii), multiply C by $1 - A_i$, that is, 1 minus the color value read from the light buffer. In step 3(b), set the color in the fragment shader to A_i instead of 0, and replace the Over operator with the following blending operation:

$$C = C_1 + (1 - C_1)C_0 \qquad (8)$$

Light Buffer Compositing for the Translucency Model

In Equation 8, C_1 is the color of the incoming fragment, and C_0 is the color currently in the target render buffer.

Next, an additional buffer is used to blur the indirect attenuation components when updating the contents of the light buffer in step 3(b). The two buffers are used in an alternating fashion, such that the current light buffer is sampled once in step 3(a) for the eye, and multiple times in step 3(b) for the light. The next light buffer is the render target in step 3(b). This relationship changes after each slice, so the next buffer becomes the current buffer and vice versa.

To sample the indirect components for the blur operation, the texture coordinates for the current light buffer, in all but one texture unit, are modified using a perturbation texture. The radius of the blur circle, used to scale the perturbations, is given by a user-defined blur angle φ and the sample distance d:

$$R = d \tan\left(\varphi/2\right) \qquad (9)$$

Blur Radius for the Translucency Approximation

In the fragment shader during step 3(b), the current light buffer is read using the modified texture coordinates. The blurred attenuation is computed as a weighted sum of the values read from the light buffer, and then blended into the next light buffer.

Figure 39-13 shows an example of translucent volume rendering using a fish CT data set. This technique is important for creating convincing images of clouds and other atmospheric phenomena (see Figures 39-1 and 39-14a). Because a separate opacity for each color component is used in step 3(b), it is possible to control the amount of light penetrating into a region by modifying the A_i values to be smaller or larger than the alpha value A used in step 3(a). When the A_i values are less than A, light penetrates deeply into the volume, even if from the eye's point of view, the material appears optically dense.

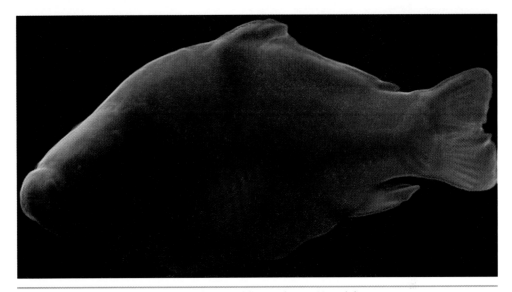

Figure 39-13. Example of Volume Rendering with Translucent Materials

Also, because an independent alpha is specified for each color channel, light changes color as it penetrates deeper into the volume. This is much like the effect of holding a flashlight under your hand: the light enters white and exits red. This effect is achieved by making the A_i value for red smaller than the A_i values for green and blue, resulting in a lower attenuation of the red component than the green and blue components.

Computing volumetric light transport in screen space, using a 2D buffer, is advantageous for a variety of reasons. Matching the resolutions of light propagation and the viewport produces crisp shadows with minimal aliasing artifacts. The method presented in this subsection decouples the resolution of the light transport from the 3D data grid, and it permits accurate lighting of procedural volumetric texturing effects, as described in the following subsection.

39.5.2 Procedural Rendering

One drawback of volume rendering is that small high-frequency details cannot be represented in low-resolution volumes. High-frequency details are essential for capturing the characteristics of many volumetric phenomena such as clouds, smoke, trees, hair, and fur. Procedural noise simulation is a powerful technique for adding detail to low-resolution volume data (Ebert et al. 2002). The general approach uses a coarse model for the macrostructure and procedural noise for the microstructure. Described next are two ways of adding procedural noise to texture-based volume rendering. The first approach perturbs optical properties in the shading stage; the second method perturbs the volume itself.

Both approaches use a small noise volume. In this volume, each voxel is initialized to four random numbers, stored as RGBA components, and blurred slightly to hide artifacts caused by trilinear interpolation. Multiple copies of the noise texture are used for each slice at different scales during rendering. Per-pixel perturbation is computed as a weighted sum of the individual noise components. To animate the perturbation, a varying offset vector can be added to the noise texture coordinates in the fragment shader.

The first technique uses the four per-pixel noise components to modify optical properties of the volume after the transfer function has been evaluated. This results in materials that appear to have irregularities. By selecting which optical properties to modify, different effects are achieved.

The second method uses noise to modify the location of the data access in the volume (Kniss et al. 2003). In this case, three components of the noise texture form a vector, which is added to the texture coordinates for the data texture lookup. Figure 39-14 illustrates how volume perturbation is used to add intricate detail to coarse volumetric models.

39.6 Performance Considerations

Texture-based volume rendering can easily push the performance limits of modern GPUs. This section covers a few considerations specific to volume rendering on GPUs.

39.6.1 Rasterization Bottlenecks

Unlike most graphics applications, texture-based volume renderers use a small number of relatively large geometric primitives. The rasterizer produces many fragments per primitive, which can easily become the bottleneck in the pipeline. In addition, unlike opaque objects, the transparent proxy geometry used in volume rendering cannot leverage the early depth-culling capabilities of modern GPUs. The rasterization bottleneck is exacerbated by the large number of slices needed to render high-quality images. In addition, the frame buffer contents in the compositing stage have to be read back every time a fragment is processed by the fragment shader or the compositing hardware.

For these reasons, it is important to draw proxy geometry that generates only the required fragments. Simply drawing large quads that cover the volume leads to a very

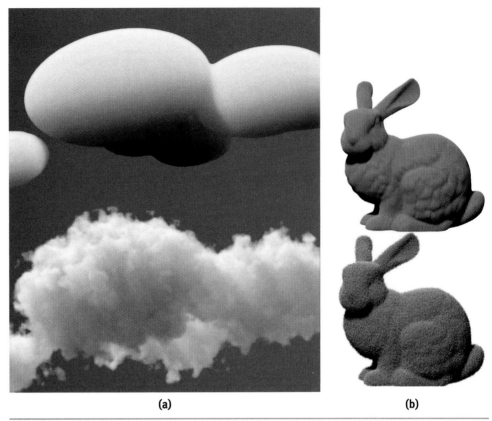

(a)   (b)

Figure 39-14. Examples of the Volume Perturbation Technique
(a) The original low-resolution data set is generated from multiple ellipsoids that define the large-scale cloud structure. (b) A fur effect is added to the "Stanford bunny" using volume perturbation.

slow implementation. The rasterization pressure is reduced by making the viewport smaller, decreasing the sample rate, using preintegrated classification (Engel et al. 2001), and by not drawing empty regions of the volume (Li et al. 2003, Krüger and Westermann 2003). Empty-space skipping can efficiently balance the available geometry and fragment processing bandwidth.

Fragment Program Limitations

Volume rendering performance is largely influenced by the complexity of the fragment shader. Precomputed lookup tables may be faster than fragment programs with many complex instructions. Dependent texture reads, however, can result in pipeline stalls, significantly reducing rendering speed. Achieving peak performance requires finding the correct balance of fragment operations and texture reads, which can be a challenging profiling task.

Texture Memory Limitations

The trilinear interpolation (quadrilinear when using mipmaps) used in volume rendering requires at least eight texture lookups, making it more expensive than the bilinear (trilinear with mipmaps) interpolation used in standard 2D texture mapping. In addition, when using large 3D textures, the texture caches may not be as efficient at hiding the latency of texture memory access as they are when using 2D textures. When the speed of rendering is critical, smaller textures, texture compression, and lower precision types can reduce the pressure on the texture memory subsystem. Efficient compression schemes have recently emerged that achieve high texture compression ratios without affecting the rendering performance (Schneider and Westermann 2003). Finally, the arithmetic and memory systems in modern GPUs operate on all values in an RGBA tuple simultaneously. Packing data into RGBA tuples increases performance by lessening the bandwidth requirements.

39.7 Summary

Volume rendering is an important graphics and visualization technique. A volume renderer can be used for displaying not only surfaces of a model but also the intricate detail contained within. The first half of this chapter presented a typical implementation of a texture-based volume renderer with view-aligned proxy geometry. In Section 39.5, two advanced techniques built upon the basic implementation were described. The presented techniques improve the quality of images by adding volumetric shadows, translucency effects, and random detail to the standard rendering model.

Volume rendering has been around for over a decade and is still an active area of graphics and visualization research. Interested readers are referred to the list of references for further details and state-of-the-art techniques.

39.8 References

Ebert, D., F. Musgrave, D. Peachey, K. Perlin, S. Worley, W. Mark, and J. Hart. 2002. *Texturing and Modeling: A Procedural Approach*. Morgan Kaufmann.

Engel, K., M. Kraus, and T. Ertl. 2001. "High-Quality Pre-Integrated Volume Rendering Using Hardware-Accelerated Pixel Shading." In *Proceedings of the SIGGRAPH/Eurographics Workshop on Graphics Hardware 2001*, pp. 9–16.

Hadwiger, M., T. Teußl, H. Hauser, and E. Gröller. 2001 "Hardware-Accelerated High-Quality Filtering on PC Hardware." In *Proceedings of the International Workshop on Vision, Modeling, and Visualization 2001*, pp. 105–112.

Kindlmann, G., and J. Durkin. 1998. "Semi-Automatic Generation of Transfer Functions for Direct Volume Rendering." In *Proceedings of the IEEE Symposium on Volume Visualization*, pp. 79–86.

Kindlmann, G. 1999. "Semi-Automatic Generation of Transfer Functions for Direct Volume Rendering." Master's Thesis, Department of Computer Science, Cornell University.

Kindlmann, G. 2003. The Teem Toolkit. **http://teem.sourceforge.net**

Kniss, J., G. Kindlmann, and C. Hansen. 2002a. "Multidimensional Transfer Functions for Interactive Volume Rendering." *IEEE Transactions on Visualization and Computer Graphics* 8(4), pp. 270–285.

Kniss, J., K. Engel, M. Hadwiger, and C. Rezk-Salama. 2002b. "High-Quality Volume Graphics on Consumer PC Hardware." Course 42, ACM SIGGRAPH.

Kniss, J., S. Premo e, C. Hansen, P. Shirley, and A. McPherson. 2003. "A Model for Volume Lighting and Modeling." *IEEE Transactions on Visualization and Computer Graphics* 9(2), pp. 150–162.

Krüger, J., and R. Westermann. 2003. "Acceleration Techniques for GPU-Based Volume Rendering." In *Proceedings of IEEE Visualization*, pp. 287–292.

Lefohn, A., J. Kniss, C. Hansen, and R. Whitaker. 2004. "A Streaming Narrow-Band Algorithm: Interactive Deformation and Visualization of Level Sets." *IEEE Transactions on Visualization and Computer Graphics* (to appear).

Levoy, M. 1988. "Display of Surfaces from Volume Data." *IEEE Computer Graphics & Applications* 8(2), pp. 29–37.

Li, W., K. Mueller, and A. Kaufman. 2003. "Empty Space Skipping and Occlusion Clipping for Texture-Based Volume Rendering." In *Proceedings of IEEE Visualization*, pp. 317–324.

Max, N. 1995. "Optical Models for Direct Volume Rendering." *IEEE Transactions on Visualization and Computer Graphics* 1(2), pp. 97–108.

Moret, B., and H. Shapiro. 1991. *Algorithms from P to NP.* Benjamin Cummings.

Rezk-Salama, C., K. Engel, M. Bauer, G. Greiner, and T. Ertl. 2000. "Interactive Volume Rendering on Standard PC Graphics Hardware Using Multi-Textures and Multi-Stage Rasterization." In *Proceedings of the SIGGRAPH/Eurographics Workshop on Graphics Hardware 2000*, pp. 109–118.

Roettger, S., S. Guthe, D. Weiskopf, T. Ertl, and W. Strasser. 2003. "Smart Hardware-Accelerated Volume Rendering." In *Proceedings of the Eurographics/IEEE TVCG Symposium on Visualization*, pp. 231–238.

Schneider, J., and R. Westermann. 2003. "Compression Domain Volume Rendering." In *Proceedings of IEEE Visualization*, pp. 293–300.

Weiskopf, D., K. Engel, M. Hadwiger, J. Kniss, and A. Lefohn. 2003. "Interactive Visualization of Volumetric Data on Consumer PC Hardware." Tutorial 1. *IEEE Visualization*.

Wittenbrink, C., T. Malzbender, and M. Goss. 1998. "Opacity-Weighted Color Interpolation for Volume Sampling." In *Proceedings of the IEEE Symposium on Volume Visualization*, pp. 135–142.

Chapter 40

Applying Real-Time Shading to 3D Ultrasound Visualization

Thilaka Sumanaweera
Siemens Medical Solutions USA, Inc.

The vast computing power of modern programmable GPUs can be harnessed effectively to visualize 3D medical data, potentially resulting in quicker and more effective diagnoses of diseases. For example, myocardial function and fetal abnormalities, such as cleft palate, can be visualized using volume rendering of ultrasound data. In this chapter, we present a technique for volume rendering time-varying 3D medical ultrasound volumes—that is, 4D volumes—using the vertex and fragment processors of the GPU. We use 3D projective texture mapping to volume render ultrasound data. We present results using real fetal ultrasound data.

40.1 Background

Volume rendering is a technique for visualizing 3D volumetric data sets generated by medical imaging techniques such as computed tomography (CT), magnetic resonance imaging (MRI), and 3D ultrasound. Volume rendering is also used in the field of oil exploration to visualize volumetric data.

Visualizing volumetric data sets is challenging. Although humans are extremely adept at visualizing and interpreting 2D images, most humans have difficulty visualizing 3D volumetric data sets. Prior to the invention of volumetric medical imaging techniques, plain 2D x-ray images ruled the field of diagnostic medical imaging. Radiologists became accustomed to visualizing and interpreting 2D x-ray images quite well. When volumetric imaging techniques were invented, the number of 2D images viewed by radiologists skyrocketed, because each volume now contained a series of 2D images or slices. The need for a more intuitive way to visualize the volumetric data quickly became apparent and led to the development of volume rendering.

Since the late 1980s, medical imaging modalities such as CT and MRI have benefited from volume rendering as a technique for visualizing volumetric data. CT and MRI data are acquired in 3D Cartesian grids, as shown in Figure 40-1a. Ultrasound data, however, is more complex, because typically ultrasound data is acquired in non-Cartesian grids such as the one shown in Figure 40-1b, called the *acoustic grid*. Therefore, volume rendering of CT and MRI is simpler than volume rendering of ultrasound data.

Say you want to get a 3D ultrasound scan of some part of your anatomy. In the clinic, a sonographer first places an ultrasonic transducer on your skin. A transducer is basically an antenna, sensitive to sound waves operating at about 1 MHz or higher. It sends out inaudible sound pulses to the body and listens to the echoes, just like radar. Just like radar, ultrasound volumes are typically acquired in a grid that diverges as you move away from the transducer into the body. To give you an idea of the nature of ultrasound images, Figure 40-2 shows a 2D ultrasound image of a fetus. You can imagine the 3D version of the ultrasound volume: a truncated pyramid or a cone, similar to Figure 40-1b.

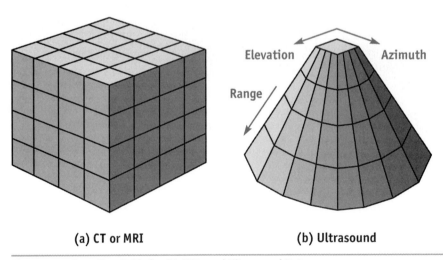

(a) CT or MRI   (b) Ultrasound

Figure 40-1. Sampling Grids for CT, MRI, and Ultrasound Data

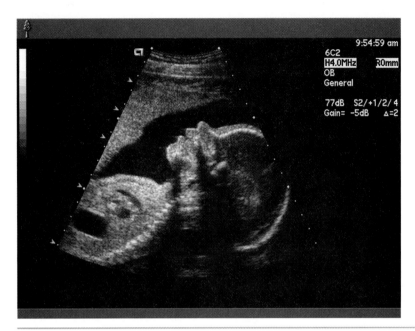

Figure 40-2. A 2D Ultrasound Image of a Fetal Head

Three-dimensional ultrasound data is acquired by an ultrasound scanner and stored in its local memory as a 3D array. The fastest-moving index of this 3D array corresponds to the distance away from the transducer, called the *range* direction (see Figure 40-1b). The next-fastest-moving index corresponds to the *azimuth* direction of the transducer. The slowest-moving index corresponds to the *elevation* direction of the transducer.

Ultrasound data can also be 4D, acquired in three spatial directions and in the time direction. You may have seen 4D ultrasound images of a fetal face acquired at an OB clinic. The number of volumes per second required for an application such as imaging a fetal face is far less than the number of volumes per second required for an application such as imaging the human heart. This is because the heart is moving rapidly and we need to acquire and volume render several 3D volumes per cardiac cycle to adequately visualize the heart motion.

Luckily, programmable vertex and fragment processors in modern GPUs, such as NVIDIA's GeForce FX and Quadro FX, have recently provided the means to volume render 4D ultrasound data acquired in non-Cartesian grids at the rates required for visualizing the human heart. A number of techniques exist to volume render 4D ultrasonic data. In this chapter, we walk through one such technique.

40.2 Introduction

Three-dimensional grid data sets, such as CT, MRI, and ultrasound data, can be volume rendered using texture mapping. A variety of techniques exists. See Chapter 39, "Volume Rendering Techniques," in this book and Hadwiger et al. 2002 for good reviews. In this chapter, we are using 3D textures. We first review how volume rendering is done using data such as CT and MRI in Cartesian grids. The sample OpenGL program `VolumeRenderCartesian.cpp` (which is on the book's CD and Web site) demonstrates how volume rendering is done using Cartesian grids. We do not go into great detail about this program here, but let's go through some basics.

40.2.1 Volume Rendering Data in a Cartesian Grid

Figure 40-3 shows the gist of volume rendering Cartesian data using 3D textures. The data is first loaded into the video memory as a 3D texture, using `glTexImage3D`. Then with alpha blending enabled, a series of cut-planes, all orthogonal to the viewing direction, is texture-mapped, starting from the cut-plane farthest from the viewer and proceeding to the cut-plane closest to the viewer. Remember, the cut-planes are all parallel to the computer screen. Let's call the coordinate system associated with the computer screen the *cut-plane space*. The data set can be rotated with respect to the computer screen. Let's call the coordinate system associated with the data set the *data set space*.

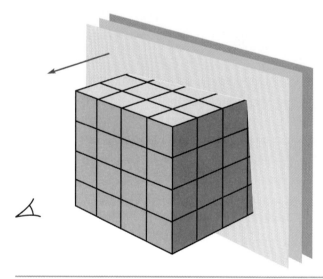

Figure 40-3. Volume Rendering 3D Cartesian Data

The content of a pixel in the frame buffer after the ith cut-plane is rendered, P_i, can be expressed as:

$$P_i = \left[1 - f(I_i)\right] P_{i-1} + g(I_i),\qquad(1)$$

where P_{i-1} is the pixel content after the $(i-1)$th cut-plane is rendered, I_i is the incoming fragment from the ith cut-plane, $f()$ is an opacity function, and $g()$ is an opacity-weighted transfer function. Both $f()$ and $g()$ are assumed to be in the range $[0, 1]$. Intuitively, this means that if the incoming fragment is opaque, the contributions from the fragments behind it are suppressed. Equation 1 can be implemented in OpenGL using alpha blending, with the blending function being GL_ONE_MINUS_SRC_ALPHA. The opacity-weighted transfer function produces the RGB values for the pixel, and the opacity function produces the alpha values of the pixel.

When texture-mapping the cut-planes, they can be specified using two different approaches: *enclosing rectangles* and *polygons of intersections*.

Enclosing Rectangles

The use of enclosing rectangles is the most straightforward way of texture-mapping cut-planes. The sample program VolumeRenderCartesian.cpp uses this technique. In this method, a series of quads enclosing the extent of the data set is drawn from back to front. You can store the coordinates of the vertices of the quads in the video memory for quick access for fast rendering. The only point to remember is to enable one of two ways to suppress texture mapping of the data outside the original data volume (that is, when any of the texture coordinates (s, t, r) is less than 0.0 or greater than 1.0). One can do this in one of three ways: (a) using clipping planes, (b) using GL_CLAMP_TO_BORDER_ARB for wrapping the texture coordinates and setting the border color to black, or (c) using GL_CLAMP_TO_EDGE for wrapping the texture coordinates and making the data values equal to 0 at the borders, as follows:

$Data = 0$ if $s = 0.0$, $t = 0.0$, $r = 0.0$, $s = 1.0$, $t = 1.0$ or $r = 1.0$.

Polygons of Intersection

This method is a bit more complex and requires you to find the polygon of intersection between a given cut-plane and the cube of data. You can ask either the CPU or the GPU (using a vertex program) to find it for you. Once you find the vertices of the polygon of intersection, you can then texture-map that polygon. This approach is faster than the other approach from the fragment program's point of view, because you are visiting only those fragments that are inside the cube of data. However, from the rasterizer's point of view, it is more demanding, because more triangles now need to be rasterized. Furthermore, each time the viewer changes the viewing direction with respect to the data set space, the program needs to recompute the polygons. If you are using the CPU to recompute the polygons, then you also need to upload the vertices of the polygons to the GPU before they are rendered, which can be time-consuming.

The sample program `VolumeRenderCartesian.cpp` uses the enclosing rectangles with clipping planes to render the cut-planes. Figure 40-4 shows a volume rendered image of a CT data set produced by the `VolumeRenderCartesian.cpp` program. You can rotate, zoom, and step through the volume when running this program. Type the key "h" when you have the keyboard focus on the graphics window to see help. The data set used for this visualization is $256 \times 256 \times 256$ voxels.

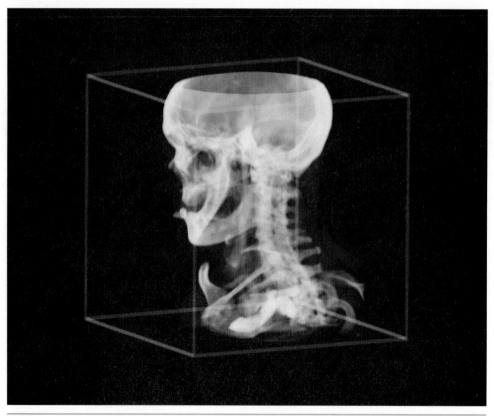

Figure 40-4. A Volume Rendered CT Data Set Acquired in a Cartesian Coordinate System

40.2.2 Volume Rendering Data in Pyramidal Grids

Now let's examine volume rendering of data acquired in pyramidal grids. There are several grids that have the property of diverging as you go into the body, including pyramidal, conical, spherical, and cylindrical grids. For simplicity, we use a pyramidal grid in this chapter because it lends itself to the kind of linear processing that GPUs are good at, as we see later. Furthermore, other types of grids, such as those shown in Figure 40-1b and Figure 40-2, can also be transformed into pyramidal grids by resampling the ultrasound data along the range direction, without loss of generality.

For explanation's sake, let's first look at two 2D cases: (a) Cartesian and (b) pyramidal grids, as shown in Figure 40-5. For each 2D grid, we acquire an ultrasound data sample at each of the grid points, forming a 2D data array. In general, ultrasound images have a lot more grid points. But here we are looking at only a 5 × 5 grid. In the Cartesian grid shown in Figure 40-5a, the vertical lines corresponding to constant s are called *ultrasound lines*. The transducer is located at the $r = 0.0$ plane. The ultrasound scanner fires each ultrasound line sequentially from left to right and samples data at each grid point to collect a 2D image. The texture coordinates (s, r) correspond to the azimuth and range directions of the transducer.

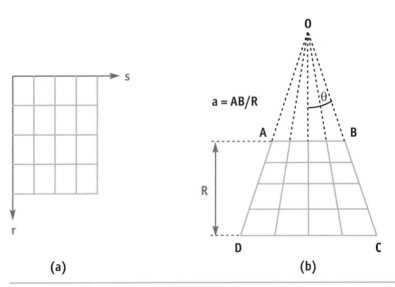

Figure 40-5. Cartesian and Pyramidal Grids in 2D

In the pyramidal grid shown in Figure 40-5b, the ultrasound lines all meet at a common point, O, called the *apex*. The extent of the transducer, AB, is called the *aperture size*. In this chapter, we use the concept of the normalized aperture size: $a = AB/R$, where R is the height of the pyramid ($0 \leq R \leq 1.0$). The angle AOB is called the *apex angle*, 2θ. We can think of the pyramidal grid as being equivalent to the Cartesian grid, with the change that the s coordinate is scaled as a function of the r coordinate, linearly. We can easily accomplish this by using projective texture mapping, as we discuss later.

Figure 40-6 shows the 3D pyramidal grid. In order to generate the correct texture coordinates for the 3D pyramidal grid, we scale the s and t texture coordinates as a linear function of r, similar to the 2D pyramidal grid. The following are the steps of this algorithm:

1. Assuming that we are using a Cartesian grid, generate the texture coordinates inside the vertex program by mimicking OpenGL's automatic texture-coordinate-generation function, glTexGen.

2. The goal is to scale the s and t coordinates, but not the r coordinate, as a linear function of r. To do this, compute the following new texture coordinates inside the vertex program:

$$q = a + 2r \tan \theta, \qquad (2)$$

$$s' = (s - 0.5) + 0.5q, \text{ and} \qquad (3)$$

$$t' = (t - 0.5) + 0.5q, \qquad (4)$$

where s', t' and q are the new coordinates.

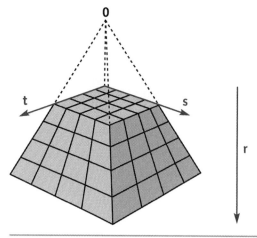

Figure 40-6. 3D Pyramidal Grid

3. Then in a fragment program, do the scaling and texture lookup in a single step using the projective 3D texture lookup instruction. Keep in mind that you need to prevent the scaling performed on the r coordinate; otherwise, you get scaling along the r direction as well, generating a pyramidal data volume that appears to stretch more and more along the r direction as you go into the body. To avoid this, simply pre-multiply the r coordinate with the scale in the fragment program:

$$r' = rq, \tag{5}$$

where r' is also a new texture coordinate. (Because this step is a nonlinear operation, we cannot do it in the vertex program, because the GPU then interpolates incorrect values for r' across each fragment.)

4. When all is said and done, the projective texture lookup instruction uses the following effective texture coordinates for texture lookup:

$$s_{proj} = (s - 0.5)/q + 0.5, \tag{6}$$

$$t_{proj} = (t - 0.5)/q + 0.5, \text{ and} \tag{7}$$

$$r_{proj} = r. \tag{8}$$

The cut-planes are specified as a series of enclosing rectangles as discussed earlier. The size of these rectangles is chosen such that they completely enclose the pyramidal grid. The sample OpenGL program, `VolumeRenderPyramid.cpp`, the vertex program, `VolumeRenderPyramidV.cg`, and the fragment program, `VolumeRender-PyramidF.cg`, illustrate our algorithm using the same CT data set used before in `VolumeRenderCartesian.cpp`. There is also an assembly version of the fragment program in `VolumeRenderPyramidF.ocg`. Now let's investigate the vertex and fragment programs.

The Vertex Program

We now go through our vertex program one line at a time, as shown in Listing 40-1 The input to this vertex program is the variable `Position`, containing the vertex coordinates. Ten uniform variables—`ZoomFactor`, `Pyramid`, `ClipPlane0-5`, `ModelView`, and `ModelViewProj`—are also input to this program. `ZoomFactor` contains the scale value used for zooming. `Pyramid` contains two parameters describing the geometry of the pyramidal grid: `Pyramid.x`, the normalized aperture size of the transducer, a, and `Pyramid.y`, two times the tangent of half of the apex angle, $2 \tan \theta$. `ClipPlane0` through `ClipPlane5` contain the equations of the six clipping planes. `ModelView` and `ModelViewProj` contain the modelview matrix in the data set space and the modelview matrix concatenated with the projection matrix of the cut-plane space, respectively.

Listing 40-1. `VolumeRenderPyramidV.cg`

```
void VertexProgram(in float4  Position   : POSITION,
                   out float4 hPosition  : POSITION,
                   out float4 hTex0      : TEX0,
                   out float  hClip0     : CLP0,
                   out float  hClip1     : CLP1,
                   out float  hClip2     : CLP2,
                   out float  hClip3     : CLP3,
                   out float  hClip4     : CLP4,
                   out float  hClip5     : CLP5,
                   uniform float4 ZoomFactor,
                   uniform float4 Pyramid,
                   uniform float4 ClipPlane0,
                   uniform float4 ClipPlane1,
                   uniform float4 ClipPlane2,
                   uniform float4 ClipPlane3,
                   uniform float4 ClipPlane4,
                   uniform float4 ClipPlane5,
                   uniform float4x4 ModelView,
                   uniform float4x4 ModelViewProj)
{
  // Compute the clip-space position
  hPosition = mul(ModelViewProj, Position);

  // Remove the zoom factor from the position coordinates
  Position = Position * ZoomFactor;

  // Compute the texture coordinates using the Cartesian grid
  hTex0 = mul(ModelView, Position);

  // Save original texture coordinates
  float4 hTex0_Orig = hTex0 - float4(0.5, 0.5, 0.0, 0.0);

  // Compute the scale for the texture coordinates in the
  // pyramidal grid
  hTex0.w = Pyramid.x + hTex0.z * Pyramid.y;

  // Adjust for the texture coordinate offsets
  hTex0.x = hTex0.x - 0.5 + 0.5 * hTex0.w;
  hTex0.y = hTex0.y - 0.5 + 0.5 * hTex0.w;
```

Listing 40-1 (*continued*). `VolumeRenderPyramidV.cg`

```
  // Clip pyramidal volume
  hClip0 = dot(hTex0_Orig, ClipPlane0);
  hClip1 = dot(hTex0_Orig, ClipPlane1);
  hClip2 = dot(hTex0_Orig, ClipPlane2);
  hClip3 = dot(hTex0_Orig, ClipPlane3);
  hClip4 = dot(hTex0_Orig, ClipPlane4);
  hClip5 = dot(hTex0_Orig, ClipPlane5);
}
```

The outputs of this vertex program are the clip-space position of the vertex, `hPosition`; the texture coordinates, `hTex0`; and the clip distances, `CLP0` through `CLP5`.

In the first line, we are computing the clip-space position of the vertex, and in the second line, we remove any scaling applied by the OpenGL program to the position coordinates. In the third line, we are computing the texture coordinates for the Cartesian coordinate system, mimicking OpenGL's `glTexGen` function. In line 4, we are saving the original content of the texture coordinates, shifted by 0.5 only in s and t directions, in `hTex0_Orig` for later use. And then comes the fun part. In line 5, we are computing the amount of stretching or scaling we have to do to the s and t texture coordinates for a given r coordinate. In lines 6 and 7, we are offsetting the origin of the s and t texture coordinates so that the scaling of s and t texture coordinates in the fragment program is performed around the central axis of the pyramid. Lines 8–13 compute the clipping values for the six planes bounding the pyramidal volume. Fragments containing clipping values less than zero are not drawn to the frame buffer.

The Fragment Program

The fragment program in Listing 40-2 takes it from where the vertex program left off. The input, `inTex`, is a variable containing the texture coordinates. There are two uniform inputs as well: `USTexture` and `ColorMap`. `USTexture` contains the 3D texture describing the 3D ultrasound volume. `ColorMap` is a color map table containing the opacity-weighted transfer and opacity functions. The output, `sColor0`, contains the fragment color.

In the first line, we are premultiplying the r coordinate with the scale. In the second line, we are looking up the texture value with the 3D ultrasound volume using projective texture mapping. In the third line, we are doing a 1D color map lookup to generate the colors to render according to the ultrasound data value.

Listing 40-2. VolumeRenderPyramidF.cg

```
void FragmentProgram(in float4 inTex : TEXCOORD0,
                     out float4 sColor0 : COLOR0,
                     const uniform sampler3D USTexture,
                     const uniform sampler1D ColorMap)
{
  // Premultiply 'r' coordinate with the scale
  inTex.z = inTex.z * inTex.w;

  // Projective 3D texture lookup
  float val = tex3Dproj(USTexture, inTex);

  // Color map lookup
  sColor0 = tex1D(ColorMap, val);
}
```

Typically, the volume rendering speed is limited by the complexity of the fragment program (that is, it's fill-rate bound). Therefore, sometimes it is better to hand-tweak the fragment assembly code to get the maximum throughput, as shown in Listing 40-3.

Listing 40-3. VolumeRenderPyramidF.ocg

```
!!FP1.0
# NV_fragment_program generated by NVIDIA Cg compiler
# cgc version 1.1.0003, build date Mar  4 2003  12:32:10
# command line args: -q -profile fp30 -entry FragmentProgram
#vendor NVIDIA Corporation
#version 1.0.02
#profile fp30
#program FragmentProgram
#semantic FragmentProgram.USTexture
#semantic FragmentProgram.ColorMap
#var float4 inTex : $vin.TEXCOORD0 : TEXCOORD0 : 0 : 1
#var float4 sColor0 : $vout.COLOR0 : COLOR0 : 1 : 1
#var sampler3D USTexture :   : texunit 0 : 2 : 1
#var sampler1D ColorMap :    : texunit 1 : 3 : 1
MOVX H0, f[TEX0];
MULX H0.z, H0.z, H0.w;
TXP  R0, H0, TEX0, 3D;
TEX  o[COLR], R0.x, TEX1, 1D;
END
# 4 instructions, 1 R-regs, 1 H-regs.
# End of program
```

In the first line, the incoming texture coordinate is loaded into one of the 12-bit fixed-point registers, H0. In the next line, the *r* component of the texture coordinate is pre-multiplied using the scale. Using 12-bit fixed-point math, we can accelerate the rendering speed significantly. In the third line, we are looking up the fragment value using 3D projective texture lookup. In the last line, we are looking up the color value of the fragment using a 1D color map lookup. And that's it!

Figure 40-7 shows a volume rendered image produced by the sample OpenGL program, `VolumeRenderPyramid.cpp`, which lets you play with the aperture size (keys "a"/"A") and the apex angle (keys "b"/"B") and see the effect on the screen. Press the "h" key to see Help.

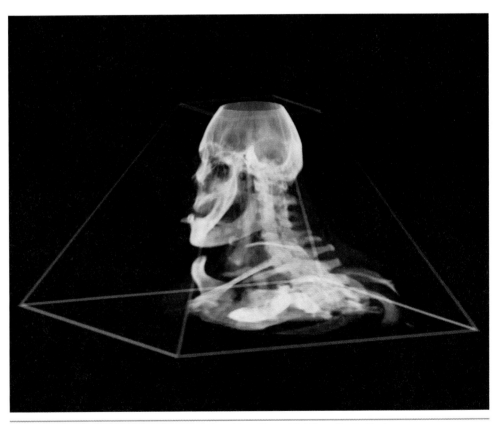

Figure 40-7. The CT Data Set Volume Rendered in a Pyramidal Coordinate System

Volume Rendering Ultrasound Data

The sample program `VolumeRenderPyramidUS.cpp` demonstrates the use of ultrasound data for volume rendering. The ultrasound data of a fetus *in utero*, acquired using an ACUSON Sequoia 512 ultrasound system, consists of $256 \times 256 \times 32$ voxels. Note that in this case, due to the special geometry of the ultrasound probe used to acquire the data, we do not need to change the t coordinate as we did in Equation 7. We only need to scale the s coordinate as a linear function. This produces a pyramidal geometry consisting of a wedge-shaped volume.

40.3 Results

Figure 40-8 shows a volume rendered image of the face of a fetus using the projective texture mapping technique outlined in this chapter. The sample program `Volume-RenderPyramidUS.cpp` produces this image using 181 cut-planes. In the movie clip VolumeRenderPyramidUS.avi, if you look closely, you can see the fetus putting its tongue out and scratching its head.

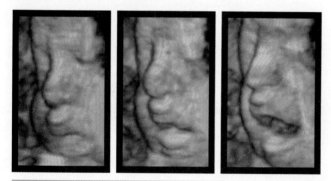

Figure 40-8. The Volume Rendered Image of a Fetal Face Using Projective Texture Mapping

40.4 Conclusion

GPUs have advanced to the point where it is possible to do volume rendering at the rapid rates required for 3D ultrasonic imaging. We have described how to do this for pyramidal grids using projective texture mapping. Using this as the framework, one can include a shading model and also reduce moiré artifacts by using techniques such as preintegrated volume rendering (Engel et al. 2001), with some frame-rate loss.

Note that Equations 6 and 7 can be implemented in a fragment program directly, without using projective texture mapping. This approach is slower compared to the approach we have taken in this chapter. This is because typical volume rendering applications are fill-rate bound, and implementing Equations 6 and 7 would require you to invert the value of r, which requires additional statements and hence runs more slowly.

Note also that we could have supplied a transfer function to the fragment program instead of an opacity-weighted transfer function, and generated the opacity-weighted color inside the fragment program by multiplying the opacity value with the color, sColor0. This would reduce the quantization artifacts at the expense of the frame rate, because it would require an additional statement.

40.5 References

Engel, Klaus, Martin Kraus, and Thomas Ertl. 2001. "High-Quality Pre-Integrated Volume Rendering Using Hardware-Accelerated Pixel Shading." *Proceedings of the SIGGRAPH/Eurographics Workshop on Graphics Hardware 2001*. Available online at **http://wwwvis.informatik.uni-stuttgart.de/~engel/pre-integrated/ paper_GraphicsHardware2001.pdf**

Hadwiger, Markus, Joe Kniss, Klaus Engel, and Christof Rezk-Salama. 2002. "High-Quality Volume Graphics on Consumer PC Hardware." Course Notes 42, SIGGRAPH 2002. Available online at **http://www.cs.utah.edu/~jmk/sigg_crs_02/course_42/course_42_notes_small.pdf**

Chapter 41

Real-Time Stereograms

Fabio Policarpo
Paralelo Computação Ltda.

41.1 What Is a Stereogram?

A stereogram is a 2D image that encodes stereo information so that, when viewed correctly, it reveals a hidden 3D scene. It all started back in the 1960s, when Bela Julesz, who worked at (AT&T) Bell Labs researching human vision—particularly depth perception and pattern recognition—created the *random-dot stereogram* (RDS). Stereograms evolved from stereo photography, in which two photographs are taken from slightly different camera positions (representing the displacement between our eyes).

41.1.1 Stereo Photography

Stereo photography is very old, dating back to 1838, but some of the old stereo cameras and stereo photograph viewers, such as the one shown in Figure 41-1a, can still be found at antique shops. The idea behind stereo photography is to take two similar photographs, but from different positions displaced horizontally (like our eyes). Our eyes are separated from each other by about 65 mm, and this disparity causes slightly different images to be presented to the brain. These differences allow the perception of depth.

In Figure 41-1a, two images (stereo pairs) are placed side by side in front of the lenses. The lenses facilitate viewing, presenting each image to each eye, respectively. The stereo pairs must be visualized so that the left photograph is seen by the left eye, as shown in

(a)   (b)   (c)

Figure 41-1. Stereo Photography
(a) Victorian stereo photograph viewer; (b) left and (c) right stereo pair images. Notice the small differences between the penguin images on the left and on the right.

Figure 41-1b, and the right photograph by the right eye, as in Figure 41-1c. If the images are swapped (with the left image viewed by the right eye and vice versa), depth perception will be inverted.

41.1.2 Random-Dot Stereograms

To generate an RDS, we start by creating an image made of random dots, as shown in Figure 41-2a. Then we duplicate the image and modify it by selecting a region and displacing it horizontally, as in Figure 41-2b (the bigger the displacement, the deeper it looks). The gaps created by moving the regions of the image are then filled with more random-generated dots, as in Figure 41-2c, and…that's it!

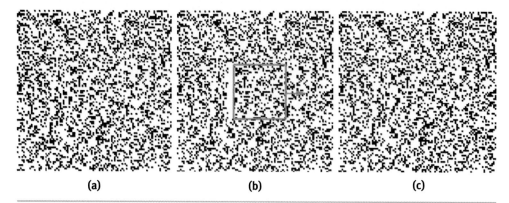

(a)   (b)   (c)

Figure 41-2. Generating an RDS
(a) Original random-dot image (left-eye image); (b) region selected and translated horizontally; (c) final image, with gaps filled with additional random dots (right-eye image).

We now have two images, the original and the copied/displaced versions. Displaying each image to each eye allows the depth perception, and the hidden 3D scene is then visible.

You can view an RDS like a standard stereo photograph. To visualize an RDS (or standard stereo photographs) using only your eyes and no extra apparatus, simply look at two images, such as those in Figure 41-3, crossing your eyes before the image plane. This makes you see four images instead of two, because each image duplicates (as if you were looking at your nose).

Changing the focus point moves the duplicated images in relation to each other, and when the center images merge, you'll see the 3D hidden scene. At the correct focus point, you'll see only three images: one in 3D at the center and two in 2D on the edges. See Figure 41-4 for a detailed explanation of how this works.

Figure 41-3. An RDS Pair Ready for Visualization
When viewed correctly, these two images will show a cube in the middle of the image.

41.1.3   Single-Image Stereograms

A single-image stereogram (SIS), an evolution of the standard RDS, requires only one image. The idea is that neighboring vertical slices of the image will match patterns, thus generating the depth perception. See Figure 41-5 (top). In an SIS, we slice the image into vertical strips, reducing the displacement needed when viewing. For example, if we slice the image into eight strips, we need one-eighth the displacement to view it. This allows the eye crossing point to be closer to the image plane, which is more comfortable to the viewer.

Focus point on image plane. See two images. Each eye sees same position in same image. No 3D visible.

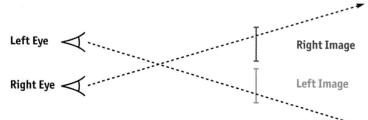

Focus point before image plane. See four images. Each eye sees different position in different image. No 3D visible.

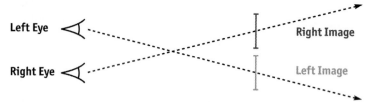

Focus point before image plane. See three images. Each eye sees same position in different image. 3D scene is visible!

Figure 41-4. Viewing a Stereo Image Pair

For an RDS, the eye crossing point must be farther in front of the image plane (that is, closer to the viewer) than in an SIS, so that the displacement of the images seen is the size of the image itself. Actually, an RDS pair works just like an SIS with two strips.

With stereo photography and classic RDS images, viewers must always cross their eyes *in front of* the image plane. But in an SIS, because the separation between the strips is smaller than the distance between our eyes, there is an alternative, more comfortable way to view the image. Viewers can cross their eyes *behind* the image plane, thereby inverting

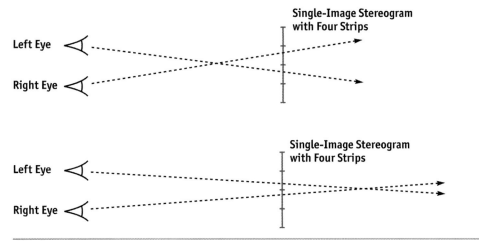

Figure 41-5. Viewing a Stereogram with Four Strips
Top: Eye crossing point before image plane; 3D scene is not visible.
Bottom: Eye crossing point after image plane; 3D scene is visible!

their depth perception but still resulting in a 3D image. See Figure 41-5 (bottom). Most popular SIS images are generated to be viewed this way.

41.2 Creating a Single-Image Stereogram

An SIS is generated from a given depth map (that is, a grayscale image with depth information) and a tile pattern (usually a colored tile image), as in Figure 41-6.

Notice in Figure 41-7 that the tile pattern is repeated and deformed, based on the depth map. If a random-dot image is used as the tile pattern, the resulting stereogram is a *single-image random-dot stereogram* (SIRDS).

41.2.1 Parameters

When creating a new SIS, we need to consider parameters: the number of strips to use; the depth factor, which can increase or decrease the depth perception (which in turn controls the amount of deformation applied to the pattern tiles); and whether to invert the depth values (white can be considered depth 0 or full-depth 1).

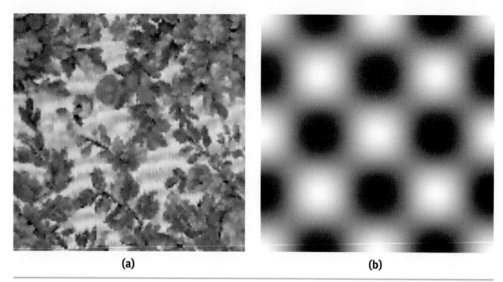

(a)   (b)

Figure 41-6. Input Images
(a) Colored tile image; (b) grayscale depth map.

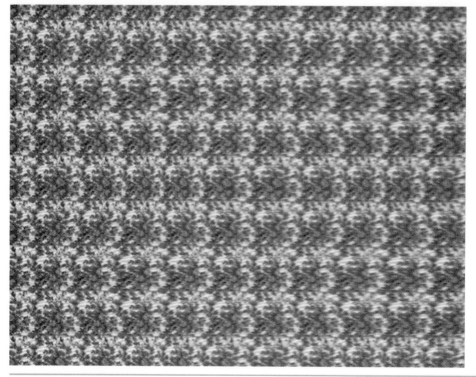

Figure 41-7. The Resulting Stereogram

Here are some of the parameters:

- Number of strips (`num_strips`): Integer value, usually from 8 to 24
- Depth factor: Floating-point value in the range 0.0 to 1.0, with 1.0 meaning full depth
- Invert depth: Boolean value indicating whether depth values should be inverted (1 − depth)

41.2.2 Rendering

To render the SIS, we start by subdividing the depth map and the result image into vertical strips. To simplify this example, we use four strips (`num_strips = 4`), but for a true SIS we would use more. We then subdivide the depth map, shown in Figure 41-8, into four strips (`num_strips`) and divide the result map into five strips (`num_strips + 1`), because we need a reference strip to start with.

This is the pseudocode for the SIS rendering:

```
select_pattern_texture();
draw_strip(0);
read_strip_to_result_texture(0);

enable_fragment_program();
select_depth_texture();
select_result_texture();

for(i = 0; i < num_strips; i++)
{
  draw_strip(i + 1);
  read_strip_to_texture(i + 1);
}

disable_fragment_program();
draw_result_texture();
```

At the beginning of the pseudocode, we simply draw the first strip, texture-mapped with the tile pattern, as in Figure 41-8a (no fragment program is needed, just normal texture mapping). We copy the strip pixels to the result texture map (using `glCopy-TexSubImage2D` to copy the region we just modified). We then have the result image, as shown in Figure 41-8b.

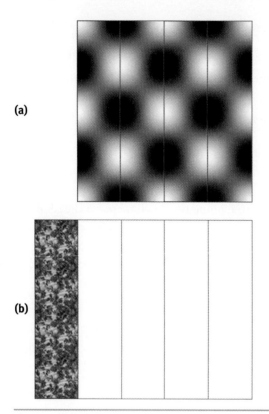

Figure 41-8. Rendering the Image
(a) Depth map; (b) result map.

Next, we enable the fragment program and set the depth map, result map, and depth factor as parameters to it. We loop, drawing the remaining four strips from the result image. For each strip we draw, we must copy its pixels to the result texture map, because each new strip uses the previous strip's image as a reference.

When drawing the missing strips from Figure 41-8b, we will be copying the content from the previous strip and displacing pixels horizontally based on the current pixel depth. For example, if a given pixel depth is 0, we will copy the exact color of the same pixel location in the previous strip. But for other depth values, we will be getting the color from the previous strip at positions in the same scan line, but displaced proportionally to its depth.

Now consider the depth map and the result map images with coordinates ranging from [0, 0] to [1, 1]. A given fragment with coordinates [x, y] uses the following computations to find the coordinates in the previous strip of the result map from where to get the color:

$$[x, y]_{\text{result\_map}} = [x + a - c, y]_{\text{result\_map}}, \quad \text{where}$$

$$a = \left[b \times \left(\frac{x}{c - 1} \right), y \right]_{\text{depth\_map}} \times c \times \text{depth\_factor},$$

$$b = \frac{1}{\text{num\_strips}},$$

$$c = \frac{1}{\text{num\_strips} + 1}.$$

41.2.3 Creating Animated Single-Image Stereograms

Because SIS images can be generated in real time using the fragment program capabilities of our GPU, we can now make an *animated single-image stereogram* (ASIS). We will use a normal 3D scene made of triangles, and use its z-buffer as the SIS depth map—which means we'll render a 3D scene from a given viewpoint and read the z-buffer contents into the depth map texture. See Figure 41-9.

(a)　　　　　　　　　　　　　(b)

Figure 41-9. Making an Animated SIS
(a) A normal rendering of a 3D scene. (b) The depth map acquired from the z-buffer contents after rendering the 3D scene.

When we use the z-buffer from a real-time rendered scene as the source for the depth map image, we can interactively move the 3D scene (or have a predefined camera animation path) and have the stereogram update every frame to reflect the changes. This produces a real-time animated stereogram (a single frame from the animation is shown in Figure 41-10).

It's difficult to visualize an animated stereogram, so look at it first without animation, and when you have a clear view of it, turn animation on. This is because you must keep your eye crossing point fixed at the correct distance while the image animates to be able to visualize the animated stereogram. People unfamiliar with stereograms will find it easier to search for the correct eye crossing point distance with a static image.

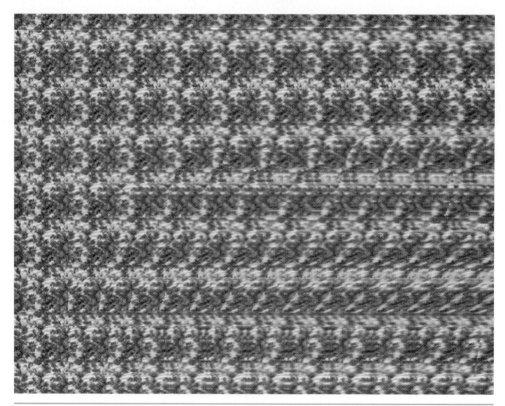

Figure 41-10. One Frame of the Animated Stereogram
Generated from the 3D scene z-buffer in Figure 41-9b.

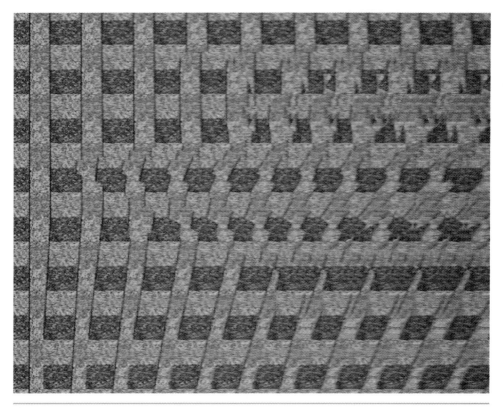

Figure 41-11. Another View with Different Color Tile
Also generated from the 3D scene z-buffer in Figure 41-9b.

41.2.4 Fragment Program

Listing 41-1 shows the fragment program used to generate the stereograms we've discussed.

Listing 41-1. Fragment Program for Generating Stereograms

```
struct vert2frag
{
  float4 pos      : POSITION;
  float4 texcoord : TEXCOORD0;
};

struct frag2screen
{
  float4 color : COLOR;
};
```

Listing 41-1 (*continued*). Fragment Program for Generating Stereograms

```
frag2screen main_frag(
  vert2frag IN,
  uniform sampler2D resmap,    // result map
  uniform sampler2D depthmap, // depth map

  // [1.0/num_strips, 1.0/(num_strips + 1)]
  uniform float2 strips_info,
  // depth factor (if negative, invert depth)
  uniform float depth_factor)
{
  frag2screen OUT;

  // texture coordinate from result map
  float2 uv = IN.texcoord.xy;

  // transform texture coordinate into depth map space
  // (removing first strip) and get depth value
  uv.x = (IN.texcoord.x/strips_info.y - 1.0) * strips_info.x;
  float4 tex = tex2D(depthmap,uv);

  // if factor negative, invert depth
  if (depth_factor < 0.0)
     tex = 1.0 - tex.x;

  // compute displace factor
  // (depthmap_value * factor * strip_width)
  float displace = tex.x * abs(depth_factor) * strips_info.y;

  // transform texture coordinate from result map into
  // previous strip translated by the displace factor
  uv.x = IN.texcoord.x - strips_info.y + displace;

  // assign output color from result map previous strip
  OUT.color = tex2D(resmap, uv);

  return OUT;
}
```

41.3 Sample Application

The sample application uses OpenGL and Cg for the fragment program support. It is a simple Win32 application, and the source code is small. To run the application, start the pStereogram.exe file. To browse the source code, open the pStereogram.dsw file in Microsoft's Visual C++. The application uses the `GL_ARB_fragment` program extension and should execute in any environment supporting this extension. Even emulator-based fragment program support will work—slowly, but it will work.

41.3.1 Application Options

The application includes several options that let you generate new and custom-made stereograms. You can load new depth maps (Ctrl+D), new tile patterns (Ctrl+T), and new 3D geometry (Ctrl+M). Image file formats supported are JPG and TGA. The application supports 3D geometry file formats 3DS and P3D.

In the View menu, you can select options such as these:

- **Texture Filtering (Ctrl+F):** This option allows smooth depth ranges. If disabled, depth values will be discontinuous and you will clearly see the gaps between depth levels (like depth stairs).

- **Invert Depth (Ctrl+I):** This option inverts the depth values (1 − depth). It works by inverting the depth image values (white turns black and vice versa). Some people feel more comfortable viewing stereograms with the eye crossing point before the image plane, some after it (as if you were looking at something inside the monitor). If you see the 3D images entering the image plane, use this option to obtain the correct image.

- **Depth Factor (<, >):** This option selects the factor for multiplying the depth values. Small factors result in shallow images. High values make very deep images. The depth factor should not be higher than 1.0, or artifacts will be generated if the depth map uses all of the available range (0.0 to 1.0).

- **Number of Strips (−, +):** This option specifies the number of strips to use. Small values generate fewer—but larger—strips, and large values generate lots of smaller strips. This will modify how close to the image plane you have to cross your eyes to get the 3D image.

- **Generate Stereogram:** When this option is selected, the fragment program is activated and you'll see the stereogram. If disabled, the fragment program is deactivated and all you see is the current selected depth map.

- **Depth from 3D Mesh:** This option makes animated stereograms possible. When enabled, the depth map used by the program is acquired from the z-buffer of the currently selected 3D mesh object render. In this mode, you can navigate the 3D scene while viewing the resulting stereogram. Some 3D scenes might include more than one camera, and some cameras might be animated, so change cameras using the number keys: "1", "2", . . . , "9". You can move through the scene interactively by using the "S", "X", and arrow keys. You can also rotate the view by clicking and dragging with the left mouse button and pan the view with the right mouse button.

41.4 References

The SIRDS FAQ. **http://www.cs.waikato.ac.nz/~singlis/sirds.html**

The Magic Eye Web site. **http://www.magiceye.com**

Thimbleby, Harold W., Stuart Inglis, and Ian H. Witten. 1994. "Displaying 3D Images: Algorithms for Single Image Random Dot Stereograms." *Journal Computer* 27(10), pp. 38–48. Available online at **http://archive.museophile.sbu.ac.uk/3d/pub/SIRDS-paper.pdf**

Chapter 42

Deformers

Eugene d'Eon
University of Waterloo

Three-dimensional modeling and animation packages offer a wide variety of deformation tools such as Deform by Lattice and Deform by Wave. These tools allow a small number of controls to warp an arbitrarily complex mesh. Deformers can be used to quickly perform advanced modeling operations, and their controls can be animated to provide powerful animation rigs. In most cases, offloading deformation calculations from the CPU onto the GPU is possible, allowing more advanced animation systems within real-time applications and providing more interactive modeling tools. In this chapter, we will explore how to offload deformers onto the GPU, with emphasis on the problem of computing normals.

42.1 What Is a Deformer?

A deformer is an operation that takes as input a collection of vertices and generates new coordinates for those vertices (the deformed coordinates). In addition, new normals and tangents can also be generated. If you want to deform a sphere, you pass the coordinates of all its vertices to the deformer and you get back a new set of coordinates. This task is perfectly suited for vertex programs, provided that the following requirements hold:

- No vertices or edges are created or deleted by a deformer.

- The deformed coordinates of a given vertex are in no way influenced by the other vertices being processed. (A vertex averaging/smoothing operation is not a deformer because it looks at neighboring vertices.)
- The deformer is deterministic. If any two vertices have the same input coordinates before the deformation, then they will have the same output coordinates. As well, if you deform the same mesh many times, you get the same result each time.

A very simple example would be a translation. A translation deformer takes an input coordinate and returns a translated coordinate. Examples of deformers found in Softimage|XSI, Maya, and 3ds max are Deform by Curve, Cage, Lattice, Bend, Bulge, Shear, Twist, and more. The Randomize deform in Softimage|XSI is not a deformer that meets our requirements because it is not deterministic. Our technique for normal computation could not be used to implement a randomize mesh deform.

Most deformers have controls: user-defined parameters that give the deformer some variation. In most cases, controls can be animated. A wave deformer has amplitude and phase controls. A lattice deformer has lattice control points.

42.1.1 Mathematical Definition

In the most general sense, we think of a deformer as a vector-valued function, $\mathbf{f}(x, y, z)$. Or if you like, a deformer is three scalar functions put into a vector:

$$\left(f_x\left(x, y, z\right),\ f_y\left(x, y, z\right),\ f_z\left(x, y, z\right) \right),$$

where f_x, f_y, f_z are the component functions of $\mathbf{f}$. This function $\mathbf{f}$ takes the coordinates (x, y, z) of a vertex and returns the deformed coordinates of that vertex. To deform a mesh, we take each vertex, input its coordinates into $\mathbf{f}$, and store the output as the new vertex coordinate. Or thinking in component form, f_x gives us the new x coordinate of the vertex with original coordinates (x, y, z), f_y gives the new y coordinate, and so on. The deformer function $\mathbf{f}$ should be defined for all real values of x, y, and z, or at least some range of such values that contains the input mesh.

Spatially dependent deformers, such as a wave, will have varied results in different coordinate spaces, so passing in object, world, or eye space coordinates to $\mathbf{f}$ will deform in object, world, and eye space, respectively.

Linear transformations such as rotations, scales, and translations are a simple subset of all possible deformers. They take as input a set of coordinates and output a new set of coordinates (in the form of a matrix multiplication, typically). Linear transformations are not a particularly interesting set of deformers, and we already know how to compute normals under such transformations. This definition of deformers includes a much larger set of operations on geometry.

Controls

The deform operation also depends on the controls of the deformer. Controls are parameters that affect the operation of the deformer. For example, the output of a wave deformer depends on the frequency of the wave, so technically the function **f** depends on a variable, say *freq*, as well. However, we will not write f(x, y, z, *freq*). Instead, we will think of *freq* as being a constant for a given deformation operation: it does not vary across the vertices of the mesh being deformed. Therefore, it will simply appear as a constant in at least one of the component functions of **f**. Likewise, for a time parameter that may be used to animate a deformer: the time parameter, *t*, will appear as a constant in **f**, because time doesn't depend on coordinates *x*, *y*, and *z*.

42.2 Deforming on the GPU

42.2.1 Formulating the Deformer

To facilitate normal computation, it will be useful to formulate the deformer in correspondence with our mathematical definition: in functional form. If we think of a simple translation of positive 2 units in the *y* axis as a deformer, then the deformer **f** is:

$$\mathbf{f}\left(x, y, z\right) = \left(f_x, f_y, f_z\right) = \left(x, y + 2, z\right).$$

If we are implementing a radial wave deformer, we might have

$$\mathbf{f}\left(x, y, z\right) = \left(f_x, f_y, f_z\right) = \left(x, y + \sin\left(\sqrt{x^2 + z^2} + \lambda\right), z\right),$$

where λ is the phase control parameter.

Note: f_x denotes the *x* component function of **f**, not to be confused with $\partial f/\partial x$.

42.2.2 Writing the Vertex Program

Once we have written down the deformer in functional form, deforming the vertices in a vertex program is very straightforward. Control parameters and possibly a time parameter are passed in as uniform inputs to the program (in the constant registers). To compute the vertex positions, we simply compute f(x, y, z) and store the result in the vertex position output. We apply the model and view transformations before or after computing **f**, depending on whether we want to deform in object, world, or view space. We may also have additional coordinate transformations to center and orient a spatially dependent deformer with respect to the object it is deforming.

What About Normals?

When we perform a linear transformation on a mesh, such as a translation, rotation, scale, or some combination of those, we know to take the matrix representation of that transformation, **M**, and transform the normals by the inverse transpose of **M** and then renormalize.[1] But linear transformations are a small subset of all possible deformers that we might want to implement in a vertex program. In general, a wave deformer can't be written in matrix form (where some constant matrix **M** gives us the deformed position by computing **Mv**) because a wave deformer is not a linear transformation. So we have no global matrix **M** to take the inverse transpose of and transform our normals with. We need a new technique for transforming normals.

42.2.3 Deforming Normals

How Would We Compute Normals in Software?

Animation packages first transform all vertices in the mesh by the deformer. Once that is done, it is possible to traverse the vertices in a second pass to recompute normals based on neighboring vertices in the new, deformed mesh. We don't have that option with vertex programs. Each vertex being processed in a vertex program has no knowledge of its neighbors, and there is no second stage where we can look around and do computations.

An Approximate Numerical Technique

An estimate for the deformed normal can be achieved by deforming three points for every input vertex. We find two new points very close to the input vertex. Add a very small multiple of the tangent to the vertex coordinates to get the first point. Add a very small multiple of the binormal to the vertex coordinates to get the second. These three points define two vectors whose cross product is the original normal (up to a normalization constant). We can then deform all three of these points by the deformer, and these three deformed points will define two vectors whose cross product is approximately the deformed normal (up to a normalization constant). The closer together these three points are, the more accurate the approximation will be, although numerical

---

1. See the "Homogeneous Coordinates" section of the *OpenGL Programming Guide* (published in book form by Addison-Wesley).

accuracy problems creep in if the points are too close together. It turns out that we can do better than this, however, and so avoid the numerical difficulties and the problem of choosing the extra points to deform.

The Jacobian Matrix

If a deformer $\mathbf{f}(x, y, z) = (f_x, f_y, f_z)$ has continuous first-order partial derivatives, then we can compute a matrix for each vertex called the *Jacobian matrix*, $\mathbf{J}$. As we know, everywhere a scalar function $f(x)$ is smooth, it is locally approximated by a straight line (a linear function: $f(x) \approx f'(a)(x - a) + f(a)$, for some real number a). Likewise, everywhere the map $\mathbf{f}(x, y, z)$ is smooth, $\mathbf{f}$ can be approximated by a linear transformation, $\mathbf{J}$, plus a translation $(\mathbf{f}(\mathbf{x}) \approx \mathbf{J}(\mathbf{a})(\mathbf{x} - \mathbf{a}) + \mathbf{f}(\mathbf{a})$, for some point $\mathbf{a}$, and $\mathbf{x} = (x, y, z)$. This follows from the generalized Taylor's theorem. The Jacobian matrix is defined as follows. Note: the Jacobian matrix is often denoted $\mathbf{D}\mathbf{f}(\mathbf{x})$.

$$
\mathbf{J}(x, y, z) = \begin{pmatrix} \dfrac{\partial f_x}{\partial x} & \dfrac{\partial f_x}{\partial y} & \dfrac{\partial f_x}{\partial z} \\ \dfrac{\partial f_y}{\partial x} & \dfrac{\partial f_y}{\partial y} & \dfrac{\partial f_y}{\partial z} \\ \dfrac{\partial f_z}{\partial x} & \dfrac{\partial f_z}{\partial y} & \dfrac{\partial f_z}{\partial z} \end{pmatrix},
$$

where all partial derivatives are evaluated at (x, y, z).

Example. Suppose we had the following deformer (where λ is a constant control parameter):

$$
\mathbf{f}(x, y, z) = \left(f_x, f_y, f_z \right) = \left(\lambda x, z^3, z - y^2 \right).
$$

Then the Jacobian would be:

$$
\mathbf{J}(x, y, z) = \begin{pmatrix} \dfrac{\partial f_x}{\partial x} & \dfrac{\partial f_x}{\partial y} & \dfrac{\partial f_x}{\partial z} \\ \dfrac{\partial f_y}{\partial x} & \dfrac{\partial f_y}{\partial y} & \dfrac{\partial f_y}{\partial z} \\ \dfrac{\partial f_z}{\partial x} & \dfrac{\partial f_z}{\partial y} & \dfrac{\partial f_z}{\partial z} \end{pmatrix} = \begin{pmatrix} \lambda & 0 & 0 \\ 0 & 0 & 3z^2 \\ 0 & -2y & 1 \end{pmatrix}.
$$

For each position (x, y, z), we now have a linear transformation matrix $\mathbf{J}(x, y, z)$ that we can use to transform vectors at that position. If we had a tangent vector $\mathbf{t}$ at (x, y, z), then the deformed tangent would be $\mathbf{J}(x, y, z) * \mathbf{t}$ (followed by a renormalize to get a unit tangent).

If we make the assumption that the vertices of the mesh are discrete samples of a smooth surface, then transforming vectors on the surface by the Jacobian matrix is valid. We can also transform normals using $\mathbf{J}(x, y, z)$ in two equivalent ways.

1. The inverse transpose of $\mathbf{J}(x, y, z)$ can be computed per vertex in the vertex program and used to transform the normal directly. If $\mathbf{n}$ is the input unit normal, then the deformed normal is:

$$\mathbf{n}' = \text{normalize}\left[\left(\left(\mathbf{J}(x, y, z)\right)^{-1}\right)^{T} \mathbf{n}\right].$$

   Notation: A^{T} denotes the transpose of a matrix A.

2. If a unit tangent vector, $\mathbf{u}$, is given per vertex, then we can generate a unit binormal $\mathbf{v} = \mathbf{n} \times \mathbf{u}$. We can transform the tangent and binormal to the deformed space, using the matrix $\mathbf{J}(x, y, z)$. Then the new, deformed normal is:

$$\mathbf{n}' = \text{normalize}\left[\left(\mathbf{J}(x, y, z)\mathbf{u}\right) \times \left(\mathbf{J}(x, y, z)\mathbf{v}\right)\right].$$

   The tangent and binormal need not actually be unit length, because the final result is normalized.

Inverting 3×3 matrices is not a particularly suitable task for a vertex program, so method (2) is generally easier to implement and faster to compute. If a tangent and binormal are not given per vertex, they can be generated either on the CPU when the mesh is loaded or in the vertex program. To generate a tangent, compute two cross products, $\mathbf{n} \times (0, 0, 1)$ and $\mathbf{n} \times (0, 1, 0)$. Select the result with the larger magnitude. The result is a tangent vector to $\mathbf{n}$. The binormal is then given by $\mathbf{v} = \mathbf{n} \times \mathbf{u}$.

Note: This technique generates discontinuous tangents and binormals across the surface and would not suffice for bump mapping and other techniques that require a continuous tangent field.

It is important to renormalize the normals, because in general normals generated with these methods will not be unit length, and most lighting equations assume unit normals.

42.3 Limitations

- Faceted meshes fail the smooth-surface assumption and will in general not give the same normals that would be achieved in software by first deforming the mesh and then recomputing faceted normals. In general, normals will vary across each face after deforming. However, in some cases this method may still create acceptable results.

- Computing the inverse of the Jacobian matrix for the purposes of transforming the normals requires that the Jacobian matrix be nonsingular at that location (that is, the determinant must be nonzero). This will be the case for most practical deformers, but it is possible to devise deformers that have ill-behaved functions that are not of maximal rank on their entire domain. At such locations, a normal cannot be computed. Both techniques described in this chapter will produce the zero vector for the deformed normal at such degenerate points. In practice, numerical errors will produce a vector very close to the zero vector, and subsequent normalize operations will generate random results.

- This method demands that the functions involved be in fact differentiable—and preferably analytically differentiable—on the domain of interest. Functions that have no known analytic derivative require using numerical derivative techniques to approximate the partial derivatives, which typically lengthen the computation greatly and are therefore highly undesirable.

- This method is limited by the length restrictions of the vertex program, especially if the Jacobian is lengthy to compute. If an object is being deformed by a series of deformers, it is probably only practical to compute the last one on the GPU. If in addition, skinning or other complex operations need to be performed in the same vertex program, then the program may have too many instructions or be too slow to compute on a large number of vertices.

42.4 Performance

As mentioned before, an alternative approximate numerical method for computing normals involves deforming three vertices for every input vertex, one very slightly along the tangent and one very slightly along the binormal. These three deformed vertices can then be used to approximate the deformed tangent and binormal, and a cross product gives the estimated deformed normal. This involves more than three times the work of deforming just the one set of vertex coordinates. In a lot of cases, computation of the Jacobian matrix can be done in fewer instructions than are required to deform two extra sets of coordinates. Expressions tend to be repeated across terms in the Jacobian, and some expressions are exactly those that were computed in computing the vertex coordinates and can be reused. This is not always the case, especially if the partial derivatives involve complicated expressions. The Jacobian method has no overhead of passing down extra coordinates and avoids most of the numerical difficulties associated with the approximate method.

Performance is a simple function of the number of instructions needed to compute the deformation. Complex deformers such as a $4 \times 4 \times 4$ lattice deform require a lot of instructions, which will limit the amount of geometry that can be deformed in real time. In each case, the complexity of the deformer, the CPU load and GPU load of the application, and the amount of geometry to be deformed will all have to be factored in to determine if deforming on the GPU is the better solution.

42.5 Example: Wave Deformer

Here we will consider a simple circular wave with vertical displacement (in the y axis) based on radial distance from the origin in the x-z plane. In functional form we have:

$$\mathbf{f}(x, y, z) = \left(f_x, f_y, f_z\right) = \left(x, \ y + \sin\left(v\sqrt{x^2 + z^2} + \lambda\right), \ z\right),$$

where v is a wave frequency control parameter and λ is the wave phase parameter. We then compute the Jacobian matrix:

$$\mathbf{J}(x, y, z) = \begin{pmatrix} \dfrac{\partial f_x}{\partial x} & \dfrac{\partial f_x}{\partial y} & \dfrac{\partial f_x}{\partial z} \\[2ex] \dfrac{\partial f_y}{\partial x} & \dfrac{\partial f_y}{\partial y} & \dfrac{\partial f_y}{\partial z} \\[2ex] \dfrac{\partial f_z}{\partial x} & \dfrac{\partial f_z}{\partial y} & \dfrac{\partial f_z}{\partial z} \end{pmatrix}$$

$$= \begin{pmatrix} 1 & 0 & 0 \\[2ex] \dfrac{\cos\left(v\sqrt{x^2 + z^2} + \lambda\right)}{\sqrt{x^2 + z^2}} vx & 1 & \dfrac{\cos\left(v\sqrt{x^2 + z^2} + \lambda\right)}{\sqrt{x^2 + z^2}} vz \\[2ex] 0 & 0 & 1 \end{pmatrix}.$$

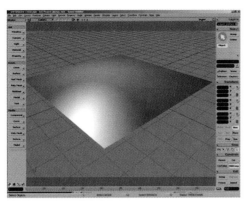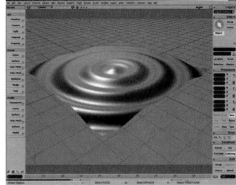

Figure 42-1. A Circular, Vertical Displacement Wave Deformer Applied to a Plane

Suppose we are deforming a vertex with coordinates $(3, 0, 4)$ and normal $(0, 1, 0)$. Let's choose a wave frequency $\upsilon = 2$, and a wave phase parameter $\lambda = 0$. We first compute the Jacobian matrix at that location.

$$
J(3,0,4) = \begin{pmatrix} 1 & 0 & 0 \\ \dfrac{\cos\left(2\sqrt{3^2 + 4^2} + 0\right)}{\sqrt{3^2 + 4^2}} 2(3) & 1 & \dfrac{\cos\left(2\sqrt{3^2 + 4^2} + 0\right)}{\sqrt{3^2 + 4^2}} 2(4) \\ 0 & 0 & 1 \end{pmatrix}
$$

$$
\approx \begin{pmatrix} 1 & 0 & 0 \\ -1.00689 & 1 & -1.34251 \\ 0 & 0 & 1 \end{pmatrix}.
$$

Next, suppose a tangent and binormal are given:

$$
\mathbf{u} = (-1, 0, 1), \quad \mathbf{v} = (1, 0, 1).
$$

Then the transformed tangent and binormal are:

$$
\mathbf{u}' = \begin{pmatrix} 1 & 0 & 0 \\ -1.00689 & 1 & -1.34251 \\ 0 & 0 & 1 \end{pmatrix} \begin{pmatrix} -1 \\ 0 \\ 1 \end{pmatrix} = \begin{pmatrix} -1 \\ -0.335629 \\ 1 \end{pmatrix}
$$

and

$$\mathbf{v}' = \begin{pmatrix} 1 & 0 & 0 \\ -1.00689 & 1 & -1.34251 \\ 0 & 0 & 1 \end{pmatrix} \begin{pmatrix} 1 \\ 0 \\ 1 \end{pmatrix} = \begin{pmatrix} 1 \\ -2.3494 \\ 1 \end{pmatrix}.$$

Then the deformed normal will be in the direction of:

$$Cross\left(\mathbf{u}', \mathbf{v}'\right) = \left(2.01377, 2, 2.68503\right).$$

Then we normalize the last calculation to get our deformed normal:

$$\mathbf{n}' = \left(0.515426, 0.511902, 0.687235\right).$$

42.6 Conclusion

We have considered a large class of mesh deformation operations and found the mathematical tools to perform such operations on the graphics hardware. The Jacobian matrix of the deformation allows us to deform normals inside the vertex program without worrying about neighboring deformed vertices. This technique is widely applicable to a number of deformation operations, keeping in mind the limitations that were observed.

Although much of this book deals with shading effects, the way that objects move and deform is just as important in creating realistic animated graphics. Currently, the quality of character animation in movies surpasses the animation in interactive graphics such as video games. This quality gap results in part from the much more sophisticated deformation techniques used in movies; most games are limited to simple skinning. We hope that over time, techniques such as those described in this chapter will help to bring the full spectrum of animation techniques to real-time productions.

Index

A

a2v structure
  in absorption simulation, 268
  in texture-space diffusion, 273
a2vConnector structure, 53
AA (application of antialiasing), 414–415
absorption, 266–272
abstraction, 537
accelerations in Navier-Stokes equations, 641
accessibility in ambient occlusion, 281
accumulate_skin function, 71
accumulated matrix skinning, 71
accumulation-buffer depth of field, 379–380
acoustic grids, 694
additive blending
  in caustics computations, 36
  for flames, 94–95
AddRef method, 507
adjacency information for shadow volumes, 145
adjacent cell images in texture bombing, 325–326
advanced GPU programming, 624
advect function, 654–655
advection
  in fast fluid dynamics simulation, 653–655
  in Navier-Stokes equations, 642, 646–648
advertising imagery, 366
after-image effect, 359
AGP connections, 633
Akenine-Moller, Tomas, 165
albedo in SBRDF, 294–295
algorithms
  binary searches, 631
  bitonic merge sorts, 628
  image-space shadow, 218
  multipass, 196
  object-space shadow, 217

aliasing. *See also* antialiasing
  of caustics, 43
  in glow, 349, 357–358
  in perspective shadow maps, 218, 239–240
  in water simulation, 18
alpha blending
  in flames, 94–95
  in glow sources, 347
  in pipeline performance, 484
  in shadow volume multipass rendering, 142
  in texture-based volume rendering, 673
  in ultrasound visualization, 697
alpha channels for glow sources, 347–348
alpha parameter, 655–656
alpha-test rejection, 96
ambient function, 177
ambient occlusion, 279–280
  hardware-accelerated, 283–284
  preprocessing steps for, 281–282
  rendering with, 284–289
  summary, 289–292
ambient terms in shadow volume rendering, 141
amplitude of waves, 8
  geometric, 14–15, 20
  light, 124
  texture, 16–17
angles in shadow volume rendering, 159
animated objects
  bounding boxes for, 495–496
  sprites
    flames and smoke in, 90–92
    implementing, 89–90
animated single-image stereograms (ASISs), 717–719
animation, 63
  for fire, 94
  for grass simulation, 111–112
    per cluster, 113–115

buffers (*continued*)
  in Cinema 4D, 570
  for circle of confusion, 377
  for glow, 359
  for Image, 454, 456–457
  for lens flares, 501
  in OpenEXR, 455–457
  in parallel reductions, 625
  for perspective shadow maps, 240
  in pipeline performance, 484
  for shadow volumes, 138, 141–142, 144–145,
     150–151, 164
  in volume rendering, 682–686
bump maps
  in Cinema 4D, 573
  in diffraction, 129–130
  in high-quality software rendering, 591, 593
  in Noise function, 78, 82–83
  parameters for
    eye vectors in, 24–27
    tangent-space basis vectors in, 23–24
  for skin lighting, 50, 52
  surface normals, 59
bundles, geometry pipe, 517
buoyancy, 660–661

C

C++ language
  half format for, 429
  image-processing framework. *See* framework for
    image processing
C4Dfx plug-in, 567
cameras
  in FX Composer, 530
  with perspective shadow maps
    light, 225–233
    virtual, 219–225
canceling waves, 125
caps, 150, 153–154
Card, Drew, 166
Cartesian grids
  in fast fluid dynamics simulation, 640–641
  in ultrasound visualization, 694, 696–698
casters, 139, 150, 159
categories of objects, 508
caustics, 31–32

approach to, 35–36
computing, 32–35
high-level shading languages for, 38–44
OpenGL for, 37
summary, 43
Cb value for screen-aligned filter kernels, 405
cell-centered discretization, 663
cells in texture bombing, 324–328
center method, 452
Cg language
  for caustics, 38
  for high-quality filtering, 392
  for SBRDF, 302–305
  for shadow volume rendering, 147–148
  for SISs, 719–720
cgConnectParameter function, 541, 544
cgCreateParameter function, 544
cgCreateProgram function, 540–541
cgCreateProgramFromFile function, 540–541
cgFragmentProgram function, 458
CgFX toolkit, 567–569
  connecting Cinema 4D to, 570–571
  lessons learned in, 578–579
  offline renderer emulation in, 573–577
  results and performance in, 577–578
  shader and parameter management in, 572–573
cgGetNamedUserType function, 541
cgProgram function, 554
cgSetArraySize function, 544
cgSetAutoCompile function, 540
cgSetParameter function, 541
chain rules in caustics computations, 39
changeZoomFactor method, 452
channel-based color correction
  curves in, 366–368
  levels in, 364–365
channels
  for glow sources, 347–348
  in OpenEXR headers, 430
checker function, 418–420
checkerboard patterns, 418–420
choppiness effect, 14
CIE colors, 371
Cinema 4D, hardware shading into, 567–569
  connecting to CgFX, 570–571
  lessons learned in, 578–579
  offline renderer emulation in, 573–577
  results and performance in, 577–578

distances
    in absorption simulation, 267
    in circle of confusion, 377
    in focus, 375
    in omnidirectional shadow mapping, 199
    sorting objects by, 493–494
`DistanceShapingParams` structure, 177
divergence-free vector field, 645
`divergence` function, 657
divergence in fast fluid dynamics simulation,
        642–643, 645, 656–657
Dolly camera movements, 530
Doom 3 game, 137–138, 162, 193, 195
`dot` function, 556
dot products, 645
Dougherty, Michael, 165
Draw stage in texture-based volume rendering,
        670–671
drawing image data, 449
`DrawPrimitive` function, 245, 355
"Dusk" demo, 64
dye fields, 660
dynamic occlusion for morph targets, 68
dynamic ranges
    normalizing, 454
    in photography, 429
dynamic shadows, 217

E

early-z optimizations, 482
early-z rejection, 487–488
`edgeDetectGPS` function, 397
edges
    in cinematic lighting, 170–171
    in constant filter kernels, 397–399
    in depth of field, 381
    in per-pixel lighting, 254
    in shadow volume rendering, 155
    in water simulation, 21–22, 27
Editor window, 506, 525–527
effect files in shaders, 602–606, 613–615
effects for games, 356–360
efficiency
    in FX Composer file formats, 513
    in texture bombing, 332
elevation direction, 694–695

ellipses in shadow volume rendering, 162
emission-absorption model, 670
emissive terms in shadow volume rendering, 141
emotions in animation, 65–66
emulating offline renderer, 573–577
enclosing rectangles in ultrasound visualization,
        697
engineering applications, 667
entering intersections in shadow volume rendering,
        150
environment lighting, 286–289
environment maps
    in Cinema 4D, 573
    for glow, 355
    for HDR images, 442
    for lighting, 49
    SBRDF rendering using, 298–305
errors
    in fragment program optimizations, 558
    in FX Composer, 532
    quantization, 17
errors of visibility in depth of field, 381–382
Euler's method, 647
`eval` function, 546
evaporation in fast fluid dynamics simulation, 661
exitant directions in SBRDF, 294
exiting intersections in shadow volume rendering,
        150
expensive code in cinematic lighting, 182
explicit texture coordinates, 27
extensible engines, 506
external forces in Navier-Stokes equations, 642
eye buffers in volume rendering, 682–683
eye direction in vertex programs, 556
eye vectors in bump-environment mapping, 24–27
eyesight in dark environments, 463

F

`f2fConnector` structure, 104
`f3texCUBE_RGBE_Conv` function, 302
`f4texRECTbilerp` function, 655
face culling, 157
face normals, 571
`faceFragmentShader` function, 59
faces in shadow volume rendering, 153
faceted meshes, 729

GPU derivatives, 405–406

GPUs

    computation on. *See* computation on GPUs

    convolution on, 351–352

    for deformers, 725–728

    and pipelines, 473, 479, 489

`gradient` function, 657

gradients

    for curves, 367

    in fast fluid dynamics simulation, 642–643, 645

    in Noise function, 75–80

    of scalar fields, 645

    in volume rendering, 675

    of wave functions, 41

gradients of p, 656

`gradwave` function, 42

grain for fire, 101, 103

granularity in Noise function, 76

graphics-API antialiasing, 414–415

graphics cards, 578

grass simulation, 107–108

    animation for, 111–112

        per cluster, 113–115

        per grass object, 117–119

        per vertex, 115–117

    object preparation for, 108–111

    summary, 120

    texture for, 109

grating, diffraction, 124–125

gravitational pull in fast fluid dynamics, 661

gray patches for gamma, 439

gray ramps for curves, 367–368

grayscale conversion, 369–370

grayscale data

    in filter kernels, 394–397

    stripe coverage for, 409

grayscale helper textures, 397

Green, Simon, 401

green color remapping, 368–369

grids

    in fast fluid dynamics simulation, 639–641, 658, 663

    in Navier-Stokes equations, 644

    in ultrasound visualization, 694, 696–698

    in volume rendering, 696–705

Gritz, Larry, 167, 175

ground planes, 148

GUIDs (globally unique identifiers), 507–508

H

`half` format, 428–429

`half` type, 454

halos of light. *See* glow

hardware-accelerated ambient occlusion, 283–284

hardware profiles, 417

hardware shading into Cinema 4D, 567–569

    Cinema 4D to CgFX connections in, 570–571

    lessons learned in, 578–579

    offline renderer emulation in, 573–577

    results and performance in, 577–578

    shader and parameter management in, 572–573

hardware-specific glow implementations, 352–355

hashing of gradients, 75–76

HDR (high-dynamic-range) environments

    lighting in, 47–49

    maps for, 290

HDR (high-dynamic-range) images

    creating and using, 441–443

    OpenEXR, 425–428

HDRShop program

    for HDR images, 441

    for high-dynamic-range environments, 48

    for image-based lighting, 317

headers in OpenEXR, 430

heat shimmer, 101–102

height

    in images, 450

    in water simulation, 7–9, 19–21

`height` function, 9, 450

Helmholtz-Hodge decomposition, 644–645

Hermite splines, 75

`Hierarchy` class, 570

high-dynamic-range (HDR) environments

    lighting in, 47–49

    maps for, 290

high-dynamic-range (HDR) images

    creating and using, 441–443

    OpenEXR, 425–428

high-frequency features

    in cube sampling noise, 81–82

    in glow sources, 348

    in volume rendering, 688

high-level languages

    for caustics, 38–44

    for morph targets, 65–67

L

Lafortune representation, 294–295, 299–300
Lambertian contributions, 317
Landis, Hayden, 280
Laplacian operators
  in fast fluid dynamics simulation, 642–643
  in Navier-Stokes equations, 648
"Last Chance Gas" demo, 205–206, 213
lat-long maps, 286
`latlong` function, 288–289
layered depth of field, 379–380
layers
  for flames, 97–98
  in z-buffer depth of field, 388
lens flares
  glow for, 356
  occlusion culling for, 499–503
lenses in focus, 375–376
`lerp` function, 148
levels in color correction, 364–365
levels of detail (LODs)
  in texture bandwidth, 476
  in texture bombing, 331
  vertex-processing, 481
lifetime, object, 510
light buffers, 682–686
light cameras, 225–233
light caps, 150, 153–154
`Light` interface, 543–544
light meters, 439
light reflections and refractions on water, 31
light rigs, 592
lighting, 552
  ambient occlusion. *See* ambient occlusion
  cinematic. *See* cinematic lighting
  diffraction. *See* diffraction
  with frustums, 251–254
  for gamers, 137
image-based. *See* image-based lighting (IBL)
  Materials panel for, 524
  in omnidirectional shadow mapping, 200–201
  for OpenEXR images, 440
  parameters for, 554
  per-pixel. *See* per-pixel lighting
  for perspective shadow maps, 233
  shader interfaces for, 542–545

shadow volume rendering. *See* shadow volume rendering
  for skin, 47–50
    fragment shaders in, 58–61
    implementing, 51
    vertex shaders in, 52–58
  skin response to, 50–51
  sources of, 552–553
  in vertex programs, 556
  in volume rendering, 682–687
`LightParams` structure, 177
`lightPos` property, 528
`LightRadius` semantic, 605
limited outputs in GPU computations, 633
line-plane intercepts, 40–42
`LINEAR` filters, 331
linear pixel values, 438–441
linear shading, 54
linear transformations, 724–728
`lineOrder` attribute, 430
liquids, simulating, 660
load balancing, 622
loading images, 451–452
`LoadOperator` class, 451
`loadVertexProgram` function, 148
lobes in SBRDF, 294–296
local forces in Navier-Stokes equations, 642
localized cube maps as backgrounds, 318–320
localizing image-based lighting, 307–311
locking resources, 478–479
LODs (levels of detail)
  in texture bandwidth, 476
  in texture bombing, 331
  vertex-processing, 481
Log panel in FX Composer, 533
`lookup` function, 441
lookup tables
  in photographic film simulation, 440–441
  in pipeline optimization, 480
  in volume rendering, 669, 689–690
loop bodies in fast fluid dynamics simulation, 650–651
looping of Gerstner waves, 14
lossless file compression, 431
low-frequency features
  in cube sampling noise, 81–82
  for glow sources, 348

ModelViewProj variable, 701
monitor gamma, 438–440
Monsters, Inc. film, 168–169
Monte Carlo sampling
  in ambient occlusion, 282
  in caustics computations, 34–35
morph targets in animation
  high-level languages for, 65–67
  implementation, 67–68
motion blur, 442
Mounier, Michael, 165
MRI (magnetic resonance imaging), 693–694
multichannel color correction and conversion,
      368–369
  color-space, 370–372
  grayscale, 369–370
multidimensional transfer functions, 675
multipass rendering
  for lighting, 553
  for omnidirectional shadow mapping, 196
  for shadow volumes, 141–144
multiple choices in texture bombing, 330–331
multiple images per cell in texture bombing,
      327–328
multiple lights, shader interfaces for, 542–545
multiple-sample antialiasing, 415
multitexturing, 233
multithreading, 570

N

nabla operator, 642–643
names
  in FX Composer connection parameters, 511
  for variables, 605, 609–610
Navier-Stokes equations
  advection in, 642, 646–648
  for choppiness effect, 14
  first realization in, 645
  Helmholtz-Hodge decomposition in, 644–645
  for incompressible flow, 641–642
  initial and boundary conditions in, 650
  Poisson equations in, 645, 649–650
  second realization in, 645–646
  solving, 644–650
  vector calculus for, 642–644
  viscous diffusion in, 648–649

voxel-based solutions for, 5
NEAREST filters, 331
negative weights for bicubic filter kernels, 400
neighbor-sample placement for glow, 352
Neumann boundary conditions, 650
night vision, 463–465
NightFilter operator, 463
ninja model, 189–192
no-ops in vertex processing, 477
no-slip conditions
  in fast fluid dynamics simulation, 658
  in Navier-Stokes equations, 650
noise and Noise function
  bumps and neighboring vertices for, 82–83
  improvements in, 78–80
  original implementation, 74–77
  in pixel shaders, 80–82
  in ray-traced depth of field, 378
  summary, 84
  in volume rendering, 688–689
  in z-buffer depth of field, 387
non-power-of-two (NPOT) textures, 454
nonverbal cues, 46
nonzero divergence in Navier-Stokes equations,
      645
normal maps
  in high-quality software rendering, 584–587,
      593, 596
  in texture waves, 16
  in water simulation, 7
normalization
  of dynamic ranges, 454
  in pipeline performance, 482
  in shader interfaces, 539–540
normalize function, 539
normalized vectors, 11
Normalizer interface, 539
normals
  in accumulated matrix skinning, 71
  in ambient occlusion, 283–284
  deformer, 726–728, 732
  in glow, 356
  in high-quality software rendering, 584
  for texture waves, 17
  in water simulation, 9–10
nPixelFormat variable, 456
NPOT (non-power-of-two) textures, 454
nrm function, 539

pluggable class factories, 508
point lights
    in omnidirectional shadow mapping, 195
    in shadow volume rendering, 159, 164
pointers to objects, 510
points
    in Noise function, 74
    in shadow volumes, 138
Poisson equations
    in fast fluid dynamics simulation, 643, 656
    in Navier-Stokes equations, 645, 649–650
Poisson-like distributions in Noise function, 76
polygon meshes, 584, 593
polygons
    in bounding boxes, 497
    in Cinema 4D, 570
    in grass simulation, 109–110
    in occlusion culling, 498
    in volume rendering, 672, 676–677
polygons of intersection, 697–698
position
    in accumulated matrix skinning, 71
    in ultrasound visualization, 701
`position` function, 65
post-projective space, 218, 221–224
post-rendering fire effects, 99
post-T&L vertex caches, 481
pow function, 365
power-of-two-size textures, 674
PowerStrip tool, 475
`powVal` function, 560
precision
    in pipeline performance, 482
    of texture waves, 16–17
`PrecomputeEnvMap` function, 301–302
preprocessors, 538
    in omnidirectional shadow mapping, 202
    in shaders, 613–614
pressure in Navier-Stokes equations, 642, 650
primitives in volume rendering, 670
priority in texture bombing, 326
PRMan, 562
procedural features in texture bombing, 326–329, 333–335
procedural rendering, 687–688
procedural texture for caustics, 38
processing in volume rendering techniques, 674–676

product rules in caustics computations, 39
profiles for filter-width estimates, 417
Project Gotham Racing game, 343
projection
    in fast fluid dynamics simulation, 656–657
    in Navier-Stokes equations, 645–646
    in omnidirectional shadow mapping, 196
Properties panel in FX Composer, 511, 528–530
proxy geometry, 670, 672, 676–677, 689–690
proxy polygons, 672, 676
pseudo-angles, 676
pseudo-random gradients, 78–79
`PSIZE` value, 414
PSMs. *See* perspective shadow maps
pull data in filter networks, 447
pure Neumann boundary conditions, 650
push data in filter networks, 447
`Pyramid` variable, 701
pyramidal grids, 699–705
pyramids, bounding boxes for, 494–495

Q

quads
    for flames, 92
    in shadow volume rendering, 155
Quake 3 game, 154, 163
quality vs. speed in high-quality filtering, 391–392
quantization errors, 17
queries
    in FX Composer, 509–510
    occlusion, 487
        operation of, 488–489
        working with, 489–493
`QueryInterface` method, 507

R

Radiance software, 442
radiologists, 693–694
rainbow maps, 127, 130–131
ramps and ramping effect
    for curves, 367–368
    for glow, 359–360
random direction sampling, 282
random-dot stereograms (RDSs), 709–711

random image selection in texture bombing, 330–331
Randomize deforms, 724
randomUV function, 324, 331
ranges
    in focus, 375
    normalizing, 454
    in photography, 429
    in ultrasound visualization, 694–695
ranks for curves, 366
raster operations (ROP)
    in bottleneck identification, 476
    in pipelines, 474–475
rasterization bottlenecks, 688–689
ray-quad tests, 37
ray theory vs. wave theory, 125
ray-traced depth of field, 378
rays and ray tracing
    in caustics computations, 33–36
    in occlusion interval maps, 209
    in shadow volume rendering, 160–161
rBeta parameter, 655–656
RDSs (random-dot stereograms), 709–711
reading OpenEXR images, 431–433
real-time environment lighting, ambient occlusion
        in, 279–280
    hardware-accelerated, 283–284
    preprocessing steps for, 281–282
    rendering with, 284–289
    summary, 289–292
real-time glow, 343–347
    convolution in, 349–352
    for games, 356–360
    hardware-specific implementations for, 352–355
    rendering sources of, 347–349
    summary, 361
real-time RenderMan conversions. *See* conversions
real-time shadows, 137
receivers, message, 511–512
reconstructions in volume rendering, 669
red, green, blue, emerald (RGBE) color filters, 404
red color remapping, 368–369
reflectance scaling, 294
reflected wave phase, 126
reflection maps, 586
reflection vectors, 48
reflections
    in cinematic lighting, 172–173
    cube-mapped, 307

in eye vectors, 24–25
of geometric waves, 20
in skin lighting, 50
on water, 21, 31
reflectPS function, 314–315
reflectVS function, 313
refractions
    in caustics computations, 32–34
    on water, 31
regions
    in focus, 375
    in shadow map antialiasing, 186
RegisterNVObjects function, 507
rejection sampling in ambient occlusion, 282
Release method, 507
remapping color channels, 366
Render panel, 515
render style for glow, 356
render-to-texture (RTT) operations
    copies, 652
    on GPU, 351
Render window, 506
renderBegin method, 449, 457
rendered texture maps, 346
renderEnd method, 449, 457
renderer contexts, 356, 608–609
rendering
    with ambient occlusion maps, 284–289
    front to back, 484–485
    glows
        contexts for, 356
        convolution in, 349–352
        sources of, 347–349
    high resolution, 497
    multipass, 141–144, 196, 553
    occlusion interval maps, 209–211
    in omnidirectional shadow mapping, 199–200
    OpenEXR images, 433–438
    ping-pong, 239
    procedural, 687–688
    SBRDF
        using discrete lights, 296–299
        using environment maps, 298–305
    shadow volume. *See* shadow volume rendering
    volume rendering. *See* volume rendering techniques
RenderMan
    for high-quality filtering, 392
    shader conversions to real-time. *See* conversions

ultrasound visualization (*continued*)
    volume rendering data in
        in Cartesian grids, 696–698
        in pyramidal grids, 699–705
ultraviolet light waves, 124
uncapped performance in shadow volume rendering, 160–161
Under operator, 681
underwater caustics, 32–35
Undo/Redo feature, 526
unit cube clipping, 225–228
unloadVertexProgram function, 148
unpack_4ubyte function, 440
UnRegisterNVObjects function, 507
update method, 452
Update stage in texture-based volume rendering, 670–672
Uru: Ages Beyond Myst, 5–6
user-defined filter kernels, 393–394
user interface, FX Composer, 514
USTexture input, 703

V

v2f structure
    in absorption simulation, 268
    in texture-space diffusion, 273
v2fConnector structure
    for fire, 104
    in skin lighting, 54
values for effect file variables, 605
variable ramping effect, 359–360
variable stripe texture, 413–414
variables
    in effect files, 605
    in shaders, 609–610
vecMul function, 55
vectors
    in bump-environment mapping parameters, 23–27
    in Cinema 4D, 571
    for deformers, 724
    eye, 24–27
    in fast fluid dynamics simulation, 639–640, 642–644, 663
    in fragment program optimizations, 560
    for morph targets, 67

normalization techniques for, 540
    tangent-space basis, 23–24
velocity
    in fast fluid dynamics simulation, 658
    in Navier-Stokes equations, 645, 650
vert2frag structure, 719
vertex branching, 481
vertex buffers, 144–145
vertex fetching, 478
vertex indices, 153–154
vertex-processing LODs, 481
vertex programs
    for absorption simulation, 268–269
    for deformers, 725–726
    in fragment program optimizations, 557–559
    vs. fragment programs, 555–556
    for pyramidal grids, 701–703
    for texture-space diffusion, 272–275
    for uberlight-like shaders, 175–181
vertex shaders
    for glow, 352–354
    for grass simulation, 112–113
    for image-based lighting, 312–313, 320
    for morph targets, 67
    for omnidirectional shadow maps, 199
    for perspective shadow maps, 238
    in pipeline optimization, 480
    in shadow volume rendering, 147–148
    in skin lighting, 52–58
    for texture waves, 17
vertex texture coordinates for glow, 355
vertexOutput structure, 312–313
vertexOutputB structure, 319
VertexProgram function, 702–703
vertical blur, 351
vertices
    in bottleneck identification, 477
    in caustics computations, 37
    in Cinema 4D, 570
    in circular waves, 11
    in deformers, 723
    in edge-length filtering, 21
    in Gerstner waves, 12–14
    in high-quality software rendering, 584, 588–593
    in pipelines, 474, 477, 480–481
    in shaders, 609, 611–612
    in skinning, 69–70

vertices (*continued*)
  in volume rendering, 676–677
  in water depth, 18–21
  in water simulation, 7, 27–28
vFilter values, 203
view-aligned planes and slicing, 676
View menu in stereogram application, 721
viewers in shadow volume rendering, 148
virtual cameras, 219–225
viscosity in Navier-Stokes equations, 642
viscous diffusion
  in fast fluid dynamics simulation, 655
  in Navier-Stokes equations, 648–649
visibility
  in depth of field, 381–382
  of lens flares, 499–501
  in occlusion interval maps, 207–209
  in per-pixel lighting, 245
    applications for, 255–256
    batches with, 246–248
    fill rates for, 255
    sets for, 248–254
    summary, 256
visibility function, 207–209
visible sets, 248, 250
vision in dark environments, 463–465
visual effects of subsurface scattering, 263–264
visualization
  of object translations, 530
  ultrasound. *See* ultrasound visualization
Vlachos, Alex, 166
volume rendering techniques, 667–668
  compositing in, 670–671, 681
  data representation and processing in, 674–676
  fragment program limitations in, 689–690
  illumination in, 675, 679–680
  lighting in, 682–687
  methods in, 668–670
  performance considerations in, 688–690
  procedural rendering, 687–688
  proxy geometry in, 676–677
  rasterization bottlenecks in, 688–689
  shadow volume. *See* shadow volume rendering
  summary, 690
  texture-based, 670–674
  texture memory limitations in, 690
  in texture-space diffusion, 275
  transfer functions in, 669–675, 678–679

  in ultrasound visualization
    in Cartesian grids, 696–698
    in pyramidal grids, 699–705
volume texture for flames, 94
VolumeRenderCartesian.cpp program, 696–698
VolumeRenderPyramid.cpp program, 701, 705
VolumeRenderPyramidF.cg program, 701, 703
VolumeRenderPyramidF.ocg program, 701, 704
VolumeRenderPyramidUS.cpp program, 705–706
VolumeRenderPyramidV.cg program, 701–703
von Neumann architecture, 622
Voronoi regions, 332, 335–337
vorticity confinement, 662–663
voxels
  for Navier-Stokes equations, 5
  in volume rendering, 668–669
vp_Diffraction function, 128–129
VS_INPUT structure, 112
VS_OUTPUT structure, 112
VS_TEMP structure, 113
"Vulcan" demo. *See* fire and flames

W

w component in shadow volume rendering, 145–146
warnings in FX Composer, 532
water
  caustics. *See* caustics
  condensation, 661
water simulation, 5
  authoring in, 18–19
    depth in, 19–21
    edge-length filtering in, 21–22
    overrides in, 21
    texture coordinates in, 22–23
  geometric waves in, 11–15
  goals and scope of, 5–7
  normals and tangents in, 9–10
  runtime processing in, 23–28
  sum of sines approximation for, 7
  texture waves in, 15–18
  wave selection in, 7–8
wave deformers, 730–732

informIT

Register
Your Book

at www.awprofessional.com/register

You may be eligible to receive:

- Advance notice of forthcoming editions of the book
- Related book recommendations
- Chapter excerpts and supplements of forthcoming titles
- Information about special contests and promotions throughout the year
- Notices and reminders about author appearances, tradeshows, and online chats with special guests

Contact us

If you are interested in writing a book or reviewing manuscripts prior to publication, please write to us at:

Editorial Department
Addison-Wesley Professional
75 Arlington Street, Suite 300
Boston, MA 02116 USA
Email: AWPro@aw.com

Addison-Wesley

Visit us on the Web: http://www.awprofessional.com

Addison-Wesley Warranty on the CD-ROM

Addison-Wesley warrants the enclosed disc to be free of defects in materials and faulty workmanship under normal use for a period of ninety days after purchase. If a defect is discovered in the disc during this warranty period, a replacement disc can be obtained at no charge by sending the defective disc, postage prepaid, with proof of purchase to:

> Disc Exchange
> Addison-Wesley Professional
> Pearson Technology Group
> 75 Arlington Street, Suite 300
> Boston, MA 02116
> Email: AWPro@aw.com

Addison-Wesley makes no warranty or representation, either expressed or implied, with respect to this software, its quality, performance, merchantability, or fitness for a particular purpose. In no event will Addison-Wesley, its distributors, or dealers be liable for direct, indirect, special, incidental, or consequential damages arising out of the use or inability to use the software. The exclusion of implied warranties is not permitted in some states. Therefore, the above exclusion may not apply to you. This warranty provides you with specific legal rights. There may be other rights that you may have that vary from state to state. The contents of this CD-ROM are intended for personal use only, unless otherwise addressed under a separate license.

NVIDIA Statement on the Software

The source code provided is freely distributable, so long as the NVIDIA header remains unaltered and user modifications are detailed.

NO WARRANTY

THE SOFTWARE AND ANY OTHER MATERIALS PROVIDED BY NVIDIA ON THE ENCLOSED CD-ROM ARE PROVIDED "AS IS." NVIDIA DISCLAIMS ALL WARRANTIES, EXPRESS, IMPLIED OR STATUTORY, INCLUDING, WITHOUT LIMITATION, THE IMPLIED WARRANTIES OF TITLE, MERCHANTABILITY, FITNESS FOR A PARTICULAR PURPOSE AND NONINFRINGEMENT.

LIMITATION OF LIABILITY

NVIDIA SHALL NOT BE LIABLE TO ANY USER, DEVELOPER, DEVELOPER'S CUSTOMERS, OR ANY OTHER PERSON OR ENTITY CLAIMING THROUGH OR UNDER DEVELOPER FOR ANY LOSS OF PROFITS, INCOME, SAVINGS, OR ANY OTHER CONSEQUENTIAL, INCIDENTAL, SPECIAL, PUNITIVE, DIRECT OR INDIRECT DAMAGES (WHETHER IN AN ACTION IN CONTRACT, TORT OR BASED ON A WARRANTY), EVEN IF NVIDIA HAS BEEN ADVISED OF THE POSSIBILITY OF SUCH DAMAGES. THESE LIMITATIONS SHALL APPLY NOTWITHSTANDING ANY FAILURE OF THE ESSENTIAL PURPOSE OF ANY LIMITED REMEDY. IN NO EVENT SHALL NVIDIA'S AGGREGATE LIABILITY TO DEVELOPER OR ANY OTHER PERSON OR ENTITY CLAIMING THROUGH OR UNDER DEVELOPER EXCEED THE AMOUNT OF MONEY ACTUALLY PAID BY DEVELOPER TO NVIDIA FOR THE SOFTWARE OR ANY OTHER MATERIALS.

More information and updates are available at:
http://developer.nvidia.com
http://www.awprofessional.com/